EVERYMAN'S CONSTITUTION

"... the gravest brutality of our time is racial inequality...."

"In the closing decades of the nineteenth century various factors —few of them creditable—combined to make our judges and legislators forget that the permanent overthrow of slavery and all its sordid by-products was, in fact, the dominant objective of the three Civil War amendments. Mr. Justice Miller spoke discerningly as observer of his times when, in 1873, he said that the 'pervading purpose' of the equal protection clause of the Fourteenth Amendment was the invalidation of all laws 'in the States where the newly emancipated negroes resided, which discriminated with gross injustice and hardship against them as a class.'"

"... the Court of the 1950's so enforced the prohibitions of the Fourteenth Amendment as to revivify the basic objective of the generation which sponsored and enacted the amendment.... The nation as a whole and the South in particular had lived for more than half a century on borrowed time."

MARK DE WOLFE HOWE
*The Garden and
the Wilderness*

EVERYMAN'S CONSTITUTION

HISTORICAL ESSAYS ON
THE FOURTEENTH AMENDMENT,
THE "CONSPIRACY THEORY",
AND AMERICAN CONSTITUTIONALISM

By *Howard Jay Graham*

WITH A FOREWORD BY

Leonard W. Levy

WISCONSIN HISTORICAL SOCIETY PRESS

The State Historical Society of Wisconsin acknowledges, with thanks, permission by the University of Chicago Press to quote from Mark De Wolfe Howe's *The Garden and the Wilderness* (Copyright © 1965 by the University of Chicago Press), and by Holt, Rinehart and Winston, Inc., to quote from Robert Frost's poems "Two Tramps in Mud Time," "Not Quite Social," and "What Fifty Said" (Copyright © 1942 by Henry Holt & Co.).

COPYRIGHT © 1968 BY
THE STATE HISTORICAL SOCIETY OF WISCONSIN
ALL RIGHTS RESERVED

PAPERBACK EDITION, 2013

LIBRARY OF CONGRESS
CATALOG CARD NUMBER
LC 68-64058

For
MARY WILSON GRAHAM
and in memory of
LOREN MILLER
1903-1967
and
HELEN GRAHAM LEMING
1908-1953

Foreword

THE YEAR 1968 marks the one hundredth anniversary of the ratification of the Fourteenth Amendment. A most fitting commemoration of that centennial is this collection of essays by Howard Jay Graham, who is surely the greatest authority on the history of the amendment. He is its Maitland, and perhaps our foremost living historian of American constitutional law as well.

The Fourteenth Amendment is the American mini-Constitution, the Magna Carta of our federal system, and the instrumentality for nationalizing civil rights. Its stirring phrases—life, liberty, and property; due process of law; equal protection of the laws; privileges and immunities of citizenship—are talismanic symbols of our constitutional democracy. Yet the amendment has had a melancholy and ironic history. Originating as the constitutional embodiment of abolitionist ideology, the amendment was primarily meant to secure the rights of man without distinctions based on race; nevertheless, for many decades the principal beneficiary of the amendment was corporate capitalism. Only in our own time has the Supreme Court construed the amendment as its framers intended.

Excepting the commerce clause, which is the basis for so much congressional legislation, modern constitutional law is very much made up of Fourteenth Amendment cases. No part of the Constitution has given rise to more cases than its due process clause alone, and its various clauses taken together account for about half of the work of the Supreme Court. The states in our federal system can scarcely act without raising a Fourteenth Amendment question. The vast majority of all cases which concern our precious constitutional freedoms—from freedom of speech to separation of church and state, from racial equality to the many elements of criminal justice—turn on the Fourteenth Amendment. The history of its interpretation is, at bottom, the story of the two great subjects that bulk largest in our constitutional law: government regulation of the economy and individual rights.

Howard Jay Graham has played an important part in the developing history of the Fourteenth Amendment. Even as he chronicled its origins and purposes, he influenced its interpretation. By no coincidence, substantive due process of law as the mainstay of decisions against the constitutionality of government regulation came to an end when Graham provided the scholarly proof that the amendment was not designed to benefit business enterprise. Similarly, when he showed that the amendment emerged from the efforts of its framers to ensure that Negroes should have the same rights as other citizens, he provided the historical basis for decisions, which rapidly followed, in support of equal rights regardless of race.

Graham's work has always reflected a sensitivity to democratic values and democratic public policy. He is a scholar whose conscience matches his scrupulous regard for historical facts. His critical intelligence is both rigorous and humane, making his study of the history of the amendment a means of unfolding its promise. In depth and precision of scholarship, he may be equalled by a few but excelled by none in the field of constitutional history. His achievement may be appreciated by considering how very little we would know about the amendment without his contribution. It consists not merely in what he has added to our knowledge by his prodigious and original research and by his superbly crafted essays; his contribution consists, too, in spurring awareness that so much new and significant can be said about an old subject, and in the sheer incitement to excellence that his fellow scholars relish from models such as Graham's.

For three decades he has published his work in law journals from coast to coast. Unfortunately, too few historians even in the field of constitutional history read the law journals. As a result Graham has not had the recognition that he deserves from the profession. He has been a scholar's scholar, operating on the fringes of the academy. A shy and modest man, handicapped by deafness, he earned his bread as a law librarian until his recent retirement. Yet he has taught a generation of teachers who have been fortunate enough to know his work. It has appeared in scattered places, and the individual essays, considered separately, have had an episodic character. They needed to be gathered together within the covers of a single volume to reveal their rare insights, their unity, and their elegance. Predictably, this book will give Graham's work the means of widening the impact that he has already made on the initiate. He is, like Lord Acton, the author of great books never written. Here, at least, is a selection of his essays in the field of American constitutional history. The Society Press does itself honor by bringing Graham's work to the larger audience that he deserves.

LEONARD W. LEVY
Earl Warren Professor of
American Constitutional History
Brandeis University

Author's Preface

THE FOURTEENTH AMENDMENT of the Constitution of the United States stands first in all but name. First in jurisdictional, jurisprudential, historical, and litigational significance. Its privileges and immunities, due process, and equal protection clauses, together with the due process clause of the Fifth Amendment, and the antecedent and related clauses of the original colonial charters and of the now-fifty state constitutions, have been the sources and the bases of at least one-third, and during certain critical periods, possibly more than one-half of our aggregate constitutional litigation. From the very start, American constitutional law has been, and in our day continues to be, a gloss on these antecedent, continuing, quintessential texts. Not since the days of the Schoolmen, in likelihood, has more been written about less, by so few (and by so many!), more authoritatively, with so much "in process," in doubt, and in limbo.

Why all this is true, what the past has held, where we stand at present, and why, are the themes and subjects of these essays.

My thesis is simply that what the United States, under these guarantees, did for itself, and for corporations, in curbing manifest and latent hostility and antagonism to corporate enterprise, 1880–1940, the United States can and must do for itself, and for still disadvantaged minorities, using the same techniques and weapons, supplying similar, and, in this case, *intended* process and protection. Our giant corporations, moreover—now rivals of the states, and in this matter, potential auxiliaries and allies of government—must also seize the initiative, and, in sheer gratitude and enlightened self interest, provide for others what others provided for them—economic opportunity, the protection of law, and the opportunity to realize to the full their inherent capacity and potential.

* * *

Constitutional history is history of a special and fascinating sort. Any book on the subject thirty-five years in the writing becomes a study in the "process" and the processes it describes. Twice or more, these essays have figured peripherally in major cases and trends. During and after this centennial year, the elaborated statements, findings, and hypotheses may be helpful again. Not only the Introduction and the Epilogue, which together provide a summary and overall view, but also Chapters 11 and 12 are here published for the first time. In the case of the other chapters, except for the correction of factual, grammatical, and citational errors, and for necessary revision of cross references, the original texts of the law review essays have been retained and reprinted in full, as follows:

Chapter 1. "The 'Conspiracy Theory' of the Fourteenth Amendment. Part I." 47 YALE LAW JOURNAL, pp. 371–403. January, 1938. Reprinted by permission of the Yale Law Journal Company and Fred B. Rothman & Company from the Yale Law Journal.

Chapter 2. "The 'Conspiracy Theory' of the Fourteenth Amendment. Part II." 48 YALE LAW JOURNAL, pp. 171–194. December, 1938. Reprinted by permission of the Yale Law Journal Company and Fred B. Rothman & Company from the Yale Law Journal.

Chapter 3. [Part I.] "Four Letters of Mr. Justice Field." 47 YALE LAW JOURNAL, pp. 1100–1108. May, 1938. [Part II.] "Justice Field and the Fourteenth Amendment." 52 YALE LAW JOURNAL, pp. 851–889. September, 1943. Both reprinted by permission of the Yale Law Journal Company and Fred B. Rothman & Company from the Yale Law Journal.

Chapter 4. "The Early Antislavery Backgrounds of the Fourteenth Amendment." 1950 WISCONSIN LAW REVIEW, pp. 479–507, 610–661. May, July, 1950. Reprinted by permission of the Wisconsin Law Review.

Chapter 5. "Procedure to Substance: Extra-Judicial Rise of Due Process, 1830–1860." 40 CALIFORNIA LAW REVIEW, pp. 483–500. Winter, 1952–1953. Copyright ©, 1952, California Law Review, Inc. Reprinted by permission.

Chapter 6. "The Fourteenth Amendment and School Segregation." 3 BUFFALO LAW REVIEW, pp. 1–24. 1953. Reprinted by permission of the Buffalo Law Review.

Chapter 7. "Our 'Declaratory' Fourteenth Amendment." 7 STANFORD LAW REVIEW, pp. 3–39. December, 1954. Reprinted by permission of the Stanford Law Review.

Chapter 8. "Crosskey's Constitution: An Archeological Blueprint." 7 VANDERBILT LAW REVIEW, pp. 340–365. April, 1954. Reprinted by permission of the Vanderbilt Law Review.

Chapter 9. "An Innocent Abroad: The Constitutional Corporate 'Person.' " 2 U.C.L.A. LAW REVIEW, pp. 155–211. February, 1955. Reprinted by permission of The Regents of the University of California and the U.C.L.A. Law Review.

Chapter 10. "Builded Better Than They Knew: The Framers,

the Railroads and the Fourteenth Amendment." 17 UNIVERSITY OF PITTSBURGH LAW REVIEW, pp. 537–584. Summer, 1956. Reprinted by permission of the University of Pittsburgh Law Review.

Chapter 13. "The Waite Court and the Fourteenth Amendment." 17 VANDERBILT LAW REVIEW, pp. 525–547. March, 1964. Reprinted by permission of the Vanderbilt Law Review.

Editorial notes have been added to revise and update, and sometimes to qualify or extend statements and interpretations. My own "then" and "now" views and judgments thus are as identifiable as those which are frequently criticized. This is embarrassing, yet altogether proper: the critic of anachronism must not spare nor ignore his own. In the case of the Conspiracy Theory at least, the humbled are in numerous and excellent company.

The editorial notes, including those at the foot of the page identified by **1968**, are an integral part of the book. They tell a research story, motivate and connect the chapters, and make for a more rigorous separation of research, hypotheses, and interpretation than sometimes has been the case with Fourteenth Amendment history.

At this point a word about bibliography may not be amiss. General readers and citizens long annoyed and handicapped by inadequate documentation of the history, enforcement, and nonenforcement of the Fourteenth Amendment are handicapped no longer. *Political and Civil Rights in the United States* (Emerson, Haber, and Dorsen, eds. Boston: Little, Brown, 1967. 3d edition. 2 vols., 2274 pp.), one of the distinguished and enlightened reference works of our time, surveys, analyzes, and documents this immense field with elaborate and well-indexed bibliographic, sociological, legal-constitutional, and chronological coverage throughout. Volume 2, furthermore, is devoted wholly to Discrimination. Treated seriatim and systematically are discrimination in protection of the person, voting, education (North and South), administration of justice, employment, housing, public accommodations, transportation, health, and welfare. The period since 1950 (since Myrdal's *An American Dilemma*); the Civil Rights Acts, 1957–1966; federal, state, and local policies and action: all are admirably covered. A compendium in the best sense, this book integrates, for each topic and major field, the history, law, literature, and social experience, with authority and references (both popular and professional) provided at each point. Everyman seldom has been so well served, and never at a more crucial time.

This volume updates and documents, far better than selective referencing possibly could do, the judicial, congressional, and administrative sides of problems here mentioned and treated. Readers are urged to make the most of this extraordinary work.

* * *

For a librarian and lipreader—a member of both groups that understand best how corporate and sociological modern research and communication are—to attempt to thank his friends and benefactors for aid extending over a lifetime is a pleasant yet nearly impossible task. Those blessed with hearing will perceive as readily as those not that *Everyman's Constitution* is a composite: a product of Law, Teaching, and Bibliography, that trinity we have so often celebrated. And because "Every man is indebted to his profession," this is doubly so. One's first thanks accordingly go to those fellow librarians, researchers, and archivists from coast to coast, who have shared, often anonymously but no less devotedly, in the larger mutual endeavor. I am proud and thankful to have served in and with this group, and to have seen and stressed, in consequence, the pluralistic, professional, even extraprofessional sides of our law and constitutionalism—of due process-equal protection constitutionalism in particular.

To the respective law reviews and publishers who have kindly granted permission to republish the materials cited above, I tender grateful thanks.

It is a further privilege to acknowledge these ineluctable obligations:

To members of the Graham-Wilson family, foremost and reverently to Anna Johnson, Roderick Morrison, and Lorena N. Graham, my deceased parents and aunt, whose love and sacrifices assured college education for five children, made scholarship precious and teaching the noblest of professions. To my sister Helen, whose life and spirit beautifully expressed and re-exemplify this.

To all my teachers, individually; especially to Emily Reed Hooper, for wakening and quickening adolescent interest in history and constitutional history; to the faculties of Whitman College and the University of Washington, for broadening and deepening undergraduate interests; to President C. C. Maxey of Whitman for an early and happy introduction to the Fourteenth Amendment.

To the University of California, Berkeley and Los Angeles, and to all who made Berkeley "home," and that wonderfully exciting place it was to work and study, 1927–1939. Specifically, to the late Professor Frank L. Kleeberger, for a clerkship-readership which

Preface

made possible not only graduate research and completion of library training, but also personal acquaintance with many of that distinguished faculty. To the late Professors P. O. Ray, Felix Flugel, Stuart Daggett, Max Radin, D. O. McGovney, and Henry Ballantine, who (with others from old Boalt and South Halls) so generously helped an inquisitive (and sometimes unregistered) student on his special projects; to Professors Charles Aikin, Lawrence A. Harper, and George R. Stewart, Samaritans all, for doing much, even more, of the same; to the faculty of the School of Librarianship, 1938–1939, for further professional preparation, often under mutual difficulties—bridged in this instance, as always, by my wife Mary's faithful assistance.

To the late Thomas S. Dabagh, Librarian, and to the Board of Trustees of the Los Angeles County Law Library for opportunities as Order Librarian, 1939–1950, and to Forrest S. Drummond, Librarian since 1950, for reassignment as Bibliographer, assuring opportunity to re-examine and catalog more fully the large rare book, constitutional, treatise, and social science collections earlier acquired, "building better" again than either of us then knew, or even could imagine.

Again, most especially, to the John Simon Guggenheim Memorial Foundation, and to Dr. Henry Allen Moe, then Secretary, for two Memorial Fellowships, the recognition and opportunities of which assured the continuance of research which otherwise might have lapsed.

To these long-standing friends: Professor Franklin Walker of Mills College and Alfred H. Kelly of Wayne State University, for counsel, recognition, and encouragement at crucial stages; to my childhood friend, Anna Lou Rosenquist, and to Professors Franklin Henry and Jacobus tenBroek, all of Berkeley, for devoted friendship and proof that handicap generally is a state of mind; to Allan M. Carson, Esq., and to my sometime colleague and collaborator, John W. Heckel of San Francisco, for patient assistance, and note-and-oral "conversations" that have meant more than they can ever know; to the late G. A. Nuermberger and his wife, Ruth K. Nuermberger, historians and friends from library school days, for counsel and happy times in Washington and Berkeley.

To these distinguished Americanists and teachers who have inspired, counseled, encouraged, and sometimes goaded, principally by their writing, reviews, and correspondence: the late Charles A. Beard, Edward S. Corwin, Loren Miller, and Mark de Wolfe Howe, master constitutionalists; Professors Dwight L. Dumond of Ann

Arbor, Willard Hurst of Madison, Charles Fairman of Harvard, John P. Roche and Leonard W. Levy of Brandeis, and C. Peter Magrath of Brown University. To Professor Levy I am further indebted for suggesting the re-publication of these essays.

To Dr. Donald Gleason, my physician, for good health.

Finally, above all: To my wife, Mary Wilson Graham—librarian, teacher, mother, homemaker—who for thirty-eight years has shared the joys of marriage and research, her teaching, our travel and home, and at last the dedication of this "family book" with two whose lives touched ours and the America we have wanted to see, most poignantly. To our daughter Anna Graham Snively, reference librarian, and our son, Dr. Donald W. Graham, research chemist, who have lived with *Everyman's Constitution* from birth, and who often took precocious delight in the stacks of "little white slips" which so long were its constituent forms.

To all, and again, I extend deepest heartfelt thanks and appreciation.

Happy and heartening to us in these days of national and human travail are these lines of Robert Frost, America's poet-mentor, and Everyman's especially since that memorable January day in 1961:

> *Only where love and need are one,*
> *And the work is play for mortal stakes,*
> *Is the deed ever really done*
> *For Heaven and the future's sakes.*
>
> . . .
>
> *The way of understanding is partly mirth.*
>
> . . .
>
> *When I was young my teachers were the old.*
> *I gave up fire for form till I was cold.*
> *I suffered like a metal being cast.*
> *I went to school to age to learn the past.*
>
> *Now I am old my teachers are the young.*
> *What can't be moulded must be cracked and sprung.*
> *I strain at lessons fit to start a suture.*
> *I go to school to youth to learn the future.*

HOWARD JAY GRAHAM
Los Angeles, California
December, 1967

Contents

Foreword	vii
Author's Preface	ix
INTRODUCTION	3
1. THE "CONSPIRACY THEORY" OF THE FOURTEENTH AMENDMENT: PART I	23
2. THE "CONSPIRACY THEORY" OF THE FOURTEENTH AMENDMENT: PART II	68
3. JUSTICE FIELD AND THE FOURTEENTH AMENDMENT	98
4. THE EARLY ANTISLAVERY BACKGROUNDS OF THE FOURTEENTH AMENDMENT	152
5. PROCEDURE TO SUBSTANCE: EXTRAJUDICIAL RISE OF DUE PROCESS, 1830–1860	242
6. THE FOURTEENTH AMENDMENT AND SCHOOL SEGREGATION	266
7. OUR "DECLARATORY" FOURTEENTH AMENDMENT	295
8. CROSSKEY'S CONSTITUTION: AN ARCHEOLOGICAL BLUEPRINT	337
9. AN INNOCENT ABROAD: THE CONSTITUTIONAL CORPORATE "PERSON"	367
10. "BUILDED BETTER THAN THEY KNEW": THE FRAMERS, THE RAILROADS AND THE FOURTEENTH AMENDMENT	438
11. "ACRES FOR CENTS": THE ECONOMIC AND CONSTITUTIONAL SIGNIFICANCE OF FRONTIER TAX TITLES, 1800–1890	494
12. "PROPHET UNHONORED": ROBERT S. BLACKWELL, TAX TITLES, AND THE "SUBSTANTIVE REVOLUTION" IN DUE PROCESS AND EQUAL PROTECTION, 1830–1880	519
13. THE WAITE COURT AND THE FOURTEENTH AMENDMENT	552
14. EVERYMAN'S CONSTITUTION: A CENTENNIAL VIEW	585
Appendixes	595
Index	621

Introduction

EVERYMAN'S CONSTITUTION: ODYSSEY FROM THE AMERICAN ILIAD

I

THIS IS A BOOK about the American Creed, the American Conscience, and the American Constitution, their relationships to one another and to the processes of Law and of History. It is a book about the forms and norms, the ways and standards of Constitutionalism; about Free Men and Freedmen; and about the Law-of-the-Land guarantee of Magna Carta and the equally fundamental and familiar clause in our Declaration of Independence.

It is a book about Persons, natural and corporate,* about Law and Rights, natural and constitutional—and again, about the relationships, the shifts, and the transmutations one to another. It is a book

---

* *Natural* "persons" are humans, men. *Corporate* "persons" are *artificial* persons created by government and law. Both natural and corporate persons hence are *legal* persons; but only since 1882–1889 have artificial corporate "persons," like natural ones, *also* been judicially treated as *constitutional* "persons" within the meaning of the federal equal protection and due process clauses. This major judicial dispensation permitted corporations (read also: *aggregated capital*) to challenge government action under clauses which for centuries had been applied solely to *men*, and originally solely to *free* men—that is, only to *natural* persons.

Controversy soon arose over the expediency of such a step; and, in the case of the Fourteenth Amendment, over whether the framers of the Amendment had foreseen or intended such a result.

Treaties and constitutions often (and necessarily) employ the same word in different senses, contexts, and degrees of inclusiveness. Thus the Fathers of 1787 spoke of Representatives and Senators, as well as slaves, as "Persons"—all without compunction or elaboration. (See the United States Constitution, Article I, Sections 2, 3, and 9, and Article II, Section 1.) The fact that corporations or shareholders never had aspired to *slave* "personality," nor even directly to a United States senatorship, did not at all preclude their lawyers from invoking *corporate personality* under the due process and equal protection clauses. Constitutional law, in short, embraces much more than lexicography.

"Natural rights" are those *fundamental moral rights* which men possess by reason of common humanity *in any ethically grounded and ordered society.*

"Constitutional rights" are rights one stage farther along—rights constitutionally defined and sanctioned, rights *enforceable by prescribed procedures of law and government.*

"Law" (herein and generally) of course embraces statutes, custom, cases, administrative action—in the fullest sense, *the administration of justice, the protection of persons and property.*

Procedural law and *procedural* due process relate to the *forms* of litigation and administration, deal generally with *how* law operates. *Substantive* law and *substantive* due process, on the other hand, deal more broadly, and with *ends*: with what law *is*, what law *seeks*, what law (and legislatures) can *do*.

3

about Process of Law and the processing of rights; about Protection bestowed by government, and protection denied; about the *due*, *un*due, and *over*due processing of those fundamental rights of life, liberty, and property; about the protection, *equal* protection, and sometimes very *un*equal protection of the laws relating to persons, liberty, and property.

It is a book about *affirmative* due process, *affirmative* equal protection, *affirmative* government and laws; about *dueness* and *duty* as moral and legal sources thereof; and about *duty* as the generator-converter of rights long affirmed and declared, which must be and are finally *affirmed* and *established* in *truth* and *in fact*.

It is a book, particularly, about human prejudice—prejudice irrational yet vincible; and about discrimination—discrimination invidious and arbitrary, corporate and noncorporate, overcome and yet to be overcome. It is a book about the groups, professional and lay, whose use and misuse, whose cultivation and construction of this key phraseology contributed to significant changes—often called and miscalled "revolutions"—in federalism, in American judicial review, in our economy and our business structure. It is a book about a marvelous fluke and an historical illusion, long known as the "Conspiracy Theory" and involving events and episodes that are fortunately unique in American legal advocacy, historiography, and constitutionalism, all three. It is a book about judges and judging, reformers and abolitionists, frontier lawyers and corporation lawyers; about what and how these groups learned from one another, and from earnest dedicated citizens; and about what we today can and must now relearn from them.

In sum, this is a book about that Anglo-American constitution-in-miniature, called here a Constitution for Everyman, *Everyman's Constitution*: the first and fifth sections of the Fourteenth Amendment to the Constitution of the United States.

The texts of these sections—familiar, yet never commonplace; fundamental, yet still misunderstood—are here reprinted in full for ready and perhaps recurring reference:

> Section 1. All persons born or naturalized in the United States, and subject to the jurisdiction thereof, are citizens of the United States and of the State wherein they reside. No State shall make or enforce any law which shall abridge the privileges or immunities of citizens of the United States; nor shall any State deprive any person of life, liberty, or property, without due process of law; nor deny to any person within its jurisdiction the equal protection of the laws.

Introduction

Section 5. The Congress shall have power to enforce, by appropriate legislation, the provisions of this article.

The purpose and the logic of Everyman's Constitution are clear the instant our minds grasp what American slavery for so long had been: a system of caste and of prejudice, of mores and of positive law, which utterly denied the protection of law and the bounties of government to members of the enslaved race, and which predicated and sanctioned that terrible, stupendous mass denial on sheer force and on a presumed racial superiority. Until those years 1863–1868, American law too had treated Afro-Americans as chattels, "property," "persons held to Service or Labour." After emancipation, until Everyman's Constitution, Negroes were still and in fact "vagabonds," "refugees," "freedmen" rather than free men—still an "inferior," stigmatized, "degraded" caste, denied, as a result of enrooted *mores* and prejudices, *any* (compare now EQUAL) *protection of the laws*; still deprived of the fundamental rights ("life, liberty, and property") without *any* (compare now DUE) *process of law*. Those parallel strikingly contrasted readings show very well how the antislavery generation reasoned; they show what those who understood slavery best and who hated it most, meant to accomplish and in fact did accomplish with these forms. Members of the antislavery generation filled that ancient void; they turned the tables completely; they uprooted the caste system as a matter of law; they bestowed the protection and introduced the *duty* to protect, both of which so long had been wanting; they ended, and in fact reversed, as a matter of law and of policy as well as of principle and creed, the myriad "abridgments," "denials," and "deprivations"— (they used even the verb forms of those nouns to do so!); they meant to cover, and they did cover, the entire ground so far as words and thought could cover it: They nationalized the fundamental rights of American citizenship and of human personality; they provided this mutually reinforcing, overlapping, triple *protection*, with *added* judicial, legislative, and executive powers and duties, both federal *and* state.

Purpose, logic, theory, were and are as clear, as sound and simple as that. Moreover, the tools and the language employed were the tools and the language Englishmen and Americans had employed in their constitutional struggles and crises from the beginning: The cloak and the majesty of citizenship; the guarantee of the law of the land and of due process of law derived from the *per legem terrae* clause of Magna Carta itself—the very germ and gene of Constitutionalism; finally, that added buttressing guarantee of the equal protection of the laws derived from the "self evident truthes—All men are created equal" phrase of the Declaration of Independence.

"Constitutionalism," in Walton Hamilton's definition, "is the name given to the trust which men repose in the power of words engrossed on parchment to keep a government in order." It is a composite, a synthesis of Law, History, and Criticism, a way of resolving conflicts by focusing and fractionating them. Very early and luckily, Englishmen learned to use primary documents and records creatively, to attenuate conflict by historicizing it, to substitute—no matter how hesitantly, reluctantly at first—"writing for fighting" and pleading for bleeding. Constitutionalism thus conceived is the art and the process of assimilating and converting statute and precedent, ideals and aspirations, into the forms and the Rule of Law—into a Fundamental and Supreme Law.

Section 1 of the Fourteenth Amendment is the culmination, the irreducible form, process, and essence of constitutionalism so conceived: a miniature, transistorized model of it and for it. The wonder, the economy of these forms: Even the name—"process"—is built in engendering both the use and the thing. Three other universals—"life, liberty, and property"—also are present and equally functional. Finally—rather from the very start in 1215—*lex terrae, per legem terrae*, the law of the land, as the prime guarantee, driver, and mover. (Just one word, Law, be it noted, for both *lex* and *jus*, statute and right, law and justice, for *supreme* law and for ordinary law. This undoubtedly is one of the secrets of our constitutionalizing process, one of the strengths, and one of the evident weaknesses too.) So, likewise, with *due* and with *equal*; everything here in two, ten, or thirty-one words, depending on the fullness of the constitutional texts quoted or cited.

Repointing and extending the matter, constitutionalism is law and government at the frontiers, law and government in the process of ordering and extending themselves, and of doing this by process and protection,* and hence dependent, for ultimate success, on the faith, the trust, and the power which men put with them and into them. Here, obviously, is the catch—not a weakness, but surely the paramount difficulty: trust and faith and reason can waver; and power easily can get lost or diverted. But in these troubled frontier

---

* The terms "process" and "protection" as employed here (and in similar passages throughout) are to be read as shorthand for "due process of law" and "equal protection of the laws." Those full phrases in turn are the acknowledged quintessentials of constitutionalism, ordered government, and principled administration of justice based on reason and freed of caprice in both the bestowal and the enforcement of fundamental rights.

Introduction

areas, such as race, where men still are learning to live by and with the law, and with their fellows and emotions, getting rid of hoary prejudices by reason and by law, "*due* process of law," and "*equal* protection of the laws," are almost the only sources and brands of constitutionalism there are or can be, at first.

These two guarantees thus have been, and are, and in this area especially, *must be*, the leading edge and spearhead of constitutionalism—reason, law, and government combined—"pushing as far ahead as it can." Due process and equal protection are natural right and natural law in the process of being converted—by this "due process"—into *enforceable* constitutional right and law.

All constitutionalists recognize and acknowledge this, but some still profess uneasiness when such "vague," "diffuse," "natural law" beginnings have to be made, and are made, in the field of race. More caution, more "neutral" principles, it is said, are necessary here. Yet is it not perfectly plain that to reason so—to renounce or denounce these ethico-moral, natural law innovations and beginnings in this *one* field, and at this date—is simply to redraw yet another color line? To subvert the remedy by the mischief? Given the chance, "need and conscience, merits and syllogisms," sufficed and worked admirably for others. Given the same chance, they suffice and work just as admirably here. Political, ethical, religious and moral principles—Creed and Conscience—working on, by, and through public, private, and judicial constructions of this quasi-legal phraseology, have innovated long and well, and protected many others. They can and must protect those whom these clauses were specifically added to protect.

No one denies or minimizes the difficulties of this enterprise. "Bootstrap constitutionalism" is the best name for it. Some difficulties are inherent in all constitutionalizing; others clearly are peculiar to this *due* processing and to this *equal* protecting of freedmen's and free men's and "persons' " rights, and "citizens' " privileges and immunities; difficulties peculiar to the overthrow and the abolition of slavery, and to eradication of its vestiges; difficulties peculiar to the sturdy pestilent character of the mass prejudice and the race prejudice which these two sections were added to counter and to liquidate.

Some constitutional jobs are harder, take longer than others. Yet one century is long enough.

"Words engrossed on parchment" remain words until "trust" is reposed in the "power to keep a government in order." Power, in short, was added: Constitutional power was amply enlarged; full enforcement power was granted to Congress by Section 5. Later, that power got disused, lost, breached. But the point is that the power was and *is* there, that the power need not have been lost, disused, nor breached. Sections 1 and 5 together make perfect sense, once we understand and face up to the problems. They made perfect sense also to that generation that knew slavery best, that faced up to it, and that understood the problems of uprooting it far better than we ever can.

The need—and the plan—was to erase the color line, to erase it the only way we too have learned it can be erased: by eroding and eradicating those discriminations and those denials of protection which themselves preserve and foster prejudice. For these purposes, and for these reasons, there were no nonsensical definitions of *race*. No litmus tests of color. Just *protection. Equal* protection. Provision that from that day forth the basic human rights and the fundamental protections of law and the bounties of government extended to *all*—extended to Everyman, as Everyman understood they heretofore certainly had not. Government finally had the power and the obligation to protect *all* as heretofore it protected only *some*. Government now had the power and the duty to assure full and progressive solutions; to wipe out "the stigmas and badges and indicia of slavery"; to deal with the enrooted prejudices and discriminations that were the most fearsome and perplexing part of slavery as a fallen and moribund, yet still pervasively rooted institution.

Evils—no less than "mischiefs"—must measure and determine legal and constitutional powers and remedies. Slavery—evil incarnate—involved millions; involved the mores, not merely of a section, but of the whole United States. The American Creed had been nudging the American Conscience, and both had been leavening conduct and innovating Constitutionalism *extra*-officially and *extra*-judicially for ninety years. Jefferson's self-evident truths, taken to mind and to heart, thus had made slavery untenable long before Emancipation. Yet Jefferson himself had died, on the fiftieth anniversary of the Declaration, July 4, 1826, still a slaveholder. "All men were created equal." But not quite yet. During the next forty years, slavery had been curbed, overthrown, finally prohibited by the Thirteenth Amendment. People first had loathed and hated its barbarisms and its degradation of man; they next had resisted its extension to the Territories; then increasingly had seen and conceded the need and the rightness of process and protection for *all* persons and for all citizens, state and national. But these, we must realize, were molar, osmotic changes; their continuation and their consummation was what mattered, what still had to be achieved and secured. This was

Introduction

the staggering task—mores, prejudices, and custom being what they were and are. Most thoughtful people, in 1866–1868, were awed by the difficulties. Many doubtless were overawed. Few could have *under*estimated the job. No man could plumb the future; Everyman surely did not, and did not try.

One phase and ideal of constitutionalism had had to advance here, and had crystalized here *ahead* of the rest—belief in the need to make this *constitutional* start which natural rights-declaratory thinking had begun and had got under way; belief also in the need to consolidate the gains, to commit and oblige and empower America to continue to *work* on these matters, to be *true* to itself and its creed. We cannot say, and do not, that Everyman yet wanted every other man to have his rights and his protection. Yet *most* of those who had *thought* about it agreed the *principle* was sound, agreed that this *constitutional* start *had to* be made. Here indeed was the problem, as it still is ours: Not how to *give* power to do these things, but how to *exercise* that power; how to follow through; how to deal progressively with this vestigial mass prejudice; how to lift, by Law's and by Constitutionalism's bootstraps—by process and protection—this crushing national incubus. How to innovate further, how to consolidate gains, how to realize constitutionally, how to actualize nationally, what we profess and what we realize as individuals. Constitutional language always and inherently is broad and general; this constitutional language, we can see, had to be, and was, especially so, for especially good and clear reasons.

We cannot say, and do not, that Everyman reasoned things out in any more precise fashion than this, or that all then held even these views. We need not even argue that a majority *yet* did. What we must believe, and do, is that it *was* the right century for *some* to have done so and to have made this start—for *all* to have done so indeed!—and that rational men, men of reason and good will, draftsmen and ratifiers, *did* think things out and *did* intend so. Or, if we still insist upon putting their thoughts and their intentions in the negative, as the Supreme Court and so many commentators so long have done, then we say simply that these thinkers and men of goodwill emphatically *did not* mean, by these two sections, to *indulge* slavery's hangover or to preserve, entrench, and perpetuate its vestigial mores, prejudices, and discriminations. Such men knew then, as well as we do now, what had to be done, and they gave those who came after them the *power* and the *duty* to do it, period.

We must underscore this final point, for it is the heart of the matter, the answer absolute, to that thoughtless, fallacious claim and rule which, more than any other, has emasculated these two sections and which accordingly has put the United States in its present plight in the matter of race relations. Reference of course is to the "State action" claim and rule—that pitiful lawyers' afterthought and absurd notion that *because* the second sentence of Section 1 begins "No *State* shall *make* or enforce any *law*," this fact *of itself* signifies that these constitutional clauses and sections were drafted and ratified to deal *only* with action by the state or by the states' subdivisions—with prejudiced actions and discriminations by *state government* in short; and that it accordingly follows that Section 5 gave and gives Congress power to enforce *only* this negative—gave and gives, in other words, no power to deal creatively with the real difficulty or with the crushing national incubus above noted.

"State action," needless to say, was and is an aberration, a syndrome of the legal mind, a retrospective invention, simple but never pure. It still is the excuse, the rationale, for state and for federal *in*action. Offered, or accepting it, we are led, but certainly not *forced* to believe, that these two sections amounted to a gigantic swindle, a mere double negative, a constitutional lawyer's verbal cat's cradle, the net intent as well as effect of which was to leave Negro rights exactly where and as they always had been—at the mercy of the states, at the mercy of prejudice and bigotry.

II

So Racism still is humanity's hangover from slavery. Certainly it is peculiarly, notoriously, the United States'. "Sturdy pestilence," in Justice Douglas' phrase—a perdurable, unendurable pestilence which after a century still threatens national integrity, security, personal and national life, *notwithstanding* these two sections added— we shall have to keep continually reminding ourselves—"for one pervading purpose. . . . the freedom of the slave race, the security and firm establishment of that freedom."

For so the Supreme Court *half* affirmed in its first construction of these clauses in the *Slaughter-House Cases* of 1873. Yet barely twenty-five years later, by that succession of disasters which culminated in *Plessy v. Ferguson*, these provisions—added out of hypercaution to assure *every* means of lifting slavery's incubus of racism—had become instead provisions which, during the next two generations, and until 1954, promoted, preserved, and virtually *licensed* that incubus.

As an admittedly unconventional, yet up-to-date and perhaps welcome recapitulation of these half-familiar cases and developments, we excerpt here a spirited examination essay written (let us suppose)

Introduction

in a course in constitutional law or political science by one of today's campus civil rights leaders—those prickly, forthright, precocious idealists justifiably proud of their kinship to Frederick Douglass, W. E. B. Dubois, Thurgood Marshall, and James Baldwin, to name only four. Asked to *Discuss, and comment on, three leading 14th Amendment 'race' cases, 1873-96*, our young leader might well oblige us with something of this order:

In the *Slaughter-Houses* the freedmen weren't even in Court. But their rights and the 14th Amendment were. Everybody got *half* slaughtered at the start: All because an association of poor white independent butchers (who'd lost their jobs to a smelly or perhaps not-so-smelly monopoly set up by a "carpetbag legislature") wanted and tried to keep on working—claimed they had a natural, and now, under the 14th, a *constitutional* right to butcher. But the Court couldn't and didn't see it that way, or let them, and shouldn't have either. Because downtown butchering and flies are bad, unsanitary, in New Orleans. . . . "The Court wanted and tried to help everybody, but this time just couldn't," you said. I get the point, and agree "the Judges talked too much, too."

Because in the *Civil Rights Cases* (1883) the slaughtering of this Amendment, and now of the freedmen, kept on—got *almost* finished in fact, using what lawyers described as, and claimed to be, "state action," and what they even persuaded 8 judges to think was real and that the framers had meant "*only* state action," but which really meant—after this decision—*no action at all by anybody*. I forgot to remind you that Congress finally had passed Sumner's Civil Rights Bill in 1875. But this already was 1883 and Justice Bradley—and all the others except Harlan of Kentucky (an ex-slaveholder, mind you: do you suppose he and they understood these things best after all?) thought that since the freedmen had to begin shifting for themselves sometime, now was as good as any. Former slaves couldn't be "special favorites of the laws"—*Forever*, Bradley meant, even if so many still were helpless and uneducated. Besides, "mere discrimination on account of race or color" never had been regarded as a "badge of slavery," not even by or within the experience of *free* Negroes *before* this Amendment, and the Judges all thought things weren't nearly so bad now, or hopefully at least, wouldn't be. . . . So all the Court and Congress could do was enforce this 14th Amendment. "Enforce what? Why, enforce the prohibition"—that "No state shall. . . ." But that couldn't, wouldn't, help anybody, and it didn't. *We* learned that quicker than the Court did.

Because finally in 1896 came *Plessy* v. *Ferguson*. "Separate but Equal!" You could be separate and segregate and *still* be equal—in trains, theaters, schools, housing, any place. Because now you had a *perfect* right—actually a *constitutional* right to be—I mean, not *equal*, but *separate* and *segregate*—especially *to be* separated and segregated! This 14th Amendment, the Waite, Fuller, and White Courts claimed, really hadn't intended anything else. Justice Brown now was blunter about it even than Bradley had been. Cautioned colored people not to be so thin-skinned. Some "merely . . . legal" distinctions "founded in . . . color" had to exist "so long as white men are distinguished from the other race by color." But what of that? Such laws were "reasonable," weren't "arbitrary" —stigmatized only those who felt stigmatized. (The feeler's *"fallacy"* the Justice called it!) . . . Sure enough, "The *object* of the Amendment *undoubtedly* was to enforce the *absolute* equality of the two races before the law. . . ." But from here on, segregation— *now constitutionally sanctioned and enforced*—constituted *absolute* equality"; "racial instincts" just couldn't be eradicated by "legislation." The Constitution of the United States, even this Amendment to it, couldn't raise *"inferiors"* up.

So for *practical* purposes, Sections 1 and 5 *were* declared *unconstitutional*. Actually it was worse even than that: For another 58 years these sections *licensed* and *promoted* what they'd been designed and added to wipe out—the color line. . . . "Confusing," *you* called it. I liked that irony. . . . *Insulting* too, to some of us.

In your final lecture you explained that "The Court has to correct its own errors," "and usually it does." Right—and sooner, faster, at least, than some! . . . So . . . What *next*? What about "state action"? *"Inaction,"* *we* call it. *The Slaughter-Houses—* that's where we see now the trouble really started, where the Court tripped itself! I'll bet you that Justices Miller and Bradley would be astonished—outraged—to see what happened. So soon. So long. . . .

Tell me, then, why did you next go on and blame everything on the draftsman, poor John A. Bingham? "He and the rest of the Joint Committee," you said, "made such a messy, curious job of it." So, too, by that reasoning—*scapegoating*, sir—did Moses and the Almighty with their decalogue! Never mind. "Counterfeit logic!" Lincoln would have nailed such talk. (Remember, *you* told us *that* slave-wife story too!)

What happened here reminds me of a scene on TV: The heavy and the sheriff . . . staring at those three picked Yale locks: "Moughtn't they a-done better goin' to Harvard?" . . . No, mister, *that* was some *more* of our trouble—too many *did* go there, and to Yale and the rest! Too many of the best lock pickers . . . because *after* 1868, almost all the "good" lawyers were on the wrong sides . . . squads of them . . . working for corporations—railroads, steamship lines, hotels—*proving* you couldn't raise "inferiors" up! . . . .

Introduction

    Professor, I sure congratulate you on this course . . . But next year tell more about state *in*action . . . about the sheriffs and the lock pickers.

III

    Were the record limited to these cases, we might indeed despair. For eighty years, the Fourteenth Amendment provided dubious, limited Protection and Process for freedmen and Negroes. But let no one infer from this that Everyman's Constitution proved a dud, or that others met with such frustrations and troubles, still less that "bootstrap constitutionalism" failed to change American mores and folkways, or to reduce longstanding, often thoroughly irrational, prejudices, or to overcome systematic "arbitrary," "unreasonable," "invidious" discrimination in *all* states of the Union.

    Due process-equal protection constitutionalism scored great and enduring successes in these fields. Just how long and how effectively it worked, to protect *corporations* that is, and ultimately to eradicate prejudice and discrimination against *them*, only readers now past middle life can know, and they only if they also know how their ancestors felt about corporations, and made corporations feel in turn.

    There was no "feelers' fallacy" here in the least, and the significant point is that no one claimed any. Without getting detailed, or clinical or morbid, let us say only that down to the 1880's corporations were among the lower forms of American political, economic, and constitutional life, were treated and mistreated accordingly, that corporation managers and lawyers felt, acted, and reacted accordingly, yet with scant, and (it seemed for long) diminishing success.

    The 1870's marked the nadir. Panic. Strikes. Riots. Decade-long depression. Higher taxes and mounting assessments for corporations. Railroad and elevator rates set by legislative fiat, and affirmed by the Supreme Court in the *Granger Cases* (1877), with Chief Justice Waite telling the roads they must seek their relief at the polls, not in the courts. Disinclination of courts, both state and national, to disturb or disrupt the political-regulatory processes of government; hence persistent refusal to overrule legislatures, or to sanction use of the new clauses of the Fourteenth Amendment to throttle regulation —such were the guiding precepts and trends.

    Due process and equal protection, the Supreme Court acknowledged, must be defined and interpreted by "inclusion and exclusion of cases." Yet *exclusion*, in practice, tended to remain the rule, where legislative discretion clearly was involved and justifiable. Mr. Justice Miller, like Chief Justice Waite, sometimes was blunt about it.

"Corporations," he quipped, "lack the human affections." And in *Davidson v. New Orleans* (1878), roundly criticizing counsel and litigants for their "strange misconceptions," and for repeated attempts to misuse due process and equal protection in particular, he dashed hopes by dicta which *seemed* to imply that neither of the two guarantees ever could or would be regarded as a limitation on the state taxing power!

So it went, and in case after case, year by year. Of the nine members of the Supreme Court, only Justice Stephen J. Field, a Union Democrat named by President Lincoln in 1863, regularly dissented in the great corporation and business regulation cases of the 1870's. To worried conservatives and leaders of the corporate bar—and to his friends like Senator Roscoe Conkling of New York—Field alone seemed alive to the dangers, to understand the problems and viewpoint of Business. And it was he who most consistently sought to extend judicial power and judicial review, to honor pleas for broader constitutional process and protection, for large property and for interstate business in particular.

For this there were good and special reasons. Field's 9th (or Pacific) Circuit already had taken its place as the corporate-judicial constitutional storm center which it would continue to be increasingly during the 1880's. Field's family, and many of his friends moreover, were acknowledged leaders in the great entrepreneurial-corporate revolution then under way: brother Cyrus, promoter of the Atlantic cable; brother David Dudley, counsel for Jay Gould and Jim Fisk in the Erie Wars; he himself, friend and confidant of the Stanford-Huntington-Hopkins-Crocker group, the Sacramento Big Four who during the 1860's had built the Central Pacific, garnering construction profits in stocks and bonds that could be fully realized only if monopoly were maintained; and who hence were locked in a titanic conflict, struggling to build a second transcontinental line, the Southern Pacific, *without* a federal bond subsidy, wholly from the earnings of the first, in order to head off and to defeat Tom Scott's and Jay Gould's Texas Pacific, which then was seeking a federal bond subsidy at every session of Congress. For such Titans, Field had unbounded respect and admiration, and he naturally was gravely disturbed by trends and opinion in his beloved California, which he usually visited each summer to hold court as Circuit Justice.

California at this date was a cauldron of hostility, prejudice, and litigation, racial as well as corporate. Hostility and antagonism to the Chinese, and hostility and antagonism to corporations—to the railroads especially for having brought in and employed so many Chinese as contract construction laborers—had merged, fused, and flared to incandescence. Finally, in 1879, had come a new state constitution, one which dismayed and frightened conservatives, which overhauled the system of taxing railroads, *and which barred corporations from employing Chinese aliens!*

Of all the casual alliances, the uneasy and unnatural partnerships, that have prospered American business and American constitutionalism, none ever was more timely, welcome, fateful, and fruitful than the one thus formed. What the freedmen and "persons of the Negro race" shortly, and *in effect,* would lose; what butchers, insurance agents, and ratepayers repeatedly had been unable to gain; this the Chinese of San Francisco and the railroads of California *together* might easily, and now did win. Chinese first; then the railroads; and eventually, of course, corporations generally. It was almost as if California's bigots—San Francisco's so-called Kearneyites and Sandlotters —had managed unwittingly to save everybody: saved the Stanford and the Huntington fortunes, and ultimately endowed a university and founded a magnificent research library. (But only after the vigorous, timely intervention of Circuit Justice Stephen J. Field and Circuit Judge Lorenzo Sawyer, both of whom were fittingly made original members of the governing board of Stanford University.)

Having vainly attacked the new state system of railroad taxation and exhausted their resources in the California courts, the railroads "removed" their cases to the United States Circuit Court and in August–September, 1882, were heard by Justice Field sitting with Judge Sawyer. Both judges held that the new assessment system denied the companies the equal protection of the laws. Judge Sawyer expressly held corporations to be constitutional "persons"; Justice Field agreed, but phrased his own opinion more narrowly and discreetly: corporate shareholders were "persons" in any event—persons whose "property" merited protection, and who must and now would receive protection. With all state and county railroad taxes for three years hanging in the balance, the counties appealed to the Supreme Court of the United States.

Now occurred one of the staged entrances, imagined climaxes, grand flukes, and unparalleled fiascoes of our constitutional and legal history—that celebrated argument, made by former Senator Roscoe Conkling in the *San Mateo* case, December 22, 1882, before the full bench in a jammed courtroom tingling with expectancy.

Conkling of course spoke as a former draftsman of the Fourteenth Amendment, and he capitalized this position fully. Almost seventeen years before he had been one of the eight House Republicans on the Joint Committee—one who, unbeknown to most (if not all of this audience) for long, and at first, had voted *against* John A. Bingham's due process-equal protection drafts! Now Conkling dramatically produced the manuscript journal of the Committee, and based an elaborate argument upon it.

In the seventeen-year interim, as New York state boss and United States Senator, as President Grant's confidant and chief of the now-beaten "Stalwarts" and "third term" forces, Conkling had posed, sulked, feuded, bullied, and browbeat his way, gaining fame, but little regard, as the great egoist, hater, and cynic of a mediocre Senate; the imperious, lavender-vested dandy with the "Hyperion curl" —transfixed for all time in 1866 by his archrival James G. Blaine, for that curl, and for "his haughty disdain, his grandiloquent swell, his majestic, super-eminent, overpowering, turkey-gobbler strut." Pure "bouffe" and "stage exaggeration," beyond even "burlesque," Henry Adams characterized him, a grossly overrated man even in the Gilded Age, a "leader" who during twenty years in Congress had left no legislative monuments whatever; a sneering, derisive wounder ("Rutherfraud Hayes," "snivel service"); still nursing insensate hatred for Blaine; and who in May, 1881, had made as galling, miscalculated, farcical an exit as any politician possibly could make. Having broken with President Garfield over "senatorial courtesy," and over the New York patronage, as earlier he had broken with President Hayes, Conkling and his junior colleague, "Me-too" Tom Platt, spitefully resigned their seats, counting on immediate re-election at the hands of a servile New York legislature. Haplessly, the demented assassin Guiteau, calling himself a "Conkling Stalwart," intervened, and fatally wounded President Garfield. On the fifty-sixth ballot thereafter, Conkling failed ignominiously of re-election. "SPOILSMAN. SPOILER. SPOILED!" were the headlines and refrain. Declining President Arthur's tender of a nomination to the Supreme Court, as in 1873 he had declined President Grant's offer of the Chief Justiceship, Conkling turned belatedly to the corporate bar, won a retainer from Jay Gould, and then, on February 8, 1882, another for $5,000 from Collis P. Huntington. Later in the year, the word went out: Roscoe Conkling would argue the great *California Railroad Tax Cases* before the Supreme Court.

The rest is history, without parallel, without recourse. How it ravelled and unravelled over eighty years is one of the threads of our book, and need not be further anticipated here. Save this one fact, very tardily perceived, yet at last unmistakable: In his briefs and argument for the railroads, Conkling did not tell the Court that he

Introduction

and his fellow draftsmen intentionally had inserted the word "person" in the due process and equal protection clauses in order to embrace or protect corporations. Coming seventeen years late, a statement—even an inference to that effect—would have been prima facie, self-exposing, self-defeating nonsense. Doctrinally and forensically, a curbed state taxing power—a taxing power curbed by the Fourteenth Amendment—and not the establishment of the constitutional corporate "person" as such, was the one indispensable point for these railroads. To get the full Supreme Court to accept, and preferably to presume this point, as Field and Sawyer had presumed it at Circuit, was the burden and the objective. And Justice Miller's *Davidson* and *Slaughter-House* dicta of course were the primary hazards and obstacles.

In his attempt to attain these ends, as will appear shortly, Conkling resorted to fraud and misquotation—reared an edifice that has taken eighty years to unlock and to level. All that need be said here is that the *San Mateo* case was not decided on its merits, but that in 1886 a statement by Chief Justice Waite appeared in the United States Reports which had the effect, without formal opinion, of declaring corporations to be "persons" within the meaning of the equal protection clause. (This statement too, we lately have learned from the Waite Papers, in likelihood was not at all what it so long appeared to be, but was, itself, the result of another fluke and misunderstanding.)

Yet fluke or not, the important thing in the 1880's, 1890's, and after, was that corporations had access to constitutional process and protection which earlier had been, once expressly, and very often tacitly, denied. "Corporations," as Mr. Justice Douglas has put it, "now [were] armed with constitutional prerogatives." Things for them, for judges and legislatures, and for business generally never would be the same again. Corporations attained this protection, it will be observed, at the very time members of the Negro race in the wake of the *Civil Rights* and *Plessy* decisions were losing out.

IV

Here was, here is, surely, contrast indeed—contrast of fortunes, contrast of remedies, most strikingly of all, contrast in treatment and in result. Process and Protection, freely and fully invoked and extended in the one field, worked wonders, raised hopes, status, and performance. Corporations, capitalizing their new protection and opportunities, improved their lot and environment, demonstrated undreamed-of capacity, countered prejudice, and finally—as everyone can see—overcame it. What many of us overlook, or forget, is that corporations gained this protection and process under (and by successfully invoking use of) that phraseology which the draftsmen had *intended* for Negroes, gained it *while Negroes usually could not gain or attain it under the same Amendment from the same governments, legislatures, and courts.* "Persons," in short, got switched. "Persons" got lost and found—and so, consequently, did the *intended* Process and Protection. And the framers it was, we shall see now more at length, who shortly got tagged with the blame in the one field, and with *both* the blame and the false *credit* (for long) in the other! "Constitutional Persons—Lost, Found, Missing," thus is the title that covers and that epitomizes the five decades of Fourteenth Amendment history from the 1890's to the 1940's.

Not merely to the naïve, nor to the deserted, 1886–1937, but to sophisticates as well, every overblown extension of economic due process to corporations, like every breach and curtailment of protection to the freedmen and their descendants, made members of the Joint Committee *look* more and more like bunglers, cozeners, or worse; and made Roscoe Conkling, that tardy claimant and unsuspected forger and talebearer, *look* more and more like Mephistopheles—seer and historian in spite of himself. John A. Bingham, by contrast—his (and the Civil War generation's) antislavery zeal, theory, and motivations now forgotten and ignored—*looked* more and more the perfect dupe, accomplice, or worse.

The passing of the antislavery generation, the steady decline in natural rights-natural law thinking, the rise of legal positivism, and the tendency to write and study constitutional history more and more from the Supreme Court and majority opinions alone, all contributed to this bizarre canonization, inversion, deracialization.

Curiously, it was none other than Senator Henry Cabot Lodge, Brahman historian and "the scholar in politics," who authoritatively assembled and certified the Conkling canon. Addressing the Senate on January 8, 1915, on behalf of his motion to reprint the Joint Committee journal which B. B. Kendrick recently had unearthed and edited, Lodge noted that 6,000 copies had been printed by Senate order in 1884. For some reason these never had circulated. A single unbound pamphlet copy of this edition remained at the Printing Office library; and no other was known. Yet leading statesmen—Fessenden, Conkling, Reverdy Johnson in the Senate, and Thaddeus Stevens of the House—had served on this committee. The Fourteenth Amendment was their handiwork, this was the record of their deliberations. "In the case of San Mateo County against Southern

Introduction 19

Pacific Railroad [Lodge continued] Mr. Conkling introduced in his argument excerpts from the Journal, then unprinted, to show that the fourteenth amendment did not apply solely to negroes, [sic] but applied to persons, real and artificial of any kind. *It was owing to this, undoubtedly, that the Court extended it to corporations."* (Italics added.)

Thus was the legend launched—from Beacon Hill and Capitol Hill, be it noted, by a Brahman historian and a Harvard Law graduate; not by "that economic determinist," Charles A. Beard.

Constitutional laissez faire had reached another of its periodic flood tides, 1908–1914. Workmen's compensation, minimum wage, child labor, utility regulation and valuation laws and orders were struck down in series. "Some things," Tories cried—too early perhaps, and too possessively—*"can't* be done in a government like *ours!"*

Myth often is the only counter to myth. So *counter*myth now began to humble and chasten. In *The Rise of American Civilization* (1927) Charles and Mary Beard made Bingham and Conkling the masterminds, the veritable swingmen of America's destiny and history. The Beards did this, moreover, at the very time that conservative majorities on the Supreme Court, overplaying the constitutional headsman, again were making the Amendment, and the Court's own powers and decisions, matters of intense controversy, threatened impasse, and ultimate stalemate.

So it finally came about—and before the end of another decade— that a mere *half* disproof of this mythic "Conspiracy Theory" sufficed to make overblown *economic-corporate* due process suddenly repugnant and untenable. More important, more significant still, findings and evidence unearthed in the course of that disproof led research on—prodded and shamed scholarship into—retracing, restudying, retrieving, and finally reconstituting, those long "lost" antislavery backgrounds, origins, and "persons" without which this Amendment had become incomprehensible, yet with which, as already shown, its phraseology and objectives are as clear as they are essential, forthright, historic, and commendable.

Step by step, in this fashion, and decade by decade—"word for word, syllable for syllable" (to requote first Bingham, then Kendrick, then the Beards!)—the draftsmanship, the "original understanding," the objectives, and above all, those *unintended accomplishments* of Everyman's Constitution got explored, and reassessed.

At the same time, that other rejected-depressed side of this now dual/split constitutional "personality" also was becoming manifest, as one by one the disasters, flukes, reversals, defeats, and frustrations came ever more clearly to light.

There thus emerged, gradually and tardily, yet in still fuller scope and detail, that stark, inescapable contrast between the *corporate* cases and trends on the one hand and the *racial* cases and trends on the other. Stronger evidence of national failure, inertia, and inversion; more striking evidence of judicial bias and historical error, could hardly be found or imagined. Historical evidence and precept thus supported—and thus sustained—the now manifest resolve of the Hughes, Stone, Vinson, and Warren Courts to intervene more actively and more effectively against *racial* discrimination—to take the initiative and to lead in this field, with full, triple *constitutional* mandate—just as the predecessor Waite, Fuller, and White Courts had so boldly and successfully done, in that other field, at only plaintiffs' urging, and by *self-construed* mandate.

V

The wonder, then, is not that the Beards nodded. Only that their Homeric nod proved so timely, so beneficial. "Personality" disorders were cleared up, quickly and finally; but the point is that *corporate gains* held good, were unaffected! Thus that "corporate miracle" can be seen today for what it truly is: The Corporate-Racial *Parable*. "Prejudice *is* vincible," just as the abolitionists said, just as the framers of the Fourteenth Amendment reasoned and intended. Process and Protection *do* work, and *have* worked, wonders. Nothing else works better. Little else worked at all. Process and Protection, so long, so fully, so successfully accorded in one field thus set the stage and underscore the precept: "Apply these same remedies. *Due* Process. *Equal* Protection. Work these cures again. At last. *Now!*"

Everyman's Constitution is uniquely, ideally suited to wipe out these scourges by its process and by its protection, just as its framers thought, just as the Supreme Court itself already has demonstrated. National history, national honor, national interest and policy—to say nothing of *inter*national and *personal*—all demand affirmative action. More than ever, it is Everyman's Constitution or none.

We are presently celebrating the centennial of the Fourteenth Amendment. This story is more timely and pertinent than ever; for all centennials tend to be confessionals and carillons commingled, just as this one is certain to be. To understand Sections 1 and 5 and their history is to gain a clearer view and grasp of what America and American Constitutionalism are and have been, what they mean to

Introduction 21

Everyman, and what Everyman alone can make them mean, be, and do.

In brief, this book studies, reconstructs, and retells the story of our constitutional Odyssey from the American Iliad. Or, to put it in more modern, or at least nineteenth-century terms, it retells the story of our constitutional derailment and *re*railment: Where and why our Fourteenth Amendment left the track; how it got routed, rerouted, turntabled, and put back on the track; what happened before, what happened after and in between; and what must happen now, and next. These are the themes, the segments, the whole of the story.

And like Chanticleer, these essays collected here observed and heralded a constitutional dawn. No one, having watched and waited for that dawn, and having worked half a lifetime deciphering the Beards' hypothesis, Conkling's argument, the antislavery backgrounds, and the frontier tax-title backgrounds, will ever claim more; but no one, I think, ought to claim less. History and Criticism *are* undervalued, indispensable parts of Constitutionalism. Scholarship *itself* is a process—a vital, primary part of *due* process.

This, then, is the conclusion and fervent wish: May these essays, as finally gathered, corrected, edited, and supplemented, contribute to that Process and that Protection they again herald and celebrate.

[CHAPTER 1]

The "Conspiracy Theory" of the Fourteenth Amendment: Part I

EDITORIAL NOTE. "Publish or perish" is a veritable campus dirge today. During the Great Depression it had a livelier beat. For a freelance writer-clerk, learning while collecting rejection slips at the University of California (after a first-prize start), the excitement of the chase soon provided the richest returns. By 1934, after receiving three-fifths of a cent a word for a longish serial on the Argonauts' Bay Bridges, 1849–1860,[1] I was encouraged to research an economic-entrepreneurial-great-law-case-history of California, 1860–1890, "The Golden Pageant." The impact of the corporation—the railroad in particular—would be the core theme. I spent two exciting years in working out the cost and construction profits of the Central Pacific-Southern Pacific promoters, covering the Big Four's correspondence at Stanford, revelling in Collis P. Huntington's letters to his associates telling of the financial and legal battles.

The *San Mateo* and related *California Railroad Tax Cases* of the 1880's were of course equally relevant to this story and to the Fourteenth Amendment. Events, furthermore, were moving to conjunction and climax. *The Rise of American Civilization* now had immense appeal and prestige. "Triumphant Business Enterprise" had faltered, and the Civil War, treated as "The Second American Revolution," had ironic bearings and overtones. Only a few skeptics, however, Zechariah Chafee[2] and Walton Hamilton[3] among them, had even questioned the Beards' thesis. Hamilton, though he soon came to regret having tagged it "the conspiracy theory," most neatly and wryly hit the mark: the Beardian account, he observed in 1932, "endows . . . captains of a rising industry with a capacity for forward plan . . . they are not usually understood to possess."

Could the Beards have been naïve, have nodded perhaps? What of

---

[1] *When the Bay Bridge Was a Joke*, SAN FRANCISCO NEWS, Aug. 27–Sept. 15, 1934.
[2] Book review, 41 HARV. L. REV., 265, 267 (1927).
[3] See Chapter 1, *infra*, n. 13.

Conkling? Bingham? *Were* these clauses an *intended* sanctuary for corporations? Or had they, perhaps, simply got taken over, misappropriated as such?

Fatefully, I first investigated, not the use which Conkling had made of the Joint Committee journal, but his and the Beards' statements which were most easily checked in the pages, and particularly in the petition columns, of the *Congressional Globe* and debates. Thus I discovered first those insurance and express company "petitions and bills" which *seemingly* corroborated the inferences Conkling *seemingly* had drawn and which the Beards, even more tautly, ambiguously, and significantly, *seemingly* had redrawn, in their accounts! (The "seeminglys," needless to say, are retrospective insights and wisdom!)

I also found, about this same time, but merely scanned, Bingham's main speeches of 1866, and, if I remember correctly, his speech on the Admission of Oregon, of 1859. But before either the petitions or these speeches could be assayed, I had also encountered, and run down, while "citation-chasing" in Charles Warren's *The Supreme Court in United States History*,[4] some equally fascinating leads and references. These suggested that Mr. Justice Field had seized on certain cases he had decided at circuit in 1874–1879 to advance his then-minority views on the scope of the Fourteenth Amendment. Later in 1882–1883 Field's opinions in these nonappealable or nonappealed Chinese habeas corpus cases had served as almost the only "precedent" and support for his circuit opinions in the *San Mateo* and *Santa Clara* cases, which extended the protection of the Fourteenth Amendment to corporations. California bigots, it appeared, had lit and held the candle for the American corporate bar. Field's "Ninth Circuit law," in any event, was timely and germane, for everyone knew, and now declared the corporate "person" to be, the linchpin of judicially-sanctioned "liberty to contract" and laissez faire.

Right at this point, and almost simultaneously, two more grappling hooks caught hold. During his last years Justice Field had systematically collected and destroyed his correspondence. Two collections, however, survived, unknown to Carl B. Swisher and most earlier biographers. Four letters written to Professor John Norton Pomeroy, and reproduced in Chapter 3, *infra*, first were recovered from Pomeroy heirs. Then at Portland, voluminously and faithfully preserved in the library of the Oregon Historical Society, I located the professional papers—the lifetime correspondence indeed—of

---

[4] Vol. 3, p. 409, n. 1.

Field's friend and subordinate, Matthew P. Deady, United States District Judge for Oregon, 1859–1893.

This was treasure beyond all reckoning: intimate personal correspondence that shortly was found to cover four episodes and matters now of vital current interest: first, the details of those Chinese habeas corpus cases, and hence of the genesis and proliferation of the Ninth Circuit Law; then Field's role in the various *California Railroad Tax Cases*; finally, and above all, the secret of Field's presidential aspirations, and the continued activity of friends in his behalf, in the campaigns of 1880 and 1884: his often-declared intent—if only he might have been nominated and elected—to enlarge the Supreme Court to twenty-one members, to pack it with twelve staunch conservatives. In this way, Field planned to reverse the *Granger*, the *Sinking Fund* and other obnoxious decisions, and make the due process clauses of the Fifth and the Fourteenth Amendments a bastion of laissez faire.

Coincidence often sharpens history and memory, and it did and does here: The day I began hauling up this treasure was "the day the Old Court went too far"! June 1, 1936: *Morehead v. Tipaldo*,[5] decided by 5 to 4 vote, with Mr. Justice Roberts as "swingman," of course held bad, as a violation of due process and as an infringement of laundryowners' and laundry workers' liberty to contract, the New York Womens' Minimum Wage Law. Earlier in the term, Court majorities had knocked out, in whole or in part, thirteen acts of Congress, much of the New Deal program. Constitutional impasse now was absolute. *Neither* Congress nor the states had power to govern. Field's Circuit Law had reblossomed, and gone utterly to seed. Almost immediately, therefore, critics were clamoring for the very nostrum which Field, in these letters spread before me, had urged and anticipated: "Pack the Supreme Court of the United States!"

Before I even could finish a three-article draft, President Roosevelt, on February 5, 1937, presented *his* Court Plan to Congress. As hurriedly, and as fully as possible, I reworked the story and submitted it first to *Harpers'*, then to the *New Republic*. . . . But it still was too dense, overtechnical: "Unbelievable without documentation." Not for Everyman.

Certainly not many free lances have had and muffed such a chance as this, or sat silent and frustrated in a hurricane's eye. To the friends who have asked, or wondered, *this* is the reason that I "gave away such treasure to law reviews."

More material now, neither was needed nor wanted. Yet more ma-

---

[5] 298 U. S. 587.

terial—the final breathtaking discovery, and a wholly fresh start—it had to be. For presently, routinely checking Conkling's *San Mateo* argument against B. B. Kendrick's edition of the Joint Committee journal, I came upon that amazing, that still almost incredible, misquotation and forgery.

By the mid-1930's, of course, the Conspiracy Theory had become daily gossip, an article of national faith and popular enlightenment. The Constitution, Due Process, Equal Protection—now were Everyman's business without doubt. *People* were "persons" too, even though sometimes not quite the "persons" corporations were. Everyone was reading, citing, quoting, *The Rise*: "Bingham, you know, and Conkling *planned* it that way . . . slipped in the corporations' joker!"

Fantasy! we should say soon enough, and warrantably, today. *Any* constitutional amendment, which must be passed by two-thirds majorities, ratified by three-fourths of the states, and *then* interpreted judicially case by case, is an unlikely enough attraction, and no shortcut at all, for schemers or cozeners. Constitutional meaning is sociological, not just verbal. Intuitive draftsmanship is apt to be duped draftsmanship. (The Electoral College, for example.) Devious draftsmanship is an absurdity. Constitutional meaning develops in "cases and controversies," and to impute foresight is to ignore this, to invert the order, to mistake result for design.

All this skeptics hinted and suggested in the 1930's, but without success. The Supreme Court had simply *made* foresight *look* too easy!

The Beards' hypothesis, it can be seen today, was a mirror and reflex of the times. Eventually also, it was an ingenious, intuitive, blessed corrective. Economic determinism, as Eric Goldman[6] and Douglass Adair[7] have pointed out, often served as the Progressive era's answer to a sterile, legal determinism. Economic interpretation of the Constitution countered economic *mis*interpretation.

The Beards' prima facie case was essentially a reduced, reversed facsimile of Conkling's—minus his misquotations. What the Beards really did was cram the whole "due process revolution," and by implication America's failure to pursue and realize the avowed racial objectives of the Civil War Amendments—sixty years of constitutional history—into this one word, "person," misreading result as a kind of perverse intent, but thereby focusing all the more mercilessly

---

[6] GOLDMAN, RENDEZVOUS WITH DESTINY: A HISTORY OF MODERN AMERICAN REFORM (rev. Vintage ed., 1959), Chapter 7.
[7] Adair, *The Tenth Federalist Revisited*, 8 WILLIAM & MARY QTLY., 48–67 (1951).

on gross and growing miscarriages. Details were left open and conjectural; law and history were compressed and oversimplified beyond reason. Not, however, beyond precedent; for Conkling and the Supreme Court both had invited this very result.

So not since Montesquieu has a misapprehension proved richer in irony or benefits. Mark well this feat and fluke, this same corporate innocent that had ushered in judicialized laissez faire, returning now to usher it out. The same legal fiction, word play, spurious presumptions, silences, and semantic confusion that so often had helped Conkling, and later the whole corporate bar and High Court, so easily to treat complex problems of business taxation, classification, and regulation as exercises in nothing but formal logic—now a Nemesis indeed. Conkling's own daring "law office history"—misread and boiled down—now the antidote-emetic for that judicially-developed, judicially-impacted laissez faire which, while not implicit in the corporate "person," had come to rest jurisdictionally, and very vulnerably, upon it. To a degree, in a manner never excelled, and none too soon, Charles and Mary Beard made Everyman his own constitutional lawyer.

This first part of the "Conspiracy Theory" thus was written easily and quickly in June–July of 1937, submitted to the *Yale Law Journal* in October, accepted in December, and published in the January, 1938, number. One week after publication, on January 31, 1938, Mr. Justice Black delivered his lone, dramatic dissent,[8] attacking the constitutional corporate "person," citing the *Yale Law Journal* and this article.

After seven years, a footnote in history!

* * * *

Four pages of Olympian prose institute and project our inquiry. In the climactic section of their climactic chapter on the Civil War as "The Second American Revolution," the Beards wrote as follows of the Fourteenth Amendment, its purposes, interpretation, and draftsmanship:[9]

"While winning its essential economic demands in the federal sphere, the party of industrial progress and sound money devoted fine calculation to another great desideratum—the restoration and extension of federal judicial supremacy over the local legislatures

---

[8] Connecticut General Life Insurance Co. v. Johnson, 303 U. S. 77, 83, 87 (1938).
[9] Charles A. Beard and Mary R. Beard, *The Rise of American Civilization*, Volume II, pages 111–114. Copyright, 1927, by The Macmillan Company, New York. Reprinted by permission.

which had been so troublesome since the age of Daniel Shays. Restoration was heartily desired because the original limitations imposed by the Constitution on the power of the state to issue money and impair contracts had been practically destroyed by adroit federal judges imbued with the spirit of Jacksonian Democracy. An extension of federal control was perhaps more heartily desired because, for nationalists of the Federalist and Whig tradition, those limitations had been pitifully inadequate even when applied strictly by Chief Justice Marshall—inadequate to meet the requirements of individuals and corporations that wanted to carry on their business in their own way, immune from legislative interference.

"In all this there was nothing esoteric. Among conservative adepts in federal jurisprudence the need for more efficient judicial protection had been keenly felt for some time; and when the problem of defining the rights of Negroes came before Congress in the form of a constitutional amendment, experts in such mysteries took advantage of the occasion to enlarge the sphere of national control over the states, by including among the safeguards devised for Negroes a broad provision for the rights of all 'persons,' natural and artificial, individual and corporate.

"Their project was embodied in the second part of the Fourteenth Amendment in the form of a short sentence intended by the man who penned it to make a revolution in the federal Constitution. The sentence reads: 'No state shall make or enforce any law which shall abridge the privileges or immunities of citizens of the United States; nor shall any state deprive any person of life, liberty, or property without due process of law, nor deny to any person within its jurisdiction the equal protection of the laws.'

"Just how this provision got into the draft of the Fourteenth Amendment was not generally known at the time of its adoption but in after years the method was fully revealed by participants in the process. By the end of the century an authentic record, open to all, made the operation as plain as day. According to the evidence now available, there were two factions in the congressional committee which framed the Amendment—one bent on establishing the rights of Negroes; the other determined to take in the whole range of national economy. Among the latter was a shrewd member of the House of Representatives, John A. Bingham, a prominent Republican and a successful railroad lawyer from Ohio familiar with the possibilities of jurisprudence; it was he who wrote the mysterious sentence containing the 'due process' clause in the form in which it now stands; it was he who finally forced it upon the committee by persistent efforts.

"In a speech delivered in Congress a few years later, Bingham explained his purpose in writing it. He had read, he said, in the case of Barron *versus* the Mayor and Council of Baltimore, how the city had taken private property for public use, as alleged without compensation, and how Chief Justice Marshall had been compelled to hold that there was no redress in the Supreme Court of the United States—no redress simply because the first ten Amendments to the Constitution were limitations on Congress, not on the states. Deeming this hiatus a grave legal defect in the work of the Fathers, Bingham designed 'word for word and syllable for syllable' the cabalistic clause of the Fourteenth Amendment in order, he asserted, that 'the poorest man in his hovel . . . may be as secure in his person and property as the prince in his palace or the king upon his throne.' Hence the provision was to apply not merely to former slaves struggling for civil rights but to all persons, rich and poor, individuals and corporations, under the national flag.

"Long afterward Roscoe Conkling, the eminent corporation lawyer of New York, a colleague of Bingham on the congressional committee, confirmed this view. While arguing a tax case for a railway company before the Supreme Court in 1882, he declared that the protection of freedmen was by no means the sole purpose of the Fourteenth Amendment. 'At the time the Fourteenth Amendment was ratified,' he said, 'individuals and joint stock companies were appealing for congressional and administrative protection against invidious and discriminating state and local taxes. . . . That complaints of oppression in respect of property and other rights made by citizens of northern states who took up residence in the South were rife in and out of Congress, none of us can forget. . . . Those who devised the Fourteenth Amendment wrought in grave sincerity. . . . They planted in the Constitution a monumental truth to stand four square to whatever wind might blow. That truth is but the golden rule, so entrenched as to curb the many who would do to the few as they would not have the few do to them.'

"In this spirit, Republican lawmakers restored to the Constitution the protection for property which Jacksonian judges had whittled away and made it more sweeping in its scope by forbidding states, in blanket terms, to deprive any person of life, liberty, or property without due process of law. By a few words skillfully chosen every act of every state and local government which touched adversely the rights of persons and property was made subject to review and liable to annulment by the Supreme Court at Washington, appointed by the President and Senate for life and far removed from local feelings and prejudices.

"Although the country at large did not grasp the full meaning of the Fourteenth Amendment while its adoption was pending, some far-sighted editors and politicians realized at the time that it implied a fundamental revolution in the Constitution, at least as interpreted by Chief Justice Taney. Ohio and New Jersey Democrats, reckoning that it would make the Supreme Court at Washington the final arbiter in all controversies over the powers of local governments, waged war on it, carrying the fight into the state legislatures and forcing the repeal of resolutions approving the Amendment even after they had been duly sealed. As a matter of course all the southern states were still more fiercely opposed to the Amendment but they were compelled to ratify it under federal military authority as the price of restoration to the Union. Thus the triumphant Republican minority, in possession of the federal government and the military power, under the sanction of constitutional forms, subdued the states for all time to the unlimited jurisdiction of the federal Supreme Court."

[CHAPTER 1]

"No state shall . . . deprive any person of life, liberty, or property without due process of law, nor deny to any person . . . the equal protection of the laws."

SECTION 1, FOURTEENTH AMENDMENT

IN AN ARGUMENT before the Supreme Court of the United States in 1882[1] Roscoe Conkling, a former member of the Joint Congressional Committee which in 1866 drafted the Fourteenth Amendment, produced for the first time the manuscript journal of the Committee, and by means of extensive quotations and pointed comment conveyed the impression that he and his colleagues in drafting the due process and equal protection clauses intentionally used the word "person" in order to include corporations. "At the time the Fourteenth Amendment was ratified," he declared, "individuals and joint stock companies were appealing for congressional and administrative protection against invidious and discriminating State and local taxes. One instance was that of an express company, whose stock was owned largely by citizens of the State of New York . . . ." The unmistakable inference was that the Joint Committee had taken cog-

---

1 See San Mateo County v. Southern Pacific R.R., 116 U. S. 138. A printed copy of the *Oral Argument of Roscoe Conkling* is preserved in a volume entitled SAN MATEO CASE, ARGUMENTS AND DECISIONS, in the Hopkins Railroad Collection of the Library of Stanford University. It is this copy which I have used and cite hereafter as CONKLING'S ARGUMENT; see Appendix I for a paged reprint of the constitutional portions of this ARGUMENT.

nizance of these appeals and had drafted its text with particular regard for corporations.

Coming from a man who had twice declined a seat on the Supreme Bench,[2] who spoke from first-hand knowledge, and who submitted a manuscript record in support of his stand, so dramatic an argument could not fail to make a profound impression. Within the next few years the Supreme Court began broadening its interpretation of the Fourteenth Amendment, and early in 1886 it unanimously affirmed Conkling's proposition, namely that corporations were "persons" within the meaning of the equal protection clause.[3] It is literally true therefore that Roscoe Conkling's argument sounded the death knell of the narrow "Negro-race theory" of the Fourteenth Amendment expounded by Justice Miller in the *Slaughter-House* cases. By doing this it cleared the way for the modern development of due process of law and the corresponding expansion of the Court's discretionary powers over social and economic legislation. Viewed in perspective, the argument is one of the landmarks in American constitutional history, an important turning point in our social and economic development.

Conkling's argument has figured prominently in historical writing since 1914 when B. B. Kendrick unearthed and edited the manuscript copy of the Journal which Conkling used in court.[4] Checking the record in the light of his major propositions, historians became convinced of the fundamental truth of Conkling's story. Repeatedly, it appeared from the Journal, the Joint Committee had distinguished

---

[2] Once as Chief Justice, *vice* Chase, in 1873; again as Associate Justice, *vice* Hunt, in 1882. Chief Justice Waite and Justice Blatchford thus both occupied seats which had been declined by Conkling.

[3] See Waite, J., in Santa Clara County v. Southern Pacific R.R., 118 U. S. 394, 396 (1886). This case involved the same questions as the *San Mateo* case argued three years before.

[4] THE JOURNAL OF THE JOINT COMMITTEE OF FIFTEEN ON RECONSTRUCTION (1914). The Journal itself is printed in Part I, pp. 37–129. The "Introduction," pp. 17–36, gives an interesting account of its history and the circumstances of discovery. It is revealed that 6,000 copies of the Journal were printed by the order of the Senate in February, 1884 (while the *San Mateo* case was still before the Supreme Court). For some unexplained reason these copies never circulated, a single printed copy of the edition being preserved in the Government Printing Office. This copy was used by Horace E. Flack in the preparation of his monograph, THE ADOPTION OF THE FOURTEENTH AMENDMENT (1908). But it was not until 1911 and the publication of Hannis Taylor's THE ORIGIN AND GROWTH OF THE AMERICAN CONSTITUTION (1911), wherein attention was directed to Conkling's argument, that the full historical importance of the manuscript was noted. It should be added that Professor Kendrick was concerned with the bearing of the Journal on matters pertaining to Reconstruction, and referred only incidentally to the later use made by Conkling. This fact explains the failure to note the discrepancies in Conkling's quotations from the Journal.

in its drafts in the use of the words "person" and "citizen."[5] Under no circumstances could the terms have been confused. Moreover, as the Committee had persistently used the term "person" in those clauses which applied to property rights and the term "citizen" in those clauses which applied to political rights, the force of this distinction seemed plain: corporations as artificial persons, had indeed been among the intended beneficiaries of the Fourteenth Amendment. Convinced on this point, historians developed an interesting theory: the drafting of the Fourteenth Amendment had assumed something of the character of a conspiracy, with the due process and equal protection clauses inserted as *double entendres*. Laboring ostensibly in the interests of the freedmen and of the "loyal white citizens of the South," the astute Republican lawyers who made up the majority of the Committee had intentionally used language which gave corporations and business interests generally increased judicial protection as against State legislatures.

What appeared to be corroboration for this viewpoint was presently found in the speeches[6] of Representative John A. Bingham, the Ohio Congressman and railroad lawyer who almost alone of the members of the Joint Committee had been responsible for the phraseology of Section One. Bingham, it appeared both from the Journal and the debates on the floor of the House, had at all times shown a zealous determination to secure to "all persons" everywhere "equal protection in the rights of property."[7] Moreover, he had evinced an extraordinary preference for the due process clause and had developed and defended its phraseology in most vigorous fashion. As no other member of the Joint Committee, or of Congress, gave evidence of a similar desire to protect property rights, and none manifested his partiality for the due process clause, it seemed logical to conclude that Bingham's purposes had in fact been far more subtle and comprehensive than was ever appreciated at the time. Bingham had been the master-mind who "put over" this draft upon

---

[5] KENDRICK, *op. cit. supra* note 4, at 50–51, 56, 60–61 for striking examples.

[6] CONG. GLOBE, 39th Cong., 1st Sess. (1866), 429, 1034, 1064–1065, 1089–1095, 1292.

[7] Originally Bingham's draft was phrased in the positive form: "*Congress shall have power* to make all laws necessary and proper to secure to all persons in every State within this Union equal protection in their rights of life, liberty and property." Later, a clause was added giving Congress power to "secure to all *citizens* the same immunities and also equal political rights and privileges." These clauses were the embryonic forms out of which the later phraseology developed. Early drafts made no mention of "due process of law." Not until the House had virtually rejected the Amendment on the grounds that it gave Congress too sweeping powers—thus compelling a change from the early positive to the present negative form ("no State shall . . .")—was the due process phraseology inserted. Bingham's early speeches reveal, however, that he had had due process of law in mind from the very beginning.

an unsuspecting country. The fact that he had tried and failed to secure the inclusion of a "just compensation" clause in Section One as still another restraint upon the States' powers over property,[8] and the fact that in 1871,[9] five years after the event, he declared he had framed the section "letter for letter and syllable for syllable" merely served to strengthen these suspicions.

Impressed by this cumulative evidence, and alive to its historical implications, Charles A. and Mary R. Beard, in 1927, developed in their *Rise of American Civilization* what is still, a decade later, the most precise statement of the conspiracy theory. Undocumented, and with conclusions implicit rather than explicit, the Beards' thesis was this: Bingham, "a shrewd . . . and successful railroad lawyer, . . . familiar with the possibilities of jurisprudence," had had much broader purposes than his colleagues. Whereas they were "bent on establishing the rights of Negroes," he was "determined to take in the whole range of national economy." Toward this end he had drafted the due process and equal protection clauses and forced them upon the Committee by persistent efforts. Quoting Bingham's speeches and Conkling's argument in support of the view that corporations had been among the intended beneficiaries of the draft, the authors concluded:[10]

> "In this spirit, Republican lawmakers restored to the Constitution the protection for property which Jacksonian judges had whittled away and made it more sweeping in its scope by forbidding states, in blanket terms, to deprive any person of life, liberty, or property without due process of law. By a few words *skillfully chosen* every act of every state and local government which touched adversely the rights of persons and property was made subject to review and liable to annulment by the Supreme Court at Washington."

Thus, while the Beards nowhere expressly state that Bingham was guilty of a form of conspiracy, this is none the less a fair inference from their account, and it is one which has repeatedly been drawn. Numerous writers,[11] accepting the Beards' account and popularizing it, have supplied more explicit interpretations. Thus, E. S. Bates, in

---

[8] KENDRICK, *op. cit. supra* note 4, at 85. Bingham made this attempt at the meeting of the Committee on April 21, 1866. The adverse vote was 7 to 5, with three members absent.

[9] CONG. RECORD, 42nd Cong., 1st Sess. (1871) Appendix, at 83–85.

[10] Vol. II, p. 111–113 (italics added).

[11] See, *e.g.*, Lerner, *The Supreme Court and American Capitalism* (1933) 42 YALE L. J. 668, 691; DAGGETT, PRINCIPLES OF INLAND TRANSPORTATION (1934) 436–437; JOSEPHSON, THE ROBBER BARONS (1934) 52.

his *Story of Congress,* declares that Bingham and Conkling in inserting the due process phraseology, "smuggled" into the Fourteenth Amendment "a capitalist joker."[12]

Despite widespread acceptance and a prestige which derives from the Beards' sponsorship, the conspiracy theory has not gone unchallenged. Numerous writers have expressed varying degrees of disapproval and skepticism.[13] Constitutional historians in particular appear reluctant to accept its implications, although they, any more than the sponsoring school of social historians, have not as yet presented their case in documented detail. One thus observes the curious paradox of a theory which cuts across the whole realm of American constitutional and economic history and which is itself a subject for increasing speculation and controversy, yet which has developed piecemeal, without systematic formulation or criticism.

How extraordinary certain aspects of this situation are may be judged from the fact that one is now left wholly in the dark as to the nature and degree of conspiratorial intent imputed to Bingham and his colleagues. Is one to believe, for example, that these men determined from the first to devise phraseology which included corporations? Or simply that they later perceived it possible, or advantageous, to do so? Again, what type of protection did the framers contemplate within the meanings of the due process phrase? Protection in the modern substantive sense? Or simply protection against arbitrary procedure? If simply the latter was intended, the "conspiracy" was scarcely worthy of the name, for to have used "person" and "due process" in this manner would have been natural for any well informed lawyer of 1866, whatever may be said of the understanding of the layman. On the other hand, to have applied due process substantively with regard to corporations in 1866 would have been a thoroughly revolutionary step, even for a lawyer. For this reason it is a substantive usage that is most consistent with the theory. In both of these issues the implied difference in motive is great; and likewise

---

12 At 233–234.
13 Louis Boudin has referred with obvious irritation to the "legendary history of the Fourteenth Amendment" and has threatened a monograph in disproof of "pseudo history" sponsored by certain "eminent historians." 2 GOVERNMENT BY JUDICIARY (1932) 404. More precise and dispassionate, Walton H. Hamilton has objected that the theory "endows the captains of a rising industry with a capacity for forward plan and deep plot which they are not usually understood to possess." *Property—According to Locke* (1932) 41 YALE L. J. 864, 875. Finally, E. R. Lewis, the most recent writer to examine the matter in the light of both the published Journal and the Congressional debates, has emerged frankly skeptical of Conkling's whole story and inclined to demand more convincing evidence. A HISTORY OF AMERICAN POLITICAL THOUGHT FROM THE CIVIL WAR TO THE WORLD WAR (1937) 28 ff.

The "Conspiracy Theory," Part I   35

the implied ambiguity in the theory. The matter of motive and intent would seem to be too fundamental an element of conspiracy to leave in so unsatisfactory a state.

It is the purpose of this article to re-examine the conspiracy theory and to determine, insofar as possible, the extent to which it meets certain essential conditions.

I. Conkling's Argument Re-examined

A priori, there are two major reasons for being skeptical of a declaration that the framers of the Fourteenth Amendment aimed to aid business interests when they devised the due process and equal protection clauses. First, as we have just seen, such a declaration virtually demands as its major condition that John A. Bingham and the other members of the Joint Committee regarded due process of law as a restraint upon the substance of legislation at the early date of 1866, whereas due process was at this time, with a few striking exceptions,[14] merely a limitation upon procedure. The theory thus presupposes that the drafters assumed what was really an extraordinary viewpoint: it endows them with remarkable insight and perspicacity. The second objection is that, as an apparent explanation of the Committee's choice of the word "person" in preference to "citizen," the theory ignores the fact that "person" was really the term employed in the Fifth Amendment, the phraseology of which Bingham simply copied. Further, in line with this last point is the fact that "persons," as a generic term and as a device employed in the original Constitution to refer to Negro slaves,[15] clearly included "persons" of the Negro race and may logically have been preferred for this reason, since grave doubt existed as to whether Negroes were "citizens," and troublesome problems of definition arose if one tried to speak of them in still more precise terms.

The obstacles which these facts throw in the way of the conspiracy theory are at once apparent. Granted that Bingham's speeches reveal a solicitude for property rights not found in the speeches of his colleagues, granted that his drafts of the Amendment were couched in much broader language than those of his associates—in language which today "takes in the whole range of national economy"—still,

---

[14] The two most conspicuous were Chief Justice Taney's dictum in the *Dred Scott* case [19 Howard 393 (U. S., 1856)] and the various dicta in the New York liquor case of *Wynehamer v. People* [13 N. Y. 378 (1856)]. For the development of due process of law before the Civil War, see Howe, *The Meaning of Due Process Prior to the Adoption of the 14th Amendment* (1930) 18 Calif. L. Rev. 583; Corwin, *The Doctrine of Due Process of Law Before the Civil War* (1911) 24 Harv. L. Rev. 366, 460.

[15] Art. I, § 2, par. 3; Art. IV, § 2, par. 3.

it hardly follows that Bingham in 1866 was thinking of corporations as the beneficiaries of his drafts, nor that he regarded due process in the modern substantive sense. He may, conceivably, have used the words "any person" merely as a sure means of including Negroes as well as whites; he may also have used "due process of law" as a sure means of guaranteeing fair trial and fair procedure to all natural persons. In fact, so long as these were the prevailing usages down to 1866 one is hardly warranted in attributing a more subtle or comprehensive purpose to Bingham without definite, positive evidence. To do otherwise is to risk interpreting Bingham's purposes in the light of subsequent events.

So long as these fundamental objections place serious obstacles in the path of the theory, the question at once arises whether the direct statements made by Conkling in 1882 are alone sufficient to sustain it. If they are not, search must be made for new evidence, and the whole problem of the circumstantial materials in Bingham's speeches must be thoroughly canvassed.

An examination of Conkling's argument properly becomes the starting point of our inquiry. To facilitate later discussion, an analytical abstract of his argument will be presented:

1. Conkling's basic proposition, inferred at the outset, was that the Committee had had two distinct and clearly defined purposes. The first of these "related chiefly to the freedmen of the South" and dealt with the "subject of suffrage, the ballot, and representation in Congress." The second was broader and far more important, namely, to frame an amendment which would secure universal protection in the rights of life, liberty, and property.[16]

2. Having drawn this division in the agenda, he now declared, and offered extensive quotations from the Journal designed to show, that before the Committee undertook the second of these tasks—*i.e.*, the task of framing what later became the due process and equal protection clauses—it had in fact "completely disposed of" and "lost all jurisdiction and power over" the first, *i.e.*, "the portion which did in truth chiefly relate to the freedmen of the South."[17]

3. His quotations from the Journal were also designed to show that the Committee had throughout its deliberations repeatedly distinguished between "citizens" and "persons," and that it had in general used "citizens" in the clauses designed to secure political rights

---

[16] CONKLING'S ARGUMENT, *op. cit. supra* note 1, at 13–15.
[17] *Id.*, at 15, 19, 20. Note the inference of the modifier "which did in truth chiefly relate." Conkling's argument abounds with such subtle suggestions of a broader and undeclared purpose.

The "Conspiracy Theory," Part I 37

and privileges (*i.e.*, in what later became the privileges and immunities clause) and had used "persons" in the clause designed to secure "equal protection in the rights of life, liberty, and property."[18]

4. He even quoted from the minutes to show that on one occasion he himself had moved to strike out of a draft "citizens" and substitute "persons."[19]

5. Most important of all, he gave his listeners to understand—even emphasized the fact—that the draft of the equal protection clause as originally reported by a sub-committee had itself specified "citizens," and it is questionable, from a close reading of the argument, whether his listeners may not have gained the impression that it was he, Conkling, who had been responsible (by the previously mentioned motion) for the substitution of "persons" for "citizens" in this clause.[20]

6. Without laboring his point, and relying on his listeners to recall that in the final draft of the Amendment the privileges and immunities clause applied to "citizens," and the due process and equal protection clauses to "persons," Conkling asked in conclusion if this record did not show that "the Committee understood what was meant" when it used these different terms.[21]

7. Apparently to remove all doubt on this score, Conkling casually added, "At the time the Fourteenth Amendment was ratified . . . individuals and joint stock companies were appealing for congressional and administrative protection against invidious and discriminating State and local taxes"—inferring that the Committee had taken cognizance of this situation and that a desire to protect corporations had been the real explanation for maintaining the distinction between "citizens" and "persons."[22]

Two features of Conkling's argument, which in many respects is a masterpiece of inference and suggestion, are now to be stressed. First, nowhere does Conkling explicitly say that the Committee regarded corporations as "persons"; nowhere does he say that the members framed the due process and equal protection clauses with corporations definitely in mind. These are simply the casual yet unmistakable impressions gained from dozens of hints, intimations, and distinctions made throughout his argument. The second feature, somewhat surprising in the light of the first, is that in his conclusion Conkling not only failed to press his points but, on the contrary, now

---
[18] *Id.*, at 17-19, 23, 24.
[19] *Id.*, at 18, 19.
[20] *Id.*, at 17-19.
[21] *Id.*, at 24, 25.
[22] *Id.*, at 25.

substantially waived them. "I have sought to convince your honors," he said, "that the men who framed ... the Fourteenth Amendment *must have known* the meaning and force of the term 'person'," and in the next sentence he spoke significantly of "this surmise."[23] Later, in his peroration, he freely admitted the difficulties of the proposition he had maintained. "The statesman," he declared, "has no horoscope which maps the measureless spaces of a nation's life, and lays down in advance all the bearings of its career." Finally, he concluded in this vein, "Those who devised the Fourteenth Amendment *may have builded better than they knew ... To some of them, the sunset of life may have given mystical lore.*"[24]

These quotations reveal an equivocal and indecisive element in Conkling's argument, and they provoke various questions. Why, if he had definite knowledge that the Joint Committee really framed the Amendment to include corporations, did he adopt this peculiar, tenuous, and indirect means of saying so? Why, after laboring to give the impression of intent, did he himself at times seem to belie that impression by use of such indecisive language? Was this simply a lawyer's caution, a desire for understatement? Was it because he felt that suggestion might here prove a stronger weapon than detail? Was it because he feared too concrete an account of unwritten history might harm his cause? Or was it because of some inherent weakness—even absence—of fact in his argument? A critical reader must puzzle over these questions and a cautious one will seek for tangible answers. In this connection several tests come to mind. Does Conkling's argument bear evidence of a scrupulous regard for facts, first in its major propositions, second in its essential details? Is it inherently consistent? Does it bear evidence of care and good faith in quotation from the Journal?

Application of these tests to the more than twenty pages of Conkling's argument leads to some startling discoveries. Not only does it appear as a result of such an inquiry that Conkling suppressed pertinent facts and misrepresented others, but it is hard to avoid the conclusion that he deliberately misquoted the Journal and even so arranged his excerpts as to give listeners a false impression of the record and of his own relation thereto. In framing a bill of particulars, the following may be set down in refutation of his major points:

1. With regard to his fundamental proposition that the Joint Committee had been charged with two distinct, clearly defined purposes and that these two purposes had at all times been kept separate

---

[23] *Id.*, at 31 (italics added).
[24] *Id.*, at 33, 34 (italics added).

The "Conspiracy Theory," Part I 39

and distinct, it is sufficient to say that Conkling himself quoted[25] a resolution in the Journal which effectively disposed of his point. This resolution, introduced in the Joint Committee by Senator Fessenden on January 12, 1866, reads as follows:[26]

> "Resolved that . . . the *insurgent States* cannot . . . be allowed to participate in the Government until the basis of representation shall have been modified, *and* the rights of all persons amply secured . . . ."

Obviously this resolution specified two tasks for the Joint Committee. But the important fact, not mentioned by Conkling and even disguised by him, was that it specified both tasks with regard to the "insurgent States." This being the case, it is hard to see how the two purposes could ever have been "separate and distinct" in the sense which Conkling contended, and harder still to believe that only those portions of the Fourteenth Amendment relating to "representation, the suffrage," etc., dealt exclusively with conditions in the South. The "insurgent States" reference practically destroys Conkling's case at the outset. His argument is rendered suspect by one of his own citations from the Journal. Only by laying emphasis upon Fessenden's use of the word "persons" in this resolution did Conkling steer listeners past this flaw in his case.

2. Auxiliary to his main proposition, Conkling was at great pains to show[27] that the text of Bingham's Amendment, which originally read "Congress shall have power . . . to secure to all persons equal protection in the enjoyment of life, liberty and property," had been dealt with by the Committee as if members had at all times regarded it as distinct in both subject matter and purpose from the other amendments dealing with suffrage and representation. His particular point in this connection was that on January 24, 1866 the Bingham Amendment had been referred to a different sub-committee than the one that had considered the other drafts. What Conkling neglected to say was that when Bingham originally introduced this draft on January 12, 1866, it had been referred, at Bingham's own motion, to "the sub-committee on the basis of representation"—the same sub-committee, in short, which received the other drafts.[28] This appears to be a damaging omission, for it suggests that Bingham himself may have regarded his draft merely as one which,

---

[25] *Id.*, at 16.
[26] KENDRICK, *op. cit. supra* note 4, at 42 (italics added). Cited hereafter as the Fessenden resolution.
[27] See note 17, *supra*.
[28] KENDRICK, *op. cit. supra* note 4, at 46.

applying to "the insurgent States," "amply secured the rights of all persons," thus, perhaps, effectuating the second purpose outlined in the Fessenden resolution.

Whether this last interpretation is warranted or not, failure to mention the fact that Bingham's draft had originally been referred to the "subcommittee on the basis of representation" led Conkling into embarrassing difficulties—difficulties from which he extricated himself only by stratagem. We need here say no more than that at one point in his argument[29] Conkling quoted this passage from the Journal:[30] "The Committee proceeded to the consideration of the following [*i.e.*, Bingham] amendment . . . *proposed by the sub-committee on the basis of representation*." Obviously, to have read the text in this form would have been to risk wiping out the very impression which he was laboring to establish, namely that the Bingham Amendment was a thing apart, and one dealt with by a separate sub-committee—the "sub-committee on the powers of Congress." If we judge by his printed argument, Conkling extricated himself from this hole by pausing after the word "sub-committee" —*i.e.*, by inserting a comma in the written text—so that the reported passage reads as follows:[31]

> "The Committee proceeded to the consideration of the following amendment . . . proposed by the sub-committee, on the basis of representation: 'Congress shall have power to make all laws necessary and proper to secure to all citizens of the United States in each State the same political rights and privileges, and *to all persons in every State equal protection in the enjoyment of life, liberty, and property*'."

By thus splitting off the final phrase, and relating it not to its proper antecedent "sub-committee" but to the text of the Amendment which followed, Conkling salvaged his case. The fact that intrinsically the Bingham Amendment had nothing whatever to do with "the basis of representation," that it thus belied Conkling's motivating phrase, was probably not perceived by his listeners for the reason that this point was inconsequential to his main argument, and that in the reading of the text he laid great stress on Bingham's use of the word "persons," thus directing thought in other channels.

3. Turning now to Conkling's second proposition, one finds the evidence almost as damaging. Again and again Conkling intimated

---

29 CONKLING'S ARGUMENT, *op. cit. supra* note 1, at 20.
30 KENDRICK, *op. cit. supra* note 4, at 54 (italics added).
31 See note 29, *supra* (italics in original).

The "Conspiracy Theory," Part I   41

that the real reason Bingham and the Joint Committee used the terms "persons" instead of "citizens" had been to include corporations. Close examination not only fails to substantiate this statement but even provides an alternative explanation. One discovers the word "persons" used in numerous contexts which suggest that the real reason for preferring the term to "citizens" was that the freedmen, as natural beings and former slaves, were unquestionably to be regarded as "persons," whereas numerous complications arose whenever one attempted to speak of them, or even to define them, as "citizens."[32]

Nowhere is this shown to better advantage than in a draft of an amendment which Conkling himself sponsored,[33] and from which, with rare audacity, he quoted in argument.[34] "Whenever in any State," he read, making clear that the text was his own, "civil or political rights or privileges shall be denied or abridged on account of race or color, *all persons of such race or color shall be excluded from the basis of representation.*" One naturally wonders whether we do not have here a clue to the intended scope of the term "persons," and to the fundamental reason for choosing it.[35] Surely the reference to "all persons of such race or color" suggests an explanation quite as plausible as Conkling's. It does not preclude the possibility of mixed or compound motives in determining the use of the term; it simply cautions against assuming that a single explanation is necessarily adequate and that other possibilities may be ignored.[36]

---

[32] Passages in the Journal (KENDRICK, *op. cit. supra* note 4, at 42–44, resolution of Mr. Williams and Mr. Conkling; at 50–51, report of sub-committee) indicate that the Joint Committee, confronted early in its deliberations with the problem of how best to refer to the Negroes, divided into two groups. The first group, led by Conkling and Bingham, preferred to use the inclusive term "persons" throughout. The second group, led by Stevens, preferred the narrower term "citizens" with an added clause defining citizenship in such manner as to include Negroes. The dangers of ambiguity in definition apparently weighed heavily in the minds of all, for when the question finally came to a vote, the Bingham-Conkling form was adopted and Stevens withdrew his motion. *Id.,* at 52–53. It was not until much later, when the final draft of the amendment was before the Senate, that the first sentence of Section 1, which now defines citizenship, was added.

[33] KENDRICK, *op. cit. supra* note 4, at 44.

[34] CONKLING'S ARGUMENT, *op. cit. supra* note 1, at 16.

[35] This view is strengthened when one discovers that on April 21, 1866, the Joint Committee approved the following phraseology as a final draft of Section 1: "No discrimination shall be made by any state, nor by the United States, as to the civil rights of *persons* because of race, color, or previous condition of servitude." KENDRICK, *op. cit. supra* note 4, at 83–85. Bingham's phraseology was finally substituted on April 28, 1866, after some surprising reversals in voting. *Id.,* at 106.

[36] Further evidence which suggests that the word "persons" may not originally have been used with any subtle or devious intent is found in the text of the Fessenden

4. Doubtless the most impressive point made by Conkling, so far as the Justices of the Supreme Court were concerned, was to the effect that Bingham's Amendment, as originally reported by the sub-committee, used the word "citizens" throughout; "persons," he emphasized by implication, appeared nowhere in the text.[37] What gave real significance to this point was that Conkling had earlier emphasized that the text as originally introduced by Bingham, and ordered referred to the sub-committee, read, "Congress shall have power . . . to secure to all *persons* equal protection in the enjoyment of life, liberty and property." Recalling this emphasis, listeners could hardly have failed to have been impressed. For not only did it follow that the sub-committee had stricken out "persons" and substituted "citizens" in this early draft of what eventually developed into the equal protection and due process clauses, but it followed further, since in the ultimate form both clauses applied to "persons," that at some stage or other—Conkling did not say when, or touch directly upon this point—the broader of the two terms had been reinstated. Obviously the mere fact of these successive deletions and insertions justified a view that the Committee had framed these clauses carefully, with utmost discrimination. And Conkling's statement regarding the joint stock companies provided a plausible reason.

To remove the underpinning from this part of the argument—and virtually from Conkling's entire case—one has to say merely that neither the sub-committee, nor anyone, at any time or under any circumstances, so far as the historical record indicates, ever used the word "citizen" in any draft of the equal protection or due process clauses. "Persons" was the term used by Bingham;[38] "persons" was the term reported by the sub-committee;[39] "persons" was the term discussed and approved by the Committee as a whole.[40] Conkling misquoted the Journal in his argument, and it is almost impossible to believe that he did not do this intentionally. The reason is that

---

resolution, *supra* note 26. It will be recalled that this resolution specified that "the rights of all persons" must be "amply secured," but that it so specified only with regard to the "insurgent States." This being the case, and in view of the advantages of referring to Negroes as "persons," it seems gratuitous for Conkling to have asked with regard to this resolution, why, if Fessenden intended only to "bespeak protection for the black man of the South, he should choose these general, sweeping, if not inapt words." One can never know with certainty whether Fessenden regarded corporations as "persons" within the meaning of this resolution, but one rather marvels at Conkling's audacity in intimating that Fessenden did.

37 See *supra*, note 20.
38 KENDRICK, *op. cit. supra* note 4, at 46.
39 *Id.*, at 51, 56.
40 *Id.*, at 60–61, 82–107.

The "Conspiracy Theory," Part I 43

he paused, repeated, and rhetorically underscored the misquoted word "citizen" so that the passage, as it appears in the printed argument,[41] reads as follows:

> "Now comes the independent article:
> 'Article —. Congress shall have power to make all laws necessary and proper to secure to all citizens of the United States, in every State, the same political rights and privileges; and to all citizens in every State'.
> "I beg your Honors to remark that the term here employed was 'all citizens in every State' . . . 'equal protection in the enjoyment of life, liberty, and property'."[42]

So long as the presumption must be strongly against a mere lapse on Conkling's part, the question necessarily arises what he could obtain by so bold a move. The reader must remember in this connection that Conkling predicated his entire case on the distinction between the meaning of the terms "citizen" and "person," and that the effect therefore was immeasurably to strengthen his hand. Another aspect of the matter is that it is questionable from a reading of the argument, particularly from the standpoint of one hearing it delivered orally for the first time, whether, in the passage immediately following, listeners may not have received the impression that Conkling himself was responsible for the substitution of the word "persons" for "citizens" in this embryo equal protection-due process clause. The reason for this belief is that Conkling went on to quote excerpts from the Journal which showed that he had himself moved to substitute "persons" for "citizens" in one draft,[43] and that he stated, but did not emphasize, that this motion to substitute was really with reference to one of the earlier quoted articles relating to representation and suffrage.[44] The question, therefore, is whether

---

[41] P. 18.

[42] It is sufficient to point out that the emphasis and underscoring eliminate the possibility of a mere verbal slip on Conkling's part in substituting "citizens" for "persons." And this appears to leave but one alternative, the possibility that Conkling really intended to emphasize the use of the word "citizens" in the first clause rather than in the second. Yet a rereading of his text with this object in mind reveals the unlikelihood of such an explanation—if for no other reason than that it requires his making not one verbal slip, but two, and that together these would have so altered his meaning as to make their delivery and oversight appear improbable.

[43] See *supra* note 19.

[44] Article B as reported in the Journal. KENDRICK, *op. cit. supra* note 4, at 50–51. Conkling had quoted Article B, and its alternative form, Article A, on pages 17–18 of his argument, but immediately after doing this he had also quoted Bingham's "independent article." Confusion might very easily arise from failure to make clear that his motion to substitute thus applied to Article B, particularly since its phraseology was of little apparent interest.

his listeners—who must have been highly impressed by his dramatic underscoring of the misquoted word "citizens," and who were probably still wondering when the word "persons" had eventually been reinstated—did not jump to the conclusion, uwarranted by a close reading of the argument, that Conkling was himself the man responsible for this change. In view of these circumstances, it can be seen that Conkling undoubtedly gained a great deal from this part of his argument. Whether, and to what extent, his gains were the result of deliberate plan and artifice can never be known with certainty—and one must recognize some of the same pitfalls in imputing plot and design to Conkling as we have already mentioned in the case of Bingham[45]—but the present writer is convinced that the foregoing evidence is most reasonably explained as a deliberate misuse of facts. To say this is not to say that the Joint Committee may not have regarded corporations as "persons"; that, indeed, is a question which depends upon many things. It is simply to say that Conkling could not prove his proposition from the Journal itself. In making the attempt, therefore, he resorted to misquotation and unfair arrangement of facts. He made free use of inference and conjecture, and above all he imposed upon the good faith of listeners who undoubtedly had a high regard for his veracity.

In summing up, it appears that the portions of Conkling's argument which rest upon quotations from the Journal of the Joint Committee by no means sustain the impressions he drew. The whole argument, in fact, is found to be little better than a shell of inference built up in the course of attempted proof of inconsequential points. Not one but both of his major propositions collapse under weight of facts which he himself cited. Misquotation, equivocal statements, and specious distinctions suggest an inherently weak case—even point toward deliberate fabrication of arguments. All in all, the showing is so poor that one is forced to consider whether Conkling's personal reputation, and the advantage which he enjoyed as the first member of the Joint Committee to produce and make use of the Journal, did not account to large extent for his contemporary success, whereas the continued credence given his argument has been the result of these factors plus the natural tendency for us today to assume foresight in those matters which are reasonably clear to hindsight, it being forgotten that as applied to historical interpretation this is often an unwarranted—even dangerous—assumption.

---

[45] There is the important difference, however, that Conkling undoubtedly had a strong motive for misleading the Supreme Court, whereas the chief question must always be whether Bingham had any motive for desiring to aid corporations.

Practically, the only point in Conkling's argument not so far discredited is his statement that "at the time the Fourteenth Amendment was ratified, joint stock companies were appealing for congressional and administrative protection against invidious and discriminating State and local taxes. One instance was that of an express company whose stock was owned largely by citizens of the State of New York . . ."[46] This is an explicit statement, and one which merits thorough investigation, but it must be stressed that by itself it is scarcely adequate proof of Conkling's point. Corporations may indeed have petitioned the Thirty-ninth Congress for relief, but alone this fact proves little. Without direct, contemporaneous evidence that the drafters of the Fourteenth Amendment devised its phraseology with corporations in mind, or at least without evidence that they regarded it as benefiting corporations, once drafted, the existence of these parallel occurrences may have been simply coincidence—a coincidence which Conkling, arguing long after the event and at a time when corporations were moving heaven and earth to broaden judicial interpretation of "persons" and "due process of law," may have shrewdly determined to capitalize. In view of the liberties he appears to have taken with other facts, in view of his temptations to stretch the record[47] and of his unique opportunities for doing so,[48] above all, in view of the dangers of relying upon purely circumstantial evidence to establish intent in cases where intent presumes an exceptional viewpoint and perspicacity, one is warranted, at least until it is proved that Bingham had a substantive conception of due process, in regarding this portion of Conkling's argument as essentially immaterial.

II. The Evidence in the Congressional Debates

It becomes increasingly apparent that the conspiracy theory can hardly attain satisfactory status until precise knowledge is had of what the framers themselves conceived to be the meaning of the language they employed. Conkling's argument and the circumstantial record of the Journal prove inconclusive and therefore inadequate on this point. It remains to assay the evidence which is found in the congressional debates of 1866.

---

[46] See *supra* note 22.

[47] *I.e.*, as a lawyer anxious to see the Supreme Court "liberalize" the Fourteenth Amendment, particularly to the extent of declaring corporations "persons."

[48] *I.e.*, as a man high in public life relating inside history for the first time, and bolstering his case—or shall we say his inferences—by citations from a manuscript journal not heretofore known to exist.

The impressive thing here, of course, is the utter lack of contemporaneous discussion of these clauses which are today considered all-important. Hundreds of pages of speeches in the *Congressional Globe* contain only the scantest reference to due process and equal protection.[49] Two opposing explanations will perhaps be offered in this connection. Critics of the conspiracy theory will doubtless hold that dearth of discussion indicates a universal understanding that these clauses were to protect the freedmen in their civil rights. Sponsors, on the other hand, may argue that silence indicates a universal misunderstanding of what were in fact the "real" purposes of the framers.

It is desirable because of this double-edged character of the argument from silence, and because of the peculiar dangers inherent in its use as a proof of "conspiracy," that we digress a moment at this point in order to avoid later confusion.

So long as intent or design is one major element in any conspiracy, and so long as silence or secrecy is the other, it readily follows that if the framers of the Fourteenth Amendment intended to benefit corporations, and yet failed to make known their intentions—which otherwise were not suspected—then the framers were guilty of conspiracy. In short, intent plus silence in a situation of this kind equals

---

[49] Aside from the Bingham speeches cited *supra* in note 6, the most important references to these clauses were in speeches by Reverdy Johnson, Democratic Senator from Maryland and minority member of the Joint Committee [CONG. GLOBE, 39th Cong., 1st Sess. (1866) 3041]; J. B. Henderson, Republican Senator from Missouri [*Id.*, at 3035–3036]; Jacob M. Howard, Republican Senator from Michigan and majority member of the Joint Committee [*Id.*, at 2766]. However, even these references are so brief as to settle nothing. Reverdy Johnson favored the due process clause but opposed the privileges and immunities clause "simply because I do not understand what will be the effect of that," inferring, of course, that he thought he understood what was to be the effect of due process. The only fragment of evidence in the *Globe* suggesting that Johnson may have had a substantive conception of due process is that on one occasion when debating the constitutionality of test oaths—*i.e.*, not when discussing due process—[CONG. GLOBE, 39th Cong., 1st Sess. (1866) 2916] he alluded to the Alabama case *In re Dorsey* [7 Port. 293 at 296 (1838)] in which Justice Ormond had held a duelling test oath to be a violation of the due course of law clause of the Alabama Constitution. This would seem to be too slender a reference to serve to link these two concepts.

The speech of Senator Henderson is more suggestive, particularly in the light of our later discoveries regarding Bingham's views. Henderson obviously regarded the whole of Section 1 as applying only to Negroes, for he criticized it as unnecessarily prolix and declared that the whole problem would have been solved by a draft prohibiting the States from discriminating against Negroes because of race or color. However, he did regard "life, liberty, and property as absolute inalienable rights" and was thus probably prepared to read into the clause his personal conceptions of justice—even though his discussion implied that he regarded the due process phrase as properly securing only notice and hearing, etc.

Howard's speech is consistent with a "Negro race interpretation" of Section 1.

conspiracy. When this formula is applied to the present case, it follows further, since the fact of silence is not questioned,[50] that the actual intent of the drafters to afford corporations relief is the only point at issue. To prove intent is to prove the conspiracy theory. But it is precisely at this point that confusion arises. Since silence, along with intent, is one of the major elements of conspiracy, there is a natural tendency to use it not only to prove the theory, but also, by a confusion of purposes and ideas, to prove intent. This is done generally in the roundabout fashion of assuming that silence is evidence of secrecy, and that secrecy in turn is evidence of intent. It is hardly necessary to point out that this is a chronic form of circular reasoning which amounts practically to using the argument from silence as a screen to mask the assumption of what one is really trying to prove. Logically, it is a pitfall which one must take particular care to avoid. Intent to aid corporations must be proved by satisfactory evidence and not derived or assumed from the mere fact of silence.

Turning now to an examination of the evidence in the *Globe*, it can be said that the speeches of Bingham[51] alone are really suggestive and worthy of analysis, although even they are found deficient in essential particulars. Stripping Bingham's arguments down to their vital points, one may list the following, particularly in their cumulative effect, as more or less favorable to the conspiracy theory:

1. Bingham deemed it to be a grave weakness that the entire Bill of Rights of the Federal Constitution and more particularly the due process clause of the Fifth Amendment applied only as a restraint upon Congress. Holding citizenship to be national and denying, therefore, that the States had ever rightfully been able to interfere

---

[50] That is, one searches the debates in Congress and in the ratifying legislatures in vain for any intimation to the effect that the Fourteenth Amendment afforded prospective relief to corporations.

[51] See *supra* note 6. It should be stated at this point that Bingham nowhere defined what he meant by "due process of law." However, the following exchange took place in the course of one of his speeches:
Mr. Rogers ... "A question. I ... wish to know what you mean by 'due process of law'."
Mr. Bingham, "I reply to the gentleman, the Courts have settled that long ago; and the gentleman can go and read their decisions."
                    CONG. GLOBE, 39th Cong. 1st Sess. (1866) 1089.
One might say in 1937 that Bingham was somewhat deceived as to the "settled" character of his doctrine.

In the peroration of this same speech Bingham spoke of "due process of law— law in the highest sense, that law which is the perfection of human reason, and which is impartial, equal, exact justice; that justice which requires that every man shall have his right; that justice which is the highest duty of nations as it is the imperishable attribute of the God of nations."

with the privileges of national citizenship—among which were the fundamental rights of life, liberty and property[52]—Bingham's first consideration was to devise an amendment which would remedy this defect.[53] It can be said with assurance that to do this was the general purpose of all his various drafts, including the early forms which provided "Congress shall have power to . . . secure to all persons in every State equal protection in the rights of life, liberty and property." A desire to curb the States, to nationalize fundamental rights, and to do this using the phraseology of the Fifth Amendment, were the hubs around which Bingham's thinking revolved.[54]

2. Bingham was emphatic at times in pointing out that the Fourteenth Amendment did not apply merely to the Southern States and to the Negroes. "It is due to the Committee," he declared on one occasion[55] when asked whether his draft "aimed simply and purely toward the protection of American citizens of African descent," "that I say it is proposed as well to protect the thousands and tens of thousands and hundreds of thousands of loyal white citizens of the United States whose property, by State legislation, has been wrested from them by confiscation, and to protect them also against banishment . . . It is to apply to other States also that have in their constitutions and laws today provisions in direct violation of every principle of our Constitution." Asked at this point whether he referred to "the State of Indiana,"[56] Bingham replied,[57] "I do not know; it may be so. It applies unquestionably to the State of Oregon." These allusions are obviously in harmony with some explicit and definite purpose.

3. Likewise suggestive of catholic motive, and of one somewhat in line with Conkling's claims, is the fact that Bingham on one occasion[58] sounded out congressional sentiment in favor of an "added . . . provision that no State in this Union shall ever lay one cent of tax upon the property or head of any loyal man for the purpose of paying tribute and pensions to those who rendered service in the . . . atrocious rebellion . . . I ask the gentlemen to consider that,

---

[52] A view which derived from Justice Washington's dictum in Corfield v. Coryell, 6 Fed. Cas. No. 3, 230 (E. D. Pa. 1823). See HOWELL, PRIVILEGES AND IMMUNITIES OF STATE CITIZENSHIP (1918) 19.

[53] This point, which recurs in Bingham's speeches, is best developed in that of Feb. 28, 1866, CONG. GLOBE, 39th Cong., 1st Sess. (1866) 1089-1090.

[54] For a more detailed analysis of the framers' purposes, see FLACK, op. cit. supra note 4, at 68-69, 81-82, 94-97.

[55] Speech of Feb. 27, 1866. CONG. GLOBE (1866) 1064-1065.

[56] Ibid. The question was put by Rep. Hale, Republican, New York.

[57] Ibid.

[58] CONG. GLOBE, 39th Cong., 1st Sess. (1866) 429.

as your Constitution stands today, there is no power, express or implied, in this Government to limit or restrain the general power of taxation in the States."

4. At one point in his argument Bingham referred,[59] though very casually, to the decision of the United States Supreme Court in "the great Mississippi case of Slaughter and another." Unquestionably this reference was to the slavery case of *Groves v. Slaughter*,[60] decided by the Court in 1841. As such, it is a reference of great potential importance for the reason that Justice Baldwin, an ardent defender of slavery, anxious to place that institution beyond the control of both the States and the Federal Government, had here, for the first time, used the due process clause of the Fifth Amendment as a means of restraining Congress' power over slaves in interstate commerce.[61] Baldwin's opinion thus applied due process in a definitely substantive sense, and it anticipated by fifteen years Chief Justice Taney's similar application in the case of Dred Scott.

A fact which seems to heighten the importance of Bingham's mention of *Groves v. Slaughter* is that in a later part of his dictum Justice Baldwin had used the comity clause (Article IV, Section 2) as the means of withdrawing the slave traffic from State control.[62] In short, Baldwin used both of the identical clauses which Bingham and the Joint Committee eventually included in Section One. The question necessarily arises, therefore, whether Bingham may not have taken his cue from Baldwin—whether, as a means of protecting all property, including of course the property of (former) slaves, he did not deliberately build upon and strengthen the No Man's Land which Baldwin originally had created for the protection of property in slaves. For a Radical Republican to have done this would have constituted a great tactical triumph, in any event, and one can readily see how, if Bingham actually sought to protect foreign corporations in the manner Conkling intimated, the stroke would have amounted to positive genius. For, clearly, in addition to strengthening the barriers of that No Man's Land which—according to Justice Baldwin at least—existed in the original Constitution with regard to property *per se*, Bingham created still another No Man's Land which surrounded and protected the "persons" who owned property. He did this simply by making the due process clause—one half of Baldwin's original system of protection—itself a restraint upon both

---
[59] Speech of Feb. 28, 1866, *id.*, at 1094.
[60] 15 Pet. 449 (U.S. 1841).
[61] *Id.*, at 514. For the historical importance of this dictum, see CORWIN, COMMERCE POWER VERSUS STATES' RIGHTS (1936) 70–71.
[62] 15 Pet. 514–516 (U. S. 1841).

the Federal Government and the States. "Persons" in consequence were thus secured in their rights of property, against both Congress and local legislatures.

What is one to conclude from the discovery that John A. Bingham, author and sponsor of the equal protection-due process phraseology, (1) aimed to secure greater protection in the fundamental rights of property; (2) intended to curb all states, including Oregon; (3) desired an "added provision" limiting the taxing power; (4) cited a case wherein substantive use had been made of due process to protect property rights; (5) even used the identical clauses in Section One which Justice Baldwin had used in this early substantive opinion?

The first point to note in answering this question is that only when one places the most favorable interpretation upon each individual part of the evidence does the whole, taken collectively, suggest that Bingham may have had the purpose which Conkling intimated in his argument. A moment's examination, however, reveals numerous points at which the evidence is inadequate to support these separate conclusions. Three in particular may be cited:

1. Bingham simply declared himself in favor of an additional provision limiting the taxing power. One cannot determine from his speeches whether he regarded his own draft as having the effect of limitation or whether he simply meant to sound out sentiment in favor of a draft which would have this effect.[63] Obviously one must not infer the former motive from silence alone, without other evidence.

2. Bingham mentioned no particular opinion when referring to *Groves v. Slaughter*;[64] he simply inferred that the case had decided that "under the Constitution the personal property of a citizen follows its owner, and is entitled to be protected in the State into

---

[63] Bingham's only reference to the need for a curb on the taxing power was made in a speech delivered January 25, 1866. CONG. GLOBE, 39th Cong., 1st Sess. (1866) 429. The day previous the Joint Committee had voted to remove the injunction of secrecy [KENDRICK, *op. cit. supra* note 4, at 56] in order that members might "announce the substance and nature of the proposed amendment" in their speeches on the floor. When this fact is kept in mind, the order and substance of Bingham's remarks suggest that his speech was in the nature of a trial balloon designed to test the sentiment in the House. **1968:** For evidence and discussion of the *apparent* (and spurious) significance of this circumstance in recent research, and for the final rationale, see editorial headnote, Chapter 13, *infra*, notes 8, 18, 19.

[64] Failure to mention an opinion is important for the reason that the Court in this case split six ways, with four opinions. Baldwin alone mentioned due process. See SWISHER, ROGER BROOKE TANEY (1936) 396-399 and 2 WARREN, THE SUPREME COURT IN UNITED STATES HISTORY (1923) 340-347, for details of this case which in many respects was prophetic of the *Dred Scott* decision.

which he goes." While these words might be construed as a reference to the comity clause portion of the Baldwin dictum,[65] the conservative course is to draw no conclusion from such meager circumstances.

3. It will be noted that Bingham justified his draft on the grounds that it protected "loyal white citizens" and "any loyal man" as well as Negroes. In short, his references are all to natural "persons," never to artificial ones.[66] Granted that a hidden motive would undoubtedly have impelled secrecy with reference to corporations, it is still true, as we have already pointed out, that secrecy is not here admissible as a proof of intent.

The chain of circumstances from which intent might be deduced thus being broken at several points, it is plain that the evidence in Bingham's speeches is not adequate proof of the conspiracy theory. It remains to linger a moment at this point, however, in order to note several features of his argument.

First of these features is a very important implication of his statement that his phraseology was designed to protect, not merely Negroes, but "the thousands . . . of loyal white citizens of the United States whose property, by State legislation, has been wrested from them by confiscation, and to protect them also against banishment. It is to apply to other States also that have in their constitutions and laws today provisions in direct violation of every principle of our Constitution."[67]

The fact that intrinsically this statement suggests that natural persons were the only objects of Bingham's solicitude must not be

---

[65] 15 Pet. 449, 515 (U. S. 1841).

[66] Bingham's most explicit statement pertaining to the word "person" was made in the course of a speech on the Civil Rights bill on March 9, 1866 [CONG. GLOBE, 39th Cong., 1st Sess. (1866) 1292]. Objecting that the bill as then drafted applied only to "citizens," and therefore discriminated against aliens, Bingham declared: "The great men who made that instrument, [the United States Constitution] when they undertook to make provision, by limitations upon the power of this Government, for the security of the universal rights of man, abolished the narrow and limited phrase of the old Magna Carta of 500 years ago, which gave the protection of the laws only to 'free men' and inserted in its stead the more comprehensive words 'no person'; thereby obeying the higher law given by a voice out of heaven: 'Ye shall have the same law for the stranger as for one of your own country'. Thus in respect to life and liberty and property, the people by their Constitution declared the equality of all men, and by express limitation forbade the Government of the United States from making any discrimination.

"This bill, sir, . . . departs from that great law. The alien is not a citizen. You propose to enact this law . . . in the interests of the freedmen. But do you propose to allow these discriminations to be made in States against the alien and stranger? Can such legislation be sustained by reason or conscience? . . . Is it not as unjust as the unjust State legislation you seek to remedy? Your Constitution says 'no person,' not 'no citizen,' 'shall be deprived of life, liberty, or property,' without due process of law."

[67] See *supra* note 55.

permitted to obscure the significance of the type of legislation which had offended him. Laws enacted before, during, and after the Rebellion by the eleven "rebel" and apparently by a few "other States," laws which inflicted "banishment" and "confiscation" upon "loyal white citizens" were the particular objects of his ire. Such laws, in his judgment, violated "every principle of our Constitution" and in giving Congress power to "secure to all persons equal protection in the rights of life, liberty and property," he doubtless meant to extirpate these abuses.

The point which we here wish to stress is that this motivation practically assures—so long as Bingham appears to have associated "equal protection" with "due process of law"—that he had a substantive conception of due process. It is hardly conceivable, at any rate, that a Radical Republican, outraged by acts of rebel confiscation—which he regarded simultaneously as denials of equal protection and due process of law—objected to this confiscatory legislation simply because it denied such traditional requirements of due process as fair notice and hearing. Inherently the circumstances suggest that it was the substance of such legislation, not merely its effects upon the procedural rights of the accused, that one invoking the clause would have attacked. Stated otherwise, circumstances point to a "natural rights" usage, and a natural rights usage is here obviously a substantive one.[68]

By a somewhat indirect and unexpected turn, one thus discovers evidence which indicates that Bingham in 1866 probably did have a substantive conception of due process of law, and did, therefore, regard the guarantee in a manner which was potentially of benefit to corporations. Paradoxically, however, the importance of this discovery is minimized, so far as its bearing on the conspiracy theory is concerned, by its own implications. Bingham used due process in a natural rights sense. He read into the clause his personal conceptions of right and justice. But the very circumstances under which he did this point to the existence of an intense and specific motivation which may very well have so absorbed his energies and interests that he gave little or no thought to the auxiliary uses of his phraseology. If one adopts this view, Bingham was a Radical Republican consumed by a determination to thwart those "rebels" and Democrats who were inclined to vent their animosity by discriminating against Negroes, loyalists, "carpetbaggers," etc. He was a crusad-

---

[68] Confirmation of Bingham's substantive conception of due process is found in his speech of March 9, 1866, on the Civil Rights Bill [see *supra* note 66] and in his speech of Feb. 28, 1866 [see *supra* note 51].

ing idealist, and it is an open question whether he was not, for this reason alone, one of the persons least likely to ponder the needs and constitutional status of corporations. A zealot is rarely so ambidextrous.

It is a merit of this simple discovery relating to Bingham's purposes that it leads to an hypothesis which can be readily and profitably checked. If Bingham regarded due process of law in a natural rights-substantive sense; if he conceived certain laws enacted by rebel and "other States" as violating "every principle of our Constitution," then conceivably, he may have outlined his views in earlier speeches in Congress. Particularly so long as the problems dealt with in these Reconstruction debates are known to have extended far back in the pre-war controversies over slavery, it is logical to expect that Bingham, a highly articulate leader who served in Congress almost continuously beginning in 1854, expressed himself freely on these matters, and that his speeches thus record the evolution and content of his thinking. Obviously it is an easy matter to inspect his speeches with an eye for clues to the origin, development, and significance of his concepts of due process and equal protection.

Bearing in mind the mystery of the declaration that his draft applied "unquestionably to the State of Oregon," and bearing in mind also the ambiguity of his allusions to the "great Mississippi case of Slaughter and another," and to the need for curbing the taxing power of the States, we can now make an investigation of this kind.

III. Bingham's Conception of Due Process of Law, 1856–1866

Three major speeches are found which shed light on these important matters. In 1856,[69] in 1857,[70] and again in 1859,[71] Bingham outlined views which not only clear up the obscurities we have noted in his later speeches but which go far toward solving the deeper problems of his motivation. Carefully checked, these three speeches reveal that Bingham did in truth conceive of due process as a limitation upon the substance of legislation—that he so conceived it as early as 1856. Yet they give no indication that he regarded corporations as "persons," nor do they indicate that his use of the due process clause was inspired by any solicitude for corporate rights. On the contrary, it appears that Bingham in his third speech in 1859 cited the due process clause of both the Fifth Amendment and the

---

[69] Cong. Globe, 34th Cong., 1st Sess. (1856) Appendix, at 124.
[70] Cong. Globe, 34th Cong., 3rd Sess. (1857) Appendix, at 135–140.
[71] Cong. Globe, 35th Cong., 2nd Sess. (1859) 981–985.

Northwest Ordinance, together with the comity clause—in short, the very clauses which seven years later he used in his final draft of Section One—as having been violated by a section in the Oregon Constitution[72] which provided:

> "No free negro or mulatto not residing in the State at the time of the adoption of this Constitution, shall ever come, reside, or be within this State, or hold any real estate, or make any contract, or maintain any suit therein . . . ."

This evidence obviously suggests that free Negroes and mulattoes —natural "persons," rather than corporations—were the original objects of Bingham's solicitude. As his speeches and drafts in 1866 give evidence of having been based upon his speech of 1859, the question necessarily arises whether Negroes rather than corporations were still the sole objects of his concern at the later date.

Read in their social and historical context, Bingham's speeches not only reveal how he came to focus upon the due process clause, but how he came to read into it this revolutionary substantive meaning. It was on March 6, 1856—exactly one year before Chief Justice Taney's opinion in the *Dred Scott* case—that Bingham, making his maiden speech in the House,[73] argued that laws recently enacted by the Kansas (Shawnee Village) legislature, declaring it a felony even to agitate against slavery, deprived "persons of liberty without due process of law, or any process but that of brute force." As this speech was delivered just two weeks after the Supreme Court's decision in the major case of *Murray v. Hoboken Land and Improvement Company*,[74] wherein counsel in arguing procedural questions had cited such germinal substantive cases as *Hoke v. Henderson*[75] and *Taylor v. Porter*,[76] and wherein Justice Curtis had distinguished in

---

[72] Article I, Section 35, Constitution of Sept. 18, 1857.

[73] See *supra* note 69. The Kansas Territorial Legislature, dominated by the pro-slavery forces and acting under a pro-slavery Constitution, had adopted verbatim the drastic Missouri slave code which *inter alia* (quoting Bingham) made it a felony "for any *free* person, by speaking or writing, to assert that persons have not the right to hold slaves in said Territory." Bingham contended that these provisions abridged "the freedom of speech and of the press as well as deprived persons of liberty without due process of law." The text of the Kansas law is given in SEN. EXEC. DOC., No. 23, 34th Cong., 1st Sess. (1856) 604–606.

[74] 59 U. S. 272 (1856). This case was argued Jan. 30, 31, Feb. 1, 4, 1856, and decided Feb. 19, 1856.

[75] 15 N. C. 1 (1833). Professor Corwin stresses the significance of this case in his article cited *supra* note 14, at 383.

[76] 4 Hill 140, 146 (N.Y. 1843). This case is famous as the first in which the New York Courts began employing the due process clause of the State constitution as a means for absorbing the doctrine of vested rights. See Corwin, *Growth of Judicial Review in New York* (1917) 15 MICH. L. REV. 297.

his opinion between legal process and due process with regard to procedure,[77] the presumption is that Bingham, seeking for a constitutional clause on which to hang his political and ethical opinions, appropriated Curtis' distinction and carried it over from procedure to substance. The fact that the Kansas laws had simply defined the felonies, and had not interfered with the procedural rights of the accused, makes it plain that Bingham's citation could have been made only in a substantive sense.[78]

The character and circumstances of Bingham's original application of the due process clause raise the question of whether he could have been the first—or among the first—to employ it as a weapon in the slavery debates, and whether, accordingly, his action did not in some manner determine the Republican Party's heavy reliance upon "due process of law" just three months later in its platform of 1856.[79] Satisfactory answers to these two questions must necessarily wait a careful search of voluminous records, but meanwhile several fragments of evidence point in Bingham's direction: (1) Bingham was colleague and protégé of Joshua Giddings, abolitionist Congressman from Ohio who in 1856 served as an influential member of the Republican platform committee, and who drafted the planks in which the due process clause appeared.[80] (2) While Giddings is known to have made use of due process in his speeches after 1856,[81] the writer has found no instance of his having done so earlier,[82] thus suggesting that Bingham's usage antedated Giddings', and that it

---

[77] 59 U. S. 272, at 276 (1856).

[78] See Bingham's own paraphrasing of these in his speech. CONG. GLOBE, 34th Cong., 1st Sess. (1856) Appendix, at 124. See *supra* note 73 for one example.

[79] The plank on Slavery in the Territories, drafted with particular reference to Kansas, declared that "our Republican Fathers, when they . . . abolished slavery in all . . . national Territory, ordained that no person shall be deprived of life, liberty, or property without due process of law; it becomes our duty to maintain this provision against all attempts to violate it for the purpose of establishing Slavery in the Territories of the United States by positive legislation . . . ." In a later passage the people of Kansas were cited as having been "deprived of life, liberty and property without due process of law." See PROCEEDINGS OF THE FIRST THREE REPUBLICAN CONVENTIONS OF 1856, 1860, AND 1864 (1893) 43.

[80] *Id.* at 22. Julian states, [THE LIFE OF JOSHUA R. GIDDINGS (1892) 335-6] "By far the most important part of the platform was written by Giddings in his library at Jefferson and is here copied," and then quotes the entire plank relating to Slavery in the Territories.

[81] See CONG. GLOBE, 35th Congress, 2d Sess., 346 (1859).

[82] Giddings' SPEECHES IN CONGRESS, published in 1853, reveal that throughout his long career as an Abolitionist leader in the House he relied on the Declaration of Independence as a secondary constitution, citing the phrase "inalienable rights of life, liberty and *the pursuit of happiness*" again and again. Yet no mention is found of due process of law either in these speeches or in those between 1852 and 1856 in the *Congressional Globe*.

may, therefore, even have inspired it. (3) Philomen Bliss, another Republican and Ohio colleague of Bingham in the 34th Congress, is known to have used the due process clause in several speeches in 1856 and 1857,[83] but in each instance it was after a similar usage by Bingham. Bingham therefore is the earliest known user, and this fact, together with his persistence, and the apparent tendency for the early usage to center in the Ohio delegation, suggests that he may well have been the evangel of due process in the modern substantive sense.

Evidence indicates that Bingham, having discovered due process of law, explored it thoroughly, perceived something of its rhetorical possibilities as a weapon in the anti-slavery debates, noted that it had been included in the Northwest Ordinance of 1787,[84] and read into the vague outlines of the phrase all the fervent idealism of a natural rights philosophy. Thus, in his second speech,[85] delivered on January 13, 1857, (still six weeks before the *Dred Scott* decision) one finds him emphasizing repeatedly that the clause applies to all "persons," not merely to all "citizens"; that "it protects not only life and liberty, but also property, the product of labor"; that "it contemplates that no man shall be wrongfully deprived of the fruit of his toil any more than his life." In this speech also, Bingham alludes to the case of *Groves v. Slaughter*—albeit to McLean's, not Baldwin's opinion;[86] and in it too he makes clear that the "absolute

---

[83] CONG. GLOBE, 34th Cong., 1st Sess. (1856) Appendix, at 553-7. Speaking two and a half months after Bingham, and on the eve of the Republican convention, Bliss leaned heavily on stock natural rights arguments, and cited the due process clause in several places. Even more suggestive of Bingham's influence is Bliss' speech of Jan. 15, 1857 (two days after Bingham's speech of Jan. 13). CONG. GLOBE, 34th Cong., 3d Sess. (1857) Appendix, at 145, 149. Here Bliss cited constitutional history and emphasized that the framers of the Bill of Rights substituted "person" for "freemen," etc.

See the speech of Rep. A. P. Granger of New York, [CONG. GLOBE, 34th Cong., 1st Sess. (1856) Appendix, at 295-7] April 4, 1856, four weeks after Bingham's first speech. This is the earliest known speech, aside from Bingham's, that employs due process of law in argument and the only one which the writer has been able to find made by a non-member of the Ohio delegation.

[84] The significance of this fact is that Congress in organizing Territories and passing enabling acts for the creation of new States frequently stipulated that these new local constitutions be "not repugnant to the Northwest Ordinance of 1787." Thus one could argue that while the due process clause of the Fifth Amendment applied only as a restraint upon Congress, the law of the land clause of the Northwest Ordinance had nevertheless been made a restraint upon these particular States. This idea seems to have been implicit (if not always clearly stated) in Bingham's arguments, and it was apparently one means of his getting round the embarrassing features of John Marshall's opinion in *Barron v. Baltimore* [7 Pet. 243 (U. S. 1833)]. The speech on the President's Message in 1857 lays considerable stress on the Northwest Ordinance, even quoting Taney's opinion in *Strader v. Graham* [10 How. 82 (U.S. 1850)].

[85] See *supra* note 70.

[86] Bingham's use of Justice McLean's opinion deserves comment. Having argued

The "Conspiracy Theory," Part I 57

equality of all and the equal protection of each" are the great constitutional ideals of American government and as such "ought to be observed and enforced in the organization and admission of new states." In point of fact, Bingham declared they were enforced: It was for this very reason that "the Constitution . . . provides that no person shall be deprived of life, liberty or property without due process of law," and that it made "no distinction either on account of complexion or birth."

In short, this second speech, likewise made with reference to the power of Congress to regulate slavery in the Territories, reveals a progressive development of ideas and a more thorough study of Constitutional history.[87] One concludes that while Bingham still applied the due process clause only with reference to natural "persons," he none the less increasingly thought of it as extending protection in accordance with his views of right and justice. Moreover, his political idealism, expressed in the "equal protection" concept, and strongly infused with natural rights philosophy, provided a reservoir of ethical and moral judgments which one might logically expect to find their outlet through the due process phrase.

It is exactly this tendency that one notes in Bingham's third speech,[88] delivered February 11, 1859, with reference to the above-quoted "no free Negro or mulatto" clause in the Oregon Constitution. Seeking constitutional sanction for his anti-slavery views, Bingham again and again relied upon "natural and inherent rights," on "sacred rights . . . as universal and indestructible as the human race," on "equality of natural rights," etc., as the cornerstone of his

---

that due process "contemplates that no man shall be *wrongfully* deprived of the fruit of his toil," Bingham had obviously laid himself open to exactly such use of the clause as Chief Justice Taney (then engaged in writing his opinion) was presently to make in the *Dred Scott* case. There is reason to believe that Bingham was conscious of this weakness, for it was in this connection that he quoted McLean's opinion: slaves were not property under the Constitution; "The character of property is given them by the local law . . . the Constitution acts upon slaves as persons, and not as property." One must immerse himself deeply in anti-slavery polemics to follow the logic of this distinction, but once the premises are granted, it is plain how due process was to be made a bulwark for slaves and abolitionists, but not for their masters. The sole difficulty, apparently, was that Chief Justice Taney was not convinced.

[87] Specifically it shows (1) a growing awareness that the due process clause specified (a) "no person" and (b) "property" in addition to "life and liberty," (2) a conviction that this meant "no man shall be wrongfully deprived of the fruits of his toil," (3) a formulated concept of "equal protection"—the very phrase which Bingham was later to use in the Fourteenth Amendment—as the lofty ideal of American government, and as the corollary, if not merely the equivalent, of due process of law. The genesis of the equal protection concept is of extraordinary interest, particularly in view of its association with due process of law.

[88] See *supra* note 71.

argument. Nor was this reliance without profound significance. Again and again he maintained that "these *natural* and *inherent* rights which belong to all men irrespective of all conventional regulations are by this Constitution guaranteed by the broad and comprehensive word 'person,' as contradistinguished from the limited term 'citizen,' as in the Fifth Article of Amendments."[89] The due process clause, in short, was the repository of natural rights.

Adding to the significance of this natural rights usage of due process, and illuminating the pressures that inspired it, is the fact that while no other member of Congress appears to have used the clause as Bingham did, a number nevertheless relied heavily on extra-Constitutional natural rights arguments in defending or condemning the provision in the Oregon Constitution,[90] and at least one member attempted to use the "Republican form of government" clause in exactly the manner which Bingham used due process.[91] Obviously these circumstances suggest that Bingham's tendencies were in no way exceptional or extreme; he had simply made a happier choice in his selection of weapons. Whereas the "Republican form of government" wording was probably too ambiguous to invite usage in such cases, the due process phraseology, containing the all-embracing terms "life," "liberty," and "property," and containing also the word "due," one synonym of which is "just," was ideally suited both for application and expansion.

One finds in this third speech also an explicit and significant clue to the type of protection which Bingham conceived. Who would be "bold enough to deny," he demanded, "that all persons are equally entitled to the enjoyment of the rights of life, liberty and property;

---

[89] (Italics not in the original.) It is impossible to determine from Bingham's speech whether he was aware as yet of the decision in the case of *Barron v. Baltimore* [7 Pet. 243 (U. S. 1833)] wherein John Marshall had declared the first eight amendments to be restraints on the Federal Government, not on the States. In 1866 this decision served as the cornerstone for Bingham's whole argument, and he cited Marshall's opinion again and again. However, the fact that his speeches in the fifties all concerned the constitutional rights of persons in the Territories, not in the States, and the further fact that the Northwest Ordinance (with its law of the land clause) had generally been made binding on the Territories at the time of their organization, may partially explain Bingham's silence regarding the *Barron* decision at the earlier date. He may simply have assumed that whatever the status of due process in the States, the Northwest Ordinance clauses applied in the Territories.

[90] See, *e.g.*, the very interesting speech of Rep. Hoard [CONG. GLOBE, 35th Cong., 2d Sess. (1859) 987] in which he said, "Is it not manifestly unjust to deny any freeborn American, guilty of no crime, the right of home in the land of his fathers? If it is admitted, as I think it must be, that such denial is unjust, then it is unconstitutional." Here surely is evidence of how strongly in need men were of some clause to give constitutional sanction to their ethical and political opinions.

[91] *Id.*, at 952 (Rep. Granger).

that no *one* should be deprived of life or *liberty but by punishment for crime;* nor *his property, against his consent and without due compensation.*"⁹²

This telescoping and virtual rewriting of the due process and just compensation clauses necessarily affords valuable insight into Bingham's mind. It is probably to be expected that anyone using these clauses in a natural rights sense will use them loosely; yet three aspects of the constitutional status of property as viewed by Bingham must be noted. First, he deems it axiomatic that a man's property must not be taken "without his consent"; property rights by his view are thus virtually absolute. Second, and not altogether surprising in the light of this first proposition, he omits all reference to the qualifying phrase that it is really "for public use . . ." that property is not to be "taken without just compensation." Third, in using "due" as a synonym for "just" in the just compensation clause, it is reasonable to suppose that conversely he may have used "just" as a synonym for "due" in the due process clause; and very likely it was in this manner that a textual factor reinforced the natural rights factor in furthering his substantive conception of due process. Stated somewhat differently, according to Bingham's view, due process probably meant just process, and inherently, therefore, it could never be limited simply to its procedural elements.

All in all, when one considers the scope and possible applications of the phraseology construed in this manner, it is apparent that Bingham from 1859 onward held views—whether he actually applied them or not—which were potentially capable, to use the Beards' phrase, of "taking in the whole range of national economy." Indeed his views are in many respects so much like those expressed by the Justices of the New York court in the revolutionary case of *Wynehamer v. People* in 1856⁹³ that one is led to speculate whether Bingham may not have been familiar with the dicta of those opinions. It seems significant at any rate that his own views should so closely parallel those which others, elsewhere, were applying to the defense of business interests then contending against legislative regulation.

---

⁹² *Id.* at 985. (Italics not in original.) Here it will be noted that Bingham is thinking (1) only of natural persons, who are, however, to be "equally" protected; (2) of liberty in the physical rather than in the present-day sense.

⁹³ 13 N. Y. 378, 391 (1856). To quote Professor Corwin's analysis: "The main proposition of the decision in the Wynehamer case is that the legislature cannot destroy by any method whatever, what by previous law was property." *Op. cit. supra* note 14, at 468. Bingham obviously regarded this proposition as axiomatic; for who would deny that "no one should be deprived of . . . his property against his consent and without due compensation?"

Two additional points must now be noted. The first is that judging by the similarity of numerous passages of rhetoric and statements of fact, the Oregon speech of 1859 appears to have served as an important source and reference in the preparation of his arguments and drafts in 1866.[94] This fact alone suggests a close link between the Fourteenth Amendment phraseology and the Oregon "no free Negro and mulatto" provision.

The second point, more or less implicit in foregoing quotations, is that several times in the course of this argument in 1859 Bingham made clear that he regarded the just compensation clause, no less than the due process clause, as a bulwark of natural and "sacred rights which are as universal and indestructible as the human race." The significance of this fact will be apparent when one recalls that Bingham's attempt to secure inclusion of a just compensation clause in the Fourteenth Amendment in 1866 has always been regarded as one of the strongest indications of an intent to aid business and corporations and thus to "take in the whole range of national economy." Now, however, it develops that he cited this same clause seven years earlier in the speech which, as we have just pointed out, appears to have been an important source of his later remarks, and which was indubitably inspired by discriminations against free Negroes and mulattoes.

Finally, perhaps the most significant thing about Bingham's Oregon speech is that he here made use, in addition, of the comity clause in order to guarantee the rights of the free Negroes and mulattoes.[95] He was able to do this because native-born Negroes and mulattoes, by his comprehensive anti-slavery definitions of citizenship, were "citizens" as well as "persons."[96]

There were two important corollaries of this proposition so far

---

[94] Thus, in his Oregon speech in 1859 [CONG. GLOBE, 35th Cong., 2d Sess. 982] Bingham quoted from Story, Rawle, Kent, and the *Dred Scott* opinions to bolster his definitions of citizenship. In his first speech delivered on Jan. 25, 1866, he quoted these identical references in the same order and connection. CONG. GLOBE, 39th Cong., 1st Sess. (1866) at 430.

[95] CONG. GLOBE, 35th Cong., 2d Sess. (1859) 984-5. Republicans used this clause to attack the Oregon constitutional provisions. See, *e.g.*, speeches by Reps. Granger and Dawes. *Id.*, at 952, 974.

[96] Bingham protected free Negroes with the shield of citizenship, but like Lincoln and others of his party he did not at this date approve of granting Negroes equality of social and political privileges. He upheld the right of States to deny free Negroes the franchise, but disclaimed the right to deny them residence, etc. The difference in Bingham's mind was between political and natural rights: "All free persons . . . born or domiciled in any free state of the Union are citizens of the United States; and although not equal in respect of political rights, are equal in respect of natural rights." *Id.*, at 985.

as Bingham was concerned. First was that those privileges and immunities to which "citizens of each state" were entitled under the comity clause of the Constitution, Bingham interpreted to be the "privileges and immunities of citizens *of the United States;*" so that the clause read: "Citizens of each State shall be entitled to all privileges and immunities of citizens (*of the United States*) in the several states."[97] This of course was the very view which he held in 1866 and which is known to have prompted insertion of the privileges and immunities clause in Section One.[98] Second, and more revealing as a clue to his later purpose in drafting Section One, was that according to his view "amongst these privileges and immunities of citizens of the United States" were "the rights of life and liberty and property and . . . *due protection in the enjoyment thereof.*"[99] Thus the due process clause and the comity clause really guaranteed the same rights, but one applied to "citizens," the other to "persons." By using both clauses in this argument, and likewise by using the phraseology of both clauses in the text of the Fourteenth Amendment in 1866, Bingham undoubtedly conceived that he was affording double protection to the "800,000" free Negroes and mulattoes from such discriminations as Oregon had put in her State Constitution. The due process clause being the repository of the natural rights of all "persons," and the comity clause the special repository of the natural rights of certain "persons" who were also "citizens," it can readily be seen that in theory Bingham had worked out an ingenious though rather complex system of constitutional protection.[100]

With these facts at hand it is now possible to formulate conclusions regarding Bingham's purposes and to note their bearing on the conspiracy theory. The striking thing is of course that in laying the foundation for conspiracy we have apparently destroyed the superstructure. Seeking confirmation for the substantive character

---

[97] *Ibid.* As pointed out *supra* [note 52]. Bingham's views derived from one possible reading of Justice Washington's dictum in *Corfield v. Coryell*, 6 Fed. Cas. No. 3, 230 (E. D. Pa. 1823).

[98] FLACK, *op. cit. supra* note 4, at 84–87. See also speech of Senator Howard, a member of the Joint Committee, CONG. GLOBE, 39th Cong., 1st Sess. (1866) 2765–66.

[99] CONG. GLOBE, 35th Cong., 2d Sess. (1866), 984.

[100] With this insight into Bingham's reasoning, and into early Republican constitutional theory in general, one inclines to moderate the view recently expressed by Professor Grant [*The Natural Law Background of Due Process* (1931) 31 COL. L. REV. 56, at 66] that Section One was "miserably drafted." "Too zealously drafted," would seem the juster phrase; like many before and since, Bingham reckoned without the Supreme Court. 1968: My bibliography of Bingham's speeches in Congress, in campaigns, and elsewhere, 1856–1875, now numbers twenty-five items (besides newspaper reportage of others). The views stressed and detailed here often were repeated.

of Bingham's conception of due process, we have really found confirmation—or apparent confirmation—of Justice Miller's "one pervading purpose—Negro race" theory of the phraseology of Section One.

We have found this by discovering that every clause which Bingham used in his drafts in 1866 really dated back from seven to ten years in his speeches,[101] and was identified, originally, with the problem of slavery in the Territories and with the controversial question of the citizenship of free Negroes and mulattoes. State and territorial provisions denying these last-mentioned "persons" the privileges of residence, and of acquiring property and making contracts, provided Bingham with what may have been merely an apparent economic motivation.

An anti-slavery polemist of the natural rights school, a man who held thoroughly Lockian views concerning the sanctity of property and the rights of all men to acquire it, Bingham hit fortuitously upon due process in 1856 and used the weapon first to protect the "liberty" of abolitionists, then to bolster Congress' power over slavery in the Territories. Chief Justice Taney's application of the same clause with reverse effect in the case of Dred Scott presumably intensified Bingham's convictions and led him farther afield. Eventually the Oregon discriminations caused him to use due process to guarantee to free Negroes as "persons" the very rights which Taney had guaranteed to slave holders as "persons." To clinch this protection, and doubtless to pay his respects to the aged Chief Justice, Bingham maintained that native born Negroes were not only "persons," but "citizens," and not only "citizens," but "citizens of the United States," and as such entitled to be protected by Congress in the enjoyment of their rights of life, liberty and property.

Four observations may now be listed:

1. Apart from its direct bearing on the conspiracy theory, this evidence illuminates the forces which brought about a revolutionary expansion of due process in America. The strong natural rights strain in our political thinking,[102] and the Lockian view of property as sacred and absolute,[103] have often been emphasized in this connection. To these, apparently, should be added the intrinsic advantages of the due process phraseology itself and the role of the slavery

---

[101] That is, the comity, due process, equal protection, and just compensation forms were all employed in these early debates. They were likewise employed in the various drafts of Section One, the just compensation clause, unsuccessfully. See *supra* note 8.

[102] See particularly Grant, *loc. cit. supra* note 100; and for an exhaustive general treatment see HAINES, THE REVIVAL OF NATURAL LAW CONCEPTS (1930).

[103] Hamilton, *Property—According to Locke* (1932) 41 YALE L. J. 864.

debates in acting as a powerful flux in welding together these diverse elements. The irresistible urge to find constitutional sanction for ethical and political opinions relating to slavery led both sides to employ the clause in a substantive sense. Perhaps but for the boomerang effect of Taney's usage in the *Dred Scott* case, due process might have undergone a much earlier and more rapid expansion.

2. A natural rights philosophy and an aversion to the spread of slavery, rather than any profound insight into the potentialities of due process, apparently provided the driving force in Bingham's usage. So far as one can judge he was originally a zealot, not a schemer, an antagonist of slavery, not a protagonist of due process and judicial review. The indications are even that like many polemists he was singularly blind to the broader implications of his stand; for during these years he was one of the sternest critics of the Supreme Court[104] and at the same time the advocate of doctrines which implied a tremendous expansion of its powers. Taken alone, this fact is obviously hard to reconcile with the view that an antidemocratic philosophy and a desire to curb popular control of property in general lay deep in Bingham's consciousness.

3. Section One of the Fourteenth Amendment may be explained in its entirety by assuming that Bingham's purposes in 1866 were similar to his purposes in 1859. Phraseology which has heretofore been abstruse, mysterious, "cabalistic," is thus rendered plausible without imputing to Bingham a desire to include corporations or to "take in the whole range of national economy."

4. While this is true, one must recognize that Bingham's views of "property" and "due process of law" were such that it would have been perfectly natural for him, had occasion ever arisen, to have applied that guarantee to protect the property of corporations. The fact that as a lawyer he spoke and thought of corporations as legal "persons" and that in professional practice he was concerned with their protection, only makes this possibility the more real.

Conclusion

If these facts point to no positive conclusion, they do at least permit one to define more accurately the possible limits of "conspiracy" and to restate its essential conditions.

Stated as concisely as possible, the question henceforth would seem to be whether Bingham in the seven years between 1859 and

---

[104] See his speech on President Buchanan's Message, wherein he denied that the Supreme Court was "the final arbiter on all questions of political power." [Cong. Globe, 36th Cong., 1st Sess. (1860) 1839]. See also 3 Warren, *op. cit. supra* note 64, at 171, 189.

1866 came to realize the full potentialities of his doctrine or whether he continued merely to apply it in defense of free Negroes and mulattoes. Phraseologically the system of constitutional protection he had invoked with reference to the property rights and earning power of Negroes was equally applicable to the protection of the property rights and earning power of corporations.[105] Did his zeal as an enemy of slavery and as a defender of the Union prevent him from seeing this fact? Did it blind him to the needs and interests of corporations? Or did his neo-Lockian fervor in behalf of the rights of property—all property, excepting that in slaves—awaken him to the possibility that corporations, since they were "persons" in common legal parlance, might also be "persons" within the meaning of the due process clause? Did Bingham come to extend to corporations—or to shareholders—the same substantive protection he extended to Negroes? In short, did Bingham's views remain static during these years? Or did they prove as flexible and dynamic as during the Fifties? Did the Civil War, which raised a host of problems relating to business and corporations, direct attention to such matters; or did it obscure and crowd out their consideration? The alternative possibilities here balance one another so nicely that even speculation is difficult; yet obviously these are the terms upon which future decision must rest. The charge of "conspiracy" can eventually be maintained only if it is shown that some force or influence caused Bingham to broaden his application of the clause to include corporations—either sometime prior to 1866, or while the Fourteenth Amendment was before the Joint Committee. Evidence bearing upon these possibilities the writer proposes to review at a later date.

———◆◆◆———

EDITORIAL NOTE. Triumphal arches are often built of and on rubble, overdecorated, and accepted on faith or favor. So it was with this one, so long attributed, so often rededicated, to Roscoe Conkling. No one troubled to examine his statements, or their pedigree. No one checked his claims or quotations. No one bothered to ask what evidence there was that judges had been influenced or persuaded by his advocacy. The corporate person was then an *accomplished fact*. The corporate person had *followed* Conkling's argument. Therefore,

---

[105] It is of particular interest to note how the chance provisions of the Oregon Constitution barring Negroes from owning property and making contracts led Bingham into a fundamentally laissez faire usage of due process which anticipated the decisions in *Allgeyer v. Louisiana* [165 U. S. 578 (1897)] and *Smyth v. Ames* [169 U. S. 466 (1898)] by nearly forty years.

the corporate person had in fact *been accomplished* by Conkling! This twisted, macaronic syllogism is no mere caricature, but rather an illuminating analogy, the more pointed for all who have tended to see only *framer* or *judicial* error in the history and interpretation of the Fourteenth Amendment!

The Conspiracy Theory thus still has interest today as a classic study in academic and popular illusion compounded of anachronism, ambiguity, social and constitutional needs, and, above all, professional surmise and assumptions.[1] Sociological "context" and "presentist" pressures[2] are seen to have weighed heavily throughout, nudging and coloring scholarship and thinking, yet also acting correctively and affirmatively in the long run.

"Prima facie cases," of course, easily and frequently become prima facie problems. "Conspiracy," moreover, is notoriously and inherently an issue which begs and fogs the processes of law and thought —too often or too easily "proved," as Mr. Justice Jackson observed,[3] by "evidence that is admissible only upon the assumption that conspiracy existed." And in this case, the Beards themselves were credited (or "tarred"[4] as Charles Beard wrote the editors of the *Yale Law Journal*) with a "conspiracy theory" they had neither specified nor named—had not, indeed, precisely formulated, much less documented. Nor had Conkling initially, for his part, done more to detail or substantiate what he really *meant* in 1882, still less what he knew or meant actually had *happened* in the Joint Committee, or in Congress, in 1866–1868. Time problems and differences—especially in the use and status of due process at these crucial dates, and as related to framer intent and judicial understanding and motivation, and hence as sustaining proof (and the burden of proof) of Bingham's or Conkling's or the Court's understanding and intent—thus were easily, and in fact continually ignored and confused.[5] Capping and

---

[1] Note simply that historians, too, projected backward to 1856–1866 and beyond the highly sophisticated modern procedural-substantive cleavage of due process, ignoring the implications of natural rights usage entirely. See, for example, my discussion *supra* p. 34, par. 2.

[2] For classic and embarrassing example, note that in the discussion of *Groves v. Slaughter* (1841), *supra* p. 49, Taney Court justices already were anticipating the Hughes Court's "No Man's Land"!

[3] Concurring in Krulewich v. U. S., 336 U. S. 440 at 453 (1948). For evidence of the unfortunate associations and connotations of the word "conspiracy," see *supra* pp. 38, 44. The dash-enclosed caveat in the latter passage shows general awareness of the problem, but general awareness was not enough.

[4] Charles Beard to Martin Goldstein, Jan. 15, 1938.

[5] For my own disregard of time values as related to due process development and burden of proof, see *supra* p. 36 (sentence ending at footnote signal 16). "Universal protection in the rights of life, liberty and property" was the way it looked in 1937; but

compounding all of this was the Supreme Court's own initial silence, and, therefore, its almost standing invitation to conjecture: no opinions whatever had got written on the crucial point, or on the merits, of the corporate "person" as such.

Little wonder, then, that hypothesis and presumption, inference and conjecture, got pyramided here, and literally ran riot; little wonder that this was such an intriguing, popular and professional skeleton (yet just whose, and in whose closet?); and little wonder that this vague murkiness remained heavy still in 1937, as is evident at various points in this essay as already noted.

The overall effect of these influences was to hide the fact that Conkling's argument had been *only incidentally* a plea for the corporate "person" as such; *primarily* it had been a plea for a curbed state taxing power.[6] But once the *Santa Clara* dictum had established and sanctioned the corporate "person" (1886), the "person" *appeared to have been* Conkling's chief objective. Solution of both the historical and the historiographical problems was long stymied by this simple disguise and illusion.

Hardly less striking is evidence of the extent of America's loss and ignorance, 1937–1938, of the antislavery backgrounds and origins of the Fourteenth Amendment. Note especially the distressing naïveté of the statements above, made with reference to Bingham's due-process usage (1856–1859): "the earliest known user,"[7] "the evangel,"[8] "hit fortuitously upon due process."[9] Real howlers, these, and written four years after Gilbert H. Barnes's *The Anti-Slavery Impulse, 1833–1843* had refocused on the abolitionists, and had shown that the organized movement had centered in Ohio—had *begun*, in fact, in Bingham's own congressional district. Yet not one of many letters received on the "Conspiracy Theory" article pointed this matter, nor did anyone else, seemingly, pursue it.[10] Such facts speak

---

query: 1882? or 1866? Note also my reference to (*i.e.*, assumption of) Conkling's "contemporary success" (p. 44). This in a paragraph stressing the dangers of contemporary assumptions! The short of it is that what Conkling said and did in 1865–1866, what he said and meant in 1882, and what he himself may have wanted or led listeners to believe he said or meant—these are different, elusive, and still very easily confused matters. For a shocking example of failure to update research and thinking on such matters, see Harvey Wish, *A Historian Looks at School Segregation*, in DE FACTO SEGREGATION AND CIVIL RIGHTS (1965), pp. 81–98 at 87, where the discussion of Bingham's draftsmanship and motivation is still hopelessly confused.

6 See Introduction, *supra* p. 17, and *infra* Chapters 9, 13, and 14.
7 See *supra* p. 56.
8 *Id.*
9 See *supra* p. 62.
10 Note, for example, how largely even Louis Boudin, in combatting the Conspiracy Theory (*Truth and Fiction About the Fourteenth Amendment*, 16 N.Y.U.L.Q.

volumes on the national mind and the public interests of even the late 1930's.[11] In retrospect, the chief contribution of this essay, obviously, was that it *did* link, however casually and fortuitously, the Fourteenth Amendment with its antislavery backgrounds. World War II doubtless interrupted and delayed academic research. Yet the war also soon refocused and catalyzed this whole problem.

REV. 19–82, Nov., 1938), concentrated his attack on economic-corporate *misuse* of due process and equal protection, rather than on racial *disuse*.

Equally impressive and significant was the failure of A. C. McLaughlin in CONSTITUTIONAL HISTORY OF THE UNITED STATES (1935) even to mention *anti*slavery use of due process. His account mentioned the *Wynehamer* and *Dred Scott* cases in discussing the 1850's, but ignored all the originating usage—usage of which he (and such contemporaries as A. B. Hart and T. C. Smith) certainly had been well aware.

[11] Not merely the law review literature, but even the JOURNAL OF NEGRO HISTORY reflects the national paucity of constitutional research and discussion at this period. Such was the price and impact of the 1877–1897 constitutional and sectional "settlement." All honor therefore to the work of the NAACP, and to the Carnegie Corporation and President F. P. Keppel for launching, in 1937, the foundation study which culminated in AN AMERICAN DILEMMA (1944, 2 vols.).

[CHAPTER 2]

The "Conspiracy Theory" of the Fourteenth Amendment: Part II

EDITORIAL NOTE. Mr. Justice Black's dissent dramatized and focused issues as never before. Both historically and doctrinally, the situation was without precedent: Fraud and misquotation had been employed in briefs and arguments addressed to the Supreme Court of the United States, in a major constitutional case, by an advocate who himself had twice declined a seat on the Court he addressed, and had gone undetected for fifty-five years; yet this same fraudulent *San Mateo* argument *reputedly* was the one on which "modern" interpretation of the Fourteenth Amendment had turned, and on which a half century of economic-corporate due process and equal protection still rested. Incredulity and consternation were mutual, general, almost palpable.

And my own predicament now was as anomalous, as vexing, as could be: Barely half the case had been presented—the negative, the sensational half (discovered last), the half that *dis*credited, if it did not utterly demolish, the Conkling-Beard thesis. Yet there now remained the original half, the affirmative evidence—those "petitions and bills" (discovered first)—which "seemingly" half-corroborated Conkling, and, in the shambles of "conspiracy," conjecture, and circumstance, "seemingly" left the Beards with the last word!

An "over-circumstanced," "misleading" case this second half was, and ultimately proved to be; just as Dean Charles E. Clark and Professor Walton Hamilton advised the editors of the *Yale Law Journal*, and they in turn argued when the article was submitted and in process. My nets had indeed got "cast too wide," the research had been "too thorough, too conscientious," and too lucky-unlucky, for my

The "Conspiracy Theory," Part II 69

or any good use! The basic difficulty, of course, was that while the weight of the evidence was unmistakably, overwhelmingly adverse, those still-unexplained circumstances—vestiges—remained incorrigibly, almost inherently suggestive of "conspiracy." Those insurance and express company "petitions and bills" not only *were there*; one kept encountering *others*—the various railroad petitions, for example—and these, too, involved the leading framers. And just what did one make of this fact: In July, 1871, the newly-passed Ku Klux Act enforcing the equal protection clause got editorially invoked by the San Francisco *Daily Alta* to protect corporate mining properties then threatened by strikers and sabotage. Barnstorming for his party in San Francisco at that moment was draftsman John A. Bingham. And Roscoe Conkling had been out there often before!

Coincidence and circumstance, in short, played hard and dirty all the way.

Part of the trouble, obviously, stemmed from the restricted character of previous research. Few "nets" of any kind had been cast for years into the antebellum backgrounds of either economic or humanitarian due process, especially since the Corwin-Haines research, and no attempt ever had been made to explore either the congressional usage and "understanding" with reference to the corporate and economic sides, nor to integrate congressional and judicial history, either before, during, or after the draftsmanship.

Lawyers, rightly enough, *called* their great books "Digests." But study of the digestive process as such, of the legal physiology—of the digestive side of due process-equal protection in particular—had got badly neglected and shortcircuited; so completely limited in fact to Supreme Court and to *post*-Civil War cases, with little or no attention to briefs, or to the bar's or the public's roles, that *any* wider approach at once ran into these difficulties, and hence clouded some matters in the course of explaining and clarifying others.

Everyone agreed, of course, that the affirmative evidence must be presented, analyzed, and interpreted, as best it might. Historical integrity demanded no less. But an *author*, unable as yet to explain such details, was under heavier constraints than were law review editors and faculty, willing simply to dismiss or ignore them.

Historiographic problems thus loomed ever larger and larger. The complexity of what so long and often had been mistaken for, and treated as, a prima facie case, now was clear, and was increasingly the challenge.

[CHAPTER 2]

IN 1866, Roscoe Conkling was a member of the Joint Committee which drafted the Fourteenth Amendment. In 1882, during the course of an argument before the Supreme Court of the United States, Conkling produced for the first time the manuscript journal of the Committee, and by means of extensive quotations and pointed comment conveyed the impression that he and his colleagues, in drafting the due process and equal protection clauses, intentionally used the word "person" in order to include corporations. A lively controversy has since been waged over the historical foundation for Conkling's statement.

Social historians have contended that the equal protection and due process clauses were designed to take in "the whole range of national economy"; that John A. Bingham, the member of the Joint Committee chiefly responsible for the phraseology of Section One, "smuggled" these "cabalistic" clauses into a measure ostensibly drafted to protect the Negro race. Others have been skeptical of this view, and have pointed out that it is pyramided on three propositions: (1) that the framers had a substantive conception of due process, (2) that as early as 1866 there existed a number of constitutional cases in which due process had been invoked in a substantive sense by corporations, (3) that the framers knew of these early cases and realized the corporate potentialities of their draft, which were not suspected by the ratifiers.

In an earlier essay,[1] the writer demonstrated the essentially false and misleading character of Conkling's argument insofar as it was based on the Journal of the Joint Committee. And although it was shown that Bingham, as early as 1856, had employed due process of law as a substantive restraint upon the legislatures, no indication was found that Bingham in these early usages ever employed the guarantee to protect other than rights of "natural persons." It was therefore concluded that the so-called "Conspiracy Theory" of the

---

The writer wishes to express his gratitude to Mr. Milton Ronsheim of Cadiz, Ohio, for answering numerous inquiries regarding the career of John A. Bingham; to Mr. D. N. Handy of Boston, for assistance in locating the rare pamphlet cited in note 66; to Professors D. O. McGovney and J. A. C. Grant, of the University of California, for a critical reading of the manuscript of the first article; above all, to Professor Charles Aikin of the University of California, for counsel and encouragement at all stages of this and other research.

[1] See Chapter 1, *supra*.

Fourteenth Amendment could henceforth be maintained only if it were proved "that some force or influence caused Bingham to broaden his application of the due process clause to include corporations—either sometime prior to 1866, or while the Fourteenth Amendment was before the Joint Committee." In this essay the writer proposes to complete the study, reviewing first the development of corporate personality down to the Civil War, and then considering whether in the light of extant cases, the framers could have regarded corporations within the terms of Section One.

I.

Due process of law underwent a phenomenal development in the early and mid-fifties; it was occasionally, though as yet unsuccessfully, employed by corporations; and it was for a time reduced to a state of extreme debility after 1857 largely as a result of its own excesses and false popularity. For an understanding of these developments, it needs to be borne in mind that as early as 1805, the University of North Carolina, a public corporation, had in effect been held a "freeman" within the "law of the land" clause of the State constitution;[2] and in the years prior to the *Dartmouth College* decision[3] the law of the land clauses of the states generally seemed destined to become bulwarks for vested corporate rights.[4] Superseded

---

[2] Trustees v. Foy, 5 N. C. 58 (1805). The constitutional text read "no freeman ought to be taken, imprisoned, or disseized of his freehold, liberties or privileges, or outlawed, or in any manner . . . deprived of his life, liberty or property but by the law of the land," and Justice Locke reasoned "that this clause was intended to secure to corporations as well as individuals the rights therein enumerated, seems clear from the word '*liberties*,' which peculiarly signifies privileges and rights which corporations have by virtue of the instruments which incorporate them, and is certainly used in this clause in contradistinction to the word '*liberty*,' which refers to the personal liberty of the citizen." *Id.* at 62.

But more important than logic for understanding of this opinion is the fact that the entire controversy was a part of the intense conflict between Jeffersonians, who were in control of the Legislature, and Federalists entrenched in the courts. See BATTLE, HISTORY OF THE UNIVERSITY OF NORTH CAROLINA, I (1912) c. 2. It would be difficult otherwise to explain why the law of the land clause was here declared a limitation "on the legislature *alone*."

[3] 4 Wheat. 518 (U. S. 1819).

[4] Trustees v. Foy, 5 N. C. 58 (1805), cited *supra* note 2, however, was not the first public corporation case under a State Bill of Rights; its staunch Federalist dogma may well have been aimed, in part at least, at the majority decision, rendered the year previously, by a Republican-controlled Virginia court in the case of Turpin v. Lockett, 6 Call 113 (1804). Here, upholding an act disestablishing the Church of England and depriving it of certain lands, Justice Tucker had reasoned "if the legislature . . . grant lands to a private person, in his natural capacity . . . such donation" would be irrevocable; but where the legislature had created "an artificial person, and endows that . . . person with certain rights and privileges" such action "must be intended

in this respect after 1820 by the neater contract clause formula, the law of the land nevertheless continued to be invoked in the class of cases involving charter changes of public institutions.[5] Eventually, in 1847, after due process of law had developed full-fledged substantive appendages,[6] and after the contract clause had begun to suffer the limitations of the *Charles River Bridge* decision,[7] a Pennsylvania court, in the case of *Brown v. Hummel*,[8] laid the foundations for renewed corporate usage. Less than two years later, in the case of *White v. White*,[9] a New York Supreme Court upheld the arguments

---

as having some relation to the community at large" and therefore if subsequently the legislature deemed the vesting act "unconstitutional, or merely impolitic and unadvised," it might amend or repeal its own act. *Id.* at 156. But note in considering the early importance of the law of the land clause in such cases, that except for the sudden death of Chief Justice Pendleton the Turpin decision would have gone against the Legislature. See *id.* at 187, "memorandum," and MOTT, DUE PROCESS OF LAW (1926) 196, n. 15.

It is well known, of course, that the law of the land clause was relied on most heavily in the *Dartmouth College Case* in the state court [1 N. H. 111 (1817)], and while the argument was rejected by Justice Richardson on the fundamental grounds of the historic meaning of the law of the land, the argument on corporate personality was nevertheless explicitly made. See SHIRLEY, DARTMOUTH COLLEGE CAUSES AND THE SUPREME COURT OF THE UNITED STATES (1879) 158–159.

5 State v. Heyward, 3 Rich. L. 389 (S. C. 1832), holding unconstitutional a statute depriving the faculty of a medical school of the right to grant degrees. "A body . . . corporate is not, it is true, *a freeman*, . . . ; yet it is composed of freemen . . . ; and of course the corporation can only be . . . deprived of any of its privileges in the same way" as a natural person. *Id.* at 411–412; Regents of the University of Maryland v. Williams, 9 Gill and J. 365 (Md. 1838).

See also Vanzant v. Waddell, 10 Tenn. 260, 270 (1829), holding that the law of the land means a general and public law, which binds every individual equally. "Were this otherwise, odious individuals *and corporate bodies* [italics added] would be governed by one rule, and the mass of the community who makes the law, by another."

6 See particularly, Hoke v. Henderson, 15 N. C. 1 (1833); Taylor v. Porter, 4 Hill 140 (N. Y. 1843).

7 11 Pet. 420 (U. S. 1837).

8 6 Barr 86 (Pa. 1847). Voiding certain statutory changes in the charter of an orphanage, the Court applied the due *course* of law clause of the Pennsylvania Constitution ["All Courts shall be open; and *every man* for an injury done him in his lands, goods, person or reputation shall have remedy by the due course of law . . ." Art. 1, § 11] to protect the interests of the original trustees, and seems even to have assumed a corporation to have been a "man" within its meaning.

Strictly construed neither this clause nor the text of the State Bill of Rights ["*In all criminal prosecutions the accused* hath a right to be heard . . . ; nor can he be deprived of his life, liberty, or property, unless by the judgment of his peers or the law of the land." Article I, § 9.] would have afforded protection even to corporate shareholders or trustees, yet in practice they early came to do so. This fact suggests caution when reasoning from a purely textual basis as to the *meaning* which the due process clause had in the minds of, say, the framers of the Fourteenth Amendment. Cumulative evidence indicates that all such clauses were used as often in their natural rights as in their literal sense; and that "property," not "due process" or "person," was the key word.

9 5 Barb. 474 (N. Y. 1849); see particularly 481–484.

of counsel who cited the dicta of *Taylor v. Porter*[10] as a basis for invalidating that section of the Married Woman's Property Act which applied to existing rights under prior marriages. And beginning in the Fifties, as a result of the expanding sphere of legislative action and more frequent collision between vested rights and various movements for economic and humanitarian reform,[11] due process of law was warped into play by corporate interests in New York, Pennsylvania, and Illinois.[12]

Foremost among the corporate contenders for an expanded interpretation of due process in New York were numerous foreign insurance companies. A fascinating story will some day be written of the struggles of these corporations to escape discriminatory and retaliatory laws relating to licenses, taxes and bonds.[13] Far back in the Twenties and Thirties Jacksonian legislatures had precipitated conflict by passage of measures designed to make insurance, like banking, a protected franchise, subject to drastic state control. Against these attempts to restrict what otherwise was a national market in a field ideally suited to exploitation by large scale enterprise, insurance companies had sought judicial approval for a system of constitutional protection, which, while it was in perfect harmony with earlier court decisions and with American "natural rights" concepts,

---

[10] 4 Hill 140 (N. Y. 1843).

[11] The intimate connection between the early use of due process and judicial predilections against such reform movements as Abolitionism, Women's Rights, and Prohibition has been noted by so conservative an historian as A. C. McLaughlin in A CONSTITUTIONAL HISTORY OF THE UNITED STATES (1935) 461–462. There is need, however, for a thorough integration of social and constitutional history in these particulars. For a suggestive treatment of the social backgrounds of constitutional developments in New York during the Fifties see 6 HISTORY OF THE STATE OF NEW YORK, THE AGE OF REFORM (1934) c. 8. For insight into the interrelations between the movement for state prohibition laws and the growth of due process, see COLVIN, PROHIBITION IN THE UNITED STATES (1926) c. 2.

[12] It is possible that the first use of due process by a private corporation may have occurred in Ohio in 1852–54, just as Bingham was making his entrance into national politics. After years of bitter partisan warfare, Democrats had in 1851 repealed all tax exemptions granted (chiefly by Whigs) to banks and other corporations. No arguments of counsel are printed in any of the test cases in 1 Ohio State Reports, but it appears from the opinions of the Democratic judges upholding repeal of the exemptions, that Taylor v. Porter [*supra* note 6] and Regents of the University of Maryland v. Williams [*supra* note 5] figured prominently in the arguments. 1 Ohio St. 622, 633–634 (1853). The general character of the cases makes it seem probable that the *due course of law* clause of the Ohio Constitution was heavily relied on by Henry Stanbery in his arguments for the companies. 1968: See Chapter 13 infra, notes 39, 64, 69.

[13] Unfortunately there is yet no adequate history of the insurance industry in the United States, nor of two closely-allied subjects, inter-state commercial retaliation and anti-corporate movements and legislation. See, however, HENDERSON, THE POSITION OF THE FOREIGN CORPORATION IN AMERICAN CONSTITUTIONAL LAW (1919) 50–63, 101–102; Whitney, *Commercial Retaliation Between the States* (1885) 19 AM. L. REV. 62.

was still fundamentally at odds with the Jacksonian era's philosophy of States' Rights and the prevailing antagonism to corporations. The companies argued in effect that since foreign corporations—or at least the shareholders of foreign corporations—had long been treated as "citizens" under the diversity of citizenship clause for purposes of suit in the Federal courts,[14] the same parties should also be treated as "citizens" under the comity clause.[15] It was hoped of course that "corporations [or shareholders][16] of each state" might thus eventually be held entitled in all States, to the "right to trade," the right "to acquire and possess property", and above all, to the right "to exemption from higher taxes and other unequal impositions," which Justice Washington had declared in *Corfield v. Coryell* to be among the "privileges and immunities of *citizens* in the several States."[17]

However ingenious as a formula for laissez faire, and as a means for virtually abolishing state lines and state control over corporations, these arguments necessarily gained little headway in Federal courts presided over by Jacksonian judges.[18] From the date of their first defeat in 1837,[19] the plight of the insurance companies grew

---

[14] Bank of United States v. Deveaux, 5 Cranch 61 (U. S. 1809); see Louisville, C. & C. R. R. v. Letson, 2 How. 497, 558 (U. S. 1844) (presumed all shareholders to be citizens of the chartering state); HENDERSON, *op. cit. supra* note 13 at 54–63.

[15] See Warren Manufacturing Co. v. Etna Insurance Co., 29 Fed. Cas. No. 17,206 (C. C. D. Conn. 1837); Bank of Augusta v. Earle, 13 Pet. 519, 585 (U.S. 1839); and particularly Webster's argument, printed more fully in 11 WRITINGS AND SPEECHES OF DANIEL WEBSTER (1903) 106, 112–115; HENDERSON, *op. cit. supra* note 13, at 54–63.

[16] Webster only argued that the *shareholders*, having gained the right to sue in the corporate name, should be granted the right to do business in the corporate name. But the broader proposition was of course the ultimate goal.

[17] 6 Fed. Cas. No. 3,230 (E. D. Pa. 1823). Counsel failed to note that Justice Washington had himself qualified these broad rights by saying that they were "subject nevertheless to such restraints as the government may justly prescribe for the general good of the whole."

[18] It is interesting to note in retrospect how fundamentally at odds the corporations' strategy was with the dominant sentiments of the period—how completely States' Rights arguments cancelled out Natural Rights arguments. In the abstract, the principles of the Corfield dictum were dear to the heart of every American; but as applied in behalf of corporations in the Thirties and Fifties they led to consequences abhorrent to all but the most doctrinaire nationalists. The logic and simplicity of the formula, together with the encouragement which the Supreme Court seemed to offer from time to time by its wavering interpretations of the diverse citizenship clause, doubtless account for the arguments' vitality, but it is plain today that since no Court could have declared a corporation a "citizen" under the comity clause without in practice vitiating all State control over corporations, there was little chance for success. It is significant that foreign corporations eventually attained protection under clauses of the Constitution that permitted more readily of judicial discretion, and involved no such universal and automatic system of *laissez faire* as the insurance companies long tried to establish.

[19] Warren Manufacturing Company v. Etna Insurance Company, 29 Fed. Cas. No. 17,206 (C. C. D. Conn. 1837).

steadily more anomalous and more acute—more anomalous because as foreign corporations the companies were in fact treated as "citizens" within the meaning of one clause of the Constitution, yet were not so treated within the meaning of another,[20] more acute because this understandable lack of consistency in judicial construction eventually gave license to new and more alarming forms of discrimination. Beginning in the Forties and Fifties State legislatures not only undertook to raise the license fees and premium taxes formerly collected, but also began experimenting with provisions that required deposit of large cash bonds—taxable in most cases—as security for resident policy holders.[21] Legitimate in principle, these requirements naturally provoked retaliation, tied up progressively large amounts of capital, restricted and at times demoralized the entire insurance business.[22]

To combat these tendencies, established companies in the Fifties turned to the State courts, using a wide range of constitutional weapons, but relying most heavily on the Comity clause, and on the hope of gaining a decision which might eventually be employed to overturn Chief Justice Taney's opinion in *Bank of Augusta v. Earle*.[23]

---

[20] HENDERSON, *op. cit. supra* note 13, at 50–76, presents the classic analysis of this paradox.

[21] See *id.* at 101–102; Whitney, *supra* note 13. Recrudescence of the ancient commercial feud between New York and New Jersey, quiescent since the Twenties, seems to have led to the bonding requirement, which soon spread to other States and found most drastic and ingenious use in the Far West during the Civil War. See *infra* note 63.

[22] It is difficult today to disentangle the motives that led to these enactments, and even more difficult to pass on the merits. In general one can say that like all such enterprises at the time, insurance companies were economically undertaxed, and real property owners were campaigning for equalization through licenses and premium taxes. Insolvencies and fly-by-night agencies were cited to justify the bonding requirements. Local promoters and ambitious capitalists stepped in, organized "wild cat mutuals" without actuarial knowledge or distribution of risks, and appealed for stiff discriminations to further their schemes. Old line companies thus suffered not merely the restriction of the market, but the discredit which failure of the "wild cats" eventually brought to the still novel principle of insurance. Caught thus between the upper and the nether stones, conservative Eastern companies had good reason for alarm, particularly since retaliation proved scarcely better than suicide.

[23] 13 Pet. 519 (U. S. 1839) (corporations not citizens under comity clause). For the companies' strategy see assembled arguments and briefs, The Fire Department v. Noble, The Fire Department v. Wright, 3 E. D. Smith 440 ff, 453 ff, particularly 458–468, 472–486 (C. P. N. Y. 1854). For evidence of how quick the Southern agrarians on the United States Supreme Court were to sense and spike the companies' move, see Justice Campbell's opinion in Marshall v. Baltimore and Ohio R. R., 16 How. 314, 352 (U. S. 1853). Apprehension that a tendency to liberalize interpretations of corporate citizenship under Art. III, Sec. 2, might favor the companies' strategy caused the Court in this case virtually to repudiate the Letson dictum, note 14 *supra*; *cf.* also Rundle v. Delaware and Raritan Canal Co., 14 How. 80 (U. S. 1852), particularly Daniels' dissent at 95; see HENDERSON, *op. cit. supra* note 13, at 60–63.

Failing in at least three attempts in Kentucky,[24] Illinois[25] and New Jersey,[26] counsel finally selected a test case in the New York Court of Common Pleas. Elaborate arguments were made under the Comity and the just compensation clauses,[27] though no mention appears to have been made of due process.[28] But before decision could be rendered in the test case, the Court of Appeals decided *Westervelt v. Gregg*,[29] which voided the Married Woman's Property Act as a denial of due process. Encouraged by this expansion, counsel for the insurance companies abandoned their Comity clause and just compensation attack in favor of a new test suit, commenced and elaborately argued on due process grounds.[30] Yet the subsequent opinion of the Court of Common Pleas took no notice of the insurance companies' new argument; and it is possible that the "law of the land" might again have undergone eclipse had it not been for passage, in April, 1855, of the New York anti-liquor law appying even to liquor on hand at the time of passage.[31] This law, held void, as a denial of due process to private persons, by several judges of the State Supreme Court as early as July,[32] remained a center of controversy throughout the year.[33] In March, 1856, following presentation of due

---

[24] Commonwealth v. Milton, 12 B. Mon. 212 (Ky. July, 1851) (overruling a favorable decision in the lower court).

[25] People v. Thurber, 13 Ill. 554 (June, 1852) (rejecting arguments that a law licensing agents of foreign companies violated the Commerce clause). Immediately following this decision, the Illinois Legislature, currently in session, passed a statute modelled on that of New York levying a tax of two per cent on all premiums collected by the agents for outside companies, the tax going to the Chicago firemen, who at this date of course were as fearless in politics as at fires. See note 42, *infra*.

[26] Tatem v. Wright, 3 Zab. 429 (N. J. Law, November, 1852).

[27] New York Fire Dept. v. Noble, 3 E. D. Smith 440 (N. Y. November, 1854) (validity of tax of two per cent on all fire premiums collected by outside companies levied in support of the New York Fire Department, at that time a chartered corporation).

[28] Possibly because in 1851, lawyers for individual private property owners in Brooklyn had been unsuccessful in an attempt to employ the earlier due process dicta of *Taylor v. Porter* and *White v. White* to contest the validity of certain special assessments for street improvements. See People v. Mayor of Brooklyn, 4 Comst. 419 (N. Y. April, 1851) [overruling decision which had invalidated the assessments as violations of the just compensation clause, 6 Barb. 209, (1849)]. No arguments of counsel are given in 4 Comstock but the due process point is covered obliquely in the opinion at 423 and 438.

[29] 2 N. Y. 202 (1854).

[30] New York Fire Dept. v. Wright, 3 E. D. Smith 453 (N. Y. 1854).

[31] COLVIN, *op. cit. supra* note 11, c. 2.

[32] People v. Toynbee, People v. Berberrich, 20 Barb. 168 (N. Y. 1855).

[33] *Cf.* Wynehamer v. The People. 20 Barb. 567 (N. Y. Sup. Ct. Sept. 1856) (law sustained). The argument of F. J. Fithian in this case, pp. 569–588, is a landmark in the development of due process of law. It shows how far the guarantee was explored prior to the Civil War and helps to explain the elaborate dicta in the Court of Appeals opinions delivered six months later.

process arguments by a former colleague[34] who had concurred in *Westervelt v. Gregg*, members of the Court of Appeals handed down the celebrated decision in *Wynehamer v. The People*.[35] Alarmed at the spread of anti-slavery, anti-liquor, and Women's Rights agitation,[36] four of the concurring judges, by dicta reminiscent of stump speeches, undertook to rally conservative opinion and to erect judicial barriers for the protection of property rights.[37] Naturally this step proved a signal for further attack on the New York insurance laws by counsel who cited the various dicta to prove that local agents for foreign companies had been denied the right to pursue a lawful calling in violation of due process.[38] But the Court of Appeals, already subject to bitter criticism for the *Wynehamer* decision, declined to intervene in favor of the corporations.[39]

While there is abundant reason to believe the Court of Appeals dicta had temporarily excited the hopes of companies' counsel, and caused the due process clause later to be argued extensively in cases before the Court of Appeals,[40] it was nevertheless on the Comity clause that chief reliance continued to be made. In Virginia in

---

[34] Amasa J. Parker, who later in the same year was the unsuccessful Democratic candidate for Governor of New York.

[35] 13 N. Y. 378 (1856). Strictly speaking, certain of the opinions here reported cover the case of The People v. Toynbee; see pp. 486–488 for the manner in which the eight Judges, six of whom concurred in voiding the law as it applied to liquor on hand, divided on the overlapping cases.

[36] See particularly the opinion of Justice Comstock, alluding to "the danger" of "theories alleged to be founded in natural reason or inalienable rights, but subversive of the just and necessary powers of government, [which now] attract the belief of considerable classes of men," and declaiming that "too much reverence for government and law is certainly among the least of the perils to which our institutions are exposed." *Id.* at 391–392. Professor Corwin has regarded these words as aimed at the Abolitionists. *The Doctrine of Due Process of Law Before the Civil War* (1911) 24 HARV. L. REV. 460, 469–471. But the target seems likely to have been broader. Comstock's attitude is the more striking because he saw plainly that judicial delimitation of legislative powers contained "germs of great mischief to society by giving to private opinion and speculation a license to oppose themselves to the just and legitimate powers of government."

[37] Justice Selden included "all vested rights to [corporate?] franchises," which otherwise might be left "entirely at the mercy of the legislature." 13 N. Y. 378, 434 (1856).

[38] See the arguments of William Curtis Noyes, 3 E. D. Smith 458–468 (N. Y. 1854), who cited particularly the *Wynehamer* opinions of Comstock and Johnson, J. J., 13 N. Y. 378, 392–393, 416–421.

[39] The opinions in 3 E. D. Smith 440, note 27 *supra*, are reported as "unanimously affirmed" by the Court of Appeals. For facts bearing on failure to appeal to U. S. Supreme Court, see note 42, *infra*.

[40] The date of arguments and decision by the high court is unknown, but since Noyes' revised brief makes effective use of the opinions in Wynehamer v. People, the date was sometime after March, 1856.

1856,[41] again in Illinois in 1859,[42] and in Wisconsin in the first year of the Civil War,[43] the battle went on, yet wholly without tangible results. The way was definitely blocked.

It was in Pennsylvania therefore, and not in New York, that the doctrine of corporate personality made its farthest advance. And it was a railroad, not an insurance company, which led the charge. Following a long struggle between the State and the Erie and North East Railroad, many of whose acts were cited as *ultra vires*, the Pennsylvania legislature in 1855 repealed the franchises of the corporation.[44] Since no provision had been made in the repealing statute for judicial proceedings to determine the fact of franchise abuse, lawyers for the company challenged the law both as an impairment of contract and as denial of due process.[45] The majority of the Court, speaking through Justice Jeremiah S. Black on January 9, 1856, took no notice of the latter point. Chief Justice Lewis however, in a dissenting opinion,[46] accepted the view that these were judicial, not legislative questions, and held that the *property of the stockholders* had been taken "without the judgment of their peers, and contrary to the law of the land established by the constitution"[47]—held in

---

[41] Slaughter v. Commonwealth, 13 Grat. 767 (Va. 1856).

[42] Firemen's Benevolent Ass'n v. Lounsbury, 21 Ill. 511 (1859) (sustaining the tax mentioned note 25 *supra*). No indication here that due process was raised, although the statute at issue was the one which had inspired Mark Skinner's brief printed in 3 E. D. Smith. See note 23 *supra*. Possibly the adverse criticism of the Dred Scott decisions accounts for failure to use the argument.

[43] Milwaukee Fire Dept. v. Helfenstein, 16 Wis. 136 (1862) (due process used by counsel at 138).

[44] See 6 GREAT AMERICAN LAWYERS (1907) 1-74; KLINGELSMITH, JEREMIAH S. BLACK 20-25.

[45] Erie and North East Railroad v. Casey, 26 Pa. 287, 293 (1856). Counsel quoted this striking dictum from Brown v. Hummel, 6 Barr. 86, 91: "*It is against the principles of liberty and common right to deprive a man of his property or franchise while he is within the pale of the constitution, and with his hands on the altar, and give it to another, without hearing or trial by due course and process of law.*" [Italics added].

[46] 1 Grant's Cases (Pa. 1856) 274.

[47] *Id.* at 290. In the conclusion of his opinion Justice Lewis seems to have relied on Article I, Section 9—("In all criminal prosecutions *the accused*") yet in the body (at p. 276) he was intent on showing that "the stockholders" were "tangible individuals"—i.e., "men"—within the meaning of Article I, Section 11. One concludes therefore that the judge was quite aware the text was hardly suited to his purposes, and that even the fiction of "looking through" to the stockholders left certain rough edges to the argument. See note 8 *supra* for texts of these clauses.

Perhaps the best illustration of the Pennsylvania Courts' tendency to disregard constitutional texts is found in Reiser v. William Tell Savings Fund Association, 39 Pa. 137. 146 (1861). Justice Lowrie, in voiding a special statute which had legalized usurious interest rates of building and loan associations, wrestled with the phraseology of Article I, Section 9 (*supra* note 8), and by sheer force of will made it apply to *civil* as well

short, that whether or not they were "men" or "the accused in criminal prosecutions," corporations were nevertheless to be granted such protection against legislatures as the judiciary might believe compatible with sound public policy.

Simultaneously with these parallel (and outwardly independent) corporate invocations of due process of law in New York and Pennsylvania, a third use occurred in Illinois which was clearly inspired by example. On February 23, 1856, just six weeks after the decision in *Erie Railroad v. Casey* (and while the insurance and liquor act cases were still pending in the New York Courts), Mark Skinner, a former judge of the Illinois Supreme Court now retained by insurance interests, wrote a brief[48] arguing that an Illinois insurance statute modelled on that currently challenged in the East was invalid as a denial of due process.[49]

Judge Skinner's brief is a striking symbol of developments that overtook due process of law in the ensuing twelve months. During this period substantive and political use of the clause broke all bounds and culminated in a costly and tragic blunder. On March 6th —within two weeks from the date of Judge Skinner's brief, within two months from the decision in *Erie Railroad v. Casey*, and almost simultaneously with the Court of Appeals decision in *Wynehamer v. The People*—Bingham delivered his maiden speech in Congress, citing the Kansas slave code as a violation of due process.[50] On April 4th, Representative Granger of New York spoke similarly,[51] followed on May 22 by Bingham's colleague, Representative Bliss.[52]

---

as *criminal* proceedings. The phraseology meant, he declared, paraphrasing to suit his argument, "no *person* shall be deprived of life, liberty, or property except by the legal judgment of his peers, or other due course or process of law. *Here, civil and criminal law, rights of property, and of life and liberty, are put in the same class. Rights of property* (and money possessed and owned is property) *and the rights of life and liberty, have the same guaranty* that they are to be tried by due course of law. But they have not the same guaranty, if the legislature may direct the court, after *civil cases* arise, or after contracts or other transactions are complete, how we shall . . . interpret the law under which they arise; *which it is admitted they cannot do in criminal cases. This section of the Bill of Rights is violated when civil and criminal rights are not both alike tried by due course of law*." (Italics added).

Edgar W. Camp errs in listing this as a corporate personality case. See *Corporations and the Fourteenth Amendment* (1938) 13 STATE BAR JOURNAL (Calif.) 12, 18 n. 25. Justice Lowrie's ingenuity was directed solely in behalf of natural persons; his decision being in favor of Reiser, the plaintiff in error.

[48] Printed in 3 E. D. Smith, 472–478 (N. Y. 1854); reprinted in a CIRCULAR TO THE INSURANCE AGENTS OF THE UNITED STATES. See note 66, *infra*.
[49] See note 25, *supra*, for history of the Illinois law.
[50] See Chapter 1, *supra*, particularly notes 73, 78.
[51] *Ibid.*, particularly n. 83.
[52] *Ibid.*

In June, Joshua Giddings, the veteran Ohio Abolitionist, drafted the Kansas-due process planks which were adopted by the first Republican National Convention at Philadelphia.[53] In the ensuing campaign, "Bleeding Kansas" and "due process of law" were the twin catch phrases of Republican orators. In November a concurring minority of the Indiana Supreme Court *assumed* a corporation to be a "man" entitled to the protection of due course of law.[54] In January, 1857, Bingham and Bliss[55] once again employed the clause—this time to bolster Congress' power over slavery in the Territories. And less than six weeks later, Chief Justice Taney, succumbing to a year of provocation, drafted the dictum in the case of *Dred Scott*[56] which hastened the Civil War and destruction of everything his opinion had been designed to preserve.

II.

We may now consider the implications of these discoveries. Manifestly, the foregoing facts, while in no way altering our conclusion that Bingham was concerned primarily with protecting free Negroes and mulattoes—that he was an idealist, in short, and an opportunist, not a schemer—nevertheless do suggest certain important secondary considerations.

The first is that so far as due process of law is concerned, Bingham's original use of the phrase in 1856 could easily have derived from, and thus have been made with full knowledge of, one or more of several earlier corporate usages. It is idle, without knowing more of Bingham's early attitude toward corporations, to speculate on the full significance of this discovery; yet it seems obvious that one cannot categorically reject the thesis that Bingham in 1866 at least regarded corporations as *included* along with natural persons, so long as there exists the possibility that he first used the clause (ten years earlier) as a result of a number of uses by corporations.[56a]

A second consideration is that the entire battery of constitutional

---

53 *Id.* at n. 79, 80.
54 Madison & Indianapolis R. R. v. Whiteneck, 8 Tanner 217 (Ind. 1856).
55 See Chapter 1, *supra*, n. 83, 86, 87.
56 19 How. 393, 450 (U. S. 1856). See SWISHER, ROGER BROOKE TANEY (1936) 476–523. Relevant here is Professor Borchard's conclusion: "If the due process decisions on substantive law prove anything, they demonstrate that the Court's judgment is the product of the will. It is the social and economic predilection which speaks." *The Supreme Court and Private Rights* (1938) 47 YALE L. J. 1051, 1078.
56a 1968: The naïveté, presumptions, and conjecture of this paragraph are conspicuous and embarrassing today. See the editorial note following Chapter 1, *supra*, especially footnotes 7–9, and the editorial note following this chapter, for basic fallacies and disclaimers.

clauses which Bingham had by 1859 evolved for the protection of free Negroes and mulattoes was virtually identical with the battery which insurance company lawyers evolved in the New York courts between 1854–1856 for the protection of foreign corporations. Due process of law, just compensation, and interstate privileges and immunities were the components of both systems. The point in this connection is not that Bingham's entire system was consciously based on that of the corporations—one can be reasonably certain that it was not.[57] It is, rather, that we are confronted with two separate lines of usage of the same set of constitutional clauses—the set that eventually finds its way into Section One. The crucial question therefore, is not what minor cross-pollenizations may have influenced the early development of the two systems, but what relations existed between the two in 1866? At that time we are certain at least that idealists intent on securing Negro rights undertook to use constitutional phraseology and concepts which corporations had already been using for a generation. Did the idealists proceed to do this without awakening the interest and participation of the business group? Was the Fourteenth Amendment a sheer windfall for Business—a product of unsolicited aid? Or was it somehow the product of joint interest and joint participation? Was it framed with reference to the needs of both Negroes and corporations? Or was it simply made up of clauses which had been *used in behalf* of both Negroes and corporations? Did Bingham, assuming now that he originally had been indifferent to, if not wholly oblivious of the use of his "system" by corporations, remain so during the months the Amendment was before the Joint Committee?[58] Did insurance company lawyers, who had proved so quick to capitalize the dicta of *Westervelt v. Gregg* and *Wynehamer v. The People* in the State courts, and who had fought stubbornly

---

[57] If only for the reason that use of the comity clause to protect free Negroes and mulattoes dated back to the Missouri Compromise [see GEORGE, THE POLITICAL HISTORY OF SLAVERY IN THE UNITED STATES (1915) 38–39, 48–51]; and that virtually every constitutional argument conceivable was employed by both sides in the Slavery debates. Recognition of the ingenuity of even the amateur constitutional lawyer throughout American history makes unnecessary the assumption that Bingham was incapable of choosing his own weapons.

[58] It must be emphasized that three months elapsed between Bingham's first speech in the House outlining in general terms the character of the Amendment, and adoption of the final draft by the Joint Committee on April 28, 1866. CONG. GLOBE, 39th Cong. 1st Sess. 429. Bingham's original positively-worded draft, "The *Congress shall have power* to make all laws . . . necessary and proper to secure to all citizens of each State all privileges and immunities of citizens of the several States; and to all persons in the several States equal protection in the rights of life, liberty and property," reached the floor of the House February 13, 1866. Even as early as December 15, 1865, the New York World had called unfavorable attention to Bingham's original draft (at

but without success for a decision holding a corporation to be a "citizen" under the Comity clause, manifest no interest when the due process-comity clause phraseology was proposed in Section One? Did foreign corporations, suffering from what they regarded as discriminatory taxation and "class legislation,"[59] exhibit any interest when Bingham on January 25, 1866, sounded out sentiment for an Amendment to limit the taxing power of the States and to prohibit "class legislation"? Finally—and we arrive now at the heart of the matter—can there be shown to have been any significant relation between the corporate activity which might be expected from the foregoing circumstances, and that which was implied to have taken place by Roscoe Conkling's remarks in 1882?[60]

Conkling, it will be recalled, at the climax of his 1882 argument before the Supreme Court, declared "At the time the Fourteenth Amendment was ratified,[61] *as the records of the two houses will show,* individuals and joint stock companies were appealing for congressional and administrative protection against invidious and discriminating state and local taxes. One instance was that of an express company, whose stock was owned largely by citizens of the State of New York who came with petitions and bills seeking acts of Congress to aid them in resisting what they deemed oppressive taxation in two States, and oppressive and ruinous rules of damages applied under State laws."[62]

Careful search of the *Congressional Globe* provides the material for a partial answer to the above questions. It appears that while Bingham and his colleagues were at work drafting the phraseology of Section One, two different groups of corporations whose lawyers had earlier made use of the component clauses "came with petitions and bills" designed to secure "congressional and administrative protection" against adverse forms of State action.

---

that time pending merely as a resolution) "Congress shall have power . . . to secure to all persons in every State . . . equal protection in their rights of life, liberty and property." See FLACK, THE ADOPTION OF THE FOURTEENTH AMENDMENT (1908) 140. It can be said confidently therefore, that from December on, corporations and their counsel had reason to be interested in the trend of events.

59 One of the arguments used by William Curtis Noyes in 1854 had been that the New York Act was "entirely unequal in effect and operates only upon a certain class of persons" [see 3 E. D. Smith 462], whereas to prohibit "class legislation" was of course an avowed object of the framers of the Amendment. See particularly, CONG. GLOBE, 39th Cong., 1st Sess., 1064, for the debate between Thaddeus Stevens and Rep. Hale.

60 See Chapter 1, *supra.*

61 Obviously, Conkling meant "At the time the Fourteenth Amendment was *drafted,*" not "ratified;" else his whole case would have fallen.

62 CONKLING'S ARGUMENT, Chapter 1, *supra.* [Italics added.]

The "Conspiracy Theory," Part II 83

First to arrive—and in such form, and under such circumstances as could hardly have failed to attract interest on the part of the framers —were petitions from insurance companies, mobilized now for an attempt to suppress and circumvent the type of legislation from which they had long suffered, and which, notwithstanding the strongly ascendant nationalism and the discredit of localistic policies as a result of Secession, had recently made alarming headway on the Pacific Coast.[63] Between March 2, 1866—two days after the virtual defeat in the House of Bingham's positively worded draft[64]—and June 8, 1866

---

[63] As reconstructed chiefly from a pamphlet-circular TO THE INSURANCE AGENTS OF THE UNITED STATES (note 66, *infra*) published February 1, 1866, it appears that while the Civil War brought a phenomenal prosperity to the industry as a whole, and a vast increase in outstanding insurance, this prosperity was marred after 1864 by enactment, first in California, then in Nevada and Oregon, of laws which had the effect not only of "cinching" Wells Fargo Express Company but of sponsoring the growth on the Pacific Coast of powerful insurance companies which—(or at least so the Eastern firms feared)—might draw their capital from the bonanza mines of Nevada.

In 1862-63 San Francisco capitalists had begun to organize home companies, and in 1864 had succeeded in inducing the Legislature to boost the cash bond required of outside concerns from $50,000 to $75,000 *in gold, and* to require *in addition to*, not in lieu of, as before, a premium tax of two per cent, etc. To catch Wells Fargo Express, a New York corporation, foreign "insurance companies" were so defined as to include "all express companies . . . engaged in the carriage of treasure or merchandise . . . and insuring the same . . ." STATS. CALIF. (1863-1864) 131-134. As in all such matters, California's statute promptly served as a model in Oregon, [ORE. GEN. LAWS (Deady & Lane, 1843-1872) 447, 616] and in Nevada [NEV. STAT. (1864-1865) 104-9].

These developments on the Pacific Coast, together with passage of similar troublesome legislation in the Midwest, and the prospect that the Southern States would shortly begin reenactment of non-intercourse laws, prompted the Eastern companies to meet in the autumn of 1865 and organize for mutual protection. For almost a year, insurance journals had been discussing the prospect of "nationalizing insurance" in the manner of the banks; and in many respects conditions were favorable. At length, steering committees formed by both the life and the fire companies decided to work for a Federal Bureau of Insurance. For supplementary sources see KNIGHT, HISTORY OF LIFE INSURANCE IN THE UNITED STATES TO 1870 (1920) 134-141; COMMERCIAL AND FINANCIAL CHRONICLE (1866) 265, 292.

While no petitions are on record, the writer has wondered if perhaps Wells Fargo was not the New York company alluded to by Conkling in argument. Mr. Harold Jonas of New York, who is completing a biography of Conkling, has suggested the counter possibility that the reference may have been to the United States Express Company, whose head was Thomas C. Platt, Conkling's political associate (and later) colleague in the Senate. In either event, it seems probable that legislation of the type enacted in California was the source of the express companies' troubles. This part of Conkling's statement, therefore, may be concluded to have had some basis in fact.

[64] Conservatives feared destruction of the States and Federal centralization; Radicals the prospect of Democratic control of Congress and the almost certain repeal, in that event, of all Reconstruction measures. For the Conservative viewpoint, see speech of Rep. Hale of New York, CONG. GLOBE on Feb. 27, 39th Cong., 1st Sess. (1866) 1064-65. Hotchkiss, in closing the debate, objected that Bingham's views were "not sufficiently radical." He wanted the Amendment redrafted to secure *constitutional*—not merely *congressional* protection—"we may pass laws here today and the next Congress may wipe them out—where is your guarantee then?" The writer suggests that this speech

84   EVERYMAN'S CONSTITUTION

—the date of final passage of the Amendment by the Senate—more than two hundred of these petitions were received in Congress "praying for enactment of just, equal and uniform laws pertaining to interstate insurances, and for the creation also of a Federal Bureau of Insurance."[65] This influx was given force by a specially-prepared pamphlet[66] which pointed out the "Necessity," the "Desirableness," and the "Equity" of congressional relief, and which quoted in full (in addition to the stock commerce and Comity clause arguments) Judge Skinner's brief arguing that an Illinois insurance law was a violation of due process. Insurance company petitions are known to have been received by at least six members of the Joint Committee,[67] and were referred in the House to the Committee on Commerce,

---

by Hotchkiss probably impressed Bingham with the expediency of adopting the negative form "No State shall . . ." In later years Bingham inferred that study of John Marshall's opinion in *Barron v. Baltimore* had prompted him to make the change [see CONG. REC., March 28, 1871, Appendix pp. 83–85.] but it seems improbable in the light of the foregoing that the influences were entirely academic.

By what the writer, in the absence of any evidence to the contrary, concludes to have been merely a coincidence, Rep. Hotchkiss on March 2nd—two days after making the above-quoted speech—submitted the first insurance company petition found in the GLOBE.

65 Of a total of 208 petitions, some bearing as many as 500 signatures, and practically all of which were submitted by Republicans in the House, nearly three-fourths are found to have been received prior to final action by the Joint Committee on Section One—in fact, the peak was reached in mid-April just prior to such action. Only petitions relating to the tariff and freedmen's rights appear to have been received in greater numbers. The petitions dropped off suddenly in mid-June, but probably only because the campaign organized in February had run its course.

66 CIRCULAR: TO THE INSURANCE AGENTS OF THE UNITED STATES (Feb. 1, 1866) [only known copy is in the Library of the Insurance Library Association of Boston]. Prepared under the direction of C. C. Hine, secretary of companies' steering committee, and one of the leading insurance publicists of the post-Civil War period, the pamphlet leaves no doubt of the origin and character of the petitions. Elaborate instructions were provided for a "write-your-Congressman" campaign; petitions and memorials (on prepared forms) were to be circulated among influential business men; conventions of agents were proposed for each congressional district. *Id.* at 7–9.

The body of the pamphlet consisted chiefly of arguments and briefs against the constitutionality of foreign corporation and non-intercourse laws; the most notable of which were those of William Barnes, Superintendent of the Insurance Department of the State of New York, (pp. 15–20); extracts from the argument of William Curtis Noyes taken from 3 E. D. Smith (pp. 26); emphasis that under New York laws "the term *person* . . . shall be construed to include *corporations* as well as individuals" (p. 27); the entire brief of Judge Mark Skinner of Chicago, holding the Illinois law of 1852 to be a violation of due process (pp. 27–30). Pages 33–52 were made up of selected articles from insurance journals in 1864–1865 proposing a National Bureau of Insurance and a National Insurance Law.

67 Conkling submitted five. CONG. GLOBE, 39th Cong., 1st Sess. 1662, March 26; p. 1727, April 2; p. 1979, April 16; p. 2049, April 19; p. 2442, May 7 (1866). Washburne, two; Morrill, one; Fessenden, one; Grimes, one; Harris, one. Bingham appears to have submitted no petitions.

whose chairman at this session was Elihu Washburne, himself a member of the Joint Committee.

In summary, one can say that these petitions were independently motivated, and merely an extension and culmination of earlier trends. It is also to be distinctly noted that a statute,[68] not a constitutional amendment,[69] was the companies' real objective. It would seem to be established, however, that the petitions came to the attention of the framers while they were engaged in drafting the Amendment. On this basis, and in the light of Conkling's remarks, a tentative conclusion may be drawn. It cannot be inferred that the Amendment was deliberately or consciously framed to assist the insurance companies or other corporations, but everything about the petitions —their source, incidence, chronology and substance—suggests that they would have been likely to raise the question of corporate status while the framers were at work.[70]

Arriving almost simultaneously with the petitions of the insurance companies—yet addressed in this instance only to members of the

---

[68] See CIRCULAR, op. cit. supra note 66, at 6. Just when the bill for a National Bureau of Insurance was presented before Congress is unknown; but such a proposal was reported by the House Judiciary Committee, June 29, 1866 [CONG. GLOBE 3490]. And previously, on June 14, the day following final passage of the Fourteenth Amendment by Congress, Rep. Lawrence of Pennsylvania, had introduced a similar bill [Id. at 3162] which received no attention on the floor of Congress. It appears that Rep. J. K. Moorhead, brother of Jay Cooke's brother-in-law and partner, was the co-sponsor (with Lawrence) of the latter bill. Here again one is struck by a unique harmony of interests, for a funding bill lay at the heart of the Cooke's entire enterprise at this date [LARSON, JAY COOKE, PRIVATE BANKER (1936) 207–214, 239–240]; and one can readily understand how a proposal to "nationalize" the insurance companies (after the manner of the national banks) by investment of a certain share of capital in United States bonds, impressed the Cookes as sound financial statesmanship.

[69] For evidence that insurance men had nevertheless considered the prospects for a constitutional amendment, see William Barnes, Superintendent of the Department of Insurance of the State of New York, Annual Report for 1864, quoted in CIRCULAR, op. cit. supra note 66 at 19. Speaking of possible relief by interstate compacts, Barnes added "Such a proceeding would . . . be undesirable and might be more troublesome . . . than a direct effort to produce an amendment of the Constitution, making the [comity clause] expressly applicable to *corporations* as well as to *citizens*."

[70] If Bingham is ever revealed to have had insurance company connections, one might attach significance to the fact that he submitted his revised draft, made up (as he emphasized) of the comity clause and the Fifth Amendment, on February 3rd, just two days after the imprint date of the CIRCULAR: TO THE INSURANCE AGENTS OF THE UNITED STATES. It must be borne in mind, however, that an *adequate* explanation for Bingham's adoption of this phraseology is found in his own earlier speeches; and in the further fact that the Joint Committee had itself been moving in that direction. For the obviously laborious evolution of the phraseology in sub-committees January 12 to 27, 1866, see KENDRICK, JOURNAL OF THE JOINT COMMITTEE OF FIFTEEN ON RECONSTRUCTION (1914) 46–58. In either case of course it is obvious that February 1 to 3 marks the focal point of two independent but historically-converging lines of usage. The question is: what sort of relations prevailed at the historical intersection?

Ohio and Pennsylvania delegations—were several petitions from the "Cleveland and Mahoning Railroad . . . asking Congress to restore" certain franchises which "had been taken away by the . . . State of Pennsylvania, thus impairing vested rights of the citizens of Ohio."[71] These petitions sought redress for repeal of charter privileges by the same State which numbered among its constitutional opinions *Brown v. Hummel* and *Erie Railroad v. Casey*. Not unexpectedly, therefore, these petitions are likewise found suffused with due process of law. They serve to corroborate our tentative hypothesis regarding the character and effect of the insurance company petitions, and the likely relations that existed between the corporate and Negro rights usages of due process in 1866. In this instance, however, it is to be emphasized that the evidence goes considerably farther: by reason of certain of its ramifications, it not only injects new life into the possibility that Bingham, in 1866, *may have prepared* all his drafts with a definite intent to aid corporations as well as natural persons; but it indicates that at least one of Bingham's colleagues, and perhaps three of the members of the Joint Committee who voted in favor of his equal protection-due process phraseology, may have done so with the understanding that its wording might prove useful to corporations that found themselves in such straits as the Cleveland and Mahoning Railroad.

Keystone of this hypothetical structure is the fact that Reverdy Johnson, the leading minority member on the Joint Committee, (who nevertheless voted fairly consistently in favor of Bingham's

---

[71] The basic facts with reference to these petitions are that in the early Fifties, Ohio promoters, led by David Tod, later war Governor of Ohio, had projected a railroad from Cleveland to Pittsburgh, through the then largely undeveloped Youngstown district. Franchises were obtained from both Ohio and Pennsylvania, and by the end of the decade the road was complete to the Ohio line. For some reason, construction lagged in Pennsylvania, and it was not until the early Sixties, when English capital became interested, and plans were laid for a unified line through to Washington under direction of the Baltimore and Ohio, that the Cleveland and Mahoning and Pittsburgh and Connellesville charters threatened to serve as means for breaking the monopoly of the Pennsylvania Railroad in the region of Pittsburgh.

By May, 1864, this threat was no longer merely apparent; and at the dictation of the Pennsylvania's managers the state legislature summarily repealed the franchises of both roads, charging failure to fulfill time clauses. Whereupon the victims resorted to the Federal courts, secured a decision in July, 1865, holding the repealer void, and commenced negotiations with Tom Scott and J. Edgar Thomson of the monopoly—only to be harassed in the state courts by a host of vexatious suits. At length, construction stalled, the Ohio promoters resorted to flank attack in Congress, stressing with great shrewdness their rival's contumacy of Federal authority. See CONG. GLOBE, 39th Cong., 1st Sess., petitions at 1905 (Moorhead), 1925 (Garfield), 2634-5; and debates at 2282, 2365-2366, 2902-2903, 2922-2925 (1866); HANEY, CONGRESSIONAL HISTORY OF RAILWAYS IN THE UNITED STATES 1850-1887 (1910) 222-223.

drafts⁷²) had in June, 1865, served as counsel for the Cleveland and Mahoning Railroad and affiliates in the cases in the Federal courts.⁷³ In that capacity Johnson appears to have made such effective use of Chief Justice Lewis' dissenting opinion in *Erie Railroad v. Casey* that Justice Grier, in voiding the repealers, did so on the ground that the company and its affiliates had been denied the due course of law guaranteed by the Pennsylvania Constitution.⁷⁴ It therefore seems likely that Reverdy Johnson, at least, must have understood that to add a due process clause to the Federal Constitution as an express restraint upon the States was to add a source of valuable protection to corporate interests. Indeed, if one assumes that Johnson recalled the gingerly manner in which Justice Grier had been obliged to apply the "due course of law" clause of the Pennsylvania Constitution,⁷⁵ some special significance might be attached to the inference of Johnson's cryptic remark, made in Senate debate, that he favored the due process clause because he knew what its effect would be.⁷⁶

Reverdy Johnson was not the only member of the Joint Committee who had close relations with the Cleveland and Mahoning Railroad. On May 30, 1866, a month after final adoption of the present form

---

⁷² Johnson even voted in favor of adding the just compensation clause [KENDRICK, *op. cit. supra* note 70, at 85], although he opposed the privileges or immunities clause and moved to strike it out in Senate debate (see *infra* note 76).

⁷³ Baltimore v. Pittsburgh and Connellesville Railroad, 2 Fed. Cas. No. 570 and 827 (C. C. W. D. Pa. 1865). For Johnson's connection with the case see CONG. GLOBE, 39th Cong., 1st Sess., 2925; STEINER, THE LIFE OF REVERDY JOHNSON (1914) 141. Technically Johnson was counsel for the city of Baltimore, a bondholder; but the case was moot. Actually the Baltimore and Ohio monopoly, for which Johnson had been counsel for forty years, stood behind both the Cleveland and Mahoning and the Pittsburgh and Connellesville roads.

⁷⁴ *Id.* at 13. Declaring the object and effect of the repealer to be to "transfer the franchises and property of one corporation, anxious . . . to complete a valuable public improvement, to another [the Pennsylvania monopoly] whose interest is not to complete the road," the Justice held the act to be first a violation of the contract clause, then of due course of law. Due process, he implied, required that the Attorney General should have instituted judicial proceedings to ascertain the facts, etc. This was precisely the point on which the Pennsylvania State Court had ruled to the contrary in Erie R. R. v. Casey, cited note 45, *supra*.

Justice Grier made no mention of due course of law in his opinion, but said merely "The principles of law . . . are . . . clearly and tersely stated by Chief Justice Lewis in his opinion to be found in 1 Grant's Cases 274 with a review of the cases and a proper appreciation of that from Iowa"—the latter of course dealing with the "law of the land."

⁷⁵ See note 8, *supra*.

⁷⁶ "I am in favor of that part of the section which denies to a State the right to deprive any person of life, liberty or property without due process of law, but I think it is quite objectionable to provide that 'no state shall make or enforce any law which shall abridge the privileges or immunities of citizens of the United States,' simply because I don't understand what will be the effect of that." CONG. GLOBE, 39th Cong., 1st Sess. 3041, June 8, 1866.

of Section One, Thaddeus Stevens, whose narrow Negro Race draft had finally been abandoned (with his own approving vote) in favor of Bingham's broader drafts,[77] undertook to jam through the House, without debate, bills for relief of the Cleveland and Mahoning and affiliated companies.[78] Failing in his immediate objective, Stevens nevertheless succeeded the following day in securing full approval of the bills by the House, after a debate in which Justice Grier's opinion had been read into the record. And voting in favor of passage on May 31, 1866—while the Fourteenth Amendment was still being debated in the Senate—were, in addition to Stevens himself, Roscoe Conkling and John A. Bingham.

III.

Many matters, of course, remain to be investigated.[79] Yet with even these shadowy glimpses into the relations existing between the framers of the Fourteenth Amendment and the corporate interests farther along in the use of the due process and Comity clauses, one is no longer at loss to suggest plausible explanations for the statements Conkling made in his argument in 1882, nor is it very rash

---

[77] Stevens' course in these matters excites speculation. After announcing [see KENDRICK, *op. cit. supra* note 70, at 83], that he sponsored an amendment whose first Section provided "No discrimination shall be made by any State, nor by the United States, as to the civil rights of persons because of race, color or previous condition of servitude" he thereupon proceeded to vote (1) in favor of Bingham's move to add the just compensation clause [*id.* at 85]; (2) in favor of adding what is now Section One as [a redundant?] Section Five [*id.* at 87] (3) against striking out the same Section [*id.* at 99]; (4) in favor of substituting Bingham's draft (stricken out as Section Five) in place of his own [*id.* at 106]. Stevens was thus the sponsor of the narrowest sort of Negro Race draft and at the same time the most consistent supporter of Bingham's ["economic?"] drafts; and ultimately, when forced to choose between Bingham's and his own, he chose Bingham's. Why? Was it to afford *double* or *triple* protection to free Negroes and mulattoes? Or was it to protect corporations? Or was it, perhaps, to do both?

[78] See CONG. GLOBE, 39th Cong., 1st Sess. (1866) 2902-2903. Strictly speaking, Stevens sponsored the Pittsburgh and Connellsville bill, while Garfield sponsored the Cleveland and Mahoning's. The latter had been introduced in the House April 30, a fortnight after the first petitions, and just two days after final and unexpected substitution of Bingham's for Stevens' draft of Section One.

[79] *Id.* at 2922-2925. The vote in the House on the Cleveland and Mahoning bill was 77 to 41, with 65 not voting. Prior to the vote, Garfield, who was in charge of debate, made plain that the Pennsylvania legislature had acted "without a hearing, without any legal process in the courts . . . by the mere force of votes . . . ." Whereupon a waspish Pennsylvania sympathizer correctly anticipated a reciprocal treatment by Congress!

Despite this strong reception in the House, however, the Garfield-Stevens bills were killed by the Senate Committee on Commerce. And here, too, hangs a circumstance. Senator Edmunds of Vermont reported the adverse action of the Senate Committee; and made clear that he in no way concurred in the result. *Id.* at 3333; see also 4288. This of itself would excite no interest, except that sixteen years later, in the *San Mateo*

to venture hypotheses regarding the motives of Bingham and his associates. It is perhaps too much to expect that any of these hypotheses can ever be proved, but each possesses the dubious merit of being consistent with the known fragments of evidence. Disregarding such problems as the burden of proof, and interpreting matters most favorably to the idea of corporate inclusion, four major possibilities may be noted, any one of which lends support to the view that the constitutional status of corporations probably was considered by the framers.

1. Wholly apart from Bingham's personal understanding of his phraseology, his original intentions in drafting it, or the relations existing between the Cleveland and Mahoning Railroad and other members of the Joint Committee, it is possible that Reverdy Johnson, in the course of the Committee's deliberations, or perhaps even in private conversation with Conkling,[80] mentioned Justice Grier's decision as among the most recent involving the due process clause, and in this manner precipitated a frank discussion of the entire problem of corporate rights. Such a discussion would in likelihood have turned on the social ends which Grier's opinion had served; and we can be reasonably certain that in this respect the leading members of both parties on the Committee were in substantial agreement as to the merits: monopoly had been frustrated, bondholders protected,

---

Case, [116 U. S. 138 (1882)] Senator Edmunds appeared as counsel for the Southern Pacific Railroad. While he made no argument as explicit as Conkling's, he nevertheless did appear as one who had served in Congress in 1866 and who was presumed to speak with authority when he declared: "There is not one word in it [the Fourteenth Amendment] that did not undergo the completest scrutiny." In his peroration he extolled the "broad and catholic provision for universal security resting upon citizenship as it regarded political rights and resting upon humanity as it regarded private rights." See p. 8 of *"Argument of Mr. George F. Edmunds"* before the Supreme Court of the United States in San Mateo County v. Southern Pacific R. R., 116 U. S. 138 (1882).

[80] Conkling's voting record on Section One is scarcely less remarkable than Stevens'. Not only did he vote repeatedly in the Committee against Bingham's drafts down to April 28th [KENDRICK, op. cit. supra note 70, at 61, 62, 98, 99], and not only did he vote for the motion tabling the draft in the House Feb. 28th, [CONG. GLOBE, 39th Cong., 1st Sess. 1094] but on January 22, he had even gone on record in debate as opposing an amendment which would "prohibit States from denying civil or political rights to *any class of persons*." [Italics added.] Such a plan, he declared, "encounters a great objection on the threshold. It trenches upon the principle of existing local sovereignty. It denies to the people of the several States the right to regulate their own affairs in their own way." *Id.* at 358. Yet on April 28 Conkling voted in favor of substituting Bingham's for Stevens' draft. KENDRICK, op. cit. supra, at 106. How is one to explain his reversal? Merely as another product of the early confusion and uncertainty over Reconstruction policy which historians have noted in the minds of many leading Radicals—uncertainty which disappeared when partisan advantage became clearer? *Id.* at cc. 4, 5, 6; BEALE, THE CRITICAL YEAR (1930) *passim*. Or is one to regard it as having some more concrete and specific base? Future research should make this clear.

"vested rights" rendered secure, and the way reopened for the economic development of important sections of the country.[81] When it is realized that framers considering the subject in this light would have been unlikely to have pursued matters further, or to have pondered the abstract problem of discretionary due process as a means for frustrating social reforms and legislation, an entirely new face is put upon the problem of "conspiracy."[82] Not only is it plain that the status of corporations under the Amendment could have been raised incidentally, and in good faith, without regard for anti-democratic or reactionary purposes;[83] but it would seem to be necessary, if one is to escape an anachronistic fallacy, to make due allowance for the character of this early usage by Justice Grier and the manner in

---

[81] It is interesting to note that Congress at this session finally passed the amended Interstate Communications bill which Garfield and other Republicans had been sponsoring since 1864 in an attempt to break the power of such State monopolies as the Camden and Amboy of New Jersey. In its original form the bill would have declared competing lines military and post roads and have given *Federal* authority to build in disregard of State charters. See HANEY, *op. cit. supra* note 71, at 157–224, *passim*. See also Congressional debate on the measure, May 5, 1866 [CONG. GLOBE, 39th Cong., 1st Sess. (1866) 2365–66] wherein Senator Sherman cites Ohio's "demand" for the Mahoning and Connellesville roads as justifying passage; and wherein Reverdy Johnson implies that "the controversy [between these roads and the Pennsylvania monopoly] is not yet settled."

In 1866, opposition to such measures as the Interstate Communications Act came chiefly from Democrats and conservatives fearful for "States' Rights" and alarmed at the trend toward "centralization." *Id*. at 1857; 2197–2199. Reverdy Johnson himself had scruples in this regard, explained in part perhaps by the fact that the Baltimore and Ohio monopoly, while endeavoring to gain a route through Pennsylvania, was resisting attempts of rival roads to break into Maryland.

Rep. Jack Rogers, the second most influential *minority* member of the Joint Committee—who also voted consistently in favor of Bingham's drafts, including the rejected just compensation clause—was during these years counsel and Congressional advocate for the Camden and Amboy monopoly in New Jersey. In the latter capacity in 1864 Rogers had even argued that an early draft of the Interstate Communications bill threatened to deprive the Camden and Amboy of its property without just compensation! CONG. GLOBE, 38th Cong., 1st Sess. (1865) 1238–1241.

[82] Inevitably, in *a priori* analysis, students of constitutional history have tended to assume that the Conkling-Beard thesis requires (1) that intent to include corporations was the primary or decisive fact operating in the selection of the phraseology, (2) that it was accordingly necessary for the framers to have *foreseen* the substantive potentialities inherent in the clause. It is now plain of course that neither point is essential to the proposition; and that the second is itself the product of serious misconceptions concerning use of due process prior to the Civil War.

It should be said, therefore, in tribute to the Beards, that whatever the shortcomings of the circumstantial evidence upon which they appear to have based their conclusions, their *fundamental assumptions* were far sounder than those of constitutional historians who often have criticized them.

[83] Even if it develops that Bingham was aware of the Cleveland and Mahoning's troubles, or that he had knowledge of effective corporate use of due process *at the time he phrased his original drafts*, it by no means follows that intent to aid corporations was primary—least of all that Section One was a mere plot to aid certain Ohio pro-

which it would have determined the attitude toward corporate personality *if* the question were raised.

2. It is not unreasonable to suppose that Bingham, an Ohioan, and the Congressional representative of a section of the State interested in the completion of the Cleveland and Mahoning Railroad,[84] knew of the company's difficulties from the first, and watched with mounting apprehension the tactics employed by its Pennsylvania rival. Thus it is possible to argue that even if Bingham originally knew nothing of Reverdy Johnson's arguments (or Justice Grier's opinion) predicated upon due process, his personal sense of justice was offended by the charter repeal,[85] and accordingly he later drafted his constitutional amendment with the definite intention of covering such cases—an intention of which Conkling somehow became aware. It is to be emphasized that additional evidence is required to *establish* the proposition in this form; yet one feels warranted in pointing out that circumstances, so far as they are known, are not inconsistent with this interpretation of Conkling's inference.

3. Another possibility is that while Bingham may have known nothing of the railroads' use of due process when he first submitted his drafts, and while he originally had no thought of aiding anyone but Negroes and natural persons, and while the corporation on its part originally intended to do no more than appeal for Congressional aid at a time when circumstances were peculiarly favorable to such aid, the presentation of the petitions and bills, and the lobby arguments incident thereto, nevertheless did make clear that the due process-equal protection phraseology was comprehensive enough to include corporations. It is quite possible therefore that a full and free discussion ensued in the Committee, or among some of its mem-

---

moters. No one reading the speeches of the idealist who in 1859 sought to safeguard the rights of free Negroes to travel and to make and enforce contracts, and to earn a decent living in the North as well as in the South, will be likely to argue that Bingham's primary—or even his incidental—purpose was ever to protect hotel corporations and factory owners from paying workers a minimum wage. Our thinking on these subjects has been too much confused by the unfortunate connotations of the word "conspiracy."

[84] Defeated in 1862, but re-elected in 1864, Bingham represented the east-central constituency adjoining that passed through by the Cleveland and Mahoning. The road then terminated at Youngstown, leaving parts of this rich coal district without direct connections with Pittsburgh.

[85] In view of Bingham's apparent readiness to apply the due process clause wherever needed to protect or advance interests he approved of, this possibility is obviously of more than academic importance. Since we know (from his vote) his reaction to the major issue, it is largely a question of whether sufficient publicity was given to the controversy in its early stages in 1864-65 to assure that Bingham, a lawyer and politician whose business was to keep informed regarding such matters, would have been likely to have learned of it.

bers, regarding the expediency of a draft which offered prospective benefits of this type.

4. The final possibility is that petitions and bills of the insurance or express companies—or perhaps the remarks of an importunate counsel or lobbyist in charge of the companies' campaign in Congress—served to direct attention not merely to the potentialities of the due process-equal protection phraseology, but also to the privileges or immunities clause. It therefore involves no strain on credulity to believe that corporate citizenship as well as corporate personality was considered by the Joint Committee; yet one wonders—if this happened to be the case—whether the framers may not have concluded, in view of repeated interpretations of the Comity clause, that there was no likelihood corporations would ever be treated as "citizens" within the meaning of Section One.[86]

All these possibilities, of course, leave a doubter with his doubts. The striking thing in this essay, as in the previous one, is the paradoxical and indecisive character of the evidence. Just as discovery of

---

[86] It is an ironic fact, suggestive in certain of its implications, that the insurance companies, which down to 1866 pioneered in the use of the phraseology employed in Section One, were almost the last to gain protection under its terms. This paradox is the more striking because these companies were naturally the first to employ the improved weapons. As early as February, 1871, the Continental Life Insurance Company of New York attacked a New Orleans agency-license ordinance which discriminated against outside corporations, counsel apparently contending that corporations were "persons" within the meaning of both Section One and the Civil Rights Act passed in enforcement thereof. United States Circuit Judge Woods flatly rejected this view, reasoning much as did Mr. Justice Black in his recent dissent in Connecticut General Life Insurance Co. v. Johnson, 58 Sup. Ct. 436 (U.S. 1938), *i.e.*, that since only natural persons can be "born and naturalized," a double standard of interpretation of the word "person" is required to sustain the argument from the present text. Insurance Co. v. New Orleans, 1 Woods 85 (U. S. C. C. La. 1870). (Inquiry of the clerk of the United States District Court for New Orleans reveals that the official record of this important case has been lost.)

The Continental Life Insurance Company began its attack on this New Orleans ordinance just two weeks after the United States Supreme Court, in Liverpool Insurance Company v. Oliver, 77 U. S. 566 (February 6, 1871) gave counsel to understand, as clearly as a court ever could, that nothing was to be gained by continued reliance on the comity clause to attack legislation of this type. Beginning with Paul v. Virginia, 75 U. S. 168 (argued in October, 1869), and continuing with Ducat v. Chicago, 77 U. S. 410 (submitted December 21, 1870, decided January 9, 1871), former Justice Benjamin R. Curtis, as chief counsel for the companies, had relied almost entirely on the commerce and comity clauses in making the long delayed appeals to the Supreme Court. This fact of itself suggests what might be assumed from Curtis' past connections with *Murray v. Hoboken*, 18 How. 272 (U. S. 1855), and *Dred Scott v. Sandford* (*supra* note 56)—namely, that Curtis' preferred strategy was to get corporations declared "citizens" rather than "persons"; and to do so, first under the comity clause, then under Section One. Apparent failure to stress the due process, equal protection, and privileges or immunities clauses in these early test cases may therefore have been simply a tactical maneuver.

the Negro rights sense in which Bingham first used due process tended to eclipse what had been regarded as his economic motivation, so now a survey of the pre-war use of due process by corporations suggests that the framers may have proceeded with greater understanding than constitutional historians have been willing to acknowledge. The impressive thing, indeed, is the cantilever nicety of the balance.

It is now plain not only that a development of corporate personality took place prior to 1866 but that Reverdy Johnson, at least, and perhaps several of his colleagues, had knowledge of certain phases of that development. Yet when this is said it must be remembered (1) that Bingham's speeches and drafts in 1866 were modelled on earlier speeches which were preoccupied with the problem of protecting *natural* persons; (2) that Conkling's misquotations from the Journal are difficult to reconcile with a clean-cut case, particularly in view of the absence of corroborating statements by other members of the Joint Committee, and since Conkling himself appears to have said nothing publicly for sixteen years.

Heightening the uncertainty and confusion inherent in the foregoing circumstances is the further fact that Reverdy Johnson, the one member of the Joint Committee who had used corporate personality prior to 1866, nevertheless failed to invoke the due process clause of the Fifth Amendment when he argued for the plaintiffs in the hard-fought case of *Veazie Bank v. Fenno*, in 1869.[87]

Obviously the foregoing evidence can be woven into different patterns. Ignoring or minimizing the first set of factors, Conkling can be portrayed as a shrewd lawyer who in his argument in 1882 capitalized earlier coincidence. Ignoring or minimizing the second set, he can be portrayed as a drafter who in 1866 figured in something akin to a "plot."

After considering the matter for two years, the writer's personal conclusion is that as long as all major conditions are fulfilled, Conkling perhaps ought to be given benefit of the doubt, even though few courts would be inclined to accept him as a disinterested or even honorable witness. Yet this acknowledges no more than that the corporation problem probably did come up incidentally in the discussions, and that no special significance was at that time attached to it one way or the other. From a study of the evolution of the phraseology in the Joint Committee the writer feels confident that Section

---

[87] 8 Wall. 533, 19 L. ed. 482 (1869). See the summary of Johnson's argument in the Lawyers' Edition, at page 483.

One was not *designed* to aid corporations, nor was the distinction between "citizens" and "persons" conceived for their benefit.

But the outstanding conclusion warranted by the present evidence is concerned with the irrelevancy rather than with the character of the Joint Committee's intentions. It is now plain that corporate personality, as a constitutional doctrine, antedated the Fourteenth Amendment, and was in fact so vital and natural a part of the self-expansion of judicial power within the framework of due process, that its postwar development was assured, whatever may have been the original objectives of the framers. The two great classes of petitions[88] in the *Congressional Globe* foreshadow and explain this result: Having simultaneously fostered the growth of corporate enterprise as well as a mighty upsurge of popular idealism, the Civil War *of itself* consummated a marriage of idealistic and economic elements in American constitutional theory.[89] In the words of Max Ascoli,[90] the Fourteenth Amendment was the "supreme celebration" of this union. It would appear largely immaterial whether those who presided at the rites were conscious of their function.

EDITORIAL NOTE. The concluding paragraph, with its metaphor, obviously begged the question, as surely as it weighted the "affirmative" evidence. Worse still, it was both misleading and erroneous to say that "corporate personality, *as a constitutional doctrine*, antedated the Fourteenth Amendment." Actually, all that *antedated* the Amendment were some scattered cases, arguments, and dicta in

---

[88] These petitions present an insight into the unique harmony of ideas and interests between petitioners seeking added protection for property rights and those seeking to secure Freedmen's rights. Side by side, and often submitted on the same day by the same members of Congress, are appeals from "Western citizens . . . for the greater protection of interstate securities," from "Iowa Quakers asking perfect equality before the law for all regardless of color," from "citizens . . . of Pennsylvania asking for amendments giving *all classes* of citizens their natural rights," from "citizens of Pennsylvania asking just and equal laws relating to interstate insurances to protect the interests of the policies."

[89] Between Radicals and racial equalitarians on the one hand, and representatives of business enterprise on the other, existed not only harmony in such general objectives as the need for expanding Federal and contracting State power, but in the very details of constitutional theory—as evidenced by the natural rights usage by *both* groups of *both* the comity and the due process clauses. Such harmonies, essentially products of the Secession and defeat of the slave interest, and of the determination of both humanitarians and northern capitalists to let nothing jeopardize the fruits of the war, stand sharply in contrast to the weakness and isolation of these same groups in the Thirties and Forties. See note 18, *supra*.

[90] INTELLIGENCE IN POLITICS (1936) 160–161.

The "Conspiracy Theory," Part II 95

which members of the bench and bar had relied on a due process clause to protect corporate property or rights. Cases and usage of this sort,[1] and the constitutional *doctrine* of corporate personality, are two different, two separate things entirely, as eventually became clear when the railroad and the insurance company usage was re-canvassed.[2] But in 1938 this point remained clouded, and neither Yale critics and skeptics,[3] nor other reviewers and commentators, pinpointed this flaw.

This period, 1866–1868, in short *appeared* to be, and in fact was, the chronological point at which the antebellum and the postbellum developments intersected historically, hence perhaps the time that ideas and usage had begun to interact and percolate. But this was far from meaning there yet had been, much less there yet had been found, or could be, an overt or articulate corporate "person" as a *constitutional doctrine*. The latter of course presumes and requires a judicial holding, not simply a hypothetical chance or prospect of one.

Those blind spots and other weaknesses are glaring, embarrassing enough today:[4] possibilities upgraded to probabilities—proof thus waived or begged; inference mistaken for fact, or equated with it; verification of *one* detail, fact, or time, accepted as corroboration of far more—all these are evident, and at several points. And once again my naïveté was characteristic of others'.

Yet the essay as a whole, and the broadening case study, did clarify and advance research, disintegrating on the one side, re-integrating on the other. The ramifying, interlocking, circular complexity of a once-simple, ambiguous hypothesis now became starkly clear, especially as I drafted and redrafted sections II and III in the effort to cover widening, or incongruous fact or circumstance. Fuzziness, gaps, flaws, and conflicts in the basic statements of Bingham and Conkling, as relied on by Hannis Taylor, Kendrick, and the Beards; a consequent unravelling of their original premises and inferences, and

---

[1] *I.e.*, as discussed *supra*, sections I and II.

[2] See *infra*, Chapter 10, and editorial note preceding Chapter 13.

[3] No one, it appears from the correspondence, really cut through the ambiguous-controversial inferences, or broke down the "seeminglys" into their divergent values and potentials, with reference to the three crucial periods 1866–1868, 1882–1886, and 1927–1937.

[4] The discussion at pp. 79–81, obviously was forced, weak, and naïf; the text at footnote 57 shows awareness of the complexity and the hazards, but the various "open" circumstances and time values still are not appreciated and not differentiated, either as applied to Conkling's argument or to the Beards'. The discussion at p. 90, notes 82–83, barely approaches a "then" and "now" contrast. Conkling is given the benefit of both doubt *and* credence-credulity.

hence also of my own; an ever-lengthening and broadening search for evidence: all this put matters in context and in question.

Beardian determinisms—"Ideas and interests"—with the latter distinctly "up"—were riding almost as high as ever; most of the "presentist pressures" earlier noted, prevailed still, and the frightened concern of conservatives as evidenced by E. W. Camp's article[5] was beginning to show just how diverse these pressures were and would be.

Therefore, a Scottish verdict, "Unproved"—in this case perhaps "unprovable"—was all that presently could be returned in the premises.

The corollary was that both corporate and humanitarian usage had to be re-explored, and a great deal more learned of each. And there now was the possibility, too, that the "conspiracy"—how that idea lingered and befogged—really had been congressional and statutory, not judicial; nothing Conkling had said or not said precluded this interpretation, and various details favored it. Senator Reverdy Johnson now, not Bingham nor Conkling, clearly seemed the pivotal figure. But Johnson himself had not used due process, neither Fifth Amendment due process in *Veazie v. Fenno,* nor (apparently) Fourteenth Amendment due process after 1868.[6] Insurance and express company interests, however, definitely had not waited sixteen years as so long presumed by the skeptics, before "exercising the corporate person." Rather, both interests had continued active in both Congress and the courts during and after ratification. As chairman of the House Judiciary Committee, Bingham had sponsored key insurance company bills, 1869–1871.[7] (This might well be the rationale?) Implications of expanded congressional power certainly had to be probed, for these were the years in which *interstate* business really had made its debut in Congress and in the courts. So far as framer understanding and intent were concerned, a secondary-intention hypothesis was the rationale that seemed best to fit the "facts" as they stood in 1938–1939.

Articles and commentaries by Louis Boudin,[8] Willard Hurst,[9] and

---

[5] See *supra* at note 47.
[6] See *supra* at note 87. Reverdy Johnson's "use" of due process, like that of the various railroads (cf. *supra* p. 91) turns out to have been insignificant indeed; see *infra,* Chapter 10.
[7] See *infra,* Chapter 3, at notes 54 and 57.
[8] See *supra,* editorial note following Chapter 1, footnote 10.
[9] Book review, 52 HARV. L. REV. 851–860 (March, 1939).

Mark Howe[10] sharpened and focused the issues; Professor Hurst's analysis was especially acute and suggestive. Interesting progress was made in pursuing these leads in May and June, 1939, but on July 1, having completed graduate library training, I entered law librarianship. A much broadened, sustained attack now became possible. Process and protection no longer were abstractions, but matters of daily interest, observation, and insight.

---

[10] As cited *supra*, Chapter 1, note 14.

[CHAPTER 3]

Justice Field and the Fourteenth Amendment

EDITORIAL NOTE. Law libraries are the receiving hospitals, laboratories, and cemeteries of a learned practicing profession. Order librarians, willy nilly, are aides, accessioners-in-chief, and factotums who, during troubled times, become professional expediters, reoutfitters en masse. During twelve years of the late New Deal–Fair Deal period, 1939–1950, it was my privilege to serve in these capacities as Order Librarian of the Los Angeles County Law Library, one of the largest American collections, and then booming in all departments. Fascinating employment this was: ordering, receiving, processing new materials, historical and current; building up constitutional and administrative law and history in particular; screening offers and lists, checking catalogs and bibliographies; scanning court reports and loose-leaf services for the latest births and burials, and the law journals for leads, trends, and commentary—all during the Law's grand demarche Right and Left, with the Conspiracy Theory articles now being generously noticed and cited; economic due process already a memory; racial protection at last on the upgrade—Myrdal's *An American Dilemma* and the declared war aims of the Atlantic Charter having shamed us good. Everyman's Constitution, in short, rising and standing, but no longer standing pat. All in all, a fascinating study of the Law's redeployment, of constitutionalism as such, and an impressive demonstration of the primacy and the flexibility of these due process-equal protection guarantees.

Wartime extracurricular activities at this date were reinforcing everyone's experience and impressions. For seven years commencing in 1939, first as reader and case selector, later as co-author of the State Constitutional Law Survey for the *American Political Science Review*,[1] I covered, one by one, in the advance sheets of the National Reporter System, the major cases which were already, or soon des-

---

1 See that REVIEW, August numbers, vols. 34–40: reader for author Charles Aikin, 1939–1942, vols. 34–36; reader for author Jacobus tenBroek, 1942–1943, vol. 37; co-author with Jacobus tenBroek, 1944–1946, vols. 38–40.

tined to be, the valves and hydrants by which procedural-substantive flows were controlled, and often reversed. On weekends, holidays, and vacations during the final war years I worked as an extra longshoreman, usually in well-integrated gangs. I thus learned that many of Eric Hoffer's and my new colleagues were quick and plainspoken, and I owe my life to one who saved us both from self-decapitation by an asphalt barrel, yet who today, despite service in two wars, and a son's services in a third, still stands among *The Petitioners*, needing, as the late Judge Loren Miller[2] so forcibly reminded us, "Supreme Court decrees to buy or rent, vote in elections, read in city libraries, loll in public parks, or swim in the ocean."

More and more during this period, judicial restraint and judicial self-restraint, judicial motivation and the judicial function generally, were matters of vigorous, often strident debate. Law and opinion were realigning, accommodating to change and circumstance. Academic interests and academic views were changing as fast as judicial. The decline and fall of economic due process had necessarily highlighted and raised questions about the rise.

In the case of my own work, Justice Field of course had got upstaged in 1937–1938 by Conkling, and six years of research had been pushed aside. Yet that story now was more pertinent than ever. To complete it, to integrate Field, the Fourteenth Amendment, and the railroad story; to fit together the racial-humanitarian and the economic-corporate "halves" and contrasts; to do the same with the pre-Civil War and the post-Civil War developments and constructions, pursuing the leads and the findings of the Conspiracy Theory monograph, combining and synthesizing the whole with the graces and the beatitudes of the "Ninth Circuit law" as the latter now stood revealed in the Pomeroy and Deady collections, and in long-neglected briefs and cases—this was my task and challenge.

Field, everyone recognized, was "the once-and-perfect" integrator and unifier of Fourteenth Amendment history; "pioneer and prophet" of judicial laissez faire—so called by E. S. Corwin as early as 1909;[3] the judge whose feud with Chief Justice Waite had racked and strained the whole Waite Court period (1874–1888). Field's presidential aspirations, his Court Plan, his steadfast defense of the Chinese, and of the Big Four's railroads, his circuit opinions establishing the corporate "person," and above all, the bearing of these

---

[2] MILLER, THE PETITIONERS: THE STORY OF THE SUPREME COURT OF THE UNITED STATES AND THE NEGRO (1966), a distinguished work providing the best general coverage.
[3] Corwin, *The Supreme Court and the Fourteenth Amendment*, 7 MICH. L. REV. 643, 653 (1909).

on the triumphs, the excesses, and the ultimate eclipse of doctrinaire economic due process, made the study of his achievements and personality more timely and interesting than ever.

Justice Black's dissent meanwhile still nettled and dismayed conservatives. In the October, 1940, number of the *American Historical Review*, A. C. McLaughlin, dean of American constitutional historians, had attempted an oblique, yet almost pointless rejoinder. Entitled "The Court, the Corporation, and Conkling," yet saying almost nothing of the latter, the essay pointed up the heavy emotional commitment and investment which many still felt and held in corporate personality and in the ancillary and buttressing doctrines, even as a now unmentionable taint exposed the hopeless shambles.[4]

A second autopsy, performed at this time by Louis M. Hacker in *The Triumph of American Capitalism* (1940), underscored these same discredibilities, indeed proved that Conkling and Bingham were harder for a once neo-Marxist to fit into such a pattern or thesis in 1940[5] than they had been for the Beards in *The Rise of American Civilization* in 1927.

Written during weekends, holidays, and vacations, "Justice Field and the Fourteenth Amendment" is an overcrowded and overloaded essay, now rather a period piece in some respects. Yet it also was a necessary first attempt to get the Fourteenth Amendment as a whole into focus as my successive studies had revealed it, and an assurance too that my six years' work between 1931–1937 would not be wholly lost. (Yet so ironically it almost was, when the original manuscript disappeared in the Marine Corps mails en route to one of the editors of the *Yale Law Journal* on duty in the Pacific.)

The four letters of Justice Field, originally written to Professor John Norton Pomeroy and edited and published in the *Yale Law Journal* in May, 1938, afford striking insight into Field's personality and motivation. Reprinted at this point, they may be read either as an introduction to the essay proper or as extended documentation for specific points later cited and quoted.

---

[4] 46 Am. Hist. Rev. 45–63 (1940).
[5] See as cited, pp. 387–392.

[CHAPTER 3]

PART ONE: FOUR LETTERS OF MR. JUSTICE FIELD

IN JUNE, 1937, the Library of the University of California acquired four letters written by Stephen J. Field, Associate Justice of the Supreme Court of the United States, to John Norton Pomeroy,[1] first Professor of Municipal Law in Hastings Law College. The letters were acquired from Mrs. Walter Schirmer, of Carmel, California, widow of John Norton Pomeroy, Jr. They are of extraordinary historical interest. They constitute an intimate record of those years during which Justice Field's friends were actively working in his behalf for the Democratic nomination as President, and during which he himself was often disheartened by the reluctance of a majority of the Supreme Court to broaden judicial review in accordance with the tenets of his laissez faire, natural rights philosophy. Requiring almost no clarification, and serving as an admirable supplement to Professor Swisher's biography, *Stephen J. Field, Craftsman of the Law*,[2] the letters are here published by permission of the University of California.

I.

SUPREME COURT OF THE UNITED STATES
Washington, June 21st, 1881.

My Dear Sir:

Some months ago I wrote to you respecting the sketch[3] of a certain person's Legislative and Judicial work, and stated that it was so strong in its award of commendation that I should hardly dare show it to my friends. However, I have shown it to many of them and all have expressed a desire that it should be put in type. So I have concluded to give it to the printer. The book of comments upon my

---

[1] See "John Norton Pomeroy," by John Norton Pomeroy, Jr., GREAT AMERICAN LAWYERS, VIII, 91–135 (Philadelphia, 1909) edited by William Draper Lewis; at 123–124.

[2] Brookings, 1930.

[3] During the winter of 1880–81, Professor Pomeroy had written the appreciative review of Justice Field's career eventually published as the "Introductory Sketch" in SOME ACCOUNT OF THE WORK OF STEPHEN J. FIELD, edited by Black and Smith, privately printed, 1881.

opinions and of extracts from them will be enlarged by additions relating to inter-State commerce, taxation, attorneys and counsellors at law, the Pueblo of San Francisco and the treatment of the Chinese in California. With your sketch prefixed the book will be valued by my friends.

But your sketch has been altered in several particulars. Much of its strong language of commendation has been omitted, and some of it has been modified, and in these respects I think the sketch will be more acceptable to others as it is to myself. The severe condemnation you expressed of the old Supreme Court of the State is also omitted. It still states—what is true—that the court did not at all times have the confidence of the public, but that this was owing to the character —intellectual and moral—of persons who are now dead. The living members of the old court are Judge Hastings[4]—the founder of your Law Department, Judge Hydenfeldt,[5] Judge Bennett,[6] Judge Burnett[7] and Judge Terry.[8] No one ever questioned the integrity or ability of Hydenfeldt and Bennett, or the integrity of Burnett or Terry. Hastings you know, and he was never regarded as a shining light. Terry had ability but his Southern prejudices and partisanship affected his judgment. The judges who brought the greatest reproach upon the bench, were Wells,[9] Murray[10] and Anderson,[11] all of whom are dead. I think the sweeping language you used would create much unpleasant feeling.

The common law of England was adopted as a rule of decision in

---

[4] Serranus Clinton Hastings, 1814–1893, Chief Justice of Supreme Court of Iowa 1848–1849; first Chief Justice of Supreme Court of California, 1849–1851; Attorney General of California, 1852–1854. In 1878 Hastings provided an endowment of $100,000 for the founding of Hastings College of the Law. See 8 DICT. AM. BIOG. 387.

[5] Solomon Heydenfeldt, 1816–1890. Associate Justice of Supreme Court of California 1850–1857. See SHUCK, A HISTORY OF THE BENCH AND BAR OF CALIFORNIA (1901) pp. 457–459.

[6] Nathaniel Bennett, 1818–1886. Associate Justice, Supreme Court of California 1849–1851. See SHUCK, *op. cit. supra* note 5, at 445–447.

[7] Peter Hardeman Burnett, 1807–1895. Judge of Supreme Court of Oregon 1845; appointed Associate Justice of Supreme Court of Oregon Territory by President Polk 1848. First Governor of California 1849–1851; Associate Justice of Supreme Court of California, January, 1857, to September, 1857. See 3 DICT. AM. BIOG. 300–301.

[8] David Smith Terry, 1823–1889. Associate Justice, Supreme Court of California, 1855–1857; Chief Justice, 1857–1859; later, as a result of affairs growing out of the Sharon Will Case, a bitter personal and political enemy of Field. See 18 DICT. AM. BIOG. 379–380; SWISHER, *op. cit. supra* note 2, pp. 321–361 ("The Terry Tragedy").

[9] Alexander Well, ?–1854. Associate Justice of Supreme Court of California, January, 1853 to October, 1854.

[10] Hugh C. Murray, 1825–1857. Associate Justice of Supreme Court of California, 1851–1852, Chief Justice, 1852 to 1857. See SHUCK, *op. cit. supra* note 5, at 435–436.

[11] Alexander Anderson, ?–1853. Associate Justice of Supreme Court of California, April, 1852, to January, 1853.

the courts by the first Legislature in April 1850. I was a member of the second one. Some changes were required in your article in consequence of this misapprehension. [See page 15.]

The statement of my views in Washburn vs. Perry,[12] the Legal Tender case in the Supreme Court of the State, and in the granger cases[13] in the Supreme Court of the United States, is not strictly accurate. Although I have always held that the States can collect their taxes in such way as they might choose—in goods, (as was formerly done in Virginia, in tobacco) or in coin or notes, and that their power in this respect could not be controlled by Congress, I did not express it in the State Supreme Court. I suggested it to Chief Justice Chase in the case of Lane County vs Oregon,[14] and he expressed my views. In the granger cases I did not place my dissent on the interference of the State Legislation with the power of Congress under the commercial clause. I have accordingly corrected your sketch in these particulars. But the general analysis of the labors of your friend remain unchanged.

Please look over the accompanying sheets and if you approve of the sketch in its present form it will be published, otherwise not. Whatever appears in print must have your sanction as it will bear your name as its author. Of course you will alter it to suit your own views if you think it necessary. Make such changes as you like bearing always in mind, if you will pardon me, that its language is already as eulogistic as justice will permit. When you have corrected it please return it to me. I will ask your early attention to this as I wish to have the matter completed before I leave for Europe this coming month. It is my present purpose to leave between the 5th and 10th of July.

On Sunday last Mr. Lloyd Tevis,[15] of San Francisco, passed several hours with me and in the course of conversation with him reference was had to the Pacific Railway Company and the want of tact in the management of its affairs. This led me to mention the letter that I wrote to Mr. Towne[16] urging the officers of the company to retain your professional services. I told Mr. Tevis of your ability as a legal writer, of your frequent communications to law journals and of your

---

[12] 20 Cal. 318 (1862).

[13] Munn v. Illinois, 94 U. S. 113; Chicago, B. & Q. R.R. v. Iowa, 94 U. S. 155; Peik v. Chicago & N. W. R.R., 94 U. S. 164; Chicago, M. & St. P. Ry. v. Ackley, 94 U. S. 179; Winona and St. Peter R.R. v. Blake, 94 U. S. 180; Stone v. Wisconsin, 94 U. S. 181 (all 1877).

[14] 74 U. S. 71 (1869).

[15] Lloyd Tevis, 1824–1899, President (1872–1892) Wells Fargo Express Company, and a former President of the Southern Pacific Railroad. See 18 DICT. AM. BIOG. 384–385.

[16] General Manager of the Central Pacific and Southern Pacific Railroads, 1883.

special study of questions in which the Railway was interested. I observed that the company would act wisely if it retained you and he agreed with me fully and added, that he would speak to the officers on his return to San Francisco and urge them to retain your services.

Mr. Tevis is a very efficient man in all matters of business, has great tact and good sense and is more likely to effect an arrangement of the kind than any person that I know of. If you will consult him on the subject—and indeed on any matters of business, you will find him of invaluable service; and he is faithful in all things.

Please let me hear from you as soon as you can conveniently examine the accompanying papers.

With kind remembrances to Mrs. Pomeroy, I am

Very truly yours,—
Stephen J. Field

Prof. John Norton Pomeroy
of University of
California

II.

Washington, D. C.
April 14th 1882

My dear Professor Pomeroy:—

Your letter of the 1st inst. was received yesterday.

I have, today, mailed a copy of the volume containing "some account of my legislative and judicial labors" to the several persons named in the list which you inclosed. As I am not acquainted with any of the gentlemen, I wrote on the corner of the book, outside, "From J.N.P."; which, I suppose, is what you desired—thus showing that it was forwarded *at your request*. I shall be glad to send a copy to any other persons whom you may suggest.

I lately met a lawyer in this city, of marked ability, Professor Maury by name, who delivers lectures in the Law School of Columbia College, & who will, probably, soon be appointed Assistant Attorney General; and he told me, that he had read the first volume of your work on Equity Jurisprudence,[17] with the greatest admiration and instruction; that he considered it vastly superior to the work by Storey on the same subject. He added, that in a late conversation

---

[17] A TREATISE ON EQUITY JURISPRUDENCE, AS ADMINISTERED IN THE UNITED STATES OF AMERICA; ADOPTED FOR ALL THE STATES AND TO THE UNION OF LEGAL AND EQUITABLE REMEDIES UNDER THE REFORMED PROCEDURE, San Francisco: A. L. Bancroft, 1881–1883, 3 vols.

he had with Judge Bradley of our Court, the Judge expressed the same opinion to him. I requested him to write a Review of the book for one of the law magazines; and he promised me to do so. I mentioned to you, in one of my letters, that I received the first volume on the eve of my departure to Europe last summer. Since my return I have been so occupied that I could scarcely find time to answer my letters. I have not, therefore, read the book, except a few pages here and there. I saw enough, however, to greatly interest me; and as soon as the Court adjourns in May, I shall give it a careful perusal: I doubt not that it possesses all the merit which characterises your writings.

I see that California is very much excited over the veto of the Chinese Bill by the President.[18] I do not wonder at it. It must be apparent to every one, that it would be better for both races to live apart—and that their only intercourse should be that of foreign commerce. The manners, habits, mode of living, and everything connected with the Chinese prevent the possibility of their ever assimilating with our people. They are a different race, and, even if they could assimilate, assimilation would not be desirable. If they are permitted to come here, there will be at all times conflicts arising out of the antagonism of the races which would only tend to disturb public order and mar the progress of the country. It would be better, therefore, before any larger number should come, that the immigration be stopped. You know I belong to the class, who repudiate the doctrine that this country was made for the people of *all* races. On the contrary, I think it is for our race—the Caucasian race. We are obliged to take care of the Africans; because we find them here, and they were brought here against their will by our fathers. Otherwise, it would be a very serious question, whether their introduction should be permitted or encouraged.

I expect to leave Washington, about the last of May or first of June, for California; and when there I hope I shall have the pleasure of spending some pleasant hours with you.

Please present my kind regards to Mrs. Pomeroy, & believe me

Very sincerely yours,
Stephen J. Field

Professor J. N. Pomeroy.

---

[18] President Arthur had vetoed the Chinese Exclusion Act, April 4, 1882.

III.

Washington, D. C.,
March 28th 1883

My dear Mr. Pomeroy:

Yesterday Mr. Wager Swayne,[19] a partner of Judge Dillon[20] of New York called to see me, and in the course of conversation he stated that he was desirous of securing for one of our law magazines a careful review of the recent decisions of the Supreme Court in the Louisiana and Virginia cases,[21] and asked me whether you would be likely to furnish an article on that subject if applied to, the usual compensation for such articles being given.

I said in reply that I thought you would. He will accordingly write to you on the subject in the course of a few days, having first inquired of the magazine editors whether such an article would be acceptable to them.[22]

The recent decisions of our Court in those cases have provoked a great deal of comment and much hostile criticism. I do not myself see how it is possible to sustain the decisions of the majority of the Court without overturning a whole line of decisions commencing almost with the foundation of the Government. However, that is a

---

[19] Wager Swayne, 1834–1902, Yale 1856. Son of Field's former colleague, Justice Noah H. Swayne. See 18 Dict. Am. Biog. 240–241.

[20] John Forrest Dillon, 1831–1914. United States Circuit Judge for the Eighth Judicial Circuit, 1869–1879. See 5 Dict. Am. Biog. 311.

[21] On March 5, 1883, the Supreme Court had decided the so-called Repudiation Cases (107 U. S. 711) involving the power of various Southern States to readjust the huge debts piled up by the corrupt carpetbag regimes in the years immediately following the Civil War. As in all Reconstruction cases, issues were hopelessly confused, and the majority opinion, written by Chief Justice Waite, denied the competency of the Court to compel States to meet their obligations. Justices Field and Harlan dissented. See William A. Scott, The Repudiation of State Debts (N. Y., 1893) Chapter VI, "Repudiation in Virginia"; Ella Lonn, Reconstruction in Louisiana After 1868, (N. Y., 1918) passim, for historical background.

[22] Professor Pomeroy's attack on the trend of constitutional interpretation as then evidenced by the majority decisions in Munn v. Illinois and Ex Parte Wall, 107 U. S. 265, 1883 (as well as in the Repudiation Cases) appeared in 17 American Law Review 684–734 (September-October 1883, "The Supreme Court and State Repudiation"). Reprinted in pamphlet form, it attracted wide attention. (John Norton Pomeroy, Jr., supra note 1, at 108.) Today the article is notable as an analysis and criticism of the tendency of the early Waite Court to interpret narrowly limitations on legislative power: to hold, as Pomeroy said, (p. 703) that these "be strictly construed in favor of the government"; that "nothing . . . be added to their express terms by implication or inference." Decrying this tendency as one both "subversive" and "erroneous," in that it left property rights subject to "injurious and communistic legislation," Pomeroy hailed Field's minority views as the hope of the future.

Stricken with pneumonia early in 1885, Professor Pomeroy did not live to see the reversal of the trends he deplored.

Justice Field and the Fourteenth Amendment 107

matter which you can better judge of when you have read the opinions.

A few days since I sent you a copy of the opinions in the Virginia cases.[23] I will today send you a copy of those in the Louisiana cases.[24] They certainly either constitute a new departure for the Court, or the profession has been greatly mistaken as to the purpose and effect of its previous decisions.

Some weeks ago, I wrote you with reference to the San Mateo tax case[25] telling you that its decision would not be made until next term, and enclosing you also certain memoranda which had been handed me by two of the Judges. Have you ever received these? They were, of course, intended only for your eye, and I should be glad to know that they have come to your hands.

I shall leave here for San Francisco about the first of June. I may perhaps stop at Carson City on the way, to hold Court for a few days there.

I shall be ready to take up any new tax cases[26] as soon as I arrive, and I hope in whatever case is tried all the facts relating to the mortgage upon the property of the Railroad Company will be shown and also the extent to which its property has been subjected to taxation throughout the State.

I take the Argonaut,[27] from San Francisco, and I—see no other California paper, except occasionally. Now and then some good friend will send me the Chronicle, containing either a direct attack or some base insinuation. But for newspaper attacks I have long since ceased to care. They do not worry me at all. As I have often said, if my opinions present the law truly they will ultimately be sustained, though accompanied with censorious criticism on all sides on their first appearance. On the other hand, if they do not present the law truly, they will ultimately go down and be disregarded, though accompanied at first with the praises of the whole commu-

---

[23] Antoni v. Greenhow, 107 U. S. 769 (1883).
[24] Louisiana v. Jumel; Elliott v. Wiltz, 107 U. S. 711 (1883).
[25] County of San Mateo v. Southern Pacific Railroad Co., 13 Fed. 145, 722, decided by Justice Field at Circuit, September 25, 1882. Appealed to the Supreme Court of the United States, argued December 19, 20, 21, 1882, decided December 21, 1885 (116 U. S. 138). See SWISHER, *op. cit. supra* note 2, Chapter IX.
[26] Numerous cases involving issues subordinate to those of the San Mateo case were on the docket of the Circuit Court in San Francisco; and were decided by Justice Field on his next visit to the city in 1883. See County of Santa Clara v. Southern Pacific Railroad Company and cases reported therewith, 18 Fed. 385. Final decision in these cases was made by the Supreme Court of the United States in May, 1886 (118 U. S. 394).
[27] A well-written organ of conservative opinion edited by Frank Pixley.

nity. Their proper place must be ultimately determined by the profession of the whole country. As for personal attacks upon my motives I care not. So long as I retain a consciousness of having endeavored to do my duty, I shall not be troubled by what others say of my action.

Please present my kindest regards to Mrs. Pomeroy whose health, I hope, has been entirely restored before this. Mrs. Field unites with me in kind remembrances both to her and her daughter.

Very sincerely yours,
Stephen J. Field

Prof. John Norton Pomeroy.

IV.

Washington, D. C.
July 28th 1884.

My Dear Mr. Pomeroy:

Your very welcome letter of June 21st was received some weeks ago. Many thanks for all the kind words and kind offers it contains.

Had my name been successful at the Chicago Convention[28] I should not have hesitated to have called upon you for the addresses to which you refer. But as that Convention has put another in nomination, my political life may be considered as substantially at an end. It is not at all likely that my name will ever again be used in connection with any political office. I had, of course, some ambition to carry out certain measures which I believed would be of great advantage to the country. Particularly did I desire a reorganization of the Federal Judiciary.[29] As now constituted it fails of the purpose of its creation. The Supreme Court is three years behind in its regular business, and its docket is increasing from year to year so rapidly that it will soon be four years, and more, before a case can be reached after it is docketed. Could I have been instrumental in reorganizing the Federal Judiciary I would have placed on the Bench able and conservative men and thus have brought back the decisions of the Court to that line from which they should not have departed and thus, as I believe, have contributed something towards strengthening and perpetuating our institutions. There were also many other measures of great importance to the country, like the improvement of the Mississippi

---

[28] Meeting in Chicago on July 8, 1884, the Democratic National Convention had nominated Grover Cleveland. Justice Field's name had been rendered unavailable as a result of party strife in California. See SWISHER, *op. cit. supra* note 2, at 300–310.

[29] Justice Field's plan for reorganizing the Federal Judiciary will be outlined in a separate article.

River and connecting it with the Lakes; the revival of our commercial marine and the revision of the tariff, to the success of which I might have contributed. But all this must be placed in the category of dreams that might have been but will not be realized.

I shall have much to say to you when we meet; particularly of the very strange action in California. Had I received the cordial support, instead of opposition of that State my candidacy, according to the judgment of my friends, would have stood great chances of success; and even without that support, had the forces of Mr. Cleveland ever given way my name would have been presented at Chicago with reasonable prospect of success. At least, so all my friends say. But I am content where I am. There at least I have no caprices to consult and no clamors to fret me.

My brother Cyrus[30] will start for Oregon by the Northern Pacific route on the 23rd of August and he has invited me to accompany him and I have accepted his invitation. We shall reach Portland about the 30th. After holding court there a few days I shall proceed to San Francisco and remain in California two or three weeks. I do not expect to hold court there more than one or two days.

With kind regards to Mrs. Pomeroy, I am,

Very sincerely yours,
Stephen J. Field

Prof.
John Norton Pomeroy.

---

[30] Cyrus W. Field, 1819–1892, promoter of the Atlantic cable. See 6 DICT. AM. BIOG., pp. 357–359.

PART TWO: JUSTICE FIELD AND THE FOURTEENTH AMENDMENT*

"It is a misfortune if a judge reads his conscious or unconscious sympathy for one side or the other prematurely into the law, and forgets that what seem to him to be first principles are believed by half his fellow men to be wrong. . . . When twenty years ago a vague terror went over the earth and the word socialism began to be heard, I thought and still think that fear was translated into doctrines that had no proper place in the Constitution or the common law. Judges are apt to be naif, simple-minded men, and they need something of Mephistopheles. We too need education in the obvious—to learn to transcend our own convictions and to leave room for much that we hold dear to be done away with short of revolution by the orderly change of law."[1]

SIXTEEN YEARS before Justice Holmes thus stated the case for tolerance and self-restraint in the exercise of the judicial veto, another jurist gifted with the power of luminous statement and self-revelation seized an opportunity to epitomize his judicial philosophy. The jurist was Associate Justice Stephen J. Field;[2] the opportunity was the occasion presented by his retirement from the Supreme Court of the United States after a record-breaking term of thirty-four and a half years.

In a touching valedictory, Field recalled that he had received his appointment from President Lincoln in 1863, that previously he had served five and a half years as justice and chief justice of the Supreme Court of California, that he had thus rounded out more than forty years on the state and federal bench. Now, past eighty-one, feeble to the point of senility, yet his appearance and mien reminding one

---

* "Any attempt to interpret trends in American constitutional history outside the frame of professed doctrine calls for the utmost wariness. Its chief impulse must be the hope of stimulating confirmation or contradiction, and especially that pertinacious inquiry into the cultural and psychological roots of legal doctrine on which very little spadework has yet been undertaken. At best we are likely to know much less of the forces that shaped the great judge and the development of his mind after he came to the Bench, than we know about distinguished statesmen. Often the intellectual history of a great judge before his appointment is largely irrecoverable." FRANKFURTER, THE COMMERCE CLAUSE UNDER MARSHALL, TANEY, AND WAITE (1937).

[1] See HOLMES, Law and the Court in COLLECTED LEGAL PAPERS (1920) 295.
[2] See SWISHER, STEPHEN J. FIELD, CRAFTSMAN OF THE LAW (1930); SOME ACCOUNT OF THE WORK OF STEPHEN J. FIELD (Black and Smith, ed., 1881).

more than ever of Michelangelo's aged figure of Moses, he concluded his valedictory with these words:

> "As I look back over the more than a third of a century that I have sat on this bench, I am more and more impressed with the immeasurable importance of this court. . . . It has indeed no power to legislate. It cannot appropriate a dollar of money. . . . But it possesses the power of declaring the law, and in that is found the safeguard that keeps the whole mighty fabric of government from rushing to destruction. This negative power, the power of resistance, is the only safety of a popular government. . . ."[3]

The gulf between two opposing conceptions of judicial duty, and between the social and political philosophies underlying them, has probably never been made clearer than in these contrasting statements of Justice Holmes and Justice Field. Here, in essence, are philosophies grounded on faith and on fear, on the premise men can govern themselves and on the premise they must be governed, on the conviction that democracy must ultimately be the preserver of the judiciary and on the conviction that the judiciary must ultimately be the preserver of democracy. In both cases the philosophies were integrations of experience and found their clearest expression in prophetic interpretations of the Fourteenth Amendment. Their very antithesis thus illumines and correlates nearly a hundred years of our constitutional history.

To Justice Holmes, a skeptic with "no belief in panaceas, and almost none in sudden ruin," an intellectual aristocrat with an Olympian faith in "a universe not measured by our fears, a universe that has thought and more than thought inside of it," the "provisions of the Constitution were not mathematical formulas." Indeed, "a constitution was made for peoples of fundamentally differing views" and "not intended to embody a particular economic theory." And because Holmes was convinced that the successful functioning of popular government presumes "the right of a majority to embody their opinions in law,"[4] he often felt it his duty

---

[3] 168 U. S. 713–17 (1897).
[4] See FRANKFURTER, MR. JUSTICE HOLMES (1931); LIEF, THE DISSENTING OPINIONS OF MR. JUSTICE HOLMES (1929), for concise (and perhaps overdrawn) statements of Holmes's philosophy. The writer is not here concerned how consistently Justice Holmes adhered to a philosophy of self-restraint (note that in only one-fourth of all cases involving invalidation of state laws under the Fourteenth Amendment during his term did Holmes disagree with his colleagues) nor how frequently and tenaciously Justice Field espoused doctrines inconsistent with his principles. See FAIRMAN, MR. JUSTICE MILLER AND THE SUPREME COURT, 1862–1890 (1939) 317, n. 5. The contrast of approaches and major premises is sufficiently clear to warrant inquiry into Field's motivation.

to uphold legislation he believed unwise. He especially mistrusted attempts to make the Fourteenth Amendment a bar to social and economic legislation. In classic dissents he repeatedly indicated his disapproval of the accordion-like process by which an "unpretentious assertion of the liberty to follow the ordinary callings . . . was expanded into the dogma, Liberty to Contract."[5] More than anything else, therefore, it was to this amazing judicial hybridization of due process of law with the economic tenets of laissez faire that Justice Holmes objected.

He obviously believed that the proliferation of substantive due process which began in the nineties and reached one of its peaks about 1910[6] was attributable in part to conservatives' mounting fear of socialism and to their conscious and unconscious desire to read into vague constitutional clauses personal predilections for individualism as opposed to paternalism in government. It is clear that he mistrusted this tendency, not because he personally believed in socialism, for he did not, but because he was convinced that in the long run judicial enforcement of laissez faire would prove mischievous and self-defeating. Modern urban industrial society presumed the progressive extension of social controls; democracy presumed their extension in accordance with popular desires. Judges, too, therefore, needed "education in the obvious"—to learn to transcend their convictions and leave room for much they held dear "to be done away with short of revolution by the orderly change of law." Resistance to change might well lead courts to immolate themselves. Hypertrophy of due process might prostrate judicial as well as legislative power. The "rule of reason," applied as a purely reactionary formula, might lead to the rule of force and unreason.[7]

The contrast between Justice Holmes, the restrained judge solicitous of the right of the majority to embody its opinions in law, and Justice Field, the advocate of "resistance" and judicial trusteeship to save the "fabric of government . . . from rushing to destruction" is manifested both doctrinally and psychologically in Field's work. It is manifested doctrinally by the fact that he laid the foundations for the doctrines whose misuse and extension "to dryly logical extremes" Holmes later deplored. To a greater or lesser degree, liberty to contract and substantive due process are rooted in dicta in Field's majority opinions of the eighties; and the whole modern

---

[5] Adkins v. Children's Hospital, 261 U. S. 525, 568 (1923).
[6] See FRANKFURTER, *op. cit. supra* note 4, App. I.
[7] See ADAMS, THE THEORY OF SOCIAL REVOLUTIONS (1913), for a statement of this thesis which may have impressed Holmes more than he was aware. *Cf.* 1 HOLMES-POLLOCK LETTERS (Howe, ed., 1941) 123-24.

interpretation of the Fourteenth Amendment rests upon his dissenting opinions in the *Slaughter-House*[8] and *Granger*[9] cases and upon opinions at circuit holding that corporations are "persons" within the meaning of the equal protection and the due process clauses.[10]

The contrast is manifested psychologically by a pervading tone of anxiety, by an almost total lack of that sense of relativity which so distinguished Holmes's opinions. Forebodings and premonitions,[11] ungrounded fears for the security of corporate property,[12] "parades of horribles," and threats of ruin[13] were familiar features of Field's opinions; and they reached an anguished crescendo in the oft-quoted passage attacking the constitutionality of the four per cent Federal Income Tax of 1895 as an "assault upon capital . . . the stepping stone to others, larger and more sweeping, till our political contests . . . become a war of the poor against the rich; a war constantly growing in intensity and bitterness."[14]

Coupled with this dark outlook was a sense of confused frustration that at times seemed to heighten anxiety and reveal a partial awareness that even the staunchest resistance to paternalistic trends might prove fruitless and self-defeating. Observation of the developing frontier made Justice Field as conscious as Henry George[15] of the parallel growth of wealth and want, progress and poverty. That he brooded over this paradox, yet was powerless to resolve it, and that failure added to his troubled state of mind is clear from an address he delivered in New York at the centenary of the Supreme Court of the United States in 1890. Appealing for an increasingly broad enforcement of all guarantees of private rights, he distilled his anxiety and dissatisfaction into one remarkable sentence:

---

[8] 16 Wall. 36, 83 (U. S. 1873).

[9] 94 U. S. 113, 136 (1877).

[10] See San Mateo County v. Southern Pacific R. R., 13 Fed. 722 (C. C. Cal. 1882); Santa Clara County v. Southern Pacific R. R., 18 Fed. 385 (D. Cal. 1883). **1968:** In the thirty years since this paragraph was written, the dissenting opinions of Justices Harlan, Holmes, and Brandeis of course have supplanted Field's as the bases of the "modern interpretation of the Fourteenth Amendment."

[11] See Juillard v. Greenman, 110 U. S. 421, 470 (1884): "From the decision of the court I see only evil likely to follow."

[12] See Sinking Fund Cases, 99 U. S. 700, 750 (1879): "The decision will . . . tend to create insecurity in the title to corporate property. . . ."

[13] See Bartemeyer v. Iowa, 18 Wall. 129, 139 (U. S. 1874): "If the state can say the owner shall give the horns and hoofs, it may say he shall give the hide and the tallow. . . . It may say that the butcher shall retain the four quarters and return to the owner only the head and the feet."

[14] See Pollock v. Farmers Loan & Trust Co., 157 U. S. 429, 607 (1895).

[15] It is interesting to note that it was during the period 1870-71, while Henry George was editor of the San Francisco Daily Evening Post that his single tax theories began to crystallize.

As population and wealth increase—*as the inequalities in the conditions of men become more and more marked and disturbing*—as the enormous aggregation of wealth possessed by some corporations excites uneasiness lest their power should become dominating in the legislation of the country, and thus encroach upon the rights or crush out the business of individuals of small means—as population in some quarters presses upon the means of subsistence, *and angry menaces against order find vent in loud denunciations*—it becomes more and more the imperative duty of the court to enforce with a firm hand every guarantee to the constitution. *Every decision weakening their restraining power is a blow to the peace of society* and to its progress and improvement. . . .[16]

That during his final quarter-century on the Court Field was thus obviously an anxious and troubled man, committed to policies whose ineffectiveness he sensed, yet to which he clung all the more tightly, is no more remarkable than that his early opinions reveal a very different motivation.[17] On the bench of California from 1857 to 1863, Field distinguished himself by his liberality with the legislature, his readiness to sustain state interference, his refusal to expand discretionary judicial review. "Frequent elections by the people," he declared in an opinion upholding the validity of a Sunday law, "furnish the only protection under the Constitution against the abuse of acknowledged legislative power."[18] The fact that such legislation interfered with economic liberty and freedom of contract impressed him hardly at all: "The law steps in to restrain the power of capital . . . not to protect those who can rest at their pleasure, but to afford rest to those who need it, and who, from the condition of society, could not otherwise obtain it." Authority for the enactment lay in "the great object of all government, which is protection. . . . To protect labor is the highest office of our laws."[19] Moreover, it is striking to note that in 1859 Field emphatically did not regard a limited due process clause of the state constitution as a limitation on the taxing power.[20]

---

[16] (1890) 24 AM. L. REV. 351, 366–67 (italics added).

[17] See SWISHER, *op. cit. supra* note 2, at 77-81.

[18] See *Ex parte* Newman, 9 Cal. 502, 527 (1858). In 1861 a similar Sunday law was upheld, Field concurring. See *Ex parte* Andrews, 18 Cal. 679 (1861). For further evidence of Field's liberality toward the legislature, see McCauley v. Brooks, 16 Cal. 11, 56 (1860); Lin Sing v. Washburn, 20 Cal. 534, 586 (1862); and McMurray, *Field's Work as a Lawyer and Judge in California* (1917) 5 CALIF. L. REV. 87, 104.

[19] See *Ex parte* Newman, 9 Cal. 502, 520, 521 (1858).

[20] See People v. Burr, 13 Cal. 343 (1859). After hearing arguments that a funding measure took property without due process of law, Field declared that "the only limitation on the taxing power was in the state uniformity clause. *Id.* at 350. It is

Justice Field and the Fourteenth Amendment 115

For some years after his elevation to the Supreme Court, Field held to his tolerant views. In interpreting the contract[21] and commerce[22] clauses of the Constitution, he was less disposed than his associates to overturn state legislation. As late as 1869, in the *National Bank* cases,[23] he voted to sustain a sweeping exercise of the Federal taxing power, not as a source of revenue, but as an instrument of social policy. In *Paul v. Virginia*[24] he shifted attention from the possible abuses of legislative authority to the need for regulating large aggregations of capital.

In short, until about 1870, in matters affecting property rights, Field was a liberal, restrained judge, tolerant of legislative innovation, who could see clearly that democratic government assumes wide margins of error and a continual clash of opinions and interests. His philosophy was not materially different from that of Justice Holmes in that he not only resisted attempts to broaden the discretionary powers of the courts, but he recognized the impropriety of making his personal views on the soundness of social legislation the criterion of constitutionality.

The obvious conclusion, therefore, is that during the Reconstruction period,[25] and through the seventies and eighties, Field reversed himself, not only on judicial first principles, but on fundamental concepts of his social and political philosophy. The mild paternalist of the fifties became the arch-individualist of the seventies and

---

true that the due process clause of the California Constitution of 1849, Art. I, § 8, was clearly limited to the protection of the accused "in any criminal case"; but it is also true that such limitations were often ignored by judges who felt need for protecting private rights. See Chapter 2, *supra*, note 47.

[21] Note his concurrence with the strict constructionist minority, in Home of the Friendless v. Rouse, 8 Wall. 430 (U. S. 1869); Washington University v. Rouse, 8 Wall. 439 (U. S. 1869); Chenango Bridge Co. v. Binghampton Bridge Co., 3 Wall. 51 (U. S. 1866). Field, of course, subsequently maintained opposition to bartering away the taxing power. The point here is not that he turned doctrinal somersaults on points of law after 1871, but that his *relative* position on the Court shifted markedly to the right with the years; before the seventies he was less inclined than his colleagues to void regulatory legislation, after the seventies, more inclined.

[22] See Gilman v. Philadelphia, 3 Wall. 713 (U. S. 1866), Justice Field concurring, Justices Clifford, Wayne and Davis dissenting. See also Steamship Co. v. Joliffe, 2 Wall. 450 (U. S. 1864), majority opinion by Justice Field, Justices Miller, Wayne and Clifford dissenting.

[23] See Veazie Bank v. Fenno, 8 Wall. 533 (U. S. 1869). Justices Nelson and Davis dissented.

[24] 8 Wall. 168 (U. S. 1869).

[25] See *Ex parte* Garland, 4 Wall. 333 (U. S. 1867); Cummings v. Missouri, 4 Wall. 277 (U. S. 1867). Justice Field wrote the majority opinion invalidating the test oaths in both cases, and his predilections against such measures probably originated as a result of his early experience in California. See SWISHER, *op. cit. supra* note 2, c. 2. See also Hepburn v. Griswold, 8 Wall. 603 (U. S. 1870).

eighties. The staunch defender of legislative power became the leader in expanding judicial review. The judge who in 1859 had given no inkling that he regarded due process as a limitation on the taxing power, in 1882 made it a limitation, not only as regards natural persons, but corporations as well.[26]

Impressed with paradoxes of this sort, and seeking a plausible rationale, Carl B. Swisher concluded in an interpretive chapter of his biography, that Field found "the menace of communism . . . no idle threat."[27] Field's vehement individualism, his allegiance to laissez faire, his pre-occupation with the rights of property and corporations, his successful efforts to broaden judicial review and make it the means of frustrating paternalistic ventures in government—all these were expressions of deep-seated anxiety for the stability and safety of social institutions. Courageous as he was in his relations with people, Field was "thoroughly fearful of attacks upon what were to him fundamental principles in the organization of society."[28]

Thus, without stressing the fact, Swisher advanced essentially the same hypothesis as a rationale for the paradoxes of Field's career that Justice Holmes had offered years before as an explanation and criticism of the general trend of judicial decision. In both instances, fear of communism and socialism was regarded as a decisive factor in the self-expansion of judicial power. This essay will present evidence corroborative of these views.

It now appears not only that fear of communism and radicalism was an underlying cause of much of Justice Field's distressed anxiety at the course of democratic government, but that this same fear was an important factor in bringing about the near-reversal in his views on judicial first principles in the years following 1870. The two historic events which served to crystallize Field's fears and affect his reorientation were the Franco-Prussian War and the Paris Commune. Like many Americans living in the chaos of the Reconstruction period, fearful that their new industrial order might be jeopardized almost at the moment of its birth, Justice Field was appalled at the recrudescence of revolution in Europe. Under the cumulative impact of successive shocks, and because his personal

---

[26] See San Mateo County v. Southern Pacific R. R., 13 Fed. 722 (S. D. Cal. 1882); Santa Clara County v. Southern Pacific R. R., 18 Fed. 385 (S. D. Cal. 1883). Legalists will point out that, strictly speaking, Field did not declare corporations persons, but rather adopted the fiction of "looking through" to the stockholders. To historians concerned with practical consequences the difference is small, and the craftsmanship is noteworthy in itself.
[27] SWISHER, op. cit. supra note 2, at 383, 429.
[28] Id. at 429.

Justice Field and the Fourteenth Amendment

experiences abroad and in California rendered him particularly sensitive to these influences, he became an apostle of reaction, determined, in his own later phrase, "to strengthen, if I could, all conservative men."[29] The evidence is clearly such as to mark the Paris Commune as an important pivot in American constitutional history, a chronological and doctrinal key both to Justice Field's career and to the historical evolution of the Fourteenth Amendment.

I.

Circumstantially, there are several major reasons for accepting this hypothesis relating to communism and socialism and for suspecting that it affords a clue to the expansion of the judicial power in the eighties and nineties.

One reason is the relation between the use and growth of substantive due process and that will to "resistance"[30] born of overpowering anxiety and insecurity which came eventually to characterize Justice Field's whole outlook. It is significant in this regard that the leading cases in which substantive due process was invoked almost without exception concerned either novel reform legislation or momentous social and partisan issues. The determination of these questions not only stirred endless controversy but invited a forensic use of any formula which disguised individual opinions and gave them the sanction and prestige of a supreme fundamental law. Due process met these requirements perfectly and was increasingly used as a weapon of last resort, as an ingenious question-beggar, as an Archimedian lever whose adjective "due" served as the fulcrum to shift ultimate responsibility for decisions upon social policy from the legislature to the courts. Its advantages lay in its extraordinary simplicity, in the universal scope of its subordinate terms, in its historic connotations as a right derived directly from Magna Carta, and above all, in its users' unconscious capitalization of the fact that in democratic, limited governments due process *as an ideal* implies more than due procedure and thus inevitably raises substantive questions.

The dangers inherent in its use were derived from its advantages, and they were foreshadowed as early as 1818, long before the advent of the due process clause of the Fourteenth Amendment. In that year Chancellor Kent stressed confidentially to the President of

---

[29] Field to Matthew P. Deady, May 17, 1886, shortly after the Haymarket Riot: "On many accounts I should be glad to go to the Pacific Coast this summer. I should like to add my voice to strengthen, if I could, all conservative men." See note 70 *infra*.

[30] See Chapters 1 and 2 *supra*, especially notes 11 and 36 of Chapter 2.

Dartmouth College that his "objections," made fourteen years before as a member of the Council of Revision, to certain changes in the New York municipal charter had been "made as a politician, not as a judge" and that he was "not clear that the doctrine laid down [and grounded on the state due process clause] was correct as applied to corporations for the purposes of government."[31] Possibly these scruples of Chancellor Kent against the extension of "law of the land" beyond historical and textual limitations contributed to Webster's and Marshall's shift in the *Dartmouth College* case to the contract clause as the major bulwark for corporate rights.

Yet during the Jacksonian period, as the number and importance of corporations increased—even in the face of growing popular hostility—conscientious judges continued to ignore phraseological limits and on several occasions indicated that their willingness to stretch the meanings of key words was prompted by general mistrust of legislative trends and policies.[32] Illustrating this tendency, and in a sense broadening and culminating it, was the epidemic of substantive use of federal and state constitutional terms that broke out in the mid-fifties. In swift succession the New York Court of Appeals invalidated on the ground of that state's due process clause a married woman's property act[33] and a drastic anti-liquor law,[34] and counsel for insurance companies and railroads attempted unsuccessfully to void state regulation and charter repeals. Republicans in Congress and on the stump brandished the due process clause of the Fifth Amendment as a weapon against slavery; and in 1857 the elderly Taney, seeking to bolster what others would destroy, vainly turned the tables on his opponents and denied Congress power over slavery in the Territories.[35] It is plain that substantive due process is a weapon born of political stress, that its use flourishes in periods of crisis and under the pressure of intense conviction. It should occasion little surprise, therefore, if counsel and judges frightened by socialism and communism fell back upon this guarantee in the troubled Reconstruction period.

Another circumstance supporting the hypothesis is implicit in Chancellor Kent's statement: "I have likewise imbibed from the stupendous events of the French Revolution an aversion to innova-

---

[31] SHIRLEY, THE DARTMOUTH COLLEGE CAUSES (1895) 270, letter of Francis Brown to Daniel Webster, September 15, 1818. See Howe, *A Footnote to the "Conspiracy Theory"* (1939) 48 YALE L. J. 1007.
[32] See Chapter 1, *supra* notes 37, 47.
[33] See Westervelt v. Gregg, 12 N. Y. 202 (1854).
[34] See Wynehamer v. People, 13 N. Y. 378 (1856).
[35] See Dred Scott v. Sandford, 19 How. 393, 450 (U.S. 1856).

tion except by cautious steps."[36] In view of the fact that conservatism and radicalism are reciprocal and self-neutralizing forces,[37] that the Terror of 1791–93 contributed to the establishment and early growth of judicial review in the United States,[38] that successive French revolutions each produced widespread psychological repercussions in this country,[39] and that the great European revolutions of 1848, occurring simultaneously with the birth of Marxism and promulgation of the Communist Manifesto, tended to combine in American minds a horror of the traditions of violence with a mistrust of such ill-fated collectivist experiments as Louis Blanc's National Workshops[40]—in view of these facts, it would scarcely be surprising to learn that fear of communism and radicalism played its part either in conditioning Field's outlook or in coloring his views on social and economic policy.

This is especially true in view of the further fact that at the time when Justice Field's opinions were veering more and more in the direction of conservatism, he had reason to be troubled by the trend of domestic affairs and by his colleagues' decisions.[41] These were the months of the Tweed Ring exposures, the aftermath of the Erie Wars and Gold Corner, and the impeachment of President Johnson —months of widespread demoralization in all departments of government, state and national—and months characterized more than

---

[36] HORTON, JAMES KENT (1939) 271, quoting an undated letter to Edward Livingston, published in (1837) 16 AM. JURIST 361, in which Kent explained his reasons for preferring the common law to codes.

[37] See WOLFE, CONSERVATISM, RADICALISM AND THE SCIENTIFIC METHOD (1923).

[38] Beveridge brilliantly sketched the influence of the French Revolution in America concluding that there was "scarcely an incident" in Marshall's private experience "but was shaped and colored by this vast series of human events." 2 BEVERIDGE, JOHN MARSHALL (1929) c. 1, 44.
For further insight, see the speeches of Federalist members of Congress in the debates on the repeal of the Judiciary Act of 1801, especially speeches of Senator Ogden, 11 ANNALS OF CONG. 171 (1851); Representative James C. Bayard, 11 ANNALS OF CONG. 627 (1851); and Representative John Rutledge, 11 ANNALS OF CONG. 746 (1851).

[39] See GAZLEY, AMERICAN OPINION OF GERMAN UNIFICATION, 1848–1871 (1926) 247; Curtis, *American Opinion of French Nineteenth Century Revolution* (1914) 19 AM. HIST. REV. 249.

[40] *Ibid.*

[41] One can hardly fail to note here how suddenly, during Reconstruction, the tides of fortune shifted for Field. A Union Democrat, bullionist, friend and brother of rising capitalist-promoters, he shared to the full the elation over Union victory and the phenomenal material successes of his time, only to see the whole suddenly threatened, after 1866, by a motley crew of Radicals, Greenbackers, and Grangers. Increasingly circumscribed in personal contacts, unfamiliar (rather than unsympathetic) with the lot of small farmers and laborers, inclined to judge eastern and midwestern legislation of the seventies and eighties by California conditions and standards of the fifties, he thus suffered equally from the handicaps of his position and experience and from the general demoralization of the times.

anything else by growing public antipathy and contempt for the policies and personnel of state and national legislatures.[42] For a War Democrat who had hoped for magnanimity toward the South, who had welcomed the Fourteenth Amendment[43] only to see it employed for what he regarded more and more as partisan purposes, who deplored the majority of the Court's refusal to invalidate the Congressional reconstruction program, they were the agonizing months of democracy's Gethsemane. Far from bringing improvement and relief from these conditions, the spring of 1871 intensified them. During this time the reconstituted Supreme Court reversed the *Legal Tender*[44] decisions, in which Field had concurred, and upheld, over his dissent, legislation authorizing confiscation of Confederates' property.[45] Legislatures in the Granger states debated and passed the first statutes that established maximum rates and regulated the businesses of grain elevators and railroads.[46] Radicals in Congress pushed through the drastic Ku Klux Klan act.[47] Finally, as if to personalize the confusion and heartbreak of the entire period, Field's elder brother and patron, David Dudley, for months under ceaseless attack for his activities as counsel for Fisk and Gould in the Erie Wars, was now engaged in a battle for his professional and moral reputation.[48] In these circumstances one can perceive a basis for acute psychological and judicial maladjustment. The precise focus is ad-

---

[42] See editorials, *San Francisco Alta*, Nov. 13, 1870 ("A legislature so tied . . . that it cannot move at all is . . . the greatest of blessings."). *Disregard of Constitutions*, Sacramento Union, Nov. 8, 1870, citing flagrant evasions of prohibitions against subsidies and lotteries.

[43] See especially, Field to Chief Justice Chase, June 30, 1866, quoted in SWISHER, *op. cit. supra* note 2, 144–45.

[44] See Knox v. Lee, 12 Wall. 457 (U. S. 1871), *rev'g* Hepburn v. Griswold, 8 Wall. 603 (U. S. 1870), decided May 1, 1871, by a 5 to 4 vote. Intra-court bitterness remained intense throughout 1870–71. See FAIRMAN, MR. JUSTICE MILLER AND THE SUPREME COURT (1939) c. 7; SWISHER, *op. cit. supra* note 2, c. 7.

[45] See Miller v. United States, 11 Wall. 268 (U. S. 1871). In his dissent Field declared that "the same reason which would sustain the authority of the government to confiscate the property of a traitor would justify the confiscation of his property when guilty of any other offense." *Id.* at 323.

[46] See letter to Chief Justice Chase, June 30, 1866, quoted in SWISHER, *op. cit. supra* note 2, at 145–46.

[47] 17 STAT. 13–15 (1871). President Grant's message of March 23, calling for suppression of the outrages in the South preceded enactment and touched off a month-long debate on the scope and purpose of the Fourteenth Amendment. See notes 86, 88 *infra*, and John Norton Pomeroy's unsigned article, *The Force Bill* (1871) 12 NATION 268.

[48] See Stickney, *The Lawyer and His Clients*, and Adams, *An Erie Raid* in HICKS, HIGH FINANCE IN THE SIXTIES (1929), which assembles materials bearing on both sides of the controversy.

Justice Field and the Fourteenth Amendment

mittedly difficult to establish with precision; yet the biographical significance is readily apparent.

The view that Justice Field's retreat from his early liberalism stemmed in part from events of 1870-71 is further supported by the circumstance that it was during this period that the equal protection, due process, and privileges or immunities clauses first clearly emerged as bulwarks of a new capitalist order. One need not assume that Field intuitively, or at the cost of great intellectual effort, discovered these potentialities for himself. For, prompted by two influential and provocative syntheses of the case law[49] and encouraged to seek the sort of substantive protection which Chief Justice Chase had invoked in the case of *Hepburn v. Griswold*,[50] lawyers throughout the nation, from California to Maine, began barraging courts with appeals against advancing state regulation[51] and Reconstruction misrule.[52] Along with the trends of usage thus established, strategists

---

[49] COOLEY, CONSTITUTIONAL LIMITATIONS (1868) (with its chapter XI "On the Protection of Property by 'the Law of the Land'"), and POMEROY, CONSTITUTIONAL LAW (1868) were both published almost simultaneously with ratification of the Fourteenth Amendment. See especially COOLEY, *supra* at 356-57, POMEROY, *supra* at 156-60. 1968: See Chapters 11 and 12 *infra*, and the editorial note preceding Chapter 13 *infra*, for clarifying data and insights with regard to the works and role of Cooley and Pomeroy.

[50] 8 Wall. 603, 624 (U. S. 1870). Clarkson N. Potter, one of the leading counsels, had raised the point.

[51] See *Ex parte* Smith and Keating, 38 Cal. 702 (1869), where counsel unsuccessfully attacked a Sacramento ordinance prohibiting music and the presence of women in saloons after midnight. See also the line of Maine due process, Fourteenth Amendment cases antedating the *Slaughter-House* decision. Opinion of the Justices, 58 Me. 590 (1871) (state due process); Allen v. Jay, 60 Me. 124 (1872) (state due process); Maine v. Doherty, 60 Me. 504 (1872) (Fourteenth Amendment); Dunn v. Burleigh, 62 Me. 24 (1873) (Fourteenth Amendment). See also Chief Justice Lawrence's opinion in Chicago-Alton R. R. v. People, 67 Ill. 11 (1873), substantially holding corporations persons "so far as necessary to protect their property and franchises against the operation of a law that . . . condemns without a trial." *Id.* at 24. Due process, both federal and state, came rapidly to the fore in the *Granger Cases* in the state courts, 1872-73. Arguments printed in 2-4 ANNUAL REPORTS OF THE ILLINOIS RAILROADS AND WARE-HOUSE COMMISSION (1872-1874) indicate that Corydon Beckwith, Chief Counsel for the Chicago and Alton Railroad and the Northwestern Fertilizing Co. pioneered the usage, though he apparently was much handicapped by Judge Woods's decision in *Continental Insurance Co. v. New Orleans*. See note 56 *infra*. Judge Drummond's decision in Northwestern Fertilizing Co. v. Hyde Park, 18 Fed. Cas. 394 (C. C. Ill. 1873), holding corporations persons within the Civil Rights Act of 1871, promised partial relief, but was immediately overshadowed by the Supreme Court's decision in the *Slaughter-House Cases*.

It was not until after the *Bartemeyer* decision that counsel again took heart. One then finds James C. Storrs, Chief Counsel for the Central Pacific Railroad, advising California subordinates to make use of the due process clause of the Fourteenth Amendment in various tax cases then pending. Storrs to S. W. Sanderson, May 17, 1874, 6 HUNTINGTON CORRESPONDENCE (1874) 175, Stanford University Library.

[52] See the ingenious argument of A. W. Shaffer in Worthy v. Commissioners, 9 Wall. 611 (U.S. 1870) (unsuccessfully employing section one of the Fourteenth Amend-

for the insurance companies which had asked Congress for relief while the Fourteenth Amendment was being drafted,[53] sought to profit by its broad phraseology. Early in the first session after ratification, John A. Bingham, drafter of section one and the chairman of the House Judiciary Committee, sponsored a bill[54] skillfully designed to extend to corporations the privileges or immunities of citizens of the United States. After Congress had rejected this measure, and after Justice Bradley's and Judge Woods's decisions in the *Slaughter-House Cases* at circuit[55] had seemed to take for granted

---

ment as a weapon to defeat the provisions of section three), and the masterpiece of research and opportunism prepared by former Justice John A. Campbell as counsel for the butchers in the various *Slaughter House* cases [State v. Fagan, 22 La. 545 (1870) and 16 Wall. 36 (U. S. 1873)]. It is interesting to note that Campbell in his arguments before the Supreme Court in 1872 and 1873 stressed the potentialities of section one as a bulwark against Communism and Socialism. See CONNOR, JOHN A. CAMPBELL (1920) 214.

[53] See Chapter 2, *supra*, n. 86.

[54] See House Bill 349, 41st Cong., 1st Sess. (1869). The text of this measure is not found in the Congressional Globe. It was repeatedly referred to, however, as a sweeping bill which extended to corporations "the privileges and immunities guaranteed by the Constitution of the United States," *i.e.*, under both the comity clause and the Fourteenth Amendment.

Apparently no serious move was made to secure passage until after the Supreme Court in Ducat v. Chicago, 10 Wall. 410 (U. S. 1871), and Liverpool Ins. Co. v. Mass., 10 Wall. 566 (U. S. 1871), had cleverly put an end to hopes of judicial relief. On Feb. 15, 1871, after the Senate had acted unfavorably on a much less sweeping substitute measure, Bingham sought House action on the same substitute. See CONG. GLOBE, 41st Cong., 3d Sess. (1871) 538, 715, 1288–90. This revised bill provided, he explained, "first, that no corporation created by any State of this Union shall be subjected to forfeiture or penalty for bringing a suit authorized by the laws of the United States. . . . Second, that being ruled to be citizens of the United States within the meaning of the Constitution to the extent that they shall be entitled as such to sue and be sued in the courts of the United States, by virtue of their citizenship under the Constitution, against the citizens of any other State, they are therefore, of necessity, within the ruling of the Court, under the protection of that provision of the Constitution of the United States which gives them in whatever State they may be found no greater disability in reference to trade and commerce than the citizens of the state in which they live."

"That, Sir," Bingham added (with reference to the first half of the statement, and in apparent hopes listeners might conclude he was speaking of the whole) "is the ruling made and adhered to by the Supreme Court of the United States for more than fifty years."

Like other skeptics, the writer has often asked, "Why, if framers of the Fourteenth Amendment intended to aid or include corporations in 1866, no evidence has been found that identifies them with such usage in the years immediately following ratification?" With reference to corporate benefits under the citizenship clause, it now appears that such evidence is at hand. Neither the circumstances of the utterance, nor Bingham's standing and abilities as a constitutional lawyer seem to the writer to be consistent with Professor McLaughlin's view that the argument just quoted indicates Bingham's ignorance of what the Court recently had held in the *Paul, Ducat*, and *Liverpool* cases. See note 57 *infra*.

[55] See Livestock Dealers & Butchers Association v. Crescent City Livestock Landing & Slaughter House Co., 4 Fed. Cas. 891 (C. C. La. 1870).

that corporations—or at least shareholders—were protected by the phraseology of section one, the insurance company lawyers turned again to the courts and sought Judge Woods's express ruling on corporate personality and citizenship. In a remarkable *volte face* that dismayed the entire insurance bar, Judge Woods ruled in *Continental Insurance Company v. New Orleans*,[56] in 1871, that corporations were neither "citizens" nor "persons" within the meaning of the Fourteenth Amendment.

Whatever may be one's views on the bearing of these facts on the problem of the framers' intentions,[57] it is obvious that there early

---

[56] 13 Fed. Cas. 67 (C. C. La. 1870). Judge Woods reasoned much as did Mr. Justice Black in his dissent in Connecticut General Life Ins. Co. v. Johnson, 303 U. S. 77 (1938), *i.e.*, that since only natural persons can be "born or naturalized" a double standard of interpretation of the word "person" in section one is required to make the due process and equal protection clauses cover corporations. So far as the framers' intentions are concerned, this argument of course ignores the fact that the introductory sentence defining citizenship was added in the Senate, and did not appear in the Joint Committee's drafts. See note 82 *infra*.

[57] Possibly unaware that Bingham had first introduced the broader House Bill 349, 41st Cong., 1st Sess. (1869), Professor McLaughlin minimizes the importance of immediate post-ratification use of section one by insurance companies. See McLaughlin, *The Court, the Corporation, and Conkling* (1940) 46 AMER. HIST. REV. 45, 50–51. He further questions whether corporate activity in Congress caused framers to consider applicability of the section to corporations.

Pending Harris L. Rubin's completion of a projected biography of Bingham, the writer is unprepared to carry skepticism so far. Evidence not only corroborates Conkling's statements with regard to the corporation petitions but reveals several possible links between members of the Joint Committee on the one hand, and between prior users of due process and current (*i.e.*, 1866) seekers after federal protection on the other. See Chapter 2, *supra*, note 20. Consequently, the writer feels that the so-called "secondary intention hypothesis" best accords with the facts as they stand: Bingham and his colleagues drafted section one to safeguard the rights of Negroes, mulattoes and Southern loyalists. Yet they probably soon became aware, by reason of the insurance company and railroad petitions, and as draftsmen obliged to consider all meanings of their texts, that "persons" as a generic term embraced corporations.

Speculation ought not to proceed much beyond this point, but Bingham's acceptance of Credit Mobilier stock in 1866 suggests that the anti-slavery zealot of the fifties was now on intimate terms with business leaders, and inclined to favor their programs. His original positively-worded draft—"Congress shall have power . . ."—harmonized nicely with the needs and aims of petitioning business interests. Together with such colleagues as Reverdy Johnson and Roscoe Conkling he probably saw no reason to oppose phraseology which offered prospects of incidental Congressional or judicial aid to beleaguered railroads and insurance companies. This conclusion is strengthened by the fact that Radicals in 1866 not only assumed Congress to have plenary powers under the Amendment but were currently solidifying their alliances with business. See BEALE, THE CRITICAL YEAR (1930). In the last analysis, therefore, belief in a secondary intent to aid business presumes little more than a decent respect for the framers' intelligence and a willingness to believe that intelligent and informed men did not rigidly compartmentalize conceptions of "persons" and "due process" but adopted prevalent conceptions which harmonized with their general views of statecraft.

Perhaps for these reasons it is difficult for the writer to accept Professor McLaughlin's view that Bingham's failure to cite decisions in which the Supreme Court had redeveloped—and while Field was in a mood to have appreciated its timeliness—a pattern of constitutional usage strikingly like the one that he eventually championed. Not only in Congress but in the courts, well-organized campaigns were under way to make the Fourteenth Amendment a shield against what many businesmen and conservatives regarded as dangerous and excessive regulation. It is no great act of faith to believe that these maneuvers came to the attention of a Justice of the Supreme Court of the United States and that he probably formulated conclusions as to their merits.

Finally, climaxing the circumstantial case, is the fact that a great social cataclysm—the first to be reported by cable and exploited by modern journalistic devices[58]—may well have been one of the decisive factors in reorienting Field's outlook. Simultaneously with the most depressing personal and national crises in the spring of 1871, the Paris Commune[59] shocked the entire world, discredited collectivist and radical programs, and produced a hysteria in conservative circles in the United States which caused such current indigenous

---

cently blasted counsel's hopes of judicial protection under the comity and commerce clauses signified ignorance of these decisions and presumably ignorance of any company plans for Congressional protection under the comity clause and the Fourteenth Amendment. Silence here might also be construed as discretion, though as the writer has pointed out elsewhere, silence in such cases is admissible neither as proof of intent, nor the lack of it.

In those railroad charter cases in which Reverdy Johnson had successfully figured as counsel just prior to his membership on the Joint Committee, and in which due process arguments had been used, it may be added that the cases were decided favorably to the railroads a few months before the Fourteenth Amendment was declared officially ratified. See Chapter 2 *supra*, note 22, and p. 75ff.; Commonwealth v. Pittsburgh & Connellesville R. R., 58 Pa. 26 (1868). Continued citation of such cases as Brown v. Hummel, 6 Pa. 86 (1847), and Erie R. R. v. Casey, 1 Grant's Cases 274 (Pa. 1856), indicates that Reverdy Johnson continued to rely on due process, although the decision turned on other points.

58 Tremendous sums were spent by the American press for cable tolls and correspondence during the Franco-Prussian War and the Paris Commune. See LEE, HISTORY OF AMERICAN JOURNALISM (1923) 328-29. Contemporary readers probably gained a sense of the immediacy of events which is difficult for jaded moderns to appreciate. Field's correspondence often glowed with fraternal pride and wonder at the miracle of the cable and telegraph; potentialities of the instruments fascinated him, and apparently he pondered deeply their significance and reports.

59 For the modern view of this complex upheaval, which uniformly emphasizes its spontaneous, heterogeneous, often chauvinistic and proletarian, but essentially non-Marxian and unsocialistic character, see Bourgin, *The Paris Commune* in 4 ENCYC. SOC. SCIENCES (1931) 63-66; MASON, THE PARIS COMMUNE (1930). Mason concluded: "The revolution of March 18th was the product of a spontaneous uprising of an exasperated populace." *Id.* at 133. Compare contemporary accounts in the New York Herald, San Francisco Alta, and FETRIDGE, THE RISE AND FALL OF THE PARIS COMMUNE (1871), all of which tended to exaggerate the role of the Internationale and Marxists in fomenting revolt.

forms of radicalism as the Granger and labor movements to be attacked as conspiracies against the institution of property.

These effects are most strikingly revealed in E. L. Godkin's editorials in *The Nation*[60] and by the repercussions of the Commune in California. Familiarity with French revolutionary backgrounds and with the Marxian thesis and program currently propagandized by the Internationale led Godkin to anticipate outbreaks which, after their first occurrence in October, 1870, during the Siege, and especially after the carnage and incendiarism that finally marked the Communards' overthrow in May, 1871, prompted repeated editorial probing of domestic affairs. Mounting labor unrest, sectional, class and partisan antagonisms, legislative and executive demoralization, the greed and lawlessness of capital—all ominous in themselves—were now viewed against still darker backgrounds. Appalled at these "unforeseen tendencies of democracy," Godkin not only flinched at the thought of increased state interference and argued that nothing could be accomplished by legislation toward reconciling capital and labor, but rebuked such humanitarians and reformers as John Stuart Mill and Wendell Phillips for their espousal of labor and land reforms which, he declared, would only encourage irresponsible fanatics to make greater demands.

This same impairment of reason and social sympathy by acts of violence is even more forcibly illustrated by the aftermath of a miners' strike in Amador County, California.[61] Bitter against "Amador Communists" who had stopped the pumps, damaging property to the value of $100,000, after failing to gain demands for a three-dollar wage and abandonment of the twelve-hour day, San Francisco's leading daily, the *San Francisco Alta*,[62] sensationalized a

---

[60] See particularly: *The French Republic*, Oct. 27, 1870; *The 'Red' Uprising in Paris*, March 23, 1871; *La Commune*, April 13, 1871; *'The Commune' and the Labor Question*, May 18, 1871; *The Objectives of the Commune*, May 25, 1871; *Communistic Morality*, June 15, 1871; *The Future of Capital*, June 22, 1871. The titles themselves, and their sequence, convey something of the impact on Godkin's thinking.

[61] See CROSS, HISTORY OF THE LABOR MOVEMENT IN CALIFORNIA (1935) 68; and the *San Francisco Bulletin*, *San Francisco Chronicle* and *San Francisco Alta*, June 23 to August 1, 1871. Violence was first reported June 23 while papers were still filled with news of suppression of the Communards. Troops were withdrawn July 15th. The Orangemen riots in New York City on July 12, 1871, in which more than 100 persons were killed and 300 wounded, likewise alarmed law-abiding citizens and excited fears of increasing social instability. (See San Francisco Alta, July 26, 1871; San Francisco Chronicle, July 15, 1871, reprinting editorials of the Chicago Tribune and New York Tribune.)

[62] The *San Francisco Alta*'s accounts, later acknowledged to have been sensationalized (see issues of July 29 and 30) were so virulent in attacks on the miners, as to lend weight to the charge that McCrellish, publisher of the *San Francisco Alta*, held a large financial interest in the mines.

drunken brawl which occurred shortly after the withdrawal of state troops from the scene of the strike and represented it as a desperate assault upon organized government and property. A remarkable editorial entitled "The Federal Authority and the Amador Conspiracy"[63] climaxed appeals for judicial as well as renewed military protection. In the editor's judgment both the Fourteenth Amendment and the Ku Klux Act gave the federal courts ample powers to deal with such violence, so that if the value of mining property were again endangered, it was their duty to exercise these powers.

These circumstances afford impressive documentation of the view that fear of socialism and radicalism may have profoundly affected Justice Field and the course of judicial history. Recurrence of revolution abroad, in conjunction with Reconstruction and the rise of the regulatory movement at home, obviously stimulated an opportunist "natural rights" use of all the clauses of Section One. Bingham's triple-reinforced but highly ambiguous phraseology[64] literally collapsed under the threat of universal usage. Obliged to deal at once with the one problem which had all but escaped the framers' attention—namely, which department of government was charged with delimiting the states' powers—the federal courts were thrust into a deadly cross-fire between Confederates and Radicals and corporations and Grangers. Statesmanship in such a situation called for curtailment of jurisdiction, and this in turn required retreat from the advanced position originally taken by Justice Bradley and Judge Woods.[65] Yet manifestly there were definite limits to judicial

---

[63] July 26, 1871. Most alarming feature of the affair in the *San Francisco Alta*'s eyes was the fact that public opinion, especially in the Amador district, supported the miners and acknowledged their grievances. Unreconciled to the discovery that it had lost its strictly "private" character, property appealed for military sanctions, and invoked aid of the recently-passed Ku Klux Klan Act and Fourteenth Amendment.

And it is here that one encounters the most puzzling—or impressive—of all circumstances: John A. Bingham, drafter of section one, returned temporarily to San Francisco from Oregon (where he had continued his stumping for the Republican ticket) on July 24th—the day of the renewed violence at Sutter Creek, the day before the newspapers' reports thereof, and two days before publication of the *San Francisco Alta*'s leader, *The Federal Authority and the Amador Conspiracy*! No substantial evidence has been found linking Bingham with this suggested use of the Fourteenth Amendment. Furthermore, it is obvious that editorial opportunism affords a perfectly adequate explanation of such usage. Numerous brief reports of Bingham's remarks do show, however, that section one—and especially the equal protection clause—constituted the core and refrain of nearly every speech. Possibly the Bingham papers hold the clue to this baffling circumstance. But a preliminary search, undertaken by Dr. Austin Hutcheson of the University of Nevada, disclosed nothing in the correspondence of the framers bearing on these matters.

[64] See Chapter 1, *supra*.

[65] That is, in the *Slaughter-House Case* at circuit, 4 Fed. Cas. 891 (C. C. La. 1870). The concluding paragraphs of Justice Bradley's dissenting opinion in the same case

Justice Field and the Fourteenth Amendment 127

caution and self-restraint. Resolve to uphold historic state powers and prestige of the courts during a prolonged national crisis could in the long run only intensify appeals for judicial protection. Ebbing respect for legislatures and mounting fears of revolt, on the other hand, progressively undermined the confidence and security which were the bulwarks of judicial self-restraint. Above all, the courts most emphatically had *not* totally rejected the doctrines of corporate personality and liberty of contract.[66] They had rejected merely the uses to which those doctrines had been put.

Our problem now is to determine the relevancy and application of these general circumstances. Did Justice Field react to the Commune in substantially the same manner as Godkin and the editor of the *Alta*? Is it likely that he learned of the Amador riot and shared the reactions of his California friends?[67] Is there anything in his correspondence that sheds light on this episode and points to its biographical importance?

Additional circumstantial, as well as direct contemporaneous, evidence suggests affirmative answers to these questions. It appears that Justice Field arrived in San Francisco on July 10, 1871,[68] five days before withdrawal of troops from the Amador mines, and was holding circuit court there when the *Alta* bore the news: MORE TROUBLE IN AMADOR. REIGN OF TERROR IN SUTTER CREEK. MASKED MINERS HUNTING FOR MINE OFFICERS. AMADOR MINE STILL IN POSSESSION OF OWNERS. BADGER SHAFT OF THE AMADOR MINE ON FIRE.

---

before the Supreme Court, 16 Wall. 36 (U. S. 1873), aimed at what he called the "argument from inconvenience," emphasize how heavily political and practical considerations weighted the majority opinion.

[66] See Justice Miller's opinion in Bartemeyer v. Iowa, 18 Wall. 129, 133 (1873); and Chief Justice Waite's dictum in the Sinking Fund Cases, 99 U. S. 700, 718 (1879), assuming corporations to be persons within the meaning of the due process clauses of the Constitution. Consider too, that the Court in the State Railroad Tax Cases, 92 U. S. 575 (1875); in the Granger Cases, 94 U. S. 155 *et seq.* (involving corporations); and in Railroad Co. v. Richmond, 96 U. S. 521 (1877), while obviously dismayed at the increasing economic and substantive usage of due process, nevertheless tacitly permitted corporations to continue raising the point. Indeed, the latter case was argued the day Justice Miller delivered his oft-quoted rebuke of due process misusers in Davidson v. New Orleans, 96 U. S. 97, 102–03 (1877). Yet the fact that the Supreme Court four years later (in 1882) permitted lengthy arguments on the point of corporate personality cautions against the view that there were no doubts or reservations in the Justices' minds in 1878–79 at the time of Waite's dictum. Probably few questions have raised more momentous and confusing problems in seemingly simple form than the questions whether corporations should be permitted to challenge state legislation under the due process clauses.

[67] It is not to be overlooked, for example, that D. D. Colton, later the business associate of Stanford and Huntington, and, intimate friend of Field, was president of the Amador Mine. See SWISHER, *op. cit. supra* note 2, at 247.

[68] See San Francisco Alta, July 10, 1871, p. 1, col. 2.

THE WAR SAID TO BE JUST COMMENCED. Under these circumstances it would have been remarkable if the *Alta*'s suggested applications of the Fourteenth Amendment and the Ku Klux Act failed to receive his earnest consideration.

The real importance of the Amador episode is indicated, however, not by these circumstances, but by a reference in a letter written six months earlier. On December 12, 1870, during the siege of Paris and shortly after the first outbreaks[69] that eventually culminated in the Commune, Field excused his neglect of a correspondent stating, "For months the stirring events occurring in Europe have absorbed my thoughts to the exclusion of almost everything else, except the duties which I have been obliged to discharge from day to day."[70]

It is not difficult in the light of his known experiences before 1870 to account for this preoccupation. Unlike most Americans, Field knew the meaning of revolution; he had witnessed it at first hand, and his life and environment had been among the best proofs of its folly.

An impressionable New England-bred law clerk of thirty-two, off for a *wanderjahr*[71] with his elder brothers and sisters, he had arrived in Paris in July, 1848, just after General Cavaignac's suppression of the barricades, the discredit and collapse of the Provisional Gov-

---

[69] American papers devoted considerable attention to an abortive assault on the Hotel de Ville led by Gustave Florens, October 31. See the telegraphic dispatches, San Francisco Alta, Nov. 5–10, 1870; editorial comment in the Sacramento Union, Nov. 5, 1870, N. Y. Herald, Nov. 4, 5, 9, 1870; and delayed accounts in the San Francisco Alta, Dec. 1–10, 1870.

[70] To Matthew P. Deady, United States District Judge, 1859–1893, and one of Oregon's most distinguished citizens. The Field-Deady correspondence consisting of 156 letters extending over the period 1865–1893 is preserved with other Deady papers in the archives of the Oregon Historical Society, Portland.

[71] See SWISHER, *op. cit. supra* note 2, at 22–23. As nearly as can be reconstructed from his *Reminiscences* and from family sources, Field sailed from New York in June, 1848, with his father; they were met in London by his brother Henry; the party proceeded through Belgium to Paris and spent several days there while the city still bore the scars of the "Bloody Days of June." After touring the provinces, and perhaps Germany, the family wintered in Paris. At Galignani's news room in December, Field read President Polk's message confirming the discovery of gold in California, but resolved to complete his travels as planned. In the spring, joined by Cyrus and family, the party journeyed through Italy, arriving in Rome just after lifting of the siege and occupation by French troops. Severe fighting was under way in Hungary when the party reached Vienna.

There is no evidence that the tour during the year of the revolutions was more than mildly exciting; but it would have been remarkable if Field, having been in Paris during Louis Napoleon's election as President and shortly after promulgation of the Communist Manifesto, had evinced no more than casual interest, twenty-two years later, in the collapse of Napoleon's Second Empire, and in the apparent resurgence of Marxism.

ernment, and its unsuccessful experiments with Louis Blanc's National Workshops. Continuing their grand tour, the Fields witnessed outbreaks in Rome and Vienna, the beginnings of German unification and Marxian socialism, the seethings and travail of a whole continent in ferment. After more than a year abroad, Field returned to New York, and sailed almost immediately for gold-rush California.[72]

During the next two decades, borne on by the exhilarations and opportunities of a rapidly growing nation, Field advanced swiftly from law clerk to Alcade, to legislator, to justice, to chief justice of the state supreme court, and finally to Associate Justice of the highest Court in the land. In 1870–71, reviewing the miracle of the frontier against embittered talk of class war and the bloody struggles of Communards and anti-Communards, the man who barely twenty years before had, penniless, walked the streets of San Francisco exclaiming, "Isn't it glorious! Isn't it glorious!"[73] turned his thoughts to the problem of ordering society to escape the horrors of revolution[74] and to safeguard institutions[75] he held dear.

More and more, beginning in the seventies, Justice Field tended to condemn, where earlier he had approved, legislation regulating the use and acquisition of property.[76] Historically considered, it was Field's tragic confusion that made the aftermath of Civil War and the conduct and program of desperate Parisians denied security, self-government, and justice, the test of democracy's validity and strength. Yet in the light of what Field had seen and experienced his confusion was not unnatural. Probably most individuals, reared in his environment, witnessing the same contrasts and suffering the

---

[72] He landed in New York, October 1, 1849; and six weeks later sailed for California via the Isthmus, arriving in San Francisco, December 28, 1849.

[73] See FIELD, REMINISCENCES (1893) 6–7.

[74] Apparently the David Dudley Fields were in Paris during the Commune. DEADY's JOURNAL, entry May 9, 1871. It is possible that their accounts or experiences intensified Field's reactions.

[75] Field's reverence for the family and marriage, and his love for children, are evident throughout his correspondence. Congratulating Deady, Oct. 19, 1866, on "the happy event which is to be," he added, "would that like good fortune was to happen to me." Writing his brother-in-law, G. E. Whitney, Dec. 16, 1869, Field asked that his new-born niece be christened Stephanie. See DEADY COLLECTION, FIELD PORTFOLIO.

[76] See his dissenting opinion in the Sinking Fund Cases, 99 U. S. 700, 750 (1879); and compare the views expressed in *Ex parte* Newman, 9 Cal. 502 (1858); and other cases cited note 18 *supra*. See also his concurrence with Justice Bradley's dissenting opinion in Railroad Co. v. Peniston, 18 Wall. 5, 38 (U. S. 1873) (wherein the minority favored exemption from state taxation of the property of federal-chartered and subsidized Pacific railroads. Note that Field earlier had concurred with the unanimous decision in Thomson v. Pacific R. R., 9 Wall. 576 (U. S. 1870) (holding the state-chartered, federal-subsidized Pacific Railroad to be taxable by the states).

same shocks and disappointments, would have reacted in much the same manner.

The historian's problem, therefore, is not merely one of explaining Justice Field's reorientation, but of undertaking to gauge its consequences. This task involves exploring the relation between Field's personal anxiety and his role as the leading apostle of laissez faire and broadened judicial review. What remains obscure, yet is plainly essential to the understanding of recent constitutional history, is the connection in Field's thought between the psychological aftermath of the Commune and the hybridization of section one of the Fourteenth Amendment with the economic tenets of laissez faire. In what ways did Field's economic motivation manifest itself? What objectives did he pursue? Is there evidence that he fostered or accelerated development of the doctrines of liberty to contract and corporate personality? Were his contributions to these doctrines indispensable? What is their ultimate bearing on Field's place in judicial history?

II.

It is obvious that before these questions can be considered the constitutional history of the post-Civil War period must be briefly reviewed, and Field's part therein critically examined. Historians have long puzzled over the paradox that the biography of the Fourteenth Amendment begins with an apparent death sentence and ends in near apotheosis. Phraseology which today has come to be literally a bill of rights in itself, a constitution within the Constitution, and a phenomenally efficient source of judicial power originally received the narrowest possible reading and was restricted in its practical application to "persons of the Negro Race."[77]

Widespread cynical opportunism in the use of the concepts was without doubt an important factor in the sudden eclipse of due process and corporate personality in the period 1871-73. Yet it is equally clear that Judge Woods's substantial about-face in *Continental Insurance Company v. New Orleans*[78] and Justice Miller's majority opinion in the *Slaughter-House Cases* would both have been unlikely but for two textual flaws which had crept unnoticed into the framers' drafts in 1866. Radical Republicans had warmed easily to the logic of Bingham's rudimentary equal protection–due process– privileges or immunities clauses; they feared only that even these

---

[77] See Slaughter-House Cases, 16 Wall. 36, 83 (U. S. 1873) (opinion by Justice Miller, speaking primarily with reference to the equal protection clause). Paradoxically, this clause was the first to be universally applied.

[78] See note 51 *supra*.

three complementary guarantees might prove worthless if Democrats regained control of Congress.[79] Conservatives, on the other hand, bitterly opposed any sweeping enlargement of Congressional power. To achieve a *constitutional* rather than mere *Congressional* protection, therefore, and to placate opponents of unitary, centralized government, Bingham shifted from his original positively-worded draft, "Congress shall have power to make or enforce all laws necessary and proper," to the present negative form, "no state shall make or enforce any law," and in the fifth section gave Congress power "to enforce the provisions of this article by appropriate legislation." Whether, in making this shift, Bingham uncritically regarded it as a clever compromise which gave Congress substantially the same powers as the original form, or whether he perceived that in evading a showdown with critics, he had merely authorized Congress to enforce a prohibition on the states, is not today apparent. Textually, the effect was a drastic reduction in the scope of Congressional power and an attendant failure of the framers to consider further what department of government should enforce the new guarantees.[80]

The same excessive zeal for multiple protection responsible for this flaw had also made for another. Was it not a curious oversight, critics argued, that the Amendment designed to clarify rights of citizenship nevertheless failed to include any definition of the crucial word "citizen"?[81] Deeming the point well taken, the Senate without extended debate[82] added to the Joint Committee's draft

---

[79] See *loc. cit. supra* note 64; FLACK, THE ADOPTION OF THE FOURTEENTH AMENDMENT (1908) *passim*. 1968: At this point—in a paragraph written in mid-1942—I commenced a recanvass of the historical evidence bearing on the text and form of Sections 1 and 5, particularly a rethinking of that judicially acknowledged yet widely evaded and denigrated (hence seemingly irrational and chimerical) "one pervading purpose of all the War Amendments." What had gone wrong? What . . . who . . . was at fault here?

The "two textual flaws" initially mentioned were of course only apparent and imagined. But that tag, pejorative and unmerited, itself speaks volumes about the problems and viewpoints of even the mid-1940's, as we began slowly to grasp the implications of the antislavery backgrounds, the significance of declaratory and natural rights thinking (and their decline), and above all the flukes and shifts (such as the last-minute addition in the Senate of the first sentence defining citizenship) which had stymied and defeated a perfectly reasonable and again discernible framer-intent. Chapters 4 to 10 *infra* will grapple with these entangled problems, and Section II of this chapter marks the rough restart.

[80] Flack concluded that Bingham and other leading Radicals regarded the change as having little effect on Congress' power—a conclusion difficult to accept until one perceives how far natural rights ideology dominated the framers' thinking. *Ibid.*

[81] *Id.* at 88. Senator Ben Wade of Ohio, an ultra-Radical, was chiefly responsible for the change.

[82] See CONG. GLOBE, 39 Cong., 1st Sess. (1866) 2869.

the present introductory sentence: "All persons born or naturalized in the United States . . . are citizens of the United States and of the state wherein they reside." No one observed, apparently, that while citizenship was thus made dual in the first sentence, only the privileges or immunities of "Citizens of the United States" were specifically protected in the second sentence against abridgement by the states! This oversight is, of course, easily explained. For years Bingham, and, indeed, all Republican opponents of slavery and of the *Dred Scott* decision, had assumed every important constitutional right to be a privilege or immunity of citizens of the United States.[83] Such had been the basic premise and the theory of the entire Amendment. They therefore could not conceive—what nevertheless plainly was the case—that a sentence added to clarify rights of citizenship, might, by its juxtaposition and inclusiveness, have the contrary effect of obscuring and jeopardizing those rights. Likewise it escaped notice that an Amendment originally regarded as necessary, and originally designed to broaden Congress's powers, ultimately passed in a form which not only fell short of clear-cut enlargement, but actually fell back on the very form which, in the case of the Thirteenth Amendment, had been regarded as ambiguous and inadequate.[84]

These defects came to light early in the Reconstruction era. They figured in Democratic attacks[85] on the Radical program in Congress and the courts. Yet it was not until early in 1871, in debates[86] over the Ku Klux Klan Act, that their potentialities were fully perceived. Ironically, responsibility for emphasizing them rests with two of the ablest and staunchest defenders of Negro rights, Senators Trumbull of Illinois and Carpenter of Wisconsin. President Grant's message advocating a Second Force Bill to cope with extra-legal suppression of Negro rights in the South had raised a host of troublesome questions. Had Congress the power to deal with these matters, to hold, in short, that the Amendment forbade denials of equal protection

---

[83] See Chapter 1, *supra*, at n. 98.

[84] Whether section two of the Thirteenth Amendment had granted Congress power to pass the Civil Rights Act of 1866 was one of the chief issues agitating Congress at the time of the drafting of the Fourteenth Amendment. Bingham himself contended that further and unequivocal enlargement of Congressional power was essential. See CONG. GLOBE, 39 Cong., 1st Sess. (1866) 429, 1034, 1064–65, 1089–95, 1292.

[85] See FLACK, *op. cit. supra* note 79, c. 5, particularly at 221–22.

[86] See CONG. GLOBE, 42d Cong., 1st Sess. (1871) 376–592 *passim*. As originally submitted the Ku Klux Klan Act of 1871, in the words of Trumbull, went to the extent of punishing offenses against the states and undertook "to furnish redress for wrongs done by one person upon another in the . . . states . . . in violation of their laws." But as passed by the House it went no further "than to protect persons in the rights . . . guaranteed to them by the Constitution and laws of the United States."

and abridgement of privileges by acts either of omission or of commission?[87]

Torrents of rhetoric and political casuistry sought to answer these questions, but an extempore exchange in the Senate between Trumbull and Carpenter epitomized the debate and reveals the sources of both previous and subsequent confusion. An idealist and ardent believer in Federalism, who was as distressed at this time by the latitudinarianism of the vindictives as he earlier had been at the cynical opportunism of the Confederates, Trumbull denied that the Fourteenth Amendment authorized Congress to protect citizens in their rights of person and property in the states. Such an interpretation, he declared, would mean "annihilation of the States." "The Fourteenth Amendment has not changed an iota of the Constitution. . . . The difference between the Senator and myself is as to what are the privileges and immunities of citizens of the United States. . . . National citizenship is one thing, and state citizenship is another. . . . Before this amendment was adopted the same obligation . . . rested upon the Government of the United States to protect citizens of the United States, as now."[88] In short, the Fourteenth Amendment was not remedial; it was simply declaratory—declaratory of what *always* had been the *real* meaning of the Constitution. Thus it "added nothing," created no rights, merely recognized and restated the inalienable, universal, indestructible rights of man.

When he was later retained to argue the validity of the New Orleans Slaughter-House monopoly before the United States Supreme Court, Senator Carpenter made telling use of these views, the expression of which he had previously prompted and criticized. It is no disparagement, indeed, to say that Justice Miller's opinion in the *Slaughter House Cases* is largely a re-synthesis of the arguments Senator Carpenter[89] derived from Trumbull. The heart and strength of both the arguments and opinion inhered in a skillful emphasis on the dual character of the Union, the expediency of maintaining the integrity of the police power and of declining to establish judicial censorship of state legislatures, and an uncanny capitalization of the view that the Fourteenth Amendment had "added nothing" to the Constitution. Basically it was the third point—the joint product of natural rights thinking and of inability to see (while judicial

---

[87] This question had arisen a year earlier. See CONG. GLOBE, 41st Cong., 2d Sess. (1870) 3611 (remarks of Senator Pool).

[88] CONG. GLOBE, 42d Cong., 1st Sess. (1871) 577. FLACK, *op. cit. supra* note 79, at 225 *et seq.* summarizes the debates. The Carpenter-Trumbull exchange occurred on April 11, 1871.

[89] See Slaughter-House Cases, 16 Wall. 36, 21 L. Ed. 394, 399-402 (U. S. 1873).

review was still incompletely established) that the *content* of citizenship is actually whatever courts will enforce—that determined the entire result. Justice Miller's *Slaughter-House* opinion—a never-ending source of amazement to his admirers—moved majestically, almost irresistibly, from the Trumbull-Carpenter premises to the practical absurdity that the Fourteenth Amendment effected no fundamental change either in the content of national citizenship or in the scope of Congressional power. It did so, of course, because Miller and four colleagues were convinced that statesmanship would best be served during Reconstruction by interpretations which upheld the legislature's capacity to govern and which at the same time restricted the discretionary powers of the courts.[90] Accordingly, these Justices freely exploited the flaws in one of the loftiest expressions of American idealism and foreshadowed the virtual emasculation of the Amendment as a bulwark of Negro rights.

The fact that Field, a states' rights Democrat who feared centralization, led the attack on the self-denying majority decision written by the Republican and nationalist Miller is further evidence of the intellectual and political confusion of the post-Civil War years. To Stephen Field, his brethren's *Slaughter-House* opinion was an offense against both reason and justice. It was not only bad law, but poor statesmanship: bad law, because it reduced the Fourteenth Amendment to an absurdity, "a vain and idle enactment which accomplished nothing," and the passage of which "most unnecessarily excited Congress and the people";[91] and bad statesmanship, because the Court construed its own powers so narrowly as to threaten leaving the South at the mercy of Negroes and carpetbaggers, and business, to the discretion of Grange-dominated legislatures. To Field these consequences were equally fearful. Throughout the seventies he stated and restated his convictions with a fervor that at times, as in his opinion in *Bartemeyer v. Iowa*,[92] in 1874, came close to exasperation and querulousness. He had no objection to—indeed concurred in—later decisions[93] restricting Congress'

---

[90] Interesting in light of the relations of Representative Bingham and Justice Miller to the Fourteenth Amendment is the fact that these two statesmen toured the Pacific Coast together in the same party in the summer of 1871 (DEADY'S JOURNAL, entry July 21, 1871, and Portland Oregonian, July 19, 1871) while Bingham was almost daily expounding his views of the Amendment's scope and purpose. See note 57 *supra.* It hardly seems possible, therefore, that Justice Miller was unfamiliar with the framers' views; yet his reading of the Amendment in the *Slaughter-House Cases* was certainly not that assumed by Bingham in 1866.
[91] 16 Wall. 36, 96 (U. S. 1873).
[92] 18 Wall. 129, 137 (U. S. 1874).
[93] See United States v. Cruikshank, 92 U. S. 542 (1876); United States v. Harris,

powers under the amendment and exploiting further the two flaws with reference to Negro rights, but he thoroughly deplored the Court majority's failure to expand the due process and equal protection guarantees in order to make the Amendment—and the Court—"a perpetual shield" against "hostile and discriminating legislation."[94] In his dissenting opinions in the *Granger* and *Sinking Fund* cases he argued for the broadest possible substantive protection and criticized both decisions as blows to the security of corporate rights.[95]

What historians and biographers have overlooked is that by the mid-seventies Justice Field was neither psychologically able nor judicially willing merely to state these views in dissenting opinions. Even as early as the *Bartemeyer* decision, the tenor of a reference to his new chief, Morrison R. Waite, suggested mounting dissatisfaction and maladjustment.[96] Prolonged economic depression, unfortunate personal investments, the failure of the Bank of California,[97]

---

106 U. S. 629 (1883); Civil Rights Cases, 109 U. S. 3 (1883). Field even dissented from the decisions in *Ex parte* Virginia and Coles, 100 U. S. 339, 349 (1880); Virginia v. Rives, 100 U. S. 313 (1880), and other of the 1880 *Civil Rights Cases*, assuming positions which would have completely destroyed the Amendment as a source of protection for the Negro Race.

[94] Slaughter-House Cases, 16 Wall. 36 (U. S. 1873). These phrases, and their counterparts, recurred in Field's opinions and at times were the articulate major premise.

[95] Field's basic premise as stated in *Ex parte* Wall, 107 U. S. 265, 302 (1883) was that ". . . all the guarantees of the Constitution designed to secure private rights, whether of person or property, should be broadly and liberally interpreted so as to meet and protect against every form of oppression at which they were aimed, however disguised and in whatever shape presented."

[96] Field to Deady, March 16, 1874: "That matter—the Chief Justiceship is at last settled. We have a Chief Justice. He is a new man that would never have been thought of for the position by any person except President Grant. He is a short thick set person, with very plain—indeed rough features. He is gentlemanly in his manners and possesses some considerable culture. But how much of a lawyer he is remains to be seen. He may turn out to be a Marshall or a Taney, though such a result is hardly to be expected. My objection to the appointment is that it is an experiment whether a man of fair but not great abilities may make a fit Chief Justice of the United States—an experiment which no President has a right to make with our Court." Interesting in this light is Circuit Judge Sawyer's report of a conversation he had had with Field the previous summer: "Upon my suggestion that if [Attorney General] Williams should not be appointed and it should not be deemed expedient to elevate one of the associate Justices to the position, the appointment ought to be made from those who had already distinguished themselves on the bench of some other Court rather than from the bar at large, or the mere politicians. He remarked that the Chief Justice ought to be a Statesman as well as a lawyer and few of them were sufficiently distinguished in that line. I do not fully appreciate the force of the suggestion. He said the Chief Justice would not be taken from the Justices of the Supreme Court." Sawyer to Deady, May 23, 1873.

[97] "I have been very much down in mind and purse since my return from Oregon. The failure of the Bank of California affected in some degree almost every one. Even so humble a person as myself has found great inconvenience following from it. My

and the continual scandals of the Grant administration, all added to his restlessness and anxiety. "God help the country when the public service and public offices are thus demoralized—whither are we drifting?" he wrote in 1876.[98] In swift succession there followed the strain of his service on the Electoral Commission[99] and the galling spectacle of President Hayes's inauguration.[100] And while overwrought and embittered at these events Field had to face the long-delayed decisions in the *Granger Cases* and the great Railroad Strike of 1877.[101] Inevitably, his relations with colleagues and subordinates suffered. Great patience and firmness were required of Chief Justice Waite in resisting Field's efforts to gain assignment of the opinion in a Pacific Railroad case[102] that involved the obligations of his

---

stocks have so shrunk in consequence that an immediate sale would cause me great loss." Field to Deady, September 26, 1875.

Judging by evidence in the Deady papers, Field suffered a high degree of loss in many of his investments; mining stocks particularly proved disappointing. Field to Deady, September 14, 1872, October 29, 1875. Late in life his straightened financial position and meager estate caused him much anxiety and embarrassment. Field to Deady, November 10, 1885, April 24, 1890, December 6, 1890.

[98] Field to Deady, April 2, 1876. The passage begins: "There is nothing new here. The very air is heavy with scandals unearthed, and rumors of greater scandals yet to be exposed."

[99] See SWISHER, *op. cit. supra* note 2, c. 10; DOYLE, *The Electoral Commission of 1877* in SOME ACCOUNT OF THE WORK OF STEPHEN J. FIELD (1881) 411. "The decision of the Commission, not to enquire into the correctness of the action of the Canvassing Boards of Louisiana and Florida was a great shock to the Country. It is the first time, I believe, that it has ever been held by any respectable body of jurists, that a fraud was protected from exposure by a certificate of its authors. I shall have much to say to you during the summer of the proceedings before that Tribunal and of its action." Field to Deady, April 2, 1877.

[100] Following the passage quoted in note 99 *supra*, Field continued: "The President, who owes his seat to the success of a gigantic conspiracy and fraud, is not finding his place a bed of roses. It is right that it should be so. He is evidently a very weak man, and hardly knows what to do. He perceives very clearly, for that has been dinned into his ears, that he and Packard [Governor of Louisiana] are twins of the same birth, and that he cannot well proclaim Packard a bastard, without impeaching his own legitimacy. And yet the people will not stand much longer bayonet rule in Louisiana. The vile wretches, who have fattened on the life-blood of that state, must be driven from their places, and its people be allowed to govern themselves, like the people of other States. What a commentary it is upon the utter demoralization of the public mind, that it can be supposed for a moment that a Governor of a State requires, for the legitimacy of his authority, the recognition of the President! He has no more to do with the matter than he has with the conduct of my family." *Ibid.*

[101] The *Granger Cases* were finally decided March 1, 1877; the great Railroad Strike occurred in July, 1877.

[102] United States v. Union Pacific R. R., 91 U. S. 72 (1875) (opinion by Justice Davis). Apparently Field had been refused the assignment because of his well-known friendship with the California railroad promoters, and because his dissatisfaction with the Government's argument might "unconsciously . . . find expression in your opinion. Once in, it would be difficult to get it out." Waite to Field, November 10, 1875, quoted in TRIMBLE, CHIEF JUSTICE WAITE: DEFENDER OF THE PUBLIC INTEREST (1938) 262.

friends, Stanford and Huntington. Throughout the Hayes administration Field confided details which left friends with an unfavorable opinion of Justice Bradley's decisive role as a member of the Electoral Commission.[103] How irascible and domineering he eventually became in relations with the subordinate judges of his circuit is evident in his remark: "It is not pleasant to find the moment one leaves the State that all the spirit and courage ooze out from the Federal judges in San Francisco."[104]

Judicial reserve, therefore, was in time overbalanced by restlessness, ambition and anxiety. During the seventies and eighties Field maneuvered to reverse the trend of judicial decision, unsuccessfully at first by sponsoring a proposal whereby membership of the Supreme Court would be increased to twenty-one; later, by the more fruitful expedient of making his dissenting opinions on the scope of the Fourteenth Amendment the constitutional law of the Ninth Circuit.

By one of the strangest paradoxes in American history, the means which President Roosevelt later would have used to eradicate laissez faire from the Constitution was originally conceived and sponsored by Justice Field as a device to assure its development. Burdened with more arduous circuit duties than his colleagues and convinced

---

[103] Several entries in *Deady's Journal* mention "long talks with Field" regarding the Electoral Commission and other matters, and on August 31, 1878, Deady observed that Field's "account of what passed between him [Field] and Bradley, when he chose the latter for the Fifth Judge on the electoral commission . . . does not redound to Bradley's credit, but the contrary." No details were given, but it was currently charged that Bradley had yielded to partisan influence. DEADY'S JOURNAL, entry August 31, 1878.

See NEVINS, ABRAM S. HEWITT, WITH SOME ACCOUNT OF ·PETER COOPER (1935) 305–400, for apparent confirmation, though judgment on this point may be suspended until publication of Charles Fairman's life of Bradley, based on the Justice's personal papers. 1968: Professor Fairman's biography remains uncompleted, but see his essay, *Mr. Justice Bradley*, in DUNHAM, ed., MR. JUSTICE (Chicago, 1956) 69–93.

[104] Field to Deady, April 3, 1890, with reference to his subordinates' indifference to his requests in matters growing out of the Sharon-Hill divorce and will cases. Parenthetically, it may be said that strain and excitement of this prolonged litigation burdened Justice Field's later years. His confidential correspondence must necessarily be read with regard for the personalities and conduct of the Terrys. See SWISHER, *op. cit. supra* note 2, c. 13; 15 AMERICAN STATE TRIALS (Lawson ed. 1926) 465. Yet his prejudices were apparent from the beginning, Field to Deady, Aug. 25, 1885, Sept. 5, 1885, and the antagonisms aroused and rekindled by the cases soon transformed him into a heated partisan of the Sharons. See Field to Deady, Feb. 2, 1888, Sept. 13, 1888, May 25, 1889, July 23, 1889, Nov. 5, 1889, April 24, 1890. Field's ablest colleagues at circuit, Deady and Sawyer, were themselves men of strong will and character, who, while sharing many of Field's social views, occasionally resented dictation and interference. "If as Field wrote and telegraphed us we are bound to follow him till reversed by the Supreme Court although every other Judge in the Circuit disagrees with him, then that Court ought to decide the question between us, when it gets the question regularly before it and thus relieve us from our exceedingly embarrassing and disagreeable position." Sawyer to Deady, Nov. 9, 1884.

that some means had to be found to expedite the vastly increased business of the federal judiciary,[105] Field in the late sixties or early seventies became the advocate of a functionalized Supreme Court.[106] Enlarged to twenty-one members, the new Court would have sat in three sections after the manner of the continental Courts of Cassation. The stressed advantage of this reform was that under it closely contested and constitutional cases could be decided by the full Court while all others could be expedited through an appropriate section.

---

[105] Field's proposals for reform of the judiciary must be viewed in the light of the burdens under which he and his colleagues labored until Congress at last passed the Act of March 3, 1891, creating the United States Circuit Courts of Appeals. 26 STAT. 826 (1891). For an excellent survey of the expansion of the Court's docket and the numerous proposals and attempts made to secure relief, see FRANKFURTER AND LANDIS, THE BUSINESS OF THE SUPREME COURT (1927) c. 2 *passim*. Many members of the bar and judiciary advocated similar or competing plans. *Id.* at 69–102. See also *Reports of the Committees on Relief of the United States Courts* (1883) 5 A. B. A. REP. 343–386.

Field seems to have been the only member of the Court who actively favored its enlargement; Justice Miller favored relief by curtailment of appellate jurisdiction; former Justice Davis worked zealously for creation of circuit courts of appeals. Functionalization (but not enlargement) of the Court was advocated in (1875) 9 AM. L. REV. 668. Circuit Judge Sawyer sponsored a hybrid plan which called for enlargement of the Supreme Court to eighteen, with the same Justices sitting from time to time as a National Court of Appeals. See (1883) 5 A. B. A. REP. 348.

[106] Field outlined his views on judicial reorganization in several letters to Deady. On March 16, 1874, immediately following the passage quoted in note 96 *supra*, relating his unfavorable impression of Chief Justice Waite, he wrote:

"Our Court has disposed of an unusually large number of cases this year and before we adjourn shall probably dispose of one hundred and fifty more. But there must be some radical change in our Court before the business, which is increasing every year can be disposed of each term. I believe I explained to you my ideas on the subject some years ago. I would have twenty-one judges, divided into three Sections of seven each and assign to one Section the admiralty, patent and revenue cases, to another Section the Equity cases, and to the third Section all other cases. If a constitutional question had to be decided before the case could be disposed of, and there was any difference of opinion among the Judges of the Section considering the case, I would have it referred to the full number for decision. By this system we could have the equivalent of three Courts of last resort, between which there would be no clashing decisions, as a different class of cases would be assigned to each Section." Field to Deady, March 16, 1874.

On October 23, 1877, he stated: "The Court has got fairly at work, but with a calendar so great as to take away all hope of disposing of it for years. I don't think that the country will long stand the present organization of the Federal Courts. Some more efficient system must be devised for the disposition of their business particularly in the Supreme Court. The system I outlined to you when in Oregon, of providing different Sections for the disposition of different classes of business is growing more and more into favor every day. But I don't think anything will be done this present session—meaning by that the extra and regular session together. I am inclined to think that the coming winter will be devoted by Congress principally to financial measures, and measures for preventing frauds in Presidential Elections. The country is pretty well disgusted with the tricks of the politicians, and is determined to have no more of such scandalous transactions as disgraced the last election. Such scenes could not take place again without a civil war." Field to Deady, October 23, 1877.

How far original sponsorship of the plan was determined by political considerations is not clear.[107] Yet it is evident that hopes of reversing majority holdings eventually colored the entire scheme. Beginning in the late seventies, they combined to push Field deeper and deeper into Presidential politics.[108] Ill-concealed dislike for President Hayes, mounting agrarian and labor unrest, particularly in California, praise for his dissenting opinions by business leaders who also saw merit in the Court plan, natural enthusiasm for his candidacy in the South—these factors made it inevitable that he sanction use of his name for the Democratic nomination. After hurried efforts of friends and brothers failed at Cincinnati in 1880, systematic preparations were laid for the campaign four years later.[109]

---

[107] Possibly Field's interest in the functionalized Court dated from his European tour or was stimulated by his brother David Dudley's knowledge of continental legal systems. An enlarged court of eighteen modeled on the French Court of Cassation, had been advocated by Senator Thurman in Senatorial debate in 1869. See CONG. GLOBE, 41st Cong., 1st Sess. (1870) 210.

It will be observed that in the first recorded reference to the proposal in 1874 Field recalled having outlined his ideas on the subject "some years ago." Subsequent references likewise indicate persistent and zealous advocacy. Sponsorship apparently tapered off and finally ceased after the Court began to adopt the Fieldian interpretations of the Fourteenth Amendment. In 1885, the Washington correspondent of the St. Louis Post Dispatch, reporting Field's contemplated retirement in 1888 on completion of twenty-five years' service, declared that Field "hopes to secure, before he retires, an increase in the number of Justices. . . . He believes in raising the number . . . to fourteen, with a quorum of six. . . . He has already talked with the President upon the subject, and has asked him to recommend such legislation to Congress." See San Francisco Morning Call, May 10, 1885, reprinting the dispatch dated April 29, 1885.

So far as the writer is aware this was the only occasion in which Field's name was publicly linked with the proposal; and no later sponsorship, either public or private, has been found. On January 26, 1880, a bill incorporating the chief features of the plan was introduced in the House by Representative Manning of Mississippi. It was indorsed in principle by a minority of the American Bar Association Committee in 1882. See (1883) 5 A. B. A. REP. 363.

[108] "You say that my name is being mentioned in connection with the presidency. I suppose you smiled at that, as I have; and would probably smile more if I should be generally taken up as a candidate. But there is little probability of that—not one chance in a thousand. Therefore, I do not give any thoughts to the subject, nor allow it to distract my sleep or trouble my digestion. Seriously, I would not give up the independence of thought and action I enjoy for the presidency for life." Field to Deady, May 31, 1879 (shortly after his dissenting opinion in the *Sinking Fund Cases* first inspired serious talk of his candidacy).

"Justice Field is largely occupied (entre nous) in putting the wires in order for the next Democratic National Convention to nominate a candidate for President. He is *not without hopes* and is doing his level best in that direction." Sawyer to Deady, September 18, 1879.

"Judge Field's 'Boom' seems to be booming quite finely just now. He is beginning to write letters on the Chinese. See Letter to General Miller in today's Call." Sawyer to Deady, March 22, 1880, alluding to an open letter wherein Field had clarified his views of Chinese immigration.

[109] Field was philosophical at defeat in 1880: "You see, by the result of the Cin-

But the forces which had propelled Field's candidacy ultimately sabotaged it. Aroused and embittered at circuit decisions which had blocked attempts to secure an economically fair assessment of the property of the Southern and Central Pacific Railroads owned by Stanford and Huntington,[110] California agrarians and workingmen inserted a plank in the Democratic state platform of 1884 "expressly repudiating the Presidential aspirations of Stephen J. Field."[111] This blow, falling, as it did, on the eve of the national convention, made a jest of Field's candidacy and inflicted wounds which never healed. Its full impact, however, was not felt until some months later when diatribes against "communist" and "agrarian"[112] enemies further betrayed the subconscious sources of Field's anxiety. Yet distress

---

cinnati Convention, that I am to be left in peace this summer—not badgered nor fretted, not abused nor vilified, not shown to have been guilty of all the crimes on earth for which I have been or ought to have been punished—in other words, I am to be permitted to maintain during the year some little of a civilized and christian character.

"My candidacy for the Presidency has been but an episode in my quiet life and will soon be forgotten. I shall remain as a good soldier at my post." Field to Deady, July 10, 1880.

Yet friends were amused that he should still circulate his unpublished recollections. "They will be ready for the campaign of '84.'" Sawyer to Deady, Aug. 2, 1880. "Field showed me a sketch of his life and an analysis of his leading opinions by Pomeroy . . . and wanted me to look it over and tell him what I think of the propriety of publishing it. . . . Talked at some length and with some feeling of the mean way the railway people of Cal. had used him about the Democratic nomination in 1880. . . ." DEADY'S JOURNAL, entry Dec. 28, 1881. See also Field to Pomeroy, June 21, 1881, *Four Letters of Mr. Justice Field, supra*.

"Field still dreams of the Presidency and may yet attain it." DEADY'S JOURNAL, entry Sept. 22, 1883.

110 See SWISHER, *op. cit. supra* note 2, c. 12.

111 Apparently Field's initial reaction was a greater consciousness of his social sympathies. "The wealthy and comfortable wonder . . . at the grumblings of the needy and are measuring the eye of the needle which the camels of old had some difficulty in squeezing through, to see what chance there is for their passage. They are not so confident of the 'good time' hereafter as they are of the condition of their bank account now. I am on the other side and would give the underfellow a show in this life. It is a shame to put him off to the next world." Field to Deady, Oct. 29, 1884. But later, after the magnitude of the humiliation at Stockton became clearer, and California supporters sought aid in the bitter fight to control local patronage, his tone changed. "I have not hesitated to explain the true situation of things in California to the President and Heads of Departments who have inquired of me respecting it. I have let them understand that the question was not whether A or B should have a particular place but whether the men of order and law, men who believed in the great institutions of society should have the ascendancy in the State, or whether the outcome of the sandlot, and the agrarian and nihilistic element should control. Having stated that the real contest was between civilization on the one hand and anarchy on the other I have left the matter to those who may feel disposed to aid either the one side or the other." Field to Deady, April 8, 1885.

112 See the letters quoted in SWISHER, *op. cit. supra* note 2, 314–16; and Field to Deady, May 17, 1886.

mingled with bewilderment and resentment was manifest in a letter which disclosed to John Norton Pomeroy the hopes which had motivated the entire venture:

> I shall have much to say to you when we meet; particularly of the very strange action of California. Had I received the cordial support, instead of the opposition of that State, my candidacy . . . would have stood great chances of success. . . .
> I had, of course, some ambition to carry out certain measures which I believed would be of great advantage to the country. Particularly did I desire a reorganization of the Federal Judiciary. As now constituted it fails of the purpose of its creation. The Supreme Court is three years behind in its regular business, and its docket is increasing so rapidly that it will soon be four years, and more, before a case can be reached after it is docketed. Could I have been instrumental in reorganizing the Federal Judiciary I would have placed on the Bench able and conservative men and thus have brought back the decisions of the Court to that line from which they should not have departed and thus, as I believe, have contributed something towards strengthening and perpetuating our institutions.[113]

Coincident with Justice Field's campaigns for the Presidency—and for an enlarged reconstituted Court—was another campaign, still less publicized and understood, which ultimately proved of greater significance. This was the development, in a series of major circuit opinions, of what subsequently came to be attacked as "the Ninth Circuit law."[114]

---

[113] Field to Pomeroy, July 28, 1884, *supra* p. 108. Field's political naïveté and his handicaps of temperament and position were also strikingly revealed in the letter written to Deady, July 16, 1884:

"My name was not presented by my friends, who thought it would be unwise, so long as the strength of Cleveland remained unbroken. Had that ever been broken, my name would have been brought before the Convention, and according to the statement of my friends, with a reasonable prospect of success.

"The action of the Stockton convention, in California did me much harm with politicians; for it seems to be an established rule with them, that a candidate must have the support of his own state before he can expect the support of a National Convention. The rule is a very unwise one; for the acts and measures which may render him popular outside of his own state, may render him unpopular there. But aside from politicians, with the thinking men throughout the country, the action of the Stockton convention did me no harm, but rather called forth tributes of regard and appreciation greater than I had ever received before.

"I am well contented with the result. Indeed, had my wishes been consulted, my name would never have been used. In my present sphere I may do some good, and after all position is only desirable as a means of doing good." Field to Deady, July 16, 1884.

See also the statement printed in *San Francisco Alta*, June 18, 1884, and quoted in SWISHER, *op. cit. supra* note 2, at 308–09.

[114] "Certain mischievous tendencies are observable in the Federal courts, which the

Long before Field's time, determined justices, dissatisfied with colleagues' decisions, had sought by well-phrased dicta to gain recognition and eventual acceptance for their minority views. How far the dissenter would go in these directions was of course determined by his self-restraint and his respect for the majority's holdings. In actual practice, by taking advantage of cases in which decisions of

---

scheme of reporting circuit court decisions according to circuits is calculated to promote. We allude to what is called the 'law of the circuit.' Certain judges, for instance . . . have certain ideas upon certain questions. It may be the circuit justice; it may be the circuit judge. More likely it is both together. They impress these ideas . . . upon their subordinates . . . and these ideas become, until reversed, what is termed 'the law of the circuit.' These ideas very often relate to questions which, from their nature, can not get to the Supreme Court,—such as questions arising in criminal prosecutions and under the writ of habeas corpus. . . . [The judges] in the Ninth Circuit . . . have certain ideas [which] . . . are alluded to as 'the law of the Ninth Circuit.' The leading characteristic of this new law is an unwarrantable enlargement of Federal jurisdiction, the erection of a general and irresponsible superintendency over the police regulations of the States, over their process of interstate extradition, and over the administration of their criminal laws. It is quite time that this matter were checked." Thompson, Book Review (1884) 18 Am. L. Rev. 535-36. See Thompson, *Abuses of the Writ of Habeas Corpus* (1884) 18 Am. L. Rev. 1-23, *Practice in Cases of Extradition* (1883) 17 Am. L. Rev. 315-49, (1883) 17 Am. L. Rev. 997-1000, (1884) 18 Am. L. Rev. 136-38, 145-47, 284-85, 321-26, 327-28, 690-92, 891-94, 1030-31, 1062-64. 26 Am. L. Rev. 113 (1892).

Thompson argued that the objection was not so much to what the judges had decided in these cases as to the fact that they had exercised jurisdiction at all. By passing on the validity of state laws and provisions of state constitutions, the federal and district judges had assumed, he maintained, a final appellate jurisdiction over the courts of the state, without reference to their rank or authority. See Thompson, *supra*, 18 Am. L. Rev. 1-23.

Thompson's campaign was thus waged chiefly with reference to the jurisdictional rather than constitutional phases of the decisions, yet he stressed the great importance of the constitutional questions in *Parrott's Chinese* case. See note 128 *infra*.

Largely in response to his agitation in the *American Law Review*, and before the American Bar Association Conventions of 1883 and 1884, Congress finally passed the Act of March 3, 1885, restoring appellate jurisdiction of the Supreme Court in habeas corpus cases. Sawyer's and Deady's opinions, especially those cited hereafter, appear to have contributed heavily to the result. See *Report of the House Judiciary Committee*, 48th Cong., 1st Sess. (1885); H.R. Rep. No. 730, 48th Cong., 1st Sess. (1885).

Insofar as criticism directed against the circuit law was based on abuse of the writ of habeas corpus, it appears to the writer that Judge Thompson ignored—perhaps for tactical reasons—the degree to which such factors as the statutory extension of habeas corpus during Reconstruction, the broad wording of section one of the Fourteenth Amendment, and the implication of the supremacy clause of the Federal Constitution combined to work revolutionary changes in the use and effect of an ancient common law writ—combined to make it, potentially—and at times in practice—the writ of error it had never been intended to be. Yet this does not preclude criticism of the manner in which Sawyer and Deady, with Field's encouragement, chose to exercise an exceedingly delicate jurisdiction. In such cases as *In re* Ah Lee, 5 Fed. Cas. 899 (D. Ore. 1880); and *In re* Lee Tong, 18 Fed. 253 (D. Ore. 1883), Deady (in Thompson's phrase) proceeded almost as if section 753 of the Revised Statutes were "a ram in the judicial fleet by which a single judge might cut the processes of the State courts in two amidships."

Justice Field and the Fourteenth Amendment 143

the circuit courts were final,[115] it was quite possible for a strong-willed dissenter to ignore and occasionally undermine majority decisions by establishing his minority views as the law of his own circuit.[116] Such occasional applications, however, appear to have had little or no constitutional significance until after 1868. In that year, to forestall an adverse decision on the constitutionality of the Reconstruction Acts,[117] a Radical-dominated Congress summarily withdrew the Supreme Court's appellate jurisdiction in all habeas corpus cases.[118] The practical and unforeseen result, of course, was to increase tremendously the freedom and discretion of the circuit Justices and their subordinates in dealing with the momentous political and economic issues of Reconstruction whenever these issues were raised in habeas corpus proceedings.[119]

And it would appear that the extraordinary dicta of the former opinion, as well as the severely criticized holdings of the latter, originated from a desire to embroider the Fourteenth Amendment.

When at length in Robb v. Connolly, 111 U. S. 624 (1884), the Supreme Court [unanimously overruling Sawyer in In re Robb, 19 Fed. 26 (D. Cal. 1884)] held the habeas corpus jurisdiction of the federal courts to be concurrent rather than exclusive, thus partially clipping the circuit judges' wings, Judge Sawyer declared himself "mortified and astonished," especially that Justices Field and Matthews had concurred in the decision. To the sympathetic Deady he confided that both Justices had expressed their approval (in advance) of a draft of his circuit opinion—Field declaring emphatically that "in any conflict [the state] court must go to the wall." "So it is now settled," Sawyer added philosophically, "that we judges on this coast have been 'elevating our horns' a little too high of late, and we must take them down." Sawyer to Deady, May 21, 1884.

It is only fair to say that federal-state issues in the *Robb* case were presented in such scrambled form that first-rate minds might easily have been confused. Yet one wonders, in retrospect, if the harvest was not partially of the Ninth Circuit judges' own sowing.

For a merciless probing of the difficulty of confining the writ of habeas corpus to purely jurisdictional matters, and the virtual necessity of permitting its use in certain instances as the equivalent of a writ of error, see *In re* Bell, 19 Cal. 488 (Cal. 1942).

[115] Notably habeas corpus cases, see note 118 *infra*; criminal prosecutions, see REV. STAT. § 697 (1815); FRANKFURTER AND LANDIS, THE BUSINESS OF THE SUPREME COURT (1928) 79, n. 107; and suits in circuit courts involving less than $5000, see REV. STAT. § 691-92 (1875); FRANKFURTER AND LANDIS, *supra* at 87-88. Prior to the Act of Feb. 16, 1875, 18 STAT. 316 (1875), decrees of the circuit courts had been final only in cases involving less than $2000.

[116] This is reputed to have been the result in Justice Nelson's circuit in the sixties with regard to foreign extradition proceedings. Compare *Ex parte* Kaine, 14 How. 103 (U. S. 1852) with *Ex parte* Kaine, 14 Fed. Cas. 78 (S. D. N. Y. 1853). See *In re* Henrich, 11 Fed. Cas. 1143 (S. D. N. Y. 1867); *In re* Farez, 8 Fed. Cas. 1007 (S. D. N. Y. 1870). See also Thompson, *Practice in Cases of Foreign Extradition* (1883) 17 AM. L. REV. 315-49, 322.

[117] See *Ex parte* McCardle, 6 Wall. 318 (U. S. 1868), 7 Wall. 506 (U. S. 1868). See also SWISHER, *op. cit. supra* note 2, at 158-63; 2 BROWNING, DIARY (1925) 191-92.

[118] Act of March 27, 1868, 15 STAT. 44, § 2 (1868), repealing relevant parts of Act of Feb. 5, 1867, 14 STAT. 385 (1867).

[119] See note 114 *supra*.

In this manner it developed that in the summer of 1874, shortly after his slighting reference to Chief Justice Waite[120] and after his vehement, almost querulous, opinion in *Bartemeyer v. Iowa*, Justice Field journeyed to San Francisco and there heard the habeas corpus case of *The Twenty-One Chinese Prostitutes*.[121]

Concluding a remarkable opinion, which already had invalidated as an infringement of treaty rights and exclusive Congressional power a California statute the purpose of which had obviously been to choke off Chinese immigration by authorizing an inspector to bar "all lunatic, idiotic . . . , crippled . . . , lewd and debauched" persons, Field declared that inasmuch as the equal protection clause applied to all "persons" rather than "citizens," the statute violated the Fourteenth Amendment as well. Since the point was judicially redundant,[122] it may be inferred that the postscriptum was added principally to make Field's *Slaughter-House* and *Bartemeyer* dissenting opinions on the scope of section one the constitutional law of the Ninth Circuit.[123]

However this may have been, the Ninth Circuit law flourished in proportion to the reverses its doctrines suffered in the Supreme Court of the United States. In the summer of 1879, after the majority's disappointing decisions in the *Granger* and *Sinking Fund*[124] cases, and while California conservatives were aghast at the regulatory agencies created by their new state constitution, Field reaffirmed and elaborated his earlier dictum. The equal protection

---

120 See note 96 *supra*.

121 See *In re* Ah Fong, 1 Fed. Cas. 213 (D. Cal. 1874). See also SWISHER, *op. cit. supra* note 2, c. 8, 211–16.

122 It is difficult to see by what line of reasoning the equal protection clause can be applied to aliens seeking admission to the United States; for the clause reads: "Nor shall any State . . . deny to any person *within its jurisdiction* the equal protection of the laws." (italics added). Logically, the Court's decision was necessary to place the Chinese women "within the jurisdiction" of California.

123 This conclusion is strengthened by the fact that Field wrote no concurring opinion expressing his view that the statute violated the Fourteenth Amendment when the Supreme Court of the United States, on writ of error to the Supreme Court of California, unanimously invalidated the statute in Chy Lung v. Freeman, 92 U. S. 275 (1876). To have done so would have emphasized the minority character of his views and might have evoked unfavorable comment on use of the equal protection clause in cases where the question before the Court was the power of the state to exclude.

124 Union Pacific R. R. v. United States, 99 U. S. 700 (1878) (Justices Strong, Bradley, and Field dissenting). Field's dissent, *id.* at 750, is of special interest viewed in relation to his Presidential aspirations and his friendship with the Central Pacific promoters. Bitterly denouncing interference with a state-chartered corporation, he argued for extension of judicial review to the point of making the "spirit of the contract clause" a limitation on Congress' powers (which in this instance had been exercised to compel a recalcitrant and mismanaged enterprise to safeguard the Government's equity).

clause, he declared in the famous *Queue* case,[125] applied to "all persons ... native or foreign, high or low"; it even shielded Chinese petty offenders from a San Francisco ordinance designed to collect cash fines under pain of clipping off queues; its implied equality of protection, moreover, embraced protection for the enforcement of contracts; its inhibitions extended to "all the instrumentalities and agencies" of state government.

As a persecuted racial minority whose treaty rights of residence and employment were repeatedly violated in western states, Chinese aliens thus succeeded in advancing, in a purely humanitarian context, the very interpretations of the key words "person," "liberty," "property," "due process," and "equal protection" which corporation lawyers had sought in vain.[126] Moreover, subordinate judges who originally had been amazed at Field's audacity and had declined to concur in his views in the *Prostitute* case,[127] now zealously fol-

---

[125] Ho Ah Kow v. Nunan, 12 Fed. Cas. 252 (D. Cal. 1879). See SWISHER, *op. cit. supra* note 2, at 216-20, SOME ACCOUNT OF THE WORK OF STEPHEN J. FIELD (1881) 394-98, for the background of this interesting case. Here again, the important point is not that Field invalidated a discreditable statute or ordinance, but rather the manner in which he rephrased dicta with an eye to emerging issues. In the *Prostitute* case he had said merely that "equality of protection implies ... equal accessibility to the Courts for the prevention or redress of wrongs and the enforcement of *rights*." Now, pressing for judicial recognition of the concept of freedom of contract, see note 124 *supra*, he substituted "for the prevention or redress of wrongs, and the enforcement of *contracts*" and laid stress on the point that "all the instrumentalities and agencies" of state government were thus inhibited (italics added).

It is also interesting to note that this appears to have been one of the few instances in which Field exercised his privilege of writing the opinion in a case handled at circuit largely by his subordinates. "Justice Field prefaced his remarks with the statement that the papers in the case were transmitted to him some time ago by Judge Sawyer [who had handled the routine matters] but he did not have time to examine the matter until the recess of the Supreme Court." San Francisco Evening Bulletin, July 7, 1879. San Francisco papers had apparently expected Judge Sawyer to hand down the decision. See San Francisco Chronicle, July 8, 1879. The fact that judicial relief almost of necessity at this date usually tended in opposite directions testifies to Field's extraordinary interest. It should be added that while not jurisdictionally grounded on habeas corpus Field's decision in the *Queue* case proved to be final—whether from statutory reasons or merely from failure of Nunan to appeal, the incomplete record fails to show. It is hard to believe that the Supreme Court would not have upheld Field, though one wonders, on the basis of Justice Miller's complaint in Davidson v. New Orleans, 96 U. S. 97 (1877), whether the majority would have relished the advertising, either of the Fourteenth Amendment, or the minority views on the scope of the equal protection clause.

[126] Compare, for example, the arguments in the various *Granger* cases, in state as well as Federal courts.

[127] "Judge Hoffman said he entirely concurred in the opinion of Judge Sawyer that neither the treaty with China, the 14th Amendment, nor any law of Congress passed in pursuance of it, had any bearing on the question before the Court." San Francisco Alta, Sept. 22, 1874. See also San Francisco Evening Bulletin, Sept. 22, 1874; BROOKS, BRIEF TOUCHING THE CHINESE QUESTION (1877) 50-51.

lowed his lead. In habeas corpus proceedings early in 1880,[128] Circuit Judge Sawyer and District Judge Hoffman invalidated the newly-enforced provision of the California Constitution of 1879 which prohibited corporations from employing Chinese.[129] Such a provision, the judges held, invaded the economic rights of both employers and employed. Due process and equal protection embraced the right to pursue lawful callings. Although the Court was apparently unwilling in the face of the decision in *Continental Insurance Company v. New Orleans* to hold with counsel[130] that corporations were "persons" within the meaning of section one, Judge Sawyer

---

On Oct. 16, 1874, Sawyer wrote to Deady: "Mr. Justice Field in my judgment overruled United States v. Miln & the Passenger Cases in his recent decision in Lewd Women case. It is true the exact point was not absolutely necessary in judgment in these cases, but the grounds upon which the first was put and the solemnly expressed opinions of the judges in the other cases cannot with any sort of propriety be called mere dicta. And I see no reason for distinguishing 'moral' from 'physical pestilence.'" Sawyer to Deady, Oct. 16, 1874.

If, as his reference to "the other cases" seems to indicate, Judge Sawyer referred to the Passenger Cases, 7 How. 283 (U. S. 1849), he apparently was confused by the multiplicity of opinions, for a bare majority of the Court therein invalidated the statutes, although nine separate opinions were written, and Taney, Daniel, Nelson, and Woodbury dissented.

[128] See *In re* Tribucio Parrott, 1 Fed. 481 (D. Cal. 1880). See also *In re* Ah Chong, 2 Fed. 733 (D. Cal. 1880), wherein Sawyer in habeas corpus proceedings held void as a violation of the Fourteenth Amendment and treaty rights a California statute prohibiting all aliens incapable of becoming electors of the state from fishing in California waters.

[129] A statute passed February 13, 1880 (Cal. Acts Amend. of the Codes, 1880, Penal § 178) in enforcement of Art. XIX, § 2 of California Constitution of 1879 made an officer of any corporation employing Chinese guilty of a misdemeanor punishable by fine and imprisonment, and provided that for a second offense the corporation should lose its charter. Parrott, president of a mine that employed 200 Chinese aliens, was arrested and convicted in a San Francisco police court February 21. His attorneys thereupon petitioned the United States circuit court for a writ of habeas corpus and elaborate arguments were made.

Sawyer had confided in a marginal note to Deady, February 15, 1880, "Yesterday both houses rushed through the anti-Chinese bill prohibiting corporations to employ them. Read three times in house on same day and the Governor hastened to sign it on same day before the ink's dry. I shall have it before long when Baker will come into play." "Baker" was Baker v. Portland, 2 Fed. Cas. 472 (D. Ore. 1879). There, Deady, in a decision later affirmed by Field, had voided (as an infringement of the implied treaty right to labor in self support) an Oregon statute of 1872 prohibiting the employment of alien Chinese on public works. See also Deady's earlier opinion in Chapman v. Toy Long, 5 Fed. Cas. 496 (C. C. Ore. 1876).

[130] The leading argument on corporate personality was made by Delos Lake, an intimate friend of Field and Sawyer, who was also counsel for the Central Pacific Railroad. See summaries in San Francisco Morning Call, March 7, 1880; Sacramento Record Union, March 8, 1880.

Obviously by 1879–80, the question of whether corporations were to gain benefits under the Fourteenth Amendment was one which could no longer be ignored on the Pacific Coast.

virtually made the *Slaughter-House* dissents the law of the Ninth Circuit,[131] and his confidential remarks[132] suggest that he was aware of the effect of his opinion.

The psychological and doctrinal significance of these Chinese cases is at once apparent. The very establishment and extension of the "Ninth Circuit law" are corroborative evidence of Field's determination to bolster the constitutional position of property. Moreover, the doctrines thus developed were the doctrines which had suffered implicit—though not explicit—rejection by the majority of the Supreme Court in the *Slaughter-House* and *Granger* cases. Assertion—either by dictum or otherwise—of a constitutional right to pursue lawful callings, to make and enforce contracts, and to conduct one's business free from extraordinary legislative demands had been prudently avoided by the majority before 1880. The later results were, therefore, anomalies which lawyers could exploit to the utmost. Chinese aliens on the Pacific Coast had rights superior to American citizens in Louisiana. The Chinese were secure in their constitutional right to work in a quicksilver mine; yet New Orleans butchers were not similarly free to pursue their hallowed calling. A California mining corporation might hire and fire as it pleased, despite legislation to the contrary; yet a midwestern railroad or a New York insurance company was required to submit to ceaseless legislative exactions. Ever ready to capitalize on such anomalies, and to reason by processes of logical extension, lawyers at last had powerful leverage in their fight to overturn *Continental Insurance Company v. New Orleans* and to remove the worst handicaps from the *Slaughter-House* decision.

Opinions differ as to the ethical and legal points raised by Justice Field's court plan and the "Ninth Circuit law." The gains and losses

---

[131] Note that Sawyer quotes Judge Swayne's dissenting opinion, Slaughter-House Cases, 16 Wall. 36, 127 (1873) to the effect that "property" signifies everything which has "exchangeable value." *Cf.* COMMONS, LEGAL FOUNDATIONS OF CAPITALISM (1924) c. 2.

[132] An entry in *Deady's Journal*, dated April 10, 1880, reads:

"Got the opinions this morning of Sawyer and Hoffman in Parrott's case and read them. Hoffman does not notice my opinions in Chapman v. Toy Long and Baker v. Portland which surprises me. It was certainly not magnanimous or kind. Sawyer does— but mincingly—I won't say grudgingly—Baker v. Portland. I had a letter from him with the opinions in which he speaks of having used my 'wedge' with his little mallet as well as he could."

The letter mentioned by Deady is missing in the files, but apparently the "wedge" was Deady's doctrine of the implied treaty right to labor in self-support, while the "mallet," which Sawyer now willingly claimed as his own, notwithstanding his original views in the *Prostitute* case, was the doctrine that the Fourteenth Amendment guaranteed to both Chinese and mine owners the right to acquire and enjoy property free from extraordinary legislative demands.

resulting from abandonment of the positions assumed by the majority in the *Slaughter-House Cases* are today so mixed that it would be difficult to criticize Field's maneuvers at circuit even if it could be demonstrated that they alone had caused the revolutionary shifts. The range of the rights embraced by due process and equal protection and the tendency of the courts continually to redefine and extend the rights demand recognition of the dual character of Field's contribution.

Similarly, if it is granted that the merits of a case and whether a court properly may substitute its judgment for the legislature's are generally the crucial questions in most constitutional debates, it is academic to criticize Field for stretching phraseological limits and for enlarging constitutional jurisdiction. Biased he obviously was, and at times, especially after 1877, lacking in judicial temperament and open-mindedness. Yet he was a slave to duty—steadfast, conscientious, almost puritanical in his resolute determination. The Reconstruction cases made him one of the leading advocates of natural rights doctrines which were possessed of great intrinsic appeal and limitless possibilities for expansion. His psychological state impelled him to explore and refine the attributes of these doctrines. In the Chinese cases at circuit he won assent to interpretations of the equal protection clause which, if they had continued to be debated in economic and political terms, might have aroused momentous controversy. Whether in these cases Field exercised more than a circuit Justice's customary freedom of expression depends upon whether the majority ever seriously believed it to be either possible or desirable *permanently* to restrict the scope of section one to persons of the Negro race, whether Field himself understood such to be the majority's intention and was thus honor-bound by it, and whether the broad phraseology employed by the drafters would have supported any attempt so to limit the section.

Fortunately, an estimate of Field's contribution, and of the importance of his circuit opinions, does not depend upon answering these questions. Whatever his motives, it is obvious that he pioneered the prevailing interpretation of the equal protection clause; he capitalized the rhetorical advantages of the Chinese cases; he probably helped as much as Cooley or John A. Campbell to fashion the forensic weapons that counsel needed. This is his great, if not an altogether lasting, achievement. It is the basis upon which his career should be judged. If, as seems likely, the threat of Court-packing has now become part of our unwritten constitution, assuring less divergence between popular desires and constitutional decisions, there is a profound, almost involute, irony in the fact that Field himself stood ready to launch this innovation.

III.

Although many of the problems of Justice Field's career and the paradoxes of his motivation may require further specialized study, one at least is now clearer and more sharply defined. This is his central role in expanding judicial power and in reading an economic content into the clauses of section one. Surveying matters broadly, and fitting facts in historical perspective, we may briefly summarize our findings.

Justice Field's important contributions to the development of the *laissez-faire* doctrine of freedom of contract, and to the establishment of revolutionary substantive due process, were essentially products of a conviction that the salvation of democracy lay in a judicial trusteeship. Judges must construe governmental powers strictly, and private rights broadly, toward the end that state interference be held to a minimum and anything savoring of the collectivist doctrines which Field associated with the violence and bloodshed of the Commune be rendered forever impossible and unconstitutional. Fortuitously, the Fourteenth Amendment was advanced as an economic and political weapon at exactly the time Field was preoccupied with this crucial problem of statecraft. Perceiving the Amendment's uses as an instrument of judicial restraint, he seized it avidly, and sought in the *Slaughter-House* and *Granger* cases to develop its capacities, but failed to convince the majority of his brethren of the expediency of such restraint. Frustrated, he sought to accomplish his purposes by singularly direct means. Failing in politics, he nevertheless succeeded, through a brilliant understanding of how the law grew and how it might be made to grow, in fostering development, through humanitarian cases unencumbered by political niceties, of those very doctrines for which skilled constitutional lawyers had before argued in vain and which they later exploited to the fullest degree.

By conditioning a state of mind which stigmatized as "Communistic" the efforts of agrarian and labor groups to control the abuses of unregulated and publicly subsidized business, the Paris Commune tragically confused American social thinking, came close to subverting the basic tenets of democracy, and set in motion forces which caused constitutional theory often to run counter to social needs. Because of this fateful anachronism, and by extraordinary conjunction of circumstances, purely "individualistic" enterprise was thus enshrined in the Constitution just as it ceased to be an economic fact; exercise of social and economic control, on the other hand, was discredited, and the motives of those sponsoring it made suspect, just as it became economically necessary and inevitable. In the light of this breach between theory and practice, it is not too much to say that the Paris Commune helped lay the foundations for a constitutional crisis which took two generations to mature and which ended only recently in repudiation of the Fieldian viewpoints.

———◆◆◆———

EDITORIAL NOTE. A query, at this point, to integrate experience and insight, history and law. An analogy in the form of a might-have-been may give us needed bearings and footing.

How much might it have helped, what a vast difference might there be, what might have been the course of American constitutional history and development, how much better and easier our situation, had the Central Pacific and the Southern Pacific railroads employed, as contract laborers to build their lines, during the 1860's, 70's, and 80's, gangs of *Negro freedmen* instead of the gangs of thousands of Chinese? Might not pestilent racism—and the exposure and the control thereof—then have taken a different, a more favorable and domestic turn? And might not the "Ninth Circuit law" then have rallied power and opinion, "process" and "protection," to the defense of Negro rights? Habeas corpus, in short—mass habeas corpus—at once and continually made available for and to this helpless minority, for and to "citizens of the United States," "persons of the Negro race"? At length California corporations prohibited from employing Negroes, and hence rallying to Negroes' defense? Corporate personality and liberty to contract developed as adjuncts, as safeguards, and reinforcements of Negro rights? "Squads of lawyers" —corporation lawyers—defending humble, illiterate freedmen, just as they defended helpless and tormented Chinese?

I ask these questions without chauvinism, earnestly and soberly, thankful for everything Justice Field and California and Nevada corporations did to defend the Chinese; and I ask readers to consider and to answer the questions in that spirit. (This analogy and might-have-been came to mind July 24–25, 1967—the days of the Detroit riots.)

The Field article in a sense was cathartic. The ambivalence and complexity of our constitutionalism had become strikingly clear. California, without Justice Field, might have gone utterly racist.

Instead, by 1943–1945—thanks again in part to his vigilance and resource—racial protection gained headway, even while economic-corporate due process declined. The "Ninth Circuit law" and various San Francisco Chinese laundry cases again lighted and pointed the way. Ordinances and regulation, fair on their face but administered, as Justice Matthews observed, "with an evil eye and an unequal hand," had got short shrift, first from Field, then from the whole Waite Court in the mid-eighties.[1] Increasingly now these precepts bore fruit: Field, for one, always had nursed his alternatives and reserves.

Even in writing about him, not only the antislavery motivation of this Amendment, but much the strongest early use made of its clauses to curb pestilent racism, got linked in ways which provided fresh insight, and made study of the pre-Civil War backgrounds needful and compelling.

Constitutionalism renews itself in part by such research. History, as institutional and social memory, is absent-minded, even capricious. But aim and significance do make their way in time.

Did they?

Everyman alone can say.

---
[1] Yick Wo v. Hopkins, 118 U. S. 356 (1886).

[CHAPTER 4]

The Early Antislavery Backgrounds of the Fourteenth Amendment

EDITORIAL NOTE. Every generation has its talismanic beliefs and phrases. For Victorians, the talisman was *Progress*—the beatitude, the certitude thereof, was an idea for all minds, seasons, and discourse. In our time, *Process* has supplanted *Progress*. Process is the conjure-word, the building block of modern unitary thought.[1] Life, law, history, and government, all have their processes; all indeed *are* processes. All get analyzed, clarified, and, in the pinches, interpreted and explained, as processes.

Law of course introduced, pioneered, and professionalized this logomachy, and American constitutionalism as before noted has institutionalized it, literally, consummately, syncretically as *due* process of law and equal protection of the laws. Englishmen first learned how to make law by remaking it; processing and reprocessing ancient writs, customs, and cases into rules, "precedent," and authority, and these finally into the "law of the land" and the Rule of Law. Americans followed through—appropriated and extended these terms and methods, and learned how to make and remake constitutions by essentially the same means. Which is to say again, that by processing and reprocessing due process of law we keep our written constitutions viable and up to date, resolving conflict or at least sublimating and reducing it.

Unquestionably, something unique and marvelous happened to American due process. Everyman's Constitution never could have been, would not now be, without it. What it was that happened, why, when, where, and how it *chiefly* happened, are the subjects and details of this chapter. If a single word and development must

---

1 See WHYTE, THE NEXT DEVELOPMENT IN MAN (Mentor ed., 1962), 10 and *passim*.

initially characterize and describe what happened, that word, we maintain, is *affirmative: affirmative* due process; *affirmative* equal protection; *affirmative* American government and citizenship were what emerged conceptually and in fact. All these for *all* persons. For every man. For every citizen, both as such. And without the old racial exemptions and equivocations. These were the aims, the postulates, the driving thoughts, the express guarantees—all backed now, and since 1868, by complete constitutional power to make them good. To make them good affirmatively, that is to say again, without the old prejudiced exceptions. *Affirmative* thus was the vital word, the vital element.

And this word and element are the key to what the United States lost—at least half-lost—in the 1880's, and the keys to what we now, so laboriously, are recovering and reconstituting.

If the idea of an affirmative due process is still strange, novel, and ambiguous today, the wonder and the irony are all the greater, for the fact is that our land was founded and our forebears nurtured and reared on *affirmative* political and constitutional thought. The familiar English and colonial sources and origins scarcely need mention. Yet one element often gets slighted. Significantly, that element is the seventeenth-century Puritan "original" of our affirmative constitutionalism: the idea of duty, of dueness and meteness, of care and responsibility, not simply, nor even chiefly personal, but rather mutual and social—a mutual self-realization by common effort, respect and striving. That was "the original" of this part of the American Creed, and that was the part the Abolitionists recovered and proselytized, the part we are again recovering and extending.

The Mayflower Compact of course comes instantly to mind here: "We . . . do mutually covenant & combine our selves togeather into a civil Body Politik, for our better Ordering & Preservation. . . ; . . . and do enacte . . . and frame such just & equal Lawes . . . as shall be thought most meete . . . for the generall Good . . . unto which we promise all due Submission and Obedience."[2] In short: government itself as an act of faith and will, of social contract, and of pledged protection and responsibility. The old Early Tudor ideas of the Commonweal and the Commonwealth[3] embraced, and extended, an affirmation of principle—above all, of *duty* personal and social, moral and legal, and all of course then religiously motivated and sanctioned.

---

[2] W. BRADFORD, PLIMOTH PLANTATION (Mass. Hist. Coll., Fourth Series), III, 89–90.

[3] See ALLEN, A HISTORY OF POLITICAL THOUGHT IN THE SIXTEENTH CENTURY (3d ed., London, 1951), 134–156.

Less familiar, yet even more revealing in evidentiary force and context, are the preambles to the earliest codes of Massachusetts Bay and Connecticut, dating from the *Body of Liberties* (1641), and repeated almost verbatim thereafter. Here is the preamble of the *General Lawes and Liberties of Massachusetts Bay* (1648):[4]

> Forasmuch as the free fruition of such Liberties, Immunities, privileges as humanitie, civilitie & christianity call for as due to everie man in his place & proportion, without impeachment & infringement hath even been, & ever will be the tranquility & stability of Churches & Comon-wealths; & the deniall or deprivall thereof the disturbance, if not ruine of both:

So began and begin the basic codes of American law. And their second paragraph in each case succinctly stated the sacred constitutional rights of Englishmen deemed mete and proper in the premises —the rights today embraced in the due process and the equal protection clauses. *Due*, in short, was a marked, loaded word from the start; so was *free*, so was *equal*. Most revealing and significant in these passages are the pregnant "dutifiers," obligors, and commitments to affirmative government, process, and protection. Note particularly the ideas implicit in such phrases as "free fruition. . ." "due to everie man in his place and proportion . . . without . . . infringement"; above all, the "ruine" likely to follow "the deniall or deprivall thereof." These are the affirmative concepts that American political thinking began with. And how much they tell us about the almost-lost affirmative content of Everyman's Constitution.

* * * *

The hard fact was that during the Populist and the Progressive eras especially, two mutual absurdities had stymied progress in race relations. Too many people too easily were persuaded that the framers of the Fourteenth Amendment "neither had said what they meant nor meant what they said." These pronounal ambiguities were allegedly willful and flagrant; but they were not the framers' at all.

There is no blacker period or page in the American chronicle than this. Nineteen hundred and eight. Forty years after ratification; a long decade after *Plessy* and "separate but equal"; four and a half decades longer still to *Brown v. Board*. Segregation insidiously hard-

---

4 See THE COLONIAL LAWS OF MASSACHUSETTS (Whitmore ed., 1889), 121. Cf. page 33 for the 1641 version. For the Connecticut version of 1650, see CONNECTICUT PUBLIC RECORDS (1851), vol. 1, p. 509.

ening and spreading. The mountaineers of Kentucky's Berea College, "a manual labor" school of antislavery vintage and tradition (enrollment 1,097; endowment $107,999), fighting almost alone, and in vain, against now *border*-state, state-enforced segregated education (extended by this decision even to private schools and colleges). And the first Mr. Justice Harlan still, and again, in lone dissent.[5] Nineteen hundred and eight. This year too a Virginia holding, one that counterpoints trends almost diabolically: a corporation composed entirely of Negro members, the state high court held, could not be a "colored person" *within the meaning of a restrictive covenant*.[6] True, undoubtedly (Virginia's corporation law at any rate played no favorites); but hardly right. For by any sound, fair, affirmative, progressive construction of Sections 1 and 5, *all* racially-motivated restrictive covenants were outlawed and bad—and so the Supreme Court would hold, forty years later.[7]

Nineteen twenty-six. (One year now to the Beards' *Rise*). Deracialization of due process now utter and complete, even in academic circles. *Due Process of Law*, by Rodney L. Mott, a 600-page treatise covering Anglo-American law, history, and cases, a work of prodigious industry, and as sterile, desiccated, frustrated, and frustrating a product of scholarship as American social science can boast. No mention whatever of the special racial bearings, associations, orientations. Six pages devoted to the Fourteenth Amendment as such, and conspiracy extended and operative now even at the level of the "subconscious." For this was the conclusion: "Finally, there seems to have been a subconscious attempt on the part of the framers and ratifiers of the Fourteenth Amendment to make it as vague as possible." "Hindsight," we can say, "with a vengeance!"

Inertia and inaction thus continued to multiply social and racial deficits, and the "framers and ratifiers" still suffered the blame. Ostensibly, the Fourteenth Amendment had known neither parentage nor birth, but like Topsy, had "just growed." John A. Bingham's speeches in Congress, 1856–1866, had been hard enough to reconcile with such biology. Other congressional speeches and debates, discovered from time to time, had strengthened my skepticism and my surmise even more. But it remained for a chance Law Library order (dated May 4, 1942) to recommence research, and ultimately to hypostasize a genealogy.

---

[5] See Berea College v. Kentucky, 211 U. S. 45 (1908), and the searing account in MILLER, THE PETITIONERS (1966), 197–216.

[6] See People's Pleasure Park v. Rohleder, 109 Va. 439 (1908).

[7] See Shelley v. Kraemer, 334 U. S. 1 (1948); Barrows v. Jackson, 346 U. S. 249 (1953).

The library order was for *The Power of Congress Over the District of Columbia*, by Theodore Weld,[8] a work which turned out to be a powerful, elaborate, natural-rights–substantive-due-process attack on the constitutionality of slavery, made by the greatest of American abolitionists, and in the year 1837! There then followed, in swift succession, discovery and study of Gilbert H. Barnes, *The Antislavery Impulse* (1933); *The Weld-Grimké Letters*[9] (1934); and *The James G. Birney Letters*[10] (1938). Then a hunch, and soon, a virtual certainty—even on the limited basis of these works—that Bingham's three-clause draft of 1866, and indeed the whole constitutional theory of his three speeches 1856–1859, actually had evolved, and had been broadcast throughout New England, New York, Pennsylvania, and the Old Northwest, during the 1830's in the course of the American Antislavery Society's first organized crusade. Collaborative research with Jacobus tenBroek, 1946–1947, fully established and extended these points, which our two complementary studies, "The Early Antislavery Backgrounds" and "The Antislavery Origins of the Fourteenth Amendment,"[11] elaborately documented, 1950–1951.

Down to 1942 I had approached the Fourteenth Amendment from the judicial and congressional interpretations and from history, largely on the corporate side, and had concentrated, like everyone else, on problems that clustered about the intended scope and the presumed meaning of the word "persons." After 1942, and increasingly after 1946, I abandoned this narrow, arbitrary, stultifying approach. Focus thereafter was on the War Amendments as a whole, on the *racial* motivations and objectives of the Fourteenth Amendment, on the due process and equal protection clauses in particular, and on all these as culminations of the organized antislavery movement and of enlightened humanitarianism generally. The time had passed when Everyman's Constitution—which Justice Miller seventy years before in the *Slaughter-House Cases* acknowledged and declared had been added for "the freedom of the slave race, and the security and firm establishment of that freedom"—any longer could be studied, much less interpreted, without regard for, without considering and comprehending the aims, tenets, and experience of those who led the United States to establish and secure that freedom.

---

8 Reprinted as Appendix A in TENBROEK, EQUAL JUSTICE UNDER LAW (1965).
9 Two vols., ed. by G. H. Barnes and D. L. Dumond.
10 Two vols., ed. by D. L. Dumond.
11 (Berkeley, U. of Calif. Press, 1951); for retitled reprint, see *supra*, n. 8.

[CHAPTER 4]

Genesis, 1833–1835

IT IS A CURIOUS PARADOX that the three constitutional amendments adopted after the Civil War, though admittedly framed for the "security and firm establishment of the freedom of the slave race,"[1] have nevertheless aroused extraordinary speculation and controversy. This, of course, is especially true of the Fourteenth Amendment.[2] The scope and interrelations of the first and fifth sections of that article, their intended impact on the federal system,[3] whether corporate persons originally were conceived of as beneficiaries by the framers (or simply became such),[4] whether the three major

---

[1] Miller, J., in The Slaughter-House Cases, 16 Wall. 36, 71, (U.S. 1873).

[2] See Chapters 1-3, supra; FLACK, THE ADOPTION OF THE FOURTEENTH AMENDMENT (1908); THE JOURNALS OF THE JOINT COMMITTEE OF FIFTEEN ON RECONSTRUCTION (Kendrick ed. 1914); WARSOFF, EQUALITY AND THE LAW (1938); Boudin, *Truth and Fiction About the Fourteenth Amendment*, 16 N.Y.U.L. REV. 19 (1938); Hurst, Book Review, 52 HARV. L. REV. 851 (1939); McLaughlin, *The Court, the Corporation, and Conkling*, 46 AM. HIST. REV. 45 (1940).

[3] Controversy over these two questions began during debates over the various Civil Rights bills, 1868–1875 (see FLACK, *op. cit. supra* note 2, c. 5) and over the Ku Klux Act (see CONG. GLOBE, 42nd Cong., 1st Sess. 376 (1871)). It was fanned by the decision in the Slaughter-House Cases, *supra* note 1, as well as by other great Reconstruction Cases including Ex parte Yarbrough, 110 U.S. 651 (1884); Civil Rights Cases, 109 U.S. 3 (1883); United States v. Harris, 106 U.S. 629 (1882); United States v. Cruikshank, 92 U.S. 542 (1876); United States v. Reese, 92 U.S. 214 (1876). It has recrudesced at nearly every attempt at anti-poll tax, antilynching, FEPC, and similar race legislation in Congress (see KONVITZ, THE CONSTITUTION AND CIVIL RIGHTS (1947); CARR, FEDERAL PROTECTION OF CIVIL RIGHTS (1947); *Federal Power to Prosecute Violence Against Minority Groups*, 57 YALE L.J. 855 (1948)) and at nearly every major case extending judicial review and Negro rights under the War Amendments, viz.: Shelley v. Kraemer, 334 U.S. 1 (1948); Screws v. United States, 325 U.S. 91 (1945); Smith v. Allwright, 321 U.S. 649 (1944); United States v. Powell, 151 Fed. 648 (1907); Ex parte Riggins, 134 Fed. 404 (C.C.N.D. Ala. 1904).

Compare *Constitutionality of Proposed Federal Anti-Lynching Legislation*, 34 VA. L. REV. 944 (1948); COLLINS, WHITHER SOLID SOUTH (1948); COLLINS, THE FOURTEENTH AMENDMENT AND THE STATES (1912) with TO SECURE THESE RIGHTS, REPORT OF THE PRESIDENT'S COMMITTEE ON CIVIL RIGHTS (1947); *State Action and the Enabling Clause of the Fourteenth Amendment*, 44 ILL. L. REV. 199 (1949); Hale, *Rights Under the Fourteenth and Fifteenth Amendments Against Injuries Inflicted by Private Individuals*, 6 LAW. GUILD REV. 627 (1946).

[4] See Chapters 1-3, *supra*, and the works by Boudin, McLaughlin, *supra* note 2; Camp, *Corporations and the 14th Amendment*, 13 CAL. STATE B.J. 12 (June-July, 1938); Howe, *A Footnote to the 'Conspiracy Theory,'* 48 YALE L.J. 1007 (1939); Hurst, Book Review, 52 HARV. L. REV. 851 (1939).

clauses restraining state action were deemed to embrace state inaction and state failure to provide the guaranteed due process and equal protection (especially in matters affecting the lives and liberty of members of racial minorities)[5]—these are questions which have been debated and redebated for many years. Eminent historians and publicists have participated in the discussions as well as lawyers, congressmen, and judges.

During recent months, controversy has waxed rather than waned. Does the Amendment's first section incorporate the *entire* Bill of Rights? Unimpressed by sixty years' holdings to the contrary, four justices in the *Adamson* case,[6] decided in June, 1947, vigorously argued that it does—that such, indeed, was not merely the intention of the framers but the understanding of the ratifiers. In a thirty-page memorandum appended to his dissent, Justice Black elaborately documented this thesis.[7] Again, in *Wheeling Steel Corporation v. Glander*,[8] decided in June, 1949, Justice Douglas, speaking now only for himself and Justice Black, chose to reopen the question whether corporations properly are regarded as "persons" under the due process and equal protection clauses.[9]

These minority views naturally have not gone unchallenged. In an article of extraordinary importance[10] which summarizes by far the most thorough study yet made of the original understanding, Professor Fairman found the evidence to be overwhelmingly opposed to

---

[5] See the materials and debates, *supra* note 3, particularly the Ku Klux debates and remarks of Senator Pool: CONG. GLOBE, 41st Cong., 2d Sess. 3611 (1870); also Justice Harlan's dissent in Civil Rights Cases, 109 U.S. 3, 26, and the remarkable opinions of Judge Jones in *Ex parte* Riggins, 134 Fed. 404 (C.C.N.D. Ala. 1904); and U.S. v. Powell, 151 Fed. 648 (1907).

[6] Adamson v. California, 332 U.S. 46 (1947), Justices Black, Douglas, Murphy and Rutledge dissenting, the latter two in a separate opinion.

[7] *Id.* at 68, 92–123.

[8] 337 U.S. 562 (1949).

[9] *Id.* at 576–581; Justice Douglas' dissent was largely a restatement of the views expressed by Justice Black dissenting singly in Conn. Gen. Life Ins. Co. v. Johnson, 303 U.S. 77, 83 (1938). Justice Black's reasoning in turn was similar to that of Judge Woods in Insurance Co. v. New Orleans, 1 Woods 85 (1870), when the issue of corporate personality, first presented to the Federal courts in 1871, was decided adversely to corporations. In an extraordinary rejoinder appended to his opinion for the majority, Justice Jackson explained, "why, in writing by assignment for the Court," he "assumed without discussion that the protections of the Fourteenth Amendment are available to a corporation. It was not questioned by the State in this case, nor was it considered by the courts below." Corporations have been held entitled to equal protection since 1886, Santa Clara County v. Southern Pacific Ry. Co., 118 U.S. 394, 396 (1886); and to due process since 1889, Minneapolis and St. L. Ry. Co. v. Beckwith, 129 U.S. 26, 28 (1888).

[10] Fairman, *Does the Fourteenth Amendment Incorporate the Bill of Rights?* 2 STAN. L. REV. 5 (1949). See also the companion article, Morrison, *The Judicial Interpretation*, 2 STAN. L. REV. 140 (1949).

the minority's thesis of full Bill of Rights incorporation. Comment generally has remained critical of the Black-Douglas interpretations.[11] If the full faith and credit clause is the "lawyers' section" of the Constitution, and the commerce clause is the economists', the Fourteenth Amendment today clearly is the historians' and political scientists' section. As such, cynics may note, it is being buried deeper and deeper in its own glosses and literature!

One of the striking things about the protracted and voluminous controversies over the Amendment has been the limited, narrow, repetitious character of much of the supporting argument. Thanks to Dr. Flack's monograph,[12] the congressional debates of 1866–1871 have been conveniently sampled and cited for years, yet with no decisive result. Similarly, speeches of Representative John A. Bingham, the Ohio member of the Joint Committee of Fifteen who is conceded to have been the chief draftsman of Sections One and Five, have been quoted and digested again and again, often to support mutually contradictory views.[13] Equally convenient and indecisive has been the "argument from silence." Repeatedly and fallaciously it is employed both to prove and to disprove intent to protect corporations; it should be obvious it is admissible for neither purpose.[14] Finally, rules of statutory construction continue to be critically applied to the first two sentences of Section One. Critics and dissenters[15] so doing generally point out that a double standard of interpretation must be employed if the key word "person" is made to embrace both natural and artificial persons in the due process and equal

---

[11] On the Adamson dissents, see 58 YALE L.J. 268 (1949); 36 GEO. L.J. 398 (1948); 46 MICH. L. REV. 372 (1948). Braden, *Objectivity in Constitutional Law*, 57 YALE L.J. 571, 589–593 (1948). On the Wheeling dissents, see Note, *The Supreme Court, 1948 Term*, 63 HARV. L. REV. 119, 139–40 (1949); Cf. 7 NAT. B.J. 372–380 (1949).

[12] THE ADOPTION OF THE FOURTEENTH AMENDMENT (1908); see also JAMES, THE FRAMING OF THE FOURTEENTH AMENDMENT (University of Illinois Press, 1956).

[13] Compare 2 BEARD & BEARD, RISE OF AMERICAN CIVILIZATION 111–113 (1927) and HACKER, TRIUMPH OF AMERICAN CAPITALISM (1940) with Boudin, *supra* note 2, *passim*; also *compare* appendix to Justice Black's Adamson dissent, *supra* note 7, with Fairman, *supra* note 10.

[14] See Chapter 1, *supra*, pp. 46–47. Even important parts of Flack's work (*op. cit. supra* note 2, at 81, 87) heavily relied on by Justice Black are shown by Professor Fairman (*supra* note 10, at 65–66) to rest on unwarrantable inferences from silence. And at times Professor Fairman's own arguments lean toward a supposition that *failure* to assert clearly and unequivocally some point which we today regard as all-important is to be taken as evidence of more than the fact of failure (*supra* note 10, at 36). The inescapable fact is simply that the 1866 evidence is too scant, taken alone, to *prove* much of anything about the framers' or ratifiers' purposes; the scope of inquiry must be broadened.

[15] See the dissents of Justice Black: Conn. Gen. Life Ins. Co. v. Johnson, 303 U.S. 77, 87 (1938); and Justice Douglas: Wheeling Steel Corp. v. Glander, 337 U.S. 562, 578 (1949).

protection clauses yet is limited only to natural persons "born or naturalized" by the first sentence defining citizenship. This last and recurrent criticism is, in a sense, typical of the whole debate, for critics generally overlook that the first sentence defining citizenship was added at the last minute in the Senate;[16] accordingly, neither it nor the argument really is germane to the primary problem, the intention of members of the Joint Committee as to use of the word "person" in what is now the second sentence of the section.

From this it appears that the air of mystery and uncertainty which still clings to the purposes of the framers and to the meaning of their handiwork in part derives from the sterile, superficial quality of the debates and the absence, until Professor Fairman's study, of really thorough historical investigation. Even Professor Fairman's research, which clarifies so much in the course of showing the balance of evidence to be overwhelmingly against Justice Black in the matter of Bill of Rights inclusion, is limited to this one exceedingly narrow issue and to the period after December, 1865. Hence, it is essentially negative in its findings. Because of this and by reason of recurring emphasis on the often muddled, unsatisfactory character of the framers' theory[17] (when tested by our modern standards and interests), it really raises an even more vital question than it answers: Does some hidden element or blind spot in our approach cause us frequently to miss or to misread the framers' whole orientation? Certainly we must, as Professor Fairman cautions,[18] beware of that sort of hindsight which inverts perspective and makes it easy to dismiss an entire Congress or generation as inept because its views and purposes are *today* less than clear. The confusion and the difficulties may be partially ours.

It is chastening in this last respect that one still searches the vast literature in vain for any systematic attempt to relate the phraseology of the post-Civil War Amendments to pre-Civil War experiences, theory, and history. The reasons are of course obvious. Debates over slavery and over the Negroes' status raged for a century; they pervaded and dominated state and national politics; they threatened and eventually disrupted the Union. It is hard, accordingly, not to regard them merely as the chaff heap of our constitutional history. To attempt at this date to winnow the relevant from the irrelevant is both a cheerless and formidable task; yet quite obviously it is one

---

[16] CONG. GLOBE, 39th Cong., 1st Sess. 2869 (1866); the addition was made at the suggestion of Senators Wade and Stewart; see at 2560, 2768.
[17] See Fairman, *supra* note 10, especially at 24–36.
[18] *Id.* at 8–9.

Antislavery Backgrounds of the Fourteenth Amendment 161

which can no longer be avoided. For it patently is absurd, once futile and threadbare controversy begins to repeat itself after eighty years,[19] to go on disregarding the antislavery origins of antislavery Amendments simply because the bulk of the evidence is so vast and diffuse. The Fourteenth Amendment is universally presumed to be the outcome of the organized antislavery movement in the United States, yet its modern history continues to be written without reference to the abolitionists. Judges and historians seek an understanding of phrases admittedly designed to secure the "freedom of the slave race" without first reexamining the tenets of the group which fought longest and hardest to establish that freedom.

The need now is to study the two major sections of the Amendment genetically and as a whole. Numerous investigations will no doubt be necessary to determine the precise meanings and motivation of the framers. The present study is frankly introductory and experimental. It is designed to call attention to certain arguments and materials which shed important light on the genesis of later forms, and which, by reason of political geography and related circumstances, bring the whole problem into sharper focus.

In an earlier study seeking confirmation for an hypothesis that John A. Bingham did indeed have a substantive conception of due process such as might have accompanied a purpose to take in the "whole range of national economy," the writer found apparent confirmation for Justice Miller's "one pervading purpose—Negro race" theory of the whole of Section One. He found this in the form of three major speeches delivered by Bingham in Congress between 1856 and 1859.[20] These three speeches were successively directed at attacking the pro-slave laws adopted by the Kansas (Shawnee Village) Legislature, at defending the power of Congress to regulate slavery in the territories, and at the problem of securing free Negroes and mulattoes the right to acquire and enjoy property and to move freely from state to state irrespective of local constitutional and legislative barriers. Toward these ends, Bingham not only employed the due process clause in a sweeping, natural rights, substantive sense, but he also employed, in the same fashion and for the same purpose, both the privileges and immunities phraseology of the comity clause[21] and the concepts of equality before the law and equal protection of the

---

[19] See *supra* notes 9 and 14.
[20] See Chapter 1, *supra*, at 45-61. For the three speeches, see CONG. GLOBE, 34th Cong., 1st Sess. appendix 124 (1856); CONG. GLOBE, 34th Cong., 3rd Sess. Appendix 135-140 (1857); CONG. GLOBE, 35th Cong., 2d Sess. 981-985 (1859). These are summarized Chapter 1, *supra*, 45-61.
[21] U.S. CONST. Art. IV, § 2.

laws derived from the Declaration of Independence. In short, it was discovered that the Ohioan and member of Congress, who is known to have been chiefly responsible for the phraseology of Section One when it was drafted by the Joint Committee in 1866, had, during the previous decade and as early as 1856–1859, employed not one but all three of the same clauses and concepts he later used in Section One.[22] More important still, Bingham employed these guarantees specifically and in a context which suggested that freedmen—free Negroes and mulattoes rather than corporations and business enterprise—unquestionably were the "persons" to which he then referred.

While evidence seemed to indicate that Bingham's constitutional theory was more highly developed than that of many of his colleagues in the fifties, the Kansas and Oregon debates also showed that other antislavery Republicans held closely related views and in fact made similar arguments. Chief among those to do so was Bingham's friend and mentor, Joshua Giddings,[23] the original abolitionist member of Congress from the Western Reserve who was known to have been responsible for the insertion of the "due process plank" in the Republican platform of 1856. Another Republican representative from Ohio, Philomen Bliss, was found to have made similar speeches.[24]

A survey of the antislavery backgrounds of the Fourteenth Amendment will not overlook these leads. State constitutional and legislative provisions discriminating against free Negroes and mulattoes are known to have been numerous in the period 1800–1860. Controversies over them extended at least as far back as the Missouri Compromise. Were the arguments and usages which Bingham employed in the fifties and sixties perhaps evolved in these prior debates? What is the explanation and significance of the observed tendency for this natural rights usage to center in the Ohio delegation? How far back does the triple clause usage extend? How and where did it originate? What were the relations between the abolitionists' use of due process *against* slavery and Chief Justice Taney's proslavery use in the case of Dred Scott? What relations, if any, did both the proslavery and antislavery uses bear to the known prewar economic-substantive uses?

Two decades of study of the organized antislavery movement in the United States have shed important light on these questions.

---

22 As a matter of fact Bingham also used the republican form of government clause and the just compensation clause in the same connection, both in 1856–1859 and in 1866, unsuccessfully in 1866. See Chapter 1, *supra*, at 58–61; JOURNALS OF JOINT COMMITTEE, *op. cit. supra* note 2, at 71, 85.

23 See Chapter 1, *supra*, pp. 30, 55.

24 *Ibid*. Speeches were also made by Rep. A. P. Granger of New York. CONG. GLOBE, 34th Cong., 1st Sess. Appendix 295–297 (1856).

Antislavery Backgrounds of the Fourteenth Amendment 163

Research begun by the late Gilbert H. Barnes and continued by Professors Dwight L. Dumond[25] and Arthur R. Kooker[26] not only has contributed to a sounder understanding of the whole abolitionist-Free Soil movement but incidentally affords clearer insight into the antislavery origins and motivation of the Thirteenth and Fourteenth Amendments.

The pioneer work in these directions was Professor Barnes' monograph entitled *The Anti-Slavery Impulse, 1830–1844*.[27] This volume demonstrated that the real strength and leadership of the antislavery militants rested less with Massachusetts and Garrisonian elements[28] and more with neglected forces and figures that centered in the Western Reserve. In its early stages particularly, it was largely the work of a devoted band of evangelists and theological students.

Professor Barnes' story has been too well told in *The Anti-Slavery Impulse*, and too well retold in briefer compass by Professors Dumond[29] and Nevins,[30] to bear abridgment here. What matters is that "this ardent host" which swept through Ohio and the Northeast and Northwest in the late thirties, "full of philanthropy and zeal," converting whole communities to abolitionism, women's rights, and temperance, had its inspiration in the Great Revival. This was the name popularly given to the evangelical campaign conducted principally in central and western New York, Pennsylvania, and Massachusetts during the period 1824–1827 by Charles Grandison Finney. A successful lawyer and a simple, forthright speaker of extraordinary power who had turned to evangelism in his early thirties, Finney was a "new measures" Presbyterian;[31] he renounced orthodox doctrines of "election," "reprobation," and "predestination" in favor of premises more nearly akin to the transcendentalism of Emerson

---

[25] See *infra* notes 44 and 51.
[26] *The Benevolent Empire*, a paper read before Amer. Hist. Assoc. Annual Meeting, Cleveland, Ohio, Dec. 27, 1947. The writer is greatly indebted to Professors Dumond and Kooker for numerous courtesies and research leads.
[27] (Appleton, 1933).
[28] See GARRISON, WILLIAM LLOYD GARRISON 4v. (1885–1889). This comprehensive and adulatory biography is one of the chief reasons Garrison's reputation has continued to overshadow that of other antislavery leaders.
For insight into the strongly practical leadership of the early movement in Massachusetts, prior to its domination by Garrison, see NEW ENGLAND ANTI-SLAVERY SOCIETY, ANNUAL REPORT, First to Third, 1833–1835.
[29] HISTORY OF UNITED STATES 319–320 (1942).
[30] 1 ORDEAL OF THE UNION 137–151 (1947).
[31] See especially his LECTURES ON REVIVALS OF RELIGION 21 (6th ed., Joshua Leavitt ed. 1835). Doctrinally the disintegration of orthodox Calvinism by the "New Measures" school in the twenties was similar to that begun thirty years earlier in New England by Unitarianism. See 2 PARRINGTON, MAIN CURRENTS IN AMERICAN THOUGHT 321–338 (1927).

and the unitarianism of Channing. Inverting Calvinist theology, preaching rather of God's beneficence and the perfectibility of man, Finney and his ardent coevangelists also employed the "revivalists" series of related sermons to sway their audiences, and it was thus they achieved sensational success in converting whole communities. Not "election," not an arbitrary act of divine grace by a jealous and wrathful God, but rather "faith by works" became the new watchword. A "revival of religion" to Finney and his group was essentially a "revival of Christian benevolence," an exercise of individual moral responsibility no less than of divine regeneration. Individually as well as socially, men must strive to bring their institutions and conduct into harmony with professed religious principles.

This "mighty impulse toward social reform" Professor Barnes shows to have first found outlet in a "benevolent Empire" of interlocking societies dedicated to promoting home and foreign missions, Negro education, Sunday schools, and temperance.[32] Later its energies were intensified and reoriented in behalf of abolition, largely as a result of the tremendous enthusiasm generated by success of the antislavery movement in Great Britain and the timely interest and support of New York merchant-philanthropists headed by Arthur and Lewis Tappan. In 1831 these two energetic and reform-bent brothers established Finney in a huge tabernacle on Broadway. By December, 1833, barely four months after Parliament's final act emancipating the slaves of the West Indies, they brought together in Philadelphia representatives of the "benevolent Empire" and, with characteristic zest, promoted organization of the American Anti-Slavery Society. This organization was modelled on its British predecessor[33] which Buxton, the Stephens, Zachary Macaulay, and Wilberforce had founded in 1823, and which had climaxed fifty years of preparatory work by mobilizing opinion and support for "immediate emancipation." The new American society had for its joint aims first, "the entire abolition of slavery in the United States," and second, "the elevation of the character and condition of the people of color" that according to individual worth they might "share an equality with whites of civil and religious privileges." "Immediate emancipation" was again to be the slogan. Physical force and insurrection were expressly repudiated; rights were to be vindicated in this country precisely as they had been in England by "moral suasion"

---

32 Kooker, *supra* note 26.
33 On British Abolition Movement see: MATHIESON, BRITISH SLAVERY AND ITS ABOLITION, 1823-1838 (1926); KLINGBERG, ANTI-SLAVERY MOVEMENT IN ENGLAND (1926).

Antislavery Backgrounds of the Fourteenth Amendment 165

and by "arguments addressed to understanding and consciences."[34]

Professor Barnes' narrative[35] describes how two Tappan-endowed theological seminaries in Ohio presently became the center of this crusade, how Philomen Bliss and scores of other young zealots who originally had taken up the cause of benevolent reform at Oneida Institute[36] now moved westward, and how in the crucial years of 1836 and 1837 this group saved the languishing antislavery movement.

The true genius of abolitionism, Professor Barnes shows to have been Theodore Dwight Weld. Indeed, this swarthy, roughly-clad, largely self-educated scion of the Dwight, Edwards, and Hutchinson families clearly emerges after a century as one of the most influential figures of his generation—a self-effacing, thrice-gifted leader, orator, and organizer whose driving energy and personal magnetism at times constituted the principle resources of the movement. Born in Hampton, Connecticut, in 1803, a Congregational minister's son, Weld grew up in central New York. Converted by Finney in 1825 while still a student at Oneida Institute, he presently was drawn into abolitionist ranks by his Jamaica-born friend and patron, Charles Stuart, a pensioned officer of the Madras Army and already a respected and seasoned veteran of the antislavery movement in Britain.

In 1831, after spectacular success both as a revivalist with Finney and later as a temperance lecturer in New York, Weld was engaged by the Tappans to promote the cause of the manual labor (self-help) colleges in general. One of his specific duties was to choose a site for a new self-help theological seminary which with Tappan support was counted on to carry benevolent reform to the entire frontier. After a twelve-month, 4575-mile journey on foot and horseback through the West, South, and Southwest during which he enlisted the interest and support, among others, of the Alabama-lawyer planter, James G. Birney, Weld returned. By early 1833 he recommended that the Tappan aid be extended to Lane Seminary in Cincinnati, an established school the president of which was the renowned Lyman Beecher. Within a year, scores of former "Oneidas" moved west. Dozens of mature, education-hungry students whom Weld had met on his travels and as a revivalist also became students at Lane, build-

---

[34] The quotations are from Articles II and III of the Constitution of the American Anti-Slavery Society, reprinted in 1 GARRISON, *op. cit. supra* note 28, at 414. See also the Society's Declaration of Sentiments reprinted in *id.* at 408–412.

[35] BARNES, THE ANTI-SLAVERY IMPULSE, 1830–1844 cc. 2, 3, and 4 (1933).

[36] Oneida Institute was the first of numerous "manual labor" or self-help schools established in the wake of the Great Revival.

ing, farming, studying, and working as missionaries and teachers among free Negroes.

The seminary in February, 1834, held a prodigious eighteen-day, forty-five hour discussion of the questions: 1. "Ought the people of the Slaveholding States to abolish slavery immediately? 2. Are the doctrines, tendencies and measures of the American Colonization Society, ... such as render it worthy of the patronage of the Christian public?"[37] As a result of this "Great Debate," as it was soon generally known, and the subsequent suppression of the antislavery society for successfully abolitionizing the college, fifty-one students led by Weld withdrew en masse. "Free discussion," they insisted in a parting manifesto penned by Weld, was not merely a "right, inherent and inalienable," it was the "duty of every rational being and free moral agent."[38] In the spring of 1835 almost the entire group transferred across state to Oberlin College which now was destined to receive both Tappan aid and Finney's services as professor of theology.[39] Weld, however, from the autumn of 1834 until 1841 devoted his full energies to abolition. At first he was a lone "agent" in the Reserve; later he selected and trained twelve "Rebels" as colleagues to extend the revivals; finally in 1836, on commission from National headquarters, he increased the number to "Seventy," thirty of whom still were from the Lane group.

It was the "Seventy's" grass roots evangelism, reaching its climax as Barnes shows in the year 1836–1837, that played a major part in undermining slavery and mobilizing latent "Free Soil" sentiment. Night after night, in churches, lofts, and schoolhouses, these revivalists concentrated as had Weld on the "sober substantial business and professional men of the community" whom Garrisonites offended.[40] "God's moral law," Christian benevolence, the egalitarian creed of the Declaration were the major themes. Slavery was a sin, a crime, a monstrous evil, and an anachronism which must be abolished immediately.

Active control of the campaign which was liberally subsidized by the Tappans lay with a brilliant group now installed at headquarters in New York. With the exception of John Greenleaf Whittier, the

---

37 BARNES, op. cit. supra note 35, cc. 6 and 7. No extended report of the Lane Debates was published, but see Stanton's letter dated March 10, 1834, later published as a pamphlet DEBATE AT LANE SEMINARY (1834); and Weld's letter to James Hall, editor of Western Law Magazine in 1 WELD-GRIMKE LETTERS 137–146.
38 STATEMENT OF THE REASONS WHICH INDUCED THE STUDENTS OF LANE SEMINARY TO DISSOLVE THEIR CONNECTION WITH THAT INSTITUTION (Cincinnati, 1834).
39 FLETCHER, HISTORY OF OBERLIN COLLEGE, 2 vols. (1943).
40 BARNES, op. cit. supra note 35, cc. 9 and 10.

Quaker poet who aided Weld in selecting and training the "Seventy," the names and roles of this group are still largely unfamiliar.[41] There was the shrewd, patient Yankee, Joshua Leavitt, trained for both law and ministry and a veteran of the temperance and seaman's aid movements. Leavitt edited the *Weekly Emancipator* and was to devote his full life to reform. The group also included Leavitt's able opposite, caustic, versatile Elizur Wright.[42] A graduate of Yale and a former mathematics professor, Wright had been enlisted by Weld when the latter abolitionized Western Reserve College in 1831, and he now was in charge of the national office and editor of annual reports. There was also Henry B. Stanton, the ironic, humorous conciliator, a former "Oneida" and Lane Rebel and second only to Weld as an orator and organizer. He was now charged with supervision of finances and was to be the strongest link between abolitionists of the East and West.[43] Also in the group was Stanton's cultured and distinguished co-secretary, Birney, the handsome, Princeton-educated former agent of the Colonization Society who personified both the hopes and strategy of the moral suasion movement. Barely a year after Weld's visit in 1831, Birney had returned to his native Kentucky, manumitted his remaining slaves, and worked for gradual emancipation. He moved on to Cincinnati when plans for an antislavery paper were frustrated. There he began at forty-three, in 1835, a career as editor, national corresponding secretary, and, in the forties, presidential nominee of the Liberty Party. This made him the most widely known and respected of the national leaders.[44] Finally there was Weld himself, a gaunt, impassioned, John-the-Baptist-like figure, his voice a whisper from overspeaking. He morbidly shunned office yet exercised an overall supervision by dint of his amazing gifts of rhetoric and intellect. Tirelessly directing the "Seventy" by day, Weld at night turned out pamphlets that became bibles of the movement, *Slavery As It Is* (1839), *The Bible Against Slavery* (1837), and the extraordinary legal argument, *The Power of Congress over the*

---

[41] For biographical data, in addition to the works cited hereafter, see DICTIONARY OF AMERICAN BIOGRAPHY; BARNES, *op. cit. supra* note 35; and the WELD-GRIMKE and BIRNEY LETTERS, *infra* note 44.

[42] The best biography of this extraordinary figure, which stresses his later career as a distinguished actuary, is WRIGHT AND WRIGHT, ELIZUR WRIGHT, THE FATHER OF LIFE INSURANCE (1937).

[43] For evidence of his oratorical powers, see FIRST ANNUAL REPORT OF THE NEW YORK YOUNG MEN'S ANTI-SLAVERY SOCIETY . . . WITH ADDRESSES 3–11 (May, 1835).

[44] On Birney, see BIRNEY, JAMES G. BIRNEY AND HIS TIMES (1890); LETTERS OF JAMES G. BIRNEY, 1831–1857, 2 vols. (Dumond ed. 1938) referred to in these footnotes as the BIRNEY LETTERS. 1968: See also FLADELAND, JAMES G. BIRNEY: SLAVEHOLDER TO ABOLITIONIST (Ithaca, 1955).

District of Columbia (1838). All three of these were prepared by Weld in a period of a few months.[45]

Sharing Weld's capacity to make missionaries of his disciples, the "Twelve" and "Seventy" enrolled scores of able, influential converts. The evidence of their activity in this regard is striking and cumulative. From Barnes, for example, we learn that Weld himself won over the Ashtabula lawyer, Joshua Giddings;[46] Weld had a peculiar fascination for lawyers.[47] From the Birney Letters, we learn that Thaddeus Stevens was an early convert of Jonathan Blanchard, the brilliantly successful member of the "Seventy" assigned to Pennsylvania.[48] These letters also reveal that Birney himself enlisted the interest and support of Salmon P. Chase.[49] Weld's correspondence discloses that Philemon Bliss, though prevented by ill health from joining the "Seventy," remained throughout a trusted advisor and collaborator.[50]

What interests one who is studying the origins and intended scope of the Fourteenth Amendment is not simply the political geography of this movement but rather the evidence, running through both the Weld-Grimke and Birney letters, of an ingenious, exhaustive, and above all, prophetic constitutional attack on slavery. The most casual reader soon observes that as the struggle broadened and deepened and conflict became not only political but sectional the

---

[45] The best source on Weld is LETTERS OF THEODORE DWIGHT WELD, ANGELINA GRIMKE WELD, AND SARAH GRIMKE, 1822-1844 (Barnes and Dumond ed. 1934) referred to hereafter as the WELD-GRIMKE LETTERS. Readers unable to cover this entire work will find evidence of Weld's extraordinary rhetorical powers in his letter to J. F. Robinson, May 1, 1836, p. 295-298; of his common sense and practicality at p. 242-244, 425-427. The three pamphlets were all published anonymously as numbers of the Anti-Slavery Examiner.

[46] BARNES, *op. cit. supra* note 35, at 82.

[47] *Id.* at 82. Even William Jay, the distinguished lawyer and judge (see *infra* note 81) and Robert C. Winthrop as well as John Quincy Adams relied on Weld for legal research which he performed brilliantly. See 2 WELD-GRIMKE LETTERS 748, 956-958. Time and again Weld converted bitter opponents. See 1 WELD-GRIMKE LETTERS 236-240 for the conversion of General J. H. Paine, later a leader of the Liberty Party in Ohio and Wisconsin.

[48] BIRNEY LETTERS, *op. cit. supra* note 44, at 456.

[49] *Id.* at 419, 469; *cf.* BIRNEY, *op. cit. supra* note 44, at 259.

[50] WELD-GRIMKE LETTERS, *op. cit. supra* note 45, at 84. See also WELD, AMERICAN SLAVERY AS IT IS 31, 35-37, 41, 43, 102, 138 (1839) for Bliss' observations on slavery while residing in Florida in 1834-1835.

Three other distinguished lawyers who affiliated with the antislavery movement during this period were Joel P. Bishop (a student at Oneida, agent of the A.A.S.S. 1835, and editor—see WELD-GRIMKE LETTERS 71 n.4); Stanley Matthews, Associate Justice, United States Supreme Court, 1881-1889, (an antislavery editor in Cincinnati in the forties—see BRENNAN, BIOG. ENCYC.); Joel Tiffany, legal author, reporter of N.Y. Supreme Court, and inventor who shared leadership of Elyria, Ohio bar with Philemon Bliss in thirties and forties (see HISTORY OF LORAIN COUNTY, OHIO 45-47 (1879)).

original ethico-moral-religious indictment gave way to one framed increasingly in legal and constitutional terms. Merely to note three of the outstanding features and premises of this attack is to perceive their possible bearing.

1. The whole antislavery crusade, we are reminded by Professor Dumond,[51] was essentially a quest for protection of the laws; its central theme and argument derived from the "self-evident truths" of the Declaration of Independence. Not the mere excesses or abuses of the slave system, but rather its denial of that protection for which *all* governments were instituted and to which *all* human beings were entitled by their humanity was what outraged the mind and conscience of leaders like Birney, Stanton, and Weld. Slavery not only "annihilated the right, the privilege, and the responsibility of self-ownership," it degraded and debased man to a chattel; it denied him the bounties of government, the attributes of personality.

2. What thus began as a campaign for protection of slaves and free Negroes presently became one to guarantee civil liberties more generally.[52] Obliged to defend even their rights to discuss slavery and to seek its overthrow by constitutional means, abolitionists focused intently on the problem of securing and enforcing constitutional rights. They were interested, not merely in their own rights, but also in those of other dissident and unpopular groups including Indians and Mormons. Protection of these rights not merely against invasions by government action but against private action and mob violence as well was the goal. "The security of life—of liberty—of civil and religious privileges—of the rights of conscience—of the right to use our faculties for the promotion of our own happiness—of free locomotion—all these," Birney contended in his letter accepting the Liberty Party nomination in 1840, "together with the defense of the barriers and outposts thrown around them by the laws, constitute the highest concerns of a government."[53] Conversely, their abridgment marked a betrayal of the purposes and functions of government —a violation of constitutional as well as natural rights. Moreover, abolitionists shared an inarticulate as well as an articulate major premise; they traditionally presumed the federal Bill of Rights to be both morally and legally binding on the states. Thus Birney, for example, disillusioned by proslave intransigence, at length came around to the view that the federal government had not merely the power

---

[51] HISTORY OF THE UNITED STATES 319–320 (1942); ANTI-SLAVERY ORIGINS OF THE CIVIL WAR c. 3 particularly pages 43–45 (1939).
[52] ANTI-SLAVERY ORIGINS OF THE CIVIL WAR cc. 3, 4. For full-length documentation on this point, see the excellent study by NYE, FETTERED FREEDOM (1949).
[53] 1 BIRNEY LETTERS 562–566. (Birney to Myron Holley *et al.*).

but the bounden duty to free the slaves and protect the great fundamental civil rights from abridgment in and by the states.[54] Affirmative congressional protection of civil rights, still a sharply controverted issue under the Fourteenth Amendment, thus is found to have been one of the major tenets of abolitionism.

3. Setting out from these bases, abolitionists eventually employed almost every conceivable clause from the Preamble to the Bill of Rights. Judging by the edited source materials, the arguments erected on the due process, just compensation, and comity clauses gained steadily in favor. They eventually merged into and buttressed the three original primary concepts of protection, freedom, and equality grounded on the Declaration. Birney's letters in particular give evidence of systematic and continuous exploitation of due process from the late thirties onward. That clause and argument tended to spearhead the whole attack on slavery in the minor party platforms of the forties and fifties.[55]

Summing up these relevant circumstances, it appears that thirty years before the Joint Committee began its labors, there centered in Ohio, western Pennsylvania, and New York—in those very districts which Bingham, Giddings, Bliss, Granger, and Stevens later represented in Congress—an evangelical, humanitarian movement. The focal point of this movement's attack upon slavery was the utter absence and denial of legal protection, not merely to the slaves and to free Negroes and mulattoes, but also to those whites who ventured to attack the "chattelization of man."

---

54 1 BIRNEY LETTERS Intro. xviii-xxii for selections from his diary and writings 1847-1851; see also his *Can Congress, under the Constitution, Abolish Slavery in the States?* Albany Patriot, June 2, 1847.

55 The legal and constitutional argument in the BIRNEY LETTERS is remarkable both in range and interest. Note especially the due process arguments at 293, 647, 758, 805-806, 835; the declaration that colored people are "citizens" at 815, and "persons" at 658 and 835; the exceptionally strong references to "natural equality of men" at 272; the composite synthesis of all these elements in the Declaration of 1848 drafted by William Goodell at 1048-1057; the various references to major law cases at 386-387 (Nancy Jackson v. Bullock, 12 Conn. 38 (1837)), at page 658, 667-670 (Birney's arguments in THE CREOLE for which Weld did much of the research), at 758 (Jones v. Van Zandt, 46 U.S. 215 (1846) in which Salmon P. Chase was of counsel). By contrast, the legal argument in the WELD-GRIMKE LETTERS is more limited, but see page 798 for the letter of Ebenezer Chapman, an Athol, Massachusetts physician, to Weld, dated October 1, 1839, urging greater emphasis on the unconstitutionality of slavery and less on its cruelties, and specifically mentioning the Declaration of Independence, the common law, the Ordinance of 1787, the Preamble, and the due process clause of the Fifth Amendment.

Cf. use of these same clauses and doctrines in the 1844 Platform of the Liberty Party (STANWOOD, A HISTORY OF THE PRESIDENCY 218, 219 (1904)); the 1848 Platform of the Free Soil Party (*id.* at 240); the 1852 Platform of the Free Democracy (*id.* at 254, 256); the 1856 Platform of the Republican Party (*id.* at 271, 272).

In the course of their organized effort to convert the country to their belief that slavery was incompatible with the American Creed and with the Christian ethic, the members of this Weld-Birney group spelled out, in the thirties and forties, an elaborate system of constitutional protection based on the very clauses and concepts which eventually were employed by the framers in 1866. An important premise of this system ultimately came to be that the first eight amendments, in whole or in part as the instant case required, were binding upon the States; Congress had, or should have, power to safeguard and enforce rights thus guaranteed.[56]

One of the active participants in the early movement, it appears, was none other than Philemon Bliss. Among its early converts were Joshua Giddings, S. P. Chase, and Thaddeus Stevens, all of whom eventually showed partiality for equal protection–due process phraseology.

What still needs to be determined is whether the orthodox Republican theory of the fifties and sixties really was that worked out and broadcast by the abolitionists twenty years earlier, whether Bingham's three-clause system was his spontaneous personal creation or simply familiar Liberty-Free Soil doctrine, whether the long-sought key to the War Amendments and to the baffling problems of their phraseology and interrelationship does not lie hidden in old abolitionist tracts and speeches.[57] Fittingly enough, the printed report of the organizational meeting of the Ohio Anti-Slavery Society dated April, 1835, holds a partial answer to these questions.

Like the Quaker philanthropists, Benezet, Woolman, and Lundy, like Franklin, Jay, Washington, Madison, and other of the Fathers

---

[56] For insight into the situations and circumstances that prompted abolitionists in this regard, see 2 BIRNEY LETTERS 649-650 (1938). Birney in 1842, outraged by recent popular persecution of the Mormons and the Cherokees, noted that in each instance "as a State was the wrong doer," (i.e. in failing to supply the due protection of the laws) these unfortunate groups were left "without redress, the *United States* having no power, even if it had the will, to restrain a sovereign State, or compel it to make reparation." This quotation, contrasted with his views five years later (*supra* note 54) dramatically reveals the dilemmas that confronted abolitionists and humanitarians who believed no less firmly than their contemporaries in state and local responsibility. By the same token, it suggests an historic basis for broadened, and at the same time delimited, application of the Amendment to avoid making "every oversight by a policeman on his beat" a matter of federal jurisdiction; notorious, flagrant and cowardly state inaction *in cases involving discrimination or persecution because of race or color* was what was aimed at above all else.

[57] Flack's research suggested, as early as 1908, that Sections One and Five constituted a single integrated system (see *op. cit. supra* note 2, at 96-97, 138-139), yet this discovery generally has been ignored and the Fourteenth Amendment construed merely as a definition of citizenship plus a series of historic but unconnected restraint clauses, plus a redundant grant of power to Congress to enforce rights which already had been entrusted to the judiciary.

of 1787, and generally in marked contrast to the Garrisonian abolitionists, the leadership of the Weld-Birney group sensed, however vaguely and imperfectly, that there were two great obstacles to emancipation. These were an irrational, yet pervasive prejudice against color and a deep-rooted fear, not only in the South, but in the North, of the consequences of setting free large numbers of Negroes who were still unprepared for freedom and who were widely believed to be incapable and even unworthy of it. In either case, the basic problem was one of winning racial respect and of promoting racial adjustment. Only a convincing and continued demonstration that popular prejudices and forebodings were unfounded, that the widely assumed Negro inferiority sprang[58] not from real differences in racial or biological or psychological endowments but from sheer lack of social and educational opportunities, could permanently abate hostility and assure a progressive solution. "Immediate emancipation," by which really was meant "emancipation immediately begun," was a goal to be achieved by moral suasion, evangelism, and education. Measures to improve the status of free Negroes—thus combatting prejudice by demonstration—constituted the heart of the whole program.[59]

In a prodigious, single-sentence paragraph of the ringing *Declaration of Sentiments* which he drafted for the delegates assembled at Putnam, Theodore Weld outlined the "Plan of Operations" grounded on these premises:

> We shall seek to effect the destruction of slavery, not by exciting discontent in the minds of slaves, not by instigating outrage, not by the physical force of the free states, not by the interference of Congress with State rights, but we shall seek to effect its overthrow by ceaseless proclamation of the truth upon the whole subject,—by urging upon slaveholders, and the entire community, the flagrant enormity of slavery as a sin against God and man, by demonstrating the safety of immediate emancipation to the persons and property of the masters, to the interests of the slave and the welfare of community, from the laws of mind, the history of emancipations, and the indissoluble connection between duty and safety—by presenting facts, arguments, and the results of experiment, establishing the superiority of free over slave labor, and

---

[58] See Wesley, *Concept of Negro Inferiority in American Thought*, 25 JOURNAL OF NEGRO HISTORY 540-560 (1940). 1968: See also DAVIS, THE PROBLEM OF SLAVERY IN WESTERN CULTURE (Ithaca, 1966); JORDAN, WHITE OVER BLACK: THE DEVELOPMENT OF AMERICAN ATTITUDES TOWARD THE NEGRO, 1550-1812 (Chapel Hill, 1968).

[59] For characteristic references to plans for bettering the lot of the free Negro, see 1 WELD-GRIMKE LETTERS, 132-135, 262; AMERICAN ANTI-SLAVERY SOCIETY, 4 ANNUAL REPORTS 32-35, 105-111 (1837); 5 ANNUAL REPORTS 127 (1838).

the pecuniary advantages of emancipation to the master,—by correcting the public sentiment of the free States, which now sustains and sanctions the system, and concentrating its rectified power upon the conscience of the slave holder,—by promoting the observance of the monthly concert of prayer for the abolition of slavery throughout the world, that by a union of faith and works we may bring our tithes into the store-house, and prove therewith the "God of the oppressed."[60]

A second paragraph revealed more specifically the projected means and ends.

We propose . . . to organize Anti-Slavery Societies throughout the State, employ agents, circulate tracts and periodicals embodying our sentiments, invoke the aid of the pulpit, wield the power of the press, and implore the Church to purge herself from the sin of slavery. . . . We shall practically testify against slavery, by giving a uniform preference to the products of free labor. We shall absolve ourselves from the political responsibility of national slave holding, by petitioning Congress to abolish slavery and the slave trade wherever it exercises *constitutional jurisdiction.* We shall earnestly seek the emancipation of our free colored citizens from the bondage of oppressive laws and the tyranny of a relentless public sentiment, and extend to them our hearty encouragement and aid in the improvement of their condition and the elevation of their character. In the employment of these means, and in the prosecution of these measures, while we seek sedulously to observe and do the command, "thou shalt not in any wise rebuke thy neighbor, and not suffer sin upon him," we trust ever to demonstrate in our intercourse with those of opposite views, that we are no less mindful of those other precepts equally imperative, "Be gentle unto all men," "Be courteous."[61]

In keeping with this declaration, Weld's lieutenants had prepared two separate committee reports. It is in the second of these, the report of the Committee on the Laws of Ohio, that one suddenly encounters what to the student still curious regarding Bingham's motives is a thoroughly arresting body of doctrine.

The first report,[62] an eloquent twenty page statement of the Committee on the Condition of the Colored Population, artfully set the stage. In precise, objective terms it detailed the measures taken by

---

[60] PROCEEDINGS OF THE OHIO ANTI-SLAVERY CONVENTION HELD AT PUTNAM (April 22-24, 1835) 10-11.

[61] *Id.* at 11. The WELD-GRIMKE and BIRNEY LETTERS for the early years 1833-1835 are also suffused with this determined optimism and supreme confidence in ability to win over the South by moral suasion.

[62] See PROCEEDINGS, *op. cit. supra* note 60, at 17-36.

the Lane Rebels and by other philanthropic-minded Ohioans to establish schools, churches, small farms, and trade apprenticeships among the 3,200 Negroes living in Cincinnati and Brown County. Stress was laid on the home missionary phases of the effort, on the eagerness of the Negroes to learn, on their proved worth and capabilities, on the steady decline in vice, crime, drunkenness, and race prejudice, and on the betterment of community and race relations generally. In short, the emphasis was on the progressive and constructive character of the whole experiment and the vast opportunities for its expansion.

Implicitly as well as explicitly, then, the second report,[63] prepared by the Committee on the Laws of Ohio, was an appeal to the American and Christian conscience. Notwithstanding the affirmative duty of all government to "promote the happiness and secure the rights and liberties of man," and despite the fact that American government was predicated on the "broad and universal principle of equal and unalienable rights," the statutes of Ohio enacted in 1807 had singled out a "weak and defenseless class of citizens—a class convicted of no crime—no natural inferiority," and had invidiously demanded their exclusion from "the rights and privileges of citizenship."

Specifically, these offensive statutes embodied four typical and recurring discriminations:

> 1. All Negroes and mulattoes were virtually prohibited from migrating to and settling in the state by the requirement that a bond be first secured of "two or more freehold sureties, in the penal sum of $500," for the guarantee of good behavior and support.
> 2. They were systematically excluded from the common occupations and callings of the community by the expedient of forbidding residents, under penalty of fine and liability for support, "to employ, harbor, or conceal any Negro or mulatto" who had not complied with the bonding requirement.
> 3. They were effectively denied use and protection of the courts by withdrawal of their right "to be sworn or give evidence" in suits at law where either party was white, "or in any prosecution instituted in behalf of the state against any white person."
> 4. They were flatly excluded from the common schools.

Detailed constitutional guarantees, it was argued, no less than the fundamental principles of government combined to condemn such action. As italicized by the committee, Article 8, Section 1 of the Ohio Constitution declared:

---

[63] See PROCEEDINGS, op. cit. supra note 60, at 36–40.

All are born *free* and *independent,* and have certain natural, inherent, inalienable rights, among which are the enjoying and defending life and liberty, *acquiring, possessing,* and *protecting property,* and *pursuing* and *attaining happiness* and *safety.*

The report continues:

Is it a mark of this *liberty* which is blazoned forth in our Constitution, as its "inherent and natural right of *all* men" that the blacks should be under the necessity of entering into a bond. . . *before* they are admitted to *acquire* and *possess* property or to *pursue* and enjoy happiness? . . . Our Constitution does not say, *All men* of a *certain color* are entitled to certain rights, and are born free and independent. . .The expression is unlimited. . . *All* men are so born, and have the *unalienable* rights of life and liberty—the pursuit of happiness, and the acquisition and possession of wealth. According to our Constitution, they have all and the same rights which others enjoy, the same right to emigrate when and where they please and the same right to *acquire* and *possess* property. [Yet there had been added to this onerous bonding requirement the further prohibition on employment of "any . . . Negro or mulatto" whose bond was unsecured.] He is denied the poor privilege of working for his daily bread. . .the white who extends him common hospitality or performs the duties of Christian charity is liable for prosecution for harboring him. . . Can there be a more flagrant and unjustifiable violation of "natural, inherent rights," . . . or one more opposed to the spirit of our constitution?

In the eyes of the committee, the fourth section of the law by which Negroes and mulattoes were virtually excluded from use and protection of the courts was plainly such a provision. Article 8, Section 7 of the state constitution guaranteed "that all courts shall be open, and every person, for an injury done him in his lands, goods, person, or reputation, shall have remedy by the due course of law, and right and justice administered without denial or delay." "But of what avail is this to the black? His property may be taken away, his person assailed, his reputation blasted . . . and unless he can produce a white witness, provided his injuror is white, he can have no redress."

Finally, broadening and deepening the argument, the committee enunciated a clear cut, almost breathtaking concept of national citizenship which is specifically linked with the comity clause of the Federal Constitution. These three crucial questions were not yet answered categorically: Who are national citizens? What are their privileges and immunities? Does the comity clause actually have reference to such citizenship and to these privileges and immunities? The report, however, greatly clarified the issues and roughly shaped and dressed what during the next few years became a cornerstone of abolitionist theory. The comity clause, it was observed, provides that "the citizens of each state shall be entitled to all the privileges and immunities of citizens in the several states."

> Who citizens are [the report continued] is a question which admits of some doubt. Neither the Constitution of the United States nor that of Ohio clearly defines [sic]. But the Constitution of the United States, in apportioning representatives and direct taxes, says, it shall be "according to their representative numbers which shall be determined by adding the whole number of *free* persons, including those bound to service for a number of years and excluding Indians not taxed, three-fifths of all other persons." From this and the fact that *freemen* are considered citizens in other countries, it appears that all *free* persons born in and residents of the United States, with the exception of Indians not taxed, are citizens, and as such, are entitled, in every state to all the privileges and immunities of citizens of these states,—and inasmuch as no state can pass any law, in contravention of the laws of the United States, which shall be binding upon any individual; we hence infer, that those enactments, in the Ohio Legislature, imposing disabilities upon the free blacks emigrating from other states are *entirely unconstitutional*.

These arguments and premises, though decidedly atypical when compared with the usual 1835 constitutional case, were by no means unique. In fact, it appears that employment of the federal comity clause in Ohio followed almost reflexively from an earlier usage in Connecticut.

In 1833 Prudence Crandall, a resolute Quakeress of Canterbury, had established a private boarding school for Negro girls, some of whom came from adjoining states. Failing in efforts to suppress her school by a suit brought under an old vagrancy and pauper law, neighbors and townsmen, rallied by colonizationists who had been alarmed at the influx of students, promptly secured passage of a new law. This measure flatly prohibited "any [private boarding] school ... for the instruction or education of colored persons ... not resident of this state," unless the founders "first obtained the consent in writing of a majority of the civil authority and also of the selectmen of the town." Threatened, arrested, jailed, and released on bond furnished by the Tappans, Miss Crandall was twice tried, and at October term, 1833, she was finally convicted of "harboring" and "boarding" Eliza Hammond, a seventeen-year-old pupil from Rhode Island.

In addition to furnishing the bond the Tappans had engaged William W. Ellsworth, son of the second Chief Justice of the United States, and the equally distinguished Calvin Goddard—two of the outstanding lawyers and statesmen of Connecticut—as defense counsel. In an elaborate charge to the jury, the distinguished Judge David Daggett, a vice-president of the local colonization society, vigorously combatted counsels' contention that free Negroes were, or could be, "citizens" within the meaning of the comity clause. It was enough in his judgment that *slaves* and *Indians* were not citizens, that members of the African race were a "degraded caste," and that in 1789 all states but Massachusetts had tolerated slavery, and that most states had continued to discriminate against colored persons in numerous ways.[64]

On appeal the Court of Errors reversed the conviction on a technicality, and the Crandall case soon developed into a major test of strength between advocates of abolition and colonization. As such, it attracted nationwide attention and became one of the means by which the colonization movement presently destroyed itself. The Ellsworth and Goddard arguments, delivered in July, 1834, and widely circulated as a tract,[65] convincingly stated the social and ethical case for equality of opportunity irrespective of race and gave strong impetus to a gradually emerging concept of American nationality and citizenship. They remain to this day among the most persuasive and prophetic, as well as the most neglected, of early constitutional arguments. Their historic significance lies partly in that fact, partly in the use made of Justice Washington's dictum in *Corfield v. Coryell*,[66] and partly in the fact that Connecticut's odious educational discrimination raised the question not merely of what rights were "in their nature fundamental" and hence "belonged of right to the citizens of all free governments" but whether race itself was a permissible basis for the accord or denial of such rights.

---

[64] See Crandall v. State, 10 Conn. 339, 341-348 (1834).

[65] REPORT OF THE ARGUMENTS OF COUNSEL IN THE CASE OF PRUDENCE CRANDALL, PLFF. IN ERROR, VS. STATE OF CONNECTICUT, BEFORE THE SUPREME COURT OF ERRORS, AT THEIR SESSION AT BROOKLYN, JULY TERM, 1834. The arguments are printed in condensed form in the official report, Crandall v. State, 10 Conn. 339, 349-353 (1834). See also STIENER, HISTORY OF SLAVERY IN CONN. 45-52 (1893); VON HOLST, CONSTITUTIONAL HISTORY 1828-1846 98, 99 (1881); GARRISON, *op. cit. supra* note 28; JAY, MISCELLANEOUS WRITINGS ON SLAVERY 34-51 (1853); McCarron, *Trial of Prudence Crandall* 12 CONN. MAG. 225-232 (1908); Small, *Prudence Crandall* 17 NEW ENGLAND QTLY. 506-509 (1940); NYE, *op. cit. supra* note 52, at 83.

[66] 4 Wash. C. C. 371, 380-381, Fed. Case 3230 (1823).

Throughout the course of their effort to establish the citizenship of free Negroes, Ellsworth and Goddard, like all of their generation, spoke and thought of state citizenship as primary. Yet as Whigs of pure Federalist extraction they also assumed, and at times vaguely enunciated, a concept of nationality. This paramount "general" or "American" citizenship, though largely derivative from state citizenship, was also shaped and conditioned by a constitutional document that declared itself to be "the supreme law of the land." One particular clause of this document, based on similar language in the Articles of Confederation, expressly secured to citizens of each state "all the privileges and immunities of citizens in the several states."

In support of their preliminary proposition—that free Negroes were citizens of their native states—Ellsworth and Goddard first argued that if Miss Crandall's students had been white their citizenship never would have been questioned.

"A distinction in fundamental rights," obviously founded solely on color, they condemned as "novel, inconvenient, impracticable."[67] Neither the common law, the Declaration of Independence, the ideas of the Fathers, nor the state constitutions sanctioned such discrimination.

Ellsworth's argument began with questions and followed with his answers:

> Who can tell proportions and trace the mixtures of blood? What shall be the scale for ascertainment of citizenship? . . . one half, one quarter, one twentieth . . . the merest trace of Negro blood? These pupils [are] human beings, born in these states, and owe the *same obligation* to the state . . . as white citizens. . . . All writers agree that allegiance demands obedience from the citizen and protection from the government. If allegiance is due from our colored population, its correlative is due from the government, viz. protection and equal laws. . . Allegiance . . . reaches . . . binds, and confers rights upon every man within its range and rightful sway. Here the free man of colour may take his position, and upon the immutable principles of justice and truth demand his political rights and aid from that government which he is bound to defend . . . *he is not a citizen to obey, and an alien to demand protection.* Nor is he of an intermediate class. His relations to society are the same as others: his absolute and relative rights, his rights of person and to things, his acquisitions of property by contract and by inheritance—and even the soil, which no alien inherits—are the same. So every requisition of the law, in its civil and criminal provisions reaches him. Every favour or right con-

---

[67] REPORT, *op. cit. supra* note 65, at 6, col. 1.

ferred on the citizens, by general legislation, reaches *him*; every requisition demands *his* obedience.[68]

Bolstering claims based on the doctrine of natural allegiance were the Charters, statutes, and Bills of Rights of the pupils' native states. These had drawn no color line; they secured the rights of "all men," of "all the people," and at times even specifically referred to "colored citizens."

Even more decisive of nondiscrimination was the comity clause of the Articles of Confederation. By it "free inhabitants of each of these states, paupers, vagabonds and fugitives from justice excepted" had been "entitled . . . to all privileges and immunities of *free citizens* in the several states." "Free ingress and regress to any other state" had been guaranteed to "the *people* of each state," and in 1778, by a vote of eight states to two, the Continental Congress had flatly rejected South Carolina's proposal that the adjective "white" be inserted between the words "free inhabitants"—Virginia alone concurring.

Could it be supposed then that on these same points a Constitution designed to "form a more perfect union," and, as Ellsworth argued, "make one nation, to the extent of the general powers of the government," did any less? The design of the abbreviated comity clause of 1787, Ellsworth continued, was

> to declare a citizen of one state to be a citizen of every state, and as such, to clothe him with the same fundamental rights, be he where he might, which he acquired by birth in a particular state. [Its] clear intent [was] to do away with the character and consequences of *alienage* among the citizens of these United States, to the extent of the reciprocity of the privileges and immunities secured, be they what they may. To *this* extent a citizen of any state is a citizen of *every* state . . . All are . . . members of one government, one state.[69]

Having thus established that "these pupils are *citizens* of their respective states," Ellsworth and Goddard next contended that "as *citizens*, the Constitution of the United States secures . . . them the right of residing in Connecticut and pursuing the acquisition of knowledge, as people of color may do who are settled here." The question, it was contended, became one of "constitutional control," of "state supremacy,"—"of the obligation of the state to abide by the Constitution as the supreme law of the land." In the words of

---

[68] *Id.* at 7, col. 1.
[69] REPORT, *op. cit. supra* note 65, at 11, col. 2.

Justice Story, the comity clause conferred a "general citizenship." As construed by Justice Washington in *Corfield v. Coryell*,[70] it secured those "privileges and immunities" which are "in their nature fundamental, which belong of right to the citizens of all free governments," specifically including the "right . . . to pass through or reside in any other state, for purposes of trade, agriculture, professional pursuits, or otherwise." By this test, the right of education unquestionably was a fundamental right—"the first . . . pillar on which our free institutions rest." Indeed, it had been conceded to be such by Judge Daggett.

In summing up, Ellsworth tightened and elaborated his argument:

> The law under consideration forbids a citizen of another state from coming here, to pursue education, as all others may do, *because* he has not *a legal settlement in the state.* It is a crime to feed him and teach him. . . . But may not a citizen remove to Ohio and there live and act as another citizen may do? . . . Can we raise a barrier against the people of Massachusetts because *they are people of Massachusetts?* . . . This power of regulating because of *alienage* is virtually a power of *exclusion,* and in this case is, in effect, and was designed so to be . . . the legislature may superintend and regulate private schools . . . , [as it might superintend and regulate] all the pursuits of its citizens, but . . . this must be done by a general and equal law. Mere *birth* in another state cannot be seized upon, as a ground of distinction, discrimination and deprivation. . . . The law must be alike and general, or there is an end of equal privileges and immunities.

> If 4th art. sec. 2, means anything, [it secures] to a citizen of New York, a right to come here, and *remain* here, if he offends against no general law; he cannot be whipped out, nor carried out of the state because he has no legal settlement: he may present the shield of the constitution, and as Paul claimed the immunity of a Roman citizen, he may claim the immunity of an *American* citizen. . . Neither present nor future poverty can strike out of the constitution the word "citizen," and a "citizen" has a universal right, title, and immunity, to a *residence,* and other fundamental rights. So the state may guard itself against thieves from without or within, by punishing them for crimes committed in our territory, or enacting *general* laws of prevention—but I deny that it can prohibit a *"citizen of the United States"* from entering this state and remaining in it, because he *has* offended elsewhere, or *may* offend again. If he has fled from justice, and is demanded, under

---

70 4 Wash. C. C. 371, 380–381, Fed. Case 3230 (1823).

the Constitution, he must be delivered up, but while he is here, unoffending, the state cannot drive him out, nor make it penal to supply his necessities here: it could, were it not for the constitution of the U[nited] States: *he is a citizen, and that is his protection.* . . . Of all, *all* citizens, I say, they are in *their* country, be they in it where they will; they have one *common tie,* one *allegiance,* and one *citizenship.*[71]

Closing the argument for the defense, Goddard elaborated[72] this ethical, nationalistic interpretation of American origins and citizenship. Free Negroes he showed to have been among the "freemen" protected both by the Habeas Corpus Act and by the first Charter of Connecticut. Textually they were embraced by the provisions of the various state Bills of Rights; actually they had been made citizens by the Declaration of Independence. "The revolution produced a change in all free inhabitants of the United States. All the citizens of the several states became citizens of the United States. They were *subjects* of Great Britain—they became *citizens* of the United States from the very nature of our government."

Nothing since the Declaration had deprived these people of their character of citizens. Rather, the Journals of Congress, the speeches of the Fathers, and the practice of the revolutionary governments revealed a widespread recognition and acceptance of Negro citizenship. The Constitution had been drafted by these same men against this background. When the word "citizen" was employed in the clauses defining the qualifications of representatives and of the president, and in the judiciary article to define jurisdiction and "secure the rights of the people generally," "language is used," Goddard said, "which is broad enough to extend to all—to cover all." This fact, moreover, was determinative. Since the Fathers obviously had not thought in terms of color, who could say that a colored man might not "go into the courts of the United States to seek justice in any of the cases there provided for"? Yet "if he go . . . , unless it is alleged on the face of the writ that he is a *citizen* of some state, according to the established doctrine, . . . his case will be dismissed. He is then a *citizen of the United States.*"[73]

In short, since the word "citizen" was unrestricted by the adjectives of race and color, and since the ideals of the Revolution and the Fathers were at odds with such restrictions, hermeneutics com-

---

[71] REPORT, *op. cit. supra* note 65, at 14.
[72] *Id.* at 24–34.
[73] REPORT, *op. cit. supra* note 65, at 30.

bined with history and ethics to support claims of Negro citizenship in the states. And Americans, *all* Americans, had first of all a *state* citizenship, and by reason of that state citizenship a *national* citizenship, the rights of which were secured by the Federal Constitution. Among the most important and "fundamental" of these rights were those of education, of ingress and egress, and of an economic opportunity for migrant citizens equal to that which the state secured to its own citizens in like situations. Virtually every state constitution in addition to securing the great natural rights, the "rights of human nature," specifically secured the rights of conscience, of education, and of religion. It was therefore presumed that the comity clause also guaranteed and incorporated these rights by reference, thus in effect nationalizing them and constituting a sort of secondary bulwark. These last presumptions, it must be added, were as yet scarcely explicit. Talk was still of federally secured privileges of state citizenship rather than of the constitutional rights of national citizens as such.[74] Nevertheless, the *concept* of national citizenship was clearly held.[75] Moreover, this concept was linked on the one hand with a belief that natural and fundamental rights were universally bestowed and on the other with the fact that *Connecticut-born* Negro children unquestionably were free to enjoy the educational privileges which were forbidden to children of their race from outside. In view of the historical evidences of Negro citizenship and with the comity clause reading simply "citizens of each state shall be entitled to *all* the privileges and immunities of citizens in the several states," it can be seen that the Ellsworth-Goddard arguments contributed powerfully to expanding the comity clause. Through this expansion, moreover, the potential content of American or national citizenship was extended by embodying therein important elements of the ideal of racial equality.

Today, the reasons why the Supreme Court of Errors of Connecticut in 1834 hesitated to accept these contentions are obvious. Miss Crandall's conviction was reversed,[76] yet the court's reversal frankly avoided the constitutional question, resting instead on insufficiency of the indictment. (Years later, however, an opinion[77] revealed that several judges had been favorably disposed toward the constitutional

---

[74] REPORT, *op. cit. supra* note 65, at 31, 32.
[75] *Id.* at 28, 30.
[76] Crandall v. State, 10 Conn. 339 (1834).
[77] Opinion of the Judges, 32 Conn. 565, footnote (1865); 4 CATTERALL, JUDICIAL CASES CONCERNING AMERICAN SLAVERY AND THE NEGRO 415–416 (1926–1927).

Antislavery Backgrounds of the Fourteenth Amendment 183

views of Ellsworth and Goddard.) "The nature and importance" of the question, "the peculiar difficulties . . . attending the construction" of the comity clause, "the magnitude of . . . interests at stake, the excitement which always attends . . . agitation . . . connected with the interest of one class and the liberties of another . . . , the jealousies . . . the expectations . . ."—all these, the court thought, signalled caution. Some of these questions, of course, would not finally be decided for a century, and indeed, some are still left undecided in the recent case of *Edwards v. California*.[78]

Despite the claims of Ellsworth and Goddard, the question was not simply one of the rights of migrants and free Negroes. As able opposing counsel made clear, it was fundamentally one of how and where (granting these nationalist-abolitionist premises) a line might be drawn that would preserve the state's police powers. The issues raised in the *Crandall* case were not only those of the great slavery cases which finally culminated in the *Dred Scott* decision. They were also those which were to be raised again in the *Slaughter-House* cases *after* amendment of the constitution had expressly incorporated—or so former abolitionists and Free Soilers believed—the nationalist-racial-egalitarian interpretations and premises which extended back thirty years to the *Crandall* case arguments.[78a]

Viewed from this standpoint, the importance of the Ellsworth-Goddard arguments can hardly be exaggerated. They mark the first comprehensive crystallization of abolitionist constitutional theory. They reveal this theory as based on broad natural rights premises and on an ethical interpretation of American origins and history. Four ideas—or ideals—are seen to have been central and interrelated: the ideal of human equality, the ideal of a general and equal law, the ideal of reciprocal protection and allegiance, and the ideal of reason and substantiality as the true bases for the necessary discriminations and classifications by government. Race as a standard

---

[78] 314 U.S. 160 (1941). Voiding a California law designed to keep out indigents from other states, the Court, speaking through Byrnes, J., elected to employ the commerce clause; only the concurring minority (Douglas, Black, Murphy and Jackson) held the right of free movement to be a right of national citizenship secured by the privileges and immunities clause of the Fourteenth Amendment; Jackson, J., noted, "This Court . . . has always hesitated to give any real meaning to [this clause] lest it improvidently give too much." Earlier cases are reviewed in Bowman, *The United States Citizen's Privilege of State Residence*, 10 B.U.L. Rev. 459 (1930).

[78a] 1968: *Any* racial classification is odious, if not always unconstitutional on its face today. How far this then-emerging rule and precept still had to go, in the 1830's, is as striking as what it owed to these early, exploratory formulations.

breached every one of these ideals, as did color. It breached them, moreover, absolutely and wholly irrespective of their then relation to the comity clause.

As skillful lawyers familiar with limits and precedents, Ellsworth and Goddard took great pains to keep their main argument narrowly phrased, to claim for free Negroes of other states only those rights granted to the free Negroes of Connecticut.[79] Yet the sweeping natural rights premises which were the cornerstones of the abolitionist indictment were not to be readily confined by such limits. *Potentially*, as opposing counsel stressed, *slaves* as well as free Negroes were their beneficiaries.

In retrospect, therefore, the special significance of the Ellsworth-Goddard argument lies first of all in its exploratory character, in its preliminary framing of constitutional issues, and in its being based on a fact situation that fell squarely within Justice Washington's dictum in *Corfield v. Coryell*, once Negro citizenship was admitted or assumed. It lies secondly in its sound perception, that race, color, and out-of-state birth were impracticable and improper grounds for alienage in a federal system. It lies finally in the perception and argument that this was doubly true in a federal system whose fundamental law included a supremacy, a comity, and an interstate commerce clause; whose national origins were universally identified with a Declaration that "all men are created equal" and are "endowed" with the "right" of "liberty," and that governments, instituted for protection, rest upon the "consent of the governed."

By sheer force of its own circumstances and the crystallizing national conscience as much as by the power of the arguments, the *Crandall* case emerges as one of the great "lost cases" of American history. It figured prominently in abolitionist writings throughout the thirties. Even though plans for an appeal to the Supreme Court of the United States failed to materialize,[80] the propaganda value of the case remained immense. In the spring of 1835, Judge William Jay, abolitionist son of the first Chief Justice and one of the founders and vice presidents of the American Anti-Slavery Society, devoted fifteen pages of his *Inquiry into the Character and Tendency of the*

---

[79] *E.g.* see REPORT *op. cit. supra* note 65, at 33.

[80] See NEW ENGLAND ANTI-SLAVERY SOCIETY, SECOND ANNUAL REPORT 14–16 (1834). It is interesting to speculate on what might have been the course of history had the question of free Negro citizenship been squarely presented to the Court in 1834 in a case involving the right of education.

The Ellsworth-Goddard arguments were of course thoroughly rehashed at the time of the Dred Scott case, 19 How. 393 (U.S. 1857); see 32 Conn. 565, footnote, quoting letter of Williams, C. J., to Bissell, J.

Colonization and Anti-Slavery Societies[81] to a slashing attack on Judge Daggett's decision.

Conclusion

Though much remains to be investigated, it already is clear that as early as 1834–1835, more than twenty years before Bingham's three speeches of the fifties or expression of Chief Justice Taney's counter views in the case of Dred Scott, lawyers and leaders of the newly organized American Anti-Slavery Society formulated and publicized a system of constitutional protection for the rights of free Negroes and mulattoes. This system was based, not merely in part, but exclusively on the same three clauses and concepts which in 1866 were to find their way into Section One! The original and immediate concern, it is to be noted, was with the *rights* of the *free Negro* and with his rights, not in the South, but in the North—in the home states of Connecticut and Ohio. The rights asserted, moreover, were those of free migration, education, and residence, of liberty to pursue the common callings, acquire homes, and enjoy the bounties and protections of government generally; these are the very rights which the courts in recent years have enforced more vigorously in race discrimination cases.[82]

The challenging questions now, of course, are the bearing and influence of this early tripartite system on the one evolved thirty years later by the Joint Committee. Restating the matter, what significance, if any, attaches to the fact that the early abolitionists grounded their constitutional case on the very forms that Bingham ultimately and by great persistence persuaded his uncertain colleagues to adopt in 1866? The problem obviously turns in part on the representativeness of the materials we have just examined. Were these Ellsworth-Goddard and Olcott Committee arguments simply isolated instances? Or were they the very core and refrain of the theory that Weld and the "Twelve" and the "Seventy" broadcast by pamphlet and revival? Did this recurrent overlapping three clause system remain merely the product of peculiar fact situations in Ohio and Connecticut? Or did it in time become a kind of rhetorical shorthand for a lay constitutional theory of great practical consequence?

---

[81] Reprinted in Jay, Miscellaneous Writings on Slavery 36 (1853).

[82] See, in addition to the Shelley, Screws, and Allwright cases cited *supra* note 3, Sipuel v. Board of Regents, 332 U.S. 631 (1948); Morgan v. Virginia, 328 U.S. 373 (1946); Steele v. Louisville and Nashville R.R. Co., 323 U.S. 192 (1944); James v. Marinship Corp., 25 Cal. 2d 721 (1944); and the useful summaries of race law developments: Berger, *The Supreme Court and Group Discrimination Since 1937*, 49 Col. L. Rev. 201 (1949); Waite, *The Negro in the Supreme Court*, 30 Minn. L. Rev. 219 (1946).

Systematization, 1835–1837

IS ANTISLAVERY CONSTITUTIONAL THEORY the key to a better understanding of the Fourteenth Amendment?

In the previous section we reviewed evidence dating back to the Ellsworth-Goddard argument in the *Crandall Case* in 1834 and to the *Report on the Black Laws of Ohio* in 1835. These and similar materials of the fifties confirmed existence of a long background of usage by antislavery forces of all three concepts ultimately employed by Bingham and the Joint Committee in 1866. Our problem now is to determine whether these arguments were representative, whether the early and later uses are demonstrably interrelated, whether the constitutional theory broadcast by antislavery "agents" in the thirties amounted to a popular constitutional shorthand which passed into daily thought and speech. Investigation of these problems should explain much about the Amendment which heretofore has been incomprehensible.

Our starting premise must not be that a few early or isolated uses could themselves have determined later phraseology. But a discovery of such uses may signify others—even a whole body of coherent theory. We know that both the later phraseology and the antecedent uses have a common base and ancestry. This fact in itself is of great importance in understanding the natural rights theory of the framers. Basic to our whole inquiry are certain prepossessions concerning the origin and foundations of government, the nature and duty of man and his relations with God, and the binding obligation of government to protect and enforce human rights in a civil society.

It was John Locke, with his exile's loathing for the arbitrary power of the Stuarts, who systematized these principles and gave them their classic statement. In 1690, Locke argued:

> All men by nature are equal . . . in that equal right that every man hath to his natural freedom, without being subjected to the will or authority of any other man; . . . being all equal and independent, no one ought to harm another in his life, health, liberty or possessions; for men being all the workmanship of one omnipotent and infinitely wise Maker . . . sent into the world by His order . . . ; they are His property . . . made to last during His, not one another's pleasure.[83] Man, not having the power of his own life, cannot by compact or his own consent enslave himself

---

[83] Locke, Second Treatise on Government c. 2 §6 (1698).

to anyone, nor put himself under the absolute, arbitrary power of another. Every man has a "property" in his own "person." This nobody has any right to but himself. The "labor" of his body and the "work" of his hands . . . are . . . his. . . .[84] Men being . . . by nature all free, equal and independent, no one can be put out of his estate and subjected to the political power of another without his own consent which is done by agreeing with other men, to join and unite into a community for their comfortable, safe, and peaceable living, . . . in a secure enjoyment of their properties. . . .[85]

Thus are political societies and governments created for the protection of antecedent human rights. Under such governments, and by the terms of the social compact, allegiance and protection were reciprocal.[86]

No man in civil society can be exempted from the laws of it . . . where there is no law there is no freedom. . . . For liberty is to be free from restraint and violence from others.[87] . . . Absolute, arbitrary power, or governing without settled standing laws, can neither of them consist with the ends of society or government, which men would not quit the freedom of the state of nature for . . . were it not to preserve their lives, liberties and fortunes.[88]

Certain genes of American constitutionalism were implicit in these sweeping natural law premises.[89] The abhorrence of arbitrariness, which is one of the elements of due process, and the composite ideal of general and equal laws, which is the core of equal protection, are both embodied in Locke's theory.

Both were given their classic American statement by Jefferson in the Declaration. Down through the Civil War the "self-evident truths" constituted for most citizens precisely what Jefferson declared them to be—political axioms. As such they were written into the state Bills of Rights[90] and were frequently used as rhetorical short-

---

[84] *Id.* at § 27.
[85] *Id.* at § 95.
[86] *Id.* at § 4.
[87] *Id.* at § 57.
[88] *Id.* at § 137.
[89] Corwin, *The "Higher Law" Background of American Constitutional Law,* 42 HARV. L. REV. 149, 365 (1928), esp. § IV; see also Hamilton, *Property According to Locke,* 41 YALE L.J. 864 (1932); BECKER, THE DECLARATION OF INDEPENDENCE (1926); SMITH, AMERICAN PHILOSOPHY OF EQUALITY (1927); WRIGHT, AMERICAN INTERPRETATIONS OF NATURAL LAW (1931).
[90] See the "self-evident truths—created equal" or "born equally free" phraseology in the preamble or Declarations of Rights of the following constitutions: MASS. CONST.

hand by statesmen. They were popularly regarded as the marrow of the Constitution itself. A generation which enshrines the document of 1787 rather than that of 1776 needs to be reminded that originally the Declaration not only was a *part* of American constitutional law, it was "the first American Constitution."[91]

This canonization of Locke and apotheosis of the Declaration no doubt arrested development of early American political and constitutional theory. Systematic thinking and criticism were retarded by stereotyped rhetoric and habits of thought. More serious was the confusion of moral with civil rights—the failure to distinguish between socially desirable ends and the steps and means necessary for their legal or constitutional attainment. Rights were interchangeably regarded as preexistent human ideals and as socially implemented and enforceable privileges or immunities. In countless arguments what ought to be was mistaken and substituted for what was. Abolitionist theory was a monument to this imprecision. The underlying dualism worked its greatest confusion where constitutional rights were at issue. On one plane was the parchment document given effect by statutes and precedents. On the other was the subjective instrument which "guaranteed" and "declared" certain antecedent natural rights. The document was thus alternately shadow and substance—an amendable legal instrument and one which, "correctly interpreted" or "declared," required no amendment! This confusion persisted and reached its climax in 1866. The important thing to remember is that the generations which indulged in these natural law flights employed language to convey thought. At the heart of their beliefs was a conviction about the nature and purpose of popular government. There was no unanimity of political views, general propositions decided no concrete cases; "certain unalienable rights," in practice were neither "certain" nor "unalienable." Yet these difficulties and disagreements were over means not ends, over minor

(1780); PENN. CONST. (1776); N.Y. CONST. (1777); DEL. CONST. (1792); CONN. CONST. (1818); VA. CONST. (1776); VT. CONST. (1777); N.H. CONST. (1784).

Perceiving the uses made of the Virginia phraseology during the Revolution other southern states omitted it as did the first Constitution of New Jersey.

[91] *E.g.*, JOHN PARRISH, REMARKS ON THE SLAVERY OF THE BLACK PEOPLE 30 (Phila. 1806); "The Constitution of the United States is the fundamental law; [its] leading features . . . are set forth in the Declaration of Independence . . . 'We hold . . . created equal.'" Parrish (1729-1807), a Baltimore Quaker disciple of Woolman and Benezet, argued that the nonintercourse resolution of 1774, the Declaration of Independence, "the Bill of Rights, the Conventions in the different states, and the Constitution of the United States" all were of one piece and effect. Any departure from their high purpose, "calculated . . . to enslave a particular race . . . after having proclaimed that all have an inalienable right to 'life, liberty and pursuit of happiness' would be ignoble and below the dignity of men."

not major premises. The dominating thought was the idea that governments were instituted for purposes of protection and "derived their *just* powers from the *consent* of the governed."

The matter that merits study is the use the antislavery movement made of these principles. By insisting that the Lockean affirmations be given universal *human* rather than restricted *racial* application, this movement laid the groundwork for substantive due process and effectively spawned the inchoate concept of equal protection of the laws. In time it successfully developed and established a new secondary constitutional principle.[92] This principle, as Congressional debates of the sixties make clear, was tacitly assumed by many at the adoption of the Thirteenth Amendment, and was regarded as implicit in the Fourteenth. It was finally made explicit, *yet only with regard to the right of suffrage*, by the additional guarantee in the Fifteenth Amendment: "The right of citizens of the United States [that is, to fundamental human rights] shall not be denied or abridged by the United States or by any State on account of race, color or previous condition of servitude," that is, shall be fully accorded and protected, irrespective of these extraneous factors.[93]

To a generation more sophisticated in draftsmanship, all this seems incredible. Yet these omissions and assumed interpolations were reasonable enough. Like the new secondary constitutional principle, they were products of the American's predilection for natural law on the one hand and of the slowly crystallizing repugnance to slavery on the other.

For eighty years historians of abolitionism have been gathering evidences of this institutional impact.[94] A five-point summary of their

---

[92] The idea that race and color were arbitrary, capricious standards on which to base denial of human rights was implicit in all abolitionist attacks on discrimination and prejudice. Yet it was when the constitutional-legal attack began to reinforce the religious one that such arguments became explicit and the concept of an arbitrary classification developed. Lawyers like Ellsworth and Goddard, Birney (see *infra* notes 249, 250), Gerrit Smith (see A.A.S.S. 3d ANN. REPT. AND PROC. 16–17) and Salmon P. Chase (*infra* note 153, at 10) helped formulate the concept and linked it with the principles of equality, affirmative protection, and national citizenship.

[93] See TEN BROEK, ANTI-SLAVERY ORIGINS OF THE FOURTEENTH AMENDMENT, [1838–1866] (1951); also see note 103 *infra*.

[94] Badly needed is a compilation of slavery debates which will chart development of both proslave and antislave constitutional theory. Useful research aids are: LOCKE, EARLY ANTISLAVERY MOVEMENT IN AMERICA TO 1808 (1908); ADAMS, NEGLECTED PERIOD OF ANTISLAVERY IN AMERICA, 1808–1831 (1908); MOORE, NOTES ON THE HISTORY OF SLAVERY IN MASSACHUSETTS (1866); POOLE, ANTI-SLAVERY OPINIONS BEFORE THE YEAR 1800 (1873); JENKINS, PRO-SLAVERY THOUGHT IN THE OLD SOUTH (1935); NYE, cited *infra* note 234; the theses of Thornbrough and O'Dell cited *infra* notes 107, 113; CLASSIFIED CATALOG OF THE COLLECTION OF ANTISLAVERY PROPAGANDA IN THE OBERLIN COLLEGE LIBRARY (Oberlin 1932). **1968:** Also DUMOND, ANTISLAVERY: THE CRUSADE FOR FREEDOM

findings helps put the organized movement, and with it Sections One and Five, in the proper perspective:

1. The Puritan and Quaker conscience, because it was unable to square slavery with the Christian ethic or with the ideals and aspirations of a colonial people who had emigrated for their own freedom, supplied the humanitarian motive power of abolitionism. In the earliest Biblical tracts and powerful Quaker and Puritan protests is evident a fusion of Lockean principles which demonstrates how deep these basic ideas of human equality, liberty, and protection run in relation to slavery.

"Though they are black," protested German members of a Germantown Quaker meeting in 1688, "we cannot conceive there is more liberty to have them slaves [than] . . . to have other white ones. . . . We should do to all men like as we will be done ourselves, making no difference of what descent or colour they are. . . . Here is liberty of conscience, which is right and reasonable; here ought to be likewise liberty of body. . . ."[95]

Twelve years later in his tract, *The Selling of Joseph*, which he addressed to the Massachusetts legislature, the Puritan elder, Judge Samuel Sewall, declared: "All men, as they are . . . Sons of *Adam*, are co-heirs, and have equal Right unto Liberty . . . *God hath given the Earth (with all its commodities) unto the sons of Adam . . . and God hath made of one Blood all Nations of Men.*"[96]

Such protests found fruition during the period 1740–1770 in the philanthropies of two Friends. Earnest, kindly John Woolman,[97] whose evangelism is recounted in his *Journal*,[98] toured the colonies from New England to Georgia converting listeners to his creed:

> It is righteousness which exalteth a nation. "Liberty is the natural right of all men equally." Color . . . availeth nothing in matters of Right and Equity; God respecteth not persons nor colors; [prejudice was simply the product of custom] the Idea of

---

IN AMERICA (2 vols., vol. 2, "A Bibliography of Antislavery in America," Ann Arbor, 1961).

[95] MOORE, *op. cit. supra* note 94, at 75.

[96] *Id.* at 83–87; the MEMORIAL, another tract, dated 1700, is reprinted in MASS. HIST. SOC. PROC. 161–165 (1863–1864). Two early Quaker tracts were similar. MOORE, *op. cit. supra* note 94, at 108. (On the Quakers and slavery, see RUSSELL, HISTORY OF QUAKERISM 246–248 (1942); also DRAKE, QUAKERS AND SLAVERY IN AMERICA (New Haven, 1950; reprint, 1965).

[97] See his *Considerations on Keeping of Negroes, Recommended to the Professors of Christianity of Every Denomination*, JOURNALS AND ESSAYS 353, 363, 367 (Gummere ed. 1922).

[98] WOOLMAN, JOURNAL AND ESSAYS 103, 147, 177, 225 (Whittier ed. 1871).

Slavery being connected with the Black Colour, and Liberty with the White.

Anthony Benezet, a Philadelphia teacher and pamphleteer,[99] was equally persuasive. "Was it not strange," he asked, "that whilst so much noise is made about the maintenance of liberty throughout the empire, this prodigious infringement" passed unnoticed? Why were "hundreds of thousands . . . equally with us . . . objects of Christ's . . . grace . . . and as free as we are by nature," so bitterly oppressed?

2. Contributing to the growth of these ideas were the political and ethical necessities of the Revolution. After 1776 conscientious and conscience-stricken colonial leaders were impelled to repudiate slavery and forge doctrinal weapons against it. These reflexive secondary effects of the struggle are documented in Moore's *Notes on the History of Slavery in Massachusetts*.[100] The colonists found themselves confronted with what Gunnar Myrdal has termed *"An American Dilemma."*[101] Principle had to determine practice, or in the end

---

[99] DICT. AM. BIOG.

[100] MOORE, *op. cit. supra* note 94, particularly at 124–150. Massachusetts towns commenced their antislavery resolutions and protests, Moore shows, as early as 1766. Numerous bills were introduced before the Revolution and Harvard students debated whether African slavery was in accord with the law of nature. After Lord Mansfield's decision in the Sommersett Case, 20 How. St. Tr. 1 (1772), freedom suits were brought by and on behalf of slaves, distinguished counsel arguing that the royal charters, the guarantee that no man could be deprived of his liberty but by the judgment of his peers, and the abolition of villeinage by English law, all supported the cause of liberty. Suits of this type were strictly private, and the jury verdicts extended only to the parties, but slavery was challenged and in some instances successfully. "As we . . . revere the name of liberty," declared citizens of the town of Leicester in May, 1773 "we cannot behold but with . . . greatest abhorrence any of our fellow creatures in a state of slavery," MOORE at 133. Three months after the Declaration the attempted auction of two Negroes captured as prizes impelled the Massachusetts House to denounce such commerce as "a direct violation of the natural rights . . . vested in all men by their Creator, and utterly inconsistent with the avowed principles on which this and the other United States have carried their struggle for liberty," MOORE at 149. On Sept. 21, 1776, Dr. William Gordon, future historian of the Revolution, quoted the Virginia Declaration of Rights and the Declaration of Independence, "If these are our genuine sentiments, and we are not . . . acting hypocritically to serve a turn . . . let us apply earnestly and heartily to the extirpation of slavery . . ." MOORE at 176. The next year, after "Sons of Liberty" had attacked slavery in the press, and towns petitioned that slaves be restored "to the enjoyment of that freedom which is the natural right of all men," a serious attempt was made at abolition by statute. Drafted by Judge Sargent of the Massachusetts Supreme Court, the bill, finally tabled, condemned the "practice of holding . . . persons in Slavery [as] unjustifiable in a civil government . . . asserting natural freedom . . . ; wherefore . . . be it enacted . . . all persons . . . are hereby entitled to all the freedom, rights, privileges and immunities . . . that . . . belong to any . . . subjects of this State, any usage or custom to the contrary notwithstanding," MOORE at 182.

[101] MYRDAL, AN AMERICAN DILEMMA (1944); see particularly Introduction p. xliii

practice would undermine and destroy principle. Having proclaimed existence of fundamental human rights, having pledged their "lives ... fortunes and sacred honor" to the cause of liberty, either Americans endeavored to live according to their creed or stultified themselves in the eyes of the world. What emerged was an ethical interpretation of American origins and institutions. The "self-evident truths," the provisions of the state Bills of Rights,[102] even the text of the comity clause of the unratified Articles of Confederation,[103] were all employed as weapons against racial discrimination and slavery.

The high points of this early movement were the decision of the Supreme Judicial Court of Massachusetts in *Walker v. Jennison*[104]

---

and pp. 214-220. A foreign observer, Myrdal noted and stressed the ethical obligations of the American Creed. The extent to which these obligations are derivative is best seen in the Revolutionary source materials. In speeches and resolutions it was sensed that arguments based on natural and inalienable rights doomed either slavery or conscience.

> The Colonists are men: the colonists are therefore free born; for by the law of nature, all men are free born, white or black. No good reason can be given for enslaving those of any color. Is it right to enslave a man because his color is black, or his hair short and curled like wool, instead of Christian hair? Can any logical inference in favor of slavery be drawn from a flat nose or a short face? . . . Liberty is the gift of God, and cannot be annihilated.

James Otis, 1764, quoted in 3 BANCROFT, HISTORY OF THE UNITED STATES 81 (1881). Thus abolitionists had only to substitute "slaves" for "colonists" in hundreds of passages, such as that of Samuel Adams "If it is an essential, unalterable right in nature, engrafted into the British Constitution as a fundamental law . . . that what is a man's own is absolutely his own; and that no man has a right to take it from him without his consent, may not the subjects of this province, with decent firmness . . . plead and maintain this natural constitutional right?" (Letter of the Massachusetts House to the British Ministry, January, 1768). See COMMAGER, DOCUMENTS IN AMERICAN HISTORY 65-66 (1948).

102 For early use of these, see note 100 *supra*. Dr. Gordon, September, 1776, (MOORE at 176).

103 Use of the comity clause was pioneered by Dr. Gordon. Attacking racial discrimination as applied to suffrage, in January, 1778, he argued it would be

> ridiculous . . . inconsistent . . . unjust . . . to exclude freemen from voting [simply because their skins were] black, tawny or reddish. [Why not disqualify the] long nosed, shortfaced, or higher or lower than five feet nine? A black, tawny or reddish skin is not so unfavorable . . . to the . . . genuine son of liberty as a tory complection [sic] . . . The disqualification militates with the proposal in the Confederation, that the free inhabitants of each State shall, upon removing into any other State, enjoy all privileges and immunities belonging to the free citizens of such State.

(MOORE at 186). Later in the year a clause in the proposed constitution specifically excepting "Negroes, Indians and Mulattoes" from the suffrage stirred the Doctor to similar remonstrance. "The complexion of the Article," he found "blacker than any African"—"an everlasting reproach upon the present inhabitants" of Massachusetts; "evidence to the world that they mean[t] their own rights only, . . . not those of mankind, in their cry for liberty."

104 Decided, 1783; see 13 MASS. HIST. SOC. PROC. 294-296 (1873-75). Excerpt in COM-

and the antislavery clause of the Northwest Ordinance.[105] Chief Justice Cushing's opinion in the Walker case, which grew out of a master's assault on a runaway slave, is especially illuminating. Later one of the original justices of the Supreme Court of the United States, Cushing had been a member of the State Convention of 1779 and had had a hand in drafting the *"All men are born free and equal"* clause of Article I. Now in 1783 he ruled that this phraseology had put an end to slavery. True, he agreed, slavery had long existed as a "usage." But

> a different idea has taken place with the people of America more favorable to the natural rights of mankind, and to that natural innate desire of Liberty, which . . . (without regard to complexion . . .) has inspired all the human race. And upon this ground our Constitution . . . by which the people . . . have solemnly bound themselves, [declares] that all men are born free and equal, and that every subject is entitled to liberty, and to have it guarded by the laws, as well as life and property—and in short, is totally repugnant to the idea of being born slaves. This being the case, . . . slavery is inconsistent with our own conduct and Constitution, and there can be no such thing as perpetual servitude of a rational creature.[106]

It begins to be clear that in justifying one revolution Jefferson, no less than Locke, unconsciously helped lay the groundwork for another.

3. After the Revolution as before, the Quakers and clergy spearheaded the antislavery movement, sustained it during adversity, and proved themselves the most militant and effective propagandists. During this period treatises multiplied, and abolition societies were organized by the Fathers. Slavery was abolished by the Vermont Constitution and, in other northern states, by legislative action applied prospectively. Churches for a time took strong stands, and because of the migration of Quakers and the Scotch-Irish southward, strong opposition to the institution developed even in Virginia, the Carolinas, Kentucky, and Tennessee. Freedom suits, petitions to

---

MAGER, *op. cit. supra* note 101, at 110. For the backgrounds, see MOORE, *op. cit. supra* note 94, at 209-221.

[105] Passed, July 13, 1787, by the last Congress under the Articles of Confederation while the Constitutional Convention was meeting at Philadelphia. The clause read: "There shall be neither slavery nor involuntary servitude in the said territory, otherwise than in the punishment of crimes, whereof the party shall have been duly convicted." See MCLAUGHLIN, CONFEDERATION AND CONSTITUTION c. 7 (1905); DUNN, INDIANA, A REDEMPTION FROM SLAVERY cc. 5–6 (1905).

[106] See note 104 *supra*.

Congress to abolish slavery in the District of Columbia, and the efforts of journalists and publicists lent an air of fervent optimism to the movement.[107]

There is no need to recount how slavery, thus challenged and undermined, made sensational recovery in the South following invention of the cotton gin, or how economics and geography realigned the sections, even to the point of reversing interests and stands and of evolving two antagonistic theories of the nature and purpose of the Union. The upshot was that the antislavery sentiment, originally strong below the Potomac and nourished by liberal humanitarianism, underwent sharp decline[108] almost simultaneously with resurgence in the North. The Horton episode,[109] controversy over Southern seamen's laws,[110] and congressional debate over Missouri's admission signalled maturing of a sectional conflict too deep to be resolved by the first two of Clay's great compromises.[111] Eventually

---

107 In addition to the monographs by MOORE, LOCKE, and ADAMS, *op. cit. supra* note 94, see the coverage of the post-Revolutionary antislavery movement in THORNBROUGH, NEGRO SLAVERY IN THE NORTH, ITS LEGAL AND CONSTITUTIONAL ASPECTS cc. 3, 4 (Thesis, Univ. of Mich. 1946); TURNER, THE NEGRO IN PENNSYLVANIA c. 5 (1910); FOX, AMERICAN COLONIZATION SOCIETY (1919); and the following contemporaneous treatises: PARRISH, *op. cit. supra* note 91; [ROBERT WALSH], . . . FREE REMARKS ON THE SPIRIT OF THE FEDERAL CONSTITUTION ON THE PRACTICE OF THE FEDERAL GOVERNMENT AND THE OBLIGATIONS OF THE UNION, RESPECTING THE EXCLUSION OF SLAVERY FROM THE TERRITORIES AND NEW STATES (1819) (a work by the Philadelphia editor which influenced the Missouri debates as well as later arguments of Birney, William Jay and Weld). STROUD, SKETCH OF THE LAWS RELATING TO SLAVERY IN THE SEVERAL STATES (1827) (an analysis of the chattel principle and legal incidents of slavery that stressed denial of protection).

108 On the recovery of slavery, the decline of the early abolition movement, and the impact of economic and sectional forces, 1810-1830, see HESSELTINE, THE SOUTH IN AMERICAN HISTORY (1947) and works there cited; EATON, FREEDOM OF THOUGHT IN THE OLD SOUTH (1940); ROBERT, ROAD FROM MONTICELLO, A STUDY OF THE VIRGINIA SLAVERY DEBATE OF 1832 (Duke, 1941); SYDNOR, DEVELOPMENT OF SOUTHERN SECTIONALISM 1819-1848 (1948); THORNBROUGH, *op. cit. supra* note 107.

109 A *cause celebre* of 1826-1827 involving a statute of the District of Columbia which authorized sale for jail fees of *suspected* fugitive slaves. Horton, a free Negro of New York, who had been arrested and threatened with sale, was saved by timely aid of abolitionist friends who capitalized the incident. See JAY, MISCELLANEOUS WRITINGS ON SLAVERY 48, 238-242 (1853); TUCKERMAN, WILLIAM JAY AND THE CONSTITUTIONAL MOVEMENT FOR ABOLITION OF SLAVERY 31-33 (1893); 3 CONG. DEB. 555 (1826).

110 See Hamer, *Great Britain, the United States and Negro Seamen's Acts, 1822-1848*, 1 J. OF SO. HIST. 1-28 (1935); H.R. REP. NO. 80, 27th Cong., 3d Sess. (1843), an important collection of documents covering the major controversies caused by enforcement of Southern laws whereunder Northern and British free Negro seamen were confined to quarters or jailed while in Southern ports.

111 The Missouri showdown, 1819-1821, powerfully catalyzed theory on both sides. With balance of representation in the Senate at stake, the nature and extent of the power to admit "new states" and the provision in Missouri's constitution prohibiting ingress and settlement of free Negroes and mulattoes prompted antislavery arguments based on the republican form of government and comity clauses. Proslavery theorists

there began the mass exodus from the South of dissident groups,[112] particularly Quakers and Scotch-Irish Presbyterians.

4. During the period 1790–1830, Ohio and the Northwest became the home of thousands of these refugees. This amalgamation of Southern and Northern antislavery elements predisposed local sentiment and fostered interest first in colonization, then in abolition. By 1830 the local antislavery argument already combined the Bible attack on the "sinfulness" of slavery with Lockean-Jeffersonian doctrines of liberty and equality.

This is made clear in Dr. Richard O'Dell's monograph, *The Early Anti Slavery Movement in Ohio*.[113] Westward along the Lakes and Mohawk, and via the Erie Canal, had come the staunch Puritan and Calvinist stocks from New York and New England; they settled generally near Lake Erie. Pushing up the western fork of the Susquehanna, or over the Forbes and Cumberland Roads from Maryland, Pennsylvania, and Virginia, then along Zane's Trace or down the Ohio, or moving slowly northward and westward through the transverse valleys from Virginia and the Carolinas, literally in flight from slavery, came potential allies. Whole "meetings" of Quakers and thousands of Scotch-Irish yeomanry, the latter often led by pastors trained at Princeton, Dickinson, or Hampden-Sydney, were part of this movement.[114]

In the vanguard from the South had been two Virginia-born, Princeton-trained clergymen educators, David Rice[115] and Samuel Doak.[116] Each had founded colleges as well as churches and in the post-revolutionary period had indoctrinated and sent forth scores

---

countered with the just compensation clause and with the doctrine of vested rights. See MCLAUGHLIN, CONSTITUTIONAL HISTORY OF THE UNITED STATES c. 29 (1935); BURGESS, THE MIDDLE PERIOD, 1817–58 c. 4 (1897); WILSON, RISE AND FALL OF THE SLAVE POWER cc. 11–12 (1872), especially at 154.

[112] See EATON, *op. cit. supra* note 108, at 234–8, 271; WEEKS, SOUTHERN QUAKERS AND SLAVERY c. 10 (1896); RUSSELL, HISTORY OF QUAKERISM 272 (1942).

[113] O'DELL, THE EARLY ANTI-SLAVERY MOVEMENT IN OHIO (Unpublished thesis, Univ. of Mich., 1948).

[114] On these migrations and the settlement of Ohio, in addition to O'DELL at c. 2, see CHADDOCK, OHIO BEFORE 1850 cc. 1, 2 (1908); WEEKS, *op. cit. supra* note 112, Smith, *The Quakers, Their Migration to the Upper Ohio*, 37 OHIO ARCH. AND HIST. SOC. QTLY. 35–85 (1928) (valuable for its maps and tables showing concentration of settlement); 2 GILLETT, HIST. OF THE PRESB. CHURCH IN THE U.S.A. 294 (1864); BIRNEY, JAMES G. BIRNEY AND HIS TIMES 431–435 (1890); DUMOND, ANTISLAVERY ORIGINS OF THE CIVIL WAR 6–8 (1939).

[115] 1733–1816. See DICT. AM. BIOG. One of the founders of Hampden-Sydney, Rice led the unsuccessful fight for an antislavery clause in the Kentucky Constitution of 1792. O'DELL, *op. cit. supra* note 113, at 47.

[116] 1749–1830, founder of the first institution of higher learning west of the Appalachians, DICT. AM. BIOG.

of disciples. Doak's proteges came from Washington College at Jonesboro in East Tennessee, Rice's from Transylvania Academy (later the University) and various pioneer pastorates in Kentucky. Arriving with Doak's and Rice's disciples in the second wave, which reached Ohio in 1800–1810, came outstanding leaders like the brothers-in-law, James Gilliland[117] and Robert G. Wilson.[118] Other Southern Presbyterians followed: the Dickey brothers,[119] Campbells,[120] Wallaces,[121] Crothers,[122] Lockhart,[123] and Rankin.[124] Methodists like the Finleys,[125] who had fled with their congregation from Kentucky and freed their slaves on arrival, were also in this wave. Baptists like the Dunlavys[126] from Virginia, Associated Reformed church leaders like David McDill[127] of Preble County, and from Pennsylvania, scores of such leaders as outspoken John Walker,[128]

---

[117] Pastor of Red Oak congregation near Ripley, Brown County, Ohio, 1805–45; one of the managers of the Ohio A.S.S., 1835. O'DELL at 53; BIRNEY, op. cit. supra note 114, at 433–434; 4 SPRAGUE, ANNALS OF AM. PULPIT 137–140 (1869).

[118] Organizer of first church in Columbus, 1806; President of Ohio University, 1824, 2 Gillett op. cit. supra note 114, at 126, 149–150; 4 SPRAGUE op. cit. supra note 117, at 122-5.

[119] William and James, born in South Carolina and Virginia, moved to Kentucky, educated there and in Tennessee, moved to Ohio 1811 and 1817, pastors at Bloomingsberg, Salem and Concord; members of the Ohio A.S.S. 1835. See O'DELL at 361.

[120] Dr. Alexander Campbell, M.D. (1769-1857), Virginia-born, removed to Ohio from Kentucky, 1803, freeing his slaves; U.S. Sen. 1810–1813; v.p. Ohio A.S.S. 1835. BIRNEY at 432, names six other Campbells who migrated from Virginia in 1796, all of whom were early abolitionists.

[121] John Wallace, a Muskingum County pastor, whom BIRNEY at 166, says was from the South, was a delegate to Ohio Anti-Slavery Society Convention, 1835, along with two other Wallaces.

[122] Samuel Crothers (1783–1856), a frontier Jonathan Edwards and leading exponent of the Bible argument, pastor of various Kentucky and Ohio churches 1809–1819, of Greenfield, Ohio, church 1820–1856; see O'DELL at 359; BIRNEY, op. cit. supra note 114, at 167.

[123] Jesse Lockhart, a native of Virginia, raised in East Tennessee and a onetime Doak student, pastor at Russellville for 40 years, O'DELL at 363. BIRNEY at 434.

[124] John Rankin (1793–1886), called the "Father of Abolitionism," born East Tennessee, moved to Ohio from Kentucky after Missouri Compromise, Presbyterian pastor at Ripley 44 years, 1822–1866; an organizer and agent of the A.A.S.S., 1835. O'DELL at 362; BIRNEY at 168–171.

[125] Rev. Robert Finley and his son, James B. Finley, who later was a pastor in Pickaway County and an Ohio A.S.S. delegate, 1835, O'DELL at 50; AUTOBIOGRAPHY OF REV. JAMES B. FINLEY 111–114 (1853).

[126] Francis Dunlavy, organizer of the first Baptist Church established in the Northwest Territory, of the Ohio Constitutional Convention, 1802, and the Ohio A.S.S. Convention, 1835. O'DELL at 54.

[127] Brought by his parents from South Carolina, 1806; O'DELL at 375 adds that the Hopewell Congregation, Preble County, was made up largely of such emigrants.

[128] O'DELL at 375–6; Hunter, Pathfinders of Jefferson County, 8 OHIO STATE ARCH. AND HIST. SOC. QTLY. 176, 186 (1899) which reports "Walker's congregation . . . anti slavery to a man."

Antislavery Backgrounds of the Fourteenth Amendment 197

were some of the other migrants. Walker became pastor of a congregation at Cadiz and one of the founders of Franklin College, a pioneer anti-slavery stronghold at New Athens.

Settling near the Ohio and its tributaries in close-knit communities, these southern and border-state elements joined forces with slavery-hating New Englanders.[129] Together they fought losing battles against the state Black Laws,[130] organized local abolition societies,[131] supported the first antislavery papers in the United States,[132] gave encouragement to the Quaker propagandists—Embree, Osborn, Bates, and Lundy[133]—heard scores of sermons on the "sin of slavery," and published and circulated a number of these works as tracts.[134] The strongholds were the Chillicothe[135] and Miami Presbyteries

---

[129] Among the New Englanders active in organizing the Ohio A.S.S., mentioned by O'DELL at 359, were Presbyterians William Gage, pastor at Pisgah and Concord, 1832-55, and Dyer Burgess, for many years pastor at Piqua and West Union. See GALBRAITH, HISTORY OF CHILLICOTHE PRESBYTERY 145 (1889); 1 BIRNEY LETTERS 155, and *infra* note 134. Also active and influential was Rev. John Monteith (1788-1868), a Pennsylvanian, first President of University of Michigan 1817-1821, pastor in the thirties at Elyria, Ohio, where he founded the first high school in the State, later a member of The Seventy. See 1 BIRNEY LETTERS 251-54; also *infra* notes 131, 142, 146.

[130] On the enactment and operation of these measures, see O'DELL at c. 5, especially at 146-178; an extended debate on their constitutionality occurred in July-August, 1829; *id.* at 324-326.

[131] See *id.* at cc. 6-9, esp. pp. 383-7, on the Quaker societies of the twenties organized in Columbiana and Monroe Counties; see also BIRNEY, *op. cit. supra* note 114 at 164. Largest of these early organizations was the Paint Creek Society which embraced parts of the Chillicothe Presbytery and eventually claimed 4000 members. Abolitionist sentiment was also strong in Medina and Lorain Counties in the north, near Cleveland. This district, later represented in Congress by Hamlin and Bliss, was settled largely by New Yorkers and New Englanders and was the center of the original Weld-Oberlin revivals; Elyria and Medina were the chief towns.

[132] See Walsh, *Three Anti Slavery Papers in Ohio Prior to 1823* 31 OHIO ARCH. AND HIST. SOC. PUB'NS. 172-212 (1921); O'Dell, *op. cit. supra* note 114 at 207-219. These three papers, all published at Mt. Pleasant, Ohio by Quakers, included The Philanthropist, founded and edited by Charles Osborn, Sept. 1817-Oct., 1818 and continued by Elisha Bates Dec., 1818-April, 1822, and the Genius of Universal Emancipation, edited by Benjamin Lundy, July, 1821-March, 1822. All phases of humanitarian reform were covered in these publications, though the antislavery theme was dominant. See also The Emancipator, published by another Friend, Elihu Embree, at Jonesboro, Tennessee, Apr. 30-Oct. 31, 1820 (reprinted 1932), the first periodical devoted wholly to antislavery propaganda. Pages 19, 21, 34, 62, 89, 94, 96, show the prime importance of the equality argument based on the Declaration of Independence.

[133] O'DELL at 207-219.

[134] Dyer Burgess published a PAMPHLET AGAINST SLAVERY, Ripley, Ohio (1827); GILLILAND, A DIALOGUE ON SLAVERY, Ripley, Ohio (1820). According to the preface, CROTHERS, STRICTURES ON AFRICAN SLAVERY (1833), was "published by the Abolition Society of Paint Valley." The writer has seen only the Crothers piece, a harsh, bigoted diatribe unlike Quaker and later immediatist works.

[135] See O'DELL, c. 9 at 359-376 and GALBRAITH, *op. cit. supra* note 129. In 1830-31 the Chillicothe Presbytery, consisting of the southwest quarter of the state, goaded the Ohio Synod to support its own previously-taken stand that slaveholding and trading were "heinous sins."

and the Short Creek Quarterly Meeting between Cadiz and Mount Pleasant in Harrison County.[136] Though the extent of antislavery sentiment at this date might easily be exaggerated, its intensity among these groups and the importance of their leadership can hardly be questioned.

5. Convincing evidence on this score is found in two publications of the mid-twenties. Both are of special interest today for their known influence on Birney, Finney, and Weld. *Letters on American Slavery*[137] was written by Reverend John Rankin, student and son-in-law of Samuel Doak and for forty-five years Presbyterian pastor at Ripley. The other work was *A Treatise on Slavery*[138] by James Duncan, pastor of a congregation in Indiana near the Ohio line. Rankin's *Letters* became an abolitionist "textbook." Its main appeal was religious and humanitarian, yet one argument was prophetic: slavery tended to tyranny and violated the principles of republicanism. Those principles had been heralded in the Declaration. Even so, the slave states, by restricting the guarantees of their due process clauses to freemen, had "created distinctions among men"; in effect they had permitted slaves to be "taken, imprisoned and destroyed" without either judgment or law.[139]

Duncan's work was a synthesis of the Biblical and natural rights arguments—a fusion of Bible and Blackstone. It not only anticipated the "moral law" and "sinfulness" attacks of later immediatists as well as Birney's shrewd integration of arguments stressing the irrepublican, antirevolutionary character of slavery, but it also flatly asserted the slaves' "natural right to be citizens and to enjoy civil protection."

> Slavery is directly contrary to the Federal Constitution; and those laws of state legislatures which ratify slavery are unconstitutional laws. The Federal Constitution declares that all men are created free, and have equal rights; . . . not . . . that that instrument, in its present form, contains an explicit reprehension of slavery; [rather] that the foundation and ground work of the Constitution, [—the Declaration of Independence, formed by] members of Congress act[ing] as representatives of the Nation and exhibit[ing] the moral ground on which the Nation could justify herself [—] condemns the practice in the most clear and explicit form: . . . "we hold these truths [etc.]" . . . the Declaration of

---

[136] CHADDOCK, *op. cit. supra* note 114, at 95; O'DELL at 61–64; SMITH, *op. cit. supra* note 114, at 79.
[137] Written, says O'DELL at 362, in 1823; printed as a pamphlet 1826; 5th ed. 1838.
[138] Vevay, Indiana (1824); repr. by Am. A.S.S., New York (1840).
[139] (5th ed. 1838), at 67.

Independence was the only federal constitution that existed in the United States until the Articles of confederation were ratified. . . .[140]

The pioneer antislavery strongholds along the Ohio, the Tuscarawas, the Muskingum, the Scioto and the Great and Little Miami, and along Short and Paint Creeks were among the first to be converted to militant immediatism by Weld or later by the "Twelve" and the "Seventy". Still later they constituted the heart of constituencies which elected Giddings,[141] Bliss,[142] Bingham,[143] William Lawrence[144] and others[145] to serve as representatives in Congress. Weld's sensationally successful agency in 1834-1835 began with lectures before the Gilliland and Rankin congregations at Ripley and continued with series before Burgess' congregation at West Union, Crothers' at Greenfield, and the Dickey brothers' at Concord and Bloomingsburg.[146]

Equally convincing proof of the continuity of the antislavery movement as a whole is found in the backgrounds and affiliations of Bingham[147] and Lawrence.[148] Following his admission to the bar in 1841, Bingham resided in the heart of the Quaker and Associate

---

[140] DUNCAN, A TREATISE ON SLAVERY 30, 53, 109–113 (1840).

[141] From 1838 until 1859 Giddings (1795-1864) represented the Ashtabula area. By 1842 abolition sentiment was so strong in this region that following censure by the House and resignation he was overwhelmingly reelected and returned to Congress in a special election. See JULIAN, JOSHUA GIDDINGS (1892).

[142] Philomen Bliss of Elyria (*supra* note 36 and *infra* notes 230, 232, 246) first ran for Congress as a Free Soiler in 1848, was elected from the Medina-Lorain district in 1854 and reelected in 1856. See DICT. AM. BIOG.; BENCH AND BAR OF ST. LOUIS 376–379 (1884). From 1843–45, E. S. Hamlin, also of Elyria, an early convert of Weld's and a political lieutenant of Salmon P. Chase, represented this same district which included Oberlin. See 2 BIRNEY LETTERS 1025. See *infra* note 227 for formation of societies in this area.

[143] For eight terms (1855–63, 1865–73) Bingham represented the 21st Ohio district, composed of Harrison, Jefferson, Carroll and Columbiana counties, including the Quaker settlements along Short Creek and the Ohio. See DICT. AM. BIOG.; J.F. BRENNAN, BIOGRAPHICAL ENCYCLOPEDIA . . . OF OHIO 312 (1880).

[144] Lawrence represented the Zanesville-Logan district in the 39th to 41st Congresses 1865-71 and in the 43rd-44th. See DICT. AM. BIOG.

[145] Including Samuel Galloway (1811–1872) an agent of the A.A.S.S. 1836, elected as a Republican to the 34th Congresses in 1854, WELD-GRIMKE LETTERS at 228. James M. Ashley, who represented Scioto County and sponsored the 13th Amendment, (DICT. AM. BIOG.; EVANS, HISTORY OF SCIOTO COUNTY 288–294 (1903); WELD-GRIMKE LETTERS at 333). Edward Wade (1803–1862) elected as a Free Soiler from Cleveland 1853–55, and as a Republican 1855–61. Ben Wade (1800-1878), law partner of Giddings and brother of Edward, Ohio's ultraradical U.S. Senator, 1851-69. See 2 BIRNEY LETTERS 710.

[146] See BARNES, *op. cit. supra* note 35, esp. n. 14 p. 238; and Weld's letters in 1 BIRNEY LETTERS 153–6, 170–3, 180–2, 246–51.

[147] BRENNAN, *op. cit. supra* note 143.

[148] DICT. AM. BIOG.

Reformed communities of Harrison County. Lawrence practiced law in Zanesville, McConnellsville and Bellfontane, all later radical strongholds. It further appears that both of these future Repubican leaders, whose relations to the War Amendments and whose interpretations[149] thereof today are of such extraordinary interest, were students at Franklin College before 1836. These were the years the Revivalist campaign was at its height. Apart from Reverend John Walker's continued association with the college, there is convincing evidence in Birney's *Philanthropist* in the spring of 1837[150] to show that it still merited its reputation as the "fountainhead of abolitionist sentiment in eastern Ohio."

The crusade launched by the Weld-Birney forces thus was anything but a spontaneous or isolated development. Its strength lay in the character of its leadership and in the receptivity of large segments

---

[149] See Bingham's speeches, CONG. GLOBE, 39th Cong., 1st Sess. 429, 1034, 1064–1065, 1089–1095, 1292 (1866); 42 CONG. REC. Appendix 81–85 (1871); BRENNAN, *op. cit. supra* note 143, at 312. Bingham's speech of 1871 was quoted at length by Mr. Justice Black dissenting in Adamson v. Calif., 332 U.S. 46, 68, 110–118 (1947). Lawrence's speeches are of vital interest today because he was one of the few congressmen who showed knowledge of Taylor v. Porter, 4 Hill 140 (1843), and other pre-war substantive due process cases. In discussing Johnson's veto of the Civil Rights Bill of 1866, Lawrence made clear that he conceived the Bill (and hence the 14th amendment later adopted to remove all doubts of its constitutionality) as embracing not merely state action but state inaction of certain kinds: "Now there are two ways," he declared in a major speech (CONG. GLOBE, 39th Cong., 1st Sess. 1832 (1866)), "in which a State may undertake to deprive citizens of these absolute, inherent, and inalienable rights: either by prohibitory laws, or *by a failure to protect* any one of them" (emphasis added). In a speech January 6, 1874, on Supplementary Civil Rights Bill number 796 (forbidding discrimination by hotels and carriers) Lawrence squarely maintained that individual invasions and state inaction were covered by the 14th Amendment. "The object of this provision [the equal protection clause] is to make all men equal before the law. If a state permits inequality in rights to be created or meted out by citizens or corporations enjoying its protection it denies the equal protection of the laws. . . . What the State permits by its sanction, having the power to prohibit, it does in effect itself." 43 CONG. REC. 412–414 (1874). For strikingly similar views of inaction in the abstract by Calhoun, see 6 WORKS OF CALHOUN 56.

[150] April 28, 1837, p. 3, col. 5 "To the Friends and Patrons of Franklin College." After alluding to recent financial and administrative difficulties and announcing the selection of Rev. Joseph Smith Jr. as president, this advertisement assured—with obvious reference to the Lane troubles—"The two Literary Societies are in good standing, and are accessible to all students. Free discussion on all subjects is allowed in them and in College, but no preference is shown to any student on the ground of either his religious or other opinions . . . By order of the . . . Trustees. Rev. John McArthur, Rev. Jacob Coon, Committee, New Athens, April 14, 1837." An ardent abolitionist and himself later president of the college, Coons had been one of the organizers and managers of the Ohio Anti Slavery Society in 1835 (Proceedings p. 41); as had Rev. John Walker of Cadiz, leader in obtaining the college its charter in 1825. See HUNTER, *op. cit. supra* note 128, at 186. From Hunter's account, p. 135–140, one concludes that Bingham and Lawrence were at Franklin during its depressed period and while dissension over slavery was at its height.

of the population. Predecessors had pioneered the struggle and made substantial beginnings. The Chillicothe and Miami Presbyteries, and the Cadiz, Short Creek, and Mt. Pleasant Quarterly Meetings were all antislavery islands—advance bases waiting exploitation.

Doctrinally the situation appeared equally favorable. Colonization was now self-discredited, even ethically repugnant. The British example inspired the world's hopes and confidence. Locke's formulas had acquired a new scope. The cardinal premises of liberty, freedom, and equality had begun to express themselves in new criteria of arbitrariness. The rise of humanitarianism, the spread of philanthropy, broader social sympathies, more enlightened views of racial differences—all continued to undermine notions of inferiority. In the mid-nineteenth century, Weld declared, it was incumbent that "persons be treated according to their intrinsic worth, *irrespective of color, shape, condition or what not.*"[151] Negroes and slaves were "persons." It was degrading to other persons if they were denied human status and refused the rights of personality. An ethical principle was at stake—the very one on which Locke had erected his state of nature and in support of which he had quoted "the judicious Hooker": "My desire, therefore, to be loved of my equals in nature, as much as possible may be, imposeth upon me a natural duty of bearing themward fully the like affection." This thought immediatists rephrased more bluntly: "We claim these rights for *all men*," declared the Rhode Island Anti-Slavery Society, "because the golden rule of righteousness requires us to do so. We claim them *for all men,* because we would have all men claim them for us."[152]

Like their predecessors, the immediatists now seized on these religious, Lockean, Jeffersonian and state constitutional premises and insisted that they be applied literally. The backwardness of the Negro race was the consequence of enslavement; yet enslavement of blacks could no more be countenanced or justified than enslavement because of red hair. Negro slavery rested on an arbitrary classification. To condone that classification was to jeopardize the rights of all men. An insubstantial distinction made in one case might easily

---

[151] 1 WELD-GRIMKE LETTERS 270.
[152] PROCEEDINGS OF ... THE CONVENTION HELD IN PROVIDENCE ... FEBRUARY, 1836 at 18. From the Society's DECLARATION AND EXPOSE, a document drafted by William Goodell (1792–1878), abolitionist editor and compiler whose overall contributions entitle him to rank with the Ohio-New York headquarters group in influence. See especially his VIEWS OF AMERICAN CONSTITUTIONAL LAW, IN ITS BEARING UPON AMERICAN SLAVERY (1844), a recasting of abolitionist theory for the Liberty Party campaign of 1844.

become a precedent for others, particularly if such capricious tests as pigmentation and hair curl gained general sanction.[153]

What was slowly changing and continuing to act reflexively on men's social outlook was their power of observation, their psychological insight, their innate sympathy and social consciousness. To this extent, as Thomas M. Cooley later observed, immediatists were "pioneers in the wilderness of political morality."[154] Their enduring contribution to our political theory and fundamental law ultimately was a theory of a paramount national citizenship which embraced the concept of due process and equal protection of the laws. Yet in working out this theory, they began, not as lawyers or constitutionalists, but as moralists and evangelists. Their basic case was a compendious Biblico-moral, ethico-religious, natural rights argument confidently addressed to their countrymen as patriots, Christians, and "free moral agents." Yet repetitious and involute as it was, its premises and basic structure remained, until about 1836, amazingly simple.

This is evidenced, not only in the Weld-Grimke and Birney letters,[155] but in *Two Lectures on the Subject of Slavery and Abolition*[156] "compiled" by Charles Olcott.[157] An early convert of Weld's,

---

[153] See Rhode Island PROCEEDINGS, *op. cit. supra* note 152, at 25, for a characteristic statement of this not ungrounded fear; abolitionists never tired of citing cases of mistaken racial identity. See Salmon P. Chase, SPEECH, ... IN THE CASE OF THE COLORED WOMAN, MATILDA ... 32 (1837).

[154] In an address in 1884, cited in KOOKER, ANTI SLAVERY MOVEMENT IN MICHIGAN, 1796–1840 (Unpublished thesis, Univ. of Mich. at 253).

[155] See note 41 *supra*. It must be stressed again that these two sources are indispensable for insight into the motivation of the movement, particularly for the years prior to 1837.

[156] Massillon, Ohio, printed for the author (1838). Its importance today lies in the fact that it is one of the few works which suggest, and at times perhaps actually record the substance and form of the revivalist argument as delivered by Weld and The Twelve and The Seventy. Within its two main divisions the presentation is sub-topical, well organized, and, granting the premises, moves inexorably to its conclusions. These were (1) "Slavery is as great a crime against the law of God as murder," (2) immediate emancipation is both righteous and reasonable. No single work so well reveals the overwhelmingly religious and Biblical character of the early appeals, the encyclopedic preparation, the skill and cogency of the rebuttals. (See esp. p. 50 ff. for these summarized "answers" to the sixteen commonest objections and alternatives to abolition; significantly it is in this "defensive" section that much of the primitive constitutional argument appears, pp. 88–89, 92–93, 116–120).

[157] Little is known of Olcott other than that at this period he contributed regularly to a now-lost paper The Advocate of Human Rights, published in Medina by his fellow townsman and co-member on the Committee on the Law of Ohio, Timothy Hudson, (5 WICKHAM, MEMORIAL TO THE PIONEER WOMEN OF THE WESTERN RESERVE 852 (1924)) and that the county seats Medina and Elyria, within easy access from Oberlin and having bars and clergy of exceptional ability, including Rev. John Monteith, the Bliss brothers and E. S. Hamlin (see notes 129, 131, 142, *supra*) exercised vital influence on the legal and constitutional argument in Ohio. This influence is clearly observable in the pages of Birney's Philanthropist; see notes 230, 246 *infra*.

Olcott was an able Medina County lawyer, a number of whose colleagues and fellow townsmen later figured prominently in the legal and constitutional attack on slavery. He here set forth for the use of antislavery lecturers an outline of the whole Revivalist argument. His views have further significance in that he was one of the two bar members of the Committee on the Laws of Ohio and thus played an important part in drafting the 1835 Report earlier discussed.[158]

As completely as Locke and Jefferson, Olcott and the Revivalists premised their case on the higher law.

> The law of nature *clearly* . . . *teaches the natural republican equality of all mankind. Nature* revolts at human slavery, is at open war with it . . . [and every sophistical argument used to justify enslavement of blacks might equally justify enslavement of whites]. The Law of God renders all Natural Rights *inalienable* . . . Liberty and right, being *good* and necessary for the welfare of Mankind are the *gifts* of God (vide James I, 17) and whatever power violates them, violates and abuses God's gift. Both the word and the works of God proclaim the existence and inalienable nature of Human Rights, and for men to deprive each other of them for any cause except crime is a . . . violation of God's law. Governments and laws are established, not to *give*, but to protect . . . rights. [They are] made to protect the *whole* of the rights of their subjects; not to annul or diminish them. Their great . . . end . . . is to preserve men's rights entire.[159]

"The black race," Olcott continued, was "not naturally inferior." It had been degraded by slavery; "differences in condition of the races have been produced by . . . artificial means." Negroes had reason, "speech, human shape, organization, features, faculties and capacity." They were endowed by their Maker with all inalienable human rights. . . . "*All Men* have the *rights* of men."[160]

It was also argued that slavery was a crime, not only against the law of God and nature, but against the common law. By Blackstone's own definition:

> This great and excellent [common] law [guaranteed] to all human beings, within its jurisdiction and under its protection, the free use of all their natural rights, in the highest perfection. I Bla. Com. 144. [Slavery was not a crime against the common law] *by that name, any more than* Tyranny is. It is called by that

---

[158] See notes 60, 61–62 *supra*.
[159] OLCOTT, *op. cit. supra* note 156, at 24–29.
[160] *Id.* at 34–36.

law *'Assault and Battery'*, *'False Imprisonment'*, 'Kidnapping' . . . 'Robbery.'[161]

In this double identification—first of the common law with the natural law, then of slavery with the crimes of false imprisonment and assault and battery—one gets valuable insight into the initial aims of the abolitionists. Clearer too are the ingenious cross-substitutions and transfers which presently were to quicken use of due process and equal protection. On the one hand, identification of the common with the higher law served to give the former all the potentialities and attributes of an overriding law of nature. It was employed again and again by American abolitionists. This was in sharp contrast with the learned and historically meticulous common law argument which Francis Hargrave and Granville Sharp had employed to convince Chief Justice Mansfield in the Sommersett Case. The latter argument was the spearhead of the antislavery movement in England.[162]

Slavery simply was institutionalized false imprisonment, an invasion of the Negroes' inalienable right to liberty by their masters' collective "lawless" acts; Negroes alone were singled out for enslavement. In due course the premised standard of equality and the premised need for legal protection were combined with the common-higher law equivalence to give yet another twist to the argument. Olcott and Revivalists contended:

> In the case of the white people of this country, all slavish violence and oppression, is now in effect, abolished by Law . . . true not by name. But the Laws . . . against assault and battery, false imprisonment . . . murder, etc., produce the same effect, as law expressly . . . against . . . slavery. If the least attempt is made to enslave a white person of any description, he or she can apply to the Law for redress, and have full and ample relief by due course of Law. They can have all the counsel and assistance necessary for this purpose. What abolitionists demand as naked justice is, that the benefit and protection of these just laws, be extended to all human beings alike, . . . and that all mankind be allowed the same legal rights and protection, without regard to colour or any other physical peculiarities. . . . The Almighty, they say, has given the same equal rights to all men alike, and it is blasphemous for one portion of the human race to deprive another of them, without

---

161 *Id.* at 30.
162 See The Case of James Sommersett, 20 How. St. Tr. 1 (1772). Only at col. 29-30 did Hargrave's argument, which was based on Sharp's research (LASCELLES, GRANVILLE SHARP AND THE ABOLITION OF SLAVERY IN ENGLAND (1928)), rely even on Lockean-natural rights principles.

crime in the portion deprived. God has made but one law or rule of conduct for man; the latter has no right therefore, to make different laws for different men. God's law is without respect to colour or other physical peculiarities, ... Man ought never to affect to be wiser than his Maker.[163]

Surveyed against subsequent developments, this is a revealing statement. All the original elements—the higher and the common law, equality, protection, and procedural due process—are here employed incidentally in a single paragraph! Moreover, they are employed together in a way which sheds light not merely on their origins and present contents but on the future course of development. Racial discrimination was repugnant both as a breach of equality and as a breach of protection. Because it was a breach of protection, it was also a breach of equality, and because it was a breach of equality, it was thereby an even greater breach of protection. Nor was this simply circular reasoning. It was rather the outcome of the triple-barreled major premise which posited the purpose of all government to be the protection of inalienable rights bestowed upon all men by their Creator. Once that compound premise was granted—and in the sixty years since 1776 virtually all Americans had *spoken* as if they granted it—the abolitionist's conclusions were unassailable. Could the country now be persuaded that racial inferiority was a myth, that prejudice itself was "vincible," that Negroes had "all . . . potentialities other humans have"? Slavery, slashed from its roots, might indeed wither away if it could. The great object and need were simply to

> *abolish the laws, customs, and practice of slavery*, and restore the *protection of the common law and all just statute laws* to the slaves; thus *making them . . . freemen* with the whites, *enjoying the same just, equal rights and privileges.* It is to *abrogate all unjust, unequal laws and customs, . . .* and *restore the supremacy of all just and equal laws within the jurisdiction, over all persons* alike, without regard to color or other physical peculiarities.[164] [All that was needed to give effect to these objects in any jurisdiction, was] a short declaratory act . . . *declaring the Common law and all just and equal statute laws to be in force over all persons . . . , without any distinction.*[165]

The rudimentary character of the early constitutional argument, and its still incidental place, are also manifest in a paragraph entitled

---

[163] OLCOTT, *op. cit. supra* note 156, at 44.
[164] OLCOTT, *op. cit. supra* note 156, at 45.
[165] *Id.* at 48; emphasis added.

"Natural Equality" which appeared in the first number of the *Anti-Slavery Record* in 1835.

> [What did abolitionists mean when they held] with the Declaration of Independence, "that all men are created equal"? [Physical equality? equality of wealth and learning?] That criminals shall not be deprived of their liberty? No. They mean, according to the plain dictates of common sense, that, in coming into this world, and going through it, all men shall have an equal and fair chance to exercise all their powers of body and mind for their own happiness. Of course, they mean that no man shall encroach upon another. That one man shall have as good a right to acquire wealth as another. That one parent shall have as good a right to the services of his own children as another. That every wife shall be in subjection to her own husband, and to no one else; and that no man shall be deprived of his liberty for an alleged crime "without due process of law." Slavery violates natural equality in all these respects; and in the last respect it is not only contrary to our Declaration of Independence, but to the Constitution of the United States.[166]

These basic ideals of liberty, equality, and protection were deemed paramount by reason of their place in the Declaration and determinative by reason of the place of the Declaration in American life and history. They were at times also linked not only with the guarantee of due process but with the equally vital presumption regarding Negro citizenship and the affirmative duty on the part of the States to protect fundamental rights of all citizens. Two early instances of Negro citizenship already have been noted—the Ellsworth-Goddard[167] argument in the *Crandall* case and the Report of the Committee on the Laws of Ohio.[168] Another instance is found in the "Particular Instructions" which accompanied Weld's commission as an agent of the American Anti-Slavery Society, probably in December, 1833.

> People of Color ought to be emancipated *and recognized as citizens, and their rights secured as such, equal in all respects to others*, according to the cardinal principle of the American Declaration of Independence. Of course we have nothing to do with any equal laws which the states may make, to punish vagrancy, idleness, and crime, either in whites or blacks.[169]

---

[166] 1 Anti-Slavery Record 8 (1835).
[167] See notes 64–72 *supra*.
[168] See notes 60, 62, 63 *supra*.
[169] 1 Weld-Grimke Letters 126.

Hardly less arresting for its illumination, is a passage of Henry B. Stanton's which contrasts the plans of the immediatists and the gradualists in May, 1835.

> The plan of the gradualist is, continue in slavery; liable, by consequence, to the abuse of despotic power. The abolitionist proposes, not emancipation *from* law, but emancipation *into* law. The one, the irresponsible control of the master, the other, the wise and benign control of the law. The one, outlawry, with its concomitants, outrage and vice,—the other, citizenship, with the dignities and immunities of manhood.[170]

A quest for law, for the protection of law, and for an end to "outlawry" and "despotic power" and "irresponsible control"—the odious distinguishing badges and incidents of slavery—these ends Stanton lumps together in the concept "citizenship." This is not the constitutional lawyer's concept, but simply "citizenship with the dignities and immunities of manhood." Here one grasps the ideal that shaped the popular meaning of "citizen" and ultimately determined its choice and content. That ideal was "emancipation *into* law" and "*the equal protection*" thereby and thereunder of all persons and citizens.

It is apparent that restraint and optimism[171] dominated the early strategy of Ohio abolitionists. Their initial appeal was not to the Constitution but to morals and religion, ethics and patriotism. Their approach was evangelical rather than political. Victory, it was assumed, certainly would be won by reason and by moral suasion by appealing to the minds and consciences of Christian Americans. Accent was overwhelmingly on *rights*, rather than on *power*, on persuasion, not force. Only incidentally, and only in arguments designed to demonstrate the expediency and righteousness of emancipation, and the "crime" and the "sin" of slavery, were legal and constitutional sanctions relied upon at all.

Moral and ethical arguments frequently were cast in legal terms; the common law was employed by Olcott with almost the same reach and effect as the higher law itself. Birney gave polished statement to the argument that slavery was incompatible with the genius of Amer-

---

[170] *Op. cit. supra* note 43, at 7.
[171] In a letter to Birney dated June 19, 1834, Weld predicted the end of slavery "in these United States within twenty years," and "within five years in Kentucky and Missouri;" also that "within two years, the free people of color in all the free States and in some of the *now* slave States will be raised to an equality of rights and privileges with the whites." 1 BIRNEY LETTERS 119; see also *id.* at 204–210 for Birney's characteristic appeal to reason and moderation.

ican institutions. Petitioners asked Congress to exercise its power to abolish slavery in the federal district and to curb the internal slave trade. The historical fact of free Negro citizenship, earlier demonstrated by Ellsworth and Goddard, and seized on by William Jay, was reemployed, in conjunction with the comity clause and other guarantees, by the Committee on the Laws of Ohio. The rudiments of later phraseology—the premised need for protection, the prescribed standard of equality, the repugnance of absolute power, the arbitrariness of race and color as determinants of individual rights— all these were present and all were at times expressly argued.[172]

However, a popular constitutional argument did not yet exist— either as applied to slavery in the states or in federal territory. Not only the indictment of slavery and the appeals for emancipation, but the defense of the free Negro were generally grounded on broad natural law premises, or on clauses of the state constitutions or of the Declaration. The latter document still far outranked the Constitution as a supreme fundamental law. The main object was to mobilize the individual *will* to emancipate rather than the social *power*.

This state of affairs presently was reversed. Social compulsion replaced individual conversion as the guiding premise. Moral suasion gave way to political action. An ethically and religiously motivated movement, concerned with recognition of Negro rights and with education of the Negro race, and which had strong roots in the South,[173] became in a short time a politically-oriented movement. This movement was wholly sectional in character and committed to eradicating slavery by government fiat.

The key to these shifts and to their catalyzing effects on constitutional theory lies in the immediatists' confusion of purpose. To undermine slavery and cut short interminable debates over expediency and methods, they had appropriated the English slogan and strategy. But by "immediate emancipation" they meant simply "gradual emancipation *immediately begun*." They hurt themselves and their chances even more by belaboring slaveholders as "mansteelers" and by tactless harping on the "sinfulness" of slavery and the certainty of Divine retribution.[174] Combined with failure to recognize that judi-

---

[172] See Olcott, *op. cit. supra* note 156, at 78–79, 85–93, 116–120, for a compact version of the early constitutional argument; note that it appears in the rebuttal section and is wholly defensive in character.

[173] O'Dell, *op. cit. supra* note 113, at 388–9, analyzes Benjamin Lundy's claims of 130 antislavery societies with 6,625 members in 1827, of which the great preponderance (5,000 members) were in the South.

[174] Here again Olcott, *op. cit. supra* note 156, affords best insight into these features of the Bible argument which infuriated and outraged the South.

cial and legislative action by the separate states (rather than by a sovereign Parliament and single court as at Westminster) drastically slowed the progress of any emancipation movement in America, these were blunders of first magnitude. After auspicious beginnings in Massachusetts and Connecticut, state judicial action ceased to be a positive force.[175]

Fears of servile insurrection, quickened by triple coincidence, probably had doomed the Weld-Birney strategy even before it could be tried.[176] In September, 1829, shortly before the start of the debates in Parliament over emancipation in the British colonies, a free Negro of Boston, David Walker, published and circulated an incendiary *Appeal in Four Articles*. This frenetic, seditious pamphlet exulted in the slaves' strength and numbers, belittled the whites, and openly called for vengeance and rapine. Copies soon appeared in at least five southern states. Hardly had alarmed legislatures begun stiffening the non-intercourse, quarantine, and anti-literacy laws to forestall such propaganda, than Garrison launched his *Liberator*.

In the second number, the editor deprecated the Walker *Appeal*. Later he repeatedly explained his basic creed of brotherhood, non-resistance, and moral suasion. Yet to the frightened, sensitive South this was worse than futile. Neither the *Liberator's* manner nor matter appeared consistent with such principles. The invective and vilification, the censure, the absence of a positive program and the refusal to consider one—all were construed as deliberate incitements to passion and violence, or as leaving no possible alternatives. Garrison, on these points, was neither consistent nor clear headed. The *Liberator* for July 31, 1831, contained a "Song, Supposed to be Sung

---

[175] Commonwealth v. Aves, 18 Pick. 193 (Mass. 1836); Jackson v. Bullock, 12 Conn. 38 (1837); 4 CATTERALL, *op. cit. supra* note 77, at 433-436 (1936). *Cf.* Hobbs v. Fogg, 6 W. & S. 553 (Pa. 1837); State v. Claiborne, 11 Tenn. 331 (1838). Aids in studying the case law of abolitionism are CATTERALL and HURD, LAW OF FREEDOM AND BONDAGE (1862) (also covers statutes). From the first, Mansfield's decision in The Case of James Sommersett, 20 How. St. Tr. 1 (1771), exercised a hypnotic influence over abolition strategy in this country; but after the Pennsylvania courts declined to follow the bold step taken by Judge Cushing in Walker v. Jennison, (see note 104 *supra*) no progress was made until in the Aves case, *supra*, the Massachusetts court in effect affirmed the earlier unreported decision, thus arousing false hopes anew. (See LOCKE, *op. cit. supra* note 94; CHARLES STUART, MEMOIR OF GRANVILLE SHARP (Am. Anti Slavery Society, 1836); WELD-GRIMKE LETTERS 397-400). Various early attacks drew limited judicial approval, *e.g.*, the dissenting opinion of Judge Mills adopting counsel's argument that a Kentucky Black law violated the Federal Comity clause and the state due course of law clause, Amy v. Smith, 1 Litt. 326, 337-48 (Ky. 1822).

[176] See SYDNOR (c. 10), EATON (cc. 4, 5), and ROBERTS (c. 1), *op. cit. supra* note 108; also Eaton, *A Dangerous Pamphlet in the Old South*, 2 J. OF SO. HIST. 323-34 (1936); APTHEKER, AMERICAN NEGRO SLAVE REVOLTS cc. 11, 12 (1943); 1 GARRISON, GARRISON 160-1.

by Slaves in Insurrection," words of which urged the bondsmen to "strike for God and Vengeance now." The South suffered its bloodiest slave revolt exactly thirty days later. In Southampton County, Virginia, Nat Turner, a literate slave who believed himself possessed of supernatural powers, fomented and led an uprising which began with murder of his master's family, and ended in slaughter of nearly sixty whites, three-fourths of them women and children. No proof has ever linked Turner's act with Garrison or Walker; and none, in view of the circumstances, could successfully have rebutted the presumptions.

The repercussion of these incidents was a vast change in attitude toward slavery.[177] After two weeks debate in January, 1832, the Virginia legislature by a single vote finally rejected proposals for gradual emancipation. This was the turning point. Thereafter public discussion of slavery grew more infrequent; protests more equivocal; slowly the movement for emancipation collapsed—literally from fear of liberated slaves. What former generations had tended to view as an evil and as a social, economic, and moral blight, now evoked passionate counter-defense. Building on arguments of the Missouri debates and on writings of such pioneer apologists as Dr. Cooper and Governor Miller, leaders developed the thesis that slavery was a boon, a "sectional and a national blessing," "not an evil, . . . a positive good," the "very cornerstone of our republican edifice." First developed locally in the South, such arguments soon were repeated in Congress.[178]

Meanwhile, legislatures continued to tighten the slave codes.[179] As leaders of major insurrections had been literate, stiffer penalties were enacted for teaching slaves to read and write. More states forbade Negro preaching. Seditious publications were more sweepingly defined. The drastic seamen's laws, first enacted in the early twenties after the Tyler Insurrection and which required free Negroes on vessels entering Southern ports to be bonded and quarantined, were

---

177 ROBERT, *op. cit. supra* note 108; WHITFIELD, SLAVERY AGITATION IN VIRGINIA, 1829–32 (1930). JENKINS, *op. cit. supra* note 94, at 65–76.

178 See JENKINS, *op. cit. supra* note 94, at 76; speeches cited *infra* note 186; 12 CONG. DEB. col. 2456 (1835) (Rep. Hammond of South Carolina). Growing intransigence of the South (1825–26) on slavery was apparent in the speeches of John Randolph and R. Y. Hayne in the debate over recognition of Haiti. See 2 CONG. DEB. col. 112–13 (1825); O'DELL at 285–6.

179 See EATON, *op. cit. supra* note 108, c. 5 and statutes there cited. **1968:** For extensive tabular indexes showing the main categories of repressive legislation added to the various state slave codes, see FARNAM, CHAPTERS IN THE HISTORY OF SOCIAL LEGISLATION IN THE UNITED STATES TO 1860 (1938). Tables pp. 326–474. Column VI, Teaching and Preaching; Column IV, Sedition; Column XI, Migration.

amended and rigorously enforced.[180] Fresh restraints were placed on migration of free Negroes. The brother of Prudence Crandall, a Connecticut physician visiting in Washington, was arrested and tried on a *common law* charge of seditious libel for *possession* of abolitionist pamphlets.[181] Vigilanteism increased, culminating in a frightful series of episodes such as the Vicksburg Tragedy of July, 1835.[182] Condoning mob action, hot-headed leaders threatened similar fates to Garrison and the Tappans.[183]

Constitutional defenses likewise were overhauled. To some Southern leaders, Calhoun's doctrines of concurrent majority and state interposition[184] seemed to offer scant protection against abolition in *federal* territory. Slavery *in the states* might be a labor system and nexus of property relations—a local domestic matter over which Congress had no powers whatever. Yet over the federal district and territories two clearly worded grants gave Congress sweeping power, (1) "to exercise exclusive legislation in all cases whatsoever over such District (not exceeding ten miles square) as may, by Session [sic] of particular States and the acceptance of Congress, become the Seat of the Government of the United States," and (2) "to dispose of and make all needful Rules and Regulations respecting the Territory . . . belonging to the United States." Potentialities of these powers seldom had been questioned; policy and expediency alone had set their bounds. Alarmed at the petitions pouring in from the converts of Weld and his co-workers,[185] Southern leaders in Congress now sought secondary bulwarks. Abolition in the District was repeatedly attacked[186] as a "violation of public faith," "unwise," "impolitic," a

---

[180] HAMER, *op. cit. supra* note 110.

[181] See THE TRIAL OF REUBEN CRANDALL, M. D., CHARGED WITH PUBLISHING SEDITIOUS LIBELS BY CIRCULATING THE PUBLICATIONS OF THE AMERICAN ANTI-SLAVERY SOCIETY . . . (1836). Crandall was tried before Judge Cranch and acquitted.

[182] Eaton, *Mob Violence in the South*, 29 MISS. VALLEY HIST. REV. 351-71 (1942); Philanthropist, Feb. 5, 1836, p. 2, col. 5; p. 3, col. 1; *id.*, Oct. 28, 1836, p. 4, col. 2-3 reprinting a rare pamphlet later used by Eaton.

[183] SYDNOR, *op. cit. supra* note 108. Philanthropist, April 8, 1836, p. 3, col. 5, Speech of Mississippi Governor to Legislature; and see note 191 *infra*.

[184] For Calhoun's position at this period, see the South Carolina Exposition and Protest, and the celebrated Fort Hill address, reprinted in 6 CALHOUN, WORKS 1-123 (1856); BURGESS (cc. 10-11), MCLAUGHLIN (c. 33), *op. cit. supra* note 111; FREDERIC BANCROFT, CALHOUN AND THE SOUTH CAROLINA NULLIFICATION MOVEMENT (1928); BOUCHER, NULLIFICATION CONTROVERSY IN SOUTH CAROLINA (1916); WILTSIE, JOHN C. CALHOUN, NULLIFIER, 1829-1839 (1949). *Cf.* Corwin, *National Power and State Interposition, 1787-1861*, 10 MICH. L. REV. 535 (1912).

[185] BARNES, *op. cit. supra* note 27, cc. 11-13; BURGESS, *op. cit. supra* note 111, c. 11.

[186] See 12 CONG. DEB. col. 2019, 2023 (1835), speeches Reps. Robertson and Wise of Virginia, Dec. 22, 1835; speech of Rep. Pickens of South Carolina, Jan. 21, 1836. These speeches were widely circulated as pamphlets and drew immediate answer by

direct threat to the Union which might be met by nullification. But just as abolitionists in their affirmative defense of free Negroes had already linked due process and inalienable rights, so now Southern strategists, anticipating Chief Justice Taney in the Dred Scott case by more than two decades, appropriated the guarantee to slavery's defense.[187] Hints of such usage had appeared in recent debates,[188] yet it was a House Committee report,[189] issued in May, 1836, under the chairmanship of H. L. Pinckney, of South Carolina, that consolidated these defenses. In doing so, it probably ended the chance of gradual emancipation.

Congress' powers of "exclusive legislation" over the District, the Report at first conceded. But this was argued to mean simply that Congress alone possessed the law-making authority. The granted power was subject to inherent limitations; it had been bestowed "for beneficial purposes only."

> The Constitution . . . does not, and could not, confer unlimited authority [over the District]. It could confer no power contrary to the fundamental principles of the Constitution itself, and of the essential and unalienable rights of American citizens. The right to legislate . . . (to make the Constitution consistent with itself) is . . . qualified by the provision that "no man [sic] shall be deprived of life, liberty or property without due process of law," and various others of a similar character. We lay it down as a rule that no Government can do anything directly repugnant to the principles of natural justice and of the social compact. It would be totally subversive of all the purposes for which government is instituted.

No republican, the report concluded, would for a minute tolerate such things as ex post facto punishment or destruction of private contracts. Justice Chase's celebrated dictum in *Calder v. Bull*, the just

---

abolitionists. See Rep. Slade of Vermont, 12 Cong. Deb. col. 2042 (1835); Weld, Power of Congress Over the District of Columbia (1838).

187 It would be hard to find clearer evidence of the costs of divorcing legal and constitutional from general history than that in all the speculation regarding the precedents and influences responsible for Taney's reliance on the due process clause, no one seems to have called attention to this legislative precedent. So completely has the case method dominated constitutional history and law review research that it may be worth noting that when the Dred Scott decision confronted the North in the late Fifties with a judicial restatement and implementation of the vested rights–due process–no containment premises of the Pinckney Report the sectional rift was complete and the electorate at large was forced to make the same decisions regarding slavery's permanency and right to expand unchallenged which had driven the original abolitionists to embark upon political action in the late thirties and forties.

188 See note 186 *supra*.

189 H. R. Rep. No. 691, 24th Cong., 1st Sess. (1836).

compensation clause, the declared purposes of the Preamble: all were cited as barriers to abolition whether in the capital or territories.

The significance of the Pinckney report can scarcely be exaggerated. Avowedly conciliatory, drafted by unionists rather than nullifiers, and hence damned for its moderation by Calhoun and his disciples,[190] it revealed all the more clearly the nature of the approaching impasse. The South was unalterably opposed to containment of slavery; yet such containment had motivated abolitionism from the beginning. Emancipation in the District was viewed as an intolerable prospect—mortally feared as a precedent—yet precisely such a precedent constituted the hope and the saving method of gradualism. Tactically, moral suasion rested on a fair hearing and on the capacity to communicate and proselytize; yet already barriers were virtually insurmountable. Nothing reveals this more clearly than the stand on "incendiary abolitionist propaganda" taken simultaneously in December, 1835, by Governor McDuffie and President Jackson.

Lashing out at attacks of "wicked monsters and deluded lunatics" whose "inflammable and incendiary pamphlets" were "calculated to seduce our slaves and excite them to insurrection and massacre," the South Carolina Governor[191] stated:

> [it is my] deliberate opinion that laws of every community should punish this species of interference by death without benefit of clergy, regarding the authors as enemies of the human race. . . . For the institution of domestic slavery we hold ourselves responsible only to God, and it is utterly incompatible with the dignity and safety of the state to permit any foreign authority to question our right to maintain it. No human institution . . . is more manifestly consistent with the will of God . . . . Domestic slavery . . . is the cornerstone of our Republican institutions. [Two peremptory demands, therefore, must be made and entertained. First there must be forthcoming from each of the other states] a disclaimer by its legislature of the existence of any rightful power, either in such States or in the United States, . . . to interfere in any manner whatever with the institution of slavery in South Carolina; [second the] immediate passage of penal laws by such legislatures denouncing against the incendiaries of whom we complain, such punishments as will speedily and forever suppress their machinations against our peace and safety.

In his message[192] to Congress two days after McDuffie's statement,

---

[190] WILTSIE, *op. cit. supra* note 184, c. 20, esp. pp. 283–6.
[191] Reprinted Philanthropist, Jan. 1, 1836, p. 1, col. 1–4.
[192] 3 RICHARDSON, MESSAGES AND PAPERS OF THE PRESIDENTS 175–6 (Govt. ed. 1896).

the President urged federal action in the same field. Bitter over "wicked," "unconstitutional" attempts to "circulate through the mails inflammatory appeals addressed to the passions of the slaves," "calculated to . . . produce all the horrors of servile war," he called on Congress for drastic penal legislation.

What such proposals meant, in abolitionist eyes, was that in addition to being refused a hearing and being denied the right—or as they conceived it, the Christian duty—to work for an end to slavery by constitutional means, they now were confronted with demands that both state and federal power be marshalled against their movement. To them this meant a choking off of discussion and a permanent freezing of a barbarous, detested institution into American life.

That zealots and philanthropists who counted themselves "free moral agents," who thrilled at thoughts of the Quaker and British examples, and who had been fired by Weld's idealism and sensational early success, ever should fail to meet such a challenge was unthinkable. The paradox of slavery "sheltered under the wings of our national eagle, . . . republican law its protector, republican equality its advocate, republican morality its patron, freemen its bodyguard," Weld's irony already had exploited in countless revivals. To slavery's annihilation of "the sacred and eternal distinction between a person and a thing . . . a distinction created by God [and] crowned with glory and honor in the attributes of intelligence, morality, accountability and immortal existence"[193] . . . now was added this ultimate error: repudiation of reason itself. God had enjoined men to probe and test institutions. American government in particular rested on the right and duty of free discussion.[194]

The momentous consequences of this proscription of discussion and cloture of persuasion in the South, the mobbings and beatings in the North, and the hurried erection of barriers designed to make slavery constitutionally impregnable in federal territory were a gradual yet virtually complete reorientation of the abolitionist movement.[195] This reorientation, greatly accelerated by the Pinckney Report, was marked by a shift from an overwhelming faith in moral suasion to a reluctant resort to political action, from efforts to convince Americans of the expediency and justice of freeing their slaves,

---

[193] The two quotations are from the Declaration of Sentiments drafted by Weld for the Ohio Anti Slavery Convention, April, 1835. See *supra* note 60, at 8–9.

[194] See Rhode Island PROCEEDINGS, *op. cit. supra* note 152, at 68–69, for a well-documented abolitionist statement on this point.

[195] DUMOND, *op. cit. supra* note 51, esp. cc. 5–6; T. C. SMITH, THE LIBERTY AND FREE SOIL PARTIES IN THE NORTHWEST (1897); KOOKER, GENESIS OF THE LIBERTY PARTY (1949 paper to be published); NYE, *op. cit. supra* note 52.

to a search for constitutional power to free them, from an evangelical drive for converts at the state and local levels where slavery and the race problem might slowly have yielded to progressive solutions, to an ever-deepening sectional struggle.[196]

These tendencies may be traced today in the pages of the Weld-Grimke and Birney letters, in a vast pamphlet literature, in annual reports of the state and national societies,[197] but most satisfactorily in the columns of Birney's *Philanthropist*. Calhoun and "positive good" theorists had fashioned a constitutional system which promised absolute protection for slavery and which ignored the constitutional reference to slaves as "persons," referring to them whenever possible as "property." These theorists also employed the "compact" and "compromises" of 1787 as a higher-law, extra-constitutional device which removed slavery from the reach not merely of state and federal legislatures but from adverse discussion and criticism.

Birney and his colleagues now formulated a counter system, one which exalted liberty and exploited the Fathers' use of "Persons." Denying all limiting force to the "compact" or "compromises," this group hailed the spirit of the Declaration, of the Constitution, and American institutions generally. They seized on the leading provisions of the state and Federal Bills of Rights as affirmative guarantees of the freedom of the slaves.

This second body of theory was a cooperative, evolutionary product, evolved defensively—or counter-defensively—in relation to definite needs and pressures.[198] Birney played a central role in its development. Lawyer, editor, publicist, he was not, like Calhoun, a profound or an original political theorist, but rather an assimilator, a systematizer. Though his personal contributions were substantial—even distinctive—and have too long been mistakenly credited to Gid-

---

[196] *Cf.* CRAVEN, THE COMING OF THE CIVIL WAR (1943); NEVINS, ORDEAL OF THE UNION (1947).

[197] Read straight through, the six ANNUAL PROC. AND REP. OF AMERICAN ANTISLAVERY SOCIETY (1833–1839) and the five ANNIVERSARY PROC. OF THE OHIO ANTISLAVERY SOCIETY (1836–1840) reveal the shift from confident evangelism to determined self defense and political action. Not until after the Pinckney Report (*supra* note 189), the "Gags" denying antislavery petitions, and the refusal of the South to countenance discussion of the issue, does one find serious interest in political movements and tactics. The THIRD ANNUAL REPORT OF THE A.A.S.S. (May 10, 1836) signed by Elizur Wright is thus the turning point and a catalog of the factors that had reoriented opinion. By the SIXTH ANNUAL REPORT OF THE A.A.S.S. (1839), the "imperative necessity of political action" caused Wright to devote much of his space to convincing the still hesitant and divided membership.

[198] For what might be termed a first draft, prepared at white heat in February, 1836, in answer to the Southern Congressional arguments that were soon to be cast into the Pinckney Report (*supra* note 189), see the *Report on the Constitution in Rhode Island*, PROCEEDINGS, *op. cit. supra* note 152, at 68–76 (1836).

dings and Chase,[199] they were essentially those of synthesis and restatement. A born conciliator who abhorred violence and radicalism as deeply as he loved the South, a moderate man both by temperament and conviction, he integrated the argument, kept it focused on vital issues, and served as a forensic quartermaster-general for the entire movement.

Birney's first objective was to gain abolitionists a hearing. Regarding himself as strategically placed between the crusading revivalists and the militant "positive good" advocates bent on insulating the South, he undertook in his first publications to answer objections. He quoted from the Society's Constitution and Declaration to show that abolitionism was not "incendiary," "revolutionary," nor "treasonable." It was not at war with the federal compact. Its advocates were committed solely to moral suasion; they repudiated violence and addressed their appeals exclusively to whites and slaveholders, never to the illiterate bondsmen.[200] President Jackson's message on the mails,[201] the great speeches of Calhoun[202] demanding immediate suppression of agitation and propaganda, the similar speeches of McDuffie,[203] Pickens,[204] and others[205]—all were reported at length and answered with respect. Sometimes these answers took the form of appended footnotes—sometimes "leaders" upholding successively the right of "Free Discussion,"[206] "The Right to Petition Congress"[207] and "The Power of Congress over the District of Columbia."[208]

The dominant theme was the right to discuss, to associate, to proselytize. Americans were morally bound as a nation to end slavery. "When we were in our utmost need," reminded Birney, "straining, not only to produce united action among ourselves, but for the good opinion and sympathy of the world, we proclaimed as a truth fundamental to all governments, *'that all men are created equal*, and pos-

---

[199] McLaughlin, Constitutional History of the U.S. 493, by implication credits Giddings with formulation of the "Municipal law theory" of slavery in the Creole resolutions of March, 1842, but these resolutions were in fact worked out using ideas developed by Birney in 1836–37. Barnes, *op. cit. supra* note 35, at 184. For Chase's indebtedness to Birney, see Hart, Salmon P. Chase 51–52 (1899). Birney received his legal training in the Philadelphia office of the reporter and statesman, A. J. Dallas, father of his Princeton classmate, G. M. Dallas.

[200] Philanthropist, Jan. 1, 1836.
[201] *Id.*, Jan. 8, 1836, p. 3, col. 5.
[202] *Id.*, Mar. 4, 1836.
[203] *Id.*, Jan. 1, 1836, p. 1, col. 1.
[204] *Id.*, Feb. 19, 1836, p. 1.
[205] *Id.*, Jan. 8, 1836, p. 2.
[206] *Id.*, Jan. 15, 1836, p. 2, col. 5; p. 3, col. 2.
[207] *Id.*, Jan. 22, 1836, p. 3, col. 1–2.
[208] *Id.*, Feb. 12, 1836, p. 2.

sess rights that are inalienable, to their *lives*, their *liberty*, and the *pursuit of happiness.*' " Yet, "this great truth" now was often dismissed as a "rhetorical flourish"; the "obvious meaning" of "those great conservatives of our government, freedom of speech and of the press," was explained away; persistent attempts even were made to gain for slavery "the peculiar favoritism of the Constitution."[209]

Under the leadership of two distinguished members of the Cincinnati bar, Judge John C. Wright and Professor Timothy Walker,[210] that city's men of property and standing recently had done much to strengthen this proslavery stand. Failing to dissuade Birney from continuing the *Philanthropist*, they prepared in January, 1836, an elaborate *Preamble and Resolutions*. The essence of this appeal was that "after a full and thorough discussion [in 1787] the compact of the Union was consummated leaving the slave states the full discretion of settling the momentous question in their own way, and in their own good time; the implied guarantee was promulgated, that slave property shall be held sacred by the Constitution and protected by the laws." Slavery must be tolerated, therefore, even if disapproved, and all agitation on the subject should cease.[211]

It was this acceptance of Southern theory that Birney did his utmost to answer. Obliged to remarshal his arguments, he addressed a series of ten articles to Judge Wright[212] in the course of which he rejected both the *Preamble's* premises and conclusion. Epitomized in his own words, his major premises were:

1. That the right to *publish opinions*—of which *speaking, writing, and printing* are but *modes*—is a natural right—derived from our Creator—belonging to us as *men*—of which no human authority can justly deprive us.
2. That wrongs growing out of the *abuse* of the right were to be restrained, as other wrongs—by the *certainty of punishment*—but, that the *right* to publish opinions was not to be subjected to *previous* restraint, from fear that it might become a wrong. . . .

---

[209] Philanthropist, Jan. 1, 1836, p. 2, col. 5.

[210] The growth of antislavery sentiment, and Birney's pioneering role therein, are evident in the fact that by 1846 Professor Walker, author of An Introduction to American Law (1837) and for years editor of the Western Law Journal, apparently accepted many of Birney's views. See editorial comment on Chase's argument before the U.S. Supreme Court in the case of Jones v. Van Zandt, 46 U.S. 215 (1846), in 4 West. L. J. 321–328 (1846).

[211] Philanthropist, Feb. 19, 1836, p. 2, col. 5.

[212] The series appeared Feb. 19 to Apr. 22, 1836, inclusive, with good epitomes on Mar. 4, 1836, and April 22, 1836.

3. That the Constitution of the United States does not by any express provision "acknowledge" the *right* of Southern slaveholders to enslave their colored brethren any more than it acknowledges the right of a foreign despot . . . to oppress his subjects . . . .²¹³

The constitutional document itself, Birney contended, actually was silent on slavery. The Fathers, like the revolutionary generation as a whole, reprobated the institution, refused even to name it, anticipated and welcomed its early decline and death. This was evidenced by the express grant of power to Congress to abolish the African slave trade after 1808. Neither convention debates on the abominations of that traffic nor the text or purpose of either the fugitive slave clause or the clause apportioning representation and direct taxes implied recognition or approval, much less a sanction or guarantee. "The Constitution of the U.S.," Birney insisted in language which soon would be paraphrased by his friend, Henry Clay, "recognizes as *property* what the several *states* recognize as property. It *guarantees* no species of property *within the states*—because the state laws are entirely sufficient for this purpose."²¹⁴ In this brief passage appears the gist of Birney's municipal law theory of slavery later popularized by Giddings and Chase.

The significance of its appearance in an argument primarily devoted to the defense of the rights of discussion and persuasion is not to be overlooked, nor is the fact that Birney's original premise was not so much that the Constitution was antislavery or even neutral as simply that it was not proslavery. Quite as ready as Calhoun to base his theory on the local law, Birney insisted that the South stand on the platform it had erected. If slave "property" existed solely by reason of state laws, it enjoyed no special federal constitutional favor. Even so far as the District of Columbia was concerned, slaves were precisely the same as houses or town lots—"all might be taken on certain conditions for the public benefit." The expediency and justice of the institution were everywhere a legitimate subject for discussion. The absolute constitutional protection claimed by Pickens for slave property, Birney stressed, was equally applicable to the slave trade. "Did the South mean to employ the compact to deny expressly granted powers?" In Birney's view there had been neither "compacts" nor "compromises" in 1787—merely an accommodation of interests dictated by patriotism and by the need and desire for union. Yet even had there been such a compact, would it have

---

213 *Philanthropist*, Mar. 4, 1836, p. 2.
214 *Id.*, Feb. 19, 1836, p. 2, col. 1.

meant, he asked, that later generations, "suffering under the arrangement, might never open their mouths against it" nor seek to moderate it by appeals to patriotism and religion? "Does it violate a bargain founded and continued in injustice, to endeavor to persuade those who have it in their power to release us from it, to do so?" The very "persuasion resorted to" was a "continual acknowledgment of the validity of the contract." And since emancipation would result in Congressional representation of all, rather than merely three-fifths of the slaves, could it be maintained that this was an infringement?[215]

More and more, the early Biblical and religious appeals with their emphasis on the sin of slavery were supplemented by those grounded in ethics and history. The revolutionary natural rights creed of the Declaration, the universality of guarantees of the state Bills of Rights, the Signers' and the Fathers' known aversion to slavery, the "color blindedness" of the Articles of Confederation, the outright prohibition of slavery in the territories by the Northwest Ordinance, and above all, the silence, the euphemisms, the circumlocutions of the Constitution—these were the recurrent and expanding points.

As Birney labored to put in more finished form his own ethical interpretations of national origins and ideals, he reprinted the *Expostulation to Congress* which the Quaker philanthropist, Warner Mifflin, had prepared in 1793.[216] He published Whittier's eloquent letter[217] to Governor Edward Everett in which the fact is stressed that Dr. Franklin, a Father as well as Signer, had, as his last public act in 1790, sponsored a petition calling on Congress to abolish slavery in the federal district. He ran columns of quotations from the antislavery writings and speeches of other leaders,[218] producing, for example, the speech in which Senator Prentiss[219] of Vermont disposed of Pickens' due process argument. He noted that in St. Louis, one F. W. Risque, an antislavery lawyer, had convinced the county court of the unconstitutionality of a recent Missouri statute which attempted to exclude free Negroes from residence.[220] He analyzed the legal disabilities of the slaves and traced them to a single source —"the *assumed* right of property" in man.[221]

Over against this *assumed* right of the slaveholder was the slaves' *natural* right to himself and his "property." Birney and the aboli-

---
[215] Philanthropist, Feb. 19, 1836, p. 2, col. 1.
[216] *Id.*, Feb. 5, 1836.
[217] *Id.*, Mar. 18, 1836.
[218] *Id.*, p. 4, col. 5.
[219] *Id.*, Apr. 29, 1836, p. 1, col. 1.
[220] *Id.*, Mar. 4, 1836, p. 3, col. 5.
[221] Philanthropist, July 1, 1836, p. 2, col. 4.

tionists denied validity of the higher law to the defense of property in slaves, yet applied it rigorously to the defense of liberty and to the rights of slaves to property. Strict empiricists as regards slave property under the Fifth Amendment, they were metaphysical in other respects, even though in these arguments they ignored the potentialities of the constitutional text and still relied only on a turning of the tables. The tendency in this respect is best shown in a brief editorial, "The Right of Property," which Birney reprinted in March.[222] This fundamental right, harped on by the opposition as the basis for its claim that Congress lacked power to abolish slavery in the capital, was at the bottom, said the editorialist, the main reason why Congress should and could absolutely abolish it there. Abolitionists too held that Congress should not disturb, that it should protect the right of private property.

> Having exclusive legislation over the District of Columbia, [Congress] should see that every person therein enjoys the *right of property*. This is the very reason why Congress should abolish slavery. The right of property is sacred. It belongs to every man. It was not given to us by government; and it cannot, justly, be taken away by government. No compact, which takes away this right, can, so far as it does so, be of any binding force. Now, shall Congress continue to deprive one-fifth part of the people of the District of their property because Virginia and Maryland did so before? No. Congress is bound immediately to protect every person in the district, in the enjoyment of everything that is his.[223]

In addition to the antithetical conceptions of "property" and the presumed overriding natural right of self-ownership, we here observe two things. One is the hint of an affirmative obligation resting on Congress and the federal government to extend the protection of the law over all persons irrespective of race and color. The other is that this concept of an affirmative duty (which obviously is linked with an inherent as well as an expressly granted constitutional power for its effectuation) was at the start asserted mainly with reference to the desirability and justice of abolition as a policy; specifically, it was a counter to the claim that Congress lacked power to abolish slavery even in the territories over which it had "exclusive jurisdiction." This doctrine of affirmative obligation itself was capable of much more, and it might (and indeed soon would) be employed against slavery in the States[224] and to the destruction or

---

[222] *Id.*, Mar. 4, 1836, p. 3, col. 4, from HUMAN RIGHTS, an abolitionist periodical.
[223] *Ibid.*
[224] Pioneering this radical theory was Alvan Stewart, a Utica lawyer. Perceiving

disregard of state lines. This must not obscure the fact that its original purpose was to secure the rights of physical liberty and self-proprietorship.

Thus it may be said that abolitionist theory, though grounded in the higher law, began conventionally in other respects and was particularly scrupulous in its regard for the state-federal division of powers. It was the sweeping universal character of its higher law premises combined with the tactical necessity of defending federal power over the District and territories that eventually promoted aberrant and eccentric theories. Once underway, however, movement in these directions was rapid, irresistible, almost polar; for granting the respective premises, the natural rights creed served equally well either abolitionists or opponents. This ambivalence contributed toward extremism and stimulated counter-developments.

Having paid his respects in the Wright series to the timorous groups who would suppress discussion of slavery in hope of placating the South, Birney immediately recovered the ground. In a third series, significantly entitled "Harmony of Measures of Abolition with International Law and the Federal Constitution,"[225] he again contended, and still by way of defending abolitionism rather than directly attacking slavery, that there had been no guarantee of the institution either in the Convention debates or in the Constitution proper. Records of the Convention and those of the ratifying conventions revealed no such purpose. The primary object had been union. Granted the Constitution conferred no power on Congress or the free states to interfere with slavery, "may we not . . . strive to convince slaveholders . . . to plead with them . . . employ moral power?"[226]

These increasingly secular yet primitive constitutional arguments soon found expression in hundreds of resolutions and declarations. At the end of every revival converts formed new societies. On such occasions they assumed their right and their duty "as American citizens"—"as enjoyers of the great instrument which guarantees our freedom"—to discuss, petition, and proselytize.

---

the possibilities of the due process clause as used by proslaveryites in the Pinckney Report; and by Birney in answering Judge Lewis (*infra* note 251 *et seq.*), Stewart in the summer of 1837 compounded an argument that at the time of its delivery at the New York State Anti Slavery Convention, Sept. 20, 1837, dismayed Birney and conservatives (1 BIRNEY LETTERS 457-9); ultimately Birney himself assumed a similar stand, see note 54 *supra*. Stewart's argument is printed in 2 FRIEND OF MAN, Oct. 18, 1837; but was omitted by Marsh, editor of his WRITINGS AND SPEECHES (1860).

[225] Philanthropist. Apr. 29, May 6, May 13, 1836, p. 2.

[226] *Id.*, May 6, 1836, p. 2, col. 1-4. Comparison with the Feb. 19, 1836, article (*supra* notes 211, 215, 216) reveals Birney's intensive study and craftsmanship.

> [We believe it] . . . our duty [declared citizens of Willoughby, Ohio] to discuss any subject . . . important to the welfare of the nation—that the Constitution of the United States protects us in so doing—that the distinction between the majority and the minority exists in the good judgment of the people rather than physical force—that republican sentiments ought to triumph over the enfuriated feelings of a mob. . . .[227]

It was in this manner that God-given, inalienable natural rights were constitutionally assimilated. "The right of free discussion," resolved the Beaver County (Pennsylvania) Anti-slavery Society in March, 1836, "is the birthright of man—guaranteed to every American citizen by the Constitution of his country—consequently it cannot be taken from him, or abridged, by any power whatsoever."[228]

By sheer repetition, and by the processes of winnowing, elaboration, and restatement, certain doctrinal forms began to fix themselves in the public mind. One of the most popular and significant of these employed the purposes of the Preamble, often in combination with the comity clause. Thus in June, 1836, citizens and shipping interests in Massachusetts, protesting against the colored seamen's laws of Georgia and the Carolinas, carried their case to the state legislature in an appeal which Birney published.[229] Such laws, ran the petition, by their presumptions against freedom and in favor of slavery, operated to

> deprive a portion of our fellow citizens of this commonwealth of the privileges and rights guaranteed to them by our federal Constitution . . . and even to the deprivation of their liberty for life —in direct violation of the avowed purposes of our union— which were "to establish justice, insure domestic tranquillity, provide for the common defense, promote the general welfare, and secure the blessings of liberty for ourselves and our posterity"

---

[227] Philanthropist, Mar. 11, 1836, p. 4, col. 1-2, reporting the organization of a new society of 32 members organized by John W. Alvord, a "Lane Rebel" and one of the original revivalists (see 1 BIRNEY LETTERS 254, 283, 292); note also the report in the Philanthropist, Mar. 11, 1836, p. 3, col. 3, of organization of three new Societies of 70-80 members apiece in Medina County, two in Lorain, and two in Harrison. See notes 131, 142 *supra* and notes 230, 232, 246, *infra*.

[228] Philanthropist, Mar. 4, 1836, p. 4, col. 2; see also the Beaver Falls resolutions, *id.*, Dec. 19, 1837, p. 2, col. 3, characteristically arraigning the Alton mob for robbing Lovejoy of "rights and privileges purchased by the blood of our revolutionary forefathers and guaranteed by the charter of our freedom and the sacred bond of our national constitution." In the same number the Cambridge (Guernsey County) Society resolved that "as American citizens . . . we . . . regard (the right of free discussion) as secured to us by . . . the United States Constitution and as dearer . . . than life itself."

[229] *Id.*, Apr. 8, 1836, p. 3, col. 4-5.

and in utter disregard of that article ... which explicitly provides that "the citizens of each state shall be entitled to the privileges and immunities of citizens in the several states."

Equally suggestive of the broadening argument were those resolutions which transferred the attack to slavery itself. They employed the same weapons and occasionally presumed that the Constitution, by its binding force, not only embraced but secured certain minimal rights of national citizenship. Most striking in this regard were the resolutions adopted at Elyria on July 4, 1836, by the Lorain County Anti-slavery Society at a meeting attended by the Oberlin faculty and at which Philemon Bliss was elected recording secretary:[230]

> Resolved: That slavery, by interfering with the rights of conscience, and restraining a portion of their countrymen from the free exercise of religious privileges, is a gross violation, not only of the laws of God, but of the Constitution of the United States, and of every state in the Union.
>
> Resolved: That to deprive the laboring class of education and especially of reading the Bible, is a gross and high handed despotism, which ought not to be tolerated in a civilized, much less a Christian community.
>
> Resolved: That we regard the Union of these States as an invaluable blessing, and in our efforts to remove slavery, we are strongly influenced by a desire to secure its perpetuity; but that one of the most important benefits of this Union is utterly destroyed when the Constitution, which binds the States together, affords no protection to the lives of citizens out of the state in which they reside.
>
> Resolved: That the people of the United States are the source of the government, and that every citizen must be chargeable with the sin of slavery who does not make appropriate efforts to do it away.

That such resolutions were ideal media for evolving and disseminating a lay constitutional theory is now plain. As early as 1836, the distinctive doctrinal feature, though often unformulated, was a belief in a national citizenship which was superior to state and which embraced the broad fundamental guarantees of the Federal Bill of Rights. Rarely was anyone yet troubled by the fact that three years earlier, in *Barron v. Baltimore*,[231] the Supreme Court had held the

---

[230] *Philanthropist,* July 29, 1836, p. 2, col. 2. E. S. Hamlin, later congressman, (see notes 142 & 157 *supra*) was elected one of the managers of the Society. The Elyria Ohio Atlas, from which the article was reprinted, was a leading abolitionist paper.
[231] Barron v. Baltimore, 7 Pet. 464 (U.S. 1833).

provisions of the Bill of Rights to restrain only the federal government. The few who were aware of John Marshall's holding simply assumed that whatever might be the positive law, the states were morally bound by the first eight Amendments, particularly since nearly all the state constitutions contained even stronger guarantees of these basic freedoms.

The propulsive forces behind this rising nationalist doctrine were proscription and suppression. Colliding not only with each other, but with the classic dilemma of democratic federalism, abolitionists and proslaveryites impaled themselves on opposite horns. That is, national power to protect dissident and reformist groups was militantly set off against local refusal to tolerate them. National coercion was an assumed antidote for state remissness and recalcitrance just as, on the opposite side, nullification and secession had first been advanced as barriers against congressional interference. As a weak and unpopular minority alarmed at threatened breakdown of local protection, abolitionists turned instinctively toward a federal power which would secure the primary rights of petition, speech, and press, even in the face of hostile local opinion. The proslavery interests, on the other hand, were fearful of the results of free discussion and equally militant. They first invoked a drastic intellectual embargo as a measure of sectional security and then demanded its extraterritorial enforcement notwithstanding the strong and positive state constitutional guarantees of the rights of communication in the South as well as in the North.[232]

In an age firmly attached to localism, abolitionists thus emerged as advocates of an increasingly nationalistic theory. This theory they fashioned from familiar clauses also employed by their opponents. The measure of their accomplishment is that this lay theory, Websterian in character and not yet fully articulating an "American" citizenship, overcame its initial handicaps within thirty years.

How much of this eventual success abolitionists owed to their enemies is indicated in an open letter addressed to Governor McDuffie in March, 1836. The letter was written by Reverend John Graham of the famed Chillicothe Presbytery. No abolitionist, Graham was an avowed admirer of McDuffie in the days when the Governor, like Calhoun, had been one of South Carolina's ultra-nationalists. He wrote as a moderate, keenly sensitive of the South's problems.

---

[232] This sharp and growing cleavage is clearly evident in a column of resolutions quoted from many adopted by the societies July 4, 1837, Philanthropist July 21, 1837, p. 3, col. 1-2. Note those of Lorain County offered by Philomen Bliss, of Medina County offered by Charles Olcott, and those from the *Cadiz Society*.

Yet he was alarmed at implications of the new "positive good" doctrines and dismayed at the ferocity of McDuffie's attacks. Particularly repugnant were the Governor's statements approving of mob action:

> Until very lately, [he remonstrated][233] our government has been considered a government of laws. The constitution of the United States, and that of each particular state, provides that the trial by jury shall remain inviolate; thus securing to every citizen charged with crime, an impartial trial before a competent legal tribunal. And accordingly, all attempts, by individuals or combinations, to anticipate or supersede the *regular legal* administration of justice, have till lately, always been regarded and treated as offenses against the state . . . this important principle lies at the foundation of the citizen's security in his person and his rights . . . . No emergency whatever, can require or justify a departure from it. . . . Whenever, therefore, any government shall make a practice of delivering over, in any case whatever, to the management of lawless and infuriated mobs, not only the "property," but the personal safety and lives, of those it should protect; no great political sagacity is required to see that its own days are . . . numbered. The connivance . . . which the numerous disgraceful assemblies and proceedings of this description have experienced, for some months past, wherever they have occurred, from the constituted authorities . . . is calculated to cause every intelligent lover of our free institutions to tremble for their permanence and stability.

It soon was evident that the mounting clamor for suppression of abolitionism, violence, and intimidation as well as the indiscreet talk condoning mob action or official conduct conniving in it constituted effective forms of propaganda.[234] Turning to excellent account by the Birney group were a whole series of episodes: the breakup of the New York Anti-Slavery Society convention at Utica by a mob headed by a sheriff and a congressman;[235] similar, equally futile attempts at suppression of Weld's revivals at Lockport;[236] repeated

---

[233] Philanthropist, Apr. 15 and 22, 1836, p. 1. The author's name does not appear in GALBRAITH, *op. cit. supra* note 129, but apparently he had at one time lived in the South, perhaps in Carolina.

[234] In general, see NYE, FETTERED FREEDOM (1949) *passim*.

[235] Philanthropist, Jan. 8, 1836; see [THOMAS] DEFENSOR (pseud.), ENEMIES OF THE CONSTITUTION DISCOVERED (1835) for a widely circulated report and exploitation of this incident.

[236] *Id.*, May 13, 1836, p. 3, c. 2. Weld organized a Society of 438 members in Lockport after this experience, and the editorial comment of the anti-immediatist Lockport editor, quoted by Birney, well reveals the boomerang effects of suppression on minds further perturbed by the problems of the condonation and connivance of local officials.

efforts by the mayor and businessmen of Cincinnati to force the *Philanthropist's* suspension, and the destruction of three of its presses within seven months;[237] the pulpit arrest of Reverend George Storrs, an antislavery agent, in New Hampshire, and his conviction and imprisonment as a "common brawler";[238] the charge of the notorious Judge Lawless advising a St. Louis grand jury to return indictments against the lynchers of a crazed free Negro only if the lynching were found to have been "the act of the few" rather than a "multitude seized by metaphysical phrenzy";[239] the persecution and banishment from Marian County, Missouri, of Dr. David Nelson, a distinguished abolitionist educator and minister;[240] the scourging of Amos Dresser, a Lane Rebel, in the public square at Nashville;[241] the tarring, feathering, and expulsion from Hillsborough, Georgia, on suspicions of abolitionism of A. W. Kitchell, a licensed minister and prominent New Jerseyan;[242] the martyrdom of Elijah Lovejoy, Presbyterian minister and editor, killed with several of his supporters at Alton, Illinois, while defending his press against the vigilantes who previously had destroyed two other presses.[243]

Pervading the defenses and propaganda based on these incidents were two themes. The first outlined the growing menace of slavery to free institutions. It reiterated the dangers inherent, not only in proscription and suppression, but in the corollary of the "positive good" doctrine which held that governments might preserve and protect slavery but never limit or abolish it. The other developed the ideas, implicit and partially formulated in the Graham-McDuffie letter, of an imminent breakdown of constitutional guarantees and a hiatus in the existing scheme of protection. In the North

---

[237] Philanthropist, Jan. 29, 1836; July 15, 1836. See [BIRNEY], NARRATIVE OF THE LATE RIOTOUS PROCEEDINGS AGAINST THE LIBERTY OF THE PRESS IN CINCINNATI (1836).

[238] Philanthropist, Apr. 29, 1836, p. 4, for incident; *id.*, June 24, 1836, p. 4, col. 5, for resolutions denouncing this "iniquitous perversion of law," "a base prostitution of the forms of judicial proceedings."

[239] *Id.*, June 17, 1836, p. 3, col. 4, headed "Supremacy of Laws" and reprinted from the Illinois Patriot.

[240] *Id.*, July 29, 1836, p. 4, cols. 1–4. On Dr. Nelson, a one-time Doak student, see 1 BIRNEY LETTERS 328.

[241] See NARRATIVE OF AMOS DRESSER (1836) for full account.

[242] Philanthropist, July 8, 1836, p. 3, col. 1, *A Dastard Outrage*, reprinted from Cincinnati Gazette, Charles Hammond's paper; *id.*, July 22, 1836, p. 2, col. 3.

[243] Philanthropist, Nov. 28, 1837, p. 2; *id.*, Dec. 12, 19, 1837, *passim*, for resolutions and editorials denouncing the perpetrators. See also Edward Beecher's distinguished NARRATIVE OF THE RIOTS AT ALTON: IN CONNECTION WITH THE DEATH OF REV. ELIJAH P. LOVEJOY (1838), an exalted defense of civil liberty which made denial of protection of law and destruction of freedom of inquiry the focal point and means of arousing thousands.

as well as the South, hostile sentiments made it increasingly clear that Bills of Rights were not self-executing but rested on local enforcement. Hence arose the anomaly that the great natural and fundamental rights of conscience, inquiry, and communication, secured *on paper* in almost every constitution, nevertheless were denied and abridged daily for want of sanctions!

Thus abolitionists groped toward the inevitable, a concept of a defect of governmental powers.[244] The premises of their natural rights philosophy, with its dualism and confusion of abstract moral rights with enforceable constitutional ones, made this a tortuous enterprise. All men by nature "possessed" these indispensable rights; all constitutions "declared" and "secured" them; it was the bounden duty of all governments "created for purposes of protection" to safeguard and enforce them. Yet the hard fact was that state and local governments were flagrantly, increasingly derelict. Nothing, southerners argued, could be done about it![245]

Challenged in this manner, Birney and his aides shifted their ground. Gradually and unconsciously, they advanced from the old position that the Federal Constitution was neutral—"or at least not proslavery"—to the more exposed, yet tactically superior stand that

[244] Commented an abolitionist editor on the expulsion of Dr. Nelson, "If American citizens against whom no breach of the law can be proven, are to be hunted down as . . . this good man, then the times [are] far more deplorable than . . . in Rome in the days of the Caesars, when the circumstances of being a Roman citizen was an ample protection against assault without a trial. The question here involved, is not in regard to abolition, but to the rights of American citizens." Philanthropist, July 29, 1836. The same theme was sounded by the Circleville (Ohio) Herald after Lovejoy's murder: "The question is not now whether the doctrine of abolition is right or the institution of slavery wrong. . . . It is whether the laws are sufficient for protection of the citizens," Philanthropist, Dec. 12, 1837, p. 2, col. 2. See NYE, FETTERED FREEDOM (1949). Leaders like Channing, Emerson, Sumner and Chase, who had little sympathy for immediatism, were drawn into the crusade via defense of civil liberties.

[245] Resolved the Vermont Anti Slavery Society, October 25, 1837, at a meeting at Montpelier at which Birney was present and spoke: "Resolved, 3d That the popular outrage, committed on the persons of northern citizens, while visiting the South relying upon the protection of Constitutions and Laws—outrages which have passed unnoticed and unpunished, either from a criminal disregard of rights or from a want of power in the proper tribunals in the authorities of the districts in which they have been [perpetrated?]; *in fine*, that the entire prostration by the lawless of the slave states of all the barriers raised by the Constitution of the General Government for the personal security of the citizens of all the states are *on their part*, a virtual, and tend to a formal dissolution of the Union." Philanthropist, Dec. 5, 1837, p. 4, col. 2. See also the resolutions of the Green Township Anti Slavery Society, Harrison County, attacking Mayor Krum and authorities of Alton for "neglecting to defend the person and property" of Lovejoy and declaring them guilty of "aiding and abetting murder and arson." "While slavery exists, our Government, free institutions and religious privileges are in eminent peril, and . . . no citizen has . . . security for life, liberty or property." Philanthropist, Dec. 19, 1837.

the document was antislavery. Constitutionalization of the natural rights argument proceeded at a much more rapid pace. No longer was the fight waged merely defensively in behalf of the right to proselytize, or counter-defensively to support sweeping federal powers over the District and territories; more and more it was fought offensively against slavery itself.

The lines of progression and transition in this regard are evident in a short leader entitled "Slavery Against the Constitution," which Birney reprinted in August.[246] "To discuss human rights," the editorialist began, "is unquestionably the privilege and duty of every human being, . . . established as such by the Constitution of the U[nited] States, and especially by the Bible, the magna charta of the church."

"That glorious republican document is not stained with the name of slavery, no distinctions of color, nor any descriptions designate a portion of the people as perpetual slaves. It calls them *persons, not things*. . . ." After restating Birney's own thesis that the "venerable framers" had left what they regarded as a moribund institution to wither and die, making only such limited concessions as "were indispensable to . . . Union," the writer moved to higher ground.

> Their primary object had been to secure life, liberty and property to each individual person . . . , colored . . . , as well as white. . . . The Constitution is at war with slavery. . . . The right of trial by jury, and that which embraces the privileges of an American citizen are at present, in the slave-holding states, absolutely worthless.

While antislavery papers and revivals echoed these arguments, Birney, renewing his attack on the Ohio Black Laws, made way for another advance. In a fourth series entitled "The Constitution of Ohio and Slavery,"[247] he once more recast the traditional arguments from silence and idealism, employing them now in combination with the Northwest Ordinance:

> It would not be just in the absence of all evidence, to presume that such men as formed the Constitution of the United States, when constructing a system of government for a portion of the country, which, it was intended should be forever 'free' and exempt from the curse of slavery, would frame it on principles

---

[246] Philanthropist, Aug. 5, 1836, p. 1, col. 1, from The Elyria Ohio Atlas. The article is signed "M." and perhaps by Rev. John Monteith (see note 129 *supra*), a close friend of Birney.

[247] Philanthropist, 1836, Oct. 28, p. 2, Nov. 25, p. 2, Dec. 9, p. 3.

directly at variance with those they already had acknowledged as *fundamental*.[248]

Examining the territorial and congressional legislation down to 1802, and finding repeated use of the terms "inhabitant" and "persons" in contexts which applied to free Negroes, Birney concluded that by the Ordinance of 1787 "all colored persons, except such as had been brought into the territory as slaves previously to its adoption, were placed in terms of entire equality as to political rights with all other persons." Such, moreover, except for a minor militia law, had been the practiced equality down to the time of the Ohio Convention of 1802. "In common with others possessing qualifications altogether unconnected with color," free Negroes had voted for members of the Constitutional Convention, had in fact been constituents of such members. Yet by the action of their representatives in that convention and by subsequent secondary action of Ohio legislatures, they had suffered loss of their highest political and civil rights.[249]

To Birney this was an anomalous and outrageous action of an agent against his principal and against his principles. It led him to launch into what is striking evidence, not merely of Birney's intellectual and professional acumen, but of the manner in which changing social and psychological attitudes toward race led abolitionists to anticipate modern constitutional principles. For what Birney here did was to formulate precisely the modern test of substantiality of purpose. He argued that by this rigorous test, race *per se* was an arbitrary standard by which to class citizens or to discriminate between them in the enjoyment of fundamental, natural, and constitutional rights.

The Ohio *Constitution*, Birney argues, in contradistinction to the various statutes enacted since, had taken from the Negroes no civil right but that of suffrage. Waiving all question of the Convention's original power to do this, he contended that the legislature might enforce this suffrage discrimination, but it might never go further and take away other rights merely on the grounds of color. Furthermore,

> Whatever act of the Legislature would be deemed an infringement of the constitutional rights of any class of white men, ought to be considered equally as an infringement of the same rights

---

[248] *Id.*, Oct. 28, 1836, p. 2, col. 2.
[249] Philanthropist, Dec. 9, 1836, p. 3, col. 4–5.

secured to the colored class, when specially directed against the latter. For they stand precisely on the same ground. If the legislature of Ohio should pass a law requiring a certain class of the citizens of South Carolina, distinguished by black eyes and black hair, . . . that on emigrating to this state for settlement, they should bring with them certificates, [register their names and provide surety bonds]—what would be thought by the freemen of Ohio, learned and unlearned, of the constitutionality of such enactment?

[These disabilities imposed upon Negroes were unconstitutional because there] is no principle or provision in the Constitution, to the maintenance or establishment of which they have an appropriate tendency; . . . because they are in . . . derogation of "Justice," because they nullify the blessings of "liberty" intended to be secured to all by the Constitution; because they destroy or materially affect rights that the state has constitutionally, declared "natural, inherent, and unalienable"; because they are totally inconsistent with "enjoying and defending life and liberty, with acquiring and possessing and pursuing and obtaining happiness and safety." . . . And because, further, [they are] inconsistent with the Constitution of the United States, which gives "to the citizens of each state all the privileges and immunities of citizens in the several states."[250]

It is clear that by December, 1836, the abolitionist argument was slowly recrystallizing around three major propositions:

First, the great natural and fundamental rights of life, liberty, and property, long deemed inherent and inalienable, were now held to be secured by *both* state and national constitutions.

Second, notwithstanding this double security, and in disregard of the obligation of governments to extend protection in return for allegiance, these rights were being violated with impunity both on national soil and in the states, (a) by the fact of slavery itself, (b) by mob action directed against those working for abolition, (c) by flagrant discriminations against free Negroes and mulattoes.

Third, race and color—"grades and shades"—whenever and wherever employed as criteria and determinants of fundamental rights, violated both the letter and spirit of American institutions; race *per se* was not only an ignoble standard; it was an irrational and unsubstantial one.

---

[250] Philanthropist, Dec. 9, 1836, p. 3, col. 4–5.

Still almost entirely unfaced were the problems of implementing this theory, of enforcing the claimed rights in a federal system, of finding some answer for the observed defects of power.

These, as matters unfolded, were the work of the new year. An extended debate which Birney carried on in the *Philanthropist* with Seth Lewis, a Louisiana district judge and planter,[251] helped bring the larger issues to focus. Lewis argued that the laws of the slave states authorized slaveholding, "that those laws are sanctioned and confirmed by the Constitution of the United States, giving to every slave owner a legal and constitutional right to the peaceable and undisturbed possession and use of his slaves," and "binding every man in the free states to respect those laws."[252]

Answering these propositions,[253] Birney restates his municipal law theory, inquiring Socratically: "Because the Constitution does not forbid slavery, when it has no rightful power over it, is it to be inferred that it sanctions it?"

He then rescrutinized the document, making the same rigorous use of the Federal Bill of Rights that he recently had made of Ohio's, and focused ultimately on the due process clause employed in Pinckney's Report:

> The Constitution contains provisions which, if literally carried out, would extinguish the entire system of slavery. It guarantees to every state in the union a republican form of government, Art. IV, Sec. 4th. A majority of the people of South Carolina are slaves; can she be said properly to have a republican form of government? It says, that "the right of the people to be secure in their *persons*, houses, papers and effects . . . against unreasonable searches and *seizures*, shall not be violated." Slaves, Sir, are men, constitute a portion of the people: Is that no "unreasonable seizure," by which the man is deprived of all his earnings [effects?] —by which in fact he is robbed of his own person? Is the perpetual privation of liberty "no unreasonable seizure"? Suppose this provision of the Constitution were literally and universally enforced; how long would it be before there would not be a single *slave* to mar the prospect of American liberty? Again, "*no* person shall be held to answer for a capital or otherwise infamous crime

---

[251] So identified by Birney in the Philanthropist, Sept. 1, 1837, p. 2; but referred to as "Judge L" throughout much of the series; apparently Lewis' first letters were submitted anonymously.

[252] Philanthropist, Jan. 13, 1837, p. 2.

[253] Philanthropist, Jan. 13, 1837, p. 2. Close study of Birney's footnotes in this number shows clearly how much the development of abolitionist theory owed to catch-as-catch-can debate.

unless on the presentment or indictment of a grand jury, except in cases arising in the land or naval forces, [sic] nor shall any person be compelled in any case to witness against himself; nor be deprived of life, liberty or property without due process of law." Art. V Amendments.

Are slaves ever honored with indictment by a grand jury? Are they never compelled "to witness against themselves"? never tortured until they lie against their own lives? never deprived of life without "due process of law"? By what "due process of law" is it, that two millions of "persons" are deprived every year of the millions of dollars produced by their labor? By what due process of law is it that 56,000 "persons," the annual increase of the slave population, are annually deprived of their "liberty"? Such questions may seem impertinent, to Mr. L., but when he shall feel that the slave is a "person," in very deed, and has rights, as inalienable as his own, he will acknowledge their propriety. Again "In all criminal prosecutions, the accused shall enjoy the right to a speedy and public trial, by an impartial jury . . . and to be informed of the nature and cause of the accusation; to be confronted with the witnesses against him; to have compulsory process for obtaining witnesses in his favor; and to have the assistance of Counsel for his defense." Art. VI of the Amendments. Take all the above provisions in connection with that clause under Art. VI, which declares that "This Constitution and the laws of the United States which shall be made in pursuance thereof" etc., "shall be the supreme law of the land, and the judges in every state shall be bound thereby, anything in the Constitution or laws of any state to the contrary notwithstanding"—and then carry them out to their full extent, and how long would it be ere slavery would be utterly prostrated? I do not say they were inserted with a specific view toward this end, but I do say, that so long as they shall stand, the Constitution of these U[nited] States will be a perpetual rebuke to the selfishness and injustice of the whole policy of the slaveholder. The provisions embody principles which are at entire enmity with the spirit and practice of slavery. How an instrument, containing such principles, can be tortured to express a *sanction* to slavery, I am yet to learn."[254]

Reassimilation of the old theory into the Bill of Rights now proceeded rapidly.[255] The various clauses *restraining* the powers of Con-

---

[254] Philanthropist, Jan. 13, 1837, p. 2. Birney continued his "Reply to Judge L" in the Jan. 20 and 27, 1837 numbers, and in the former demonstrated his forensic powers by brilliant caricature of the South's efforts to suppress discussion of slavery.

[255] Resolutions and petitions still were the chief media in evolving this system of constitutional shorthand. Similarity of the revivalists' lectures from place to place, their widespread circulation of the Philanthropist and printed tracts, Birney's own speaking tours all contributed to resulting stereotypes. The significance is apparent

gress began to be popularly regarded as *sources* of Congressional power. The initial premise in this regard was that the provisions of the Bill of Rights were not *rights*, they were *guarantees*, and guarantees customarily presumed the intent and capacity, as well as the duty, to make them good.

An open letter to his Congressman from an unnamed abolitionist in Batavia[256] reveals the hold and spread and reach of these ideas:

> The very Constitution of the United States is attempted to be distorted and made an ally of domestic slavery. That Constitution was established, not by the *citizens* or *voters*, but by *"the people"* of the United States to secure the blessings of *liberty* and establish *justice*. The Union . . . was formed for the same great purposes, . . . yet we have been told that petitioning for *liberty* endangers this Union, that the partnership will be dissolved by extending to all the very right it was intended to secure.
>
> Slavery in the District of Columbia violates the most important and sacred principles of the Constitution . . . I speak not of the mere *letter*, but of the *principles* . . .—of the *rights* it guarantees, of the *form*, in which the guarantee is expressed. The 5th Amendment declares "no person shall be deprived of life, *liberty* or property without due process of law." This petition informs you free men in the District . . . have been first imprisoned, and then sold for their jail fees. [Suppose, he continued, this had happened to American seamen in a foreign port]. Would not Congress upon petition enquire into the fact and redress the wrong if it existed? Would not you, Sir, be one of the foremost in repelling the insult to our seamen and punishing the aggressor? Would you not consider it your *duty*—your *official* duty to do so? And yet you have no power to discriminate in the object of your protection—a colored sailor is entitled to the *protection* of his country's laws, and Constitution, and flag, and honor, as well as a white one,—he is as much entitled to that protection in Washington city beneath the flag of his country and while he reposes under the tower of the

in resolutions adopted Feb. 4, 1837, by the Anti Slavery Society of Cadiz (later to be Bingham's home town). "Resolved that while the advocates of emancipation are charged by slaveholders and their abettors, with endeavoring to destroy this Union, they themselves are the very men who are outraging it by destroying its basis, *viz*— the Constitution of the United States, which declares that 'no law shall be made abridging the liberty of speech or of the press' and also that 'the citizens of any one State, [sic] are entitled to all the privileges and immunities of citizens in the several States' and further that 'no person shall be deprived of life, liberty or property without due process of Law.'" Philanthropist. Mar. 10. 1837. p. 3, col. 4. See also resolutions adopted by a Pittsburgh, Pennsylvania meeting, *id.*, April 28, 1837, p. 4, col. 3, wherein the supremacy clause is used to bolster the first Amendment as a *"limitation"* on the States.

[256] Perhaps John Joliffe, a local antislavery lawyer, who was a close friend of Birney.

Capitol as he is at *Qualla Balloo* or Halifax, or anywhere on the face of the earth. And all should be protected with equal and exact justice, whether sailors or laborers—citizens or soldiers: if so, you are bound to enquire into the alleged abuses, and if they exist to redress them.

Quoting in order the Fourth and First Amendments, then the just compensation and the cruel and inhuman punishment clauses, the writer next contended that had the framers meant to exclude colored persons from the protection of these guarantees they would have done so in express terms. As the Amendments stood, they "repealed all former parts of the constitution inconsistent with their *principles and spirit.*"[257]

The subjects over which Congress have control may be divided into two kinds, one involves questions of policy or expediency—the other the preservation of the *rights* of the people and the integrity of the Constitution. Over the latter class of subjects you have *no discretion*. If one or more of the people be oppressed, as they owe you allegiance—you owe them protection. It is not a question of *expediency* but of *right*, and no consideration whatever can excuse you if all the means of redress in your power be not in good faith promptly adopted. You have no more *right* to lay a petition like this on the table . . . than a judge in open court has a *right* to treat with similar contempt a petition of *habeas corpus* when presented even by a slave—or by the friend of the slave. *Oppression* is alleged to exist, the sacred provisions of the Constitution have been and are now trampled underfoot—men entitled to your protection are . . . deprived of ALL *their rights* by mere brute force—their friends petition you for redress—for their protection. The same obligations that require a judge upon a petition for habeas corpus to issue the writ and inquire into the facts and do justice to the applicant without respect to his color or condition requires you to do so . . . . You are bound . . . to restore to him all his rights and place him like other persons under the protection of the Constitution of his country.[258]

Another letter, written by one W. S. Andrews of Boston to the *Emancipator* and reprinted by Birney,[259] is equally suggestive. Andrews' proposition was that the Preamble of the Constitution together with the Declaration of Independence had been adequate to abolish slavery in the District of Columbia without any congressional act.

---

[257] Philanthropist, Jan. 27, 1837, p. 3, col. 2.
[258] Philanthropist, Jan. 27, 1837, p. 3, col. 2.
[259] *Id.*, Oct. 6, 1837, p. 4, col. 3.

True, the declaration is made in the name of the people of the United States, "for ourselves and our posterity," and therefore it may be said it was intended to be restricted in its application to the people who adopted the constitution and *their* posterity, viz: the *white* population of the United States. But though this may be the letter of the preamble, . . . it cannot be the spirit . . . . Slavery was . . . constitutionally and legally abolished in the District of Columbia as soon as it was ceded to the United States and the laws of Virginia and Maryland ceased to operate with it—and the district became subject to the control of Congress, who were bound to look to the principles promulgated in the national compact and the Declaration of Independence as their landmarks of power, and rules of duty; and that Congress consistently with these principles had no right by any of their acts, to recognize slavery as still existing within the District, or to make any laws for its continuance, but were bound to consider it as having been abolished by the spirit of the national constitution as the State of Massachusetts did her own Bill of Rights.

Thus by October, 1837, the date of Birney's retirement as editor of the *Philanthropist*, the motivating premise of abolitionism already was coming to be this: Americans' basic civil rights were truly national, but in practice their basic civil liberty was not. By acts in support and in toleration of slavery and by failure to protect the friends of the enslaved race, the states and the federal government all abridged, and all allowed to be abridged, the dearest privileges and immunities of citizenship. Humanitarianism had attempted to soften race prejudice and meet this challenge squarely but had been frustrated. Failure left no alternative but political action and the instinctive answer that government had the power to do what the governed had the job to do. The answer to denied power and to defective power was the concept of an inherent power derived from the standing duty to protect. The gist of it was that because allegiance and protection were reciprocal—i.e. ought to be reciprocal— because the government protected its citizens abroad without discrimination, and because the text of the Federal Bill of Rights gave no warrant for discrimination, Congress was duty bound *not* to discriminate. It must do "equal and exact justice" irrespective of race. It had no other choice. It lacked power to discriminate between those persons who were equally entitled to protection. It was duty bound also to remove such discriminations as existed. Implicitly, and morally, these same obligations rested on the states; yet respect for the constitutional division of power here introduced conflict. Few were yet ready for the extreme proposition that Congress might *constitu-*

tionally abolish slavery *in the states*. The original form, as shown by the Andrews and Batavian communications, was more often that Congress was duty bound to hear petitions to abolish slavery, or that slavery had been abolished in federal territory by the force of the Preamble and Declaration. Because the great natural rights were now also national constitutional rights, they began to generate and carry with them— *even into the states*—the power for their enforcement.

Conclusion

If this evidence still falls short of a decisive answer to the riddle of the Fourteenth Amendment, it at least clarifies issues and suggests leads for investigation.

It now is beyond doubt that the evangelical abolitionists anticipated members of the Joint Committee by a full thirty years in developing the privileges and immunities–due process–equal protection phraseology as a bulwark for the rights of free Negroes and slaves. The regional strongholds of this early doctrine included constituencies later represented by Bingham, Stevens, Conkling, Harris, Morrill, Howard, Washburne, Boutwell and Fessenden[260]—the leading Republican members of the Joint Committee. The rhetoric is known to have been broadcast widely through the North by circulation of abolitionist propaganda and later by means of party platforms.

It further appears that even before 1840 abolitionist theorists had begun to evolve, through the early comity clause-due process usage, the concept of a paramount national citizenship. The federal government, it was at first assumed, then argued, had not only the *power*, but the *duty* to protect the fundamental rights of life, liberty and property wherever and whenever those rights were abridged, either by state action or by flagrant state inaction. To buttress further this double comity clause-due process safeguard, and to give fullest possible expression to underlying Lockean ideas of human equality and of the universal need for legal protection, the antislavery theorists also developed and repeatedly employed in their arguments the equal protection concept derived from the "all men are created equal" premise in the Declaration of Independence. By this third concept the users meant first, the citizen's right to *protection*, secondly, his right

---

[260] For concise biographies of these and other members of the Joint Committee of Fifteen, see Kendrick, *op. cit. supra* note 2, at 154–197. Fessenden's father, General Samuel Fessenden, the leading abolitionist of Maine, was a national vice-president of the American Anti Slavery Society, and the Liberty Party's candidate for governor in 1845 and 1847. A staunch Whig during this period, the younger Fessenden rejected his father's abolitionism. 1968: See JELLISON, WILLIAM PITT FESSENDEN (Ph.D. dissertation, University of Virginia, 1956).

to *equality* of *protection*; these two related rights were also among his rights as a "person" as well as among his most precious "privileges and immunities as a *citizen of the United States."*

The challenging issue is whether this theory of the thirties is the theory of the Fourteenth Amendment—whether the Ellsworth-Goddard-Olcott-Birney concept of a paramount national citizenship, ethically derived, racially non-discriminatory and triply reinforced, was that held by Bingham and the Republican leadership. It would seem quite possible for Bingham to have absorbed the *Philanthropist* rhetoric and doctrine while still a student at Franklin College. Or he may have done so indirectly and unconsciously in the forties through the scores of elaborate arguments and paraphrases repeated in pamphlets, speeches, and party platforms. Except for the Franklin College connection, much the same possibility exists with reference to other committee members and to the Civil War generation generally. It should occasion little surprise if men, accustomed to a lifetime of using the three-clause phraseology in a sweeping natural rights sense as a bulwark for Negro rights and as a weapon against slavery, consciously or unconsciously fell back on the phraseology when confronted with the problem of safeguarding those whose rights they had so long espoused. Those rights then rested precariously on the Thirteenth Amendment and on military government. Investigation of individual committee members' backgrounds and studies of the spread and popularization of abolitionist theory by means of party platforms may be expected to clarify these matters. Already Professor Nye's study of the civil rights phases of the antislavery crusade brings the problem into sharper focus.[261] The obvious need now is a searching survey of constitutional theory. Our contribution herein has been to shift attention from the opinions of sophisticated constitutional lawyers and judges to the importance of underlying mass opinion and propaganda. Lay ethical and moral opinions were the matrix of the War Amendments. Courts and legislatures eventually were overruled by force of arms and public sentiment. It follows that the scope of historical inquiry must now be broadened and familiar doctrines must be studied in their popular, not merely their legal, context.

That this lay antislavery constitutional theory was extremely heterodox is clear. It was not primarily the product of minds trained in rigorous case analysis or statutory construction. It confused moral with civil and constitutional rights. It made the Declaration of Inde-

---

[261] NYE, *op. cit. supra* note 52, particularly cc. 2, 4, 5, 6.

pendence the basic constitutional document, the Preamble the heart of the Constitution, the Federal Bill of Rights a *source* rather than a *limitation* of power. It either blissfully ignored or was wholly unaware of the Supreme Court's decision in *Barron v. Baltimore*. Historically, it seems irreconcilable with Justice Black's hypothesis that complete nationalization of civil rights in this manner affords escape from "subjective natural law."[262]

Notwithstanding all this, the theory still has its merits and appeal. It rests on an ethical interpretation of our national origins and history which most Americans today proudly accept as a challenge and an ideal. Its orientation is the orientation of the Supreme Court in recent years.[263] Even its dilemmas and dangers are those seen to be inherent in a popular government of federated and separated powers.[264] Above all, viewed against its backgrounds, it helps us understand why military and constitutional sanctions were gained for racial non-discrimination as a national policy *before* education could thoroughly undermine belief in the weakening concept of racial inferiority. We see now that this was not the method or the preference of the abolitionists. Of all groups they had perhaps the staunchest faith in reason and moral suasion. It was rejection and frustration of that faith that successively called into play political, military, and finally, constitutional power. On this theme we may close. Eighty years of tortured progress in race relations underscore the tragedies of war and the failures of Reconstruction. They thus also remind us what Weld and Birney wanted and tried to teach a heedless generation: *All* men must be accorded the *rights* of men. Race and color are ignoble standards by which to judge human character and worth.

---

[262] The consistency and uniformity to be gained by full rather than selective Bill of Rights incorporation were strongly urged by Justice Black in his Adamson dissent unmindful possibly of the problems inherent in hidden natural rights backgrounds. "To pass upon the constitutionality of statutes by looking to the particular standards enumerated in the Bill of Rights and other parts of the Constitution," he declared, "is one thing; to invalidate statutes because of application of 'natural law' deemed to be above and undefined by the Constitution is another." (See note 6 *supra*, at 91–92). Yet so far as we can see now, was it not in all likelihood the very prevalence of natural law thinking and the susceptibility, not only of this three clause epitome, but of virtually the entire Bill of Rights to natural law interpretations, that led to the widened popularity and hence eventually to reincorporation by amendment? Subjectivity and objectivity apparently are two sides of the same popular and judicial coin. Like the Court's self denying ordinance and nonconcern with expediency, natural law is now a pillar, now a reproach, in the endless round of argument. Cf. Braden, *Objectivity in Constitutional Law*, 57 YALE L.J. 571 (1948).

[263] For comprehensive surveys, see Waite, *The Negro in the Supreme Court*, 30 MINN. L. REV. 219–304 (1946); Berger, *The Supreme Court and Group Discrimination Since 1937*, 49 COL. L. REV. 201–230 (1949). **1968:** See especially MILLER, THE PETITIONERS: THE STORY OF THE SUPREME COURT OF THE UNITED STATES (New York, 1966).

[264] See *supra* pp. 647, 649–650.

EDITORIAL NOTE. What would America have been without this organized antislavery movement? What would American constitutionalism have been? From Theodore Weld and the Grimkés and the Birneys to Martin Luther King and the Supreme Court; from The Twelve and The Seventy to the Fourteenth Amendment and the continuing question whether we really mean it; from that fateful, early, ill-considered rejection of the ethico-moral-humanitarian appeal and argument to the ultimate continuing constitutionalization—the due processing and the equal protection of the rights of "all men" who are "created equal" and "endowed by their Creator with certain unalienable rights"—what would America have been and be without this? What would American law and history and historiography have been and be?

And the disturbing thing was that all this had got so nearly, so completely lost. After 1890 judicial review and judicial supremacy had taken over in fact. Since then they had been "passing off," as the English say, as very nearly the whole of constitutionalism. Academically, history and political science had missed and slipped as badly as law and jurisprudence. All had "gone clinical"—got busy with the aches and fevers, the corporate pains and excesses—and neglected the racial side, neglected the genetics, the embryology and obstetrics, almost entirely.

Everyone saw, and many, of course, deplored, the "Due Process Revolution"[1]—that gradual shift from procedure to substance; all saw what vast changes it had entailed, and especially the ease with which courts increasingly had substituted their views of "reasonableness" (*i.e.*, policy and expediency) for the views of legislatures. Successive scholars traced the role and the importance of the "higher law," and of natural-law conceptions in the shifts and process; but few extended the Corwin-Haines research and insights, either doctrinally or historically.

So when all was said and done the written history of the Fourteenth Amendment still began in 1866–1868, and more and more was it preoccupied with cases and events of the late 1870's and 80's —with the majority opinions of the Waite Court. The inarticulate national premise was that the United States had solved its race problem: solved it by ignoring it, by ignoring now even the manner and

---

[1] See BEARD, CONTEMPORARY AMERICAN HISTORY (1915), for seminal discussion.

the cases in which it began ignoring it. Accepting the Supreme Court's emasculation of Everyman's Constitution; acquiescing in denial of congressional power to act; accepting an "expedient" sectional Compromise of 1877 as if it were holy writ and a decision for all time. The fact that generation after generation of many of the freedmen's descendants were thus condemned to a culture of poverty and ignorance, and that this so-called sectional "accommodation" and "settlement" of 1877–1897 differed very little in its social premises and consequences, with respect to race, "citizenship," and protection, from that which the *Dred Scott* decision had vainly sought to establish in 1857, was generally ignored.

And the end was not yet. Fortuitously, intra-Court divisions and doctrinaire positions taken prematurely with reference to the intentions of John A. Bingham and other draftsmen and ratifiers of 1866–1868, now again bedeviled judicial construction,[2] and even carried over into academic scholarship,[3] with distinguished members of the Stanford and the University of Chicago law faculties (Charles Fairman and Stanley Morrison, and William W. Crosskey, respectively) the viziered champions of feuding principals. How it happened that four of the ablest members of the Court (Justices Jackson, Frankfurter, Black, and Douglas) ever got thus arrayed will make a sad, instructive chapter of judicial history eventually. The immediate and two-fold result was another sterile debate over another peripheral issue ("Does the Fourteenth Amendment Incorporate the [Full] Bill of Rights?"); and a debate that stirred and muddied constitutional waters just as the great problems had begun to clear. Semantics, side issues, and details of judicial craftsmanship thus deflected and re-absorbed both academic and judicial energies and attention. Negatives "proved" negatives; arguments from silence "answered" arguments from silence; axes and lances were broken, but no new ground—no lost ground—was recovered.

Worst of all, Charles Fairman's long-promised biography of Mr. Justice Bradley, author of the majority opinion in the *Civil Rights Cases*[4] (1883), based on the Bradley Papers, was put aside, and the chapter dealing with Bradley's leadership of the Waite Court and his special responsibility for policy in racial matters was left untreated. Consequently it was not until 1963–1965 that C. Peter

---

[2] Adamson v. California, 332 U. S. 46, decided by five-to-four vote (June 23, 1947); discussed Chapter 4, *supra*, notes 10, 11, and 14; see also Chapter 7, *infra*, note 80, for criticism.

[3] *Ibid.* For updated bibliography on Bill of Rights incorporation, see POLITICAL AND CIVIL RIGHTS IN THE UNITED STATES (3d ed., 1967, 2 vols.), vol. 2, pp. 1379–1380.

[4] 109 U. S. 3 (1883), discussed in the Introduction, *supra*, pp. 10–11.

Magrath and John P. Roche, using the Bradley Papers (finally on public deposit in the New Jersey archives), revealed that in 1871 Bradley himself had taken the strongest possible stand on the scope of the equal protection clause, a stand as strong as Harlan's and squarely at odds with Bradley's final positon.[5]

While this debate over Bill of Rights incorporation was raging, Jacobus tenBroek and I were completing our studies, and more than once we were twitted, derided, dismissed and suffered as "the students, the historians of constitutional might-have-been" by a number of law school and legal "positivists." ("Might-have-been, indeed, and precisely!" we say again today. And under just what *present* conditions?) We were the pair who had "resurrected the Abolitionists," "revived old fallacies," "disturbed judicial and constitutional peace." Disturbed an 1877 "settlement."

At this point, then, another query, another might-have-been, to give Everyman needed bearings, courage, and refooting: Where might we have been by now had an editor of the *Harvard Law Review*, a student of Professor Frankfurter's, discovered, in 1933, Weld and Birney and *The Antislavery Impulse* (G. H. Barnes' book *and* the materials on which the Barnes-Dumond research was based)? Where might we be today had that editor got that brilliant, restless, seminal mind reading and thinking—reading Weld's "affirmative" arguments and Birney's *Philanthropist* editorials, and watching the theory and wording of Sections 1 and 5 crystalize thirty years before the actual drafting?[6]

There are no determinisms in law and history. Only chances and mischances, opportunities and missed opportunities. Good fortune and bad. Blind spots, judicial and national.

---

[5] See Chapter 13, *infra*, notes 14, 15, and 17.

[6] See especially the materials summarized in this chapter, *supra*, and reprinted *in extenso* as Appendixes A–D of tenBroek, Equal Justice Under Law.

[CHAPTER 5]

Procedure to Substance: Extrajudicial Rise of Due Process, 1830–1860

EDITORIAL NOTE. Abolitionist constitutional theory—the antislavery "trilogy" or "trinity" of the 1830's which became Sections 1 and 5, 1866–1868—had proved a revelation. Yet its discovery confuted and complicated as much as it clarified. American due process and modern equal protection had not long remained simply judicial formulae and concepts—if ever they had been "simply" such. "Modern," "American," "substantive" due process had gained its original impetus—its real lead and start—as *racialized, affirmative* due process; had gained this long before the Civil War; had gained it, above all, *extra*judicially, and almost wholly *ante*-judicially. Laymen's, reformers', and freedmen's hands and stakes in this pioneer racial "processing" were obvious. And the implications were shattering: Affirmative due process and antebellum due process both still were novel enough. *Extrajudicial* due process and *antebellum* equal protection were rankly, frankly heretical. (Much, if not most, constitutional protection, of course, began so—as "mere" dissent or as petitioning which needed to make its way, and which did. Everyman's Constitution gains in respect and grandeur as we realize, as we appreciate that fact.)

"Procedure to Substance" thus was an act of near-temerity—an impulsive, half-exclamatory description, not of "The Emperor's New Clothes," but of what might be called the American Judiciary's "originall" due process robes. "Judicial usurpation," "self-expansion of judicial power," "judicial revolution," now, in some respects at least, were cast in doubt and in limbo, exposed as the anomalies they always had been. This, accordingly, was one essay that almost wrote itself, as I stopped merely on successive weekends to test my hypothesis by checking the law reviews and the Court reports of the 1840's to see what they might reveal about burgeoning due-

Procedure to Substance   243

process usage and natural-rights thinking at the time of that pioneer landmark substantive due-process case of *Taylor v. Porter* (1843).

Except for "The 'Conspiracy Theory'," and thanks especially to Alpheus T. Mason and William T. Beaney, "Procedure to Substance" has become the most widely known, cited, and quoted of these essays—the form, indeed, in which findings of "The Early Antislavery Backgrounds" have gained notice and assimilation. The essay thus marks an important stage in the broadening of research and of the basic reinterpretation.

[CHAPTER 5]

THAT DUE PROCESS OF LAW has undergone dazzling metamorphosis in the United States is venerable law review learning.[1] That the transition from procedure to substance, which began to gain momentum about 1890, eventually changed the scope and form of judicial review and recast relations of the three branches of both state and federal governments is equally familiar.[2] Let it be added immediately, therefore, that our purpose in this chapter is not to attempt another exercise in judicial taxidermy. Nor is it to rehearse and reargue the familiar phases of the "due process revolution."

---

[1] See Corwin, *The Doctrine of Due Process of Law Before the Civil War*, 24 HARV. L. REV. 366, 460 (1911); 1 SELECTED ESSAYS CONSTITUTIONAL LAW 203 (1938); CORWIN, LIBERTY AGAINST GOVERNMENT cc. 3-5 (1948); Haines, *Judicial Review of Legislation in the United States and the Doctrine of Vested Rights and of Implied Limitations on Legislatures*, 3 TEX. L. REV. 1 (1924); retitled, 1 SELECTED ESSAYS CONSTITUTIONAL LAW 268 (1938); Hough, *Due Process of Law Today*, 32 HARV. L. REV. 218 (1919), 1 SELECTED ESSAYS CONSTITUTIONAL LAW 302 (1938); Grant, *Natural Law Background of Due Process*, 31 COL. L. REV. 56 (1931); Howe, *The Meaning of Due Process Prior to the Adoption of the 14th Amendment*, 18 CALIF. L. REV. 583 (1930); Hamilton, *The Path of Due Process of Law* in THE CONSTITUTION RECONSIDERED (Read ed. 1938); MOTT, DUE PROCESS OF LAW (1926); Shattuck, *The True Meaning of the Term "Liberty" in Those Clauses in the Federal and State Constitutions which Protect "Life," "Liberty," and "Property,"* 4 HARV. L. REV. 365 (1891), 2 SELECTED ESSAYS CONSTITUTIONAL LAW 185 (1938); Warren, *The New "Liberty" Under the Fourteenth Amendment*, 39 HARV. L. REV. 431 (1926); 2 SELECTED ESSAYS CONSTITUTIONAL LAW 237 (1938).

[2] See HAINES, AMERICAN DOCTRINE OF JUDICIAL SUPREMACY c. 15 (2d ed. 1932); Collins, THE FOURTEENTH AMENDMENT AND THE STATES (1912); Cushman, *Social and Economic Interpretation of the Fourteenth Amendment*, 20 MICH. L. REV. 737 (1922), 2 SELECTED ESSAYS CONSTITUTIONAL LAW 60 (1938); Brown, *Due Process of Law, Police Power, and the Supreme Court*, 40 HARV. L. REV. 943 (1927), 2 SELECTED ESSAYS CONSTITUTIONAL LAW 94 (1938). **1968:** See also two recent Harper Torchbooks, both edited with distinguished introductions by Leonard W. Levy: AMERICAN CONSTITUTIONAL LAW: HISTORICAL ESSAYS (1966); and JUDICIAL REVIEW AND THE SUPREME COURT: SELECTED ESSAYS (1967).

It is rather to challenge certain basic assumptions, to point out oversights and astigmatisms which mask and blur some of the most significant phases of due process–law of the land history. If emphasis is to be mainly on popular usage and on lay conceptions of these two constitutional phrases, it is with no thought of denying their fundamentally legal character, nor of questioning the final responsibility which judges today must have for construction of these as well as other constitutional guarantees. Iconoclasm, so far as it exists, is directed, not at the fruits or character of judicial review, but at prevailing conceptions of the setting in which review operated, and the neglect of contributions made by extra-judicial forces during the formative period. How the due process phraseology gained great popular currency—how it originally came to be employed by the Civil War generation, rather than precisely what it meant, overall, to the framers and ratifiers of 1866, is our chief concern in this essay.

From the time of Professor Corwin's path-breaking articles[3] the prevailing view of American due process development has been that, except for perhaps a dozen major cases—generally treated as "sports" or mutations—pre-Civil War use and understanding of the phrases "due process of law" and "law of the land" were overwhelmingly procedural. That is to say, they were in accord with ancient English origins. Casebooks and law review contributions without number have plotted these landmarks—*University v. Foy*,[4] the Tennessee cases,[5] *Hoke v. Henderson*,[6] *Taylor v. Porter*,[7] *Wynehamer v. People*,[8] and *Dred Scott v. Sandford*.[9] Occasionally intermediate or secondary landmarks have been added to narrow the gaps in the otherwise jagged skyline. But these efforts at continuity rarely have changed the picture, and almost never the conclusions or the assumptions. The peaks still rise majestically from a broad procedural plain. Connecting ranges are shrouded and obscure. The fracturing upthrust through and from the procedural strata was sharp, sporadic, unpredictable. Above all, the primitive shaping force was judicial craftsmanship. Learned, strong-willed judges—men like Ruffin,

---

[3] See, in addition to the works cited *supra* note 1, his *Extension of Judicial Review in New York*, 15 MICH. L. REV. 281 (1917).

[4] 5 N.C. 58 (1805).

[5] Vanzant v. Waddel, 2 Yerg. 259, 271 (Tenn. 1829); State Bank v. Cooper, 2 Yerg. 599 (1831); Tate v. Bell, 4 Yerg. 202 (1833); Officer v. Young, 5 Yerg. 320 (1833); Jones Heirs v. Perry, 10 Yerg. 59 (1836); Budd v. State, 22 Tenn. 483 (1842).

[6] 15 N.C. 1 (1833).

[7] 4 Hill 140 (N.Y. 1843).

[8] 13 N.Y. 378 (1856).

[9] 19 How. 393, 450 (U.S. 1856).

Bronson, Taney—judges with the powerful minds and temperaments of creators, marshalled their dicta and syllogisms, "divided the light from darkness, called the light Day and the darkness Night," and from "waste and void" fashioned the peaks and firmament. Their basic stuffs of creation were the natural rights-higher law prepossessions common to American political thinking down to the Civil War. Lockean premises regarding liberty and property guided the syllogisms. Once the original extra-constitutional doctrine of vested rights was no longer able to canalize the volcanic forces, and once the contract clause had begun to suffer the repressive effects of the *Charles River Bridge* decision,[10] due process of law and law of the land clauses became the vents out of which the lava intermittently poured.

Always central to, and underlying this legal cosmology—truly a "Great lawyers" theory of Creation—has been the premise that throughout the formative period due process remained essentially, predominantly procedural. Contemporaneous substantive use and understanding were meager at best, even by lawyers; laymen of course lacked not only insight but interest. Not until the post-Civil War period was there any general appreciation of the grandeurs and wonders of due process substantively conceived.

The conventional views in this regard have been admirably summarized by the late Professor Haines.[11]

> Prior to the adoption of the Fourteenth Amendment to the Federal Constitution, due process of law was of little significance in American constitutional law, as a standard to test the validity of legislative acts. For about three-quarters of a century after the introduction of the term in the first state constitutions, it was seldom used as a basis for the protection of either personal or property rights. Few legislative enactments were held invalid as contravening due process of law, and some of the most important attempts to define the phrase were made in dicta in cases upholding the validity of the laws attacked. Several attempts were made to give force and meaning to the term, such, for instance, as those of North Carolina and of the Tennessee courts, but with relatively little success. Then a renewed effort was made by the courts of Massachusetts and of New York to construe due process of law into a general limitation on legislative powers, but this effort met with only meager acceptance until changes in economic and political conditions after 1860 favored extensive expressed and implied restrictions on legislative powers. On the whole, the interpretation

---
[10] 11 Pet. 419 (U.S. 1837).
[11] Haines, *supra* note 1.

of the phrases "due process of law" or "the law of the land" prior to 1870 had placed few restrictions on legislatures which were not merely procedural in character and had merely suggested ideas or principles which under a different environment were soon to be received favorably. Due process of law and other implied limits on legislative powers were slowly interpreted so as to serve as adjustable standards for the maintenance of the principles of the new conservatism.

More guarded, yet obviously of the same conviction, was the late Judge Hough:[12]

> That all men of that day [1856, the date of the Supreme Court's procedural definition in *Murray v. Hoboken*] had no conception of due process other than a summary description of a fairly tried action at law, is not asserted; but I do submit that reports before the Civil War yield small evidence that there was any professional conviction that it was more than that.

And speaking of Thomas M. Cooley's role in preparing the ground for substantive interpretations by his treatment of the early cases in the first edition of *Constitutional Limitations,* 1868, Benjamin Twiss concluded: "Previously this clause had been looked upon almost universally as only a procedural guarantee."[13] One might quote many more statements to the same effect. The conclusion has taken its place almost as an historical axiom.

Naturally, therefore, certain corollaries have been drawn. Perhaps most important is what might be called the "perversionist thesis." Because, under pressure of economic usage after the Civil War, interpretations eventually departed so radically from prewar understandings, it has been argued that both the due process and equal protection guarantees were misapplied. Especially were they perverted when used to engraft onto the Constitution the postwar laissez-faire doctrine "liberty to contract"[14] and its interference runner, corporate personality.[15] Nor have the critics of the modern laissez-

---

12 Hough, *supra* note 1 at 223; 1 SELECTED ESSAYS CONSTITUTIONAL LAW at 306. Note that Judge Hough, by confining his statement to the "reports" and "professional opinion" seems to make allowance for extra-judicial factors. Professor Corwin and other writers likewise have been well aware of abolitionist use of due process, and occasionally have alluded thereto, but no one, to the writer's knowledge, has seriously examined the extent of influence.

13 TWISS, LAWYERS AND THE CONSTITUTION 26 (1942). This admirable work, with Professor Hurst's GROWTH OF AMERICAN LAW (1950), is one of the few which have focused attention on the guiding role of the bar in constitutional construction.

14 For the doctrinal growth, see Pound, *Liberty of Contract,* 18 YALE L.J. 454 (1909), 2 SELECTED ESSAYS CONSTITUTIONAL LAW 208 (1938).

15 For the history of this development, see *supra*, Chapters 1–3.

faire applications stopped here. Still assuming a fundamentally non-economic and procedural usage prior to 1866, they have at times argued that the framers and ratifiers of the Fourteenth Amendment could scarcely have foreseen, much less intended, that the word "person" might be construed to include corporations. That the due process and equal protection clauses as a whole might be employed to overturn social, economic, or administrative regulation was scarcely dreamed of in 1866—such has been the thesis.[16] To assume otherwise, in the words of Walton Hamilton,[17] would be to endow the drafters, and the "captains of a rising industry with a capacity for forward plan . . . which they are not usually understood to possess."

Thus, the narrow procedural beginnings of the clause have been used, not only to attack later "perversions," but to question the very possibility of awareness in 1866 that due process might eventually become a formidable weapon against legislative power. Far from being academic matters, it is plain that these assumptions about the character of pre-Civil War due process go to the roots of some vital constitutional problems.

It has seemed to the writer that several *a priori* considerations alone are enough to raise cautionary doubts about these assumptions. First is the fact that law review constitutional history seldom has been institutional history; the political juices, and even the chronology, generally are lost in extracting the rules. More and more, what we get is the story of a few major cases; then ultimately merely a truncated analysis of the prevailing appellate opinions. Thus, almost inevitably in this process, far too little attention is paid to, and far too little allowance is made for, the general public's stake and participation in vital constitutional decisions. Furious public debates are eventually boiled down to neatly stated rules. Constitutional law, in more senses than one, emerges as digested politics!

Serious enough at any time, this source of potential error could be deadly when applied to the formative period. For the Constitution then was plastic; many clauses were wholly uninterpreted, others barely outlined. Judicial review was in its infancy. Issues were wide open, authorities meager or non-existent. Not until 1819, for example, was even the *Journal* of the Federal Convention published.[18]

---

[16] Boudin, *Truth and Fiction About the Fourteenth Amendment*, 16 N.Y.U.L.Q. REV. 19 (1938).

[17] Hamilton, *Property—According to Locke*, 41 YALE L.J. 864, 875 (1932), 2 SELECTED ESSAYS CONSTITUTIONAL LAW 115, 126 (1938).

[18] JOURNAL, ACTS AND PROCEEDINGS OF THE CONVENTION ASSEMBLED AT PHILADELPHIA . . . 1787 (1819). YATES, SECRET PROCEEDINGS AND DEBATES OF THE CONVENTION ASSEMBLED AT PHILADELPHIA . . . 1787 . . . INCLUDING THE "GENUINE INFORMATION" . . . by LUTHER MARTIN was published in Albany, 1821.

Madison's *Debates* came a full twenty years later.[19] It was 1833 before the Supreme Court, in *Barron v. Baltimore*, held the Bill of Rights inapplicable to the states.[20] And as late as 1845 we find the whole Illinois Supreme Court apparently unaware of Marshall's decision.[21] Yet during this period occurred the great constitutional debates. One after another came those on the Missouri Compromise, the Tariff, Nullification, the Bank Charter, and above all, the interminable crises and debates over Slavery. Nor were these passive television shows. The *Annals*, the *Register of Debates* and the *Congressional Globe* were read cover to cover by thousands, and excerpted in hundreds of papers; every crossroads had its debating society. Public law and politics were indeed democracy's lifeblood.

Here obviously are signals for caution. A nation that desiccates its history in the course of extracting and studying its law risks feeding itself pap. Yet more and more, constitutional history is written as if interpretation of the Constitution always had been solely the business of lawyers and the prerogative of judges. Because in the course of a century the law of the Constitution has become a highly technical field—the province and specialty of an elite, and the public responsibility of judges alone—like conditions are assumed to have prevailed in Madison's day. The faith of Jefferson and his generation in free discussion by a free press and free yeomanry ought to be warning enough against such conceits.

With reference to our problem of the character of early due process usage there are two other factors which make these considerations seem even more vital. One is the strong natural rights orientation of our early constitutional law,[22] the other, the inherent textual

---

[19] MADISON PAPERS (Gilpin ed., 1840).

[20] 7 Pet. 242, 247 (U.S. 1833).

[21] Rhinehart v. Schuyler, 7 Ill. 375, 414 (1845). After quoting the due process clause of the Fifth Amendment, and noting "the words 'due process of law' have been shown to correspond in meaning to the words 'law of the land' . . . in our state constitution," the majority opinion declared "Now, as the constitution of the United States, in this respect is obligatory upon all the States of the Union, is it not strange" if plaintiff's contention be sound and " 'due process of law' means trial judgment and execution [in a tax sale case] that of all these states, from the foundation of the government up to the present time, Tennessee and Illinois alone should have made the discovery that they were violating the constitution of the United States, which is everywhere admitted to be the Supreme law of the land . . . ." See *infra* text of notes 60–61. 1968: See Chapters 11 and 12 *infra*, pp. 494–503 especially, for ramifications of this case of Rhinehart v. Schuyler.

[22] See HAINES, REVIVAL OF NATURAL LAW CONCEPTS (1930); and WRIGHT, AMERICAN INTERPRETATIONS OF NATURAL LAW (1931); Corwin, *The Basic Doctrine of American Constitutional Law*, 12 MICH. L. REV. 247 (1914), 1 SELECTED ESSAYS CONSTITUTIONAL LAW 101 (1938).

advantages which the due process clause enjoyed as an artful question beggar and as a lever in the hands of those trying to shift final responsibility for social decisions from the legislatures to the courts. Little need be said about the natural law foundations. They repeatedly have been demonstrated, and are now universally conceded. Substantivized due process is essentially constitutionalized natural law.[23] Thus the "due processing" of the law of nature has been a basic theme of law review writing.

Much less commonly noted have been the advantages of the due process guarantee itself. Unlike the contract clause and the later restraint wording of the Fourteenth Amendment, the original due process guarantee of the Fifth Amendment—as well as the due process-law of the land phraseology of most of the state constitutions—made no reference to law making or law passing. A user thus could side-step the really touchy issues and concentrate on the merits, or, if preferable, on abstract justice. Moreover, the word "person" obviously embraced all mankind: "life," "liberty," and "property," virtually all human affairs. Finally, the categorical prohibition is stated in a form that is even more impressive to the uninitiated than to professionals. More than any other single clause of the Constitution, it seems *on its face* to guarantee, so far as any such provision can, both universal and personal justice. No doubt the principal reasons are that one synonym of "due process" is "just" process, and one popular connotation of "law" is "right and equity." The ideal or substantive element thus is inherent in the terms. If an intelligent child or layman is asked the meaning of these phrases he almost invariably replies: "It guarantees you a square deal." "It means you can protect your rights against anybody." "It protects human rights and freedom."

Now all this is relevant to the matter at hand. *If* this is the natural import of these phrases, and if in the early days of our Republic citizens were intensely, and at times fanatically excited about such issues as slavery, women's rights, and the evils and profits of the liquor traffic, and if the zealots who became most wrought up over these matters were not only highly literate and articulate but a bit on the stiff-necked, cantankerous side, both as to the maintenance of their rights and the salvation of those who disagreed with them, then surely, we may suspect that these hardy individuals, if no others, came naturally and effectively to the use of a weapon ideally suited

---

[23] See, in addition to the works cited *supra* note 1, Grant, *The "Higher Law" Background of the Law of Eminent Domain*, 6 WIS. L. REV. 67 (1931), 2 SELECTED ESSAYS CONSTITUTIONAL LAW 912 (1938).

to their needs. If so, it seems quite likely that there was considerable substantive "due processing" of natural law, and powerful pressure was exerted for expansion of judicial review—far more indeed, than has generally been credited.

Recent studies of the antislavery backgrounds of the Fourteenth Amendment offer strong support for this hypothesis.[23a] They suggest that the twin forces in the rise and growth of substantive due process were (1) the "common sense" lay interpretations conceived and broadcast by these dedicated, highly articulate reformist and counter-reformist groups—mainly Abolitionists and anti-Abolitionists; (2) the ease and persistence with which such elements in their thinking and propaganda, not only exploited prevalent Lockean, natural rights interpretations of the key words "life," "liberty" and "property," but also benefited by the inherent textual advantages of the phrase "due [i.e. just] process" as a means of "constitutionalizing" their earlier natural rights arguments. Due process thus was snatched up, bandied about, "corrupted and corroded," if you please, for more than thirty years prior to 1866. For every black letter usage in court there were perhaps hundreds or thousands in the press, red schoolhouse and on the stump. Zealots, reformers, and politicians—not jurists—blazed the paths of substantive due process.

What a thoroughly professional job of it they did is evidenced by the fact that at a very early date due process became an element in a constitutional trinity. By the late thirties it already was a part of the three-clause system which was to be employed thirty years hence by the drafters of Section One. Moreover, the drafters of that section—Bingham, Stevens, Conkling, Washburne, Fessenden, Morrill, Howard, Blow, and perhaps others—were men who in their youth and early manhood are known to have been thoroughly exposed to this doctrinal system.[24]

The story has its beginning deep in colonial history. Ethics, religion, political theory, all contributed to the ultimate pattern. Before

---

[23a] See Chapter 4, *supra*; TENBROEK, THE ANTISLAVERY ORIGINS OF THE FOURTEENTH AMENDMENT (1951); 2d., enl. ed., retitled EQUAL UNDER LAW (N.Y., Collier, 1965). Citations hereafter are to the paging of the first edition.

[24] Brief biographical data on members of the Joint Committee is given in KENDRICK, THE JOURNAL OF THE JOINT COMMITTEE OF FIFTEEN ON RECONSTRUCTION c.2 (1914). Regarding Stevens and Bingham see Chapter 1, *supra* and note 27 *infra*. Fessenden was the son of the Abolitionist leader of Maine (see Chapter 4 *supra*, at 236, note 260). Blow was a member of the antislavery family responsible for freeing Dred Scott and pushing his case (see HOPKINS, DRED SCOTT'S CASE 14, 180 (1951)). Morrill grew up in Vermont; Conkling and Harris in New York; Grimes in New Hampshire; Boutwell in Massachusetts; and Washburne in Maine—all regions where organized abolitionist activity was strong from the thirties on.

the Revolution, Quakers and Puritans attacked slavery as a violation of the social compact and Christian ethic. After 1776 the "self-evident truths" put a much keener edge on all such pleas. "That all men are created equal . . . [and] endowed by their Creator . . . with . . . unalienable rights [of] Life, Liberty, and pursuit of Happiness" became one of the cornerstones of nearly every antislavery argument. What emerged was an ethical interpretation of our national origins and history. In 1783, for example, Chief Justice Cushing cited the "All men are born free and equal" clause of the Massachusetts Bill of Rights and declared slavery "inconsistent with our conduct and Constitution."[25] Four years later Congress passed the Northwest Ordinance outlawing slavery in the territories. During this period the "self evident truths," the provisions of the state bills of rights, even the text of the comity clause of the still unratified Articles of Confederation[26] were all employed as weapons against slavery and race discrimination. By the 1820's, moreover, slavery's utter absence and denial of legal protection had been fully explored by critics both North and South. The dominating thought that governments were instituted for protection and derived their just powers from consent of the governed already had begun to make slavery untenable.

Tremendous reach and impact were given to these doctrines, and the whole movement accelerated, by organization, in 1833, of the American Antislavery Society. Taking as a model the British society, which, after a fifty year campaign, had just succeeded in forcing Parliament to abolish slavery in the West Indies, the sponsoring group of philanthropists headed by the wealthy Tappan brothers, launched one of the most extraordinary campaigns in American history. Soon a well educated, dedicated group of antislavery "agents" or evangelists, employing both religious revivals and a well-financed pamphlet campaign, were at work abolitionizing whole communities in Ohio, western New York and Pennsylvania. "Immediate abolition" was their slogan, moral suasion the strategy, conversion of doubters and "sinning slaveholders" the tactic. Under leadership of the brilliant orator and organizer, Theodore Weld, and the converted Alabama slaveholder, James G. Birney, success in the North was sensational. Appeals were directed at the leaders in each community. Lawyers in particular were recruited, and Weld and Birney and their agents were responsible for enlisting a host of influential antislavery leaders—Joshua Giddings, Philemon Bliss, Salmon P. Chase, Thaddeus

---

[25] See Chapter 4, *supra* at 191–193.
[26] *Ibid.* The use was in 1778 by Dr. Gordon, later historian of the Revolution; see MOORE, NOTES ON THE HISTORY OF SLAVERY IN MASSACHUSETTS 186 (1866).

Stevens, the Wades, among others.[27] The range of the agent-lecturers' argument was likewise amazing—the Common law, the Bible, history, Constitution and economics were all covered, often in the course of a two weeks' revival. Weld's disciples literally talked down and routed their opponents, foot and horse.

High idealism distinguished the early campaign, as did strict regard for constitutional requirements. Originally the hope was to achieve abolition in many states by judicial decisions based on the *Sommersett*[28] and *Aves*[29] precedents. Congress was flooded with petitions appealing for abolition in the Federal District and territories. Yet in the South action was to await the force of enlightened opinion, as slaveholders and yeomen were gradually converted. To hasten and reinforce these changes, and to demonstrate the irrationality of race prejudice and the prevailing beliefs in Negro inferiority, free Negroes in the North were given schooling and vocational training. Discriminatory "Black laws," particularly those denying free migration and access to schools, thus became prime targets.

In 1834 a brilliant opening attack was launched on the statute which barred non-resident Negro children from private boarding schools of Connecticut. Defending Prudence Crandall,[30] a Quakeress convicted of violating the act, were W. W. Ellsworth and Calvin Goddard, both leading lawyers and statesmen of Connecticut, hired by the Tappans. In the course of their arguments Ellsworth and Goddard first elaborated a concept of paramount national citizenship within the meaning of the comity clause, using the even-then familiar natural rights dicta of Justice Washington's opinion in *Corfield v. Coryell*.[31] Next, they beautifully synthesized the whole early ethical interpretation case against Negro discrimination. The ideals of human equality, of a general and equal law, of reciprocal protection and allegiance, of reason and substantiality as the true bases for necessary discriminations and classifications by government—all were employed to give both form and substance to the defense of Negro rights.

---

27 See Chapter 4, *supra* at 168, for details regarding influential converts; Thaddeus Stevens, for example, later to be a member of the Joint Committee, was enlisted by Jonathan Blanchard, one of the A.A.S.S. agents assigned to Pennsylvania; Chase was enrolled by Birney, and Bliss and Giddings by Weld.

28 Sommersett's Case, 20 How. St. Tr. 1 (1772) wherein Chief Justice Mansfield held slavery incompatible with the Common law of England.

29 Commonwealth v. Aves, 35 Mass. (18 Pick.) 193 (1836).

30 Crandall v. Connecticut, 10 Conn. 339 (1834). The Ellsworth-Goddard arguments, summarized in this official report, were printed verbatim in a pamphlet; see Chapter 4, *supra* at 176-185, for analysis and discussion.

31 4 Wash. C.C. 371, 380-381, 6 Fed. Cas. 546, No. 3230 (E.D.Pa. 1823).

The Ellsworth-Goddard arguments made no reference to due process, and little to slavery. Yet they mark a basic crystallization of abolitionist constitutional theory. Two of the three elements—equal protection and a nascent concept of national citizenship—were given polished statement. A year later, at the founding of the Ohio Antislavery Society—in preparation for launching their state campaign—Weld's lieutenants submitted a report on Ohio's Black laws.[32] These odious statutes, enacted in 1807, excluded Negroes and mulattoes from common schools, limited use of their testimony in court, interfered both with migration and livelihood. Against the infringement of livelihood the report cited and itself italicized Article Eight, Section One of the Ohio Constitution: "*All* are born *free* and *independent*, and have certain natural, inherent, and inalienable rights, among which are the enjoying and defending life and liberty, *acquiring, possessing*, and *protecting property*, and *pursuing* and *attaining happiness* and *safety*." Against the provision which virtually excluded Negroes from use and protection of the courts, they pointed to Article Eight, Section Seven: "All courts shall be open, and every person, for an injury done him in his lands, goods, person, or reputation, shall have remedy by due course of law, and right and justice administered without denial or delay." Finally, the restraints on ingress and egress were declared gross violations of the federal comity clause and of the privileges and immunities of national citizenship. Throughout, stress was on the denial, to Negroes and mulattoes, of protection of the laws, and on the outrageous inequalities of treatment as between Negroes and whites.

The significance of these arguments in Connecticut and Ohio inheres in the fact that they were anything but happenstance. It is true they originally were directed against the Black laws of the North; that at the outset they were used to prove merely the expediency and justice of abolition. By 1836, however, abolitionists had been thrown on the defensive. Obliged to defend, first their right to proselytize, then the power of Congress to abolish slavery in federal territory, leaders combed the constitutions and digests for support. Moreover, the proslaveryites' counter-offensive was itself suggestive: in both the congressional debates and the Pinckney report[33] of 1836 the due process clause of the Fifth Amendment was set up as an absolute barrier to abolition in the Federal District. This sweeping vested rights

---

[32] PROCEEDINGS OF THE OHIO ANTISLAVERY CONVENTION HELD AT PUTNAM 36-40 (April 22-24, (1836). See Chapter 4, *supra* at 172-176.
[33] H. R. REP. No. 691, 24th Cong., 1st Sess. (1836); discussed in Chapter 4, *supra* at 212-213, note 189, and TENBROEK, *op. cit. supra* note 23a, at 16-17, 79.

usage of the clause—a perfect precedent for Chief Justice Taney's blunder twenty years later—touched off furious debate over slaves as "persons" versus slaves as "property." Abolitionists of course read the phrase as "No person shall be deprived of his self-ownership and earning power;" slaveholders as, "No person shall be deprived of his slave property."

With the Pinckney report as the turning point, battle now thickened. Their hopes of a gradualist solution frustrated, denied use of the mails, and even liberty of speech and press, antislavery militants began to discover for themselves the full potentialities of due process. Overnight the phrase became a battle cry—employed not only in defense of abolitionist rights to speak and write and petition, but also counter-offensively against slavery itself.

For those wishing to trace the steps by which abolitionist leaders explored the substantive content of the guarantee, Birney's editorials and articles[34] in the *Philanthropist* (1836-37) and Professor tenBroek's chapters[35] offer a fascinating study, not only for the light they throw on the evolution of abolitionist constitutional theory, but for insight they afford into the similar use of the same premises by other groups currently and later. An able lawyer, trained in the Philadelphia office of A. J. Dallas, Birney was one of the first to spell out the affirmative protections which abolitionists now began to argue were implicit in the Federal Bill of Rights. To understand these contentions one must remember that Marshall's decision in *Barron v. Baltimore* was barely three years old, its significance not yet generally known or appreciated even by some state judges.[36] Moreover, since practically all state constitutions contained similar guarantees, and above all, since men possessed such inherent and inalienable rights irrespective of guarantee by government, abolitionists regarded the holding as academic. Thus the upshot was simply that various clauses *restraining* the powers of Congress began to be popularly regarded as sources of congressional power to enforce civil rights nationally. It was reasoned that provisions of the Bill of Rights were guarantees; and guarantees customarily presumed intent, capacity, and duty to make them good.[37] From the late thirties this was familiar abolitionist doctrine; moreover, as Dr. tenBroek shows,[38] the more radical

---

[34] See Chapter 4, *supra* at 215ff.
[35] *Op. cit. supra* note 23a, cc.1-3.
[36] See *supra* note 21.
[37] See Chapter 4, *supra*, at 232. **1968:** We sense how *affirmative* constitutional thinking gained scope and impetus once ethical considerations became operative in the field of race.
[38] *Op. cit. supra* note 23a, c.3, especially at 43-48, 54-67; see also Chapter 4, *supra* at 220, note 224.

theorists, like Alvan Stewart, even began to find in due process a source of congressional power to abolish slavery *in the states*.

During this period, simply as an incident of the intensive revival compaigns, equal protection-due process-privileges and immunities theory became the core of thousands of abolitionist petitions, resolutions and lectures. Now one, now another of the elements was accented, depending on the need and circumstances, but in an astonishing number of cases two or three parts of the trilogy were used.[39] The whole thus became, even before 1840, a form of popular constitutional shorthand.

After that date even stronger forces enter the picture. First were the compilers and synthesizers—pamphleteers and journalists like Tiffany and Goodell and Mellon who wrote the articles and treatises on the "Unconstitutionality of Slavery" which Dr. tenBroek analyzes so well.[40] Others annotated copies of *Our National Charters*,[41] setting down after each clause or phrase of the Constitution and the Declaration (much as Birney had done in his early articles) the anti-slavery arguments and doctrines gleaned "both from reason and authority." Such materials, broadcast by the thousand, reprinted, condensed and paraphrased, were themselves powerful disseminators.

It was the minority party platform, however, that gave abolitionist theory its most concise, effective statement.[42] Drafted generally by Salmon P. Chase or Joshua Giddings, these documents, first of the Liberty and Free Soil parties in the forties, then of the Free Democracy and Republican Party in the fifties and in 1860, all made use, in slightly varying combination, of the cardinal articles of faith: human equality, protection, and equal protection from the Declaration, and due process both as a restraint and a source of congressional power. Such consistent repetition, of course, testifies both to the nature and extent of previous distillations and to the power and significance of current ones. That historians—both general and constitutional—have almost completely ignored the party platform as a source for understanding the Fourteenth Amendment itself testifies to serious oversights and misconceptions.[43]

---

[39] *Id.* at notes 227, 232, 255 for examples.
[40] *Op. cit. supra* note 23a, c.3 and 86–91.
[41] GOODELL, OUR NATIONAL CHARTERS: FOR THE MILLIONS (1863); on the Fifth Amendment, due process and *Taylor v. Porter*, see pp. 74–75.
[42] See TENBROEK, *op. cit. supra* note 23a, especially c.6, n.3, for relevant planks; 1 STANWOOD, HISTORY OF THE PRESIDENCY (1928) for full texts of platforms.
[43] Even MCLAUGHLIN, CONSTITUTIONAL HISTORY OF THE UNITED STATES (1935) makes no reference to the significance of the due process planks. Writers occasionally have noted the Republican plank of 1856, but rarely those before and after.

With the essence of antislavery theory thus finding expression in treatises and party platforms it was only natural that it be increasingly employed in congressional debate and on the stump. Known uses by men like Bingham and Bliss in the fifties can now be viewed in proper perspective. Far from being isolated or creative instances, they probably reflected merely a more intensive exposure or conditioning. Bingham, for example, is known to have attended Franklin College, an abolitionist stronghold near New Athens, Ohio, in 1836–37. This was during the period the Ohio crusade was at its height. Later, he practiced law in Cadiz, where prevailing antislavery sentiment was exceptionally strong. Indeed, we today find record of petitions and resolutions adopted by the Cadiz societies in 1837 which employed the identical due process-comity clause phraseology for which Bingham, thirty years later, showed preference in his drafts.[44]

Finally, one is better able to understand Chief Justice Taney's catastrophic use of due process in the *Dred Scott* case. That he should revive the doctrine of the Pinckney report was quite as natural as that his heresy be furiously proclaimed and combatted, and ultimately overcome by forces unleashed by the abolitionists' broader usage.

What would seem to be the implications of these discoveries? Are we not obliged to consider whether, in the attempt to avoid certain notorious pitfalls of historical interpretation, legal scholarship has not lapsed into errors almost as serious? Skepticism apparently has magnified the obstacles to early due process usage, mistaken its character, even overlooked its real foundations. Grant that the pioneer users could scarcely have forseen post-Civil War developments, much less have been guided or benefited by them. Does it follow that they lacked incentive and grounds for interest; that arguments *ad hominem* were scorned, or, if made, that they were insignificant?

Our thinking on these matters has gone aground on the very rocks it would avoid. Hindsight has projected backward the current, yet highly artificial, distinction between procedure and substance. And it has missed almost entirely the significance of the then universal belief in natural and inalienable rights. Concerned with only a few major cases, and with prevailing opinions in those, with little attention to the briefs, and often none to chronology, assuming public apathy and indifference to follow as a matter of course because due process *today* is a highly technical field, and even then was an ancient one, we have emasculated both the law and lawyers and con-

---

44 Chapter 4, *supra* at 200, 232, and especially notes 150, 255.

Procedure to Substance 257

jured up some strange anachronisms: "Bible and Blackstone," "hammer and tongs" counsel and their circuit riding judges—often armed only with a Kent or Story, and arguing mainly from Locke, the self-evident truths and the Preamble—such men still supposedly approached problems of legislative power and judicial relief with the nice distinctions of a third-year class dissecting *Taylor v. Porter*. Yet these were the days when the cleaver did duty as scalpel, and both amputees and surgeons were concerned more with self preservation than with scarless sutures. Modern rule-minded lawyers and connoisseurs of technique therefore must make heroic efforts to understand the primitives. Starting points in this regard are simply (1) the natural rights philosophy and limited government premises were controlling, not the historic limits of the clause; and (2) that any natural rights-natural justice usage was potentially (if not actually) a substantive usage. If the facts of a case, on modern analysis, reveal it as strictly procedural, well and good. But no such sophisticated nonsense need be imputed, for example, to the Tennessee counsel and judges who seized on Justice Catron's dictum in *Vanzant v. Waddel*,[45] using it time and again in the thirties and forties, to kill outrageous special acts. If we are obliged to make assumptions regarding the mental set and motivation of such pioneers, it seems far more likely they were conscious of that clause in the Tennessee Constitution which declared "non-resistance against arbitrary power and oppression, is absurd, slavish, and destructive to the good and happiness of mankind,[46] than they were of any shadowy distinctions between procedure and substance. No introspection, little hesitancy, no divining rods were needed by these counsel and judges confronted with the practical problem of doing justice as they saw fit. For in addition to the usual narrow law of the land clause taken bodily from Magna Carta, the Tennessee Constitution contained the same wording which the Ohio abolitionists used against their Black laws. "[A]ll courts shall be open; and every man, for an injury done him . . . shall have remedy by due course of law, and right and justice administered without sale, denial, or delay."[47] Obviously this guarantee of judicial redress, which appeared also in the Constitution of Pennsylvania,[48] was a powerful factor in encouraging strong use of the due process-due course-law

---

[45] *Supra* note 5. Paraphrasing Webster's *Dartmouth College* definition, Catron had declared "The clause 'law of the land' means a general and public law, equally binding upon every member of the community."
[46] TENN. CONST. Art. I, § 2 (1836).
[47] *Id.* Art I, § 17.
[48] PA. CONST. Art. IX, § 11 (1838).

of the land concept as a weapon against legislative excesses. Equally important were the preambles and opening sections of many of the state bills of rights. In various forms, these repeated the Lockean-Declaration of Independence postulates regarding human freedom and equality, and man's inherent and inalienable rights of "acquiring, possessing and protecting property."

In short, it may be said that the most expansive interpretations of due process did not flow from the sparse Magna Carta-Fifth Amendment wording. They emerged from the broader state clauses related to (and used in conjunction with) sweeping Lockean phraseology which gave free wheeling to such premises as "Due process requires judicial process . . . reasonableness . . . equality of protection . . . substantiality of purpose." Thus the due process funnel originally was inverted. Dicta and holdings were caught from numerous guarantees, pooled under the one heading, which in time became shorthand for a whole reservoir of concepts.

That something of this sort is the heart of the matter is evident when we take a look at the early law journals and reports. Observe, for example, what is found regarding due process as understood and discussed in 1843–45, immediately after Judge Bronson's opinion in *Taylor v. Porter*.

The *Western Law Journal*, edited in Cincinnati by Timothy Walker, carried a fierce, rambling debate on the subject of "Curative Statutes" or "Retrospective Laws" dealing with the Ohio legislature's power, just denied by a divided Supreme Court,[49] to validate married women's conveyances defective for want of proper acknowledgments. Fifty pages, scattered through three numbers,[49a] of attack, counter-attack, rebuttal, rejoinder were written by two able lawyers in a roundhouse argument that speaks volumes. G. M. Tuttle defended the clumsy legislative shortcut as the necessary price of preventing Elizabeth Zercher from avoiding her contract; Simeon Nash ignored the sharpers as the necessary price for maintaining a doctrinaire's hostility to all retrospective laws. In some respects the

---

[49] Good v. Zercher, 12 Ohio 364 (1843). The decision was followed and affirmed in numerous other cases 1844–47 (Meddock v. Williams, 12 Ohio 377 (1843); Silliman v. Cummins, 13 Ohio 116 (1844); Robb v. Lessee of Irwin, 15 Ohio 689, 704 (1846)) but finally was overruled in December, 1847, after arguments by Henry Stanbery, Rufus King and Thomas Ewing, Chestnut v. Shane's Lessee, 16 Ohio 599, 611 (1847).

[49a] The controversy began in the January, 1845, number of 2 WESTERN L.J. with simultaneous publication of *Remarks on . . . Good v. Zercher* by G. M. Tuttle, at 154, and *The Constitutionality of Retrospective Statutes* by Simeon Nash, at 170. Nash's article was continued in the February number, at 197; his *Reply to the Review of Good v. Zercher* appeared in March at 257. Tuttle's rejoinder, published in the September number, at 534, concluded the debate.

Procedure to Substance 259

performance merits inclusion in a *Readings in Jurisprudence.* Even Tuttle, who clearly saw and exposed the fallacies whereby the Court and Nash elevated existent acts into constitutional limitations, and who stood staunchly on the positive law as the determinant of what actually is "property" protected by the Constitution, became so ensnarled in his natural rights rhetoric that his case was weakened and undermined.[50] Nash, on the other hand, chided Tuttle for relying on higher law premises, blissfully unconscious of his own!

Yet Nash knew his Ruffin, Kent, and Bronson; he was destined for the Bench and already could improvise with the best of them:[51]

> I deny that such a law, if law it may be called, is passed in reasonable exercise of legislative authority. It not only operates retrospectively and thus contradicts the essence and nature of law, but in thus attempting to deprive one man of a vested right for the benefit of another, it violates the natural and unalienable rights of humanity; rights which are superior to and beyond the reach of any earthly authority whatever. What these rights are is settled by the constitution itself. . . . The first section . . . declares that every person has a natural right of possessing and defending property and [the 7th] that for an injury to his property, or his personal rights he shall have a remedy by due course of law. The right of possessing and acquiring property is not only declared inviolate, but the courts are required to remain ever open to afford a speedy remedy, by due course of law, to every person for an injury done him in his person or property. How then can the legislature deprive him of this right to appeal to the courts for a remedy, for what was at the time an injury to his property as vested in him by law, by enacting that what *was* an injury to his property, or person, is not injury, and shall be so adjudged by the courts. What was once an injury to him in his person or property must ever remain such; and no authority known to our constitution can alter its character.

Then comes the clincher, as italicized by Nash himself.[52]

> The *private* property of one man cannot be taken for the *private uses of another* in any case. It cannot by *a mere act of the legislature* be taken from *one man,* and vested in *another directly;* nor can it, by the *retrospective operation* of laws be indirectly

---

[50] *Id.* at 157–159, 537–539; *c.f* Nash, *supra* note 49a at 177, 263–265.
[51] *Id.* at 177–178.
[52] *Id.* at 179. Nash incorrectly cited 3 Greenleaf 290 as the basis for this passage. Actually he quoted C. J. Mellen's opinion in Kennebec Purchase v. Laboree, 2 Me. 253, 267, 2 Greenl. 275, 290–291 (1823)—a strong use of Lockean state constitutional clauses which itself supports our thesis regarding such phraseology. He also cited *Taylor v. Porter* as authority for these same propositions.

transferred from one to another; or subjected to the government of principles in a court of justice, which must necessarily produce that effect.

Next, turn to the *American Law Magazine*, the oracle of Philadelphia lawyers, which carried a thirty-page anonymous article in July, 1843, entitled "The Security of Private Property."[53] The thesis is implicit in the title: man's happiness and progress have been in direct proportion to the security accorded property. Property, moreover, is timid, unstable—"in need of every parchment barrier which has been or can be thrown around it." "In a republic, where the legislature . . . is annually elected, and where . . . legislation partakes . . . of the passions and impulses of the moment, it is important to inquire into the extent of the power possessed by the majority, to encroach upon the fruits of honest industry, or interfere with the proprietor in his free and undisturbed possession and enjoyment."[54]

Promising beginning! And the author revealed immediately what was on his mind: "The right of eminent domain"—a power of sovereignty—and incidentally the subject of *Taylor v. Porter*! Lengthy quotations then followed from Grotius, Rutherford, Pufendorf, Burlamaqui, Vattel, and Kent—all stressing the bounds of the power and its limitation to "cases of urgent state necessity, or obvious public utility."

Chief Justice Gibson had gone astray, alarming the property-conscious. Three years before, speaking for the Pennsylvania court in *Harvey v. Thomas*,[55] he upheld an act of 1832 which authorized construction and outlined procedure whereby owners of property along railroads or canals might build connecting roads or sidings, the eminent domain power being expressly conferred for "public or private use." Neither the propriety nor grounds of the decision were questioned. Pennslyvania did indeed have, said the author, quoting the Chief Justice, "an incalculable interest in her coal mines; nor will it be alleged that incorporation of railroad companies for the development of her resources . . . would not be a measure of public utility; and it surely will not be imagined that a privilege constitutionally given an artificial person, would be less constitutionally given to a natural one."[56]

The grievance was rather the unparsimonious language in which

---

[53] 1 AM. L. MAG. 318.
[54] *Id.* at 319.
[55] 10 Watts 63, 36 Am. Dec. 141 (Pa. 1840). COOLEY, CONSTITUTIONAL LIMITATIONS 357, 531 (3d ed. 1874) contrasted *Taylor v. Porter* and *Harvey v. Thomas*.
[56] *Harvey v. Thomas, supra* note 55 at 66–67, 36 Am. Dec. at 144.

Procedure to Substance

the Chief Justice, near the close of his opinion, had sustained the power as applied to private, that is, quasi-public use: the just compensation clause was a limitation, "and the [sovereign] right would have existed in full force without it." Hence, there was "nothing in the Constitution to prevent" such legislation.

The remaining half of the article therefore, was an implied rebuke to the Chief Justice. More than that, it was a searching exploration of the due process-law of the land phraseology, both as to constitutional texts and cases (including elaborate quotations from *Hoke v. Henderson* and the Tennessee and South Carolina landmark cases, ending with a review of the early New York eminent domain cases from which *Taylor v. Porter* had been synthesized just a few months before).

The writer began by acknowledging that the state governments, unlike the federal, are governments of general powers.[57]

> Yet what are the general powers of government in a civilized society? Is there no *lex legum*, independent of express constitutional restrictions? It may be a wide and dangerous door to open to judicial discretion, to say, that they shall apply to the question of validity or invalidity of legislative acts, the general principles of just government as laid down by the most eminent jurists and text writers. Yet suppose the legislature to pass a law arbitrarily depriving a citizen of life or liberty, without fault or crime on his part, must we look to the constitution for an expressed disaffirmance of such a power?

If so, he continued,

> There exists a disaffirmance of it, clear, positive, and unequivocal in the words of magna carta transferred into the bill of rights of every state of the Union which has a bill of rights, and standing out in bold relief in the . . . constitution of Pennsylvania.

After quoting the full texts, and Coke's familiar elucidation:

> The same provision which secures our lives and liberties against an arbitrary exercise of legislative power, and there is no other, extends to our property.

Following brief reference to other clauses deemed potential bulwarks, he continues:[58]

> Fortunately these broad positions of the Supreme Court of Pennsylvania are not sustained by the current of American decisions.

---
[57] *Supra* note 53, at 334–335.
[58] *Id.* at 337–338.

Then follows the elaborate case analysis, ending:

> The authorities might be multiplied. It is consoling to find the sound positions of the general writers thus practically enforced through an independent judiciary; and the reader of this article will lay it aside with the reflection that the liberty of the republican states of America will owe their perpetuity to their courts, executing the supreme will of the people against acts of tyranny and oppression, whether proceeding from the executive or the legislature.

It would be interesting indeed to know who was the author of this remarkable piece. It was written, during the very months when the New York Court was hearing and deciding *Taylor v. Porter*, or shortly thereafter.[59] One feels safe only in suggesting that, whoever he was, he could hardly have been surprised or disappointed when he learned of Judge Bronson's opinion. And across the line in New York, Judge Bronson must have welcomed, and perhaps wondered a little, at such timely support. Only those who have missed the implications, and indeed our whole thesis, will need to consider correspondence or telepathy!

Finally, turn to the cases from Illinois, at the December term, 1845. How far, how fast, did the magic spread? Or was it endemic, indigenous?

Rhinehart v. Schuyler[60] held the revenue laws of the State of Illinois, from 1823 to 1829 inclusive, constitutional, and held further that the registry laws did not apply to patents or deeds emanating from the state or the United States. An auditor's deed, therefore, was admissible in evidence, without proof of its execution, and without showing that it had been regularly acknowledged and recorded, as required in cases of conveyances affecting only the interests of private individuals.

The report runs sixty-eight pages, with a three-to-two decision, two judges not sitting, and a strong dissent. "Judgment entered De-

---

[59] *Taylor v. Porter* was decided "Jan. term, 1843"; and volume four of Hill's *Reports* was published late in 1843 or early in 1844 and is digested in 7 MONTHLY LAW REPORTER 481 (January, 1845). Since the author of *The Security of Private Property*, supra note 53 (July, 1843) made no reference to the case, when he had every reason for doing so, one concludes he was unaware of it. The strong reliance on continental authors, together with the *lex legum* argument in favor of general jurisprudential authority, suggest Peter Stephen du Ponceau, 1760–1844, the eminent Franco-American lawyer of Philadelphia, as a likely author. *Cf.* the similar *lex legum* ideas advanced in his DISSERTATION ON THE NATURE AND EXTENT OF THE JURISDICTION OF THE COURTS OF THE UNITED STATES (1824) p. 126–132; and see BAUER, COMMENTARIES ON THE CONSTITUTION, 1790–1860 (1952) for a recent biographical sketch.

[60] 7 Ill. 375, 2 Gil. 473 (1845).

cember term, 1843; opinion of the court not delivered until the present term"—two years later! There are twenty pages of briefs and arguments: N. H. Purple, A. Williams, J. Butterfield were all fighting to overturn tax laws and titles twenty years old or more; three of the ablest lawyers in the state—O. H. Browning, S. T. Logan, E. D. Baker, all friends of Lincoln (and Logan, his partner),[61] staved off chaos by a single vote. Due process was the spearhead of the attack—obviously inspired by reconstitution of the Court. *Taylor v. Porter* and *Hoke v. Henderson* were both heavily relied on by Williams, who never had heard of the goose and golden egg.[62] Laws of nineteen states out of twenty provided for summary tax sales, and most of them made tax deeds prima facie evidence of title. Even the minority bowed out, confining dissent to the valuation requirement.

In short, due process was condemned to vegetate a while longer, not from ignorance of its potentialities, but from overdemonstration and abuse of them.

CONCLUSION

Obviously there have been blind spots in evaluations of the factors responsible for the shifts in due process. Widespread popular and forensic use of the guarantee did not depend on, nor wait upon, either a correct appreciation of historic meanings or the *judicial* discovery of substantive values. Reluctance to endow corporation lawyers and drafters of the Fourteenth Amendment with intuition and foresight has obscured the fact that in many of these matters intuition and foresight were not required.

Far from deriving from professional usage of the clause, public use—and misuse—preceded, stimulated, and at times unquestionably conditioned use by the Bench and Bar. Perhaps in some cases our premises need to be almost inverted. Generally speaking, political, party platform and congressional uses have been assumed to have derived from the judicial,[63] whereas evidence clearly points

---

[61] *Id.* at 377, 390, 2 Gil. at 476, 491 (Browning); *id.* at 387, 2 Gil. at 488 (Baker); *id.* at 389, 2 Gil. at 491 (Logan). Baker's argument that the "law of the land" meant a "law as defined by Blackstone and Demosthenes," and Logan's contention that the principle of separation of powers had been "proclaimed hundreds of years ago at Runnymede" dramatize the handicaps of blackletter research at circuit. Fortunately, soundness of public policy and common sense counted most heavily with such men.

[62] *Id.* at 382, 2 Gil. at 482 (Williams).

[63] Originally, in discussing the Bingham-Bliss use of due process in the slavery debates of the fifties, the writer so assumed: see Chapter 1, *supra*, notes 79–83; he herewith recants. Granted strong natural law premises and habits of thought, the professional compulsions of law and politics were about equally efficient as triggers of due process usage. Cross-fertilizations undoubtedly were common, but need not be assumed.

as often in the opposite direction. Idealism and opportunism, both born of the almost universal reliance on natural rights principles, gave due process its tremendous popularity and built on its inherent advantages.

Declining public interest in constitutional law, the current trend toward judicial self-limitation, the modern tendency toward more sophisticated forms of natural rights thinking, all combine to make these facts a bit difficult to grasp. Yet in so far as the public's contributions are concerned, there should be little cause for wonder. Laymen rarely have needed lessons from lawyers or judges to uncover and exploit a nice rhetorical question beggar. And it is no reflection on due process to acknowledge that the clause was one of the neatest, as certainly it is still one of the noblest formulas of this type ever devised. Why wonder then, at these parallel uses and explorations by the public and judiciary? Together they simply give a new twist to Professor Powell's celebrated dictum: "Much of the logic and rhetoric of constitutional law may be peculiar; but it is not peculiar to constitutional law."[64] Americans may be proud and thankful to discover, certainly in these times, that broadened and discretionary due process, far from being an excrescence or tool of ambition, is in reality so deeply enrooted in our national consciousness that its judicial achievement was quite as much a result as a cause of widespread popular usage.

EDITORIAL NOTE. "Anachronized" history fudges on its age, confuses its own thinking and development. By 1950-1953, nothing was clearer than that the history of American due process and equal protection during the nineteenth century had got thoroughly anachronized; anachronized not only by jurists, but by historians and by Everyman as well. Indeed, these two garblings clearly were related: the early antislavery usage and the racial-humanitarian expansion and coverage before the Civil War had got forgotten and eclipsed during Reconstruction, just as the economic and corporate usage began to quicken and proliferate first in lawyers' briefs, then in the court reports, finally in academic-popular discussion and history. Extension and expansion of usage thus ultimately culminated in an inversion of protection and coverage. Everyman's own absent-mindedness at length afflicted even historians. The threads of earlier

---

[64] Powell, *The Logic and Rhetoric of Constitutional Law*, 15 J. PHIL. PSYCH. AND SCI. METHOD 654 (1918), 1 SELECTED ESSAYS CONSTITUTIONAL LAW 474, 487-488 (1938).

constitutional thought not only were severed; they were now mistied and misjudged. And these blunders became reflexive and cumulative.

For one thing, the study of constitutional history and protection had waned and narrowed to a study of the *majority* opinions of the Supreme Court of the United States. Antebellum constitutional theory now went unstudied; slavery's constitutional theory was forgotten. Year by year, in both courses and casebooks, fewer post-Civil War race cases were covered. Three of those cases, as observed, were riddled with misconceptions and worse. Only passing reference now was made to the first Justice Harlan's dissents. Before long, the Justices and critics alike were debating whether the Fourteenth Amendment had "incorporated" the *full* Bill of Rights. It was unreal; an echo, indeed, of an echo, for no one even pretended that *all* the clauses and guarantees of the Bill of Rights ever could or would be enforced against the states in the twentieth century.

Such was the national stance, 1950–1954. Everyman was getting uneasy. The United States was again at war. The armed forces tardily had been integrated;[1] the white primary[2] and restrictive covenants[3] outlawed. More than ever, "Separate but equal"[4] shamed, sullied, and compromised America's conscience and integrity.

---

[1] For summary coverage and basic documentation of this delayed development, see GREENBERG, RACE RELATIONS AND AMERICAN LAW (1959), 355–370; POLITICAL AND CIVIL RIGHTS IN THE UNITED STATES (3d ed., 1967, 2 vols.), vol. 2, pp. 1880–1883; Billington, *Freedom to Serve: The President's Committee on Equality of Treatment and Opportunity in the Armed Forces, 1949–50*, 50 J. NEGRO HISTORY (1966).

[2] Smith v. Allwright, 321 U. S. 649 (1944), overruling Grovey v. Townsend, 295 U. S. 45 (1935). For basic documentation, see POLITICAL AND CIVIL RIGHTS IN THE UNITED STATES, vol. 2, pp. 1481 ff.

[3] Shelley v. Kraemer, 334 U. S. 1 (1948); Barrows v. Jackson, 346 U. S. 249 (1953). For history and commentary, see POLITICAL AND CIVIL RIGHTS IN THE UNITED STATES, vol. 2, pp. 2019 ff.; VOSE, CAUCASIANS ONLY: THE SUPREME COURT, THE NAACP, AND THE RESTRICTIVE COVENANT CASES (1959).

[4] 163 U. S. 537 (1896).

[CHAPTER 6]

The Fourteenth Amendment and School Segregation

EDITORIAL NOTE. The sociology of law, and the sociology of inquiry and research, are intricate and ramifying beyond belief. And the social forces responsible for constitutional growth and development are by far the most intricate of all. Litigational, bibliographic, and research interests wax and wane, lag, interfere, and consolidate, subject to every vicissitude and influence humanity is heir to. What law emerges, when and how; what such law holds, "means," and protects, thus depend in part on chance factors, and on the reapplications. Always, too, on the bar's, and on the courts' reading matter; or, as the professionals put it, "on the research."

Input, modern programmers continually say, determines and conditions *output*.[1] English common lawyers and parliamentarians learned and applied this centuries before anyone else heard of it. It appears likely, indeed, that two determinative factors in the rise of English parliamentary constitutionalism—in the emergence of that Stuart Constitution fashioned from Lancastrian "precedent" —were the highly selective, professional character, and the equally ruminant, regurgitative character, of the records used and reused by common lawyers and parliamentarians from the start. These, contrary to common belief, rarely were the full, official, "royal" or chancery records which historians know, celebrate, and work with today. Rather, they were simply and chiefly lawyers' own notes, abstracts, and "digests." The medieval year-books and statutes[2] alike often got preserved only in this form; that is, as and in professional compilations, notes, "commonplaces." Printing fortuitously froze all this; and during the Tudor-Stuart period, further accentuated

---

[1] For a lucid statement of the relations of cybernetics and law, see Mermin, *Computers, Law, and Justice: An Introductory Lecture*, 1967 WIS. L. REV. 43–87.

[2] Richardson and Sayles, *The Early Statutes*, 50 L. Q. REV. 201–223, 540–570 (1934).

these professional biases, habits, and trends[3] until the Stuart kings were left baffled and hamstrung—victims of an ex parte, over-edited, constricted professional record.

Socially and constitutionally, the results have not always been so benign. Just how narrow, ruminant, regurgitative legal records and research can be and are; how far the law's physiology and metabolism are controlled by its diets—and vice versa—are professional bywords and secrets. The law's indexing and self-manipulative, self-focusing powers always have been extraordinary—professionally the best by far, until recently. Yet law's astigmatisms and displacements are equally notorious, as already observed. The constitutional bearings and significance of this tend to get overlooked. Yet the dangers of inbreeding, of over-abstraction and selectivity, are as obvious and as great as the advantages. The fact is that only the *adversary character* of common-law litigation, and of our American common-law constitutionalism, ever has made this system tolerable, or workable at all. And the sobering realization is that this adversary system for so long could do, and did, nothing whatever for American slaves, Negroes, or Indians. These groups, in short, represented the prima facie exceptions—the chief, if not sole instances, in which adversary jurisprudence—process and protection—broke down, failed utterly, and from the start—owing, of course, to a unique, pestilent, racial hostility and prejudice. And of course it is *because* of this that we today have Everyman's Constitution—and that we have not yet made proper use of it.

When members of a *race*, or of a *class*, can not, and do not, plead their own case, who pleads for them? Who calls attention to their plight, and problems, and needs? Counsel for the California railroads, we saw, did this for the Chinese. And it was Mr. Justice Field who made these pleadings good. But no one ever spoke "for Logan" —for the American Indian. And for long only Justice Harlan spoke for the freedman, and against Jim Crow.

Not until the 1930's, therefore, was even the National Association for the Advancement of Colored People in a position to launch the concentrated, continuous, strategic defense and attack needed to realize the process and protection that had been contemplated. This

---

[3] On the Englishing of English law in relation to constitutionalism, see generally Graham, *"Our Tong Maternall Maruellously Amendyd and Augmentyd": The First Englishing and Printing of the Medieval Statutes at Large, 1530–1533*, 13 UCLA L. REV. 58–98 (1965), and earlier works there cited, notes 15 and 74; Graham, *The Englishing of English Law*, MOREANA: BULLETIN THOMAS MORE, No. 11 (Angers, France), 27–32 (1966).

"new" NAACP program[4] was projected and launched by leaders who established, directed, and operated with brilliant success, "the largest co-operative law office" and the most needed research and re-education program in American history.

American constitutional history, understandably, figured constantly in the planning and in the execution of this whole enterprise. "Law office history," of course, early became a pejorative term, but only from excess, and excess was not the problem here. "Law office history" as such can educate and liberate as well as direct and constrain. And lately it has.

In the study and the construction of Everyman's Constitution, so much so long had been lost, forgotten, evaded, obscured, contorted, and misrepresented in the various "inclusions and exclusions" that these major NAACP planning and strategy sessions—and eventually the briefs and arguments that were issued and addressed to the courts—were much needed and much welcomed seminars in American history, economics, political science, and political ethics. And finally, to be sure, in 1952–1955, in social psychology, in segregated American education as well. After fifty-five years, *Plessy v. Ferguson* was on the skids, nationally, constitutionally insufferable.

On June 16, 1953, just a month after I had received a Guggenheim Fellowship for further work on the Fourteenth Amendment, and shortly after the Supreme Court had requested a full rebriefing and reargument of the *School Desegregation Cases*, I received a telegram from Mr. Thurgood Marshall (now happily Mr. Justice Marshall). Would I join in preparation of working papers on the history and adoption of the Fourteenth Amendment for use of counsel engaged in the requested rebriefings?[5] Alfred H. Kelly of Wayne State University was re-assaying "framer intent" and the "original understanding" as revealed by the congressional debates and state ratifications. A buttressing paper was needed which would summarize the "Antislavery Backgrounds" and the "Antislavery Origins" and related research, and which would relate the drafts and the Amendment to the broader streams of constitutional theory and history.

The first two months of the Guggenheim Fellowship year thus were spent, not on further study of the insurance company and

---

[4] See generally, GREENBERG, RACE RELATIONS AND AMERICAN LAW (1959), *passim*; Appendix B, *NAACP Legal Defense Cases Before the Supreme Court*, a list, 1915–1958; and VOSE, CAUCASIANS ONLY (1959).

[5] See Kelly, *The School Desegregation Case*, in QUARRELS THAT HAVE SHAPED THE CONSTITUTION (1964) 243–268.

The Fourteenth Amendment and School Segregation 269

railroad maneuvers in Congress and in the courts, 1865–1890, as planned, but happily working eighteen-hour days preparing a 35,000-word survey, summary, and abridgment of previous work. From that memorandum,[6] two law review essays then were drafted. The first, "The Fourteenth Amendment and School Segregation," here reprinted, appeared while the cases were before the Court. It was satisfying good fortune indeed, for a lay bibliographer who had counted his compensation in footnotes and in dissents, to have finally contributed a thirty-page supplement ("An Analysis of the Political, Social, and Legal Theories Underlying the Fourteenth Amendment"[7]) to the main brief of the major constitutional case of our time.

The *School Cases* were decided May 17, 1954, with scant reference to the historical rebriefings or to framer intent or original understanding. Rather, political and judicial ethics, social psychology—what the equal protection of the laws means, and must mean, in our time, whatever it may have meant to whomever in 1866–1868—these were the grounds and the essence of Chief Justice Warren's opinion for a unanimous Court.

Affirmative constitutional protection, in short. *Affirmative equal* protection.

Psychoanalysis of draftsmen and ratifiers, and obeisance to a dead past, can provide no Constitution for Everyman in this century. That is the argument here.

---

[6] Graham, *The Purpose and Meaning of Sections One and Five of the Fourteenth Amendment: The Historical Evidence Reexamined* (NAACP mimeograph, 1953), 73, 25.

[7] Brief for Appellants, pp. 199–234, Brown v. Board of Education of Topeka, No. 1, Oct. term, 1953, 347 U. S. 483 (decided May 17, 1954).

[CHAPTER 6]

ONCE AGAIN intense interest and scrutiny are focused on the Fourteenth Amendment. The immediate occasion is the decision now pending in the *School Segregation Cases*.[1] Held over from the 1952 term at the Supreme Court's request, these five cases were

---

[1] Supreme Court of the United States, October, 1953 Term, docket numbers 1, 2, 4, 8, 10: *Brown v. Board of Education of Topeka; Briggs v. Elliott; Davis v. County School Board of Prince Edward County; Bolling v. Sharpe; Gebhart v. Belton.* The corresponding docket numbers of the cases, 1952 Term, were 8, 101, 191, 413, 448.

rebriefed and on December 7–9, 1953, elaborately reargued upon a series of five questions framed by the justices. The five queries[2] dealt with the purpose of the Amendment, the intent of framers and ratifiers, and the respective powers, under Sections One and Five, of Congress and the Judiciary. The first two questions sought "evidence" of the intention with regard to the school segregation issue. Question three related to the Court's existent powers under the text of the Amendment, regardless of framer-intent, in case historic evidence proved unclear or indecisive. Questions four and five concerned the judicial mechanics for ending segregation "assuming it is decided that segregation in public schools violates the Fourteenth Amendment."

A Rip Van Winkle, awakening from an eighty-year nap, would pinch himself in disbelief at these developments. The Fourteenth Amendment,[3] he would exclaim, had been drafted in 1866 to make the former slaves citizens—to remove doubt about constitutionality of the Civil Rights Act of that year. That Act in turn, drawn by Senator Trumbull,[3a] had been designed to secure to the freedmen actual as well as nominal freedom, to root out slavery's "badges and incidents," to outlaw public race discrimination.[4] The Fourteenth Amendment—universally understood as "embodying" or "incorporating" this bill—and hence as reconstituting the powers of the Federal government to the extent needed to erase the color line from American life—was ratified in 1868. Five years later, in the *Slaughter-House Cases*, the Supreme Court declared that the "one pervading purpose" of the Amendment, and indeed of all three War Amendments, had been "the freedom of the slave race [and] the security and firm establishment of that freedom."[5] One can

---

[2] 345 U. S. 972 (1953) (memorandum decision).

[3] Basic monographs and articles on the history of the Fourteenth Amendment and its major clauses are: FLACK, THE ADOPTION OF THE FOURTEENTH AMENDMENT (1908); KENDRICK, JOURNAL OF THE JOINT COMMITTEE OF FIFTEEN ON RECONSTRUCTION (1914); Fairman, *Does the Fourteenth Amendment Incorporate the Bill of Rights? The Original Understanding*, 2 STAN. L. REV. 5 (1949); Frank and Munro, *The Original Understanding of the "Equal Protection of the Laws"*, 50 COL. L. REV. 131 (1950); McLaughlin, *The Court, the Corporation and Conkling*, 46 AM. HIST. REV. 45 (1940); Boudin, *Truth and Fiction About the Fourteenth Amendment*, 16 N.Y.U.L.Q. REV. 19 (1938); WARSOFF, EQUALITY AND THE LAW (1938); TENBROEK, THE ANTISLAVERY ORIGINS OF THE FOURTEENTH AMENDMENT (1951); CROSSKEY, POLITICS AND THE CONSTITUTION IN THE HISTORY OF THE UNITED STATES vol. 2, c. 31–32 (1953); and Chapters 1–5, *supra*.

[3a] WHITE, LIFE OF TRUMBULL (1913).

[4] See TENBROEK, *op. cit. supra* note 3, c. 9–12; FLACK, *op. cit. supra* note 3, c. 1; and Chapter 7, *infra*.

[5] 16 Wall. 36, 71 (U. S. 1873).

imagine Rip's puzzlement therefore on learning that since 1896,[6] this Amendment, securing to all "persons" the "equal protection of the laws," had nonetheless sanctioned racial segregation in public schools, transportation, amusement, etc. Chide us, this awakened sleeper well might, for proof *he alone* had been napping!

Assuredly a sensitive American with an eye to the headlines as well as histories[7] would have a very bad time bringing the old gentleman down to date. These are the darkest chapters in our past: Gradual, systematic breakdown of Reconstruction; betrayal of the South and Negroes alike; vindictive partisanship, reckless Executive-Legislative warfare; shameless exploitation of sectional hatreds and Negro suffrage; at length, military rule at dead end, sectional stalemate, the freedmen and Negro race jettisoned through this "separate but equal" cynicism, with its evasions and insulting defenses.

To convey this—the combined substance of Reconstruction history and of Myrdal's *An American Dilemma*[8]—to one who had experienced the thrill of Emancipation and shared the hopes and idealism of the Trumbulls, would be a harrowing task. To undertake it now, when every headline is a reminder of farflung American interests, and of the necessity for moral leadership in a world only one-third of whose population is white, would be a sobering, depressing experience for any citizen.

The initial reaction, after incredulity, at national frustration and failures of this magnitude, is anger, and search for historic villains

---

[6] Plessy v. Ferguson, 163 U. S. 537 (1896); two excellent recent critiques are Hyman, *Segregation and the Fourteenth Amendment*, 4 VAND. L. REV. 555 (1951); Ramsmeir, *The Fourteenth Amendment and the "Separate But Equal" Doctrine*, 50 MICH. L. REV. 203 (1951).

[7] For "revisionist" views and bibliographies, see also Beale, *On Rewriting Reconstruction History*, 45 AM. HIST. REV. 807 (1940); Williams, *An Analysis of Some Reconstruction Attitudes*, 12 JL. OF SOUTHERN HIST. 469 (1946); BUCK, THE ROAD TO REUNION, 1865–1900 (1937); RANDALL, THE CIVIL WAR AND RECONSTRUCTION (1937); COULTER, THE SOUTH DURING RECONSTRUCTION (1947); DUBOIS, BLACK RECONSTRUCTION (1935); BEALE, THE CRITICAL YEAR (1930). An indispensable bibliographic aid on the legal side of civil rights history is POLITICAL AND CIVIL RIGHTS IN THE UNITED STATES (Emerson and Haber, eds. 1952) [3d ed. 1967]. 1968: Major recent works include: DEWITT, THE IMPEACHMENT AND TRIAL OF ANDREW JOHNSON (reprint of 1903 edition, Stanley I. Kutler, ed., Madison, 1967); DESANTIS, REPUBLICANS FACE THE SOUTHERN QUESTION (Baltimore, 1959); MCKITRICK, ANDREW JOHNSON AND RECONSTRUCTION (Chicago, 1960); Rindleberger, *Abandonment of the Negro during Reconstruction*, 35 JOURNAL OF NEGRO HISTORY 88 (1960); FTANKLIN, RECONSTRUCTION AFTER THE CIVIL WAR (Chicago, 1967); THOMAS and HYMAN, STANTON: THE LIFE AND TIMES OF LINCOLN'S SECRETARY OF WAR (New York, 1962); BROCK, AMERICAN CRISIS: CONGRESS AND RECONSTRUCTION, 1865–1867 (New York, 1963); Cox and Cox, POLITICS, PRINCIPLE AND PREJUDICE, 1865–1866: THE DILEMMA OF RECONSTRUCTION AMERICA (New York, 1963); DONALD, THE POLITICS OF RECONSTRUCTION, 1863–1867 (Baton Rouge, 1965).

[8] (1944).

or scapegoats. Thaddeus Stevens and Charles Sumner, the leading "Ultra-Radicals" and "Vindictives"; Andrew Johnson, the vain, pugnacious little President, as courageous (and occasionally as right) as he was inept, have served in countless histories and speeches in this regard. So have innumerable lesser, general fry—"Abolitionist fanatics," "Black Republicans," "Grant Stalwarts," "Carpetbaggers," "Scalawags" and the rest. And on the other side, their opposites, the "unrepentent Rebels, Traitors and Secesh" that figured in stump speeches for fifty years.

Our generation fortunately has outgrown such history. The Civil War and Reconstruction now are uniformly viewed as failures of statesmanship and of resource on both sides. Fanaticism was no monopoly of abolitionists. Slavery was not a "positive good"; nor its abolition "evil," nor protection of freedmen's rights "unconstitutional and unnecessary." On the other hand, neither were immediate Negro suffrage and military government the panaceas naive and designing men pretended. Negation and polarized programs at length brought both sides to near disaster. Reunion was largely at the expense of the Negro Race.[9]

Constitutional history barely has begun to benefit from this revisionism. Indeed, the whole subject has fallen on evil days. Once a favored form of American history, today it is the most neglected. McLaughlin's volume,[10] published in 1935, is still the latest general coverage as such. Constitutional *Law*, of course has split off as a discipline in its own right—abstruse, technical, increasingly viewed and taught merely as a system of rules with little regard for political and social context.[11] The residue obviously is difficult to manage. Even monographic treatments and judicial biographies have grown fewer. A widening gap is thus created, not only by differential rates of institutional growth, but by shifts of research interest as well.

An undesired consequence is that Americans generally are losing touch with a vital part of their past—and are doing so despite tre-

---

[9] This view is taken now in nearly all modern discussions, but corrective judicial interpretation still lags. For brilliant revisionary studies of the so-called "redemptionist" movement, see WOODWARD, THE ORIGINS OF THE NEW SOUTH (1951); and for the politics of the Reconstruction settlement of 1877, the same author's REUNION AND REACTION (1951).

[10] MCLAUGHLIN, A CONSTITUTIONAL HISTORY OF THE UNITED STATES (1935); KELLY AND HARBISON, THE AMERICAN CONSTITUTION; ITS ORIGINS AND DEVELOPMENT (1948) and SWISHER, AMERICAN CONSTITUTIONAL DEVELOPMENT (1943) are admirable academic works; the writer is here speaking of the decline of the subject in the popular sense. Professor Crosskey's *tour de force*, cited *supra* note 3, promises to quicken popular interest in the subject.

[11] For exploration of some of the consequences, see Chapter 5, *supra*.

mendous emphasis, in colleges and secondary schools, on American history and government. Constitutional democracy rests, in the long run, on popular understanding of its bases and operations. It is evident, therefore, that this growing neglect of constitutional history, and our tendency to build up arrearages of research and understanding, are by no means healthy signs.

In so far as popular—and even professional—understanding is concerned, one finds proof of this in the present status of the Fourteenth Amendment itself. That Amendment, as mystified Van Winkle[12] re-

---

[12] Once briefed, however, Van Winkle proved sharp indeed. The following fragment, found among his papers with the abbreviated title, "Reargt. School Seg. Cases?," suggests that he even for a time toyed with the notion of appearing *amicus curiae* opposite his eminent fellow-New Yorker, John W. Davis, Counsel for the State of South Carolina, and dean of the American corporate bar. From the references to Roscoe Conkling's argument it is plain the old libertarian took a sardonic layman's view of some matters not heretofore lightly treated either by judges or historians:

"Were we called upon to appear before your Honors in the role of counsel for corporations seeking protection as persons under Section One, challenging what even corporations apparently at times can feel to be 'invidious and discriminating legislation,' we should be obliged to make an embarrassing admission. We should have to admit that not one word ever has been found, either in the speeches of the framers, the debates of the 39th Congress, or the proceedings of the ratifying legislatures, which expressly declares, or otherwise clearly indicates, that even *one individual*, of all that extensive group, then 'contemplated or understood' corporate 'persons' to be embraced within the protection of Section One. An impenetrable barrier of silence—absolute and inscrutable—prevails here. To maintain the corporate proposition, therefore, we perhaps should be obliged to rest our case, as did that famous advocate and upstate New Yorker, Roscoe Conkling, when he appeared before this Court in 1882, wholly upon circumstantial grounds. We might be obliged to use, as was he, the Journal of the Joint Committee of Fifteen that drafted the Amendment,—and perhaps also some inference and conjecture [Chapter 1, *supra*, pp. 30–45] to show that corporations had come within the purview of the framers. We might well despair of that task—as might even our distinguished adversary, Mr. Davis himself, at this date. [See *Conn. Gen. Life Ins. Co. v. Johnson*, 303 U. S. 77, 83 (1938); *Wheeling Steel Corp. v. Glander*, 337 U. S. 562, 576–581 (1949).]

"But we all know that this corporate point, happily, has been foreclosed now for nearly 67 years. Not merely foreclosed, but substantially waived: In 1886, Conkling and his associate counsel were again prepared to make their extremely circumstantial argument, in a second series of *Railroad Tax Cases* involving the issues earlier left undecided when the first series had been withdrawn. At the outset of this second series of arguments, Chief Justice Waite announced from the bench, *in the only statement ever made by the full Court in deciding this crucial matter*: 'The court does not wish to hear argument on the question whether the provision in the Fourteenth Amendment to the Constitution, which forbids a State to deny to any person within its jurisdiction the equal protection of the laws, applies to these Corporations. We are all of the opinion that it does.'

"We today are beset by no difficulties or handicaps of evidence in these *School Cases*. The Congressional debates are almost too voluminous. . . .

"We will show, as predecessor counsel and historians have shown many times the past 85 years, that the Fourteenth Amendment was designed to be a bulwark for the rights of the Negro race; that it was designed to prohibit *all public* discriminations based upon race and color alone: that it was designed to wipe out what the Civil War

minded us has been a part of our Constitution eighty-five years. That it was adopted and ratified to remove all doubt about national power to protect the freedmen and to assure progressive removal of the discriminations, denials and abridgments in rights that had been a part of the slave system is generally conceded. Such has been the affirmed judicial view since 1873.[13] In 1908, moreover, Flack published his monograph, *The Adoption of the Fourteenth Amendment,* summarizing the debates in Congress and in the ratifying legislatures. Numerous works have recovered much of the ground since.[14] All agree regarding the racial motivation of the Amendment. In the meantime, however, certain collateral and secondary problems have become points of controversy. Two in particular have persisted at the judicial level: One, what framers and ratifiers contemplated or understood with regard to corporate persons;[15] the other, whether

---

generation rightly called the 'badges and indicia' of slavery, its hateful 'vestiges and appendages.' School Segregation, we submit, comes in this category.

"On these points, happily, our evidence is abundant; and the authorities are virtually unanimous. The ante-bellum history, the Congressional debates, the researches and writings of Flack, Fairman, Frank, Graham, Boudin, tenBroek, and Crosskey, whatever their different emphases, and whatever the doubts or disagreements on secondary details, clearly and unanimously support our position."

The notes break off abruptly at this point. Close reading shows of course that although militantly anti-separate-but-equal, the orientation here is not anti-corporate. As some of his other memoranda made clear, Van Winkle felt that " 'Due process' and 'equal protection', not 'person', are the key words." "Query: Aren't they ample enough for anybody?" To renege on corporate personality at this date was by his view "Pretty close to infanticide. . . . Remorse inevitable, then perhaps another brood —or at least another *brood of fictions.*" See the pre-Civil War history of the diversity of citizenship clause, and McGovney thereon, *A Supreme Court Fiction,* 56 HARV. L. REV. 853 (1943). Finally, he concluded with the observation, "Calvinists haven't always thought so highly of legislatures, or had such occasion to, as people 1932–195?"

Elsewhere, Van Winkle gave hearty endorsement of the punched card project, proudly noting that IBM had made itself right at home in his native Catskills. The writer wishes to express his indebtedness to Dr. Van Winkle for numerous insights and suggestions.

13 The calamitous effects of a caste system which really was consolidated and constitutionally condoned a full generation after Reconstruction (see WOODWARD, *op. cit. supra* note 9, at 209–212 and Chapter 7 *infra*) have too long obscured this fact, as has the lush economic use made of the Amendment. Yet Justice Miller's majority opinion in the *Slaughter-House Cases, supra* note 5 and Justice Bradley's majority opinion in the *Civil Rights Cases,* 109 U. S. 3 (1883) both are strong expositions of the Negro Race motivation of the Amendment. It often is overlooked in this regard that Justice Bradley himself nominally accepted the "badges and incidents" thesis of Trumbull and Harlan. See also the strong Negro Race statements in *Shelley v. Kraemer,* 334 U. S. 1, 21 (1948); *Buchanan v. Warley,* 245 U. S. 60, 76–77 (1917); *Strauder v. West Virginia,* 100 U. S. 303, 306–7 (1880). Our fears and sextants, not stars, have thrown us off course. Corrective action is a simple matter.

14 See note 3 *supra.*

15 *Connecticut General Life Insurance Co. v. Johnson,* 303 U. S. 77, 83 (1938); *Wheeling Steel Corp. v. Glander,* 337 U. S. 562, 576 (1949).

The Fourteenth Amendment and School Segregation 275

Section One was intended to incorporate the Bill of Rights to the extent of making *all* the first eight Amendments binding upon the States.[16] Significantly, both of these controversies resulted in combing and recombing of debates for evidence to support two sets of diametrically opposed positions.[17] Research of this type necessarily has been piecemeal, with attention focused on the one narrow point, and to the neglect or subordination of larger purposes.

The upshot is that after nearly a half-century of research and debate judges and historians are still unagreed about two fundamental questions concerning the Amendment's purposes. Dismayed or not, the Court meantime, by its first two questions in the *School* cases,[18] directed that another minute search be made—on another narrow point—and again in a manner that tends to lost sight of the Amendment's broader objectives.

Furthermore, framer-intent, as a criterion in these matters, obviously has had a distinctly hit-and-miss application. So much so, indeed, that one wonders whether, in asking Negro counsel to search for and present evidence of framer-intent on this specific issue of school segregation the Court remembered that no such request ever had been made—or ever could have been made—with regard to countless matters and fields over which it previously had extended the Amendment's protection. Absolutely nothing, for example, is found in the debates on whether sound trucks[19] or picketing[20] are to be regarded as constitutionally privileged free speech. There is nothing on "reasonable" rates of return for public service companies.[21] In fact, no one ever has found a single word in the main debates suggesting that framers and ratifiers "contemplated or understood" corporations to be "persons" under the due process and equal protection clauses. Yet this last, most vital point was conceded by the Court, without formal opinion, and with the matter of framer-intent substantially waived, exactly 67 years ago![22]

---

[16] *Adamson v. California*, 332 U. S. 46 (1947).
[17] On the corporate personality issue, see Chapters 1-2, *supra*; and as an example of the diverse interpretations drawn therefrom, see HACKER, THE TRIUMPH OF AMERICAN CAPITALISM 388-392 (1940), and FAIRMAN, MR. JUSTICE MILLER AND THE SUPREME COURT 187-189 (1939). On the incorporation of the Bill of Rights problem, see Justice Black's historical appendix, *Adamson v. California*, 332 U. S. 46, 68, 92-123 (1947) and Fairman, *supra* note 3, and the companion article by Morrison, *Does the Fourteenth Amendment Incorporate the Bill of Rights?* 2 STAN. L. REV. 140 (1949).
[18] See notes 1 and 2 *supra*.
[19] *Saia v. New York*, 334 U. S. 558 (1948). *Kovacs v. Cooper*, 336 U. S. 77 (1949). See also *Railway Express Agency v. New York*, 336 U. S. 106 (1949).
[20] *Thornhill v. Alabama*, 310 U. S. 88 (1940).
[21] *Smyth v. Ames*, 169 U. S. 466 (1897).
[22] *Santa Clara County v. Southern Pacific Ry. Co.*, 118 U. S. 394, 396 (1886) (equal

On the other hand, the evidence in the debates is overwhelming that racial discrimination *very broadly conceived* was the framers' target.²³ Added *constitutional* power thus was tapped for this very reason and an attempt at a minute (or even broad) taxonomy of discriminations was understandably avoided.²⁴ As Bingham put it, "You do not prohibit murder in the Constitution; you guarantee life in the Constitution."²⁵ And so, it was with "liberty" and "protection," and above all, *equal* protection."

No doubt these are matters to which the Justices are now devoting serious consideration. It is appropriate therefore, before turning to the central difficulty that bedevilled draftmanship and early interpretation of the Fourteenth Amendment—to say nothing of our own ability to perceive and fully comprehend the framer's purposes—to call attention to one vital objection to this whole prevailing approach. Manifestly, the trend at both the judicial and historical levels has been toward a narrow antiquarianism. Facts are being determined and treated in isolation, one at a time, and virtually out of their contexts. Where we should now be synthesizing our knowledge of the Fourteenth Amendment, we go on fragmentizing it, pulverizing it, compartmentalizing it. This obviously can get us nowhere. The orbits of inquiry are too restricted; the purposes too narrow, too disconnected. Results naturally are indecisive; and can only be increasingly so. Law office history and search—and *re*-search!—of this type could go on forever to no clear result—could become as sterile and negative as medieval scholasticism. Indeed, "constitutional scholasticism" would seem an excellent name for the trend. For even if applied evenhandedly this method is open to serious objection. It tends to make 1866 the decisive date in American history; it gives rise to innumerable searches of records for guidance that simply isn't there; it leads to obscurantism and conjecture; almost inevitably it transforms the humble "argument from silence" into both a murderous and a suicidal weapon.²⁶

---

protection clause); *Minneapolis and St. L. Ry. Co. v. Beckwith*, 129 U. S. 26, 28 (1889) (due process clause).

23 See Chapter 4, *supra*; Chapter 7, *infra*; also TENBROEK, *op. cit. supra* note 3; Frank and Munro, cited *supra* note 3.

24 See Chapter 7, *infra* at 300, 304, 313.

25 CONG. GLOBE, 39th Cong., 1st Sess. 432 (1866).

26 A national conference, or an hour of professional soul-searching on "The Use and Misuse of the Argument from Silence" might have beneficial results. Fifteen years ago in 47 YALE L. J. 386–387 (Chapter 1, *supra* at —), the writer probed this problem and won numerous converts. Backsliding however has been frequent, and at times the writer himself has been sorely tempted. Resolution in these matters would be effectively aided by a truly comprehensive, multi-dimensional analysis of the debates.

If we are interested in arriving at the purpose and meaning of our Fourteenth Amendment, in so far as that meaning can be determined from what was said by those who sponsored and ratified it, 1866–68, there is a simple and decisive way of doing so. The debates are extensive, but not unlimited; they simply call for systematic analysis and for *complete, detailed tabulation* of findings rather than for mere *reading, summary,* and *selective quotation.* Above all, the speakers' positions and remarks ought to be correlated with various background data, and the whole coded and analyzed with reference to all significant points and relationships.[27]

The modern, efficient way to do this is by coordinate or punched card analysis. If the eyesight and energy expended in the course of the reading and searches on each successive narrow point that has arisen had been directed along these lines, we today should have a complete permanent index covering every major issue and problem included in the debates, and one that would point up significant interrelationships, not only of the framers' ideas and objectives, but of the influences and affiliations responsible for them. With the Fourteenth Amendment today the constitutional cornerstone of civil liberties in the States,[28] and with hundreds of thousands of dollars to be expended in the next few years by the Fund for the Republic,[29] on studies of their definition and enforcement, it would seem that this long overdue project must presently be undertaken.

It is interesting to note in this respect that exploration of antislavery backgrounds[30] meanwhile has begun to afford a clearer picture of what framers of the Fourteenth Amendment were driving at, and why they employed the phraseology they did. How the equal protection–due process–privileges-immunities trilogy crystallized from primitive natural rights theories and from earlier constitutional forms; how, during the long antislavery crusade, it became a form of shorthand for, and spearhead of, the Federal Bill of Rights; how at last in 1866 it won full-fledged constitutional status as a kind of universal common denominator, is a thrilling story that need not be repeated here. The heart of it is that the framers' three-clause system represented a thirty-year winnowing and synthesis of the antislavery, anti-race discrimination argument. Religious, ethical, historical ap-

---

[27] The writer has prepared a draft schedule of a number of points and issues which in his judgment should be covered in such an analysis. He will welcome the views and suggestions of others on these matters.

[28] See works cited note 3 *supra*; REPPY, CIVIL RIGHTS IN THE UNITED STATES 103 ff. (1951) and especially c. VI "Group Discrimination and the Constitution."

[29] Newsweek, June 8, 1953, p. 60, col. 1.

[30] See especially Chapter 4, *supra* and TENBROEK, *op. cit. supra* note 3.

peals constituted its original forms. At the outset, the Lockean philosophy of antecedent and inalienable rights (which colonial leaders had employed so effectively in the Revolution) simply had been given a new twist. Americans, it was argued, had to live up their Declaration. "All men" had to mean *all men*; "Governments . . . instituted to secure these rights" of "life, liberty and the pursuit of happiness"; and governments "deriving their *just* powers from the *consent* of the governed" had to bestow protection, and to bestow it equally, irrespective of race and color, or the "self-evident truths" became self-evident mockery.

Thus, from the very beginning the antislavery movement was fundamentally a quest for *protection* of the laws. Slavery was ethically repugnant, not simply because it chattelized man, but because it repudiated the very purpose of government and arbitrarily denied to some humans its protections solely on the basis of skin color.

This double-headed concept and standard of equal protection of the laws, ethically derived from Lockean theory, from the Declaration and from the comity clauses of the Articles of Confederation, as well as from the State and Federal Bills of Rights, was already well synthesized by the 1830s.[31] It was spelled out fully and given its most persuasive statement in two of the early documents of the organized antislavery movement: first, in the Ellsworth-Goddard argument in the *Crandall Case*,[32] wherein local Black Laws in Connecticut denying out-of-state Negro children rights of education were successfully challenged; then in repeated attacks by the newly-formed Ohio Antislavery Society on similar Ohio laws which denied free Negroes rights of residence, livelihood, court testimony and education.[33] In both of these instances strong use was made of the federal comity clause, and of a nascent concept of a "general" or paramount "American" or "national" citizenship. In the Ohio attacks, moreover, the due course of law clause of the State Constitution also was employed. Thus by 1835 all three elements of our modern Fourteenth Amendment trinity are found linked together and used actively against racial discrimination and in behalf of the rights of the free Negroes of the North.[34]

---

[31] Chapter 4, *supra passim*.
[32] 10 Conn. 339, 341–348 (1834); see Chapter 4, *supra* at 176, especially n. 65.
[33] *Id.* at 171–176.
[34] It is impossible to overstress the fact that the antislavery movement merely was the largest part of an anti-race discrimination movement. The discriminations against free Negroes, and those against Indians for example, were as vigorously attacked as slavery, and for the same reason: race and color were arbitrary, irrational bases for distinctions in men's rights. This fact obviously has tremendous bearing on the

The Fourteenth Amendment and School Segregation 279

This, however, is barely half the story. The most fascinating part of it is how this primitive constitutional argument got broadcast[35] over the land—reiterated, expanded, winnowed, and clarified—until by 1866 it served the Civil War generation as a form of constitutional shorthand—an ethico-legal common denominator designed to accomplish *within* the Constitution and through the courts, precisely what, for the past thirty years, it had accomplished as a "higher law," *above* the Constitution, and *in the minds of those* who had crusaded so long against slavery and against racial discrimination. One can sense immediately the hazards and the obstacles to this sort of constitutional transsubstantiation, and these are treated at length in the following chapter.[36] The point here is that this powerful "antislavery impulse" radiated outward from central and western New York in the early and mid-thirties.[37] It was a part of a "revival of religion" led by Charles G. Finney, an able lawyer turned evangelist, and by Theodore Weld, then still a student at Oneida Institute and ultimately one of the most influential men of his generation. Backed by New York philanthropists who in 1833 organized the American Antislavery Society, and aided by dedicated groups of students attracted by his leadership and personality, Weld and his "Oneidas" moved westward. During the mid- and late-thirties they converted thousands in Ohio, west Pennsylvania and New York to their "benevolent reforms"—temperance, women's and Negroes' rights, and above all, to "immediate emancipation"—i. e., emancipation *immediately begun*. By means of revivals, pamphlets, newspapers; by "declarations," resolutions, petitions, they broadcast their ethico-moral-religious-constitutional argument, abolitionizing whole communities.[38]

Such success however, soon generated reaction, and reaction brought about reorientation.[39] Denied access to the Southern and border States; maligned and attacked as subversives and seditionists by proslave forces fearful both of emancipation and of slave insurrec-

---

scope and purpose of both the Thirteenth and Fourteenth Amendments. Yet our tendency, almost from the first in construing the Amendments has been to think of slavery simply as chattelization, and to ignore the broader motivations. 1968: The blindspot today is *custom*—our failure to sense that the problem which plagued the draftsmen of the antislavery generation, as it still plagues ours, was how to reach and uproot the mores and vestiges of slavery. To pretend that powers were not granted to reach and correct custom is to insult our ancestors. The problems of defective power, of state action and inaction, are of *our* making, not theirs.

[35] See note 30 *supra*.
[36] See Chapter 7, *infra*, at 295.
[37] See BARNES, THE ANTISLAVERY IMPULSE (1933).
[38] *Ibid.*; also DUMOND, THE ANTISLAVERY ORIGINS OF THE CIVIL WAR (1938).
[39] *Ibid.*; BARNES, *op. cit. supra* note 37.

tions, obliged to defend even their own rights to discuss and to proselytize, the American Antislavery Society leaders and their movement soon were left with no alternative but political action. This alternative they at first accepted reluctantly, then exploited brilliantly. First in the Liberty Party of 1840-44,[40] then in the Free Soil Party of 1848,[41] and the Free Democracy of 1852,[42] leaders like Salmon P. Chase[43]—original converts of the Weld group—wrote into their platforms and speeches and resolutions these very concepts of protection and of equal protection derived from the Declaration of Independence and guaranteed by the paramount national citizenship of the comity clause and by state and federal due process. Such arguments of course were now no longer limited merely to proving the expediency and justice of abolition, but were turned against slavery and all its works. At length, after repeal of the Missouri Compromise by the Kansas-Nebraska Act, the new Republican Party, taking its stand now against *extension* of slavery, appropriated *in toto* and repeated in its own platforms and in countless speeches of its members and leaders, 1854-60,[44] this identical rhetoric and theory. Old texts thus were refurbished and given rebirth. So, at long last, the rejected stones came to stand at the head of the corner.

Nothing better ties all these developments together, or better reveals their true character and significance, than a speech made in the House in 1859 by John A. Bingham.[45] Bingham of course was the Ohio representative who just seven years later was destined to draft Sections One and Five of the Fourteenth Amendment. At this date he represented the 21st District which had been thoroughly abolitionized by the antislavery evangelists in 1835-37 while he himself was attending Franklin College near Cadiz. Franklin then had been second only to Oberlin as an antislavery stronghold. Indeed, we find records of petitions and resolutions of the Cadiz antislavery societies couched in the very phraseology for which Bingham, now in 1859, and later, manifests his preference. Moreover, his speech is made

---

[40] The relevant planks are quoted in TENBROEK, *op. cit. supra* note 3, at 119-121; see also STANWOOD, HISTORY OF THE PRESIDENCY 218 (1904).
[41] *Id.* at 240.
[42] *Id.* at 253-254.
[43] See HART, SALMON P. CHASE 51-52 (1899). A thorough study of Chase's role in the antislavery movement would itself do much to set the War Amendments in clearer perspective.
[44] See STANWOOD, *op. cit. supra* note 40, at 271-272, 291-294 for the due process and other antislavery constitutional theory in the Republican Platforms of 1856 and 1860. Note Planks 2, 8, and 14 of 1860.
[45] See DICT. AM. BIOG.; BRENNAN, BIOG. ENCYCL. . . . OF OHIO 312 (1880); Chapter 4, *supra*, n. 149, 150, 255.

against a provision in the Oregon Constitution of 1857[46] which was almost a repetition of the hateful Ohio Black laws: "No free Negro or mulatto not residing in the State at the time of the adoption of this Constitution, shall ever come, reside or be within this State, or hold any real estate, or make any contract or maintain any suit therein . . . ."

Bingham first contended[47] that these provisions violated the Federal comity clause and the rights of "citizens of the United States." "Who are citizens of the United States? They are those, and those only, who owe allegiance to the Government of the United States . . . [They are] all free persons born or domiciled within the jurisdiction of the United States, and aliens naturalized under the laws of Congress."

> I invite attention to the significant fact that natural or inherent rights, which belong to all men, irrespective of all conventional regulations, are by this Constitution guaranteed by the broad and comprehensive word "person," as contradistinguished from the limited term citizen—as in the fifth article of amendments, guarding those *sacred rights* which *are* as *universal* and *indestructible* as the human race, that "no person shall be deprived of life, liberty, or property, but by due process of law, nor shall private property be taken without just compensation." And this guarantee *applies* to all citizens within the United States. [Italics supplied.]

Against infringement of "these wise and beneficent guarantees of political rights to the citizens of the United States as such, and of natural. They may not *rightfully or lawfully* declare that the the supremacy clause.

> There, sir, is the limitation upon State sovereignty—simple, clear, and strong. No State may *rightfully*, by Constitution or statute law, impair any of these guaranteed rights either political or natural. They may not *rightfully or lawfully* declare that the strong citizens may deprive the weak citizens of their rights, natural or political . . .

> This provision [excluding free Negroes and mulattoes] seems to me . . . injustice and oppression incarnate. This provision, sir, excludes from the State of Oregon eight hundred thousand of the native born citizens of other States, who are, therefore, *citizens of the United States*. I grant you that a State may restrict the exercise of the elective franchise to certain classes of citizens of the United States, to the exclusion of others; but I deny that any State

---

[46] Art. I, § 35.
[47] CONG. GLOBE, 35th Cong., 2d Sess. 981-985 (1859).

may exclude a law-abiding citizen of the United States from coming within its territory, or abiding therein, or acquiring an enjoying property therein, or from the enjoyment therein of the "privileges and immunities" of a *citizen of the United States.* What says the Constitution:

"The citizens of each State shall be entitled to all privileges and immunities of citizens in the several States." Art. 4, Section 2.

Here is no qualification . . . The citizens of each State, all the citizens of each State, *being citizens of the United States,* shall be entitled to "all privileges and immunities of citizens of the several States." Not to the rights and immunities of the several States; not to those constitutional rights and immunities which result exclusively from State authority or State legislation; but to "all privileges and immunities" of citizens of the United States in the several States. *There is an ellipsis in the language employed in the Constitution, but its meaning is self-evident,* that *it is "the privileges and immunities of citizens of the United States" that it guarantees* . . .

[S]ir, I maintain that the persons thus excluded from the State by this section of the Oregon Constitution, are citizens by birth of the several States, and therefore *are citizens of the United States,* and as such are entitled to all the privileges and immunities of citizens of the United States, amongst which *are* the rights of life and liberty and property, and their due protection in the enjoyment thereof by law; . . .

Who, sir, are citizens of the United States? First, all free persons born and domiciled within the United States—not all free white persons, but all free persons. You will search in vain, in the Constitution of the United States, for that word white; it is not there. You will look in vain for it in that first form of National Government—the Articles of Confederation; it is not there. The omission of this word—this phrase of caste—from our national charter, was not accidental, but intentional. . . .

This Government rests upon the absolute equality of natural rights amongst men. . . .

Who, . . . will be bold enough to deny that all persons *are equally entitled to the enjoyment of the rights of life and liberty and property, and that no one should be deprived of life or liberty,* but as punishment for crime; nor of his property, against his consent and without due compensation? . . .

The equality of all to the right to live; *to the right to know;* to argue and to utter, according to conscience; to work, and enjoy the product of their toil, is the rock on which that Constitution rests— ... The charm of that Constitution lies in the great democratic idea which it embodies, that *all men, before the law, are equal in respect to those rights of person which God gives*, and *no man or State may rightfully take away*, except as a forfeiture for crime. Before your Constitution, sir, *as it is*, as I trust it ever will be, all men are sacred, whether white or black. . . . [Italics supplied throughout.]

Surely, this speech alone is enough to put Sections One and Five in clearer perspective. All the clauses and concepts that Bingham and the Joint Committee were to employ seven years later are employed here. Protection and equal protection, due process of law, and a paramount national citizenship attained by removing the "ellipsis" from the comity clause, are all expressly relied on. They are relied on, moreover, to combat the type of racial classification, and racial discrimination, that were incidents of slavery, and which had been attacked by these forms repeatedly in the quarter century since their use in the *Crandall* arguments and in the Ohio Antislavery Society report on the state's Black Laws. (Indeed, use of the comity clause in this manner extended back to similar use in the debates over Missouri's admission to the Union, 1819–21,[48] and even to use, in 1778, of the comity clause of the still-unratified Articles of Confederation.)[49] It is interesting to note, furthermore, that although this speech was made two years after the *Dred Scott* decision, Bingham not only does not follow that decision, he does not even acknowledge or mention it; he simply disavows any color line as a basis for citizenship of the United States; he regards Milton's rights of communication and conscience, including the right *to know—to education*—as one of the great fundamental natural "rights of person which God gives and no man or state may *rightfully* take away," and which hence are "embodied," also, within, and secured by, "the great democratic idea that all men before the law are equal." In short, the concept and guarantee of the equal protection of the laws is already "embodied" in the Federal Constitution of 1859, notwithstanding the *Dred Scott* decision; this same concept, moreover, embraces "the equality of all . . . to the right to know"; and above all, there is no color line even in the Constitution of 1859!

It is the bearing and significance of this inherent and inalienable rights argument—("fundamental rights of person which God gives and no man or state may rightfully take away")—that calls for con-

---
[48] See MCLAUGHLIN, *op. cit. supra* note 10, c. 29; BURGESS, THE MIDDLE PERIOD, 1817–58 c. 4 (1897).
[49] See Chapter 4 *supra* at n. 103.

sideration. Patently, what we are witnessing in this speech of Bingham's—so typical of thousands in the five decades 1819-66[50] is a gradual constitutionalization of an ethico-moral argument or ideal. Slavery—with its theories of racial damnation, racial inferiority and racial discrimination—was inherently repugnant to the American Creed and the Christian ethic. This fact was being rapidly and increasingly sensed. As men sensed it, they fit it into the only political theory they knew: Governments existed, not to *give*, but to *protect* human rights; allegiance and protection were reciprocal—i. e., *ought to be reciprocal*; rights and duties were correlative—i. e., *had to be correlative* if Americans ever were to live with their consciences and to justify their declared political faith.[51]

Let us note well this point, for it is precisely the problem we still are faced with, and it is one of the keys to understanding the Fourteenth Amendment: Ethical and religious opinions were here molding and remolding constitutional doctrine. Moral premises were being translated into legal and constitutional premises—i. e., *enforceable rights*. This was being done by a "due processing" and an "equal protecting" of the Law of Nature. It was going on, as yet, largely in the public, rather than in the judicial mind, but let us not condemn it on that account. (Paraphrasing the familiar: "Is not every human a judge?") What these men were doing was using the sanctions of a "higher"—i. e., ethico-moral law—to defeat and override the claims of an arbitrary, barbarous, positive law. Now in doing this they of course got themselves into some logical and semantic difficulties. Bootstrap arguments often tend—or end—so! Yet without bootstrap arguments to give scope to men's conscience and idealism, and to their sense of justice or injustice, surely the law would have remained poor and barbarous indeed.[52]

It is strange and unfortunate so little attention has been paid to

---

[50] The report and pamphlet documentation of the American Antislavery Society crusade alone is huge; add to it items broadcasting the constitutional argument, the repetition by speeches, petitions, resolutions, editorials, literary society debates, etc., *over a period of two generations, throughout all the non-slave States*, and one perceives that the three-clause system of Section One was no spontaneous or fortuitous creation.

[51] See Chapter 4, *supra* at 191, 227ff., for characteristic statements and evidence showing the evolution of this ethical interpretation of American origins and destiny.

[52] For interesting recent discussions of the relations of the "is" and "ought" in law, cf. FULLER, THE LAW IN QUEST OF ITSELF (1940); CAHN, THE SENSE OF INJUSTICE (1949); STONE, PROVINCE AND FUNCTION OF LAW (1946) c. VIII "Natural Law," especially pp. 227–238; COHEN, ETHICAL SYSTEMS AND LEGAL IDEALS (1933). PATTERSON, JURISPRUDENCE: MEN AND IDEAS OF THE LAW 230–243 (1953) has a useful hornbook discussion and bibliography of the "Principles of Morality as Sources" of law. See also, *id.* at 358–375, §§ 4.15–4.17 on "Natural Law."

this phase of the antislavery conflict. It perhaps is the classic example of moral and ethical revision of the law and of creative popular jurisprudence and constitution making[53]—at least in the nineteenth century. "Hearthstone opinions"[54] in this process obviously were far more vital and determinative than judicial opinions.[55] Constitutional Law here was growing at the base rather than at the top. The change in the *ethos* determined the change in the *leges*, and the continuous interactions runs to the heart of both history and politics. Furthermore, our own generation is now bedevilled by similar problems, and is nervously groping toward affirmative re-declarations of human rights with a view toward eventual sanctions at the international level. It would seem very much worthwhile, therefore, to re-examine this experience and learn from it all we can.

Despite this high relevance, our attitude toward those responsible for the Civil War changes has tended toward indifference and hypercriticism. In part, this is a natural result of the Reconstruction debacle—(though certainly the worst failures of that period arose not from constitutional idealism, but from the lack or the loss of it). Hence, we still are more inclined to criticize the framers' "miserable draftsmanship,"[56] or speculate on their possible cunning, or even

---

[53] A great deal has been written of the Higher Law and Natural Law content of American constitutional decisions—cf. the familiar of Corwin, Haines, Wright, Grant, and Commager—but the fascinating and elusive relations between the popular matrix and the judicial impress are almost untouched. See however, POUND, THE FORMATIVE ERA OF AMERICAN LAW 16 (1938); and note 51 *supra*.

[54] This happy phrase was discovered in a speech made by Rep. James F. Wilson during debates on the Thirteenth Amendment. The tenacious hold and blight of slavery, he said, extended "From hearthstone opinions to decisions of the Supreme Court of the United States . . ." CONG. GLOBE, 38th Cong., 1st Sess. 1201 (1864).

[55] On the role of *anti*slavery "hearthstone opinions" in expanding due process, see Chapter 5, *supra*.

[56] For one example among many, see Grant, *The Natural Law Background of Due Process*, 31 COL. L. REV. 56, 66 (1931); or witness almost any modern law students' class discussion. Such criticism originated in the widening gap between known intent and judicial interpretation after the *Slaughter-House* decision; it has persisted and increased in recent years as our capacity to appreciate the formerly-powerful hold of natural law theories has inevitably declined.

A related astigmatism is the view, well expressed by MOTT, DUE PROCESS OF LAW 166 (1926), ". . . there seems to have been a subconscious attempt on the part of the framers and ratifiers of the Fourteenth Amendment to make it as vague as possible." The writer submits that this is hindsight with a vengeance. Possibly the shift from positive to negative form—*i. e.* moving the phrase "Congress shall have power . . ." from Section One to Section Five was dictated in part by fancied cleverness, but the antislavery backgrounds, wholly ignored by Flack and only recently rediscovered, certainly explain the rest of the draft, and incidentally expose our own long-fallacious approach to the Amendment (*i. e.* the mistaken older view that it was simply a fortuitous combination of restraint clauses plus a redundant grant of power to enforce rights already entrusted to the judiciary).

ulterior purposes,[57] than to consider exactly what it was they had to contend with. Another factor undoubtedly has been that natural rights-higher law thinking is no longer in vogue today.[58] Indeed, it is a red flag to a law school-drilled generation. Admittedly, old imprecisions and manifest preferences for clumsy "universals"[59] in place of today's sharp analysis have been further barriers to interest and understanding.

All we need to do, however, to purge ourselves of this bemused superciliousness toward those responsible for the Civil War constitutional changes is to consider for a moment exactly what these men had been up against. One perceives immediately that they had had to contend with one of the most difficult and confusing problems in politics and jurisprudence—the problem of the "irresolvable" conflict between the moral and the positive law—the political-legal equivalent of the scholastics' irresistible force and immovable body! In the extreme form and terms, such a problem obviously is unsolvable, except verbally. Yet in practice it rarely is so. Solution depends ultimately upon a fact situation, and hence upon the extent to which the irresistible forces does move the immovable body—or vice versa. Politics and government are essentially accommodation and compro-

---

[57] Cf. the perennial fascinations of the "Conspiracy Theory"; see note 3 *supra*, the works of Graham, Boudin, McLaughlin, and references therein cited.

[58] This statement obviously needs some qualification. The rapid decline of naked natural rights thinking was made possible, and perhaps inevitable, by the Fourteenth Amendment. No one officially has deplored this development. What we too often fail to appreciate is that only these thin cloaks of substantive due process and equal protection conceal and disguise our own nakedness. Our new enthusiasm for Constitutional positivism, therefore, is at times pretty smug. This was another thing that irked Van Winkle. "Intellectual prudery", he called it. "What we need now in this School Segregation business is some 'Mote and beam jurisprudence.' For seventy years everyone else has *benefited by this ambiguity and free-wheeling discretion. Must only the Negroes continue to be victims of it?*"

[59] For an interesting use of sweeping Blackstoneian "absolute rights of personal security, personal liberty and personal property," followed by embarrassing attempts to delimit them by muddled distinctions, see the speech of Rep. James F. Wilson, House sponsor of the Civil Rights Act of 1866, CONG. GLOBE, 39th Cong. 1st Sess. 1115–1119 (1866). Wilson was a conscientious and able leader, but the law he had learned out of Blackstone and Kent as a harness-maker's apprentice from the age of thirteen, simply was inadequate for the purposes at hand. The writer submits that it is either snobbery or lack of imagination to conclude from such difficulties that these men had no clear idea of what they were trying to do. The trouble is simply that our greater sophistication in the complexities of a federal system tends to distract us from their perfectly clearcut anti-race discrimination purposes. Nearly any modern law student is better equipped than these men were to deal with many phases of such a problem. But the beginning of wisdom here is to stop judging men and intent by reading history backward to 1866 and to start reading it forward to that date. The Reconstruction and post-Reconstruction shambles of the Fourteenth Amendment necessarily are poor aids for its interpretation.

mise. It is only the most fiercely and intensely held moral convictions that ever approach the uncompromisable, or rise Phoenix-like from repeated defeats, as did the Abolitionists. Positive law itself has a dual nature. It is *both* printed texts and human behaviour. When irreconcilable opinion intervenes as a third force, polarizing the two, arraying one against the other, we have trouble. Representative government is a means of minimizing this danger. The slavery conflict marks the one utter failure in American history—the unique case where ethico-moral opinions ultimately proved uncompromisable; or, to speak more accurately, where sectional interests and taboos so rigidified, stratified, and hamstrung the federal system as to render articulated compromise and reform impossible.

From the first, of course, both sides regarded the slavery struggle as one *of, by,* and *for* Law. The difficulty was over the nature and sources of law. Was slavery *legal*, or was it not? All hands agreed slavery to be supported in each of the slave States by a body of statutes and decisions. But that did not satisfy anti-slavery men. Nor would it have satisfied many of us. Slavery was wrong: Ethically, morally, outrageously wrong—the wrongest, most barbarous, anachronistic institution in the civilized world.[60] Hope originally lay for its peaceful eradication—for progressive change and attrition of the positive law through education and moral suasion. Christianity and patriotism were both powerful potential levers and solvents. Their efficacy, however, presumed and required open channels of discussion and appeal—appeal to reason and to conscience.[61]

Now in contrast, consider what actually occurred: cotton profits and politics, combining with morbid fears of slave insurrection, first had introverted, then isolated the South, withdrawing the institution from discussion and criticism, and at length—in abolitionists' eyes —blasphemously apotheosizing it, declaring it constitutionally sacred and beyond reach—a "positive good."[62] Such claims were depressing and offensive enough, even when made solely with reference to slavery *in the States*. When eventually expanded (through repeal

---

[60] See NEVINS' lucid Chapter 5, "Slavery in a World Setting" in THE EMERGENCE OF LINCOLN (1950) (also his earlier discussions in Chapters 13-15 in his ORDEAL OF THE UNION [1947]), for an account and view of the institution on the eve of the War. Nevins' conclusion merits pondering today (with reference to slavery's *vestiges*): "But the time had come when the country, however reluctantly, must face a plain fact: if the United States was really to be the last, best hope of mankind, it could not much longer remain a slaveholding republic" (p. 168).

[61] See Dumond, *op. cit. supra* note 38; NYE, FETTERED FREEDOM (1949).

[62] See Chapter 4 *supra* 210ff., especially p. 213. JENKINS, PROSLAVERY THOUGHT IN THE OLD SOUTH (1935).

of the Missouri Compromise and by the *Dred Scott*[63] decision) to remove all limits upon slavery in the Territories, they became intolerable. The impasse now was complete. Slavery, wrong as ever, had been put beyond reach, made unassailable, impregnable.

Now the point is that the "higher law" always had afforded the one psychological and doctrinal escape from such an impasse. It was essentially an ethical draft on the future for the benefit of the present—an unconscious borrowing from men's ideals to civilize their law and humanize their politics. It was the one means of reconciling facts and ideals abstractly in the hope of doing so prospectively. Slavery and race discrimination were unconstitutional by a "higher law" than the Constitution. *Ergo*, the higher law ought to *become* the Constitution.[64]

To modern-trained positivists who are inclined to reject this solution, and to dismiss it as logically "naive and unsound," it is only fair to issue this challenge: How would we, believing slavery to be morally wrong and ethically indefensible, have attacked it and attempted its overthrow by *peaceful means within a federal system so effectively controlled by pro-slave forces as to remove the institution from reach and even from constructive discussion?*

How indeed! The silence soon is shattering, and it is shattering simply because the alternatives—for antislavery Whigs and Democrats particularly—are seen to have been surrender and condonation on the one hand and resort to this unsatisfactory higher law-"court of last appeal" on the other. To be candid about it, then, the higher law was a forensic and educative device; it was the safety valve that prevented antislavery men from "blowing their tops." Our generation has been unduly smug about the matter largely because we have lacked the insight to see that—fortunately—we have escaped any such intense and irreconcilable positive law-moral law conflict in our own times. (Prohibition of course compares here as a grim joke to high tragedy. Moreover, it was so susceptible to repeal by mass evasion that the example itself underscores the differences.) War crimes undoubtedly are the nearest modern approach, and indeed a very significant one: For here again, conscience leavened and innovated the positive law, rather than confess its own impotence.[65]

---

63 19 How. 393 (U. S. 1856).
64 The research of Professors Dumond, Nye, Jenkins, and Eaton *op. cit. supra* notes 38, 61, and 62, points up the fact that the fatal blunder in the slavery struggle was the proscription of persuasion and conversion.
65 See CAHN, *op. cit. supra* note 52, at p. 30, citing R. H. Jackson, Trial of War Criminals, Dept. of State Pub. #2420 (1945), p 7. ". . . the test of what legally is crime gives recognition to those things which fundamentally outraged the conscience

The Fourteenth Amendment and School Segregation 289

We can epitomize the matter by saying that ordinarily law grows interstitially and metabolically. Yet it always is a product of men's higher faculties and social challenges. When these challenges are increased to inordinate levels, responses are apt to be likewise increased. And when the challenge is an ethico-moral challenge, the law itself ultimately must grow in ethical and moral content; it will do so creatively if it is unable to do so metabolically.

If this view be taken, it is plain that the trouble throughout the long struggle over slavery was not so much that there was this inevitable dualism between moral and civil rights, but that the necessities of the case demanded that men speak these two jurisprudential languages in the same breath. That is, *forensically*, rights needed to be—and were—interchangeably regarded as pre-existent ideals and as socially implemented and enforceable privileges or immunities. On the one plane stood the parchment constitution, given effect by statutes and precedents; on the other, the subjective instrument which "guaranteed" and "declared" certain antecedent natural rights. The document thus was alternately shadow and substance—an amendable legal instrument, and one which, "correctly interpreted" or "declared," required no amendment.

Now this dualism is inherent and inevitable in natural law theory. Indeed, Professor Fuller[66] has defined natural law as a body of thought that tolerates just such confusion for the sake of its ethical advantages. Hence the dualism persisted, and it reached its climax in 1866. From our present viewpoint, it would have helped, surely, if men had perceived then, as clearly as we do today, that when *amending the Constitution* it is best to eschew declaratory theories. To do otherwise, is to put an impossible strain upon the legal vocabulary; for definitions break down and overlap, and communication and straight thinking become almost impossible.[67] The point is that these men did not, and the Civil War generation could not eschew such theories, because until after 1865 that generation rarely had known nor used any other! Thus the antislaveryites' dualism—or if one wishes to be snobbish about it, confusion—really was inherent in their necessary job of "due processing" the Law of Nature and in "protecting" and "*equal* protecting" the rights of *all* human beings without regard for race or color.

It thus can be said that moral and ethical opinions were the matrix of the War Amendments. The texts and forms themselves, however,

---
of the American People and brought them finally to the conviction that their own liberty and civilization could not persist in the same world with Nazi Power."
[66] See *op. cit. supra* note 52, at 5.
[67] See Chapter 7, *infra*.

evolved under tremendous counter pressures. These identifying facts alone stamp the three amendments as unique parts of our Constitution. In geological terms, the three amendments are the "youngest," grandest parts of the document. The forces that produced them,[68] moreover, still are growing today, both by accretion and through deep-seated internal changes and pressures. We must remember, too, that these "peaks" arose cataclysmically in the sixties, because misguided men so misjudged their relation to these very facts and forces.

May it not be laid down as axiomatic, even, that the concept of equal protection of the laws, in racial matters, can no more be held today to its mid-nineteenth century bounds than due process of law could be held—perhaps we had better say here, *returned*—to that curiously imperfect understanding of it had by King John and his Barons at Runnymede. Indeed, what happened to old *"per legem terrae,"* 1215–1953,[69] would seem to be the answer absolute to those who now are offering us their depressing pictures of a cold, sterile, static equal protection—one cast forever in an 1866 mold;[70] just as what happened to that classic and carefully fitted volcanic plug of due process, after *Dred Scott*,[71] ought to be warning enough to the self-styled "militants" who again are bravely trucking up their cement and mixers for another filling of these same craters. Law and ethics, these men bluntly tell us, are separate fields. So indeed they are. But spare America the day again when both together do not determine the meaning of equal protection of the laws.[72]

---

[68] *Id.* and the works of Graham and tenBroek, cited note 3, *supra.*

[69] See Chapter 5, *supra*, and Chapters 11 and 12, *infra.*

[70] There were many reasons why men's understanding of equal protection, as applied to educational matters, was imperfect in 1866. There were few Negro schools of any kind at that date. Slave codes for generations had denied education to slaves. After 1835, in most slave states, it was a crime to teach *any* Negro—slave or free—to read or write. (See HURD, LAW OF FREEDOM AND BONDAGE [1862].) Negroes were barred from public schools of the North, and still widely regarded as "racially inferior" and "incapable of education." Even comparatively enlightened leaders then accepted segregation in schools. To argue that this means we today are bound by that understanding and practice is to transform the mores and laws of slave code days into constitutional sanctions impossible to be cast off or even moderated.

[71] See note 63 *supra.*

[72] It is an unpleasant fact to remember that the constitutional protection accorded the Negro Race was vitiated and progress in race relations delayed a full two generations (1897–ca. 1930) because overburdened, poorly prepared, and at times negligent or incompetent counsel, *fighting single-handedly and at random a discrimination against an individual client*, proved no match for a battery of railroad, steamship or associated State counsel in the crucial cases 1875–1896. This situation, fortunately unique in our law, obviously is a powerful argument for reopening many of these issues and for accelerating revisionism. "Jim Crow" too often gained entrance by something very close to default or left-handed social favoritism.

Equal protection of the laws, as we can see, and as Jacobus ten-Broek[73] has shown at much greater length, meant first of all the *full* protection of the laws. Mind: not *"separate* but equal," therefore, but *"full and* equal" was the protection conceived and accorded. It was only by one of the strangest perversions of the English language on record that the word "separate" was warped into use as a synonym for "full" and the disjunctive substituted for the conjunctive.[74] That "but" alone is the giveaway—a thorn in the mind and conscience of every American to whom it is not also an insult.

No Americans today ask or expect segregated Court systems or legislatures. If a state Constitution provided for such, including a "separate but equal" Supreme Court, no man would venture to suggest that Negroes and whites were thereby "equally protected." Why? Because the very concept is odious. Yet the main reason it is more odious in this one instance than in the others is that 85 years of toleration[75] and 57 of pretense[76] have blunted our sensibilities to "separate but equal" in these other areas. The racial standard is the sole basis for the distinction in either case.

Suppose that we grant for sake of argument, what no one is obliged nor disposed to grant—that an outright majority of the framers and ratifiers of *1866–68* did regard race segregation, in *their* public schools, as a peculiar form of race discrimination—as one which *in their* judgment, would remain unaffected by the Fourteenth Amendment. Does it follow—dare it follow—we *today* are bound by that imperfect understanding of *equal protection* of the laws? Must we,

---

[73] *Op. cit. supra* note 3, at 176–180, 222. Both the Freedmen's Bureau and Civil Rights Bill of 1866 secured the Freedmen "full and equal benefit of all laws," the former in Section 7, and the latter in Section 8. The Civil Rights bill was of course passed over President Johnson's veto; and the Fourteenth Amendment was drafted and adopted to remove all doubt about Congress's power in the premises. Virtually every speaker in the debates on the Fourteenth Amendments—Republicans and Democrats alike—said or agreed that the Amendment was designed to embody or incorporate the Civil Rights Act. *"Full and equal"* therefore is strictly the canonical reading. See Chapter 7, *infra.*

[74] *Plessy v. Ferguson, supra* note 6.

[75] Early post-ratification interpretation of the Thirteenth and Fourteenth Amendments was quite in harmony with their purposes. See not only the Bradley-Woods decision at Circuit in the *Slaughter-House Cases,* 4 Fed. Cas. 891, No. 2,234 (C. C. D. La. 1870), but also Judge Woods' decision in *U. S. v. Hall,* 22 Fed. Cas. 79, No. 15,282 (C. C. S. D. Ala. 1871) holding even that Congress had power to reach state inaction. See also the Thirteenth Amendment-Civil Rights Act cases: *U. S. v. Rhodes,* 27 Fed. Cas. 785, No. 16,151 (C. C. D. Ky. 1866); *Matter of Elizabeth Turner,* 24 Fed. Cas. 337, No. 14,247 (C. C. D. Md. 1867). For the factors that deflected interpretation, see Chapter 7 *infra.* See also Chapter 13, *infra* at notes 14 and 17, for recent discoveries concerning Justice Bradley's early views; their present significance is noted in Chapter 14, *infra* at note 12.

[76] See *id.* for *Plessy v. Ferguson, supra* note 6, in historical perspective.

and our children, obliged to live in a world, and assume moral leadership in a world, only one-third of whose population is white, where racism daily is becoming more menacing and hateful, and a stain upon our national honor, must we accept that understanding? Must we *enforce* that understanding? For all time? Regardless? Can one generation fetter all that come after it? Freeze standards of ethics? Rigidify law? Did the generation that struck shackles from slaves, somehow shackle our minds? Our conscience? Our common sense?

To ask such questions, is to answer them. The Doctrine of Changed Conditions, applicable in constitutional cases, certainly has special force and validity in this type of situation. Law cannot exist in a vacuum. The *equal* protection of the laws must always be, in part, an ethical and moral concept. It must grow in relevance and fulfillment with "the felt necessities of the times, . . . prevalent moral and political theories, intuitions of public policy"[77]—*ours* and our childrens'; as well as our ancestors'.

Law office history, willy-nilly, is a confining, proscriptive enterprise. One never would suspect, for example, from the State briefs and arguments in the present *School Segregation Cases*, that our Fourteenth Amendment had any ethical or moral content at all. Still less, that the spirit and text must sometimes determine intent. Much of the current pro-segregation argument reduces simply to this: that because the Civil War generation still practiced discrimination, it could never have intended to abolish it. Here again, Van Winkle's research stands us in good stead. Such a demoralized, emasculated equal protection, he pointed out, certainly was not the brand originally offered to the Supreme Court. Roscoe Conkling, indeed, was most emphatic on these matters. The determinative point, Conkling declared, when arguing for extension of the Amendment to corporations *regardless of framer intent*, was the plain meaning and spirit of these words. "The true question, in exploring the meanings of the Fourteenth Amendment, is not, in a given case, whether the framers foresaw that particular case and acted in reference to it—the inquiry is, does the case fall within the expressed intention of the Amendment. All the cases compassed by the letter of the language, must be included, unless obviously repugnant or foreign to its spirit and purpose."[78]

After quoting the celebrated declaration to this effect, made by

---

[77] HOLMES, THE COMMON LAW 1 (1881).
[78] *Oral Argument of Roscoe Conkling* [in *San Mateo County v. Southern Pacific Railroad*, 116 U. S. 138 (1882)] pp. 31-32.

Chief Justice Marshall in the *Dartmouth College Case*,[79] Conkling developed the point at some length, then concluded:[80]

> Man being human, and his vision finite, it is well that saving ordinances need not be shrunken in their uses or duration to the measure of what the framers foresaw. . . .
> Truths and principles do not die with occasions; nor do they apply only to events which have cast their shadows before.
> The statesman has no horoscope which maps the measureless spaces of a nation's life, and lays down in advance all the bearings of its career. . . .
> All that wisdom and science in legislation can do, is to establish just principles and laws; this done, every case which afterwards falls within them, is a case for which they were established. . . .
> Those who devised the Fourteenth Amendment . . . builded not for a day, but for all time; not for a few, or *for a race*; [emphasis added] but for man. They planted in the Constitution a monumental truth. . . . The truth is but the golden rule, so entrenched as to curb the many who would do to the few as they would not have the few do to them.

May this persuasive eloquence, honored by a unanimous Supreme Court in 1886,[81] soon take on new lustre and significance.

———◆◆◆———

EDITORIAL NOTE. In constitutionalism, as in war and politics, some matters are too important and fundamental to be left wholly to professionals. Due process and equal protection are surely among them, and so it has been from the first.

Due process of law, we perceive, began as a lawyer's term of art. But even in pre-Civil War America it came to be, and rightly, something more. Included in the Fourteenth Amendment, it continued to be a great deal more; but not, as we have seen, for advancement of these *intended racial* objectives. In practice and effect, Process got deflected, de-racialized, by nonuse and disuse. It may have been over-sanguine to have assumed in 1868 that newly freed slaves at once could, or for long would, assert and defend their own rights. But who, in these summers of the 1960's, will argue that freed slaves and their descendants ought not to have been put in that position; still less, that congressional power granted by the amendment (to

---
[79] 4 Wheaton 518, 644–645 (U. S. 1819).
[80] *Supra* note 78 at 33–34.
[81] *Santa Clara County v. Southern Pacific Ry. Co.*, 118 U. S. 394, 396 (1886).

provide the needed federal support and protection during the interim) ought not to have been honored, fully and nationally, instead of being, as we know it was, emasculated by the Supreme Court in the *Slaughter-House, Civil Rights,* and *Plessy* decisions, to name only three.

The worst that can be charged against the antislavery movement, and the Civil War generation which drafted and ratified Everyman's Constitution, is that they assumed, not lightly, but as a matter of course, that affirmative and progressive programs would be launched and continued under this Amendment which had obliged and empowered such. No one, in short, anticipated the Lost Century, nor even a lost half-century. No one dreamed that American law and scholarship would so wholly lose their way, and their momentum, nor that so conscientious a scholar as R. L. Mott would think for an instant that framers and ratifiers, "subconsciously" or otherwise, had made the amendment as "ambiguous as possible."

How Everyman's Constitution got tortured and tormented in construction, how law and opinion ever got so confused and disoriented are problems that now demand further notice and clarification.

[CHAPTER 7]

Our "Declaratory" Fourteenth Amendment

EDITORIAL NOTE. The law student who defined a "declaratory statute" as "one that states law without making it—without making any, I mean," poses and exposes the jurisprudential, semantic, and logical problems dealt with in this chapter. Slippery and troublesome they are and were. In the course of preparing the NAACP memorandum I came to realize, more clearly than before, how much the history and interpretation of the Fourteenth Amendment had been affected by the decline of natural rights–natural law thinking after the Civil War, and of course also by the passing of the antislavery militants.

Consider simply what is apt to happen once sober constitutional lawyers and senators of the United States begin talking, as our law student did, not about statutes or about the common law, but about Everyman's Constitution itself!

It seems to be doubtful whether Senator Matthew H. Carpenter, one of the truly gifted lawyers of the Reconstruction era, ever was sober. And Senator Lyman Trumbull, chairman of the Senate Judiciary Committee and draftsman of the Freedmen's Bureau and Civil Rights Acts, 1865–1866, may never have been drunk. Yet their colloquy in the Senate, in April, 1871, which is the pivot of this chapter and one of the pivots of Fourteenth Amendment history, makes us realize how easy "declaratory thinking" is for lawyers, and how much confusion it can work. Remembering the "compromises" and the evasions of Reconstruction, it also is clearer just how these developed, how leadership flagged, then lost its way. The antislavery idealists were dying off and losing heart. Others, like Matt Carpenter, were lending immense talents to save the likes of that "smelly New Orleans Slaughter-House monopoly." "The BANDED BUTCHERS ARE BUSTED" he had wired co-counsel at word of the decision,[1] probably

---
[1] See THOMPSON, MATTHEW H. CARPENTER: WEBSTER OF THE WEST (1954), 102. For a revealing in-depth study of the *Slaughter-House Cases*, see Franklin, *The Founda-*

never dreaming that the freedmen, as "citizens of the United States," would be busted as well. The fact was that by 1871, Everyman's Constitution was less the intended racial bulwark than a set of locks to be picked and sprung. Mr. Justice Miller, the beau ideal of advocates of judicial self restraint and Marshallian "common sense construction," one of the great American judges beyond doubt, in this instance slipped and failed miserably. His *Slaughter-House* opinion is a sad affair when one senses what really happened.

Yet it must never be concluded that "declaratory thinking" is bad as such. On the contrary, it is one of the oldest, sacred springs of constitutionalism—one of the means by which common lawyers and parliamentarians *generated* constitutional coverage and protection as surely as they here dissipated it.[1a] Even Magna Carta (1215) was thought and said to have been "declaratory" of an earlier law—dipped and sanctified in a still more ancient pool.[2] And provisions of the proposed federal Bill of Rights, some of the Fathers argued in 1789, were "purely" or "merely" declaratory—needed or unneeded, as one viewed the specific clauses and expediencies.

Declaratory thinking thus is another of the games lawyers do and must play. Like the addition to Section 1 of the first sentence defining citizenship, and like Bingham's shifting of the grant of congressional power from Section 1 to Section 5, it became one of the loopholes by which the Amendment was riddled, stripped of racial force and content. But my continued use herein of the words

---

tion and Meaning of the Slaughterhouse Cases, 18 TULANE L. REV. 1–88, 218–262 (1943). Marke, *The Banded Butchers and the Supreme Court*, 12 N.Y.U. LAW CENTER BULL. 8–13 (1964), a popular account, errs occasionally on important details.

[1a] Significantly, similar "declaratory confusion" developed in Stuart England: "The declaratory form" in which the Petition of Right had been drawn up, Holdsworth observes (5 HISTORY OF ENGLISH LAW [1945] 454) "concealed a logical defect"; accordingly it could be argued, and soon was, that "no change [had been made] in the law." This made higgling evasion easy for King Charles and his advisors. Holdsworth continues: " 'There was no new thing granted,' said Finch, C.J., in the *Case of the Ship Money*, 'but only the ancient liberties confirmed.' This argument had been foreshadowed in the king's speech at the prorogation of 1628: 'The profession of both houses in the time of hammering this Petition, was in no way to trench upon my Prerogative, saying, they had neither intention nor power to hurt it. Therefore . . . I have granted no new, but only confirmed the ancient liberties of my subjects.' " *Id.* vol. 6, 106–7, n. 7.

Surely these parallels dramatize a fundamental problem and neglected side of constitutionalism.

[2] How the introduction of printing, and the printing of common lawyers' notebooks and digests after 1480, by catching English law at near midpoint (400 years after the Conquest), fostered this professional attitude and way of thinking of an older, mythic, and hypothetical law, is one of the phases of constitutionalism greatly in need of exploration—and one I hope to treat in a monograph, "The Englishing of English Law." See Chapter 6, *supra*, p. 267, note 3.

"flaws" and "loopholes"³ in this way, it is clear now, was incorrect and unfortunate. The flaws and loopholes were not in the Amendment as such, but were products of a Reconstruction society still willing and able to sacrifice the slave race, to defer protection during the Reconstruction crisis and by the Reconstruction "settlement" of 1877. But who dreamed, who supposed such a "settlement" must or would last till the 1950's.

This is the second essay prepared from the NAACP memorandum. *Affirmative* due process and *affirmative* equal protection, as earlier stressed, are preferable terms today for bridging the years and helping us to grasp the constitutional thought of 1866–1868. Yet for a generation bred to a legal positivism, a "declaratory" Fourteenth Amendment also is a revelation. Case-hardened teachers of constitutional law have acknowledged that Justice Miller's *Slaughter-House* opinion lost its appeal, never has seemed the same again, once one sees through the stratagems. Like our young Civil Rights leader earlier, I believe that Miller⁴ and Bradley, of all judges, would be most flabbergasted by our present impasses and predicament: "Nobody planned it this way. Nobody decided it, nobody wants it. . . . Matt! Quick, we need you again!" The famous voice rings strong and true.

For all their differences, Miller and Field were great friends. One senses why. Both were Lincoln nominees, strong Unionists, defenders of minorities. Both loved and venerated the common law and the Constitution; both devoted their lives to the understanding and exposition of both, *in the light of their times.* Above all, both hated and resisted arbitrariness and arbitrary power, in the law or out of it.

---

³ See Chapter 3, *supra*, p. 131, note 79, and Chapter 7, *infra*.

⁴ Note especially Justice Miller's outrage at state *failure to protect* freedmen and southern loyalists (as evidenced in his letters of February 6, 1866, and August 29, 1869, with the searing references to the Memphis and New Orleans "massacres"); FAIRMAN, MR. JUSTICE MILLER (1939), 190–193. Like Justice Bradley in 1871 (see Chapter 13, *infra*, p. 565), Justice Miller too here postulated state and federal governments (and all branches thereof) as at last having both the power and the duty to protect, and to protect equally, "persons" and "citizens" in their fundamental rights—to protect against mobs, "massacres," state inaction, custom, as well as against infractions by Black Codes. To conclude less is to ignore the depth of Miller's feeling, to make a mockery of the antislavery generation's empathy and integrity. Professor Fairman, it seems to me, took too little notice of these references. I find it difficult therefore to follow his conclusion that Justice Miller's "great opinion in the Slaughter House cases was of a piece with his whole view of the public policy of Reconstruction." (FAIRMAN, 193.)

Justice Miller and Justice Bradley were distinguished judges—passages and positions in the *Slaughter-House* and *Civil Rights* opinions notwithstanding. Those passages and positions, as later extended, spelled disaster racially and departed from views both judges had held. It is time today to see and stress this.

[CHAPTER 7]

A "DECLARATORY CONSTITUTIONAL AMENDMENT" is today almost as baffling and incongruous a concept as an "unconstitutional constitution." By definition the Constitution is the ultimate—the "fundamental and supreme"—law. To *amend* it is to revise it and change it, not to discover or "declare" an antecedent meaning, much less to define or redefine some pre-existent natural right or rights.

Axiomatic as this is today, it often was squarely otherwise with our ancestors. They were disciples of John Locke,[1] that sturdy theorist of the "Glorious English Revolution" of 1688 whose "natural rights" theories were re-employed in the next century to justify the American Revolution.[2] Indeed, the "self-evident truths" of the Declaration of Independence were most felicitously phrased by Thomas Jefferson, but the fountainhead of Jefferson's ideas was Locke's *Second Treatise of Civil Government*.[3] In that work Locke had premised an original social compact made by men in a state of nature for their secure protection and enjoyment of those "eternal," "God-given" rights of "life, liberty and estate" that existed anterior to government and indeed independently of it. Moreover, from 1776 to the end of the Civil War virtually all Americans continued to think of human rights as "natural," "inherent," and "inalienable."[4]

---

[1] For Locke's pervasive influence on American political and constitutional theory, see 1 PARRINGTON, MAIN CURRENTS IN AMERICAN THOUGHT 189 (2d ed. 1930); ROSSITER, SEEDTIME OF THE REPUBLIC (1953); WRIGHT, AMERICAN INTERPRETATIONS OF NATURAL LAW (1931); Hamilton, *Property—According to Locke*, 41 YALE L.J. 864 (1932).

[2] An excellent, fully documented account is contained in ROSSITER, *op. cit. supra* note 1, at 139–47, cc. 13–14.

[3] See BECKER, THE DECLARATION OF INDEPENDENCE (1951); BOYD, THE DECLARATION OF INDEPENDENCE (1945); DUMBAULD, THE DECLARATION OF INDEPENDENCE AND WHAT IT MEANS TODAY (1950).

[4] The natural rights orientation of antislavery theory is redocumented in NYE, FETTERED FREEDOM: CIVIL LIBERTIES AND THE SLAVERY CONTROVERSY (1949); TENBROEK, THE ANTISLAVERY ORIGINS OF THE FOURTEENTH AMENDMENT (1951) at 62–63, note 20; and Chapter 4 *supra* at notes 91, 140. Antislavery men regarded the Declaration of Independence as "The First American Constitution" and often employed it as an overriding "higher law." For example: "Will anyone . . . pretend that there can be *constitutional or legal slavery* in any State . . . where our American 'Declaration' of self-evident truths and inalienable human rights is to be regarded as holding the authority of CONSTITUTIONAL LAW." GOODELL, VIEWS OF AMERICAN CONSTITUTIONAL LAW IN ITS BEARING UPON AMERICAN SLAVERY 139 (1844). For instances of similar usage, see TENBROEK, *op. cit. supra* at 62–63 n.20.

The current political theory was that governments were organized and that constitutions were framed to *protect*, not to *give*, human rights. Constitutions and amendments, therefore, were declaratory, even though by definition they were also fundamental and supreme law.

Obviously there was a pregnant source of confusion. Two concepts were overlapping and struggling for mastery. A written constitution that was itself a "higher law" was competing with, and must somehow be articulated with, another "higher law." An impossible strain was put on words and ideas. Straight thinking and effective communication were to prove difficult. And it was readily conceivable that thinking and communication might break down entirely if, when amending the constitution, men failed to agree exactly what it was they were doing; or if, having amended it, they began disagreeing about what it was they had done.[5] Under either of these conditions, and certainly under both, a constitutional amendment could prove a chimera or, to employ Justice Field's classic phrase, "a vain and idle enactment."[6]

The purpose of this essay is to show that as a matter of fact this is what happened when, during and after the Civil War, Americans for the first time in sixty years did amend their Constitution. It will be shown that the Fourteenth Amendment, like the Bill of Rights[7]

---

[5] The potentialities are clear in many passages of antislavery argument written a full generation before the Fourteenth Amendment. For example, Goodell contended that slavery was not, never had been and never could be constitutional. He looked to the time of its end, "when these matters will be better understood—when legislative and judicial halls will be occupied in the national task of *learning, declaring* and *applying* . . . the great principles of *eternal, immutable* LAW, rather than in vain attempts either to CREATE or to ANNUL it. . . . When will men see that . . . paper constitutions can only *teach* and *declare*, not *originate*, the fundamental principles of civil government!" GOODELL, *op. cit. supra* note 4, at 154.

On the role and decline of natural law theory in the United States, see MERRIAM, A HISTORY OF POLITICAL THEORIES (1924); WRIGHT, *op. cit. supra* note 1; Corwin, *The "Higher Law" Background of American Constitutional Law*, 42 HARV. L. REV. 149, 365 (1929).

[6] Slaughter-House Cases, 16 Wall. 36, 96 (U.S. 1873) (dissenting opinion).

[7] Professor Crosskey's thesis that the Tenth Amendment was "truly declaratory" and "not intended to effect *any change*" in the original Constitution, is another reminder that declaratory constitutional theory did not begin or end in 1866. See CROSSKEY, POLITICS AND THE CONSTITUTION c. 22 and pp. 701-2 (1953). Madison and others in 1789 spoke and thought of the provisions of the Bill of Rights as declaratory of the Constitution and human rights generally. See 1 ANNALS OF CONG. 437-38 (Madison), 737 (Gerry) (1789). Note that the term used throughout was "*declaration* of rights" and that controversy developed over the relation of the Amendments to the Constitution proper. *Id.* at 708, 709, 714, 754. Fortunately, however, the Amendments followed so soon after ratification of the original Constitution that men then and later were still inclined to think of the resulting documents as a unit. This fact tended to forestall such confusions as later developed in the case of the "declaratory"

which the Fathers added to the original Constitution in 1791, was regarded by its framers and ratifiers as declaratory of the previously existing law and Constitution. Naturally the confusion that arose over the Amendment's purpose was effectively exploited. Ultimately it became the touchstone of the decision in the *Slaughter-House Cases*,[8] and hence an important factor in emasculation of the Amendment in cases involving protection of the Negro. The fact that the *School Segregation* decision[9] marks a recovery and realization of the framers' purposes makes this an appropriate time for analysis of one of the strangest episodes in the history of political ideas and ideals: The Rise and Fall of Affirmative Declaratory Constitutional Theory.

I. Antislavery Backgrounds

The intellectual paternity and lineage of the key phrases of the Fourteenth Amendment[10] have been greatly clarified in recent years.[11] More and more Section One is seen to have been a synthesis of the three clauses and concepts which spearheaded the organized antislavery movement's constitutional attack on slavery and racial discrimination.[12] By the mid-1830's the privileges and immunities phraseology of the original Comity Clause, together with the guarantee of due process from the Fifth Amendment and from the state bills of rights, and above all the concept of full and equal protection of the laws derived from the "self-evident truths" of the Declaration,

---

Fourteenth Amendment—and such as seem to be chronic in Professor Crosskey's own hindsighting and thesis-riding. See Chapter 8, *infra* at 339, 354.

8 16 Wall. 36 (U.S. 1873).

9 Brown v. Board of Educ., 347 U.S. 483 (1954).

10 "Section 1. All persons born or naturalized in the United States, and subject to the jurisdiction thereof, are citizens of the United States and of the State wherein they reside. No State shall make or enforce any law which shall abridge the privileges or immunities of citizens of the United States; nor shall any State deprive any person of life, liberty, or property, without due process of law; nor deny to any person within its jurisdiction the equal protection of the laws.

". . .

"Section 5. The Congress shall have power to enforce, by appropriate legislation, the provisions of this article."

11 See Chapters 1-6, *supra*. Basic works on the Fourteenth Amendment are FLACK, THE ADOPTION OF THE FOURTEENTH AMENDMENT (1908); KENDRICK, JOURNAL OF THE JOINT COMMITTEE OF FIFTEEN ON RECONSTRUCTION (1914); WARSOFF, EQUALITY AND THE LAW (1938); Boudin, *Truth and Fiction About the Fourteenth Amendment*, 16 N.Y.U.L.Q. REV. 19 (1938); Fairman, *Does the Fourteenth Amendment Incorporate the Bill of Rights? The Original Understanding*, 2 STAN. L. REV. 5 (1949); Frank and Munro, *The Original Understanding of "Equal Protection of the Laws,"* 50 COL. L. REV. 131 (1950); McLaughlin, *The Court, The Corporation and Conkling*, 46 AM. HIST. REV. 45 (1940).

12 TENBROEK, THE ANTISLAVERY ORIGINS OF THE FOURTEENTH AMENDMENT (1951). See Chapter 4, *supra* at 186, 189.

had already taken their place as a system of constitutional shorthand. This shorthand was the essence of an oral and pamphlet argument that had been tirelessly propagated by evangelists of the American Antislavery Society.[13] There is no need to repeat here the story of how, under the leadership of Theodore Weld and James G. Birney, this band of zealots abolitionized much of Ohio, western Pennsylvania and New York, and parts of New England. The important fact is that the privileges and immunities–due process–equal protection trilogy which had begun to emerge by 1834-35,[14] and which received its first general broadcast in the evangelical and pamphlet campaigns in the years 1835-37,[15] eventually found its way into the Liberty, Free Soil, and finally the Republican party platforms from 1840 until 1860.[16] In catch-phrase form it gained great currency, and during the great slavery debates of 1854-61 it became the staple rhetoric of a generation of speakers[17]—men like Salmon P. Chase,[18] Joshua Giddings,[19] the Wade brothers,[20] John A. Bingham,[21] Thad-

---

[13] Exploration of the antislavery bases of the Fourteenth Amendment was prompted and facilitated by BARNES, THE ANTISLAVERY IMPULSE, 1830-1844 (1933); DUMOND, THE ANTISLAVERY ORIGINS OF THE CIVIL WAR IN THE UNITED STATES (1939). These works in turn were based on edited primary source collections: LETTERS OF JAMES GILLESPIE BIRNEY, 1831-1857 (Dumond ed. 1938); 1 LETTERS OF THEODORE DWIGHT WELD, ANGELINA GRIMKÉ WELD AND SARAH GRIMKÉ, 1822-1844 (Barnes and Dumond eds. 1934). See also JENKINS, PRO-SLAVERY THOUGHT IN THE OLD SOUTH (1935); NYE, FETTERED FREEDOM: CIVIL LIBERTIES AND THE SLAVERY CONTROVERSY (1949).

[14] See Chapter 4, *supra*.

[15] *Id.*

[16] For relevant planks, see TENBROEK, THE ANTISLAVERY ORIGINS OF THE FOURTEENTH AMENDMENT c. 6 (1951); Chapter 4, *supra*. For full platforms, see 1 STANWOOD, HISTORY OF THE PRESIDENCY cc. 18, 20, 21 (1928).

[17] For evidence and causes of this striking continuity in abolitionist theory, see Chapter 4, *supra* at (accounts of the Ellsworth-Goddard and Ohio Antislavery Society arguments of 1834-35) (Birney's various arguments in The Philanthropist, 1836-37).
The work of the Weld-Birney group was constitutionally and politically oriented; that of the Garrisonians was not—indeed was vehemently antipolitical. This difference explains the progressive deflation of Garrison's role and the increased emphasis on the Weld-Birney group's evangelism and pamphleteering as the key to the theory of the War Amendments.

[18] 1808-73; United States Senator from Ohio, 1849-55; Governor of Ohio, 1855-60; Secretary of the Treasury, 1861-64; Chief Justice of the United States, 1864-73. Chase was enlisted in the organized antislavery movement by Birney, and wrote the Liberty, Free Soil and Free Democracy party platforms from 1844 to 1852. See HART, SALMON PORTLAND CHASE 51-52 (1899); SMITH, THE LIBERTY AND FREE SOIL PARTIES IN THE NORTHWEST 139-40 (1897); WARDEN, THE LIFE OF CHASE 338 (1874); LETTERS OF JAMES GILLESPIE BIRNEY, 1831-1857 469 (Dumond ed. 1938).

[19] 1795-1864; member of the United States House of Representatives for Ashtabula and Jefferson Counties, Western Reserve, 1838-59. Giddings, an early convert of Weld's, was one of the original antislavery leaders in the House and drafter of the due process clause in the Republican platform of 1856. See BARNES, THE ANTISLAVERY IMPULSE 1830-1844 82 (1933); JULIAN, THE LIFE OF JOSHUA R. GIDDINGS 335-36 (1892).

[20] Edward Wade, 1803-66; member of the United States House of Representatives

deus Stevens,[22] Justin S. Morrill,[23] James M. Ashley,[24] all of whom rose to power with the Republican Party and a number of whom, along with lesser figures like Philemon Bliss[25] and Samuel Galloway,[26] were actually converts or even members of the Weld-Birney group. From first to last the campaign against slavery was one predicated on Lockean theories of government. The stupendous evil and wrong of slavery was that it denied men the protections and the bounties of government solely because of skin color.[27] It was a form

---

from Ohio, 1853–55 (as a Free Soiler) and 1855–61 (as a Republican). Benjamin Wade, 1800–1878; United States Senator from Ohio, 1851–69; law partner of Joshua Giddings.

[21] 1815–1900; member of the United States House of Representatives for the Twenty-first District of Ohio, 1855–63, 1865–73. The Twenty-first District included the strongly antislavery Quaker settlements around Cadiz. See BRENNAN, BIOGRAPHICAL ENCYCLOPEDIA OF OHIO 312 (1880).

[22] 1792–1868; member of the United States House of Representatives for the Lancaster District of Pennsylvania, 1849–53, 1859–68. Stevens, an antislavery convert, was Radical Republican leader in the House and a member of the Joint Committee of Fifteen on Reconstruction. LETTERS OF JAMES GILLESPIE BIRNEY, 1831–1857 456 (Dumond ed. 1938).

[23] 1810–98; member of the United States House of Representatives from Vermont, 1855–67; United States Senator from Vermont, 1867–98; member of the Joint Committee of Fifteen on Reconstruction, 1865–67. In an undated letter to Charles Sumner, written in October or November, 1865, Morrill sketched a proposed constitutional amendment: "Say all citizens of the U.S. resident [in] said States are equal in civil rights immunities & privileges *and* equally entitled to protection in life liberty & property[;] in granting the elective franchise no distinction shall be made on account of race, des[c]ent or color[;] & all laws in contravention of these rights, immunities & privileges are null and void. . . ." SUMNER PAPERS (unpublished manuscript in Harvard College Library). Note that this letter was written just before the Joint Committee began its work. **1968:** A correction: The undated letter from the Sumner Papers here cited and quoted was *not* written by Justin S. Morrill, the Joint Committee member and Republican who represented Vermont in the House (and later the Senate, 1867–1898). The letter was written by Lot M. Morrill (1813–1883), U. S. Senator from Maine, 1861–1869, and later Secretary of the Treasury. Both Morrills were early Republicans of antislavery backgrounds, Yankees born and bred; only Lot M. Morrill was a lawyer. Authorship of the letter also is misattributed in JAMES, FRAMING OF THE FOURTEENTH AMENDMENT (1956) 30.

[24] 1824–96; member of the United States House of Representatives from Ohio, 1859–69. Ashley was an early sponsor of the Thirteenth Amendment in the House. 1 LETTERS OF THEODORE DWIGHT WELD, ANGELINA GRIMKÉ WELD, AND SARAH GRIMKÉ, 1822–1844 333 (Barnes and Dumond eds. 1934).

[25] 1813–89; Judge, Ohio Circuit Court, 1848–51; member of the United States House of Representatives from the Elyria-Oberlin District of Ohio, 1855–59; Chief Justice of the Dakota Territory, 1861–63; Associate Justice of the Missouri Supreme Court, 1868–72; Dean of the University of Missouri Law School, 1872–89. Bliss was one of Weld's earliest disciples, but was forced out of the movement by ill health. See *id.* at 84.

[26] 1811–72; member of the United States House of Representatives from Ohio, 1855–57. Galloway became a member of the Weld-Birney evangelical group in 1835. See *id.* at 228.

[27] The idea that race and color were arbitrary standards on which to base denial of human rights was implicit in all abolitionist attacks on discrimination and prejudice. But it was after the constitutional-legal attack began to reinforce the earlier

of legalized outlawry at odds not only with natural right, but with such constitutional affirmations of natural right as secured every "person" against deprivation of his "life, liberty and property without due process of law"; as held "all men" to be "born" or "created free and equal" and all "governments" to derive their "just powers from the consent of the governed"; as declared "citizens of each State [including free Negroes] entitled to all the privileges and immunities of citizens [of the United States] in the several States."

What was taking place was one of the most subtle and evanescent of all the possible changes in law and government, a transubstantiation of values from the ethical to the civil and constitutional plane.[28] It was a delicate, uneven and above all a continuing change —a "constitutionalization" of the old law of nature. In modern terms, under our system of government, it meant that there was under way a large-scale shift from general, abstract and really hypothetical rights to specific, concrete and enforcible constitutional ones, from moral rights to rights defined judicially through the processes of inclusion and exclusion and eventually constituting the "essence of a scheme of ordered liberty."[29] In 1866, however, the potential role and responsibility of the courts was far less clear than it is today when judicial review is so highly developed. Probably few framers or ratifiers of 1866–68, even those whose views were most nearly as characterized, faced the problem of implementation squarely or presciently.[30] One can see how history and natural rights

---

religious attack that such arguments became explicit and the concept of an arbitrary classification began to take form. Lawyers like Ellsworth, Goddard, Birney, Gerrit Smith and Chase helped formulate the concept and linked it with the principles of equality, affirmative protection and national citizenship. See AMERICAN ANTISLAVERY SOCIETY ANN. REP. AND PROCEEDINGS 16–17 (1836); CHASE, SPEECH IN THE CASE OF THE COLORED WOMAN, MATILDA 32 (1837); The Philanthropist, Dec. 9, 1836, p. 3. See also TENBROEK, THE ANTISLAVERY ORIGINS OF THE FOURTEENTH AMENDMENT 14–18 (1951); and Chapter 4, *supra*.

28 See Chapter 6, *supra*.

29 Palko v. Connecticut, 302 U.S. 319, 325 (1937).

30 The debates on Section One of the Fourteenth Amendment are almost wholly silent on the problem of enforcement of the rights secured. This silence doubtless resulted in part from political considerations, BEALE, THE CRITICAL YEAR 201 (1930); KENDRICK, JOURNAL OF THE JOINT COMMITTEE OF FIFTEEN ON RECONSTRUCTION cc. 3–6 (1914); in part from the assumed primacy of Congress in such enforcement, FLACK, THE ADOPTION OF THE FOURTEENTH AMENDMENT 55–96 (1908); but also from sheer inability to foresee or consider the detailed use or application of drafts which had begun as an affirmative grant of power to Congress, yet which in the end, out of fear of Democratic return to power, took the form of a constitutional restraint on the states, leaving the problem of enforcement open. Hence it often is impossible today to tell even what Bingham, the chief author, was thinking in these connections. He spoke repeatedly of the power needed to reach state officers who had violated their constitutional oaths. See CONG. GLOBE, 39th Cong., 1st Sess. 156–59, 428–33,

concepts themselves prevented this: The quest had been for acceptance of the principle, not its enforcement. Enlarged judicial responsibility was for the most part implicit in the antislavery generation's position, just as was the acceptance of evolving standards of public ethics and protection in matters pertaining to race. Thus the old mystery of how framers ever could have employed such ambiguous, sweeping, general language to accomplish their purposes yields to the insight that, given the conditions and predilections that accompanied the purposes, the framers scarcely could have done otherwise. The drafters were not itemizing a simple contract; they were trying to live up to one and broaden its social base. Words and phrases in such circumstances are not logarithms. Indeed, to speak of "draftsmanship" in some respects falsifies the whole problem. Bingham and the other framers really were trying to convert ethical into political power, and moral into constitutional rights.[31] Section One was the mechanism designed to effect this transmission from the "ought" to the "is." A great deal of "play" had to be left in such a constitutional device. Hence it became subject to the operation of many extraneous factors and for a time during Reconstruction the machinery ceased to function because political "friction" and intellectual "slippage" dissipated the ethico-moral energies.

II. The Framers' Problem

Slavery is so odious a concept today that we are apt to forget that essentially it was a system of race discrimination and a denial of the protection of law.[32] Slavery rested on and sanctioned prejudice; it made race and color the sole basis for accord or denial of human rights. Human chattelization was the worst aspect of it, but the

---

1089–94, 1290–93, 2541–44 (1866). At first this apparent obliqueness of approach is incomprehensible. Then one senses that Bingham, like all Unionists, was still thinking largely about the "crime of secession" and of how to prevent and punish it in the future, rather than about property rights or about broadened judicial review as has so often been presumed.

31 Chapter 4, *supra*, at 236–237.

32 This was the antislavery cry from the beginning. "What Abolitionists demand as naked justice is that the benefit and protection of these just laws be extended to all human beings alike . . . without regard to color or any other physical peculiarities," OLCOTT, TWO LECTURES ON SLAVERY AND ABOLITION (1838); "To abolish slavery is to proclaim and *enact* that innocence and helplessness . . . are entitled to *legal protection* . . . Protection is the *CONSTITUTIONAL RIGHT of every human being under the exclusive legislation of Congress who has not forfeited it by crime.*" WELD, THE POWER OF CONGRESS OVER THE DISTRICT OF COLUMBIA 41, 42 (1838). See also BARNES, THE ANTISLAVERY IMPULSE, 1833–1844 (1933); DUMOND, THE ANTISLAVERY ORIGINS OF THE CIVIL WAR IN THE UNITED STATES (1939); TENBROEK, THE ANTISLAVERY ORIGINS OF THE FOURTEENTH AMENDMENT (1951); Chapter 4, *supra*, at 186, 189–194.

racial criterion affected every phase of life and human contact. The institution stigmatized even those fortunate enough to have escaped it, and its associations continued to stigmatize those who had been emancipated from it. This was the fundamental problem faced by the framers of the Fourteenth Amendment. Slavery had been ended, but the roots and forms of prejudice and discrimination lay untouched. Prejudice was "vincible," as old antislavery men had declared, but the remedy required education,[33] a continuous showing of the unworthiness of *any* classifications based *solely* on race and color. Therefore both time and governmental power were necessary. Full and equal protection of the laws had to be achieved in fact.[34]

How was this to be accomplished? How were the "badges and incidents" of slavery to be rooted out? After ratification of the Thirteenth Amendment there were three schools of thought regarding the power arrangements needed for the task. One school regarded the Thirteenth Amendment as having done the job and the Freedmen's Bureau and Civil Rights Bills as clearly authorized by it, if not already authorized by the war power or by inherent Constitutional power. The second school, of which John A. Bingham soon emerged as leader, regarded still another amendment as indispensable. A third group, though denying the need for another amendment, admitted one to be a salutory precaution. All three groups were united regarding the affirmative character of protection and regarding the equality of protection that must ultimately result. The difficulty and difference were over shifts in the traditional federal-state division of power, shifts that were linked to this problem and to Reconstruction generally. What had been the nature of the War?[35] Precisely what had the War decided?[36] How were its decisions to be

---

[33] This had been the cardinal premise of the American Antislavery Society's original campaign. For its leaders' plans and strategy for combating race prejudice by education of the free Negroes, see BARNES, *op. cit. supra* note 32; Chapter 4, *supra* at 164ff.

[34] On the Reconstruction period, see BUCK, THE ROAD TO REUNION, 1865-1900 (1937); COULTER, THE SOUTH DURING RECONSTRUCTION, 1865-1877 (1947); DUBOIS, BLACK RECONSTRUCTION (1935); RANDALL, THE CIVIL WAR AND RECONSTRUCTION (2d ed. 1953); RANDALL, CONSTITUTIONAL PROBLEMS UNDER LINCOLN (2d ed. 1951).

[35] On the lack of legal precision in both congressional legislation and administrative policy during the Civil War, and the extent to which the civil nature of the conflict made such confusion inevitable, see *id.* at 69-73, 514-16. The view that the conflict had been both a public war and a rebellion continued to bedevil thinking during Reconstruction.

[36] As examples of the troubled answers of leading Unionists and lawyers, see the letter of Judge I. S. Redfield of Vermont, addressed to Senator Foot, Sept. 30, 1865, quoted in HURD, THEORY OF OUR NATIONAL EXISTENCE 269, 444 (1881), stressing subordination of the states as the decisive outcome. See also John Jay's letter to Salmon P. Chase, Jan. 5, 1867, published in CHASE, DIARY AND CORRESPONDENCE 518 (1903), ex-

expressed?[37] What was to be the basis of Reconstruction?[38] Natural rights theory was no open sesame for these problems. Partisan advantage lurked behind every proposal.

The War had established the permanence of the Union, the subordination of the states, the denial of any claimed right of secession, and emancipation. These were the obvious decisions. Yet only emancipation had been constitutionally sanctified by the Thirteenth Amendment. In practice the freedmen's rights rested precariously on the war power. The Freedmen's Bureau created by Congress in March, 1865,[39] had "assumed . . . a general guardianship of the emancipated race"; supervised relief; co-ordinated charitable and educational enterprises; dealt with controversies in which freedmen were involved; strove to promote stability of settlement, occupation and family life.[40] Its powers were broad and its administration under General O. O. Howard enlightened and generally fair to members of both races; yet it was a tentative agency with little legislative guidance in matters of policy.[41] Meanwhile, especially in the Deep South, many provisions of the old slave codes had been re-enacted in cleverly contrived "Black Laws." "Persons of color" still were to be restricted in their rights of movement, contract, testimony and ownership. New "vagrancy laws" were ominous supplementary controls.[42]

---

pressing the hope of old antislavery men for a broad interpretation by the Supreme Court of the Thirteenth Amendment—one which would hold that the Amendment had "destroyed the only exception recognized by the Constitution to the great principle of the Declaration of Independence and that . . . all persons [now] . . . stand upon an equal footing—& that all state legislation establishing or recognizing distinction of race or colour are void."

[37] The words of one conscientious congressman, Representative Broomall of Pennsylvania, spoken on January 27, 1866, CONG. GLOBE, 39th Cong., 1st Sess. 466 (1866), illustrate the anxieties and doubts: "The great political problem of the day, the problem on the right solution of which will depend the well being of our country for ages is, what shall we do with the people lately in rebellion? . . . [W]ho shall decide it . . . Congress, the courts, or the Executive, or some or all of them?" One aspect of this problem was "can we intrust the negroes unaided to the rule of their late masters?"

[38] See BEALE, THE CRITICAL YEAR (1930). COULTER, THE SOUTH DURING RECONSTRUCTION, 1865–1877 (1947), is an admirable analysis of the psychological and political motivations.

[39] 13 STAT. 507 (1865).

[40] See DUNNING, RECONSTRUCTION, POLITICAL AND ECONOMIC, 1865–1877, 32 (Hart ed. 1907).

[41] Id. at 34.

[42] See DUBOIS, BLACK RECONSTRUCTION (1935); FLACK, ADOPTION OF THE FOURTEENTH AMENDMENT 20–21 (1908); RANDALL, CIVIL WAR AND RECONSTRUCTION 724–30 (1937). The texts of many of the "vagrancy laws" are reprinted in McPHERSON, POLITICAL MANUAL FOR 1866 29–44 (1867).

The Freedmen's Bureau and Civil Rights Bills of 1866 were Congress' initial answer to these challenges. On January 5, 1866, Senator Trumbull,[43] as Chairman of the Senate Judiciary Committee, introduced a bill[44] to extend the powers and territorial sphere of the Bureau which was otherwise due to expire one year after the end of the war. The cushioning effect of federal military power would be continued indefinitely, or until the situation stabilized. The Civil Rights Bill,[45] also drafted by Trumbull, was designed to assure to the freedmen, through judicial action, the same protections against discriminatory "Black Codes" and similar invasions, that the Freedmen's Bureau secured by bureaucratic enforcement. Thus the one bill supplemented the other and suggested the means for its eventual replacement. As evidence of the tremendous hold of Justice Washington's dictum in *Corfield v. Coryell*[46] upon men's thinking in these matters, Trumbull drafted the first section of his Civil Rights Bill with an eye to those rights which the Justice had declared to be "fundamental; which belong, of right, to the citizens of all free governments. . . ."[47] As finally adopted, the first section read:

> . . . [A]ll persons born in the United States and not subject to any foreign power, excluding Indians not taxed, are hereby declared to be citizens of the United States; and such citizens, of every race and color, without regard to any previous condition of slavery or involuntary servitude, except as a punishment for crime whereof the party shall have been duly convicted, shall have the same right, in every State and Territory in the United States, to make and enforce contracts, to sue, be parties, and give evidence, to inherit, purchase, lease, sell, hold, and convey real and personal property, and to *full and equal benefit* of all laws and proceedings for the security of person and property, as is enjoyed by white citizens, and shall be subject to like punishment, pains, and penalties, and

---

[43] Trumbull is one of the neglected leaders of the Civli War period. See WHITE, THE LIFE OF LYMAN TRUMBULL (1913). In his speech of January 19, 1866, he expressed the view that the Thirteenth Amendment had abolished "absolutely all provisions of the State or local law which make a man a slave. . . . With the destruction of slavery necessarily follows the destruction of the incidents to slavery." Included in the overthrow were "all badges of servitude," and among them the laws "devised . . . for the purpose of degrading the colored race, of keeping the negro in ignorance." CONG. GLOBE, 39th Cong., 1st Sess. 319-22 (1866). See also *id.* at 474, for similar views expressed in debates on the Civil Rights Bill.
[44] Sen. 60, 39th Cong., 1st Sess. (1866). See CONG. GLOBE, 39th Cong., 1st Sess. 129, 184 (1866).
[45] Sen. 61, 39th Cong., 1st Sess. (1866).
[46] 6 Fed. Cas. 546, No. 3,230 (C.C.E.D. Pa. 1823).
[47] *Id.* at 551.

to none other, any law, statute, ordinance, regulation, or custom, to the contrary notwithstanding.[48] [Emphasis added.]

Section Two provided:

> ... [A]ny person who, under color of any law, statute, ordinance, regulation, or custom, shall subject, or cause to be subjected, any inhabitant of any State or Territory to the deprivation of any right secured or protected by this act, or to different punishment, pains, or penalties on account of such person having at any time been held in a condition of slavery or involuntary servitude, except as a punishment for crime whereof the party shall have been duly convicted, or by reason of his color or race, than is prescribed for the punishment of white persons, shall be deemed guilty of a misdemeanor, and, on conviction, shall be punished by fine not exceeding one thousand dollars, or imprisonment not exceeding one year, or both, in the discretion of the court.[49]

It is in the congressional debates upon these measures[50] that we begin to see why the Fourteenth Amendment came into being and what it was designed to accomplish. Three major speeches reveal the dominant trends of thought in Congress. Furthermore, they show more clearly than anything else, by their differences and disagreements upon the power issue and by their unity of opinion upon the substantive rights-race discrimination issue, the theory that ultimately found expression in Sections One and Five of the Fourteenth Amendment.

Congressman James F. Wilson of Iowa, Chairman of the Judiciary Committee and House sponsor of the Civil Rights Bill, was representative of the group that thought the war power, the naturalization power, the Thirteenth Amendment, and above all, Congress' *inherent* powers for the protection of a paramount national citizenship adequate for the job. Wilson seems to have been ignorant of *Barron v. Baltimore*;[51] but as if to underscore the insignificance of such ignorance he relied instead on the old concepts of "great fundamental civil rights, which it is the true office of government to protect"— Blackstone's rights of personal security, personal liberty and personal property. In his eyes these "inalienable possessions of both Englishmen and Americans" ought to be, could be and were protected by

---

[48] 14 Stat. 27 (1866).
[49] Ibid.
[50] The debates are summarized in Flack, The Adoption of the Fourteenth Amendment c. 1 (1908).
[51] 7 Pet. 243 (U.S. 1833). Ignorance or disregard of this decision was by no means uncommon in the pre-Civil War period. See Rhinehart v. Schuyler, 7 Ill. 375, 2 Gil. 473 (1845), discussed in Chapter 5, *supra*.

the Civil Rights Bill. "Our Constitution is not a mockery; it is the never-failing fountain of power. . . ."[52] All the rights enumerated in the Bill were derived from these three Blackstonean rights. The war power, the naturalization power, the Thirteenth Amendment, the Comity Clause, and *Corfield v. Coryell*—all were cited and relied on.[53] Finally Wilson concluded with this statement of the inherent powers theory:

> I assert that we possess the power to do those things which Governments are organized to do; that we may protect a citizen of the United States against a violation of his rights by the law of a single State; that by our laws and our courts we may intervene to maintain the proud character of American citizenship; that this power permeates our whole system, is a part of it, without which the States can run riot over every fundamental right belonging to citizens of the United States; that the right to exercise this power depends upon no express delegation, but runs with the rights it is designed to protect. . . .[54]

Bingham, who had imbibed his antislavery theory at Franklin College during the Weld-Birney crusade,[55] was more sophisticated in his views of the federal-state division of power. He agreed with Wilson as to ends, but challenged the means. His remarks are among the clearest indications of what he and his colleagues sought to accomplish in drafting Sections One and Five of the Fourteenth Amendment:

> I know that the enforcement of the bill of rights is the want of the Republic. I know if it had been enforced in good faith in every State of the Union the calamities and conflicts and crimes and sacrifices of the past five years would have been impossible.
> But I feel that I am justified in saying, . . . the enforcement of the bill of rights, touching the life, liberty, and property of every citizen of the Republic within every organized State of the Union, is of the reserved powers of the States. . . . Who can doubt this conclusion who considers the words of the Constitution: "the powers not delegated to the United States by the Constitution, nor prohibited by it to the States, are reserved to the States respec-

---

[52] CONG. GLOBE, 39th Cong., 1st Sess. 1118 (1866). See also Wilson's remarks. *Id.* at 1294–95. Other speakers who took this view were Broomall, *id.* at 1262–65; Thayer, *id.* at 1151–53, 1270–71; and Shellabarger, *id.* at 1293. All these speeches were by men raised in Pennsylvania and Ohio while the antislavery crusade was at its height, and all are full of talk of "fundamental rights," reciprocal allegiance and protection, and equality and due process.
[53] *Id.* at 1118–19.
[54] *Id.* at 1119.
[55] See Chapter 4, *supra.*

tively, or to the people?" The Constitution does not delegate to the United States the power to punish offenses against the life, liberty, or property of the citizen in the States, nor does it prohibit that power to the States, but leaves it as the reserved power of the States, to be by them exercised. . . . I honor the mover of this bill for the purpose he seeks to attain, which is to compel the exercise in good faith by the States of this reserved power. . . . But I ask that it be enforced in accordance with the Constitution of my country.[56]

Bingham found no fault with the Civil Rights Act's introductory clause defining citizenship. That was "simply declaratory of what is written in the Constitution, that every human being born within the jurisdiction of the United States of parents not owing allegiance to any foreign sovereignty is, in the language of your Constitution itself, a natural-born citizen. . . ."[57] The remainder of the Bill's first section Bingham regarded as declaring "there shall be no discrimination of civil rights among citizens of the United States in any state of the United States. . . ."[58] Could Congress declare this by simple enactment? He concluded:

> I say, with all my heart, that [the First Section] . . . should be the law of every State, by the voluntary act of every State. The law in every State should be just; it should be no respecter of persons. It is otherwise now, and it has been otherwise for many years in many of the States of the Union. I should remedy that not by an arbitrary assumption of power, but by amending the Constitution of the United States, expressly prohibiting the States from any such abuse of power in the future.[59]

---

[56] CONG. GLOBE, 39th Cong., 1st Sess. 1291 (1866).
[57] *Ibid.*
[58] *Ibid.*
[59] *Ibid.* Bingham's speech stressed that the Due Process Clause of the Fifth Amendment applied to all "persons," not simply to all freemen as in the Magna Carta; and he suggested that the use of the more comprehensive term precluded discrimination between citizens and aliens in the adminstration of justice: "If the Bill of Rights, as has been solemnly ruled by the Supreme Court of the United States, does not limit the powers of States and prohibit such gross injustice by the States, it does limit the powers of Congress and prohibit such legislation by Congress." *Id.* at 1292.
Bingham derided the tendency of his colleagues to assume that general language such as that used in the Freedmen's Bureau and Civil Rights Bills applied only to the rights of the freedmen "for the time being in the late insurrectionary States. . . . It applies to every State in the Union . . . and is to be enforced in every State . . . until . . . repealed." *Ibid.* Because Congress was embarking on this permanent and momentous policy of enforcing equality in civil rights irrespective of race and color, because the war power at best was merely transitional, because the original federal-state division left the vast field of property and personal relations—including these racial aspects—to the states, Bingham insisted another amendment to be both necessary and desirable. *Ibid.*

Representative William Lawrence of Ohio was typical of the group that thought another amendment desirable but not necessary. A scholarly former judge, Lawrence bolstered his point with citations[60] ranging from the Statute De Natis Ultra Mare of 25 Edward III and Lord Coke, to *Taylor v. Porter*[61] and Attorney General Bates' opinion of 1862 on citizenship.[62] Like Bingham, he represented one of the districts abolitionized in the 1830's, and had attended Franklin College while the Weld-Birney crusade was at its peak.[63] His theory too was heterodox. He did not share Bingham's view that constitutional amendment was indispensable. Indeed, he leaned heavily on declaratory theory and inherent national power. He agreed with Wilson that the Bill's definition of citizenship—essentially that of Section One of the Fourteenth Amendment—was "unnecessary, but nevertheless proper, since it is only declaratory of what the law is without it":[64]

> There is, then, a national citizenship. And citizenship implies certain rights which are to be protected, and imposes the duty of allegiance and obedience to the laws.
> There is in this country no such thing as "legislative omnipotence." . . . Legislative powers exist in our system to protect, not to destroy, the inalienable rights of men.[65]

After a long review of the military government situation and evidence showing the freedmen's need for protection came quotation and citation of the Comity Clause, Kent, *Corfield v. Coryell*, and *Prigg v. Pennsylvania*.[66] Lawrence continued:

> Certainly, then, in aid of article four, section two . . . Congress has large incidental powers to enforce its observance, so essential to preserve the national life and the means of national existence. . . .
> . . . [I]t must be clear that this bill creates no new right, confers no new privilege, but is declaratory of what is already the constitutional right of every citizen in every State, that equality of civil rights is the fundamental rule that pervades the Constitution and controls all State authority.[67]

After analyzing the civil and penal provisions of the Civil Rights

---

[60] *Id.* at 1832-37.
[61] 4 Hill 140 (N.Y. 1843).
[62] 10 Ops. Att'y Gen. 382 (1862), answering a query from Salmon P. Chase, Secretary of the Treasury.
[63] See 11 Dictionary of Am. Biography 52-53 (Malone ed. 1933); Chapter 4, *supra*.
[64] Cong. Globe, 39th Cong., 1st Sess. 1832-37 (1866).
[65] *Id.* at 1832-33.
[66] 16 Pet. 539 (U.S. 1842).
[67] Cong. Globe, 39th Cong., 1st Sess. 1836 (1866).

Bill, he then added: "The whole question of the power of Congress to enact this bill is resolved to this: When the Constitution recognizes and secures rights which are denied by State laws, may Congress declare it a crime to execute or enforce unconstitutional laws, to deprive a citizen of a constitutional right?[68] Lawrence's answer was "Yes."[69]

In the light of this evidence a hypothesis may be formulated about the framers' purposes in 1866. No one reading the debates carefully will question the framers' devotion to federalism, even the extreme Radicals'. Bingham's quotation from de Tocqueville—"Centralized government, decentralized administration"[70]—is a revelation. But these men also were determined to do something about the vestigial discriminations and denials which they regarded as "badges and incidents" of the slave system.[71] Race discrimination, broadly conceived, was the framers' target, but their natural rights–declaratory theory led them to use broad, sweeping language to accomplish specific, historically defined ends.[72] When it developed in the debates

---

[68] *Ibid.*

[69] *Ibid.* For other typical statements by congressmen who held the Fourteenth Amendment to be unnecessary, but a desirable precaution, see those of Thayer, *id.* at 1153; Broomall, *id.* at 1262; and Farnsworth, *id.* at 2539.

[70] *Id.* at 1292.

[71] See especially Trumbull's views. *Id.* at 319. Similar views are expressed by Representative Cook, *id.* at 903; Senator Poland, *id.* at 2961; Senator Yates, *id.* at 3036; and Representative Julian, *id.* at app. 56.

[72] As is so often the case in Reconstruction matters, one finds illumination in the words of James A. Garfield. The future President was born in 1831, and represents the second generation of antislavery leaders. Speaking on the Freedmen's Bureau Bill, Feb. 1, 1866, *id.* at app. 64, 67, Garfield not only made use of both the Due Process and Comity Clauses, but took unmistakably nationalist and declaratory positions:

"In reference to *persons*, we must see to it, that hereafter, personal liberty and personal rights are placed in the keeping of the nation; that the right to life, liberty, and property shall be guaranteed [sic] to the citizen in reality as they now are in the words of the Constitution, and no longer left to the caprice of mobs or the contingencies of local legislation. If our Constitution does not now afford all the powers necessary to that end, we must ask the people to add them. We must give full force and effect to the provision that 'no citizen [sic] shall be deprived of life, liberty, or property without due process of law.' We must make it as true in fact as it is in law, that 'the citizens of each State shall be entitled to all the privileges and immunities of citizens in the several States.' We must make American citizenship the shield that protects every citizen, on every foot of our soil."

See also the strongly nationalist work, TIFFANY, GOVERNMENT AND CONSTITUTIONAL LAW (1867). Joel Tiffany, with William Goodell, was one of the leading antislavery theorists and pamphleteers of the 1840's who did so much to popularize the thesis of the paramount national citizenship. See TENBROEK, THE ANTISLAVERY ORIGINS OF THE FOURTEENTH AMENDMENT 49–50, 86–91 (1951). Tiffany wrote this volume before the drafting of the Fourteenth Amendment and while serving as reporter of the New York Supreme Court. His work reveals the same soaring nationalist and natural rights–declaratory theory as the pamphlets of the 1840's. *Id.* at 194, 312–13, 371–72, 397–98. Because of these ties, the work is a valuable aid in understanding the form and phrase-

on the Civil Rights Bill that there still was doubt about federal power in this regard, they went through the whole amendatory process again to forestall that doubt forever.[73]

III. THE FRAMERS' SOLUTION

Both the Freedmen's Bureau and Civil Rights Acts were vetoed by President Johnson.[74] Only the Civil Rights Act received the necessary two-thirds vote for immediate repassage and enactment.[75] Because of doubts engendered by the President's vetoes, by the traditional tenets of federalism and by the fear and dread that a defect of power might later be claimed, the Republican congressional leadership sponsored a second constitutional amendment to remove any vestige of doubt regarding power of the national government to protect the civil rights of Negroes and southern loyalists. The Fourteenth Amendment marked a "reconsummation"[76] of the crusade to root out the "badges and incidents" of slavery.

Ten members of the Joint Committee of Fifteen which drafted the Amendment are known to have grown up in states which were exposed for years to antislavery constitutional theory.[77] Bingham was chief architect and draftsman of the crucial sections. From the beginning his idea was to cling to familiar concepts and theory, to eradicate the "badges and incidents" of slavery by using the same weapons that had proved so effective against slavery itself. Like the attitude of the original Fathers toward slavery in the Constitution of 1787,[78] he carried his aversion to race discrimination to the point of refusing even to name it. Rather than deal nakedly with so degrading a con-

---

ology of the Fourteenth Amendment even though that Amendment is unmentioned in the text.

[73] Passage of the Civil Rights and Freedmen's Bureau Bills by large majorities is evidence that the Fourteenth Amendment was added out of hypercaution.

[74] See, *e.g.*, 8 RICHARDSON, MESSAGES AND PAPERS OF THE PRESIDENTS 3596–3611 (1898).

[75] CONG. GLOBE, 39th Cong., 1st Sess. 916–17, 1679–81 (1866).

[76] See tenBROEK, THE ANTISLAVERY ORIGINS OF THE FOURTEENTH AMENDMENT 181–224 (1951).

[77] See FLACK, THE ADOPTION OF THE FOURTEENTH AMENDMENT c. 1 (1908); KENDRICK, JOURNAL OF THE JOINT COMMITTEE OF FIFTEEN ON RECONSTRUCTION (1914). The ten members with antislavery backgrounds were Stevens, Bingham, Fessenden, Conkling, Harris, Boutwell, Grimes, Morrill, Washburne and Blow. It is not implied that these men were themselves abolitionists; merely that like most of their generation who supported the Civil War they absorbed much of the Free Soil constitutional theory and rhetoric.

[78] The Fathers studiously avoided reference to "slaves." They employed the euphemism "persons" in the Fugitive Slave, Slave Trade, and Slave Representation Clauses. See 2 FARRAND, RECORDS OF THE FEDERAL CONVENTION 415–16 (1911). Abolitionists never ceased capitalizing on the Founders' aversion to slavery. See, *e.g.*, LIVERMORE, OPINIONS OF THE FOUNDERS ON NEGROES AS SLAVES, AS CITIZENS, AND AS SOLDIERS (1862).

cept, Bingham and his colleagues preferred to enjoin the states from such conduct by use of the constitutional phraseology that had been employed to maintain racial rights in the past. "You do not prohibit murder in the Constitution; you guarantee life in the Constitution."[79] This statement by Bingham shows what was in his mind. He and the Congress ultimately used restraint forms, but the substantive rights were still defined by use of affirmative concepts such as equal protection, due process and privileges and immunities. Congress and the courts thus were to have broad discretion to work out affirmative solutions.[80]

---

[79] CONG. GLOBE, 39th Cong., 1st Sess. 432 (1866).

[80] Recently, chief interest has focused on whether the Fourteenth Amendment was intended to incorporate the Bill of Rights. Actually debate must be confined to whether there was a *generally understood* intent for *full* incorporation. Bingham's and Howard's speeches on the Fourteenth Amendment leave no doubt that two of the purposes of the framers were "enforcement of the Bill of Rights" and a consequent annulment of Barron v. Baltimore, 7 Pet. 243 (U.S. 1833). Flack assumed it must follow that there had been a specific, well reasoned and widely held intent to enforce and incorporate the Bill of Rights *in toto*. FLACK, *op. cit. supra* note 77, at 94-97. Justice Black and the minority in Adamson v. California, 332 U.S. 46, 68, 92-123 (1947), likewise premised that incorporation in 1866 meant all clauses of all eight Amendments.

This sweeping conclusion, however, is doubtful on several grounds: (1) Pre-Civil War usage makes it clear that varying importance was attached to different amendments during the long antislavery crusade. To constitutional sophisticates, *Barron v. Baltimore* was a real obstacle, but in actual practice its handicapping effects had been limited to cases involving the guarantees of free speech and press, unreasonable searches and seizures, due process and just compensation, and fair trial and criminal procedure. (2) Owing to this reason and the prevailing natural rights philosophy it seems likely that the necessity and desirability of full versus selective incorporation went almost unconsidered in 1866. (3) Professor Fairman's thorough examination of the evidence in the state ratifying conventions confirms the view that the entire Bill of Rights was not incorporated. Fairman, *Does the Fourteenth Amendment Incorporate the Bill of Rights? The Original Understanding*, 2 STAN. L. REV. 5, 68-132 (1949). (4) In his detailed paraphrase of the Bill of Rights made in his opening speech on the Fourteenth Amendment in the Senate, May 23, 1866, Senator Howard of Michigan omitted reference to the grand jury guarantee of the Fifth Amendment, as well as to both religious guarantees of the First Amendment, and to the guarantee of the Seventh Amendment to trial in civil suits. See CONG. GLOBE, 39th Cong., 1st Sess. 2765 (1866), quoted in FLACK, *op. cit. supra* note 77, at 85 n.47. A great deal might be made of these omissions, since they include the guarantees which have presented the greatest obstacles to arguments in favor of full incorporation, had not Senator Howard also omitted *all reference to all guarantees of the Fifth Amendment—including due process*, the clause through which selective incorporation has been effected!

Thus the controversy over incorporation of the Bill of Rights seems to be largely an academic matter when historically considered. The only real controversy has been over whether *full* incorporation was desired and intended; and if so, whether that specific intent was generally understood. On both scores the natural rights thinking and theories of the day obscured the problem and probably precluded a precise intent with reference to full incorporation. Bingham said four times in his speech of February 28, 1866, that his object was "enforcement of the Bill of Rights." CONG. GLOBE, 39th Cong., 1st Sess. 1089-90 (1866). But this does not necessarily mean that he meant *every* clause of *each* of the eight Amendments. The odds appear heavily against any such intent,

He employed these broad affirmative concepts in preference to equally broad, mistrusted phrases like "race or color" in order to avoid any implied recognition or tedious taxonomy of discriminations. And who are we to say that this is not preferable to equally broad, ambiguous, negative concepts like "race discrimination" or "discrimination on account of race or color"? Apparently it never has occurred to those who deride the draftsmanship of Section One that when they suggest that something approaching Stevens' "race or color" form[81] should have been used, they themselves are guilty of the very "clean slate" declaratory states of mind that misled the framers. Innocence, in short, can be defined either prospectively or retrospectively. Given the pressures that riddled the present text and the anthropological and practical uncertainties of "race and color," a lively parlor game can be played, drafting and construing an "unmistakable" amendment of a specifically racial type. For example, the first player accepts Stevens' draft: "No discrimination shall be made by any state, nor by the United States, as to the civil rights of persons because of race, color or previous condition of servitude."[82] Then another player poses a question designed to dramatize the anomalous character of the *Slaughter-House* actions and the disastrous effects which those actions had on the Amendment's interpretation: What would have happened had the first test case been brought by a group of albino circus acrobats who contended that their right to livelihood had been denied by a law (passed perhaps at the instance of rival attractions) which had prohibited acts of albinos on the ground that their eye defects made them a public hazard? If this is deemed fanciful, assume that *Parrot's Chinese Case*,[83] involving validity of a provision in the California Constitution of 1879[84] prohibiting corporations from employing Chinese,

---

even though Bingham indicated in his speeches (*ibid.*) that his amendment was designed to overrule *Barron v. Baltimore*. Likewise, Senator Howard's own paraphrase seems to indicate selective rather than full or automatic incorporation.

All that is certain is that "the great fundamental rights" were meant to be nationalized and to be applied and enforced without regard to race or color. Speaker after speaker in Congress recognized and declared that one purpose of the Amendment was to "constitutionalize" the Civil Rights Act. *Barron v. Baltimore* and the reserved powers of the states had been cited as obstacles to the Act; the Fourteenth Amendment was designed to overcome them. In the last analysis, the courts were left free to incorporate, to enforce, to declare.

[81] As introduced by Stevens, December 5, 1865, *id.* at 10: "All national and State laws shall be equally applicable to every citizen, and no discrimination shall be made on account of race and color."

[82] KENDRICK, JOURNAL OF THE JOINT COMMITTEE OF FIFTEEN ON RECONSTRUCTION 83 (1914).

[83] *In re Parrott*, 1 Fed. 481 (C.C.D. Cal. 1880).

[84] CAL. CONST. Art. XIX, § 2 (1879).

had been the first case, with the action brought, as it was, by the corporations rather than the Chinese. Is it not apparent that many of the problems were inherent in the objectives and in opportunistic abuse of such phraseology, not in the form of draft alone?[85]

Bingham's original drafts were in positive form—for example, "Congress shall have power to make all laws . . . necessary and proper to secure to the citizens of each State all privileges and immunities of citizens in the several States, and to all persons in the several States equal protection in the rights of life, liberty, and property."[86] In this way he proposed to correct the defect he had noted and which had plagued antislavery men from the first. In the course of the debates, however, opposition developed. Conservatives opposed this form as needlessly broad, as one that gave Congress overriding power in every field.[87] Radicals, on the other hand, objected that what a Republican Congress enacted, a Democratic Congress might as easily repeal. Some form of ironclad *constitutional* protection was their demand.[88] In response to these criticisms, Bingham reexamined Marshall's opinions in *Barron v. Baltimore*[89] and *Lessee of Livingstone v. Moore*.[90] The Chief Justice had said[91] that if the drafters of the Bill of Rights had intended to make its provisions binding upon the states, they would have adopted the form used in the re-

---

[85] The Slaughter-House decision, 16 Wall. 36 (U.S. 1873), has so long been an accepted cornerstone of our law that it often is overlooked or forgotten that the first constructions placed on the Fourteenth Amendment in the federal courts, like those construing the Civil Rights Act, were quite in harmony with the broad congressional purposes. See not only the Bradley-Woods decision at the circuit level in the Slaughter-House Cases, 15 Fed. Cas. 649, No. 8,408 (C.C.D. La. 1870), but also Judge Wood's decision in United States v. Hall, 26 Fed. Cas. 79, No. 15,282 (C.C.S.D. Ala. 1871). The *Hall* case, decided just after the congressional debates on the Second Force Bill of April 30, 1871, even acknowledge that Congress had power to reach state inaction. "Denying includes inaction as well as action, and denying the equal protection of the laws includes the omission to protect, as well as the omission to pass laws for protection. The citizen of the United States is entitled to the enforcement of the laws for the protection of his fundamental rights, as well as the enactment of such laws." *Id.* at 81.

[86] Introduced and reported to Congress on February 26, 1866. CONG. GLOBE, 39th Cong., 1st Sess. 1034 (1866). See KENDRICK, JOURNAL OF THE JOINT COMMITTEE OF FIFTEEN ON RECONSTRUCTION 61 (1914).

[87] See particularly the speeches of Representative Hale of New York, CONG. GLOBE, 39th Cong., 1st Sess. 1061-66, 1094 (1866); Representative Davis of New York, *id.* at 1083-87; Representative Raymond of New York, *id.* at 1092; and Representative Conkling of New York, *id.* at 1095. See also FLACK, THE ADOPTION OF THE FOURTEENTH AMENDMENT 57-59 (1908), for summaries of these debates.

[88] See particularly the remarks of Representative Hotchkiss of New York. CONG. GLOBE, 39th Cong., 1st Sess. 1095 (1866).

[89] 7 Pet. 243 (U.S. 1833).

[90] 7 Pet. 469 (U.S. 1833).

[91] Barron v. Baltimore, 7 Pet. 243, 250 (U.S. 1833).

straint clauses of the original Constitution: "No State shall. . . ." As he later explained,[92] Bingham acted on this suggestion. After the debates of January–February, 1866, he shifted to the final negative or restraint form, adding Section Five to give "Congress . . . power to enforce" the three restraint clauses on the states. In the course of this added consideration and change the equal protection clause evolved into a separate guarantee, and both judicial-constitutional and congressional protection were achieved. It was Bingham's conviction, moreover, that thereby he greatly increased the Amendment's strength. Everything it originally accomplished, it still accomplished —and judicial-constitutional protection besides. Apparently this was a generally accepted view among congressmen.[93]

The Journal of the Joint Committee records only the wording of the various texts and the individual votes thereon. It is evident from these, however, that other Republican members originally were reluctant to adopt Bingham's phraseology.[94] It was in and out of committee several times in various forms.[95] Ultimately, however, Bingham's persistence paid off. The most reasonable explanation is that no one could find a better common denominator than these old phrases which had been used in party platforms, petitions and resolutions from 1835 on. Thus the decisive points in favor of Bingham's drafts probably were two: (1) Their antislavery, antirace-discrimination backgrounds people understood, or thought they understood; and the framers in turn believed that the people knew and understood what this language meant. It had been used so long and often in a variety of situations and contexts, both for freedom and against slavery, that it was the text of widest appeal. (2) The texts allowed both Congress and the courts a broad discretionary base in enforcing and securing Negro rights. Numerous remarks show that congressmen mistrusted "race and color" as indefinite;[96] that they assumed protection would be long and difficult.[97] Hence discretion and choice were essential, but it was to be the discretion and choice essential to a working out of the problems of race discrimination. In short the

---

[92] CONG. GLOBE, 42d Cong., 1st Sess. 83–85 (1871).

[93] See FLACK, THE ADOPTION OF THE FOURTEENTH AMENDMENT 76, 94–97, 232–37 (1908).

[94] See, for example, the uncertain and erratic course of Stevens with reference to Bingham's drafts, noted in Chapter 2, *supra*; and in KENDRICK, JOURNAL OF THE JOINT COMMITTEE OF FIFTEEN ON RECONSTRUCTION 83, 85–99 (1914).

[95] See KENDRICK, *op. cit. supra* note 94, at 85–87. See also FLACK, *op. cit. supra* note 93, at 60–68, for a summary of the committee balloting on the major texts.

[96] See, *e.g.*, Representative Raymond's views. CONG. GLOBE, 39th Cong., 1st Sess. 483 (1866). See also Representative Broomall's more detailed discussion. *Id.* at 433.

[97] Men like Trumbull had few illusions regarding the time element. See *id.* at 319–22, 474.

phraseology was historically limited and defined. So limited and defined, it created a new constitutional right which both Congress and the courts had power to enforce. This right was the right to be free from publicly administered or enforced racial discrimination in the enjoyment of any of one's other constitutional rights, state or federal.

A single change was made in Section One after it had been reported by the Joint Committee. This was the addition of the first sentence defining citizenship. Critics had argued it was strange that an amendment designed to clarify rights of citizenship and in fact embody the Civil Rights Act, nevertheless failed to include a definition of the crucial word "citizen."[98] To the Joint Committee's draft the Senate added, without debate,[99] the present introductory sentence: "All persons born or naturalized in the United States, and subject to the jurisdiction thereof, are citizens of the United States and of the State wherein they reside." This was merely an improved statement of the definition in the Civil Rights Act; it points up further the close interrelation between that Act and the Amendment.

Significantly, no one observed that while citizenship was made dual in this first sentence, only the privileges or immunities of "citizens of the United States" were specifically protected in the second sentence against abridgment by the states. The reason for this apparent oversight is that ever since Birney's day, opponents of slavery had regarded all the important "natural" and constitutional rights as being privileges or immunities of *citizens of the United States.* This had been the cardinal premise of antislavery theory from the beginning, and this had been the underlying theory and purpose of Section One from the beginning. The real purpose of adding this citizenship definition was to remove any possible or lingering doubt about the freedmen's citizenship. The *Dred Scott* decision,[100] though overruled by events, still reposed in the books. It needed to be officially buried. An elaborate opinion by Attorney General Bates in 1862[101] had declared all freedmen of color born in the United States to be citizens of the United States. Bates also had declared that there was no class of persons intermediate between citizens and aliens. This statement had been explicit enough for most antislavery men, and characteristically they regarded the opinion as declaratory of

---

[98] Senators Wade of Ohio and Stewart of Nevada were chiefly responsible for the addition. See *id.* at 2560, 2768, 2869. See also the views of Trumbull and Reverdy Johnson. *Id.* at 504–5, 528–29, 1775–81. Tardiness in adding the definition testifies eloquently to the still remote, hypothetical character of judicial review.
[99] *Id.* at 2869.
[100] 19 How. 393 (U.S. 1857).
[101] 10 Ops. Att'y Gen. 382 (1862).

what "always had been the true law."[102] Yet there remained another aspect of the matter. Taney in *Dred Scott* had regarded state citizenship as primary and national citizenship as derivative.[103] Antislaveryites generally had taken the opposite view: national citizenship was primary with derivative state citizenship resting on domicile.[104] This second view had been vindicated by the War. So, with almost no discussion and purely out of hypercaution, the first sentence of Section One was added at the last minute in the Senate.[105]

IV. THE FRAMERS' NEMESIS

The purpose and import of this addition are so clear today, as they also were so clear to those who made and approved them in Congress in 1866, that it is almost inconceivable they ever were misunderstood. Yet misunderstood and misconstrued they presently were by Justice Miller's opinion for the majority in the *Slaughter-House Cases* of 1873.[106] Justice Miller's whole opinion was based upon the fact that although the first sentence of the Fourteenth Amendment makes "All persons born or naturalized in the United States . . . citizens of the United States and of the States wherein they reside," the second sentence secures only the privileges and immunities of citizens of the United States from abridgment by states.[107] This distinction, Miller and the majority held, signified that citizens' fundamental rights to protection of life and property had been left untouched by the Amendment and hence remained, as always, in the hands of the states.

To reach the conclusion of Justice Miller and the majority, one must disregard not only all antislavery and all anti-race discrimination theory from 1834 on, but one must ignore virtually every word said in the debates of 1865–66. Moreover, one must assume that at

---

[102] See the statements of Representative Lawrence, CONG. GLOBE, 39th Cong., 1st Sess. 1832 (1866). The most elaborate discussions of citizenship occurred in the Senate. See *id.* at 504–5, 528–29, 1775–81, 2560, 2768, 2869.
[103] Scott v. Sanford, 19 How. 393, 405–6 (U.S. 1857).
[104] See ROCHE, THE EARLY DEVELOPMENT OF UNITED STATES CITIZENSHIP (1949); TENBROEK, THE ANTISLAVERY ORIGINS OF THE FOURTEENTH AMENDMENT (1951); Chapter 4, *supra*.
[105] See CONG. GLOBE, 39th Cong., 1st Sess. 2560, 2869 (1866).
[106] 16 Wall. 36 (U.S. 1873).
[107] *Ibid*. There is nothing in Miller's opinion which indicates he was aware that the definition of citizenship had been added later and was not a part of the Amendment during the debates in Congress. He stressed the "change in phraseology" between sentences one and two of the Section, but close reading shows he meant that the phrase "citizens of . . . the States" had not been repeated in the second sentence after its use in the first. *Id.* at 72–73.

the last minute the whole Republican Congress suddenly abandoned its previously held and declared views on the Amendment's purpose, and consciously created this distinction—a distinction that left the Negroes' rights exactly where they always had been, at the mercy of the states. Above all, this was done without a single Republican or antislaveryite announcing his change of heart or the reasons therefor. Justice Field was guilty of the (for him) mildest sort of understatement then, when in his dissenting opinion he objected that Justice Miller's interpretation made the privileges and immunities clause "a vain and idle enactment," one "which accomplished nothing."[108] It may be readily conceded that the addition of the first sentence had created a potential loophole—the very one Justice Miller seized on and used so effectively in his opinion. But that loophole was beyond the imagination of framers and ratifiers. To men who for thirty years and more had believed in a paramount national citizenship,[109] it was inconceivable that adding a sentence to define such citizenship ever could be twisted into an intent to do otherwise. In their eyes the whole object of Sections One and Five was to nationalize and enforce the privileges and immunities of "citizens of the United States."[110] Privileges and immunities of citizens of the United States embraced —as a result of the constitutionalizing of the Civil Rights Act—a constitutional right of *every* citizen to be free from public race discrimination.[111] In view of the unmistaken and the unmistakable pur-

---

[108] *Id.* at 96.

[109] See Chapter 4, *supra*, at 177–184. Nationalization of the major and fundamental civil rights and putting the full power and authority of the Federal Government behind their enforcement had been implicit in antislavery theory as far back as the Ellsworth-Goddard argument in the *Crandall* case (1834) and the Ohio Antislavery Society's report on the state black laws (1835). See Argument of Counsel, Crandall v. Connecticut, Sup. Ct. Err., July Term, 1834 (the arguments are printed in condensed form in the official report, Crandall v. State, 10 Conn. 339, 348–53 [1834]); Proceedings, Ohio Antislavery Convention Held at Putnam 10–11 (April 22–24, 1835).

[110] The congressional debates on the Fourteenth Amendment add little but confirm much regarding its real purpose and meaning. Speaker after speaker regarded Section One as axiomatic and beyond challenge. See, *e.g.*, Cong. Globe, 39th Cong., 1st Sess. 2464 (Representative Thayer), 2468 (Representative Kelly), 2510 (Representative Miller), 2539 (Representative Farnsworth) (1866). See also Bingham's major speeches on the Amendment. *Id.* at 156, 428, 1089, 1290, 2541.

[111] In the final debates on the Joint Committee draft, practically every speaker of both parties either stated or clearly implied that Sections One and Five were designed either to incorporate and "constitutionalize" the Civil Rights Act, or to correct the defect of power existing under the pre-War Constitution as construed in *Barron v. Baltimore*. See *id.* at 2459 (Representative Stevens), 2461 (Representative Finck), 2462 (Representative Garfield), 2465 (Representative Thayer), 2467 (Representative Boyer), 2498 (Representative Broomall), 2500 (Representative Shanklin), 2502 (Representative Raymond), 2511 (Representative Eliot), 2530 (Representative Randall), 2538 (Representative Rogers), 2542 (Representative Bingham). **1968:** A disclaimer obviously is in order here: Race discrimination superficially and facilely categorized into "private"

poses of the Civil Rights Act with regard to race discrimination, the meaning and purpose of the Fourteenth Amendment are placed beyond question.

That the nationalistic declaratory theory of 1866 might soon be employed against their own program and partisans was suspected by few, if any, of its sponsors. Yet the first use of Bingham's three-clause system was not *against* the revived "Black Codes" by or on behalf of the freedmen, but by former "Rebels," independent butchers seeking overthrow of that New Orleans slaughter-house monopoly chartered by a reputedly corrupt Carpetbag government.[112] The ironies of this situation are evident enough. It remains to be seen how the

(permissible) and "public" (impermissible) has long been the face and corollary of "state action," hence segregation's current redoubt and apologia—pseudo-evidence and "proof" (for some) of Joint Committee "incompetence," the very heart, in short, of that cat's-cradle interpretation of the privileges-immunities clause. These constructs of course were and are self-vitiating—not merely indefensible but ignoramus in misusing the Senate's addition of a reinforcing citizenship definition to eviscerate protection for the freedmen as "citizens."

It is time to point out flatly and finally that simply *because* these framers intended to reverse and liquidate slavery's policies and vestiges—never to preserve or indulge them; *because* they initially loaded everything into a conception of *paramount national* citizenship (with Negroes finally made national citizens by birthright along with everyone else); *because* these (and the Senate) draftsmen's common sense matched their altruism and their federalism and their natural rights prepossessions, *they* were the last men in the country to split hairs and quibble over what usages and vestiges were "public" and what "private"—over what "badges and indicia" derived from "custom" and what from the Black and slave codes. These men, we say—Joint Committeemen and Senators alike—used language and granted powers accordingly. That unholy pit of "state action" was dug later, advertently and inadvertently, by others; it is a product of chance, fluke, pretense, above all, national inertia—no part at all of this Amendment designed to correct *any* and *every* "defect of power" in our government which otherwise might stymie *racial* adjustment and *racial* protection.

Self liberation from this catatonic "state action" trance therefore is easier then many imagine. Under no rules of either logic or history can that first sentence of Section 1 —added out of hypercaution *after* the substantive theory had been worked out, added to *define* citizenship explicitly and to *remove* a threatened ambiguity and to *strengthen* the Amendment—under no defensible construction, surely, can such a definition longer be twisted to justify and maintain a spurious suddenly-reneged and final framer-intent to continue the very hateful, bankrupt antebellum theory which had caused all the trouble and set the amending process in motion a second time, 1865–1866. To leave unrepudiated the *Slaughter-House misinterpretation* of the privileges-immunities clause —*as it affects the Negro race*—is to ignore a generation of antislavery usage, much of it by these Joint Committee members themselves.

The Supreme Court, we may be reasonably sure, is coming to recognize this. The Court now needs the support of enlightened opinion to rid the law of these relics and stratagems forever. Hopefully, the Holmes Devise histories will speed this rectifying process. The *Slaughter-House* corner, in particular, must be resquared with history and remortared in fact, to vindicate constitutional processes and integrity.

The Senate debates are equally emphatic and convincing. See *id.* at 2766 (Senator Howard), 2768 (Senator Wade), 2896 (Senator Doolittle), 2961 (Senator Poland), 3037 (Senator Yates), 3041 (Senator Johnson).

[112] See LONN, RECONSTRUCTION IN LOUISIANA AFTER 1868 42–44 (1918).

addition of that first sentence defining citizenship—a change designed to *bolster* the Amendment—became the innocent loophole for its emasculation.

Two scenes or episodes serve in this respect. The first is recapitulative and corroborative. The setting is the Massachusetts State House. The locale precludes dismissing this incident as "backwoods jurisprudence" or "frontier legislative confusion." Yet one complaint of the majority of this staunchly Republican committee, reluctantly opposing immediate ratification of the Amendment, was that Section One was already in the Constitution![113] It was there in the form of the Preamble, the Comity Clause, the Republican Form of Government Clause, and the First, Second, Fifth, Sixth and Seventh Amendments—all quoted, and all relied on precisely as antislavery men had relied on them for two generations. Fairly construed, the report contended, these provisions would secure everything the first section would. The Committee found it "difficult to conceive, how, . . . taken in connection with the whole tenor" of the Constitution, the original clauses could have been put more clearly. By "any fair rule of interpretation, these provisions cover the whole ground of section first."[114] Furthermore, Attorney General Bates' opinion declaring Negroes to be citizens had rendered definition of citizenship unnecessary. More significantly, in the eyes of the Massachusetts Republicans, "The definition of citizenship 'of the state wherein they reside' is of no effect *as none of the provisions of the Amendment profess to apply to persons as citizens of a State.*"[115] [Emphasis added.] True, the Equal Protection Clause was not in the Constitution in these very words, yet denial of equal protection of the laws would be a "flagrant perversion of the . . . personal rights" guaranteed by the Comity Clause and by the Amendments earlier noted. The Committee concluded that "this first section is, at best, mere surplusage"; and that furthermore,

> it is mischievous inasmuch as it is an admission, either that the same guarantees do not exist in the present Constitution, or that if they are there, they have been disregarded, and by long usage or acquiesence [*sic*], this disregard has hardened into a constitutional

---

[113] MASS. HOUSE DOC. NO. 149, pp. 2–4 (1867). See also FLACK, THE ADOPTION OF THE FOURTEENTH AMENDMENT 186–87 (1908).
[114] MASS. HOUSE DOC. NO. 149, p. 3 (1867).
[115] *Id.* at 4. "Further, we are not aware that there has been any decision, or that there is any agreement among legal authorities as to what constitutes citizenship of a State, apart from citizenship of the United States." *Ibid.*

Our "Declaratory" Fourteenth Amendment

right; and no security can be given that similar guarantees will not be disregarded hereafter.[116]

Indeed, a strange and illuminating prophecy!

Precisely the same complaint had been registered in congressional debate,[117] but when we find it within earshot of Dane Hall and Professors Washburn, Parker and Parsons, we conclude that these are not simply matters of jurisprudential sophistication. Nicety of legal analysis is a function of the complexity of the legal order. By the same token, sharp appreciation of the pitfalls inherent in the meaning of "constitutionality," "unconstitutionality," "law" and "amendment" comes most naturally to those who have had the benefits of well-established tradition in these fields. This appreciation was what the Civil War generation lacked, and it lacked it because judicial control still was largely hypothetical, because the Constitution had not been amended since 1804, because law as a whole was much simpler, and because the natural rights–social compact theory still dominated nearly everyone's thinking.[118]

Scene two is laid in the United States Senate, April 11, 1871: an *extempore* exchange between three Republican Senators, Trumbull of Illinois, Carpenter of Wisconsin, and Edmunds of Vermont. By this time the American federal system had jammed its gears. The Vindictives' program had boomeranged. Reconstruction was at near-impasse. Squarely in the middle, federal courts were swamped by threatened misuse of the new Amendments and laws.[119] President

---

[116] *Ibid.*

[117] See, for example, the statements of Representatives Kelly and Farnsworth. CONG. GLOBE, 39th Cong., 1st Sess. 2468, 2539 (1866). Senator Henderson stated: ". . . [T]his section will leave citizenship where it now is. It makes plain only what has been rendered doubtful by the past action of the Government. If I be right in that, it will be a loss of time to discuss the remaining provisions of the section, for they merely secure the rights that attach to citizenship in all free Governments." *Id.* at 3031. See also the remarks of Senator Poland. *Id.* at 2961. And see Bingham's two statements: "I do not admit and never have admitted that any State has a *right* to disenfranchise any portion of the citizens of the United States. . . . I favor this amendment [now Section Two of the Fourteenth] as a penalty *in aid of the rights guaranteed by the Constitution as it now stands.*" *Id.* at app. 57. [Emphasis added.] "No State ever had the *right*, under the forms of law or otherwise, to deny to any freeman the equal protection of the laws or to abridge the privileges or immunities of any citizen of the Republic, although many of them have assumed and exercised the power, and that without remedy." *Id.* at 2542. [Emphasis added.]

[118] Our law school-trained generation has found it increasingly difficult to understand the pre-Civil War generation for precisely these reasons.

[119] See, e.g., Worthy v. Commissioners, 9 Wall. 611 (U.S. 1870); Northwestern Fertilizing Co. v. Hyde Park, 18 Fed. Cas. 393, No. 10,336 (C.C.N.D. Ill. 1873); Insurance Co. v. New Orleans, 13 Fed. Cas. 67, No. 7,052 (C.C.D. La. 1870); Butchers' Ass'n v. Slaughter House Co., 4 Fed. Cas. 891, No. 2,234 (C.C.D. La. 1870); *Ex parte* Smith and Keating, 38 Cal. 702 (1869).

Grant had just called for a second Force Bill to cope with extralegal suppression of Negro rights.[120] The problem of quasi-public action and invasions had arisen, not in the contemplated or familiar form of discrimination by carriers, theaters and inns, but in the infinitely more tangled context of Southern whites fighting misrule and military government.

Trumbull, a Senator who personified scruple and conscience, had drafted the Civil Rights Act of 1866 to put down the "Black Codes"; but he flatly declined to go along on the latest proposal.[121] Informally he surveyed the constitutional system, including the recent changes, and then denied that the Fourteenth Amendment authorized Congress to protect citizens in their rights of person and property in the states. Recalling the various steps previously taken—emancipation, the Thirteenth Amendment, and the Civil Rights and Freedmen's Bureau Acts and their repassage over the President's vetoes—his mind and talk drifted irresistibly into the declaratory mood.

In Trumbull's view the Thirteenth Amendment had worked the really great change; it had ended slavery and enabled Congress to pass the Civil Rights Act. But that Act "did not undertake to protect those who had been slaves, nor whites, in particular rights; but declared that the rights of the colored people should be the same as those conceded to the white people in certain respects, which were named in the act."[122] Further, the definition of citizenship in the Civil Rights Act simply had been "declaratory of what the law already was." "Every person born within the jurisdiction of a nation must be a citizen of that country."[123] But formerly the slave-controlled American Government had not dared concede Negro citizenship because, for example, Pennsylvania's free Negroes might have gone to Carolina and there "enjoy[ed] all the rights and immunities of a citizen of Carolina. . . ."[124]

After the Civil Rights Act, Trumbull recalled, some minds had remained uneasy. To settle the question "once and forever," the citizenship definition had been reinserted in the Fourteenth Amend-

---

[120] 7 RICHARDSON, MESSAGES AND PAPERS OF THE PRESIDENTS 163 (1872). See 17 STAT. 13 (1871) for text of resulting KKK Act.

See also John Norton Pomeroy's unsigned article, *The Force Bill*, 12 NATION 268 (1871), in which Pomeroy, obviously influenced by the senatorial debates of April 11–14, 1871, stated that the Fourteenth Amendment made the Bill of Rights binding on the states and that Section One was "declaratory of the meaning of the Constitution and introduced no new principle or rule." *Id.* at 268–70.

[121] CONG. GLOBE, 42d Cong., 1st Sess. 575–80 (1871).
[122] *Id.* at 575.
[123] *Ibid.*
[124] *Id.* at 576.

ment. But in his opinion that addition had not changed "the fact that after the abolition of slavery, and after the authority of the States to deprive persons of liberty ceased, every person born in the United States was a citizen of the United States."[125] Phrase by phrase Trumbull proceeded through Section One. Distressed at the course of Reconstruction, he found refuge and comfort in the fact of national citizenship, but shrank from the problem of implementing it. In his view the Privileges and Immunities Clause of the Fourteenth Amendment had not changed the old Comity Clause at all. It merely was a repetition of the Comity Clause "in a little different language."[126]

This last statement proved too much for Senators Edmunds and Carpenter. Section One, Edmunds rejoined, had nationalized citizenship; it had changed entirely "the description of the class of persons who are entitled to protection. [It] provides that the citizens of the United States, whether they are citizens of any particular State or not, shall have universal citizenship in the United States."[127]

MR. TRUMBULL. That is true; but it is limited in another respect to an infringement by law.

MR. CARPENTER. . . . Are not the privileges and immunities of every citizen of the United States put on a par in every State of the Union?

MR. TRUMBULL. . . . The Senator . . . asks if they are not protected in all the privileges and immunities of citizens of the United States. Undoubtedly; but we have not advanced one step by that admission. The fourteenth amendment does not define the privileges and immunities of a citizen of the United States any more than the Constitution originally did.

MR. CARPENTER. If my friend will allow me, I heard him say a moment ago that there were some things so plain in this country that they need not be in the Constitution, and I claim this to be exactly illustrative of that remark. There are certain privileges and immunities of American citizens that are recognized in every State of the Union and by every American as being peculiarly and especially the privileges of an American citizen, and that Constitution means to protect those, or else it is mere idle talk and protects nothing.[128]

This was a shrewd way of epitomizing the 1866 attitude; and Carpenter's tacit reading of the declaratory blanks had been shared

---
[125] *Id.* at 575.
[126] *Id.* at 576.
[127] *Ibid.*
[128] CONG. GLOBE, 42d Cong., 1st Sess. 576 (1871).

by thousands then and during ratification. Moreover, Trumbull's reply shows that he still held to this declaratory view, yet with what a difference! The clash of these two able and honest minds was prophetic to the point of revelation:

> Mr. Trumbull. The protection which the Government affords to American citizens under the Constitution as it was originally formed is precisely the protection it affords to American citizens under the Constitution as it now exists. The fourteenth amendment has not extended the rights and privileges of citizenship one iota. . . . The fourteenth amendment has not defined what the privileges and immunities of citizenship are. Was not Martin Van Buren . . . or James K. Polk just as much a citizen, and a native-born citizen, of the United States before the fourteenth amendment as the Senator from Wisconsin is to-day? . . . They were citizens, and they were clothed with all the rights of American citizenship, and the Federal Government was bound to protect them in whatever immunity and privilege belonged to them as citizens of the nation; but that did not have reference to the protection of those persons in individual rights in their respective States, except so far as being citizens of one State entitled them to the privileges and immunities of citizens in every other.
>
> Mr. Carpenter. I should like to interrupt my friend once more, if he will allow me to do so.
>
> Mr. Trumbull. Certainly.
>
> Mr. Carpenter. I understand him to maintain that a colored man born in Massachusetts, under the old Constitution, was a citizen of the United States.
>
> Mr. Trumbull. That was my opinion, but not the opinion of others.
>
> Mr. Carpenter. . . . The Senator says the colored man born in Massachusetts was a citizen of the United States under the old Constitution. If he moved from Massachusetts into South Carolina he did not carry with him the rights of citizenship of the State of Massachusetts, and the Constitution in South Carolina only protected him in the rights which belonged to a colored citizen of that State. If these rights which we are now speaking of are the rights of an American citizen, apart from the citizenship of the State, and they were protected by the old Constitution, then, whatever those privileges and immunities were, they would have been the same in South Carolina as they were in Massachusetts; and yet we all know that every privilege that can be assigned to a man —the right to be a party in court, the right to be a witness—all those privileges which are personal, and which pertain to every free man everywhere, were denied to that citizen just as soon as he got into South Carolina, and the Constitution of the United

States did not reach him and did not profess to reach him. It simply said to South Carolina, "You shall give this colored man coming from Massachusetts just as much right as you give the colored men of South Carolina." The Constitution now says to South Carolina, "You shall no longer enforce a law that abridges the privileges of any citizen."

Mr. Trumbull. The Senator is entirely mistaken. This Constitution says no such thing as that a State shall not abridge the privileges of any citizen. It speaks of citizens of the United States, and you have not advanced one step in the argument unless you can define what the privileges and immunities of citizens of the United States are. If the Senator from Wisconsin had honored me with his attention when I commenced, he would have observed that I stated at the commencement that this national Government was not formed for the purpose of protecting the individual in his rights of person and of property.

Mr. Carpenter. That is what I understand to be the very change wrought by the fourteenth amendment. It is now put in that aspect and does protect them.

Mr. Trumbull. Then it would be an annihilation entirely of the States. Such is not the fourteenth amendment. The States were, and are now, the depositaries of the rights of the individual against encroachment.

Mr. Carpenter. And that Constitution forbids them to deny them, and authorizes Congress to legislate so as to carry that prohibition into execution.[129]

Obviously Trumbull and Carpenter were thinking of different facets of the same problem. Or perhaps it would be more accurate to say that in the three years since ratification the original problem had got out of hand; it had developed facets far beyond those conceivable in 1866. Carpenter's mind still was on the problem that had existed then. Trumbull's was on the current scene, grappling with a deepening crisis, unconsciously using old declaratory concepts and ambiguity to find a way of avoiding what he regarded as a fatal collision between state and federal authority. This became clearer as the dialogue continued:

Mr. Trumbull. If the Constitution had said that the privileges and immunities of citizens of the United States embraced all the rights of person and property belonging to an individual, then the Senator would be right; but it says no such thing. In my judgment, the fourteenth amendment has not changed an iota of the

---

[129] *Id.* at 576–77. See also the Trumbull-Edmunds exchange, *id.* at 693–94, for repetition and elaboration of these points.

Constitution, as it was originally framed, in that respect. I take the Senator's case of the colored man in Massachusetts. That colored man in Massachusetts before the fourteenth amendment was adopted, in my judgment, was a citizen of the United States as well as a citizen of Massachusetts. That was my opinion about it then; and this amendment carries out what I believed to be the law of the land at that time. However, as I have already explained, others took a different view in consequence of the existence of slavery which they held to be the normal condition of the colored man. The people of the southern States always insisted that slavery was not established by statute law. Some of them insisted that the colored man was a slave by nature. They did not look to statutes to make him so. This amendment simply carries out the provisions of the law, as I understood it before, and makes it certain that all persons of whatever color born in the United States are citizens.

The difference between the Senator from Wisconsin and myself is, as to what are the privileges and immunities of citizens of the United States. I insist that the privileges and immunities belonging to the citizen of the United States as such are of a national character, and such as the nation is bound to protect, whether the citizen be in foreign lands, or in any of the States of the Union. The Government of the United States protects the citizens of the United States to the same extent in Carolina or Massachusetts as it protects him in Portugal or in England. National citizenship is one thing, and State citizenship another; and before this constitutional amendment was adopted the same obligation, in my judgment, rested upon the Government of the United States to protect citizens of the United States as now.[130]

After this colloquy Trumbull proceeded with his analysis of Section One, clause by clause, repeating and elaborating his views. Presently he maintained that congressional power under Section Five of the Amendment was limited to providing for judicial enforcement of the three restraint clauses. Congress' powers were no more and no less than it had exercised in the Judiciary Act of 1789 for the enforcement of the Contract and Ex Post Facto Clauses! This stand involved Trumbull in another illuminating exchange:

> Mr. Carpenter. The prohibition in the old Constitution that no State should pass a law impairing the obligation of contracts was a negative prohibition laid upon the State. Congress was not authorized to interfere in case the State violated that provision.

---

[130] Cong. Globe, 42d Cong., 1st Sess. 577 (1871).

It is true that when private rights were affected by such a State law, and that was brought before the judiciary, either of the State or nation, it was the duty of the court to pronounce the act void; but there the matter ended. Under the present Constitution, however, in regard to those rights which are secured by the fourteenth amendment, they are not left as the right of the citizen in regard to laws impairing the obligation of contracts was left, to be disposed of by the courts as the cases should arise between man and man, but Congress is clothed with the affirmative power and jurisdiction to correct the evil.

I think there is one of the fundamental, one of the great, the tremendous revolutions effected in our Government by that article of the Constitution. It gives Congress affirmative power to protect the rights of the citizen. . . .

MR. TRUMBULL. . . . [L]et me say . . . that the authority of the United States was just as positive under the Constitution, as originally framed, as it is under the fourteenth amendment. . . .[131]

What was vested in the Government of the United States [under its original powers]? The power to carry out the clause declaring that no State should pass a law impairing the obligation of contracts. This was a power conceded by the people to the Government of the United States when they made it, and with that concession went along the power to make all laws necessary and proper to carry it into effect.[132]

Whether he was conscious of it or not, Trumbull's position thus became equivocal. To be sure, he read the Ex Post Facto and Contract Clauses of the old Constitution not merely as restraints on the states but as sources of power to the extent that under the Necessary and Proper Clause Congress *always* had been able to provide for judicial enforcement. But this circumstance he now endeavored to make determinative of the *amended* Constitution simply because the same restraint form ("No State shall . . .") had been re-employed in Section One! The whole approach was crippling, formalistic. It denied the scope and impact of the very Amendment his own civil rights program had prompted.

Carpenter, on the other hand, was not trying to hedge or limit the congressional power. The 1866 formulae still were fresh and meaningful in his mind. So too, apparently, were echoes of the old higher law and inherent, inalienable rights premises which had been used so often to make the Bill of Rights and other restraints sources of congressional power, and which had caused so

---

[131] *Ibid.*
[132] *Id.* at 578.

many to think of both Sections One and Five as "merely declaratory." Trumbull's last remark itself signaled a return to these old inherent power concepts. Rejoined the sardonic Carpenter:

> As I now understand his construction of the old Constitution, the authority conferred on Congress to pass laws to execute the powers conferred on the Government included the power to pass laws which should prevent the States from doing the things which they were prohibited from doing by the Constitution. With that admission, I do not think the fourteenth article, or any article, could add anything to the old Constitution. But I never heard of that construction before; and while I am not ready to make an affidavit that is sound, it is satisfactory for all the purposes of this bill.[133]

Trumbull ignored this irony and proceeded with his exposition. Reiterating his view that the original Constitution had given the Federal Government power to enforce constitutional restrictions on State action—for example, the restriction forbidding impairment of obligation of contract—he declared:

> ... I want to say to the Senator from Vermont that not only in regard to that right, but in regard to all the rights secured by the fourteenth amendment, however extended, in time of peace, the courts are established to vindicate them, and they can be vindicated in no other way. Sir, the judicial tribunals of the country are the places to which the citizen resorts for protection of his person and his property in every case in a free Government.
> Mr. EDMUNDS. Suppose they fail?
> Mr. TRUMBULL. If they fail by reason of organized opposition, resort, as in the case I supposed, and to which the Senator from Vermont agreed, is had to force, if necessary, in order to give the protection. ...
> But, sir, I am not willing to undertake to enter the States for the purpose of punishing individual offenses against their authority committed by one citizen against another.[134]

Presently retained to uphold validity of the New Orleans slaughter-house monopoly, Senator Carpenter made telling use of these views before the Supreme Court.[135] That Trumbull's position

---

[133] CONG. GLOBE, 42d Cong., 1st Sess. 578 (1871).
[134] *Ibid.* Speaking defensively and wholly extemporaneously, Trumbull was woefully lax in his use of such terms as "rights" and "powers." *Compare* the interpolations of Senators Edmunds and Thurman, *with* Trumbull's muddled statement immediately following the passage quoted in the text. *Ibid.*
[135] Trained in the office of Rufus Choate, Carpenter was recognized as one of the ablest constitutional lawyers in the country during the Reconstruction period. See

and contentions had struck him as novel, inconsistent and confused is obvious. That he himself had provided the best answer to them also is clear. This is true both with regard to what the Fourteenth Amendment accomplished and had been designed to accomplish, and what he in 1871 sensed to have been a confused, unlawyerlike way of regarding the prewar Constitution. Moreover, Trumbull's position certainly held no appeal to Carpenter as a Grant Stalwart. But that Trumbull's viewpoint, and even the Illinoisan's ambulatory, imprecise manner of thinking and talking about rights under both the old Constitution and the new, harmonized perfectly with Carpenter's present needs is hardly less clear. They afforded a simple, daring means of reducing at a single blow the edifice John A. Campbell[136] was endeavoring to build on the Privileges and Immunities Clause to support the independent butcher's right to a livelihood.

Thus in the argument before the Supreme Court in January, 1872, and again on reargument[137] in February, 1873, some startling propositions were advanced. They were advanced, however, in most innocent and attractive form. A great deal was heard about the integrity of the police power, about legislatures' historic and sweeping control over offensive, unsanitary trades and occupations, about the expediency of maintaining such power intact. Then casually began the discussion that eventually helped to turn the Fourteenth Amendment inside out.

> Taken in the broadest sense, this provision would prohibit any state from abridging any existing privileges of any citizens of the United States, or from enforcing any law already enacted which abridges any privileges or immunities of citizens. It operates as a repeal of all laws which abridge privileges or immunities of citizens.[138]

This meant, Carpenter and his colleagues continued—still "taking

---

FAIRMAN, MR. JUSTICE MILLER AND THE SUPREME COURT 116 (1939), for Miller's revealing characterization; also Cassoday's sketch in 7 GREAT AMERICAN LAWYERS 495-536 (1909); FLOWER, LIFE OF M. H. CARPENTER (1883); Ashley, *Matthew Hale Carpenter as a Lawyer*, 6 GREEN BAG 441 (1894).

[136] 1811-89; Associate Justice of the Supreme Court of the United States, 1853-61; see CONNOR, JOHN A. CAMPBELL 204 (1920), for two commentaries on Campbell's role in the *Slaughter-House Cases*. See also TWISS, LAWYERS AND THE CONSTITUTION 42-62 (1942); Hamilton, *The Path of Due Process of Law* in THE CONSTITUTION RECONSIDERED 170-75 (Read ed. 1938). Campbell's briefs and arguments are summarized in 21 L. Ed. 395-99 (1873).

[137] See *id.* at 399-402 for the briefs and arguments of Carpenter and other counsel for the defendants in error.

[138] 21 L. Ed. 401-2 (1873).

it broadly"—that "this Amendment will have the following results: Repeal all laws imposing license fees . . . ; all laws regulating . . . lawful employments, . . . offensive or dangerous trades and articles . . . ; all [liquor, lottery, Sunday and labor laws; all chartered privileges]."[139] It would "bring within the jurisdiction of this court all questions relating to any of these kindred subjects, and deprive the Legislatures and State courts of the several States from regulating and settling their internal affairs."[140] This was indeed "taking it broadly," and as Carpenter added, "The letter killeth."[141]

"There is no occasion," he continued, "to give such broad significance to the words 'privileges and immunities.'" Various illustrations next were offered of "departures" from so "literal" a construction of constitutional provisions. Then:

> The phrase "privileges and immunities of citizens" is not used for the first time in this Amendment. The original Constitution provided "that the citizens of each state shall be entitled to all privileges and immunities of citizens in the several states." The privileges and immunities here contemplated are those which are fundamental, as, for instance, the right of going into any state for the purpose of residing therein; the right of taking up one's residence therein, and becoming a citizen; the right of free entrance and exit, and passage through; the protection of the laws affecting personal liberty.
> See *Corfield v. Coryell*, 4 Wash. C.C. 381. . . .[142]

Presumably the cryptic reference to those privileges and immunities "which are fundamental" alluded to Justice Washington's dictum in *Corfield v. Coryell*. It will be observed, however, that the paraphrase was very gingerly made; it carefully omitted some of the most relevant Lockean theory.[143]

Finally came the momentous proposition—ambiguous as the Prophet, false as Judas, but unquestionably an inspired rephrasing of the confused, declaratory position Trumbull had taken in 1871: "There is no reason for giving any more extensive signification to this phrase, as used in the Amendment, than was given to it as used in the original Constitution."[144]

---

139 *Id.* at 402.
140 *Ibid.*
141 *Ibid.*
142 *Ibid.*
143 No reference was made to the following parts of Justice Washington's dictum: "Protection by the government; the enjoyment of life and liberty, with the right to acquire and possess property of every kind, and to pursue and obtain happiness and safety. . . ." 6 Fed. Cas. No. 3,230, at 551–52 (C.C.E.D. Pa. 1823).
144 21 L. Ed. 402 (1873).

No more, indeed! The Constitution had been re-amended in 1866. It had been re-amended, among other reasons, *to assure national powers over persons and property in the States in so far as necessary to reach and prevent race discrimination.* There was a general understanding that the Fourteenth Amendment "embodied" or "incorporated" or "declared" the Civil Rights Act of 1866. That Act in turn had been drafted around Justice Washington's dictum in *Corfield v. Coryell.* The Act's intent had been to assure that the "privileges and immunities" which Justice Washington had stated to be "fundamental and to belong, of right, to citizens of all free governments," should in fact no longer be denied to Negroes, or to anyone, on account of race or color. Fitting all this together, the least that the Fourteenth Amendment can be said to have accomplished was this: By defining national citizenship and constitutionalizing the Civil Rights Act, which had been designed to end discrimination in fundamental rights based upon race and color, the Amendment secured and protected a constitutional right to be free from all such discrimination in the exercise of any of one's other rights, state or federal. For practical purposes, a *new* constitutional right was created. Sections One and Five reallocated power in the Federal Government to make absolutely certain that the "privileges and immunities" which Justice Washington had stated to be "fundamental" when they still were simply the privileges and immunities of *"citizens of the several States"* were in practice treated as "fundamental" and as "privileges and immunities of *citizens of the United States."*

It is true that the *Slaughter-House* decision did not directly involve Negro rights. But certainly Negro rights were indirectly involved. The Trumbull-Carpenter premise, once planted and once appropriated by Justice Miller as the basis for his *Slaughter-House* opinion, emasculated one of the three clauses of Section One, and thus appreciably narrowed the scope of the Amendment's protection. This was especially true since post-ratification history and theory naturally tended to accent the importance of Negro citizenship, just as prewar antislavery theory had tended to accent equal protection and due process. The precariousness of the situation first became evident in the Trumbull-Carpenter exchange. It was made even clearer in Carpenter's briefs and arguments in the *Slaughter-House Cases.* There racial *equality* was conceded to be the purpose of the Amendment;[145] but it was already an ambiguous and precarious

---

[145] "The design establishing this amendment . . . was simple and well known. It was to assure all citizens and persons the same rights enjoyed by white citizens and

equality because it was so far withdrawn from the sheltering aegis of national citizenship and everyone was left to make his own federal-state division of the old "fundamental privileges and immunities of citizenship." Justice Miller's *Slaughter-House* opinion presently made the division as if the Constitution had never been amended.[146]

V. Conclusion

All things considered, this is one of the strangest, most baffling self-deceptions in history. The tried and, to the antislavery generation, necessary philosophy of natural rights, in addition to impelling use of broad, sweeping terms to accomplish fairly precise and limited ends, led men to take a declaratory view of the amending process—just as they had taken that view of the Freedmen's Bureau and Civil Rights Bills, of Bates' opinion on citizenship, of the Emancipation Proclamation and similar measures. To their way of thinking, the Fourteenth Amendment was declaratory of what *always* had been the "true" meaning of the Constitution, declaratory of the view that slavery and race discrimination had no place in the Constitution and were outlawed by it.

Confusion this was, confusion of the "is" and the "ought." Men were left without adequate points of reference; they did not agree about what their old Constitution meant because they never squarely faced the problem of who decided what it meant. Naturally they failed to agree and to talk meaningfully about what their amendments meant or did. Many thought and talked as if an amendment "changed nothing," "added nothing" to the Constitution.[147] They talked of states' police powers left intact in every particular; they talked of what their Constitution "rightfully" meant.[148] And during Reconstruction this talk and thinking were turned against them disastrously. Intellectual confusion thus crippled and frustrated an effort that ought to have been steady and continuous. The sectional

---

persons. Every citizen should enjoy the same rights as white citizens. Every person should enjoy the same protection of the laws as white persons." 21 L. Ed. 395, 402 (1873).

146 See Slaughter-House Cases, 16 Wall. 36 (U.S. 1873). Note that Justice Miller here used the dual definition of citizenship and Ward v. Maryland, 12 Wall. 418 (U.S. 1870), in addition to the *Corfield* dictum, to define as privileges and immunities of state citizenship the very rights that Trumbull, Bingham *et al.* nationalized to the extent of prohibiting racial discrimination.

147 See Trumbull's views. CONG. GLOBE, 42d Cong., 1st Sess. 577 (1871).

148 See, *e.g.*, Bingham's speech of 1859, CONG. GLOBE, 35th Cong., 2d Sess. 981, quoted and discussed in Chapter 6 *supra* at 281-283; note also Bingham's two statements quoted in note 117 *supra*.

settlement of 1877 rationalized the confusion;[149] the demands of subduing a continent seemed to sanctify it; eventually the *Plessy*[150] catastrophe came perilously close to institutionalizing it.

Happily the framers of Section One in their abundant caution provided a way out of this impasse; litigants and courts presently discovered it, and the recent *School Segregation* decisions[151] mark its full and unanimous acceptance. Equal protection of the laws today embraces the right to be free from public racial discrimination in the enjoyment of one's other rights. Modern due process incorporates the most vital guarantees of the Bill of Rights, precisely as Birney and Weld in their exploratory uses presumed.[152] By these means we have moved to secure and protect what was meant to be secured and protected. Such a process—due and overdue—and such protection—*full and equal*—will continue unabated. "Our Constitution *is* color-blind."[153] As the work begun by the Jays, the Ellsworths and the Chases[154] moves ever nearer fruition we need argue no more whether "the Constitution always has been so." Declaratory theory has served its purpose.

EDITORIAL NOTE. An oversanguine paragraph, this last? Certainly an unfulfilled paragraph, a nationally humiliating one.

What happened? What failed to happen? Why? Wherefore?

Cynics have stock answers, and sociologists sober ones: War industry, mechanized agriculture, urbanization of impoverished and illiterate Negroes, automation, ghettos, mass unemployment, flight

---

[149] See WOODWARD, REUNION AND REACTION c. 2 (1951).

[150] Plessy v. Ferguson, 163 U.S. 537 (1896). "[E]nforced separation of the two races stamps the colored race with a badge of inferiority . . . solely because the colored race chooses to put that construction upon it." *Id.* at 551.

[151] Brown v. Board of Educ., 347 U.S. 483 (1954).

[152] See The Philanthropist, January 13, 1837, p. 2. See also tenBroek, THE ANTISLAVERY ORIGINS OF THE FOURTEENTH AMENDMENT 21-23 (1951); Chapter 4 *supra* at 215ff.

[153] Mr. Justice Harlan, dissenting singly in Plessy v. Ferguson, 163 U.S. 537, 559 (1896).

[154] For the role of the first, third and sixth Chief Justices of the United States and their families in the abolition of slavery and establishment of equal protection of the laws, see TUCKERMAN, WILLIAM JAY, AND THE CONSTITUTIONAL MOVEMENT FOR THE ABOLITION OF SLAVERY (1894); REPORT OF THE ARGUMENTS OF COUNSEL IN THE CASE OF PRUDENCE CRANDALL (1834); HART, SALMON PORTLAND CHASE (1899). This role is discussed in Chapter 4, *supra*.

to the suburbs. In short, *de facto* segregation, neutralizing—within twenty years—both the *Restrictive Covenant* and the *School Desegregation* decisions. A "color-blind Constitution" at last, yes. But with a color-blind technology, and a color-blind illiteracy: folkways that hardened and that continued to re-cripple.

But these of course were the accepted, the uncalculated risks of the lost century and half century.

History takes no excuses; mass frustration accepts few alibis. America's moral imperatives remain what we made them in 1776, what we remade them in 1866–1868. Everyman in his heart knows this.

[CHAPTER 8]

Crosskey's Constitution: An Archeological Blueprint

EDITORIAL NOTE. The interdependence and the interactions of law and history and the legal profession's often selective use and processing of history have been recurrent points and themes of our discussion. Another theme and problem, equally vital, touching and pointing both, has been "framer intent," "the intentions of framers and public," that hypothetical "original understanding," which draftsmen and ratifiers of the Fourteenth Amendment are presumed to have had of their constitutional handiwork. Just how far *constitutional* construction ever properly depends on such factors; just how far it can, or must, or should do so, are hardy, gritty, flinty issues indeed.[1] Lawyers and legal doctrinaires in and of all ages have used intent as a mask and blind, and often as a discretionary or toggle switch, to control, rectify, and justify their claims, preferences, and decisions. The opted use or nonuse of such a device itself, of course, affords a commodious and congenial discretionary base; and the chosen facts and history relied on can handle matters nicely from there.

What everyone disparages as "law office history" is still a game that nearly everyone plays.[2] Modern constitutionalism pretty clearly would have been, and doubtless pretty soon would be, impossible without it. Once Everyman grasps this fact, his own role, stake, and play, are professionally and profitably improved and assured. The late Carl Becker, in one of the most delightful of essays, "Everyman

---

[1] "The present has a right to govern itself, so far as it can. . . . Historical continuity with the past is not a duty, it is only a necessity."—HOLMES, COLLECTED ESSAYS, 191.

"The case before us must be considered in the light of our whole experience and not merely in that of what was a hundred years ago. . . . We must consider what this country has become in deciding what that amendment has reserved."—HOLMES in Missouri v. Holland 252 U.S. 416, 432–434 (1920).

Note especially the discussion of framer intent, history, and extrinsic aids by Jacobus tenBroek, cited *infra*, note 20.

[2] See Paul Murphy, *Time to Reclaim: The Current Challenge of American Constitutional History*, 69 AM. HIST. REV. 64–79 (1964).

His Own Historian,"³ marked off the whole field and established the ground rules. But it remained for a professor of constitutional law, William W. Crosskey, to go on from there, to raise the historical odds, and to challenge historians and laymen alike to a game they scarcely could believe, or lose. In an immense two-volume polemic entitled *Politics and the Constitution in the History of the United States*, published in 1953, Crosskey pretended to derive a new, sound, and viable construction of our Constitution from what the Fathers "really" intended—professedly, basing it all, in short, on the "original understanding," on the intention of framers and ratifiers. "Back to 1787–1791!" "Back to 1866–1868!" were the pretended rules and precept. And it was all elaborated, advanced, and defended with a deadpan seriousness, authority, and learning that were wonderful at times to behold.

General historians, surprisingly enough, failed to rise to this challenge.⁴ Readers who have followed our story and argument thus far; who sense that constitutions are "made for ages to come," as John Marshall declared; who reflect on how that objective best can be assured and accomplished; who have seen that Everyman's Constitution, and the equal protection of the laws, especially, never can depend on the 1868 "understanding" alone, whatever that understanding may have been; such readers will find in the following essay grist and food for thought aplenty. These issues are inherent and fundamental, and must always be. Everyman's Constitution presumes and intended—we say here with Professor Crosskey—precisely that!

---

3 In 37 Am. Hist. Rev. 221–236 (1932).
4 But see other reviews cited *infra*, notes 9 and 15.

[CHAPTER 8]

COULD IT BE fortunate that so much of history is a closed, or at least a forbidden, book? Otherwise might we not squander our resources reliving and refighting the past? The present soon would be unendurable, the future an endless re-marshalling yard for causes stretching back to antiquity.

If the first volumes of Professor Crosskey's study* invite this somber opening reflection, it is not that his achievement is unimpressive.

---

* Politics and the Constitution in the History of the United States. By William Winslow Crosskey. Chicago: University of Chicago Press, 1953, 2 vols. Pp. xi, 1410.

Here, undeniably, is a work in the great tradition of controversial writing. Few lawyers—and certainly fewer historians—ever willingly have assumed greater burdens of proof. Yet fewer still have contrived a more ingenious *tour de force*, or written with greater verve and clarity. *Politics and the Constitution* may be a mistaken, and many will say, a misdirected book; yet it unquestionably also is a challenging one—an intellectual achievement destined to leave a mark on scholarship for years to come.

I

Professor Crosskey's thesis and plan are outlined in an introductory chapter, Our Unknown Constitution. This, by itself, perhaps is as breathtaking a piece of academic iconoclasm as has appeared since Spengler. The Fathers, it is first hinted, then in the 600,000-word body elaborately argued, did not establish the sort of balanced federal system that three leading members of the Convention—Hamilton, Madison, and Jay—assured the country they had established when the document was up for ratification. They created instead almost the exact opposite—a unitary, centralized government in which Congress was to be supreme and the states—potentially at least—might be gradually reduced to little more than French *départements* or English counties. Far from being merely the coordinate branch of a national government endowed with special and enumerated powers, Congress received in addition wide "plenary" and "general" legislative powers. Delegation, in short, was both specific and general, precise and elastic. Above all, it was intended that Congress be the supreme department, and the government as a whole, a unitary, centralized system. Hence, neither the tripartite separation nor the federal-state division was conceived to have anything like the significance each eventually assumed.

Throughout his study Professor Crosskey stresses the merits and simplicity of a government of this type. "So, if the Constitution were allowed to operate as the instrument was drawn," he argues in his concluding chapter, "the American people could, through Congress, deal with any subject they wished, on a simple, straightforward, nation-wide basis; and all other subjects, they could, in general, leave to the states to handle as the states might desire." (p. 1172). Earlier, he has assured us that "By 'a general national legislative authority' is not meant a power to supplant the legislature of any particular state. The state legislatures were, in general, continued for local state legislation. The general power apparently intended to be given to Congress was a general power of nation-wide legislation; a power to deal with matters, less than nation-wide, that transcended the competence of a single state; and a power to deal even with matters confined to a single state when of concern to any other state, or states, or to the nation." (p. 363n.)[1] Congress, in short, would somehow simply peel off its powers as needed, and there would be little if any nonsense about either adequacy or form.

Disregarding what certainly are some very loose ends in the outlined mechanics of federalism,[2] a most interesting doctrinal parallelism exists here—one that Crosskey himself has not yet stressed. In 1785, James Wilson, two years later one of the principal members of the Federal Convention and eventually one of the original Justices of the Supreme Court, spoke of the powers of the old Congress under the then-existing Articles of Confederation, in the following language:

> "Though the United States in congress assembled derive *from the particular states* no power, jurisdiction, or right, which is not expressly delegated by the confederation, it does not thence follow, that the United States in congress have *no other* powers, jurisdiction, or rights, than those delegated by the particular states.
>
> The United States have general rights, general powers, and general obligations, not derived from any particular states, nor from all the particular states, taken separately; but resulting from the union of the whole: . . .
>
> To many purposes, the United States are to be considered as one undivided, independent nation; and as possessed of all the rights, and powers, and properties, by the law of nations incident to such.
>
> Whenever an object occurs, to the direction of which no particular state is competent, the management of it must, of necessity, belong to the United States in congress assembled. There are many objects of this extended nature."[3]

It is quite evident that Professor Crosskey's thesis has features in common with this so-called "Wilson Doctrine" of inherent, general and unenumerated Congressional powers. Yet there are also pointed

---

[1] *Cf.* pp. 358–60. See also p. 387 (Marshall's "indefensible dictum" regarding enumerated powers in *Gibbons v. Ogden*).

[2] The implication—and indeed the inarticulate, tactical premise—often is that, given the Crosskeyan reinterpretations, the Supreme Court would be spared troublesome problems of linedrawing and umpiring the federal system. See the various caustic remarks on judicial "inclusion and exclusion" (c. 2 and p. 317), and the running attack on Justice Frankfurter, *passim*.

[3] *Considerations on the Power to Incorporate the Bank of North America*, in 1 THE WORKS OF JAMES WILSON 549, 557–58 (Andrews ed. 1896). The "Wilson Doctrine" is historically important in that it provided the jurisprudential base for Theodore Roosevelt's "New Nationalism"; as such it was expressly offered to and rejected by

differences. Wilson, of course, was speaking of congressional powers under the drastically narrow Articles of Confederation; Crosskey, of powers under the Constitution. Moreover, Wilson, a Scottish-trained jurist of the Age of Enlightenment, saw nothing anomalous in a concept of inherent powers: arrangements of that order existed simply as part of, or in the nature of things. Our generation of course cannot endure such nudity of mind. Crosskey's proposition therefore is not offered or argued as an abstract principle of jurisprudence or of natural law, but rather as a matter of historic fact and framer-intent. The burdens that James Wilson was willing and able to leave to God, Professor Crosskey today must shoulder himself. He does so to the extent of shifting them to the broad back of the eighteenth century and of members of the Constitutional Convention. In short, the argument of *Politics and the Constitution* reduces tacitly to this: the leadership and majority of the Convention of 1787 held substantially Wilsonian views of the nature of Congressional powers and delegation. Our constitutional document therefore, whether regarded today as embracing inherent powers or not, at least bestows on Congress large general and unenumerated powers in addition to those specifically enumerated. It does this, because that was the Framers' collective intention. To be sure, no Framers themselves ever quite put it that way, and some of them, notably Madison, later and repeatedly said precisely the opposite. Even James Wilson, during his nine years as a member of the Supreme Court, never repeated his Wilson Doctrine.[4] And of course John Marshall, the last and greatest of the Federalists, in what generally is regarded as his master opinion—*McCulloch v. Maryland*,[5] the very cornerstone of American constitutionalism—

---

the Court in Kansas v. Colorado, 206 U.S. 46, 27 Sup. Ct. 655, 51 L. Ed. 956 (1907). For contemporaneous discussion, see Alexander, *James Wilson, Patriot, and the Wilson Doctrine*, 183 NORTH AM. REV. 971 (1906); the Wilson Memorial addresses in 55 AM. LAW REG. 13 (1907); Lindsey, *Wilson versus the "Wilson Doctrine,"* 44 AM. LAW REV. 641 (1910). For fuller bibliography, see Konkle, *James Wilson*, in 15 ENCYC. SOC. SCI. 425 (1935).

[4] See Lindsey, *supra* note 3; and Cushman, *The National Police Power Under the Commerce Clause of the Constitution*, 3 MINN. L. REV. 289, 381, 452 (1919), reprinted in 3 SELECTED ESSAYS ON CONSTITUTIONAL LAW 36, 40 (1938).

In his Lectures on Law, delivered in 1792, Wilson pointed up this "striking difference between the constitution of the United States and that of Pennsylvania. . . . The latter institutes a legislature with general, the former, with enumerated, powers." 2 WORKS OF JAMES WILSON 56 (Andrews ed. 1896). But he added, "The powers of congress are, indeed, enumerated; but it was intended that those powers, thus enumerated, should be effectual, and not nugatory. In conformity to this consistent mode of thinking and acting, congress has power to make all laws, which shall be necessary and proper for carrying into execution every power vested by the constitution in the government of the United States, or in any of its officers or departments." *Id.* at 59.

[5] 4 Wheat. 316, 4 L. Ed. 579 (1819).

himself officially expounded the doctrine that the Federal Government is one of enumerated powers. Yet all such evidence to the contrary notwithstanding—and Crosskey recognizes there is a great deal of it, though he avoids showing us how much—our Constitution really created a federal government of "plenary" and "general" as well as enumerated powers.

The mood and thought of our introductory paragraph, therefore, emphatically are not Crosskey's. His hostages are irrevocably pledged to history even though the eighteenth century obviously is to be a pretty tough bargainer. What was thought and done, not just what was said, must be determined, and this book is avowedly an attempt at a full and unanachronistic re-construction (p. 7).

In Crosskey's view, the Commerce Clause was to have been the keystone of the new edifice. Destruction of that clause, and the courts' related refusal to construe the Common Defense and General Welfare Clauses[6] as a direct substantive grant of power to Congress—both promoted and abetted by the Jeffersonian party—soon left our Constitution a shambles, hardly a caricature of what the Convention intended. Simultaneously, gradual shifts in word meanings overlaid and disguised these developments.

The Federal Government today thus finds itself needlessly hamstrung—powerless to deal effectively with problems like employers' liability, fair labor standards or anti-trust legislation. Worse still, the nation is denied the obvious benefits of a uniform federal commercial code and corporation law. "States Rights" doctrine thus consistently lost every battle but the last one and is today almost as deeply and offensively entrenched as ever. Actually Congress has—as it always has had, and was intended to have—full power to regulate even *intra*-state and local trade (c. 2).

By Crosskey's "unitary view of the national governing power," the whole Constitution is of a piece with this theory. Following the brilliant salvaging operation performed on the Commerce power, (cc. 2–9) he goes on to find "oblique internal evidence" in the other clauses to substantiate his thesis that Congress possesses power to regulate all the "gainful activities the American people carry on." (p. 521). Conventional views to the contrary are attacked at great length, and a breath-taking reconstruction of the Tenth Amendment[7] blasts that obstacle aside.

---

[6] For Crosskey's "substantive" rehabilitation of this clause, and for his criticism of both the Hamiltonian and Madisonian restrictive or purposive interpretations, see c. 14, The Constitutional Context as It Relates to the General Legislative Power of Congress. This transitional chapter is an excellent epitome of the thesis and methods.

[7] C. 22, The Tenth Amendment and the National Powers. Words frequently mean

Volume 2 is essentially an alibi explaining why these interpretations never have been realized and a sustained quadruple attack on the Supreme Court for sins both of omission and commission. The Court, says Crosskey, at a very early date surrendered both its supremacy and its independence with reference to state and common law. It thus in effect abdicated its responsibilities as the supreme juridical head of the country in matters pertaining to commercial law, conflicts, etc. (cc. 23-26). In recent years this process has gone to unbelievable and disastrous lengths in such cases as *Erie Railroad v. Tompkins*.[8] Simultaneously with these early developments, the Court established itself as "the special and peculiar guardian" (p. 1161) of the Constitution and of private rights against the other two departments, expandiing judicial review far beyond anything conceived by the Fathers or required by the nature of the government; and this too has worked badly (cc. 27-29). Thirdly, the Court destroyed the originally-intended restraints on state power, especially by refusal to interpret the first eight Amendments as binding on the states as well as on the Federal Government.[9] Finally, capping the record, the Supreme Court made exactly the reverse error after the Fourteenth Amendment had made the Bill of Rights binding on the states for a second time. That is, by its wholly unwarranted development and interpretation of substantive due process and equal protection, the Court now *over*-restrained the states and set itself up as a censor in the field of social and economic legislation, instead of employing the Amendment to protect Negro rights and civil liberties generally (cc. 31-32).

As Crosskey himself puts it in his concluding chapter:

"Viewing that record as a whole, it is apparent the Justices, over the years since 1789, have very generally done things they ought not to have done, and, quite as generally, left undone the things they ought to have done; and, further to pursue the language of the Book of Common Prayer, it does truly seem that, in their discharge of this important function, there has been no health in them" (p. 1161).

---

just what Professor Crosskey wants them to mean. There nevertheless were some Anti-Federalists—and even Federalists—who in *1788-89* stubbornly or callously refused to accept his "technical" meaning of the word "reserved" as defined in the cited *1820* ed. of Sheppard's *Touchstone* (p. 77, 80). *Cf.* Crosskey 701, 1352 nn.63-64, and examples cited *infra* note 30.

[8] 304 U.S. 64, 58 Sup. Ct. 827, 82 L. Ed. 1188 (1938). For Crosskey's critique, see pp. 912-37.

[9] C. 30. *Cf.* Professor Fairman's documented article-review of this chapter in 21 U. of Chi. L. Rev. 40 (1953).

Ironically, there is nothing messianic about Professor Crosskey or his theory, even though under the circumstances, one would almost expect that there might be. For the upshot of what he is telling us is that it has taken a century and two-thirds, plus two decades of research, to get the Constitution back on the tracks, headed the way the Framers intended. It amounts to a sanguine act of faith, therefore, to disregard such obstacles and continue to base theories of constitutional government on the intrinsic meaning and intent of the document as historically discoverable. Time and distance can not be operating in our favor, but error has been shown for what it is, and *"True"* intent and *"True meanings"* are at last known. Truth and intent therefore ought to serve us henceforth. Professor Crosskey's faith is staunch and personal. Indeed, some readers will wonder at his rejection of a "Higher Law." Yet the positivism is everywhere as strong and explicit as is criticism of the Supreme Court. Curiously, severest censure is reserved for the Court's decision in *Erie Railroad v. Tompkins,* here condemned as "one of the most grossly unconstitutional governmental acts in the nation's entire history" (p. 916). Yet it was in that case that Justice Brandeis, for the majority, moved to correct what appeared to be, on the basis of Mr. Charles Warren's studies[10] of manuscript drafts of the Judiciary Act of 1789, a century-old misreading of the first Congress' true intent!

Paradoxes of this sort help make *Politics and the Constitution* the fascinating, provocative work it is. There is nothing timid nor equivocal in these pages. Understatement is an all but unexampled virtue. Categoricals like "unquestionably," "absolutely certain," "there can be no possible doubt"; helpers like "the absolute constructional necessities of the situation"—one which on its face proved something less than "absolute"; compulsives like "must have known" and "must have understood"—are scattered six and twelve to a paragraph, sometimes in sequences that cancel out bewilderingly. There also are Professor Crosskey's strong partisan preferences.[11] It might be unfair to call them more than that, but if it ever should develop that his ancestors were Federalists, this book will be a telling new argument for inheritance of acquired characters.

---

[10] Warren, *New Light on the History of the Federal Judiciary Act of 1789*, 37 HARV. L. REV. 49 (1923); *id.* at 49-52, 81-88, reprinted in 3 SELECTED ESSAYS ON CONSTITUTIONAL LAW 1246 (1938). Nowhere does Professor Crosskey discuss or analyze the important textual changes in the drafts of Section 34 of the Judiciary Act, which Mr. Warren discovered and presented; see instead pp. 627 and 902.

[11] Treatment of the Jeffersonians is a page out of the period itself. See entries in index and especially p. 779. Even the defects in the "mischievous" and "vicious" [Federalist] Judiciary Act of 1789 are attributed to Anti-Federalist maneuvering. (pp. 610 ff. and 756).

What we are given, in cantos scattered through the entire work, is another version of the Creation and Fall of Constitutional and Judicial Man. Alexander Hamilton, Gouverneur Morris and James Wilson alternate as Seraphim; Thomas Jefferson doubles as Lucifer and Satan; James Madison—"The Apostate" who faithlessly promoted an Era of Good Feeling rather than stand true and lonely with the Essex Junto—is Jefferson's sinister accomplice. Paradise [was] Lost in 1800. It has not been regained by our latter day penitence and tinkering. (p. 1170). It will only be regained when the resurrected Federalist Host returns to rout the forces of Darkness and Evil. Professor Crosskey's Puritanism is as pure and poetic as Milton's. He scarcely pretends to be writing history; he revels in "delving" (p. 13, cf. p. 6) into it and using it. The argument throughout is that of a lawyer's brief. Even the organization is selctive, forensic, dictated wholly by personal interest, never by chronology, never by the immense body of evidence some readers would like to see systematically and publicly assayed.[12]

The work thus leaves one fascinated and perplexed. None will deny the Gothic splendor of argument, the wide ranging research and intellectual passion, nor the sweep and symmetry of the parts—at least in the first volume. As a work of rhetoric, *Politics and the Constitution* compares with Spengler's *Decline of the West*, and has the same air of truculent dogmatism and infallibility.[13] Purely as an intellectual creation, it is more impressive still. One is reminded of the controversial works of the Reformation. And here of course is the rub: Forensic genius and intellect alone are not enough, for if they were, Thomas More's *Dialogue of Heresies*[14] would be one of the world's classics. Any *tour de force* is a fixed, hazardous enterprise, vulnerable generally beyond its maker's insight.

The issue, therefore, is not whether Professor Crosskey has produced a work of art. Unquestionably he has. It is not whether he has provided a brilliant resynthesis and rationalization of our constitutional law. Again, obviously he has. His "unitary view of the Consti-

---

[12] To call POLITICS AND THE CONSTITUTION a "commentary" on the document, as some have done, is misleading. Rarely does Professor Crosskey attempt systematic elucidation, or summarize existing knowledge, or assemble and weigh evidence pro and con. To get any systematic idea of the historical evidence and judicial opinion, one must keep at hand THE CONSTITUTION OF THE UNITED STATES OF AMERICA (Corwin ed., 1953) (SEN. DOC. No. 170, 82d Cong., 2d Sess.) and standard monographs. The adversary character of legal proceedings ordinarily serves as a corrective for law office history. As an historian, Professor Crosskey temporarily is trading on a broad *ex parte* margin.

[13] Note, for example, the treatment of Justice Miller, pp. 315, 1127; and Justice Frankfurter, *passim*.

[14] Reprinted in MORE, ENGLISH WORKS (Campbell and Reed ed. 1931).

tution" is neat, and to many, considering the problems and alternatives we face today, will appear attractive indeed, *limited to the ends Professor Crosskey foresees.* As a re-thinking of alternatives, and as a re-channeling of precedents, this book would be a superb job.[15] Were the United States starting from scratch, had Professor Crosskey been appointed the Supreme Court's special master to overhaul the works and develop a new plan of simplified constitutional practice in accord with modern needs, certainly we all should have to honor both his hardihood and his achievement.

This, however, is not the measure of Professor Crosskey's purpose. As already noted, his argument is not based on mere expediency, nor on persuasively-argued social and constitutional advantages. It is grounded on history; and parts of it are offered as history. (p. 6). We are not told merely that this might have been, or ought to have been. We are told that it was intended to be. Skeptics will wonder that any thesis-rider's own preferences could have been so perfectly divined by the Fathers; and cynics will go even further. Given our tendency to read history backward, to find what we look for, and to overlook what we please, several questions arise. What are the basic premises of *Politics and the Constitution?* What of that apparent antithesis in the title? In short, is this another *Dialogue of Heresies,* or is it potentially one of the wonders of all time: an *archeological* blueprint for Twentieth Century America?

II

First, some credits, debits, and historiographical notes.

Part III, the heart of the book, is a ten-chapter exposition of Crosskey's "Unitary View of the National Governing Powers." The "Scheme of Draftsmanship" (c. 13) of the Constitution as a whole is considered in the light of accepted eighteenth century rules of documentary interpretation. (pp. 369–84). This of course is largely an ultra-sophisticated modern version of the Abolitionists' premise that the Preamble, properly construed, is a part of the Constitution[16]—the

---

[15] For appreciative reviews, see Durham, *Crosskey on the Constitution: An Essay-Review* 41 CALIF. L. REV. 209 (1953); and those of Krash, Clark and Hamilton in 21 U. OF CHI. L. REV. 1, 24, 79 1953) (*Politics and the Constitution—A Symposium*). It is interesting to note that most favorable reviewers devote more space to Crosskey's *doctrinal objectives,* which they approve, than to his supporting arguments and methods. Many readers might thus be willing to "concur in the result"; but if that is to be the choice, why not leave out labored framer-intent and squarely face the issue as one of constitutional power and expediency?

[16] See, *e.g.,* GOODELL, VIEWS OF AMERICAN CONSTITUTIONAL LAW 40-43 (1844); GOODELL, OUR NATIONAL CHARTERS 5, 13 (1860).

part which defines the objectives and which must therefore help determine the scope. Accordingly, all powers granted the Federal Government and all limitations placed on the states, have to be construed to "form a more perfect Union, establish Justice . . . and secure the Blessings of Liberty to ourselves and our Posterity." One need not be so acute a lawyer as Professor Crosskey to see that this phrasing, at least in combination with the Necessary and Proper and Supremacy Clauses, is all anyone needs to fashion a commodious national power. Doubtless many citizens, distressed at the mounting complexity of our constitutional doctrine, and accepting, if not yet reconciled to its apparently inevitable freedom of decision and "subjectivization," will see gains, or even wisdom, in this turn to simpler, more flexible forms. It will be noted also, that the prescribed tonic is one that can be marketed and taken in much less than these bottle-sized doses.

Most ingenious of all perhaps is Crosskey's 100-page analysis of the Fathers' reasons for enumerating Congressional powers (pp. 409–508). Some powers, he shows, had to be enumerated because in dividing up the undifferentiated legislative-executive-judicial powers belonging to the old Congress under the Articles of Confederation, it was essential to indicate those to be regarded as legislative (c. 14). Others had to be enumerated because under standing English law and amendatory acts of Parliament, they customarily were regarded as executive powers derived from the royal prerogative (c. 15). A third miscellaneous group had to be enumerated for reasons inherent in particular circumstances. (c. 16). It is apparent, therefore, that in general the purpose of enumeration was to make clear what powers Congress was to *have*, not what powers it was *not* to have as against the states. Crosskey lays great stress on this point, which of course is the very heart of his thesis: Enumerated congressional power does not at all preclude general congressional power. In fact, it is a condition of it. The judicial rule to the contrary is simply another instance of the tales and "sophistries" propagated by James Madison until at length they have become accepted articles of constitutional faith. (p. 12). By this neat and arresting section, the groundwork of Crosskey's thesis is laid, and laid moreover on much the same lines as the Wilson Doctrine.

Here again, it is not necessary to accept the full interpretations to pay tribute to virtuosity. Despite question begging (pp. 406–07, 674), pyramided inference (p. 680) and the apparent assumption that anything in Blackstone must have been known and recalled at appropriate times by members of the Convention,[17] even a skeptical reader

---

[17] Much of Chapters 15–16 rests on this premise; see pp. 411, 546.

soon is prepared to concede that drafting the Constitution, given these eighteenth-century political and legal backgrounds, was a more subtle, complex undertaking, particularly for skilled lawyers, than generally has been presumed. Just how many members of the Convention were as sophisticated as Crosskey believes is the real question, for here again we are given neither direct proof nor testimony. Perhaps from the nature of the case none is possible. But even without it, these chapters stand as brilliant analysis and historical reconstruction, and will be read and debated for years by students of both historiography and law.

Probably the most remarkable chapter in *Politics and the Constitution* is that on the Contracts Clause (c. 12). An extreme example of Crosskey's positions and methods, it is the concluding part of a section designed to buttress his thesis that the Commerce Clause actually was intended by the Convention to give Congress power even over intra-state and local trade—"over the entire complex of gainful activities which the American people carry on." The basic proposition is that the "True Meanings" of the Imports and Exports, the Ex Post Facto, and the Contracts Clauses never were perceived by the Supreme Court, even though several early Justices were former members of the Convention. In fact, all three clauses soon were judicially emasculated, and this in turn has tended to obscure both the nature and extent of the Commerce power. By no means all this section is heterodox, though in Crosskey's view, interstate trade barriers were the real target of the Imports and Exports Clause. (c. 10). Newspaper usage is cited to show that in their true eighteenth-century meanings both "imports" and "exports" embraced products from other states as well as from abroad. Consequently, a restraint on the states' power to "lay any Impost or Duties" on imports or exports without the consent of Congress except as needed for inspection laws, must properly be viewed as an intended buttressing of the national Commerce power. Likewise, the two Ex Post Facto Clauses were intended by their drafters to prohibit all retrospective legislation, both state and national, civil and criminal. But here again the Court presently overruled the Convention, holding these clauses to prohibit only restrospective criminal laws, thus defeating the framers' obvious purposes to outlaw paper tender and debtors' stay legislation (c. 11).

The Contracts Clause, in Crosskey's view, was the perfect capstone for this interlocking four-clause system as originally conceived. Above all, it was the means by which the national Commerce power was made "sole and exclusive." Far from prohibiting merely state

Crosskey's Constitution

impairment of contracts previously formed—as judicially construed —the Contracts Clause really was intended by its framers to apply to all contracts. Moreover, its "literal effect" (p. 355) was to crystallize, as of 1787, "all pre-existing state laws on the subject of contracts," stopping the clock as of that date, and leaving the states free to diminish, but never to increase, their regulations in this field. No direct evidence whatever is adduced in support of what Crosskey, in one of his rare understatements, acknowledges as "This somewhat arresting meaning of the Contracts Clause." Its meaning, he declares, is "obvious." Moreover,

> "its obviousness* is very greatly increased when the eighteenth-century meaning of the Ex-post-facto Clauses is known. That meaning of the Ex-post-facto Clauses was, on the basis of the evidence presented in the preceding chapter, undoubtedly known* to the men of the Federal Convention; and since those men, and those of them, particularly, who originated the Contracts Clause, in the Committee of Style, were, in the main, highly skilled and careful lawyers, it seems preposterous to suppose* that this obvious* and undeniable* meaning of the Contracts Clause was not known to, and intended by them. And if they did know and intend* that meaning of the Contracts Clause, it is certain* they must have intended* to end state power, for all practical intents and purposes,* over the whole subject of the law of contracts. Of this, no reasonable doubt* seems possible,* and since a governmental system, with no part or branch having any effective power over the subject of contracts, would, very certainly, have been a great anomaly, the only reasonable conclusion* is that the skilled lawyers of that final committee must have supposed* there was a full and adequate power over contracts conferred by the Constitution on Congress" (p. 355; asterisks added).

After the reader has recovered his footing and counted those little asterisks, he begins to wonder: Does not this situation and argument presume, logically and historically, that almost the first, and certainly an indispensable, act of the new government of 1789 had been one "for the national regulation of contracts"? At any rate, some sort of stand-by or holding regulation?

If Professor Crosskey has discovered as much, or has even found serious proposals for such, he certainly owes readers the information immediately. James Madison, we know from frequent reminders, was given at this date to "bluffing" (pp. 406–07) and to carelessness, but it strains credulity to think that even he, or, if he, that other members of the Committee on Style and Detail, several of whom also served in the first Congresses,[18] ever would have jeopardized the economic and commercial life of the new Republic, or the powers of the new national government in this vital field. Or, if they did, that some anxious insider or troubled litigant would not soon have reminded them—or at least have capitalized on their oversight. Remember, these men were "highly skilled and careful lawyers." And as Crosskey elsewhere reminds us, they were capable of expressing themselves and their every idea perfectly. Yet here we have them indulging in this strange four-clause circumlocution, when what they really meant to say was: "The Commerce power shall be sole and exclusive." Fortunately everything worked out all right, because not a soul in the land ever noticed the error—not even a Philadelphia Tory lawyer.

It must be acknowledged in this regard of course, that Professor Crosskey has not yet clearly defined his positions with reference to the nature of "sole and exclusive" versus concurrent power of Congress in this field.[19] As noted earlier in the quoted paragraph stressing the flexibility of his theory, he seems to presume that virtually all delegated Congressional power was regarded by the Fathers as concurrent, and thus to be shared with and by the states until Congress acted; yet Congress was not to supplant the state legislatures, "which were, in general, continued for local state legislation." It must be remembered, however, that the members of the Convention in 1787 could not foresee later judicial rules regarding the "Silence of Congress," and that many such rules Crosskey himself at various times attacks as the root of error and evil. Here again therefore, it is virtually impossible *for us today, in wrestling with these problems, not* to reason anachronistically. Yet does not this doctrinaire "intent school"[20] of constitutional construction require exactly that?—unless the intent rule itself is to be an *avowed* anachronism? At bottom, it is this conflict and anomaly that makes *any* "Back to 1787," "Back to the true and original intent" campaign such as Professor Crosskey is here re-organizing appear such an utterly hopeless, dubious enterprise. Surely our burdens today are heavy enough without adding to

---

[18] One-half the Senate, and eight members of the House in the first Congress had been members of the Convention—*i.e.*, 20 of the 55 Framers served in the first Congress. See HART, THE AMERICAN PRESIDENCY IN ACTION: 1789 70 n.91 (1948) and authorities there cited. In addition, Jay, Rutledge, Wilson, Paterson and Ellsworth served on the Supreme Court, Paterson until 1806. Ellsworth was the leading draftsman of the Judiciary Act of 1789.

[19] *Cf.* the discussion in the following passages: 1172, 363, 318-20, and 358-60.

[20] For an excellent critique, see tenBroek, *Admissibility and Use by the United States Supreme Court of Extrinsic Aids in Constitutional Construction*, 26 CALIF. L. REV. 287, 437, 664 (1938); 27 CALIF. L. REV. 157, 399 (1939).

them this sort of extravagant exercise in historical mirror-writing and mirror-reading. Professor Crosskey attacks Justices Holmes and Brandeis and their followers for "reasoning anachronistically about the Common Law," and so getting us bogged in the morasses of *Erie v. Tompkins* (p. 910). Yet his own book is shot through with just such anachronisms[21]—as any such book must be. We all need to ponder Kierkegaard's maxim: "Life [and Law and History] can only be understood backwards. But [they] have to be *lived* forwards."

The extremely circumstantial and conjectural character of much of Professor Crosskey's argument[22] leads one to wonder how far he is willing to see such methods employed. It would be very simple, indeed, using these techniques, to "prove" that framers of the Fourteenth Amendment contemplated and understood the word "person" in the Due Process and Equal Protection Clauses to include both corporations and natural persons.[23] It would be no trouble at all to build up a *nineteenth*-century glossary showing that corporations, since Coke's time, had been regarded as artificial "persons"; were spoken of continually as such by lawyers, judges, and even laymen; that members of the Joint Committee so spoke of them; that incidents occurring while Section One was in draft raised the problem of constitutional status. Nor would the objection that all this is irrelevant because corporations cannot be "born or naturalized," and hence a double-standard of interpretation is required for the two main uses of "persons" in Section One, be hard to counter: Over the years distinguished courts and lawyers had disregarded far narrower, more precise constitutional texts in order to extend to corporations and shareholders benefit of state due process. One such case was *Brown v. Hummel*.[24] Its progeny were used in 1865 by Reverdy Johnson (who a year later was one of the drafters of

---

[21] Like all practical men, the Framers thought concretely, and largely in relation to the problems of their own day. To seek solutions for many of our problems in the solution the Framers found for theirs is like looking to Goodyear (the vulcanizer of rubber) and Duryea (inventor of the horseless carriage) for the solutions to modern traffic problems. The Framers created a going concern—and presumed that posterity's common sense would equal theirs.

[22] The Contracts Clause "must have known" argument, discussed *infra*, is extreme, but by no means unique; see *e.g.*, pp. 563–64, 679–80, 772. And after chapter on chapter of the "glossary" argument, roaming over two continents and through two centuries, what is one to make of the following *caveat* (made with reference to the Corwin-Haines treatment of the colonial precedents for judicial review): "It should be remembered that evidence remote in time, or place, from the Federal Convention is of little relevancy." (p. 1368).

[23] In fact, this was exactly what Roscoe Conkling attempted. See Chapters 1–2, *supra*.

[24] 6 Barr 86 (Pa. 1847).

Section One)—used, moreover, in a successful defense in the federal courts of the rights of one of the very corporations (later in 1866) found petitioning Congress for relief. The framers were men of large views, well aware of the meaning of words; they are known from their votes to have sympathized with these petitioning corporations. *If all this is true,* they *must have known* and *must have intended* to do precisely what Roscoe Conkling in his celebrated argument in the *San Mateo*[25] case intimated they did.

One gathers from his general positions on corporate personality (p. 43) and from his attitude toward judicial construction of the Fourteenth Amendment (cc. 31-32) that Professor Crosskey would be little impressed by this argument. His disapproval and skepticism would be wholly warranted. All we have done—all he has done in analogous cases—is to weave a web of conjecture and inference. Men and ideas are placed on the same street corner, so to speak, or in the same city, during the same year—or even during the same century—and the inference is then drawn that they inevitably were linked, or were mutually recognized or recognizable. But contiguity and simultaneity of this order are not highly persuasive. At best they are not proof, but merely the first conditions of proof. Roscoe Conkling simply made artful use of the synapse-jumping, conclusion-hopping abilities of the human mind. And it is hard to see how such use can be more validly applied to 1787 than to 1866.

The point is merely that some of Professor Crosskey's records are playable on either side. Moreover, there is enough question-begging (pp. 679-80) and *non-sequitur*[26] in his own positions to make one patient and sympathetic with the Supreme Court. Three hundred and fifty volumes written over a century and a half by nearly a hundred different justices, largely from the materials presented in the briefs and arguments, pretty obviously are a rich mine of "sophistry" and anachronism as well as of authority. Yet pretty plainly too these are occupational hazards. The difficulties are inherent in the enterprise, and they are doubly inherent in that of Crosskey. It is as easy to prove too much as too little.[27] It is easy to believe at first that what seems most vital to us today in Blackstone or Mansfield was

---

[25] San Mateo County v. Southern Pacific R.R., 116 U.S. 138, 6 Sup. Ct. 317, 29 L. Ed. 589 (1885).

[26] P. 406: Madison's membership on the Committee that drafted the Preamble and the Common Defense and General Welfare Clause makes it "utterly impossible" to believe that the views he expressed in *Federalist, No. 41*, were "candid."

[27] After a highly circumstantial section (cc. 18-19) intended to show that the Framers shared views of the common law and general jurisprudence predisposing them toward keeping a very tight rein on the state courts, we learn (p. 610) that "some of

known and recalled at the appropriate moment in the Convention; that those petitions referred to by Conkling bulked large in the framers' minds; that the word "reserved" in the Tenth Amendment was "a technical legal word . . . use[d] to indicate the creation of a *new* interest, *never previously existing as such*, in respect of *a thing conveyed*,"[28] and *not* as a synonym for "retained." It is easy, that is, until we get into the jungle of these men's minds and times—until we discover that they were not always as preoccupied with these matters,[29] nor as consistent, as we assumed; that "reserved" for example, also is found used in many contexts as a synonym for "retained" in the discussions of the *proposed* Bill of Rights![30]

One reluctantly concludes therefore that Professor Crosskey's positions simply are too over-extended for his methods. As a lawyer he prefers to argue within the four corners of the document and its clauses (p. 1173). As an historian, willy-nilly, and one assaulting long-accepted positions, he has burdens of proof that cannot be met by inference or four-corners reasoning. Many of his arguments have been advanced and rejected by the courts over the years.[31] They never were presented as a "unitary view," nor as a coherent system because the judicial process is not adapted to that method, nor need we especially regret the fact. Historiographically, therefore, Professor Crosskey's own book seems a powerful answer to his thesis.

---

these powers never have been enjoyed, in practice, by our national courts"; moreover, that the [Federalist] Judiciary Act of 1789 was "diabolically contrived" to limit the national jurisdiction and render the federal courts unpopular, and that "it is hard to doubt that these unwise features . . . were a result of maneuvers by the Anti-Federalist minority in Congress." (p. 756). See also pp. 554-55 *re* Full Faith and Credit Clause.

[28] P. 701; see *supra* note 7, *infra* note 30.

[29] The disinterest that business lawyers and leadership seem to have taken in the draftsmanship of Section One of the Fourteenth Amendment, even while simultaneously appealing to Congress for relief and for expansion of the national jurisdiction, suggests that not everything clear to hindsight is equally clear to foresight. And the reason is clear enough when one gets into these men's correspondence and problems. Insurance leaders, for example, were so preoccupied with agency agreements, policy suits, incendiarism, etc., that most of them gave little or no thought to the opportunities that presently became so obvious and important. This apparent human blindness is one of the most heartening facts in life. Problems generally are simpler and nearer of solution than they appear—unless we begin refighting our whole constitutional history!

[30] See, for example, THE FEDERALIST AND OTHER CONSTITUTIONAL PAPERS 538, 549, 551 (Scott ed. 1894) (James Winthrop, *Agrippa Papers*); *id.* at 774 (James Wilson); *id.* at 870 (R. H. Lee). The same papers are printed in PAMPHLETS ON THE CONSTITUTION (Ford ed. 1888) and ESSAYS ON THE CONSTITUTION (Ford ed. 1892). (These usages of "reserved" were discovered incidentally, and no attempt has been made to verify or disprove Crosskey on such points).

[31] The Wilson Doctrine, for example; see *supra* note 4.

III

The major jurisprudential premises of *Politics and the Constitution* are the same nice dichotomy that has served so many masters of forensics:

1. First and last, our Constitution is a legal document. It was drafted by superb lawyer-statesmen—men supreme in their mastery of law and expression. Their text is crystal clear, needs only to be taken literally and as a whole to make perfect sense. Constitutional meaning really is intrinsic (p. 390). Even the first section of the Fourteenth Amendment, which quite needlessly has befuddled the courts and which some students[32] lately have attempted to clarify by reference to its antislavery origins and backgrounds and to the prevalent natural rights usages and concepts, is "clear in itself, or clear when read in the light of the prior law." (p. 1381). "[T]he ultimate question is not what the legislatures meant, any more than it is what Congress or the more immediate framers of the amendment meant: it is what the amendment means." (*Ibid.*). Scholars and judges who ignore this cardinal fact do so at their peril. (*Ibid.*).

2. Words and texts of course do sometimes have to be construed. Here again the problem is one of arriving at the "true meaning" of texts and language, or the "true intent" of the framers. To do this we simply "delve into" American history and build up our "specialized dictionary of . . . eighteenth-century word-usages, and political and legal ideas . . . needed for a true understanding of the Constitution" (p. 5). . . . Scholars and judges who ignore this cardinal fact also do so at their peril.[33]

These two complementary halves are joined neatly together in one sentence in Crosskey's introduction: throughout the long inquiry ahead, he assures, "the conclusive piece of evidence will be the Constitution itself, read as our specialized dictionary of words and ideas will require"[34] (p. 12).

The declared approach to fundamental law and its history thus is frankly, even sternly, ambivalent. Equally vital in their bearing and importance are several of Professor Crosskey's more detailed premises about the character and direction of early American govern-

---

[32] See tenBroek, The Antislavery Origins of the Fourteenth Amendment (1951); Chapter 4, *supra*.

[33] See *passim. Enumeratio unius est exclusio alterius.*

[34] One is reminded of the late Professor Becker's words, An "argument subtle but clear, deriving the nature of an act from the intention of its makers, and the intention of its makers from the nature of the act. . . ." Becker, The Eve of the Revolution 133 (1918).

ment. Indeed, five of these more or less tacit assumptions deserve to be briefly noted:

1. The Constitutional Convention at Philadelphia was a fairly homogeneous group, and had behind it a reasonably united country. No immediate need exists, therefore, for analysis of the history and politics of that time. Economic and sectional differences of course did exist, but they assumed little real importance until later. Hence, they are secondary to the main business, which is to determine what the constitutional text itself means. After that has been done, these auxiliary matters can be considered.[35]

2. The "true meaning" of the Constitution is the meaning it had —avowed or not—to those strongly nationalist leaders, who as members of the Committees on Detail and Style, hammered out the final legal phraseology. These men—Rutledge, Wilson, Ellsworth, Randolph and Gorham of the Committee on Detail, and Johnson, Hamilton, Gouverneur Morris, Madison, and King, of the Committee on Style, together with James Wilson (pp. 673, 1335–36), consummate draftsmen and statesmen all—were more or less free agents, able to exercise their best judgment without detailed accounting to the people; and that is precisely what they did. Our problem today is to discover what their intended meanings were, even where not explicit, and that of course is the purpose of the eighteenth-century glossary and rules of construction.

3. Though the views of the remaining members of the Convention,[36] and of the people and ratifiers as such, are of little practical consequence today (p. 1381), the historic and legal meaning of the Constitution nevertheless was fixed, virtually for all time, save for processes of amendment and *correct* judicial construction, by the formal acts of approval and ratification.[37] Professor Crosskey thus takes both a pietistic and a somewhat cynical view of the constitutional contract. In fact, his scorn for the Jeffersonians obviously derives in part from their outrageous success. They soon came to regret some of their bargains, denied and haggled over others, yet still found overwhelming popular, congressional, and even judicial support!

4. The United States in 1787 were a nation well-suited to strong, highly centralized government. This premise, to be sure, is almost wholly implicit. It would seem to follow, however, from the reverence shown throughout for the extreme nationalist wing of the

---

[35] See p. 1174; also c. 1.

[36] Crosskey promises a full reexamination of the Convention debates and proceedings in future volumes.

[37] *Cf. passim*, the criticism of judicial emasculation and "sophistry."

Convention.[38] These men were the true statesmen and knew exactly what was good for the country. The fact that they gave it this highly centralized government must mean that in their judgment and Professor Crosskey's, that government was well-suited to the needs and desires of the time.

5. The American Congress, which includes most of the ablest politicians in the land, has somehow been the unfortunate victim of a century and two-thirds of "politics" and of "sophistical" interpretations of its powers—many of them made or concurred in by its own members. Congress never has found its true place, nor risen to its full stature in our constitutional scheme, largely because of various "warping influences"—specifically judicial emasculation and misconstruction of congressional powers, combined with outrageous judicial favoritism for the states and an unwarranted assumption that the judiciary alone is the guarantor and guardian of popular rights.[39]

It is fairly evident there is enough historical criticism and political theory submerged in these premises to occupy doctoral candidates for years.[40] Premises 1–3 can be left for specialists in jurisprudence or to historians of the Revolutionary-Federalist periods.[41] Numbers 4 and 5, however, are of a different order. Premise 4, in particular, assumes positions quite at odds not only with sound administrative principles and practice, but with the common understanding of our early history and society.[42] Professor Crosskey evidently is convinced

---

[38] Note, too, the premises in the sections on the Judiciary Acts of 1789 and 1801 (e.g., pp. 610–18, 754). Cf. WHITE, THE FEDERALISTS c. 38 (1948), (especially p. 483). See infra notes 44:45.

[39] See Crosskey's dedication (p. v), and pp. 4, 12–13 and c. 2.

[40] Since Professor Crosskey must steel himself to this prospect in any event—which is by no means unwelcome now that nearly every Justice's constitutional opinions are scissor-syllabied a dozen times or more by candidates on as many campuses even before the Justice has left the Bench—we suggest: "Crosskey on Constitutional Power"—i.e., is power an entity, concrete, everlasting, self-renewing, or does it have to be articulated with "Politics" to give us constitutional government? Does the Republican form of Government Clause still mean what it meant in 1787? (pp. 522–41). If so, then: "Crosskey on Political Questions," "Crosskey on Non-Enforceable Constitutional Provisions" (i.e., just which Electoral College is our not-too-Alma-Mater today—that of 1787, or 1952?). Above all, "Crosskey on Undisclosed, Denied (p. 712) and Unperceived Framer-Intent"—in short, "Crosskey's 'Conspiracy Theory'" and "Crosskey's Psycho-Analytical Interpretations. . . ." The possibilities are exciting and endless.

[41] Meanwhile, see tenBroek on framer-intent and extrinsic aids, supra note 20. See also the following standard historical works: HART, THE AMERICAN PRESIDENCY IN ACTION: 1789 (1949); JENSEN, THE ARTICLES OF CONFEDERATION (1940); JENSEN, THE NEW NATION: A HISTORY OF THE UNITED STATES DURING THE CONFEDERATION (1950); NEVINS, THE AMERICAN STATES DURING AND AFTER THE REVOLUTION (1924); WHITE, THE FEDERALISTS (1948); WHITE, THE JEFFERSONIANS (1951); and the histories of Henry Adams, McMaster and Channing.

[42] See especially WHITE, THE FEDERALISTS cc. 1, 15–16 (Post Office), cc. 30–32 (fron-

that his eighteenth-century blueprint not only is adequate for our own day, but was as well (or even better) suited to the Fathers'. This means, of course, suited to the needs and interests of four million artisans, farmers and merchants, thinly scattered along a coastal fringe a thousand miles in length, frontiersmen moving constantly westward, hacking their way through hostile Indian territory, for the most part still without decent roads and bridges, restless, land-hungry men, fiercely individualist in thought, starting their federal administrative system virtually from scratch, as yet without adequate post or coinage, dependent on uncertain sea and river communications, men jealous of authority, rent by sectional conflicts and by state prejudices and rivalries over trade, war debts and western lands.[43]

It means, in concrete terms, that in 1787, when there was not even a turnpike between Philadelphia and Baltimore, or New York and Boston, and either journey still took from five to seven days, men nevertheless were thinking about running the country from Philadelphia. It means that while President Washington was fretting over official dispatches that had taken nearly sixty days to reach Governor Randolph in Richmond,[44] or General St. Clair on the Ohio,[45] and after Hamilton's whiskey excise had boomeranged and 15,000 reluctant militiamen had had to be dispatched on a two-months' march from Philadelphia to Pittsburgh to secure the national authority,[46] statesmen had courted more of this sort of thing.

Does Professor Crosskey really mean it? Does he really think a national contracts law was conceived—or conceivable—for such a society? Or perhaps merely for ours?

And does he believe that the Jeffersonian wave of 1800 was an unmitigated disaster for the American people? That it threw the nation off course, hampered conquest of the continent and creation of stable, enduring government?

---

tier government and law enforcement), c. 38 (communications) (1948) and similar chapters in WHITE, THE JEFFERSONIANS (1951).

[43] See works cited *supra* note 41.

[44] "On October 3, 1789, he [Washington] sent dispatches from New York to Governor Randolph of Virginia which failed to arrive until November 30." WHITE, THE FEDERALISTS 191 (1948), citing 30 WASHINGTON, WRITINGS 477-78.

[45] St. Clair doubled as Indian Superintendent and as Governor of the whole Northwest Territory. In 1790 he had not a single clerk, managed Indian affairs without an office and with the help of two deputies and two interpreters. Marriage-, ferry-, tavern-, and Indian trader-licenses were a burden in themselves, and, together with land and tribal affairs, apparently account for the disinterest in a federal contracts law on the Ohio. See WHITE, THE FEDERALISTS cc. 30, 38 (1948).

[46] See BALDWIN, WHISKEY REBELS (1939); 2 MCMASTER, HISTORY OF THE PEOPLE OF THE UNITED STATES 41, 190-203 (1928).

Historical speculation is idle stuff. But national achievements are not. What happened following overturn of Hamilton's System? What accompanied the nefarious repeal of that statesmanlike Federalist Judiciary Act of 1801? (pp. 758-63).

It is a strange story of national misfortune: 1803. The Louisiana Purchase and the continent rounded out. 1805-07. Continued strong, though scarcely consistent Jeffersonian opposition to a federal program of roads and canals.[47] The Cumberland or National Road reluctantly commenced. Construction simple enough, but routing and location a nightmare of state-community rivalry, dictation and "logrolling": Maryland v. Pennsylvania; Uniontown v. Washington, Pennsylvania; Washington v. Wheeling; Wheeling v. Steubenville and so on across Ohio and Indiana to Vandalia, finally reached, 1838.[48] *Meanwhile,* 4000 miles of turnpikes completed in New York alone by 1821; 1800 more in Pennsylvania; and other states in proportion; by 1830 practically all main arteries turnpiked, wholly by state and private enterprise.[49]

1808. Secretary of the Treasury Gallatin's Report on Internal Improvements,[50] a farsighted plan for a $20,000,000 national system of canals and postroads to be built over a decade—destined only to gather dust in congressional committees. *Nevertheless,* 3,326 miles of canals constructed by 1840, at a total cost of $125,000,000, all built by state and private capital.[51]

1817. Madison's puzzling flip-flop on federally-sponsored internal improvements: "With a degree of inconsistency extreme even for him," as Professor Crosskey puts it (p. 234), the President vetoed the program he had initiated—the so-called "Bonus Bill," sponsored by, of all people, Calhoun, and one which was to have been financed from the $1,500,000 bonus received from the Bank of the United States for its charter. *Nevertheless,* the 364-mile, seven-million-dollar Erie Canal, built by New York State *alone* during the next eight years: and another 2,000 miles constructed in the country during the Thirties, inspired by the New Yorkers' example.[52]

---

[47] For the doctrinal and legislative history of the Internal Improvements controversy, see Corwin, *The Spending Power of Congress,* 36 HARV. L. REV. 548 (1923), reprinted in 3 SELECTED ESSAYS ON CONSTITUTIONAL LAW 565 (1938).

[48] YOUNG, POLITICAL AND CONSTITUTIONAL STUDY OF THE CUMBERLAND ROAD (1902), especially pp. 20-55.

[49] See TAYLOR, THE TRANSPORTATION REVOLUTION, 1815-60 (1952) (an excellent, fully documented work); and DURRENBERGER, TURNPIKES (1931); LUXON, NILES' WEEKLY REGISTER (1947) (indexes and summarizes material in that magazine).

[50] AMERICAN STATE PAPERS: MISCELLANEOUS I, 724 (1834); 3 McMASTER, *op. cit. supra* note 46, at 473-75; WHITE, THE JEFFERSONIANS c. 31 (1951).

[51] TAYLOR, *op. cit. supra* note 49, at c. 3.

[52] *Ibid.*

1822. President Monroe's veto of the Cumberland Road repairs bill.[53] 1830. President Jackson's veto of the Maysville Road appropriation, on grounds of inexpediency rather than defect of power (Jackson was impressed by bills for $106,000,000 for local improvements pending in Congress, with petitions and memorials received for another hundred millions).[54] In short, the Improvements half of Clay's "American System" challenged and aborted in his own state. *Yet*, a decade later, in 1840—barely fifteen years after construction of the first railroad in England—3,300 miles of completed track in the United States, against 1,800 for all Europe. The Philadelphia-Baltimore-New York trade rivalry—quickened of course by the Erie Canal—stoked state competition and established the national pattern: by 1838, $43,000,000 of state debts attributable to railroad subsidies—with county and municipal aid perhaps greater, and half the early railroads' original construction capital estimated to have come from public sources.[55]

The heart of it is simply that even Federalist Congresses didn't do the things Professor Crosskey's historical theory demands; because they couldn't do them.[56] Jeffersonian and Jacksonion Congresses didn't do them, and weren't permitted to do them, because leaders sensed it fortunately was unnecessary to do them.

Historical causation is quite as complex as speculation is futile. It can be very plausibly argued however, that Americans got these things so soon, and in such generous measure, *because* the thousands of state and local rivalries and drives were capitalized and given outlet directly, not dammed up or dragged before Congress to fester and exacerbate sectional and local feelings as had the Cumberland Road. It can be argued very logically that our whole "Transportation Revolution" of the pre-Civil War period would have been utterly stymied had it been left dependent on affirmative action by Congress. It can be argued that the Union stood in the end because

---

[53] 2 RICHARDSON, MESSAGES AND PAPERS OF THE PRESIDENTS 142 (1904).

[54] 2 *id.* at 482 (veto message of May 27, 1830); 2 *id.* at 97, 120 (annual message of Dec. 1, 1834).

[55] TAYLOR, *op. cit. supra* note 49, at c. 5, especially pp. 92-96, and authorities there cited.

[56] "The improvement of roads and bridges was within the grasp of the technical knowledge of the period. Time and money and resolution were required, and all were available. But the Federalist years ran their course with no action on a matter that some saw already to be a national problem." WHITE, THE FEDERALISTS 487 (1948). For the history of one of the main early and largely unsuccessful attempts at Federalist promotion (development of the Potomac), see SUNDERLIN, THE GREAT NATIONAL PROJECT: A HISTORY OF THE CHESAPEAKE AND OHIO CANAL (1946). This project dated from 1785, and George Washington was one of the original backers, yet *state* charters, *state* permission and *state* legislation were sought.

economics knit and held the sections together, even as politics was throwing them apart.

The plain fact is that "States Rights" during the period 1790–1830 was not the sterile, negative, futilitarian dodge it so often is today, or so often later became where slavery and race problems were involved. This is dramatically shown in Professor Hartz' study of the internal improvements situation in Pennsylvania.[57] The popular notion that this period was one of laissez faire and non-interference is here demolished as pure myth. State and local government activated the whole improvements program; constitutional theory and economic practice were rich, varied, and closely interwoven. It is gross falsification to presume that States Rightism *then* meant inaction and evasion. Federalism worked precisely because state policy was vigorous and affirmative. The states were willing and able to do the jobs, and did them, spectacularly.

Congress, on the other hand, was not able to do them, could not get down to them, did not know how to deal with them, had neither reason nor means to tackle them. Furthermore, Congress' deficiencies in these respects sprang less from constitutional scruples or uncertainty, than from sheer economic and political geography or arithmetic. There is no occasion whatever to make Jefferson, Madison and Jackson, or the Taney and Chase Courts, villains, or the American people their dupes or accomplices—least of all Congress the innocent victim—in order to explain this situation. Several examples will reveal why.

River steamboating gave Americans their first real taste of "Commerce among the States."[58] By 1820 seventy vessels were operating in the West alone; during the Thirties and Forties the steamboat dominated internal transport. Frightful boiler explosions occurred with monotonous regularity. *Gibbons v. Ogden*[59] of course had given Congress its cue in 1824. Clamor for congressional action began in that year. Bills were introduced and considered in every Congress. State and municipal regulation was a farce—unconstitutional by any test. Yet not until 1838 did Congress manage to pass even a token act, and that one of the strangest specimens ever: Some well-meaning provisions for lifeboats and unspecified navigation lights;

---

[57] HARTZ, ECONOMIC POLICY AND DEMOCRATIC THOUGHT, PENNSYLVANIA, 1776–1860. (1948) (one of the most illuminating syntheses yet made of American constitutional and economic history).

[58] See HUNTER, STEAMBOATS ON THE WESTERN RIVERS (1949), especially c. 13, The Movement for Steamboat Regulation, an elaborately documented account that would enliven many class discussions of federal regulation and government and business.

[59] 9 Wheat. 1, 6 L.Ed. 23 (U.S. 1824).

for periodic inspections of boilers, hulls and machinery; yet with no requirement for hydrologic tests; with the choice of inspectors entrusted to the federal district judge, and with each inspector operating solely on his own, and dependent on fees for income.[60] Not until another fourteen years, and more than a hundred fatal explosions later, did Congress finally pass the Act of 1852 licensing engineers and pilots, and creating a coordinated, supervised inspection service.[61]

On its face, this evidence alone pretty strongly intimates that the historic flabbiness of the Commerce power, and indeed the want of attractive symmetry in the whole Congressional torso, is traceable to something besides the limitations and distortions of the Supreme Court's modern "interstate theory" of Commerce. Something more than Madisonian and judicial "sophistry," and changes in word meanings, is indicated here.

Samuel F. B. Morse, inventor of the telegraph, tried for years to interest Congress in his invention. A $30,000 appropriation for an experimental line from Washington to Baltimore demonstrated the feasibility and pointed up the relation to the postal system. Editors and statesmen urged federal action. Morse repeatedly offered his patents for about $100,000. Yet the crucial Baltimore-New York extension bill failed to pass the House in 1844. The Mexican War intervened. Private capital took over, lines crossed and crisscrossed the country, 1846–50, and spanned it, 1863. This was all done in a "wonderful era of methodless enthusiasm"[62]—and utter Congressional absentmindedness. Postmasters General continued unsuccessfully to urge Congressional purchase and development for a while in the Forties to protect the Government's original stake. Then as the local lines merged and systems consolidated, the public and editors began calling for effective regulation. "Postal power," "Commerce," "Commerce among the States," "Commerce between the States," "interstate Commerce"—all were adequate and all apparently were urged. Yet not until 1862 did Congress finally move; then simply to pass the Pacific Telegraph Act,[63] subsidizing the transcontinental line. By 1866, Western Union having emerged as the "nation's first great industrial monopoly and its largest corporation,"[64] Congress clarified rights across the public domain and

---

[60] 5 STAT. 304–06 (1838).
[61] 10 STAT. 61–75 (1852).
[62] See THOMPSON, WIRING A CONTINENT (1947) (another fine study deserving a place on administrative and constitutional law reading lists).
[63] 12 STAT. 489–98 (1862).
[64] THOMPSON, op. cit. supra note 62, at 442.

secured the Government's right to purchase lines at appraised value. But not until many years and many hearings later was there any real national regulation.

Pretty evidently here too, something more than "warping influences" (pp. 12, 1174) and shifts in the meaning and judicial interpretations of "regulate," "Commerce," "among," "the States" is involved. No one will deny that the legislative and constitutional status of corporations is crucial today; and certainly the telegraph companies were among the earliest buttonholers and nosethumbers in Washington. But why pick on the Supreme Court, and its *Pensacola* doctrine (pp. 41-45)—Professor Crosskey's only reference to the telegraph business!—as a cause and example of letting corporate business run riot? Why give the idea that the Federal Convention intended to regulate intrastate commerce *in 1787* when Congress could not, would not, and did not regulate even *inter*state commerce until *after 1860*?[65] Why present these as matters of naked constitutional power, and hence of "judicial sophistry," when they obviously and mainly were matters of political expediency, sectional and corporate interest, rivalry and politics? Why divorce constitutional law from the history and circumstances that explain it? Why complain that Congress has been shortchanged judicially when so much of the trouble was and is that Congress is a representative body and there were and are a terrible lot of competing interests and viewpoints to represent? Why ignore, for example, that for years Congress was unable even to set a uniform gauge for railroads because each competing road naturally wanted its own—and this fight was no place for a congressman! That the same was true of failure to legislate on bridges across the Ohio at Wheeling[66] in the Fifties, and again across the Mississippi in the Sixties.[67] Congress gallantly bowed out of these fights, then eventually crowned the winners. It simply was the Cumberland Road situation over again, with the stakes higher and weapons sharper.

Our conclusion is simply that Professor Crosskey's brand of "Politics" is not the staple American article. Too exclusive a diet of case

---

[65] A useful aid in studying the later silences and inaction of Congress under the Commerce power over railroads is REGULATION OF INTERSTATE COMMERCE HISTORY OF BILLS AND RESOLUTIONS INTRODUCED IN CONGRESS . . . 1862-1911 (Briggs Comp. 1912); see also, HANEY, A CONGRESSIONAL HISTORY OF RAILWAYS IN THE UNITED STATES (1908-1910).

[66] See Pennsylvania v. Wheeling and Belmont Bridge Co. 13 How. 518, 14 L. Ed. 249 (U.S. 1852), 18 How. 421, 15 L. Ed. 435 (U.S. 1856).

[67] See 2 HANEY, *op. cit. supra* note 65, at c. 18. Correspondence of members of the 39th Congress contains many interesting letters from outraged constituents in the states bordering the Mississippi on the tardiness of national action.

law and the *Annals*, and too little attention to news columns, has given him a jaundiced view of history, and a strange one indeed of Congress. Congress, in reality has been an indispensable national undertaker, but a very chary, reluctant *entrepreneur*. It seldom has needed to go looking for corpses or trouble. If Crosskey is not the first to tempt it, he at least is the first to make temptation retroactive. Whether that is an anachronism, and if so, whether it is ours or his, of course depends partly on whether one postulates a Living Constitutional Document or a dead one. Again and again, Crosskey pillories the "Living Document" school (pp. 1171–72); but many, if obliged to refight these battles, will at least be obliged for that choice of weapons. Time has become a confused and confusing subject in this generation, since it now really is Space-Time. But for all that this still is a workaday world. To many, John Marshall's "We must never forget it is a *constitution* . . . we are expounding"[68]— "a Constitution meant to endure for ages to come"—seems a simpler, sounder, more heartening premise and approach than any appeal for constitutional mortmain, whether judicially or academically derived or enforced. "The earth belongs to the living," and so does the American Constitution.

Pretty clearly the ultimate, decisive limitation on national legislative power always has been geographic-political, not constitutional. It is inherent in the size of our country, in the economic and sectional diversity, in the competing interests and varying degrees of social and economic development. These are what really have given content to "Commerce"—and more often withheld it. What we need most is not another reraking of the case law and its "sophistries," but a real synthesis of the case law and the Congressional Silences. Professor Crosskey has been psychoanalysing the Fathers when he ought to have been showing us what really defeated Clay's American System and what made Webster's and Lincoln's tasks so difficult.

Such a synthesis would have provided a better footing, and a much more convincing reconstitution of the national authority than does so much of the *ex parte* brief we are here offered. For it *is* true beyond question that many factors did conspire during the early periods to limit and obscure national legislative powers—at times to the point of waste and atrophy. The prolonged stalemate over slavery, so often here stressed, was but one of them. Constitutional positions by themselves, however, seldom were consistently taken or maintained—nor can they be in any intricate or protracted social

---

[68] McCulloch v. Maryland, 4 Wheat. 316, 406, 4 L. Ed. 579 (U.S. 1819).

or constitutional controversy. Abolitionist theory was nationalist in its protection of civil rights; "states rights" on northern personal liberties laws, mixed on the problems inherent in fugitive slave rendition. And pro-slave theory was quite as tangled and inconsistent. Railroad lawyers took nationalist positions on federal aid for their own road; states rights on aid for their rivals! Professor Crosskey not only ignores these situations, but is ready to use virtually any legal argument, regardless of its origins, if the *doctrine itself* suits his immediate purpose. Indeed, the tactic of "using the devil as a character witness" probably never has been pushed farther than in these pages.[69]

Beard's "Economic Interpretations" of a generation ago[70] were welcome reactions from just this sort of sterile hyper-legalism and partisanship in constitutional history and interpretation. If Professor Crosskey now insists on another vacuum repack of our early case law and congressional argument we undoubtedly are in for another round of the corrective. Heaven help us: we barely have ceased refighting the Civil War, and now we are to go back to 1787! Boiler explosions meanwhile have been superseded by others. Minds like Professor Crosskey's simply are too few to waste on this business. What we need and want now is his version of *Paradise Regained*.

What, indeed, *is* a Constitution?[71] That is the basic question this book raises. Was and is the document a writ of mandate from the Committees on Detail and Style? Or was it—is it—something of an act of faith and trust and accommodation on the part of many groups and viewpoints through our whole history? Was it not a series of compromises *in pursuit* of union, an agreement at times intentionally vague and openended, a rough floor plan, not a perfected set of

---

[69] See pp. 189, 223 [use of Winthrop's Anti-Federalist Agrippa papers on the scope of the Commerce power; and many similar uses in cc. 8, 9, 23 (pp. 683–85)]. One sometimes wonders what Professor Crosskey would think of an avowedly historical argument that made use of the American Liberty League lawyers' logic, citations and "scare-talk," at times to beat down the more moderate constitutional positions taken by the Solicitor General, and always with the object of establishing a *super-New Deal* construction of national power. Yet essentially this is what we often have here. Is it history, or a parlor game?

[70] BEARD, ECONOMIC INTERPRETATION OF THE CONSTITUTION OF THE UNITED STATES (1913), ECONOMIC ORIGINS OF JEFFERSONIAN DEMOCRACY (1915), THE RISE OF AMERICAN CIVILIZATION (1927) (Mary R. Beard, co-author).

Crosskey has a field day exposing Madison's apostasy and sponsoring of the Virginia and Kentucky Resolutions of 1798. No reference is found to the States' Rights resolutions of the Federalists in the Hartford Convention, 1815. "Bluffers"?

[71] *Cf.* Hamilton, *The Constitution—Apropos of Crosskey*, 21 U. OF CHI. L. REV. 79, 91–92 (1953).

drawings—much less of architectural specifications—a process, in short, not simply a lawyers' document.

What it seems to me Professor Crosskey really is telling us is that constitutional government must always be effective government, and that our government today is not as effective as it once was, as it needs to be, as it can be. The world has changed; local action and local responsibility are not the sovereign rules they once were; too often they merely are excuses for inaction and evasion. More and more of our problems are national, but too many of our solutions are not. Where there are obvious advantages in uniformity and consistency, and where speed of travel and communication have destroyed the historic and geographic case for localism *per se*, and tend to leave it a mere fetish, we need to re-examine our premises and conclusions,[72] bring our theory up to date—just as the Fathers themselves did between 1776 and 1787.[73] As citizens we must face the fact that the Transportation and Communication Revolutions have erased state lines for many purposes. Willy-nilly, Congress is now the forum; it must act as responsibly and efficiently as state and local government once did. Given our traditions, and given the size and diversity of the United States, this creates tremendous challenges and obligations. Geography or not, we must think and act in national terms, exploiting more effectively the new means of communication, education and enlightenment. So basically, our crisis is not a crisis of constitutional power so much as it is one of public imagination, insight and action. Our problems have been pooled increasingly for two generations, but our solutions have not been, nor are they now.

Much of this is simply implicit in Professor Crosskey's argument. Could that be why it is so persuasive? The thought thus comes like a flash: And is *that* the explanation? Is *Politics and the Constitution* really a parable—a masterpiece of constitutional impressionism— a mirror and a sermon in the form of a brief? Stranger things have happened in the world of books and faith: Veblen, we know, delighted in professional *scherzos*. Tolstoi wrote *War and Peace* ostensibly to prove the *illusoriness* of free will. Job thought his afflictions unbearable and peculiarly his own. And Saint Thomas More wrote another book besides the *Dialogue of Heresies—Utopia*.

Like the Sphinx and Congress, Professor Crosskey speaks in riddles and shouts in silences.

---

[72] For example, Agrippa's premise, 1788: "All human capacities are limited to a narrow space." THE FEDERALIST AND OTHER CONSTITUTIONAL PAPERS 554 (Scott ed. 1894).

[73] Corwin, *Progress of Constitutional Theory Between the Declaration of Independence and the Meeting of the Philadelphia Convention*, 30 AM. HIST. REV. 511 (1925).

EDITORIAL NOTE. Constitutional meaning is inescapably, irretrievably sociological. Too many, if not most, "original understandings" have originated in modern minds and times unawares, not in the Fathers' nor the framers'. This is inevitable, and often fortunate, even if gratuitous. Were it otherwise, Magna Carta would be a feudal document still. That the "original understanding" or "intent" of King John and his barons at Runnymede is *not* the measure of Magna Carta's coverage, *not* the measure of due process and protection today, is the answer categorical to all who at this date would have us make 1866–1868 the terminal or the crucial measure for Everyman's Constitution, whether by research or by introspection. So long as men read and reason, so long as they have courts and grievances, no fundamental document or guarantee of this order will remain static or terminal. This is the fact, the rule, the strength, the principle of constitutionalism, not the weakness.

Historians rightly have begun to deplore misuse of history in constitutional cases and interpretation.[1] The precept is one which merits more rigorous example than the debates over the Conspiracy Theory, and over the Bill of Rights incorporation, have supplied.

---

[1] See generally, HOWE, THE GARDEN AND THE WILDERNESS (1965); WIENER, USES AND ABUSES OF LEGAL HISTORY: A PRACTITIONER'S VIEW (Selden Society Lecture, London, 1962); Hurst, *The Role of History*, in SUPREME COURT AND SUPREME LAW (Cahn, ed., 1954), 55–64; Wyzanski, *History and Law*, 26 U. CHI. L. REV. 237 (1959); Roche, *Expatriation Cases*, 1963 SUP. CT. REV. 325; Wofford, *The Blinding Light: The Use of History in Constitutional Construction*, 31 U. CHI. L. REV. 502–533 (1964); Kelly, *Clio and the Supreme Court: An Illicit Love Affair*, 1965 SUP. CT. REV. 119–158.

[CHAPTER 9]

An Innocent Abroad: The Constitutional Corporate "Person"

EDITORIAL NOTE. Preparation of the NAACP memorandum, redrafting the two essays therefrom, and the review of Professor Crosskey's work delayed and altered my research plans considerably. But at last, during the two and a half months from November, 1953, to January, 1954, I worked continuously, first at the National Archives, then at the major eastern libraries, on the contemplated projects and materials. The object of this trip was to cover the relevant bills, petitions, journals, and other sources bearing on the draftsmanship and the motivation, racial undoubtedly, but just *possibly* economic too, of Sections 1 and 5; then, if possible from this sifted evidence, to reach a verdict on all that once had got so blithely tagged the "Conspiracy Theory."

Considering the number of bills, petitions, principals, and possibilities I had pre-listed (using the congressional journals and debates) this was a tall order, and for a time it kept getting taller. Shortly I came to realize, as do all who dig far into either business or government archives and manuscripts, that real prophets were just as rare and elusive a century ago as they are today. And this was perhaps doubly, mutually, true of prophets long *presumed* to have been out of their respective elements. *Profits* were what interested these lobbyists, promoters, and capitalists; one could find no support here for any of the *presumed* judicial guarantees or shortcuts. "Protection" was repeatedly sought, to be sure, and of this there had been two varieties—*ad valorem* and governmental—but in not many of these cases had *parity* or *equality* proved attractive, or even sufficient, in itself. The main trouble—though it took some time to see this (prejudices and presumptions lingering as they do)—was that the variety or the brand of constitutional (and even of congressional) protection which insurance companies had sought, and sought even *after* the Fourteenth Amendment (pursuing it still, and with wonted zeal), was that same hopeless brand, based on the *old* comity clause—based on corporate *citizenship*, in short, not on corporate *personality!* And not on the Fourteenth Amendment. In this corporation field, even after 1868, the innovators really had been the despairing, the exhausted.

The upshot was that this second-round research, as extended and assimilated during the next three years, produced no tangible support for—but rather eventually a clear disproof of—what so long had been loosely termed "the Conkling-Beard hypothesis." This conclusive disproof came vexingly slow, but the adverse evidence and the trends were marked and cumulative. Even the modified or "secondary intention" hypothesis (which had theorized that a possible interest in congressional legislation, or in an expanded congressional power, sought by or for the benefit of railroads or insurance companies, might have afforded some slight basis for Conkling's ambiguous, titillating allusions) soon appeared to be more and more a mirage of ill-digested conjecture and overpatterned circumstance.

Working off and through the various records, cases, petitions, bills, committee actions; examining particularly the leading insurance journals and the strategy and arguments of the various corporations, I was impressed repeatedly by the divided, conflicting, uncertain leadership on both sides, business *and* congressional, and by the overwhelming primacy in *all* minds of the racial and the Reconstruction problems.[1]

Though an utter fiasco from start to finish, that drive of the northeastern insurance companies for a national bureau of insurance—*i.e., for* federal regulation—remained the most fascinating and complex side of the story. Remained such, because Elizur Wright, whom we remember as one of the great abolitionist leaders of the 1830's and 1840's[2] and now in the 1860's the leading American actuary—justly honored in our time as "the Father of Life Insurance"—here again appeared as a leading protagonist. A thoroughly Brandeisian figure he was, too—still two generations ahead of his time, a man who made no secret of *his* crusade for what others saw as a potent, unwelcome medicine indeed. It soon became apparent, however, that the decisive clue, and indeed the key, to this problem was the fact that the companies' strategy had continued to be based on corporate

---

[1] For the final resolution of these matters, see Chapter 13 and Appendix II *infra*.

[2] See Chapter 4, *supra*, notes 42–43, and the biography there cited; also the Wright Papers in the Library of Congress, Manuscript Division, and in the Baker Library, Harvard University.

citizenship, and on congressional relief, even *after* the Fourteenth Amendment had come into force. The texts of important bills were lacking, however, and it was some time before other evidence more than made good that lack.[3]

As these matters were clarifying, and while the eastern railroad and insurance company jigsaws—the 1865–1871 stories—were fitting together (as blanks), it became clear that the most promising sector for attack meanwhile would be a resurvey of that "Ninth Circuit law" which had culminated in the *California Railroad Tax Cases,* and in the constitutional corporate "person." This of course was where the research had started. Twice in twenty years the wheel had come full circle. For neither the two Conspiracy Theory essays nor the one on Justice Field had covered the Central and Southern Pacific railroads' situation, arguments, and strategy. Nor had these essays covered more than the heart of even Conkling's constitutional argument. Meanwhile, economic due process had suffered eclipse, and Negroes at last seemed set to receive the intended process and protection. A behavioristic account of the rise and debut of the corporate "person" thus now had double relevance. Eventually two chapters would have to cover the 1865–1871 situations, but even these would be more valuable once the corporate "person" had been set in full perspective.

Much of this basic research analysis had been performed in the 1930's; but the inwardness and the chanciness of the Chinese-railroad symbiosis never had been fully worked out or shown. Here surely, and to better advantage than anywhere in our books, were manifest the dynamic power and the potential of due process and equal protection *where the will and the need were one*; where a persecuted Chinese minority, a half-cornered railroad, and a vigilant, courageous judge—a sometimes curiously myopic one—together made history, and remade it.

The constitutional corporate "person" thus beckoned a second time, and a re-exploration of these matters corrected many old astigmatisms. For how curious, how irrelevant in such contexts as these, is that stale, naïve rhetoric that pretends to be able to cleave "human rights" from "property rights," or "procedural" due process from "substantive."

This is one of the points that must recur to all who keep wondering and asking "What happened to American due process?" and "What failed to happen to American racial equal protection, 1880–1940?" Not "conspiracy," we say; not *foreplan* by business, or even

---
[3] See note 1, *supra.*

for it. Just a remedied lack of foreplan; and on the neglected racial side, not intended judicial discrimination, not inhumanity, or indifference; rather incomprehension, lack of insight. Not a lack of empathy, but—in the case of the freedmen at least, and for so many of their families, after 1877—lack of counsel, lack of pleaders, lack of habeas corpus, lack of the ballot, lack of education, lack of friends at court, and certainly lack of corporate allies and defenders.

Justice Harlan's lone, impassioned dissent in the *Civil Rights Cases* of 1883, and Justice Field's circuit opinions establishing protection for the Chinese and for the Central and Southern Pacific railroads, thus spell out and highlight both the problems and the differences.

[CHAPTER 9]

That invisible, intangible, and artificial being, that mere legal entity, a corporation . . . *John Marshall.*

Corporation . . . an innately despotick word . . .
John Taylor of Caroline.

The most important invention of our age is very probably the corporation . . . *Chester I. Barnard.*

CORPORATIONS have played a double role in American life.[1] They have been alternately—even simultaneously—angels and devils of both our economy and politics. There is no need to labor this fact. Nor will it do, at this date, to picture American Telephone and Telegraph or United States Steel as Cinderellas. Yet the shades of President Andrew Jackson and Nicholas Biddle, for example, must

---

[1] Much of the development is uncharted: fifty jurisdictions have been promoters' meat and historians' and economists' poison. Only recently have genetic factors been objects of serious study. Basic and indispensible works include:

(1.) Historical-legal: CADMAN, THE CORPORATION IN NEW JERSEY: BUSINESS AND POLITICS, 1791–1875 (1949); DAVIS, ESSAYS IN THE EARLIER HISTORY OF AMERICAN CORPORATIONS [to 1800] (1917); DODD, AMERICAN BUSINESS CORPORATIONS UNTIL 1860, WITH SPECIAL REFERENCE TO MASSACHUSETTS (1954) (a definitive analysis of the national case law viewed against New England statutory development); HANDLIN AND HANDLIN, COMMONWEALTH, MASSACHUSETTS, 1774–1861 (1947); HARTZ, ECONOMIC POLICY AND DEMOCRATIC THOUGHT: PENNSYLVANIA, 1776–1860 (1948) (a brilliant synthesis of economic and constitutional history); LIVERMORE, EARLY AMERICAN LAND COMPANIES: THEIR INFLUENCE ON CORPORATE DEVELOPMENT (1939); Handlin and Handlin, *Origins of the American Business Corporation,* 5 J. ECON. HIST. 1, 369 (1945).

(2.) Statistical studies of incorporation as related to business cycles, legislation and charter policy: EVANS, BUSINESS INCORPORATIONS (1948); Kessler, *A Statistical Study of the New York General Incorporation Act of 1811,* 48 J. POL. ECON. 877 (1940); Kessler, *Incorporation in New England, 1800–1875,* 8 J. ECON. HIST. 43 (1948).

marvel at the changes Time has brought.[2] "Born twelve decades too soon," one might imagine the Philadelphia banker musing—but never Old Hickory!

Equally (if not still more) incredulous at these far-reaching shifts of attitude and fortune, must be the wraiths of several California worthies: Denis Kearney, Charles Crocker and Leland Stanford, among others. Kearney, it will be remembered, was that tireless agitator of San Francisco's Sand Lots in the depressed 1870's—a rich-brogued Cato with a scorpion tongue, who often marched of an evening to the magnates' mansions on Nob Hill. There he harangued his followers: "The Chinese . . . The Corporations . . . The Southern Pacific Railroad . . . must go!"[3] Several long-forgotten anti-corporate clauses of the California Constitution of 1879—including one prohibiting corporations from employing Chinese[4]—owed their original pinch to the fury of Kearney's attack on "these soulless, blood-sucking monsthurs."

(3.) Economic-legal analysis: BERLE AND MEANS, THE MODERN CORPORATION AND PRIVATE PROPERTY (1948); COMMONS, LEGAL FOUNDATIONS OF CAPITALISM (1924); Timberg, *Corporate Fictions: Logical, Social and International Implications*, 46 COL. L. REV. 533 (1946).

(4.) Constitutional Status: HENDERSON, THE POSITION OF THE FOREIGN CORPORATION IN AMERICAN CONSTITUTIONAL LAW (1918); WRIGHT, THE CONTRACT CLAUSE OF THE CONSTITUTION (1938); Farage, *Non-Natural Persons and the Guarantee of "Liberty" Under the Due Process Clause*, 28 KY. L.J. 269 (1940); Chapters 1-2, *supra*; Green, *Corporations as Persons, Citizens, and Possessors of Liberty*, 94 U. OF PA. L. REV. 202 (1946); Howe, *A Footnote to the Conspiracy Theory*, 48 YALE L.J. 1007 (1939); Robbins, *The Private Corporation, Its Constitutional Genesis*, 28 GEO. L.J. 165 (1939); Sholley, *Corporate Taxpayers and the Equal Protection Clause*, 31 ILL. L. REV. 463, 567 (1936-37); Wilkinson, *Is a Corporation Always Entitled to Due Process of Law?*, 26 GEO. L.J. 132 (1937).

2 Anti-corporate opinion and movements are a virgin field for research. Jackson's War of the Bank did much to canalize and fix public antagonism in the United States. Moreover, such sentiments never were confined to the uneducated: some of the strongest, anti-corporate, anti-bank views in American history are found in the writings of John Adams. See 2 DAVIS, *op. cit. supra* note 1, at 307-308, quoting 8 ADAMS, WORKS 660, 10 *id.* at 375, 9 *id.* at 638. These reflected the risky, speculative character of early trading companies, the unpopularity of chartered monopolies, the social memory of the Mississippi Bubble and similar failures. For evidence of early American antagonism, see SCHLESINGER, THE AGE OF JACKSON (1945); TAYLOR, ED., JACKSON V. BIDDLE (1949); Sellers, *Banking and Politics in Jackson's Tennessee, 1817-1827*, 41 MISS. V. HIST. REV. 61 (1954).

3 See CAUGHEY, HISTORY OF CALIFORNIA c. 25 (1940) and works there cited; CROSS, HISTORY OF THE LABOR MOVEMENT IN CALIFORNIA (1935); SWISHER, MOTIVATION AND POLITICAL TECHNIQUE IN THE CALIFORNIA CONSTITUTIONAL CONVENTION OF 1879 (1930).

4 See CAL. CONST. 1879, Art. XII, Corporations, passim; Art. XIX §§ 2, 3, prohibiting employment of Chinese by corporations or on public works respectively. PENAL CODE § 178, Cal. Code Amdts. 1880, c. 3, p. 1, enacted in execution of this article was invalidated, *In re* Tiburcio Parrott, 1 Fed. 481 (C.C. Cal. 1880), and repealed, Cal. Stat. 1905, c. 492, § 1, p. 652; see *infra* note 88.

Thirty years before, at the time of the Convention of 1849, there had been those who felt and spoke similarly.[5] The Golden State, they predicted, would have no truck with corporations. Even banks were unneeded and unwanted in a land where specie was so plentiful.[6] Now, a century later hundreds of banking corporations in California, including the eight-billion-dollar five hundred-branch Bank of America, the world's largest![7]

The initial point is that the use Americans have made of the corporate device is strangely at odds with this historic mistrust of corporations and "Big Business." The outcome is anomalous any way one views it. General Motors made and sold products to the value of ten billions in 1953; its net income alone was $600 millions; its assets five billions.[8] AT&T today has 700,000 employees and more than a million and a quarter stockholders.[9] Prudential Insurance Company wrote five and a half billions of life insurance in 1953, has more than $43 billion in force, and 30 million policy holders.[10] Its 1953 premium income of $1.3 billion was unmatched by the tax collections of even New York or California and its total income of $1.8 billion was one-sixth the total tax collections of *all* the 48 states![11] Sears Roebuck's 709 stores and branches sold nearly three billions of goods in the past year.[12] The 200 largest American corporations made sales of $21.8 billion in 1942; $51 billion in 1951.[13] There probably are more than three-quarters of a million *active* corporations in the United States today.[14]

Increasingly, it would seem, the average American works for a corporation, trades with corporations, owns stock in corporations. Yet for all this he traditionally has viewed the corporation with misgiv-

---

5 See CAL. CONST. 1849, Art. IV, §§ 31–36, especially § 36 making stockholders "individually and personally liable"; and GOODWIN, ESTABLISHMENT OF STATE GOVERNMENT IN CALIFORNIA c. 8 (1914) and the 1849 Constitution Debates there cited.

6 See CAL. CONST. 1849, Art. IV, §§ 34–35 (chartering of banks prohibited, and banking corporations denied power of issue, legislature commanded to prohibit such issue). Banks might be formed under general laws for deposit of gold and silver!

7 See JAMES, BIOGRAPHY OF A BANK (1954).

8 Los Angeles Daily News, March 10, 1954.

9 A. T. & T. Co., ANNUAL REPORT, 1953.

10 PRUDENTIAL INSURANCE CO., ANNUAL REPORT, 1953.

11 See BOOK OF THE STATES, 1954–55, 226 (1954); tax collections of the 48 states equalled $10.542 billion in 1953, with California in the lead with $1.139 billion.

12 Newsweek, April 5, 1954, p. 76.

13 STATISTICAL ABSTRACT OF THE UNITED STATES, 1953, Table 544, p. 485.

14 *Id.* Table 386, p. 361: 623,570 corporate income tax returns were filed in 1950, and this number included only active corporations operating for profit. **1968:** Though the "corporate miracle" today requires less notice than the "corporate parable," for a current updating and supplementation of these figures, see *The Fortune Directories*, 75 FORTUNE (no. 7, June 15, 1967), 196–231.

ings, often with downright antagonism.¹⁵ Emotionally our attachment still is to small enterprise and individual proprietorship. We long for simplicity. We fear bigness—we mistrust its power, its regimentation, its complexity. Yet we also plainly want bigness. We feel that we need it; above all, we irresistibly patronize it. Like some perverse paranoid spouse, we obviously have, during a good share of our national history thoroughly mistrusted, feared, and at times hated and reviled a partner we have been neither able nor willing to live without.

Corporation lawyers long since have grown philosophical over this situation. Like their brethren of the divorce courts, they make a very good thing of it. The basic dualism, they remind us, is institutional —inherent in the enterprise itself. Corporations, as Justice Miller once observed, are persons wanting the human affections.¹⁶ They rarely have been popular; they have been needed and tolerated rather than loved. Historically, the public's attitude generally has waivered between restriction and indulgence.¹⁷ Jeffersonians and Jacksonians waged furious debates over chartering and rechartering the Bank. Then came the conflicts over legislative charters and promotional policies generally; later, struggles over regulation of railroads, utilities and "Trusts"; more recently, over chain stores, monopoly and fair trade practices. In every instance, these have been see-saw battles—waged within and for the public mind, quite as much as between rival economic and interest-groups.

The complexities of a federal system and the opportunities of a national market soon enough heightened both the drama and the stakes. From the start, the origin and nature of corporations made them subject to strict state and local control. Yet their potentialities and the character of their operations tended to put them within the orbit of the national commerce and the national judicial power.¹⁸

---

15 *Cf.* BRANDEIS, THE CURSE OF BIGNESS (1935); GALBRAITH, AMERICAN CAPITALISM: THE CONCEPT OF COUNTERVAILING POWER (1952); LILLIENTHAL, BIG BUSINESS: A NEW ERA (1953); and the symposium-review of the two latter works in 49 N.U.L. REV. 139–194 (1954); also KAPLAN, BIG ENTERPRISE IN A COMPETITIVE ECONOMY (Brookings Institution 1954), an objective, up-to-date, and on the whole, favorable survey.

16 United States v. Union Pacific R.R., 98 U.S. 569, 620 (1878).

17 See Professor Goebel's introduction to LIVERMORE, *op. cit. supra* note 1, at ix.
Incorporation has become so universal a privilege in the United States it often is regarded as a right, as is the privilege of doing business in such form. *But cf.* Justice Brandeis dissenting in Liggett Co. v. Lee, 288 U.S. 517, 541 (1933). On the early public law status of the corporation, see the works of DODD, HARTZ, HENDERSON, WRIGHT, Graham, Howe and Robbins cited *supra* note 1.

18 See HENDERSON, *op. cit. supra* note 1, c. 2–4, and DODD, *op. cit. supra* note 1, at 14–57, 171–181 for accounts of how the early enterprise of foreign corporations impelled courts to extend the right to sue, hold property, etc.

So, too, did inclinations of management in a day when the commerce power was asserted chiefly for promotional purposes and when the judicial power constituted the last bulwark against restrictive state regulation and control.[19] Centripetal and centrifugal forces thus were in delicate balance. Legislative economic policy during the formative period generally has been pictured as laissez faire in nature, yet actually it was far more complex.[20] There always were two sides to each of these three coins—corporation, state and nation; "heads" and "tails" rarely were consistently called by, or fell for, any of the leading players. Indeed, this circumstance itself contributed to the prejudice and to emotional confusion. The very corporations spawned by and waxing fat on public subsidies, for example soon were fighting public regulation. Yet earlier the people themselves had voted the subsidies, and unquestionably wanted what they had subsidized. The "sharpers" and "jobbers," the "monopolists" and "robber barons,"[21] most often simply were the men whose enterprises a decade or two before had been thought too risky for investment and hence worthy of public aid. Gratitude and consistency became all but lost virtues—virtues demanded only of opponents; and this was as true of the public's positions as of corporate managers' and promoters'.[22]

Cupidity, therefore, to no less a degree than federalism, early assumed a hand in shaping the constitutional role and status of the corporation. Legislatures generally had issued the charters and often rendered aid in the first instance; state and federal courts took over increasingly thereafter. Because cupidity has a broad solid base, and because nineteenth century legislatures and corporate promoters, whatever their limitations, certainly were representative in this, the judiciary from the first had a great deal to do—and it did it! What it eventually did, of course, in dealing with corporate rights and status, was to hold that corporations were artificial "persons" *in the constitutional sense*, under the Fourteenth and the Fifth Amendments, as ever since Coke's[23] day they had been in common legal

---

19 See WRIGHT, *op. cit. supra* note 1, for Contract Clause history.

20 See especially HANDLIN and HARTZ, *op. cit. supra* note 1, for Massachusetts and Pennsylvania policy down to 1860; KIRKLAND, MEN, CITIES AND TRANSPORTATION (1948); PIERCE, RAILROADS OF NEW YORK: A STUDY OF GOVERNMENT AID (1953); TAYLOR, THE TRANSPORTATION REVOLUTION (1952).

21 On the social functions of the early railroad promoters and the difficulties of easy moralizing, see Cochran, *The Legend of the Robber Barons*, 74 PA. MAG. OF HIST. AND BIOG. 307 (1950).

22 *Ibid.*

23 Case of Sutton's Hospital 10 Co 23, 32b; see 1 BL. COMM. *469ff.; KYD, CORPORATIONS (1793-1794).

parlance. States were thus forbidden to deprive any [corporate] person of property without due process of law [or] deny to any [corporate] person the equal protection of the laws."[24]

It is a matter of special interest to Californians that the holding on the latter of these points was first made in two tax cases involving assessment of the Southern Pacific Railroad. The first case,[25] covered taxes due from San Mateo County, and was decided by Justice Field and Circuit Judge Sawyer in September, 1882. The second[26] involved assessments of Santa Clara County, and was decided by the same judges a year later. For various reasons, no formal opinions ever were rendered by the Supreme Court on the point of corporate personality when the circuit decisions were appealed, 1882–1886. At the time of the *Santa Clara* appeal in the latter year, Chief Justice Waite declared merely that the Court did not wish to hear reargument on the point for the reason that all the Justices then agreed corporations were "persons" within the meaning of the Equal Protection Clause.[27] The Field-Sawyer opinions thus today stand as the highest —indeed in most respects the only—authoritative judicial statement and justification of the corporate constitutional "person." This fact alone adds immeasurably to the interest and importance of both cases. Controversy has raged for years over whether framers of the Fourteenth Amendment, in 1866, really intended to cover and aid corporations.[28] Almost no attention has been paid however, to a number of equally fundamental questions. The purpose of this essay is to consider the nature, basis and significance of corporate personality as a constitutional doctrine. Framer intent, on which so much detective work has had to be done, and which still is far from clear, is presently left open. Focus will be rather on the logical, semantic and politico-social ramifications. Why is corporate personality important? What briefly has been its derivation and influence? How, in the main, has it been justified and attacked? These are our

---

For an analysis of the various leading definitions and views of the nature of a corporation, see TAYLOR, PRIVATE CORPORATIONS §§ 15, 23–24 (5th ed. 1905).

[24] Corporate personality under the Equal Protection Clause dates from the Waite dictum, 1886, Santa Clara County v. Southern Pac. R.R., 118 U.S. 394, 396 (1886), under the Due Process Clause of the Fourteenth Amendment, from 1889, Minneapolis and St. Louis R.R. v. Beckwith, 129 U.S. 26, 28 (1888).

[25] County of San Mateo v. Southern Pacific R.R., 8 Saw. 238, 13 Fed. 722 (C.C. Cal. 1882).

[26] The Santa Clara Railroad Tax Case: County of Santa Clara v. Southern Pacific R.R., 9 Saw. 165, 18 Fed. 385 (C.C. Cal. 1883).

[27] Santa Clara County v. Southern Pacific R.R., 118 U.S. 394, 396 (1886).

[28] See Chapters 1-2, *supra*; Boudin, *Truth and Fiction About the Fourteenth Amendment*, 16 N.Y.U.L.Q. REV. 19 (1938); Hurst, Book Review, 52 HARV. L. REV. 851 (1939). See also note 38 *infra*.

immediate problems. The approach is behavioristic and analytical. The object is to view the doctrine in constitutional perspective.

I

Conventionally considered,[29] corporate personality is an extremely simple doctrine—one that involves construction of only a single word, and then nothing more than a minor interpolation or transfer of meaning. "Person" is construed *in the constitutional sense* exactly as it often is in daily speech. Corporations for centuries have been called artificial or legal "persons." Countless statutes, decisions[30] and treatises so speak of them; therefore, so the argument runs, the constitutional term ought to be—and is—given its inclusive, generic construction.

This of course substantially reduces the doctrine to a bit of word play, a constitutional and judicial pun or *double entendre*—a pun, it is conceded, that really grew up, certainly one that blazed its way through American briefs and reports, but nevertheless just a pun. Many words, these apologists continue, are something of acrobats and dual impersonators. Those in the Constitution and in constitutional discussion are no exceptions. In fact, nothing here is half as spectacular as Professor Powell's celebrated triple play after the Supreme Court crisis of 1937—"A switch in time saved nine." Yet exactly the same potentialities of language are in evidence, even if not perhaps so brilliantly illuminated. The whole argument over corporate personality thus is dismissed as a tempest in a semantic teapot. The fact to be faced, it is said, is simply that corporate personality is a matter of constitutional definition and syllogism. Intrinsically, it is as simple and natural and useful a contrivance as an omelet or the lever or the wedge.

Now this, it may be added, is a feigned or imagined simplicity,

---

[29] See Camp, *Corporations and the Fourteenth Amendment*, 13 CALIF. STATE B. J. No. 6, p. 12 (1938); and other comments inspired by Justice Black's dissent in Connecticut General Life Ins. Co. v. Johnson, 303 U.S. 77, 83 (1938), viz. Martin, *Is a Corporation a "Person"?*, 44 W. VA. L.Q. 247 (1938).

A vast literature treats of the corporate person in the juridical, legal and philosophical sense as distinguished from the constitutional problem. For concise summaries and bibliography on the "fiction" theory of Savigny and Salmond and the "realist," "organic," or "entity" theory of Gierke and Maitland, to mention only the leading schools, see FRIEDMANN, LEGAL THEORY 396 (3d ed. 1953). The writings of Hallis, Dewey, Radin, and Cohen all illuminate phases of group personality as a philosophical and juridical concept. See also, RICHMOND, PERSONALITY AS A PHILOSOPHICAL PRINCIPLE (1900).

[30] The cornerstone in California is Douglass v. Pacific Mail Steamship Co., 4 Cal. 304, 306 (1854): "The word 'person' in its legal signification, is a generic term, and was intended to include artificial persons," opinion by Chief Justice Murray; Heydenfeldt and Wells, JJ., concurring.

one both spurious and deceptive, compounded and double-decked. So regarded, corporate personality is another of those semantic and constitutional icebergs. It floats serenely enough—on a tremendous submerged base; buoyancy is achieved by a mental displacement almost as great as the hydraulic. Indeed, it is much as if World Federalists, impatient at muddle and delay, were to argue that the clause, "Congress shall have power to raise and support armies" empowers Congress forthwith to create *international* armies—ignoring completely for the moment all broader constitutional implications as well as the significance of every word except "armies." The trouble in both cases is that the key word—"armies" or "persons"—is construed *in vacuo*. In the case of the Due Process Clause moreover, the construction is made wholly in retrospect, and no attention whatever is paid to the other qualifying words, "be deprived of life, liberty or property without due process of law." Or, if occasionally they are noted, the observation then is that surely no objection can be made to granting corporations "*due* process of law" or "*equal protection* of the laws." The word "person" thus is split off. Its meaning is arrived at either solely on the basis of the word itself, or according to the layman's literal, ethical and common sense reading of the phrases "due process of law" and "equal protection of the laws." Actually, of course, "due process of law" originally was a technical phrase with a fairly definite legal meaning. Barring a few exceptions, it remained so judicially until after the Civil War.[31] "Due process," therefore, rather than "person" or "property"—plainly was the controlling term in 1866; yet this fact is conveniently and completely ignored.

Moreover, history has uttered its own devastating commentary on this type of constitutional syllogism. Abolitionists tried for years to get slaves regarded as "persons,"[32] as slaves obviously were; and corporation lawyers likewise failed during the pre-Civil War period, in efforts to use the fiction of corporate citizenship under the Diversity Clause to attain corporate citizenship under the Comity Clause.[33]

---

[31] See Shattuck, *The True Meaning of the Term "Liberty" in Those Clauses in the Federal and State Constitutions Which Protect "Life", "Liberty" and "Property"*, 4 HARV. L. REV. 365 (1891); Corwin, *The Doctrine of Due Process of Law Before the Civil War*, 24 HARV. L. REV. 366, 460 (1911) and other works cited Chapter 5, *supra*, note 1.

[32] For recent treatments of the role of the constitutional theory of the anti-slavery movement in shaping modern concepts of due process and equal protection, see Chapters 4-5, *supra*; TENBROEK, THE ANTISLAVERY ORIGINS OF THE FOURTEENTH AMENDMENT (1951).

[33] See HENDERSON, *op. cit. supra* note 1; DODD, *op. cit. supra* note 1, at 36, 150-154; and Chapter 2, *supra*, at 73ff.

Nothing was wrong with the premises or syllogisms in either of these efforts. The difficulty was rather with the social result; logic and inference often are inadequate or unpopular in constitutional construction.

Had the basic constructional problem been anywhere near as simple as apologists' reasoning makes it out, it is plain there would have been no eighty-year delay in formally advancing the argument. A due process guarantee stood in the Fifth Amendment as a limitation on the Federal Government from the year 1789; most state constitutions contained similar guarantees; public corporations were held to be "freemen" and "persons" as early as 1805;[34] loose popular or "natural rights" construction of due process clauses began in the 1830's and continued for years.[35] Occasional public corporations or shareholders of private corporations were *presumed* to be "persons"; and beginning in the 1840's Pennsylvania courts disregarded the narrow wording of their state due course of law clause and held private corporations entitled to its protection.[36] Yet the fact is that no one has so far found a single instance, before 1871, where personality of a *private* corporation was explicitly urged as a constitutional doctrine, either in court or out.[37] This gestation period of eighty years, with another decade and a half for parturition, itself belies the facile view that the problem is one simply of terms and logic. Raw materials for levers and omelets and wedges, to pursue proponents' analogy, lay about the earth for centuries, their potentialities ignored. So it was to some degree apparently, with these components. Need and appetite alone at any rate were not decisive.

Constitutional doctrines nearly always have been viewed in polarized light: Vision and perception depend a great deal on the cast or color of one's spectacles. Corporate personality has proved no exception in this regard. Generally speaking, editors and historians[38]

---

[34] Trustees v. Foy, 5 N.C. 57 (1805). For discussion of this and other public corporation cases, see Chapter 2, *supra* n.4 and 5; Howe, *supra* note 1; and Dodd, *op. cit. supra* note 1, at 37, 150–154.

[35] See Chapters 1–2, *supra*.

[36] See Brown v. Hummel, 6 Barr 86 (Pa. 1847); Erie and North East Railroad v. Casey, 26 Pa. 287, 293 (1856), discussed Chapter 2 *supra*. On further investigation it appears that the significance of these cases and dicta, and their bearing on the 1866 draftsmanship is easily exaggerated.

[37] Professor Dodd apparently found none, see Dodd, *op. cit. supra* note 1, at 156, nor has the writer in a search of likely counsels' briefs. Natural rights thinking and terminological affinities may have led an occasional counsel to suggest the point before 1871, see note 46 *infra*, but if so, the usage was as abortive as it was spontaneous.

[38] See Bates, The Story of Congress 233–234 (1936); 2 Beard and Beard, Rise of American Civilization 111–113 (1927); Faulkner, Political and Economic History of the United States 416 (5th ed. 1952); Hacker, The Triumph of American Capitalism 387–392 (1940); Hacker and Kendrick, The United States Since 1865 (3d ed. 1939); Hu-

have been as inclined to overplay its importance, as the legal profession has to minimize it. The doctrine thus often is heralded as the major pivot in a series of changes which are said to have ultimately revolutionized both the scope and character of judicial review and the constitutional position of large property.[39]

Corporate personality, it is contended, greatly enhanced the power and economic authority of the Supreme Court simply by expanding the Court's jurisdiction and discretion. Moreover, in producing these results, corporate personality substantially reversed the position of *all* corporations in their relation to government. That is to say, once corporations were declared persons they were able to challenge the validity of any action adversely affecting their interests; from agencies traditionally presumed subject to strict legislative control, they were transformed overnight into agencies able to compel government to justify its regulations affecting them. Judges in turn were more readily able to substitute their own views of social and economic policy for those of Congress and the state legislatures. Where beforehand corporate business could challenge only such action as conflicted with the more specifically-worded Commerce or Contracts Clauses, after 1886 it was possible for almost any law to be attacked, and of course a great many more laws were judicially overthrown.[40] Hence, it is argued, holding corporations to be persons entitled to due process of law and to equal protection of the laws was in practice tantamount to two constitutional amendments, wordable substantially as follows: 1) "Corporations are free to challenge any governmental action opposed to their interests." 2) "The Supreme Court is empowered to review all governmental action—State and Federal—pertaining to corporations and to veto any such action deemed arbitrary or unreasonable." Practically speaking, it

---

BERMAN, AMERICA, INCORPORATED 15 (1940); JOSEPHSON, THE ROBBER BARONS 52 (1934); WEBB, DIVIDED WE STAND: THE CRISIS OF A FRONTIERLESS DEMOCRACY, c. 3 (1937); Edward T. Lee, Should the Fourteenth Amendment . . . Be Amended? (address to the Gary, Indiana Bar Association, Nov. 20, 1936); Morgan editorial, *Human Liberty and the New Feudalism*, 28 J. NAT. EDUC. ASSN. 1–4 (Jan. 1939).

[39] See especially the works by BEARD, Lee, and WEBB, *supra* note 38; also Smith, *Decisive Battles of Constitutional Law XV: The Revolution*, 10 A.B.A.J. 505, 509 (1924).

[40] See Appendix I, "Cases Holding State Action Invalid Under the Fourteenth Amendment" in FRANKFURTER, MR. JUSTICE HOLMES AND THE SUPREME COURT 97–137 (1938); also Appendix II *id.* showing geographic distribution of the state action invalidated.

See also COLLINS, THE FOURTEENTH AMENDMENT AND THE STATES Appendix C "Statistical Summary of Opinions Delivered Under the Fourteenth Amendment, 1868–1910," p. 183, Appendix E "Chronological Table of Cases Decided by the Supreme Court of the United States Under the Fourteenth Amendment," pp. 188–206, and Appendix F, a summary graph interpreting the above data, p. 207 (1914).

was quite as if all laws and regulations pertaining to corporations were *presumed* to be hostile or discriminating until the judicial branch ruled to the contrary.

Patently, the basic shortcoming of this counter or historians' view is that it confuses institutional with doctrinal factors. It virtually ignores the former and attributes to corporate personality *per se*, many of the constructional changes based on other words, and some of which certainly were inherent in the operation of judicial review itself. It is plain enough today at any rate that almost any clause of the Bill of Rights can undergo rapid substantive elaboration with attendant expansion of the courts' role and powers. Recent examples are the freedom of speech and freedom of religion clauses of the First Amendment, particularly as they bear on picketing, public education, and loyalty programs. Once society and government reach a certain stage of complexity—or perplexity—cases arise that force the judiciary, as the department having the last word in our system, to draw its line between claims based on the Constitution of Powers and those based on the Constitution of Rights. This is what happened recently in the free speech and picketing cases;[41] and it was what happened in the 1880s with regard to substantive due process, equal protection and corporate personality. In looking back on these developments, laymen and historians have been bedazzled and taken in by corporate personality *per se*. Like the butterfly fresh from the chrysalis, here was an inherently spectacular change, yet one that really was part of a maturing cycle. Numerous interrelated changes were involved. Virtually every word in the Due Process and Equal Protection Clauses had to be stretched and remolded.[42] "Property" —heretofore *tangible* property—had to be equated to "earning power" or "exchange value"; or, as one of the pioneer Southern Pacific Railroad briefs put it, in a truly inspired and prophetic typographical error, the phrase had to be read as "deprived of . . . *profit* without due process of law."[43] "Deprived" in turn, had to mean, not a *physical taking*, as heretofore, but rather consequential "diminution" or "impairment" of exchange value. Above all, "due process

---

41 See Jones, *The Right to Picket—Twilight Zone of the Constitution*, 102 U. OF PA. L. REV. 995 (1954) for a stimulating treatment.

42 See the penetrating analysis of a distinguished economist in COMMONS, *op. cit. supra* note 1.

43 See Creed Haymond, January 1882, in Central Pacific R.R. v. State Board of Equalization, 60 Cal. 35 (1882), Calif. Supreme Court Records, Vol. 694, Leaf 229, p. 48 printers' numbering: "The word 'person' in the phrase 'nor shall any State deprive any person of life, liberty or profit without due process of law' in Amendment XIV, includes corporations as well as natural persons."

of law" and "equal protection of the laws" had to be construed as full-fledged substantive limitations on legislatures—with the words "due" and "equal," in particular, read as authorizing a then still quite revolutionary judicial review of the *expediency, propriety, and justice* of legislation.[44] For us today to ignore these changes, or to lump them all together and attribute them to an enlarged construction of the word "persons," is to miss the real point and drama. Indeed, it is to repeat, in reverse, the very fallacies and pretense that masqueraded in the original arguments and opinions on corporate personality in the Eighties.

Potentially, corporate citizenship under the Privileges or Immunities Clause of Section One might have served almost as effectively as corporate personality under the Due Process and Equal Protection Clauses.[45] Moreover, had the Supreme Court squarely reversed Justice Field's *San Mateo* and *Santa Clara* holdings on the point of corporate personality, sustaining instead the views which Judge Woods expressed in *Insurance Company v. New Orleans*,[46] it seems quite likely, given the operative social pressures, the same results still might have been attained simply by suits in the names of individual shareholders of the corporation (*i.e.*, natural persons)—assuming of course that the vital and primary changes had occurred in the meaning of the other words.

II

This introductory survey points up a major fact about the corporate constitutional "person." Extreme formalism and superficiality have marked discussion from the beginning. Logic and a perfunctory appeal to expediency or history generally have carried the load—and carried it in both directions! Leading opinions are terse, general, evasive. Often they have rested on misapprehensions as to fundamental facts. Briefs and oral arguments are quite as strikingly inadequate. Some are scarcely above the byplay in a legal argument beween laymen.

There is nothing extraordinary in this. Simple concepts invariably prove the most elusive—simple only in what they presume or reject or disguise. Corporate personality is a perfect example of such protective coloration. Functionally and psychologically, affirmatively

---

[44] See the familiar works of Haines, Corwin, Mott, Hamilton and others cited in Chapter 5, *supra*, at 243, note 1.
[45] See Hamilton, *The Path of Due Process of Law in* THE CONSTITUTION RECONSIDERED (Read ed. 1938).
[46] 1 Woods 85, 13 Fed. Cas. 67, No. 7,052 (C.C. La. 1871).

and negatively, it has been used in syllogisms as a formula for results. Essentially it is an instrumentalist doctrine. Men began to use it once they perceived its advantages and saw clearly what they needed and wanted. Later, others deplored its use, and more recently, critics have urged its abandonment, for nearly opposite reasons. Yet here again, the reasons often are left largely implicit.

Precious little in the early history of the doctrine suggested its ultimate approval and importance. Indeed, the judicial record opens with flat, summary rejection. Moreover, the sharp challenge and criticism levelled in 1938 by Mr. Justice Black,[47] and again in 1949 by Justice Douglas[48] (with his colleague's concurrence) are essentially restatements of a stand originally taken by Circuit Judge Woods in 1871. During the period 1871-82 the rule that corporations were *not* to be regarded as constitutional "persons" theoretically was the law of the land. Actually it was more honored in the breach than in the observance. Woods' opinion in *Insurance Co. v. New Orleans* thus is our logical starting point. Counter views that ultimately prevailed, and the modern dissents, can best be weighed against this original.

Setting and backgrounds are vital: The Civil War decade witnessed a huge increase in the number and power of American corporations.[49] Organization under general laws rather than by special charter had by this date begun to be the rule rather than the exception. War contracts and war loans acted as a forcing house for business and banking. Consolidation of railroad and telegraph lines into trunk systems proceeded rapidly in the East; state and federal subsidies soon stretched transcontinental lines to the Pacific. Tariffs fostered enterprise, and an expanding economy literally fed on its own growth.

This tremendous upsurge of economic activity triggered as well as reflected a mounting nationalism. States Rights brakes were released. Government became a promotive and catalyzing force. As one field after another—manufacturing, railroads, telegraphs, banking—demonstrated the beneficial effects insurance and express leaders (particularly those of the old line companies of the Northeast) saw an opportunity for their own salvation.[50] Year by year for decades their businesses had been fair game for the foreign corpo-

---

[47] Connecticut General Life Insurance Co. v. Johnson, 303 U.S. 77, 87 (1938).
[48] Wheeling Steel Corporation v. Glander, 337 U.S. 562, 576-581 (1949).
[49] See DODD, *op. cit. supra* note 1, for legal development to 1860. For statistical studies of incorporation and the relationships between legislation and increasing use of the corporate device, see EVANS and Kessler, *supra* note 1.
[50] See Chapter 2, *supra*.

ration laws of states-rights-minded legislatures. Discriminatory taxes and licenses had protected home companies. In a business that needed a national market for maximum sales and risk distribution, this was bad enough. Far worse were the bond and deposit laws that froze capital while sheltering "wildcat" local companies whose failure in turn discredited the whole industry. Against such threatened paralysis and "balkanization," the Eastern concerns repeatedly invited state courts to accept the same ingenious formula that Webster originally had offered (and Taney had rejected) in the foreign corporation cases of 1839.[51] A corporation, it was there argued, already was treated as a "citizen" for purposes of suit in the federal courts under the Diversity Clause of the Constitution. So it also ought to be treated, the argument continued, under the Comity Clause. The hope was that "corporations [or shareholders] of each state" might thus eventually be held entitled in all states, to "the right to trade," the right "to acquire and possess property," and above all to the right "to exemption from higher taxes and other unequal impositions," which Justice Washington had declared in *Corfield v. Coryell*,[52] to be among the "privileges and immunities of *citizens* in the several States." During the period 1840–60 a formula which so neatly erased state lines and stripped states of all power over foreign corporations naturally met with a cool reception. Soaring war nationalism and Republican supremacy thus had raised a tantalizing hope. Moreover they suggested a fresh tack to the harassed companies: First, a drive for Congressional legislation, modelled on the National Bank Acts, to "nationalize" insurance; then—or perhaps simultaneously—another try in the Supreme Court for acceptance of the Diversity-Comity Clause alchemy, or in the alternative, a decision holding insurance to be "commerce among the States."

Point by point, 1865–1871, this program failed utterly. First a national petition drive proved abortive. Agents obtained thousands of signatures; Congress was urged to enact "just and equal laws pertaining to interstate insurances"; bills were introduced at every session calling for a Federal Insurance Bureau and for national certification as an alternative to state controls. Yet Congress showed virtually no interest.[53]

Judicially, defeat was even more decisive. In a unanimous decision, November 1, 1869, less than three weeks after argument, the Su-

---

[51] *Ibid.* See also Dodd, Henderson, and Green, *supra* note 1; Swisher, Roger B. Taney c. 18 (1935); McGovney, *A Supreme Court Fiction*, 56 Harv. L. Rev. 853, 1090, 1225 (1943).

[52] 6 Fed. Cas. 546, No. 3230 (C.C. E.D. Pa. 1823).

[53] See Chapter 2, *supra* notes 63–69; Chapter 3, *supra* note 54.

preme Court in *Paul v. Virginia*[54] held that corporations were *not* "citizens" and that insurance was *not* "commerce." On January 9 and February 6, 1871, the doors thus slammed were barred and bolted.[55]

It was at this nadir of fortunes and strategy that counsel for the Continental Life Insurance Company of New York first expressly raised the point of the corporate constitutional "person" under Section One. The attack was made against a New Orleans ordinance of December 6, 1870, which had charged foreign companies double the $250 license fee required of locals. Unfortunately briefs in the case are missing.[56] Circumstances make clear however what inspired the action. Six months earlier, in June 1870, Mr. Justice Bradley, sitting on circuit with Judge Woods, had given a broad, liberal construction to Section One, and had permitted an *association* of New Orleans butchers who had been put out of business by a specially-chartered slaughter-house monopoly to claim the Amendment's protection.[57] The Court held the monopoly not to be a police measure, but rather one that deprived the associated butchers of their constitutionally-protected right to pursue a lawful calling. Only the Privileges or Immunities Clause was mentioned in the opinion, but Bradley, accepting the positions taken in arguments by former Justice John A. Campbell, expressly held the "equal protection of the laws" and the "right to pursue a lawful calling" both to be among the "privileges or immunities of citizens of the United States."[58] To the harrassed insurance companies, this was encouragement enough. Without delay, the Continental's counsel, James B. Eustis and Robert Hutchinson, invoked the protection of all three major clauses. The case was heard by Circuit Judge Woods,[59] an Ohio Republican recently appointed by President Grant. Yet again the companies

---

[54] 8 Wall. 168 (U.S. 1869).
[55] Ducat v. Chicago, 10 Wall. 410 (U.S. 1871); Liverpool Insurance Co. v. Massachusetts, 10 Wall. 566 (U.S. 1871).
[56] Insurance Co. v. New Orleans, 1 Woods 85, 13 Fed. Cas. 67, No. 7,052 (C.C. La. 1871); information from Clerk of the U.S. District Court, New Orleans. Any inclination the insurance companies might have had to take an appeal from Judge Woods' decision was reduced by the Louisiana Supreme Court's ruling in City of New Orleans v. Salamander Insurance Co., 25 La. Ann. 650 (1873), that under the revised revenue law of 1871 payment of a *state* license fee exempted companies from the municipal license. (See note appended to Insurance Co. v. New Orleans, 13 Fed. Cas. No. 7,052 at 69.)
[57] Livestock Dealers and Butchers Ass'n v. Crescent City Livestock Landing and Slaughter House Co., 4 Fed. Cas. 891, No. 2,234 (C.C. La. 1870), rev'sd 16 Wall. 36 (U.S. 1873).
[58] See CONNOR, JOHN A. CAMPBELL (1920) and TWISS, LAWYERS AND THE CONSTITUTION c. 3 (1942); Hamilton, *supra* note 45.
[59] See "William B. Woods," 20 DICT. AM. BIOG. 505 (1936).

were disappointed: Woods ruled adversely on every count. It was well established, he said, that corporations were not "citizens." Were corporations "persons"?

The Court's answer was simple and emphatic:

> The word "person" occurs three times in the first section . . . "All persons born or naturalized in the United States"—"nor shall any state deprive any person of life, liberty or property," etc.—"nor" shall any state "deny to any person within its jurisdiction the equal protection of the laws." The complainants claim that this last clause applies to corporations—artificial persons. Only natural persons can be born or naturalized; only natural persons can be deprived of life or liberty; so that it is clear that artificial persons are excluded from the first two clauses just quoted. If we adopt the construction claimed . . . , we must hold that the word "person," where it occurs the third time . . . , has a wider and more comprehensive meaning than in the other clauses . . . where it occurs. This would be a construction for which we find no warrant in the rules of interpretation. The plain and evident meaning of the section is, that the persons to whom the equal protection of the law is secured are persons born or naturalized or endowed with life and liberty, and consequently natural and not artificial persons. This construction of the section is strengthened by the history of the submission by Congress and the adoption by the states of the 14th amendment, so fresh in all minds as to need no rehearsal.[60]

Outwardly, the question at this date was simple enough to be decided by four-corners reasoning, with only a bolstering reference to history—"history so fresh in all minds as to need no rehearsal."

Yet Judge Woods evidently was unaware that the citizenship definition had been added the last minute in the Senate.[61] His "born or naturalized" argument, therefore, hardly was germane; certainly the constructional problem, so far as it related to the drafters' original intent, could not be determined by any such offhand analysis of the two juxtaposed sentences. Six months earlier, neither Justice Bradley nor Judge Woods had raised any objection to the Butchers Association claiming the benefits of Section One for its members. From his concurrence with Justice Bradley, it would seem that Judge Woods may have assumed they might do so. Fifteen years later, moreover, both judges were members of the Supreme Court when it unanimously accepted the corporate constitutional person.[62] This

---

[60] 1 Woods 85, 13 Fed. Cas. 67, No. 7,052, 68 (C.C. La. 1871).
[61] CONG. GLOBE, 39th Cong., 1st Sess. 2869 (1866).
[62] Santa Clara County v. Southern Pac. R.R., 118 U.S. 394 (1886); see note 191 *infra*, for Sanderson's argument.

vacillation suggests that Judge Woods may have been less assured than his opinion indicated—that he may even have remained so.

In his celebrated dissent of 1938,[63] Mr. Justice Black assumed positions similar to those of Judge Woods, and defended them on much the same grounds. "Neither the history nor the language of the Fourteenth Amendment," he contended, "justifies the belief that corporations are included within its protection." The "historical purpose" of the phraseology had been that set forth by Mr. Justice Miller in the *Slaughter-House Cases*[64]—protection of the freedmen, and of the colored race generally. Ratifying electorates and legislatures never had been told of any broader purpose. "The records of the time can be searched in vain for evidence that this Amendment was adopted for the benefit of corporations." True, Conkling had made his belated argument in the *San Mateo Case*, and four years later the Court had acquiesced. But "a secret purpose on the part of the [drafting] Committee, even if such be the fact . . . would not be sufficient to justify any such construction. The history of the Amendment proves that the people were told that its purpose was to protect weak and helpless human beings and were not told that it was intended to remove corporations in any fashion from the control of state governments."[65]

Justice Black then argued the text of the Amendment to be equally at odds with such a purpose. He substantially repeated Judge Woods' analysis, stressing again the unwarranted interpolations and double standards of construction necessary to make persons cover corporations in some instances but not others. Congress significantly had failed to employ the precise term "corporation."[65a]

> The judicial inclusion of the word . . . has had a revolutionary effect on our form of government. The states did not adopt the Amendment with knowledge of its sweeping meaning under its present construction. No section of the Amendment gave notice to the people that, if adopted, it would subject every state law and municipal ordinance, affecting corporations, (and all administrative action under them) to censorship of the United States courts. No word in all this Amendment gave any hint that its adoption would deprive the states of their long recognized power to regulate corporations. . . . I do not believe that the Fourteenth Amendment had that purpose, nor that the people believed it

---

[63] Connecticut General Life Insurance Co. v. Johnson, 303 U.S. 77, 83 (1938).
[64] 16 Wall. 36 (1873).
[65] 303 U.S. 85–87 (1938).
[65a] *Id.* at 87–88.

had that purpose, nor that it should be construed as having that purpose.[66]

In the most recent judicial attack upon the doctrine, Mr. Justice Douglas, dissenting for himself and Justice Black in the case of *Wheeling Steel Corporation v. Glander*,[67] in 1949, succinctly restated the arguments from language and history. It required "distortion," he contended,

> to read "person" as meaning one thing, then another within the same clause and from clause to clause. It means, in my opinion, a substantial revision of the Fourteenth Amendment.

The sound construction was that of Judge Woods in *Insurance Company v. New Orleans*. The Waite dictum in the *Santa Clara* case was wrong and should be overruled. Like Justice Black before him, Justice Douglas thought this question one of expediency, and for the people, not the courts, to decide:

> If they want corporations to be treated as humans are treated, if they want to grant corporations this large degree of emancipation from state regulation, they should say so. The Constitution provides a method by which they may do so. We should not do it for them through the guise of interpretation.[68]

These three opinions—written, it must be remembered, over a period of nearly eighty years—make up the judicial case against the corporate constitutional "person." The negative argument has been strikingly uniform and tenacious. Always it purports to analyze Section One as a whole. Yet it invariably disregards the fact that the first sentence defining citizenship in terms of "persons born or naturalized" did not appear in the three-clause text originally reported by the Joint Committee, but rather was added later in the Senate. The argument also stresses that "life" and "liberty" are joined with "property" in the Due Process Clause in a manner which requires either that the meaning of the word "person" be restricted throughout to human beings or else a varied application must be given the word within the clause: i.e., "no *natural* person shall be deprived of life, liberty, or property"; "no *artificial* person . . . of property."

---

[66] *Id.* at 89–90.
[67] 337 U.S. 562, 576 (1949).
[68] *Id.* at 581. Justice Douglas reiterated these views in his ALMANAC OF LIBERTY 321 (1954). See also his Cardozo Lecture, STARE DECISIS 9–10 (1949):
> "Thus without argument or opinion on the point, the *Santa Clara case* becomes one of the most momentous of all our decisions. . . . Corporations were now armed with constitutional prerogatives."

The core limitation in the Woods-Black-Douglas thesis however is supplied not by text, but by history. "Citizen" and "person," it is said, were intended to mean, and ought to mean, only citizens and persons of the Negro race. Such a construction admittedly involves an interpolation, but it is an interpolation, proponents say, which is justified and supported by history. The assumption is that all will be settled if history determines meaning. Experience of course suggests otherwise, as will be made clearer shortly. But the more fundamental difficulty is that this argument rests on the very inconsistency it attacks. For the *definition of citizenship* in Section One never has been, and cannot possibly be, restricted to persons of the Negro race. No one ever has proposed that it be, least of all Justices Douglas and Black. Since this is the case, and so long as the Negro race limitation has to be ignored in the first sentence, and can only be applied in the second, the rule of construction is no more satisfactory than the one it aims to supplant. Unquestionably this was one of the flaws that doomed Justice Miller's construction in the *Slaughter-House* cases.

So when the chips are down neither the four-corners analysis nor the judicial-notice-to-be-taken-of-history approach is, or can be, decisive. Both are seen to involve inherent difficulties and contradictions, and to rest on a construction of "person" which cannot be consistently applied to the textual framework. The negative case therefore rests at bottom on little more than theories of strict construction, of adherence to rigorous standards of judicial self-restraint, and (in the case of Justices Black and Douglas) to obviously strong, yet largely unelaborated views about the "revolutionary effect" which "judicial inclusion of the word . . . has had on our form of government." By this view, state legislative and administrative action pertaining to corporations has been subjected to "judicial censorship," and corporations have been "emancipat[ed] from state regulation." Such premises in turn presumably rest on views of corporations as autonomous business units, and on certain value judgments about the preferred size and number of such units and their relations to the coordinating powers of government.

Justices Black[69] and Douglas[70] consistently have taken the strongest stand for civil liberties; on several occasions they have main-

---

[69] Frank, Mr. Justice Black (1948).
[70] See Epstein, *Economic Predilection of Justice Douglas*, 1949 Wis. L. Rev. 531; *Justice Douglas and Civil Liberties*, 1951 Wis. L. Rev. 125; Irish, *Justice Douglas and Judicial Restraint*, 6 U. of Fla. L. Rev. 537 (1953).
See also Professor Pritchett's surveys, The Roosevelt Court: A Study In Judicial Politics and Values, 1937–1947 (1948); Civil Liberties and The Vinson Court (1954); Wood, Due Process of Law, 1932–1949 (1951).

tained that the Fourteenth Amendment was designed to incorporate the *entire* Bill of Rights, and that the Supreme Court should so hold.[71] Both Justices supported judicial elaboration of "freedom of speech" to include picketing; both dissented most frequently from the less libertarian trends of the Vinson Court, including those upholding legislative restrictions and limiting the constitutionally protected economic pressure incident to picketing.[72] Yet both Justices remain opposed to the corporate constitutional "person" and evidently are convinced that restrictive interpretation is desirable here even though the Court in recent years has so narrowed constructions of "economic" due process and substantive equal protection in the business field that corporate personality is now only of academic or hypothetical importance.[73]

It would appear therefore that the Black-Douglas positions are essentially a phase of the "preferred position" or "double standard" in constitutional construction.[74] Modern liberals often have favored a preferred position for basic First Amendment freedoms. Legislative or administrative action restricting freedom of speech or assembly must be held to stricter standards than action regulating property or its acquisition. The reason is simply that communication is the life blood of a free society; political processes will function best if such channels are open.

Pro-labor groups of course have gone further and insisted that picketing itself be viewed as essentially or even wholly as communication. Such assignment and predilections have been fiercely opposed by conservatives. Picketing, it is rejoined, is far more than free speech; it is a powerful economic weapon. To mistake it as constitutionally protected free speech is to yield an undesirable autonomy to organized labor, to shield labor from the coordinating powers of government, to shift presumptions of constitutionality, and to insulate activities that should be kept under strict social control.[75]

---

[71] See Adamson v. California, 332 U.S. 46, 68, 92–123 (1947); Chapter 7, *supra. Cf.* Kauper, *The First Ten Amendments*, 37 A.B.A.J. 717 (1951); Morrison, *Does the Fourteenth Amendment Incorporate the Bill of Rights?: The Judicial Interpretation*, 2 STAN. L. REV. 140 (1949).

[72] See the analyses cited *supra* notes 69, 70.

[73] On the Supreme Court's recent interpretation of due process, see WOOD, *op. cit. supra* note 70. *Cf.* Ballantine, *Tattered Ensign?: Due Process of Law Today Nationally*, 24 N.Y.S. BAR BULL. 103 (1952); Paulsen, *Persistence of Substantive Due Process in the States*, 34 MINN. L. REV. 91 (1950); *State Views on Economic Due Process*, 53 COL. L. REV. 827 (1953).

[74] On the origins and course of the doctrine, see PRITCHETT, *op. cit. supra* note 70, at 32–36, 242–243, 249; *cf.* Kauper, *supra* note 71.

[75] For moderately critical views of the doctrine, see Gregory, *Picketing and Free*

There is an Olympian irony in these reversed positions. Tables obviously are very easily turned. And the plain truth is that they have been: the corporate constitutional "person" tardily won his spurs in the Eighties by this very sort of broad constructionism and presumption shifting. Simple syllogistic reasoning and formulae can be nicely adapted to any cause—granted the premises and the social needs and trends to support them. Roscoe Conkling and his colleagues in the *San Mateo Case* emphatically were not labor lawyers. Indeed, their basic proposition proved of dubious benefit to labor—until corporations began to defend labor's rights[76] and labor itself began to incorporate. Whether these two respective camps realize it and relish it or not, "Picketing as free speech" and the "Corporation as a constitutional person" are something of brothers under the skin.

Yet this is not the cream of the jest. For in the search for assumed intrinsic meanings of Section One *via* purely four-corners reasoning many of the difficulties noted in the Woods-Black-Douglas opinions also inhere in the pro-corporate personality argument! Justices Black and Douglas already have pointed to a number of these. Others will be noted as discussion proceeds—as will the delight that the Railroad's lawyers found in similar forays and rebuttals. The heart of the matter is simply that *both* the anti-corporate and the pro-corporate personality arguments are cast largely in negative terms. Each camp prefers to exploit the difficulties and contradictions in opponents' constructions, rather than build on the limitations inherent in its own. The silences and the ambiguities of Section One are a source of mutual aid and comfort. What the framers *meant* to say, but didn't; how much more clearly they *might have said* what opponents contend or mistakenly assume to have been said—this also is the heart and substance of the affirmative arguments now to be considered. For a profession that over several centuries has built up elaborate rules of evidence, burden of proof, and statutory construction, and which traditionally is rigorous in use of logic and self-criticism, this is an amusing, though somewhat frustrating, performance. One begins to suspect that much more is at stake here than appears on the surface.

Speech, 26 A.B.A.J. 709 (1940); Teller, *Picketing and Free Speech*, 56 Harv. L. Rev. 180 (1942). *Cf.* Jones' rationale cited *supra* note 41.

[76] *But cf.* the anomalous position of the American Civil Liberties Union, a corporation, in Hague v. C.I.O., 307 U.S. 496 (1939), where the Court permitted only the individual respondents to maintain suit and claim protections of "liberty" under the Due Process Clause, notwithstanding corporate use of "liberty" in Grosjean v. American Press Co., 297 U.S. 233 (1936). See the documented criticism of the Court's position by Farage and Green, *supra* note 1.

An Innocent Abroad 391

It is obvious, at any rate, that it hardly will do for critics to condemn the Black-Douglas positions and arguments out of hand. Corporate personality, as will now appear, got its start in the Eighties from just such avowedly "liberal" and "latitudinarian"[77] constructions of Section One, and by demonstrating the weaknesses of the narrow Negro race rule rather than the inherent strength of its own.

III

Here again, a swift sketch of backgrounds is indispensable for the understanding of events. The years 1871-1882 witnessed a momentous struggle over the scope and meaning of the Fourteenth Amendment. In the *Slaughter-House Cases*[77a] a bare majority of the Court gave Section One the narrowest construction possible, first emasculating the Privileges or Immunities Clause by an ingenious *coup de main* originally suggested by Senator Trumbull two years before,[78] then going on to require that the entire section be construed in the light of the "one pervading purpose" of all three Reconstruction Amendments—namely, "the freedom of the slave race and the security and firm establishment of that freedom."[79] "Person," therefore, impliedly meant "person *of the Negro race.*" Justices Field, Bradley and Swayne, for the minority, fiercely attacked these positions, then and later, arguing in effect for broad Lockean conceptions of the "right to pursue the lawful callings" as one of the "fundamental rights" or "privileges" secured both to "persons" and "citizens," and both as "liberty" and "property."[80] These were the positions Justice Bradley and Judge Woods had taken in the *Slaughter-House* cases at circuit.

Justice Miller's majority interpretation of the due process and equal protection phrases, of course, stood during the Seventies; yet not without further challenge. Maine courts,[81] for one, repeatedly

---

[77] See Justice Field's premise, *Ex parte* Wall, 107 U.S. 265, 302 (1882): "all the guarantees of the Constitution designed to secure private rights, whether of person or property, should be broadly and liberally construed. . . ." For background and ramifications of this dictum, see Chapter 3, *supra*.
[77a] 16 Wall. 36 (U.S. 1873).
[78] See Chapter 7, *supra*.
[79] 16 Wall. 36, 71 (U.S. 1873).
[80] *Id.* at 83, 111, 124 for the Field, Bradley and Swayne dissents. See also Bartemeyer v. Iowa, 18 Wall, 129, 137 (U.S. 1874) for a vigorous restatement of Field's views as a member of a concurring minority.
[81] See the interesting line of cases which began before the *Slaughter-House* decision: Opinion of the Justices, 58 Me. 590, 595 (1871); Allen v. Jay, 60 Me. 124, 138 (1872); Maine v. Doherty, 60 Me. 504 (1872); Dunn v. Burleigh, 62 Me. 24 (1873); Portland v. Bangor, 65 Me. 120 (1876); Pearson v. Portland, 69 Me. 278 (1879).

applied the guarantees to persons other than Negroes when invalidating state legislation. Editors and publicists meanwhile lauded and advertised dissident and protestant views.[82] Most important of all, Mr. Justice Field, sitting at circuit, shrewdly made his *Slaughter-House* and *Bartemeyer*[83] minority views the law of the entire Pacific Coast.[84] This was done in a series of non-appealable habeas corpus decisions involving rights of Chinese aliens to fair treatment and livelihood.[85] Obviously few cases could have been better contrived to erode and undermine the *Slaughter-House* majority's intended restriction of Section One to persons *of the Negro race* than these Ninth Circuit judges' staunch defense of another persecuted *racial* minority.[86]

Moreover, a near climax developed in 1879 when the new California Constitution, as previously mentioned, prohibited corporations from employing Chinese. (Here surely is one answer to neat "human rights"–"property rights" dichotomies, and to the fetching belief a "double standard" or "preferred position" will long solve

---

[82] For quotations showing the unpopularity of the *Slaughter House* and *Granger* decisions in the Seventies and Eighties, see 3 WARREN, SUPREME COURT IN UNITED STATES HISTORY 261-266, 303-306, 316 (1922). Justice Field's minority opinions in the *Slaughter-House* and *Bartemeyer* cases were reprinted and widely circulated as tracts.

[83] See note 80 *supra*. The vehemence of Field's concurring opinion, and the apparent weakening of Justice Miller's *Slaughter-House* views in this case, *see* 18 Wall. 129, 133 (U.S. 1874), served to re-alert corporate counsel to the potentialities of the Fourteenth Amendment. J. C. Storrs, Chief Counsel of the Central Pacific Railroad, wrote immediately to his colleague, S. W. Sanderson, urging use of the Due Process Clause in various tax cases then pending. 6 HUNTINGTON-HOPKINS CORRESPONDENCE 174 (1874), in Stanford University Library.

[84] Considering its importance in undermining the *Slaughter-House* majority, remarkably little attention has been given to what critics in the Eighties denounced as "The Ninth Circuit Law." For a short documented account, see Chapter 3, *supra* (1943). Justice Field's subordinates agreed thoroughly with his views on the scope of the Fourteenth Amendment: Circuit Judge Sawyer wrote District Judge Deady, June 19, 1873, expressing the belief that Justice Miller's *Slaughter-House* opinion had eliminated him as a possible Chief Justice, replacing Chase recently deceased: "In my opinion, Miller is clearly wrong in that opinion; and I do not see how he could have made such a blunder, or how Hunt, Davis and Strong could have concurred in his view. . . . Field's opinion is able and Bradley's brief and pithy." (Deady Papers in Oregon Historical Society Library.) Yet originally Sawyer and Hoffman were amazed at Field's audacity in making his dissents the law of the Circuit, and declined to go along. See Sawyer to Deady, Oct. 16, 1874, quoted Chapter 3, *supra* at n.127. Later, both judges became staunch converts. See note 88 *infra*.

[85] The fact that Congress had made habeas corpus decisions non-reviewable by the Supreme Court, Act of March 27, 1868, 15 STAT. 44, § 2, following the decision in *Ex parte McCardle*, 6 Wall. 318 (U.S. 1868), 7 Wall. 506 (U.S. 1868), see SWISHER, STEPHEN J. FIELD CRAFTSMAN OF THE LAW 158-163 (1930), provided the closed-appellate basis for the Ninth Circuit Law. See Thompson, *Abuses of the Writ of Habeas Corpus*, 18 AM. L. REV. 1-23 (1884).

[86] For the role of the Chinese as pathfinders for corporations, and for equal protection as the spearhead of due process, see *supra* note 84.

such problems: Law and society breed their own categories.) Early in 1880, San Francisco corporation lawyers, among them Field's good friend Delos Lake, argued *Parrott's Chinese Case*[87] before Judges Sawyer and Hoffman. The odious and onerous anti-employment provision, they contended, not only infringed the alien's treaty rights and rights to equal protection and to pursuit of calling and livelihood as persons under the Fourteenth Amendment, but it also deprived the *corporations* of their correlative rights to due process of law and to equal protection of the laws because corporations too were "persons" within the meaning of Section One! Though, in the face of *Insurance Company v. New Orleans*, Judges Sawyer and Hoffman were themselves unwilling to go so far—and it was quite unnecessary that they should—the judges eagerly[88] voided the state constitutional provision as a violation of the aliens' right to labor and property—under both existent treaties and the Fourteenth Amendment. The corporate "person" clearly was on his way out of hibernation!

Life had been slow during the Seventies, yet never wholly extinct. At any time of course the Supreme Court might itself have elected to stand on *Insurance Company v. New Orleans*, perhaps ending the matter then and there. Yet courts are understandably reluctant to self-limit discretion and maneuverability; hence the door remained slightly ajar. Walking the narrow judicial line between annoyance and sufferance, corporate counsel simply went on *presuming* corporations to be persons and made due process arguments on the merits as best they were able.[89] During the Seventies these arguments were

---

[87] *In re* Tiburcio Parrott, 1 Fed. 481 (C.C. Cal. 1880). For summaries of Lake's argument, see *San Francisco Morning Call, Alta Californian*, March 7, 1880; *Sacramento Record-Union*, March 8, 1880. Lake also was an attorney for the Central Pacific; he died shortly before the *San Mateo* arguments.

[88] The day following passage of the bill Judge Sawyer confided to Judge Deady, "I shall have it before long when Baker will come into play." "Baker" was Baker v. Portland, 2 Fed. Cas. 472, No. 777 (C.C. Ore. 1879), a case in which Deady had voided a similar Oregon statute as a violation of treaty rights, relying in part on his own earlier opinion in Chapman v. Toy Long, 5 Fed. Cas. 497, No. 2,610 (C.C. Ore. 1876). Two months later Deady lamented in his *Journal* (April 10, 1880) that Judge Hoffman's opinion in the *Parrott* case had failed to "notice" his *Baker* and *Toy Long* opinions." "Sawyer does—but mincingly—I won't say grudgingly [notice] *Baker v. Portland*. I had a letter from him with the opinions in which he speaks of having used my 'wedge' with his little mallet as well as he could." This letter is missing in Deady's correspondence in the Oregon Historical Society, but the "wedge" of course was the treaty right to labor in self-support, while the "mallet" was the right under the Fourteenth Amendment of Chinese, and prospectively of corporations, to acquire and enjoy property—that is to say, "everything having exchangeable value," for Sawyer in his *Parrott* opinion, 1 Fed. 481, 506 (C.C. Cal. 1880), quoted with approval that definition from Justice Swayne's dissent in the Slaughter-House Cases, 16 Wall. 36, 127 (U.S. 1873); *cf.* COMMONS, *op. cit. supra* note 1, c. 2.

[89] Due process arguments were extensively made by lawyers for the corporations in

invariably and often curtly rejected,[90] but at times the Court's reasoning and dicta also seemed to presume corporate eligibility for due process and equal protection *in some form*.[91] Consciously or uncon-

---

the various Granger cases in both the state and federal courts. Arguments printed in 2–4 ANNUAL REPORT OF THE ILLINOIS RAILROAD AND WAREHOUSE COMMISSION (1872–1874) suggest that Corydon Beckwith, Chief Counsel for the Chicago and Alton Railroad, was one of the pioneers. Though necessarily much handicapped by Judge Woods' decision in *Insurance Co. v. New Orleans*, such arguments even gained limited judicial recognition. See Chief Justice Lawrence's opinion in Chicago-Alton R.R. v. People, 67 Ill. 11 (1873), substantially holding corporations persons "so far as necessary to protect their property and franchises against operation of a law that . . . condemns without a trial." *Id.* at 24. See also Judge Drummond's decision in Northwestern Fertilizing Co. v. Hyde Park, 18 Fed. Cas. 393, No. 10,336 (C.C. N.D. Ill. 1873) holding corporations within the Civil Rights Act of 1871. Both of these developments immediately preceded the Supreme Court's decision in the *Slaughter-House Cases* and were, of course, damped off thereby. The question is whether, and if so, how far the damping off was desired and intentional on the part of the Court.

[90] Use and misuse of due process in general was repelled most forcibly by Justice Miller in the Slaughter-House Cases, 16 Wall. 36, 80–81 (U.S. 1873), and in the non-corporate case, Davidson v. New Orleans, 96 U.S. 97, 103–104 (1878). In the former, Miller did everything possible to sap misuse of the phrase outright: "Under no construction . . . we have ever seen, or any . . . we deem permissible, can the restraint imposed by . . . Louisiana be held . . . a deprivation of property [without due process of law]." Four years later, in *Davidson*, counsel were again admonished, but the growl now belied the bite: "Some strange misconceptions" existed regarding scope of the provision. It had reposed unused in the Fifth Amendment for a century. Yet lately it had become the means for testing "in this Court the abstract opinions of every unsuccessful litigant in a state court of the justice of the decision against him, and of the merits of the legislation on which such a decision may be founded." Yet Miller went on to add, that it manifestly was impossible for the Court to define this phrase in advance. Resort must be had to the "gradual process of inclusion and exclusion." As matters developed the process was indeed both "due" and "gradual," for the Court patiently heard counsel for a railroad company employ the clause again that very day! See note 102 *infra*.

[91] In neither the *Granger* nor the Illinois Railroad Tax Cases, 92 U.S. 575 (1875), for example, was objection raised to corporate use of due process. This of course does not signify judicial approval of the corporate person—merely the absence of strong individual disapproval in those cases. It goes almost without saying that so long as the issue of the constitutional corporate person was not squarely joined in any case in the Seventies after *Insurance Co. v. New Orleans*, the significance of its tacit use and non-rejection is a very dubious and problematic matter. One clue or answer might lie in such abstract and unguarded dicta as Justice Hunt's in speaking for the Court in Home Insurance Co. v. Morse, 20 Wall. 445 (U.S. 1874) and relied on heavily in the Railroad briefs in the *San Mateo* case: "A corporation has the same right to the protection of the laws as a natural citizen, and the same right to appeal to all the courts of the country. The rights of an individual are not superior in this respect to that of a corporation." *Id.* at 455. Such language is open to countless interpretations and extensions, and can later be made as specific or as general as desired. Yet read together with Chief Justice Waite's dictum in the Sinking Fund Cases, 99 U.S. 700, 718 (1879), it is hard to escape the conclusion that the judicial will to see justice done to all, including corporations and shareholders, simply was stronger and more persistent than any innate doubts or caution about the judicial capacity or propriety of such a commitment. Surely few Americans would have it otherwise.

sciously, counsel and judges in state courts repeatedly showed similar tact and discretion.[92]

Socially as well as professionally there were excellent reasons for this mutual caution and deference. The Seventies saw a further rapid maturing of both the economy and judicial review. Large scale enterprise continued to transform the country. Sectional, partisan, and departmental antagonisms still cast ominous shadows. Times were hard, with great unrest and unemployment. Legislative morale and standards were both abominable and deteriorating; corruption and cinch legislation were widespread. The so-called Granger[93] laws, moreover, had forced a showdown on the regulability of "private" property, vindicating legislative power,[94] yet also leading Justice Field—supported now only by Justice Strong—to restate[95] his doctrinaire laissez-faire views and to *assume*, along with counsel[96] and *his brethren of the majority*, that corporations might at last plead the benefits of the Due Process Clause.

In short, a nation which already had committed its destinies to limited, representative, federal government; to judicial review; and finally and increasingly of late, to corporate enterprise, obviously had some tough, complex decisions to make—and these very soon![97]

---

[92] See, for example, the due process arguments made in the *Granger* and *Illinois Railroad Tax Cases* in the state courts, see TWISS, *op. cit. supra* note 58, c. 4 for summaries and Chief Justice Lawrence's dictum, quoted *supra* note 89. Holdings often were unfavorable. See 1 MONTHLY WESTERN JURIST 70 (June, 1874), reporting the decision of Judge Zane of the Circuit Court of Sangamon County in *People of Illinois v. Chicago and Alton Railroad Co.*—Fourteenth Amendment and Civil Rights Act of 1871 apply to natural persons only; see also *id.* at 186 for a related case in Judge Drummond's U. S. Circuit Court.

[93] See BUCK, THE GRANGER MOVEMENT (1913); Fairman, *The So-Called Granger Cases*, 5 STAN. L. REV. 587 (1953); Miller, *Origins of the Iowa Granger Law*, 40 MISS. V. HIST. REV. 657 (1954).

[94] Munn v. Illinois, 94 U.S. 113 (1877). See Hamilton, *Affectation With a Public Interest*, 39 YALE L.J. 1089 (1930); McAllister, *Lord Hale and Business Affected With a Public Interest*, 43 HARV. L. REV. 759 (1930). Both articles are reprinted in 2 SEL. ESSAYS ON CONSTITUTIONAL LAW (1938).

[95] Dissenting in Munn v. Illinois, 94 U.S. 113, 136 (1877); and Chicago, B. & Q. R.R. v. Cutts, 94 U.S. 155, 183 (1877). See *id.* at 186 for passage attacking the *Munn* decision as "practically destroy[ing] all the guarantees of the Constitution . . . invoked by counsel for the protection of the rights of the railroad companies." Of what avail, Field asked, was the "constitutional provision that no state shall deprive any person of his property except by due process of law, if the state can, by fixing the compensation which he [sic] may receive for its use, take from him all that is valuable in the property?"

[96] For arguments of counsel, including former Chief Justice Lawrence (*supra* note 89) presuming corporate personality, see Winona etc. Ry. v. Blake, 24 L.Ed. 99, 100 (1875).

[97] The strong pro- and anti- approaches to the constitutional corporate person have tended to obscure the degree to which the Supreme Court's problem was one of fitting the corporation into the institution of judicial review as a whole and as that

Courts and judges were torn between traditional solicitude for corporate and property rights on the one hand, and deference to the police power on the other. If not yet explicitly, at least implicitly, the constitutional and public law status of the corporation became ever more insistent and central.

In this environment, phrases like "due process of law" and "equal protection of the laws" began to assume spectacular new dimensions. All the possibilities shown before 1866, and during the slavery debates,[98] now were manifest in defense of business and property. Such trends and results were at first highly irksome to judges like Chief Justice Waite[99] and Justice Miller.[100] On several occasions Miller berated counsel for "strange misconceptions" of due process.[101] Yet he himself displayed many of the same "natural rights" predilections; and on one occasion, in 1879, sat patiently through another "misuse" of due process—and by corporate counsel at that—on the very same afternoon,[102] apparently without the slightest disposition

---

institution had developed prior to 1880. Historians like BEARD and WEBB, *op. cit. supra* note 38, have made the outcome appear largely one of passive accommodation on the part of the courts to the desires of Business. Yet this is gross distortion. Once the pre-Civil War constitutional status of the corporation is seen in the large as surveyed by HENDERSON and DODD, *op. cit. supra* note 1, and once the significance of Professor Corwin's emphasis on the police power-vested rights dichotomy in the pre-Civil War law is grasped, it is clear that the corporate constitutional person, together with substantive due process-equal protection, was the one doctrine that stood to preserve the Court's historic powers and discretion and enable it, at the same time, to safeguard the public interest. It often is overlooked that the Court rejected the automatic and unworkable system of *laissez-faire* implicit in corporate citizenship under the Privileges or Immunities and Comity Clauses and accepted this alternative that enabled the judiciary to continue doing its job. Surely it would be less than fair to assume that the Court either could or should have pursued a course which would have amounted to abdication of its functions. Moreover, the unfortunate accompaniments of corporate personality were in large part the result of 1) failure of Congress to overhaul the federal appellate system in a period of rapid business expansion, see FRANKFURTER AND LANDIS, BUSINESS OF THE SUPREME COURT c. 2 (1927), 2) imprudent interpretations of what constituted due process or equal protection rather than of who properly were regardable as "persons." The vital point is that due process and equal protection were the two clauses that possessed maximum flexibility and that flexibility was the *sine qua non* of post-Civil War review given the pre-War developments. Moreover, the recasting of due process in the United States had itself begun long before the War, and the courts on the whole followed, rather than lead, the procession. See Chapter 5, *supra*. These facts must be borne in mind in assessing the overall statesmanship of the doctrine we are considering.

98 See Chapters 1–5, *supra*; and TENBROEK, *op. cit. supra* note 32.
99 See TRIMBLE, CHIEF JUSTICE WAITE: DEFENDER OF THE PUBLIC INTEREST (1938).
100 See FAIRMAN, MR. JUSTICE MILLER AND THE SUPREME COURT (1939).
101 See note 90 *supra*.
102 Railroad Co. v. Richmond, 96 U.S. 521 (1878), was argued the same day (January 7, 1878) that Miller spoke for the Court in Davidson v. New Orleans, 96 U.S. 97 (1878).

to cut this gordian knot! More significantly still, Chief Justice Waite, in the *Sinking Fund Cases*[103] (possibly after some prodding by Justice Field?[104]) stated emphatically in a dictum that by the Due Process Clause of the Fifth Amendment, "The United States . . . are prohibited from depriving persons *or corporations* of property without due process of law."[105] Just a year later, in 1880—and at the very moment of the resurrection of the corporate person in *Parrott's Case*, and of the first affirmative use of the Fourteenth Amendment by the Supreme Court in the *Virginia Civil Rights Cases*[106]—Judge Thomas M. Cooley lent the prestige of his name to a similar dictum: "It cannot be necessary at this day to enter upon a discussion in denial of the right of . . . Government to take from either individuals *or corporations* any property . . . rightfully . . . acquired. . . . It is immaterial in what way the property was lawfully acquired . . . it is enough it has become private property, and it is then protected by the law of the land."[107]

Meanwhile the Supreme Court was undergoing one of its sudden and periodic changes of personnel.[108] Between November, 1877, and March, 1882, Justices Davis, Strong, Swayne, Clifford, and Hunt were succeeded respectively by Justices Harlan, Woods, Gray, Matthews and Blatchford. The four latter changes occurred during the fifteen months, December, 1880, to March, 1882; and of the five, four were of Judges who had made up the various majorities in the *Slaughter-House*, *Granger*, and *Sinking Fund Cases*.[109]

Finally, these events were paralleled by a deepening crisis in the affairs of the Central Pacific and Southern Pacific Railroads. Here again the immediate cause was the new California Constitution, in which a coalition of Kearney's Workingmen's Party with representatives of disgruntled agrarians had played so decisive a part.[110] Not only had an elective railroad commission been created, with full investigative and regulatory powers over rates and service,[111] but railroads operating in more than one county were henceforth to be

---

[103] 99 U.S. 700, 718 (1879).
[104] See TRIMBLE, *op. cit. supra* note 99, and Chapter 3, *supra* note 102.
[105] 99 U.S. at 718.
[106] Strauder v. West Virginia, 100 U.S. 303 (1880), and two other cases decided March 1, 1880.
[107] Detroit v. Detroit etc. R.R., 43 Mich. 140, 147 (submitted January 20, decided April 7, 1880).
[108] See 3 WARREN, *op. cit. supra* note 82, at 482.
[109] Miller, Strong, Hunt, Davis and Clifford comprised the *Slaughter-House* majority; Waite, Miller, Bradley, Davis, Hunt, Swayne and Clifford, the *Granger* majority; the *Sinking Fund* majority was the *Granger* grouping with Harlan in place of Davis.
[110] See SWISHER, *op. cit. supra* note 3.
[111] CALIF. CONST. 1879, Art. 12, §§ 21-23.

assessed as a whole by a State Board of Equalization—also elective—with the values prorated to the counties[112]—and not figured simply at the cost of scrap iron, rollingstock and right of way by naive county assessors as before. Finally, such railroads were denied the privilege, extended by the constitution to individuals, of deducting the amount of their mortgages[113]—the good reason being that the railroads, unlike other property, were mortgaged for *more* than cost, yet still paid handsome dividends, while their bonds were, of course, held largely out of state, and by the federal government.

Beginning in 1880, the Companies' assessments and tax bills soared[114] and railroad counsel rapidly exhausted, one by one, their resources in the state courts.[115] Finally, in January, 1882, the state supreme court upheld[116] both the assessment and mortgage deduction provisions, overruling due process and Fourteenth Amendment arguments by reference to *Insurance Company v. New Orleans.*

It was at this critical point that the Railroads removed their cases to the federal courts. On February 8, Roscoe Conkling, only recently resigned from the United States Senate, received a $5,000 retainer from the Railroads.[117] Evidently plans were afoot even at this date to carry the cases through to the Supreme Court. An army of counsel began recasting and elaborating the various briefs used before the state judges. Came August, and the cases were attentively heard[118]

---

[112] *Id.* Art. 13, §§ 9–10.

[113] *Id.* Art. 13, § 4.

[114] $6,000 per mile had been the assessed valuation in Nevada and on many sections of the line in California prior to the new Constitution. See 10 HOPKINS, CORRESPONDENCE 179–189, and HOPKINS, DOCUMENTS 40 (Stanford University Library) for correspondence showing the manner and degree of the Railroad's control, 1869, and for 1872–73 tax memoranda. Tables showing the various railroad assessments, 1880–1887, are in the PROCEEDINGS, ASSEMBLY JUDICIARY COMMITTEE, 28th Sess. cited *infra* note 119.

[115] For a concise summary of this complex litigation, dated Dec. 1, 1882, see CALIF. STATE BOARD OF EQUALIZATION REPORT, 1881–82, 11–19. The leading appellate cases are People v. Supervisors of Sacramento County, 59 Cal. 321 (1881); San Francisco N. Pac. R.R. v. State Board of Equalization, 60 Cal. 12 (1882).

[116] Central Pacific R.R. v. Board of Equalization, 60 Cal. 58 (1882). After this decision, suits for taxes were begun by the state and counties on April 22, 1882; the Railroad's answer was filed May 25, 1882; on June 30, 1882, the test cases were removed to the Federal court, Justice Field accepting jurisdiction in County of San Mateo v. Southern Pacific R.R., 13 Fed. 145 (1882). See especially pp. 149–152 wherein Field set up targets and resynthesized his dicta from the earlier Ninth Circuit Chinese opinions.

Previous to the raising of the constitutional question in the San Mateo case, the Railroad had exhausted its defenses in the Federal court. See Huntington v. Palmer, 7 Saw. 355, 8 Fed. 499 (C.C. Cal. 1881). Throughout Railroad counsel offered to "compromise" the cases at 60% of the amounts due; but state and county officials (other than Sacramento county) refused.

[117] See U. S. PACIFIC RAILWAY COMMISSION, *Testimony,* SEN. EXEC. DOC. NO. 51, 50th Cong., 1st Sess. 4795 (1887) (Hereinafter cited U.S. PAC. RY. COMM.).

[118] See notes 157, 158 *infra.*

An Innocent Abroad 399

by Justice Field and Circuit Judge Sawyer, sitting in San Francisco.

For all who are seeking insight into the forces and ideas that reshaped the Fourteenth Amendment and judicial review in the Eighties, these arguments[119] hold an absorbing interest. Indeed, they often are a revelation, with a drama and logic all their own. An entire volume could scarcely do them justice. The fallacies and lopsidedness of the economics soon are baldly apparent. Cynicism and smugness are sometimes appalling. Viewed in perspective and in context, the corporate "person" shrinks into insignificance beside the values and premises being purveyed in its name. The themes therefore often are of decidedly less interest than the counterpoint. History beyond question here becomes a powerful aid to understanding.

One after another skillful counsel devoted themselves to reviving and activating the Fourteenth Amendment—not primarily for the benefit of corporations, of course, but to realize the purposes of the framers!

What was taking shape is made clear in a passage from the argument of Creed Haymond,[120] a draftsman of the original California codes, and one of the most astute of the Railroad's Machiavellis at Sacramento. Haymond hammered mercilessly on the broad, unqualified character of Section One. Any affirmative *intent* to limit its protection to the Negro race, he insisted, would have been expressed unequivocally. Yet

> neither the word "negro" nor the phrase "colored citizen" was inserted in that amendment. Great men and great lawyers participated in its enactment. Men like Conkling and Edmunds, and Bingham, its author, men . . . well versed in the mysteries of the language . . . and if they had intended to narrow its meaning in this respect, I submit . . . they would have said: "No State shall make or enforce any law which shall abridge the privileges or immunities of *colored citizens* of the United States, nor shall any State deprive any *negro* of life, liberty or property without due

---

[119] A convenient collection is ARGUMENTS AND DECISIONS, COUNTY OF SAN MATEO V. SOUTHERN PACIFIC RAILROAD in Stanford University Library (hereinafter cited ARGUMENT). The arguments of railroad counsel before the Supreme Court of the United States are reprinted in PROCEEDINGS OF THE COMMITTEE ON THE JUDICIARY REGARDING RAILROAD TAX SUITS, CALIFORNIA LEGISLATURE, ASSEMBLY, 28th Sess., Journal Appendix, v. 8, no. 3 (1889) (hereinafter cited PROCEEDINGS). Pages 77–111 reprint Conkling's argument; pp. 111–20; George F. Edmunds'; pp. 120–143, S. W. Sanderson's. Page references hereafter are to the Stanford copies of the Circuit Court arguments, to the Judiciary committee reprint of the Supreme Court arguments; and to the constitutional portions of CONKLING'S ARGUMENT as reprinted Chapter 1, *supra*, with original paging shown.

[120] Haymond, ARGUMENT, *supra* note 119.

process of law, nor deny to any negro within its jurisdiction the equal protection of the law."

If the object and purpose of that amendment had been what my friends on the other side claim it to be, how easy would it have been to have made the language conform to that intention. We may concede that the occasion of the amendment was the protection of that unfortunate and unhappy race. All general laws have for their occasion some special circumstance; but the language of general laws is necessarily broad and comprehensive, and they may —indeed, always do—include cases other than those which were the cause of their enactment.[121]

Haymond concluded with the reminder that in the *Dartmouth College Case*[122] John Marshall had refused to adopt a restrictive interpretation of the word "contracts." Instead, the Chief Justice adopted one which proved a bulwark of corporate rights for two generations. The force of analogy and precedent could hardly have been made clearer.

The ablest, most forcible, and certainly the *key* argument was made by John Norton Pomeroy,[123] since 1879, first Professor of Municipal Law in Hastings Law College. Pomeroy already was widely known as a legal scholar and writer. From the moment of his entry into the compact professional community of San Francisco, he had grown steadily in rank and influence. Friendship with Justice Field developed as a matter of course. Letters written by the Justice reveal a growing intimacy and esteem.[124] During the winter of 1880–81, Pomeroy prepared the appreciative "Introductory Sketch" of Field's career which later was published in the biography designed to promote the Justice's Presidential aspirations.[125] Field in turn recommended Pomeroy's employment to Mr. Lloyd Tevis, a friend high in the counsels of the Stanford-Huntington group. At this same date (June, 1881) Field confided to Pomeroy that he also had written Mr. A. N. Towne, General Manager of the Central Pacific and Southern

---

121 *Id.* at 17–18. For the speciousness of such arguments, see Chapter 7, *supra*.
122 4 Wheat. 518 (U.S. 1819).
123 See Pomeroy, *John Norton Pomeroy* in 8 GREAT AMERICAN LAWYERS 91 (1909); Chapter 3, *supra*, *Four Letters of Mr. Justice Field*; Leary, *John Norton Pomeroy, 1828–1885; A Biographical Sketch*, 47 LAW LIB. J. 138 (1954) (a bibliography of works by and about Pomeroy). "Points and authorities" for the Railroad also were submitted to the Circuit court by McAllister and Bergin; oral arguments were made by T. B. Bishop of Garber, Thornton & Bishop, and T. I. Bergin. All touched on the corporate person, but added nothing to points otherwise covered. All are preserved in printed form in ARGUMENT, *supra* note 119.
124 See Chapter 3, *supra*.
125 *Id.* at 101.

Pacific Railroads, "urging the officers . . . to retain your professional services."[126] Sometime thereafter, Pomeroy had been retained by the companies, apparently for four months at a salary of $10,000 per year.[127] The elaborate brief and argument thus commissioned naturally are of extraordinary interest.[128]

Pomeroy's thesis was simple. "The grand object" of the Fourteenth Amendment had been to "protect life, limb and liberty of all natural persons, and the *property* of all persons, whether natural or legal." This thesis he developed fully, elaborating positions he had assumed as far back as 1868[129] while the Amendment was being ratified. The framers, in his view, had perceived and corrected a grave defect in the American Constitution:

> The prohibitions of the early series of the Amendments, (1-8), . . . were addressed to the United States Government alone, . . . not to the States. States might, by unjust legislation or administration, invade the personal and property rights of individuals in many ways and the wrong . . . be wholly without the jurisdiction of the United States Courts or Legislature. . . . [S]uch State legislation had been repeatedly upheld by the United States Supreme Court, because there was nothing in the . . . Constitution to prevent it, . . .
>
> This grave evil, this strange omission . . . often [had] been noticed and deplored. . . . To remedy [it], Section one . . . was drawn in . . . broad comprehensive terms; . . . the remedy is perfect, the omission is completely supplied . . . [Emancipation undoubtedly was the occasion for the passage; protection of the freedmen one of the leading motives.] . . . But the language of the Amendment . . . and the whole . . . political history of the country demonstrate . . . that its interpretation was not intended to be *confined* to the protection of the blacks.[130]

---

[126] *Id.* at 103-104.

[127] See 8 U.S. PAC. RY. COMM., *Testimony, supra* note 117, at 4727. The Commission's audit of the Legal Expense Account of the Central Pacific Railroad here shows "J. W. Pomeroy, services, Oct. 2, 1882, $3333.33." The reference undoubtedly is to J. N. Pomeroy. Ten thousand dollars per year was the amount paid by the Railroad to Haymond, W.H.L. Barnes, W.W. Stow, Delos, Lake, McAllister, and Bergin and others of its senior legal staff. Wilson and Wilson drew $12,000 yearly and S.W. Sanderson, chief counsel, $24,000. See *Ibid.* Pomeroy also received $2500, Oct. 1883 for his services on the *Santa Clara Case; id.* at 4734.

[128] Pomeroy, ARGUMENT, supra note 119. Pages 21-33 cover the corporate person, and 84-95 equal protection.

[129] See POMEROY, AN INTRODUCTION TO THE CONSTITUTIONAL LAW OF THE UNITED STATES §§ 235-238 (1st ed. 1868). It has been overlooked that here, and also in two articles, *The Force Bill*, 12 THE NATION 268-270 (1871), and *Rights of Citizens*, 12 THE NATION 335 (1871), Pomeroy expressed the view that the Fourteenth Amendment was declaratory and made the Bill of Rights binding on the states.

[130] POMEROY, ARGUMENT, *supra* note 119, at 21-24.

In the teeth of the prevailing Miller-Waite constructions, this was strong meat. Yet Pomeroy was no more disposed to face the fact than were his associates or the judges he addressed. It was true, he conceded, that the Supreme Court majority originally had taken a "much narrower" view; "The construction proposed by Justice Miller ha[d] very naturally been approved by a few of the State Courts." But that construction, he argued, had "been finally abandoned, the views of the *Slaughter-House* minority had gained increasing support. Of this the Maine[131] and Ninth Circuit Chinese[132] holdings were adduced as proof (with gaps and bare spots landscaped with extra and irrelevant citations). Finally, in a labored section the 1880 *Civil Rights Cases*[133] and *Missouri v. Lewis*[134] were hailed as evidence that the Supreme Court itself had at last "wholly abandoned the theory that [the Fourteenth Amendment] was designed [simply] to protect the negro citizens." Rather, the Amendment's scope and operation had been "extended" "to *all* persons, and to all State legislation wrongfully invading the rights of any persons."[135]

Certainly this was an argument such as could have been made only before a very uncritical, sympathetic Court. Pomeroy of course was correct in this view that Congress had intended to nationalize the major civil rights, securing these to all persons regardless of race.[136] It was equally true that the text of Section One was a tremendous embarrassment to all who would limit it solely to one race. Furthermore, the Maine and Chinese cases were *prima facie* evidence that Miller's Negro Race interpretation was beginning to give way, even if it was not yet utterly doomed.

Very shrewdly Pomeroy had insinuated the notion—challengable, but nevertheless prophetic—that once

> the narrow interpretation confining the Amendment to the protection of negroes is abandoned, *then there is no possible limit at which its operation can be stopped short of the broad, comprehensive meaning which I have given.* If the language is not confined to negroes, it must extend to *all* persons, and its field of operation

---

131 See note 81 *supra*.
132 See notes 84–86 *supra*. The major Chinese cases, aside from those cited *supra* notes 4 and 88, were *In re Ah Fong*, 1 Fed. Cas. 213, No. 102 (C.C. Cal. 1874); *Ho Ah Kow v. Nunan*, 12 Fed. Cas. 252, No. 5546 (C.C. Cal. 1879), discussed Chapter 3 *supra*.
133 *Strauder v. West Virginia*, 100 U.S. 303 (1880).
134 101 U.S. 22 (Argued March 3, 1880 by G.F. Edmunds and J.F. Black for the plaintiff; decided April 12, 1880).
135 Pomeroy, ARGUMENT, *supra* note 119, at 28.
136 See Chapter 7, *supra*.

must be identical with that of the Fifth Amendment and of similar guarantees in the State Constitutions.[136a]

Here again, the strategy was not to attempt to justify corporate personality on its merits, but simply to *assume* that corporations were persons or property—convenient little bundles of property like money or tools—and that no sensible person ever had thought or held or wanted it otherwise! Thus

> While Justice Bradley [in *Missouri v. Lewis*] was laying down these rules, and protecting the equal rights of all *persons* under the Fourteenth Amendment, can it be supposed that he tacitly excepted corporations from the operation of his general language?[136b]

Again

> Can it be pretended that a statute might deny to the corporations, or to any class of the corporations in the same situation and under the same circumstances, the right to resort to these Courts for redress, and that such a statute would be valid because it did not violate the Fourteenth Amendment?[136c]

Without corporate personality, property was defenseless, expropriation and chaos were certain. With it, the way would be safe and clear:

> [I]f corporations are not embraced within the guaranties of the Fourteenth Amendment, then the States may so legislate as to deny to all corporations, or to any class of them, such as railroads, . . . [their rights and] property without due process of law, and against such legislation there would be no redress, no protection, no prevention. In short, the States might with impunity confiscate the thousands of millions of capital invested in the railroads of the country. The Fourteenth Amendment may prove to be the only bulwark and safeguard by which to protect the great railroad systems of the country against the spirit of communism which is everywhere threatening their destruction or confiscation.[136d]

IV

Justice Field's circuit opinion,[137] written largely from these briefs, is an extremely interesting and subtle document. We are concerned here of course only with those sections touching the vital issue:

[136a] *Id.* at 22. Pomeroy's italics.
[136b] *Id.* at 32. Pomeroy's italics.
[136c] *Id.* at 32-33.
[136d] Pomeroy, ARGUMENT, *supra* note 119, at 33.
[137] The Railroad Tax Case: County of San Mateo v. Southern Pacific Railroad, 8 Saw. 238, 13 Fed. 722 (C.C. Cal. 1882).

> Is the defendant, being a corporation, a person within the meaning of the Fourteenth Amendment, so as to be entitled, with respect to its property, to the equal protection of the laws? The learned counsel of the plaintiff, and the Attorney-General of the State, take the negative . . . and assert with much earnestness that the amendment applies, and was intended to apply, only to the newly made citizens of the African race, and should be limited to their protection. . . .
>
> Though the occasion of the Amendment was the supposed denial of rights in some States to newly made citizens of the African race, and the supposed hostility to the Union men, the generality of the language used extends the protection of its provisions to persons of every race and condition against discriminating and hostile State action of any kind. . . .
>
> The argument that a limitation must be given to the scope of this amendment, because of the circumstances of its origin, is without force. Its authors, seeing how possible it was for the States to oppress without relief from the Federal Government, placed in the Constitution an interdict upon their action, which makes lasting oppression of any kind by them under the form of law impossible.[138]

The protections of the Contracts Clause, Field went on, had not been confined to commercial contracts impaired by stay and tender laws such as the Fathers unquestionably had in mind. In the *Dartmouth College Case* Marshall had extended the protection to executed contracts such as charters. And Marshall there had said: "The case being within the words of the rule, must be within its operation likewise, unless there be something in the literal construction so obviously absurd or mischievous, or repugnant to the general spirit of the instrument, as to justify those who expound the Constitution in making it an exception."[139]

> Following that authority [Field continued] we cannot adopt the narrow view . . . and limit . . . application . . . of the Fourteenth Amendment to . . . members of the enfranchised race. It has a much broader application. It does not, indeed, place any limit upon the subjects in reference to which the States may legislate. It does not interfere with their police power. . . . They can legislate now, as they always could, to promote the health, good order, and peace of the community, to develop their resources, increase their industries, and advance their prosperity; but it does require that

---

[138] *Id.* at 257, 259, 260, 13 Fed. at 738, 740, 740.
[139] 4 Wheat. 518, 644 (U.S. 1819).

in all such legislation, hostile and partial discrimination against any class or person shall be avoided; that the States shall impose no greater burdens upon any one than upon others of the community under like circumstances, nor deprive any one of rights which others similarly situated are allowed to enjoy. It forbids the State to lay its hand more heavily upon one than upon another under like conditions. It stands in the Constitution as a perpetual shield against all unequal and partial legislation by the State, and the injustice which follows from it, whether directed against the most humble, or the most powerful; against the despised laborer from China, or the envied master of millions.[140]

Field was explicit and emphatic that the War Amendments had brought this to pass. The Fourteenth, he implied, had made guarantees of the Federal Bill of Rights binding upon the States. As Judge Cooley had put it, "The first ten [Amendments] took from the Union no power it ought ever to have exercised; . . . the last three required of the States the surrender of no power which any free government should ever employ."[140a] Accordingly, Field concluded, "It would . . . tend to defeat the great purpose of the late amendments if to any of them we should give the narrow construction for which counsel contend."[141]

With the Miller-Waite *Slaughter-House-Granger* battery neutralized, Field marched ahead. Private corporations, were, he admitted, artificial persons. But "they consist of aggregations of individuals united for some legitimate business." In California they were formed under general laws for any purpose for which individuals might lawfully associate themselves. Any five or more persons might form themselves into a corporation. As a matter of fact, nearly all enterprises requiring large capital were undertaken by corporations. After a ringing passage recounting the uses and accomplishments of the corporation, its necessity and ubiquity in the modern world, Field declared:

> There are over five hundred corporations in this State; there are thirty thousand in the United States, and the aggregate value of their property is several thousand millions. It would be a most singular result [he continued] if a constitutional provision, intended for the protection of every person against partial and discriminating legislation by the States, should cease to exert such

---

[140] 8 Saw. at 261–262, 13 Fed. at 741.
[140a] Cooley, General Principles of Constitutional Law 202 (1880).
[141] 8 Saw. at 263–264, 13 Fed. at 743.

protection the moment the person becomes a member of a corporation.¹⁴²

Such a conclusion was unacceptable—indeed unthinkable.

On the contrary, we think it is well established by numerous adjudications of the Supreme Court of the United States, and of the several States, that whenever a provision of the Constitution, or of a law, guarantees to persons the enjoyment of property, or affords to them means for its protection, or prohibits legislation injuriously affecting them, the benefits of the provision extend to corporations, and the Courts will always look beyond the name of the artificial being to the individuals whom it represents.¹⁴²ᵃ

This is artful rhetoric. *Constitutional* corporate personality is equated with *statutory* and *treaty* corporate personality. Then constitutional corporate personality impliedly is "well established" by "numerous adjudications" drawn wholly from the statutory and treaty fields. Yet the "Corporations-are-persons" premise is not pressed to conclusion; rather, only the minimal claim or technique of "looking through the corporate form" to the shareholders as natural persons. That is to say, Field employed the technique so long and effectively used by judges and counsel prior to the Civil War in the analogous corporate *citizenship* cases under the Diversity Clause.¹⁴³

Finally, Field turned to the narrow and equivocal use of the word "person" in the Fifth Amendment. He conceded that this phraseology, which he quoted, seemed to apply only to natural persons:

> No others can be witnesses; no others can be twice in jeopardy of life or limb, or compelled to be witnesses against themselves; and, therefore, it might be said with much force that the word person there used in connection with the prohibition against the depri-

---

142 *Id.* at 264–265, 13 Fed. at 743–744. Justice Field here greatly underestimated the number of corporations. The reporter noted in a footnote, *id.* at 265, 13 Fed. at 744, that there were over 5000 corporations in California alone. Reliable figures however are unavailable for this period. In 1880 there were 8397 certificates of corporation on file in the office of the San Francisco County Clerk alone, but this presumably included many dead corporations. See J. Hoffman's opinion, *In re* Tiburcio Parrott, 1 Fed. 481, 486 (C.C. Cal. 1880).

142a 8 Saw. at 256, 13 Fed. at 744.

143 See Dodd and Henderson, *op. cit. supra* note 1; and McGovney, *supra* note 51, at 874, 1234. In the early corporate personality and citizenship cases it was less often contended that corporations were persons or citizens than that "citizens [or persons] do not lose their rights when acting in a corporate capacity." See, for example, William Curtis Noyes' statement to that effect in his argument in Fire Dep't v. Wright, 3 E.D. Smith 453, 457 (C.P.N.Y. 1854), in the industry's curious attack on taxes levied on foreign insurance companies for the benefit of local fire departments.

vation of life, liberty and property without due process of law, is in like manner limited to a natural person. But such has not been the construction of the Courts. A similar provision is found in nearly all the State Constitutions; and everywhere, and all times, and in all Courts, it has been held, either by tacit assent or by express adjudication, to extend, so far as their property is concerned, to corporations. ["Everywhere, and at all times, and in all Courts, . . . by tacit assent or express adjudication!" Not even an inkling of *Insurance Co. v. New Orleans!* Rather, an assertion that Americans *always* had presumed or held corporate property to be protected by the due process clauses!] And this has been, [he continued] because the property of a corporation is in fact the property of the corporators. [Here again, be it noted, insistence only on the narrower, safer proposition!]¹⁴⁴

Then followed an argument *ad hominem* which throws light not only on Field's orientation, but on the forces already tugging at the meanings of "deprived" and "property":

To deprive the corporation of its property, *or to burden it*, is in fact, to deprive the corporators of their property *or to lessen its value.* Their interest, undivided though it be, and constituting only a right during the continuance of the corporation to participate in its dividends, and on its dissolution to receive a proportionate share of its assets, *has an appreciable value*, and is *property in a commercial sense*; and *whatever affects the property of the corporation* necessarily affects the *commercial value of their interest.* If, for example, . . . a corporation created for banking purposes acquires land, notes, stocks, bonds, and money, no stockholder can claim that he owns any particular item of this property, but he owns an interest in the whole of it which the Courts will protect against unlawful seizure or appropriation by others, and on the dissolution of the company he will receive a proportionate share of its assets. Now, if a statute of the State takes the entire property, who suffers loss by the legislation? Whose property is taken? Certainly the corporation is deprived of its property; but, at the same time, in every just sense of the constitutional guaranty, the corporators are also deprived of their property.¹⁴⁵

It was true, he conceded, that "the prohibition against the deprivation of life and liberty," did not apply to corporations. "Nor do all the privileges or immunities of citizenship attach to corporations," *Paul v. Virginia*¹⁴⁶ definitely had settled it that corporations were not "citizens."

---
¹⁴⁴ 8 Saw. at 267-268, 13 Fed. at 746-747.
¹⁴⁵ *Id.* at 268-269, 13 Fed. at 747 [Emphasis supplied].
¹⁴⁶ 8 Wall. 168 (U.S. 1869).

After these not more than sporting concessions, came the final flourish and resynthesis:

> Decisions of State Courts, in harmony with the views we have expressed, exist in great numbers. But it is unnecessary to cite them. It is sufficient to add that in all textwriters, in all codes, and in all revised statutes, it is laid down that the term person includes, or may include, corporations, which amounts to what we already have said, that whenever it is necessary for the protection of contract or property rights, the Courts will look through the ideal entity and name of the corporation to the persons who compose it and protect them, though the process be in its name. All the guarantees and safeguards of the Constitution for the protection of property possessed by individuals may, therefore, be invoked for the protection of the property of corporations. And as no discriminating and partial legislation, imposing unequal burdens upon the property of individuals, would be valid under the Fourteenth Amendment, so no legislation imposing unequal burdens upon the property of corporations can be maintained. The taxation, therefore, of the property of the defendant upon an assessment of its value, without deduction of the mortgage thereon, is to that extent invalid.[147]

This is an interesting, and in some respects a masterly argument—not only for what it says, but for what it fails to say. At the articulate level the themes already are familiar: Corporations, we are reminded over and over, commonly are referred to as "persons." Section One of the Fourteenth Amendment extends its protection against state action to persons. Corporations in any event really are made up of persons. Inarticulately: society and property are threatened by waves of oppressive, "hostile and discriminating legislation." It is of vital importance that the property of corporations be more fully protected against this menace. The Fourteenth Amendment—or, more specifically, its Due Process and Equal Protection Clauses, will serve admirably in this regard, once the *Slaughter-House*–Negro Race limitations are overthrown.

Thus nowhere does Field categorically answer his initial question whether the defendant Southern Pacific Railroad, being a corporation, is a "person" within the meaning of Section One. The whole trend of the argument is in the affirmative. The headnote of the case declares that "private corporations are persons within the meaning of the first section of the Fourteenth Amendment," and Judge Sawyer's lengthy buttressing opinion so holds.[148] Yet Field, for all his

---

147 8 Saw. at 269–270, 13 Fed. at 747–748.
148 8 Saw. at 281–311, 13 Fed. at 757–781.

categorical rhetoric, stops just short of reversing Judge Woods. In any event, courts can and will look through the ideal entity and protect the parties in interest. So be it! Far more important than any quibble over "person" was the scope of the substantive protection to be accorded corporate *property*:

> All the guarantees and safeguards of the Constitution for the protection of property possessed by individuals may, therefore, be invoked for the protection of the property of corporations. And as no discriminating and partial legislation, imposing unequal burdens upon the property of individuals would be valid under the Fourteenth Amendment, so no legislation imposing such unequal burdens upon the property of corporations can be maintained.[149]

It is easy today to see the blindspots in this remarkable opinion.[150] A hundred million dollar corporation was viewed as "property" not a whit different than a ten dollar gold piece. Rails, ties, graded real estate and rolling stock costing an average of $30,000 per mile (but mortgaged for upwards of $40,000 and earning large dividends even on that inflated debt)[151] were no different, for purposes of taxation, than a $5,000 farm mortgaged at fifty per cent! To change the railroad's mode of assessment, in order to get at going concern value, if

---

[149] 8 Saw. at 269-270, 13 Fed. at 748.

[150] For the associations and backgrounds that shaped Field's thinking, see SWISHER, STEPHEN J. FIELD, CRAFTSMAN OF THE LAW (1930) especially c. 9 and 14; and Chapter 3, *supra*.

[151] See note 155 *infra*, for details of the Railroad's mortgage. The Southern Pacific Railroad extending down the San Joaquin Valley from the Bay Region to Los Angeles and then eastward, was built by the Stanford-Huntington group in the Seventies and early Eighties. It was constructed for strategic reasons to forestall Tom Scott's Texas Pacific and to protect the associates' monopoly of California and transcontinental traffic. It was built without a federal bond subsidy, but for a princely land grant, solely from the construction- and operating profits of the Central Pacific. Terrain was favorable, except in the Tehachipis, and costs were comparatively low. The rub was that bond financing was possible, if at all in the depressed Seventies, only on a completed line. The associates' resources thus were strained to the utmost; the oppressive strategic construction in turn led to rate and tax policies that were economically indefensible as well as politically inept. Thus the valuation claimed for tax purposes in the Seventies generally was from $6,000 to $12,000 per mile; yet when rate regulation threatened the figure jumped to $60,000 or $100,000 per mile. Justice Field, familiar with the builders' exertion, and admiring their achievement of a completed, unsubsidized road, overlooked such tactics, or regarded them as part of the social cost—as indeed they were. But farmers and merchants, stuck with all the traffic would bear, saw things differently: the richest, most valuable property in the West proposed to go tax free or to dictate its own assessments.

On the promotional, construction, and tax history of the Central Pacific-Southern Pacific system, see DAGGETT, CHAPTERS IN THE HISTORY OF THE SOUTHERN PACIFIC RAILROAD, (1922); GALLOWAY, THE FIRST TRANSCONTINENTAL RAILROAD (1951); U.S. PAC. RY. COMM., *supra* note 117. The writer is preparing further studies in these fields.

the change threatened to diminish dividends and if the same rules and modes were not applied to all property regardless of differences in the extent of mortgages and operation, was precisely the same as stealing a locomotive, destroying a bridge, or damaging a snowshed or station. It was "hostile" and "discriminatory" action.[152] Justice Field and Judge Sawyer[153] naturally felt that men who had undertaken and accomplished the things that their friends Stanford and Huntington had accomplished ought to be allowed a very free hand by governments and legislatures. Even their *prospective* earnings ought to be treated as pretty much their own. To change rules of taxation therefore was bad faith, "hostility."

Today we can comprehend this attitude without accepting it. Our reasons for viewing it critically are largely pragmatic and historical. One need not be an economist nor an accountant to see that there definitely was more to the Central Pacific's operations and balance sheets than the promoters or the lawyers or Justice Field then saw. To equate gold pieces or farms mortgaged at fifty per cent with a railroad mortgaged at 100 to 150 per cent of cost (but which still earned an average of nearly three millions a year above taxes and interest)[154] was at best a rule of the thumb economics. To say, as Justice Field did in his *San Mateo* opinion, that the mortgage on the Southern Pacific road "exceeds $3,000 per mile," when in fact it exceeded $40,000 per mile and aggregated nearly $32,000,000—an amount approximately double the full assessed value—certainly was to betray either gross ignorance or an unmerited faith in the Railroad's briefs.[155] To treat the railroad corporation as a "person," and to ex-

---

[152] *Cf.* the phraseology of the *San Mateo* opinion, 8 Saw. 238, 260, 277–278, 13 Fed. 722, 740, 754, the latter requoted in the *Santa Clara* opinion, 9 Saw. 165, 196–197, 18 Fed. 385, 406. Both opinions bristle with the words "spoliation" (p. 191, 402), "arbitrary" (pp. 196, 405), "unequal and oppressive burdens" etc. in speaking of state action impliedly analogous to taxation of the Railroad's mortgage.

[153] On Field's friendships with the Railroad proprietors, see SWISHER, *op. cit. supra* note 150, c. 9 and pp. 116, 243–244, 257. For the Sawyer-Stanford friendship, see 2 BANCROFT, CHRONICLES OF THE BUILDERS OF THE COMMONWEALTH 46–47, 60 (1891), and notes preserved in the "Lorenzo Sawyer" folder in the Bancroft Library of the University of California, Berkeley. Sawyer was first President of the Trustees of Stanford University, and Field an appointed member of the Board.

[154] See 8 U.S. PAC. RY. COMM., *Statement 29*, *supra* note 117, at 4658–4659. Until completion of the Southern Pacific, when the situation was reversed, the Southern Pacific was leased to and operated by the Central Pacific. *Statement 29* shows that the C.P. carried to profit and loss an average of $2,900,000 annually for the five years 1878–1882.

[155] See Field's opinion, 8 Saw. 238, 246, 13 Fed. 722, 729: "The indebtedness secured exceeds $3,000 a mile," a figure apparently taken unquestioned from the Railroad's briefs and one later repeated to the Supreme Court by Conkling, ARGUMENT, *supra* note 119, at 100: "The assessment . . . appraised the actual value of these properties

tend to it "All the guarantees and safeguards of the Constitution for the protection of property . . . possessed by individuals"—in an age when economic thinking, description and analysis were this imprecise—certainly was to do more than to prevent legislatures from "imposing unequal burdens." Social benefits and advantages there were too, of course—stability and security of corporate property, and all the rapid growth and expansion ensuing therefrom.

The Field-Sawyer opinions were handed down on September 25, 1882.[156] Just a month before, while counsel still were making their arguments, Judge Sawyer had written his friend and colleague, Judge Deady of Oregon:

> We have been listening a whole week to elaborate discussions upon what constitutes "due process of law," in levying a railroad tax, and whether the railroads under our new and blessed constitution in this state enjoy "the equal protection of the law." It will take two days more at least to finish the argument, then we shall be called upon to incubate over the subject, and then—well, then, the newspapers I suppose, will take a turn at the judges. All the railroad taxes in the state hang in the balance. Of course it will be hard on the state, and still harder on the counties, if this clumsy instrument upon being weighed in the balance should be found wanting.[157]

---

at $16,500 per mile of road. The mortgage amounts of $3,000, or thereabouts, per mile of road. Can anything be more simple than to deduct $3,000 from $16,500, unless it be more simple to deal with totals—make one sum of it—and deduct $2,133,000 from $11,739,915?" This passage reflects the care or scruple with which Conkling prepared his arguments.

From the reference in Field's letters quoted *infra* at notes 206 and 207, it appears that the Supreme Court's decision in the *San Mateo* case was withheld and that Justice Field was requested to hear additional cases and evidence in the summer of 1883 because these discrepancies came to the attention of other members of the Court. In any event the true extent of the Railroad's mortgages came out in the *Santa Clara* briefs and was correctly stated in Field's opinion, 9 Saw. 165, 179: $30,898,000 in bonds then outstanding on 711 miles of road, or approximately $43,500 per mile. At these dates 620 miles of the Central Pacific lines in California were mortgaged for $27,752,-000, or $44,760 per mile, PROCEEDINGS, *supra* note 119, at 145. This was from five to ten millions more than the assessed valuations which the Central Pacific contested in the various tax cases; so if the Railroad's contentions and the Field-Sawyer decisions denying the Legislature's power to adopt a different rule for railroad mortgages ever had been upheld by the Supreme Court, the carriers would have gone tax free. As matters developed, the California tax laws at this date were so loosely drawn and administered that the Supreme Court was able to overturn the assessments on technicalities. See FANKHAUSER, FINANCIAL HISTORY OF CALIFORNIA 305–310 (1913), for summary of outcome and settlements, 1882–1897. Accordingly Field and Sawyer never were sustained on the substantive issue of the mortgage exemption.

[156] See *San Francisco Chronicle*, September 26–27, 1882.
[157] Sawyer to Deady, August 26, 1882 (Oregon Historical Society).

Two days before the decision, Sawyer wrote again:

> I am up to my ears in cases of great importance. We shall decide some important Railroad Tax Cases next week of vast interest to our people as it involves the validity of all the taxes upon railroads in the state under the 14th Amendment of the U.S. Constitution. Every county in which there is a road has a suit all transferred. If we upset the taxes won't there be a howl?[158]

Matters developed much as Sawyer anticipated. California's state and county tax system was thrown into chaos; and it remained in that state for years.[159] The immediate response of the press was more temperate than Sawyer had expected. Two days after the decision the San Francisco *Chronicle* pointed the issue: The Central Pacific, it said, was mortgaged for more than it was worth, except as "a monopoly able to charge what it pleased for transportation:"

> If corporations are at liberty to mortgage their property *ad libitum* to non-residents, and nobody disputes it, and if the non-resident holder of the mortgage cannot be reached for taxes by the state in which the mortgaged property lies, it is certainly the corporation that has the private mortgage at a disadvantage, and not, as the decision argues, the other way.[160]

For the nonce however, the public generally was more concerned with tax burdens than with technicalities. At first little attention was paid in California to corporate personality as such. This was not the case however, outside the state. Lawyers and conservatives were quick to hail the decision as one of the most important in years.

> If confirmed by the Supreme Court [said *The Independent*] it will add greatly to the protective usefulness of the Fourteenth Amendment. It will impose a restriction upon the taxing power of the States, adopted to guard against the abuses of power, and promote the general interests of justice among the people.[161]

---

[158] Sawyer to Deady, September 23, 1882 *id.*

[159] See FANKHAUSER, *op. cit. supra* note 155, and PROCEEDINGS, *supra* note 119; also CALIF. ATTORNEY GENERAL, SPECIAL REPORT ON RAILROAD TAX CASES (1893).

[160] San Francisco Chronicle, Sept. 27, 1882, p. 2, col. 2; *cf. id.* December 20, 1882 (devastating editorial criticism of the *New York Tribune's* naiveté; and exposure of the Railroad's and Tribune's talk of mortgages at $3,000 per mile: the amount is nearer $40,000 per mile; the assessed valuation $16,500 and the magnate's claimed worth of the road $60,000 etc.).

[161] November 30, 1882. See also Moore, *Corporate Taxation*, 18 AM. L. REV. 749, 753 (Sept.–Oct. 1884): corporations should stand on the same footing as individuals etc. and if sustained the *San Mateo* opinion will be a great boon.

The most significant comment appeared in the New York *Tribune* the very morning before Conkling began his argument before the Supreme Court. "Constitutional questions of the gravest moment," the editor declared in a leader entitled Civil Rights of Corporations, were involved in these pending cases. Natural persons' mortgages were deductible; those of the Southern Pacific Railroad were not. The question whether the distinction violated the Equal Protection Clause was one that embraces, "so far as we can discern, corporations of all kinds throughout the country." After a brief summary of the Circuit decisions, the editorial concluded:

> If these positions shall be permanently established . . . the results may be to give corporations a resort to Federal Courts wherever they think that State laws operate unequally against them, and to give a like privilege to taxpayers complaining that a State system of taxation is not equal and uniform.[162]

Two weeks later the *Tribune* printed Field's Circuit opinion in full, accompanied by a second editorial that shows how ingeniously these issues were viewed and presented:

> Can the State discriminate against partnerships? Can it guarantee certain rights to two citizens separately, but withdraw them when these citizens conduct their business together? Can it tax the individual only on what he owns, but if he puts his capital into a partnership, tax him then both on what he owns and what he owes?
> Stated in their simplest form, and without the use of words likely to arouse any prejudice on either side, such are some of the questions now at issue in the great California railroad tax cases . . .[163]

"Of such far reaching importance and . . . so sure to mark a great stage in our jurisprudence" were these cases, that Field's opinion was printed in full on another page.[164] Were the Circuit Justice ultimately to be upheld,

> the law will continue to guarantee to capital invested in partnerships or associations or any form of corporate effort the same rights it would have if managed separately by individual owners.
> The line of Justice Field's argument is novel, yet strongly fortified by high precedents. He finds the right to overturn a State law discriminating against capital invested in partnerships, in the

---
[162] *New York Tribune*, December 19, 1882, p. 4, col. 3.
[163] *Id.* January 3, 1883, p. 4, col. 4, editorial "The California Railroad Tax Cases."
[164] *Id.* at 7–8.

Fourteenth Amendment . . . which forbids any State to deny to any person within its jurisdiction the equal protection of the laws. . . . California has denied such equal protection to the person investing his capital in partnerships—refusing to him the right it allows every other taxpayer, of deducting his debts from the property on which he is to be taxed. Therefore its tax is unconstitutional, and its process for collection cannot be enforced. The opinion embraces many other interesting features; but this is its essential point. Grant this—which to the lay mind will surely seem equity, if not law—and the decisions of the Circuit Court must stand, while the Sand Lots Constitution must succumb.[165]

Corporations, in short, simply were partnerships! Hair-raising doctrine, this would have been, advanced on other occasions, or openly in court, yet unquestionably comforting and serviceable indeed in its present framework.

V

Aside from Conkling's dramatic use—and misuse[166]—of the manuscript Journal to convey an impression that he and his colleagues on the Joint Committee had drafted Section One with an eye to the status of corporations, arguments before the Supreme Court in December, 1882, added comparatively little to what had been said and resaid in California. This, however, is not the measure of the arguments' importance. As already noted, no formal opinion ever recorded the grounds or reasoning on which the Supreme Court accepted corporate personality. Three years after the *San Mateo* arguments, i.e., in January, 1886, Chief Justice Waite orally announced that the Court then unanimously conceded corporations to be persons within the meaning of the Equal Protection Clause.[167] Because of this passive acquiescence—which was commented on in the 90's as most extraordinary procedure for the decision on so vital an issue[168]—the arguments in December, 1882, constitute the last affirmative word on the corporate constitutional "person." The structure

---

165 *Id.* at p. 4, col. 4. On corporations as "partnerships," see DODD, *op. cit. supra* note 1, at 25–26, n.35, for interesting early cases not involving the scope of legislative authority.

166 See Chapter 1, *supra*, especially pp. 38–45.

167 Santa Clara County v. Southern Pacific R.R., 118 U.S. 394 (1886).

168 See 62 Am. St. Rep. 165, 168 (1898): "It is somewhat remarkable that a question of such paramount importance should have been determined by the Supreme Court of the United States without any statement on its part of the reasoning influencing its decisions. . . ."

of the arguments, and the response thereto in the form of questions from the Bench, thus become matters of extraordinary interest.

Not all the briefs, and none of the oral arguments, of counsel for the appellants have been preserved. Judging from what is available,[169] Attorney General Hart and the counsel for the counties made only limited, perfunctory opposition to corporate personality *per se*. They planned their appeal around the integrity of the state taxing power, and on a defense of the mode of assessment and mortgage deduction. They apparently had little taste for maintaining so difficult and abstract a position as one which would deny a corporation the right to plead that it had been denied "the *equal* protection of the laws."[170] This reluctance of course is not surprising. The complex power-balance and relationships—*i.e.* judicial-legislative and federal-state, which today bulk so large in discussions of corporate personality—were then scarcely evident, or were at best academic and hypothetical. The appellants had a far-flung, complex case as it was; but they had a relatively unfettered taxing power with which to defend it.[171] Hence they chose to rely largely on *Insurance Co. v. New Orleans*—which, after all, had been the unchallenged case law down to the Field-Sawyer opinions. It still was from a *court* of equal rank.

In consequence of this strategy Southern Pacific counsel had things pretty much their own way on the "personality" issue. There was little exploration of whole segments of the problem;[172] much of the time the two batteries of lawyers were talking about wholly dif-

---

[169] Associated Press coverage was extraordinarily extensive. See *San Francisco Chronicle*, December 21, 1882, p. 3, col. 5–6; December 22, 1882, p. 3, col. 5; *San Francisco Morning Call*, December 20, 1882, p. 3, col. 3; December 21, 1882, p. 3, col. 3, for summaries of arguments including that of former Chief Justice Rhodes, 1821–1918. For a biographical sketch see Johnson, 26 CAL. STATE BAR J. 425 (1951). Rhodes and Sanderson sat together on the Supreme bench 1864–1870, and Rhodes continued to sit until 1880. The argument of D.M. Delmas in the *Santa Clara* case, 1886, preserved in his SPEECHES AND ADDRESSES (1901) is a restatement of the Hart-Rhodes-Barstow position in the *San Mateo* case.

[170] See the SPEECHES AND ADDRESSES, *supra* note 169, at 196–197, for evidence of how much was conceded in this respect.

[171] Natural rights limitations made relatively slower headway against the taxing power than in other fields. Note the comparative recency of the cases in Maguire, *Taxing the Exercise of Natural Rights*, HARVARD LEGAL ESSAYS TO J.H. BEALE AND SAMUEL WILLISTON 273–322 (1934).

[172] Herein is perhaps the main source of the confusion that disguised and oversold corporate personality: the sheer lopsidedness of talents, resources and pressures at the Railroad's command. Not judicial bias, but disproportionate briefing and social emphasis, better prepared counsel who explored the risks of arbitrary legislation much more effectively than their overburdened opponents could hope to explore the character and necessity of legislative classification—these were among the things that tipped the balance.

ferent matters. Yet the *Tribune* editorial itself suggests the importance conservatives already attached to the case; it records a sense of anticipation which proved to the fullest degree justified.

For three days Railroad counsel hammered[173] at the *Slaughter-House*-Negro Race barrier; repeatedly they equated the constitutional with the statutory and common law "person;" they capitalized Chief Justice Waite's *Sinking Fund* dictum—Conkling in particular, playing it with superb effect. And at every opportunity surmise, conjecture and hypothesis created a mood of suspense and threatened spoliation.

Conkling's opening argument was of course the high spot.[174] Before a packed courtroom he made his dramatic and astonishing appeal. First, a short preliminary statement; then, producing the manuscript from which he already had misquoted in his printed brief, he gave the Justices to understand—by innuendo and quotation—that the Joint Committee had from the first had two separate, distinct purposes. One "did in truth chiefly relate to the freedmen."[175] But it, and its main components—"suffrage, the ballot and representation in Congress"—had been "disposed of before the Committee reached the language on which today's argument proceeds."[176] Very artfully he intimated that one purpose of the Due Process and Equal Protection Clauses had been protection of large property. Corporations had been petitioning Congress for relief at the time. The inference was that the Committee had taken cognizance of their appeals.[177] At the climax of this section, Conkling repeated the mis-

---

[173] Senator George F. Edmunds of Vermont, who had served in the 39th Congress also argued for the Railroad. He supported Conkling's position, saying, PROCEEDINGS, *supra* note 119, at 114: "There is no word in the Fourteenth Amendment that did not undergo the completest scrutiny." To argue that the word "person" must be confined to the Negro race, was like arguing that the word "freeman" in Magna Carta ought to be restricted to the Barons at Runnymede. *Ibid.* Edmunds too received $5,000 for his effort, see 8 U.S. PAC. RY. COMM., *supra* note 117, at 4639, 4796, parts of which made a deep impression on Field, see quotations in *Santa Clara* opinion, 9 Saw. at 185-6, and a marked copy of Edmunds' argument bearing Field's signature preserved in the records of the *San Mateo Case* #2807 in the United States Circuit Court in San Francisco.

[174] The Associated Press dispatches recorded an interest in the case and arguments greater than in any since the Electoral Commission of 1877. See note 169 *supra*, especially the Chronicle, Dec. 22, 1882, for a vignette of Conkling.

[175] Conkling, PROCEEDINGS, *supra* note 119, at 84. (original paging p. 15.)

[176] *Ibid. Cf.* Chapter 1, *supra*.

[177] 1968: Needless perhaps to say, this paragraph-discussion of Conkling's ARGUMENT still suffers from the same misapprehension which clouded the Beards' and nearly everyone's view once the corporate "person" had followed soon after that ARGUMENT and hence appeared to have been the primary object and even consequence of it. But all this, we see now, was trick perspective, sheer illusion. Conkling's real objective, and the Railroads', as stressed in the *Introduction* and in Chapter 13, *infra*,

quotation he had made in his brief, substituting "citizen" for "person" in one of the early drafts of the primitive Due Process and Equal Protection Clauses.[178] Listeners who were aware that in the final drafts the word "citizen" was employed only in the presumably non-economic Privileges or Immunities Clause, whereas the term "person" was used in the final Due Process and Equal Protection drafts, thus were left with the impression that this change had been made intentionally to cover corporate "persons." As a matter of fact "citizen" *never* had been employed in any of the due process-equal protection drafts; "person" had been used throughout. This part of Conkling's argument was a deliberate, brazen forgery.[179]

"The word used" he went on, "to denote those embraced in the Amendment is 'persons'." "In instances without number—it may be said uniformly"—corporations had been "held to be within the designation 'persons'." Suppose that colored men in Louisiana acquired a theater, operated it as a partnership, and so were protected against the confiscation of their property. Suppose they later incorporated. "Can it be that the ... Courts would say the right of protection was lost by the act of incorporation, and might be revived again by resuming a co-partnership name?"[180]

But in the peroration of this part of his argument, Conkling took no chances on intent alone. He had sought, he said, to convince the Court that drafters and ratifiers "must have known" the meaning and force of the term employed. But waive the point—"turn away from this surmise to the real question to be answered."[181] Would any one dare suggest that Americans

---

had to be, and indeed was, a curbed state taxing power, and for *that* purpose, an opening up of the Fourteenth Amendment, an overturning or a by-passing of the narrow Negro-Race interpretation, and specifically of Justice Miller's dicta in the *Slaughter-House* and *Davidson* cases. Conkling's innuendo and misquotations were directed to these broader ends, not to the corporate "person" as such. His listeners in 1882, on their part, accordingly were *not* put to the hazard of hearing (or of having to assume) that the corporate "person" itself had been the *doctrinal* be-all and end-all of the framers' intention—a preposterous position or inference, which, taken ten or fourteen years late, certainly would have raised some questions and judicial eyebrows. Given this scalpel, I leave readers the pleasure of finding and dissecting these not-so-old astigmatisms. See Chapter 13, *infra*, for the final discussion and rationale.

[178] Conkling PROCEEDINGS, *supra* note 119, at 86. The "persons" section of Conkling's oral argument appears as pp. 12-35 of the original edition filed December 19, 1882, with the Supreme Court. It is reprinted as Appendix I, *infra*, with original paging indicated. The corresponding section of printed brief is part "Third," pp. 106-111. (U.S. Supreme Court Library, File of Copies of Briefs, October Term, 1885 v. 6).
[179] See Chapter 1, *supra*; Chapter 13, *infra*.
[180] Conkling, PROCEEDINGS, *supra* note 119, at 92-93; (original paging p. 31).
[181] *Id.* at 93. (p. 31 original paging).

when engrafting the fourteenth amendment upon the Constitution, omitted, only because they forgot it, to say that citizens might be stripped of their possessions without due process of law; provided only the spoliation should be under pretense of taxation and the victims robbed in a corporate name?[182]

If so, let them ponder two facts: One, that Congress in reenacting the Civil Rights Bill after adoption of the amendment "declared, in effect, that the shield of 'equal protection of the laws' extended to *taxes, licenses* and the like."[183] Two, that Chief Justice Marshall in the *Dartmouth College* decision had laid it down as a principle of construction that a constitutional provision such as the Contracts or Due Process Clause was not to be restricted in its application to the existing wrong or circumstance that inspired it. Said Marshall:

> It is not enough to say that this particular case was not in the mind of the convention when the article was framed, nor of the American pepole when it was adopted. It is necessary to go farther, and to say that, had this particular case been suggested, the language would have been so varied, as to exclude it, or it would have been made a special exception. The case being within the words of the rule must be within its operation likewise, unless there be something in the literal construction so obviously absurd or mischievous or repugnant to the general spirit of the instrument, as to justify those who expound the Constitution in making it an exception.[184]

After a page of glowing eloquence in elaboration of Marshall's theme, Conkling played his ace:

> Before passing to another head of my argument, I . . . remind the learned Chief Justice and the Court, of the language of the Court speaking through him in the Sinking Fund Cases. Clearly the language . . . assumes that corporations are within the protection of the fourteenth amendment.[185] Here it is, . . . "The United States

---

[182] *Id.* at 94. (p. 32 original paging).
[183] *Ibid.* Conkling here referred to the fact that the Civil Rights Act of 1870 had added the words "taxes, licenses and exactions of every kind and none other" to the original phraseology of Section 1 of the Civil Rights Act of 1866. *Compare* 16 STAT. 144, c. 114, § 16, May 31, 1870, *with* 14 STAT. 27, c. 31, § 1, April 9, 1866.
   This argument too made a strong impression on Justice Field and was noted in his opinion in the *Santa Clara* case, 9 Saw. at 188. He had been aware of it and indeed stressed it in July, 1882, when taking jurisdiction in the *San Mateo* case, see 13 Fed. 145, 151. 1968: The significance and basis of this part of Conkling's argument are reassessed Chapter 13, *infra*.
[184] 4 Wheat. 518, 644–645 (U.S. 1819).
[185] Conkling, PROCEEDINGS, *supra* note 119, at 95.

... *equally with the States* ... *are prohibited from depriving persons or corporations of property without due process of law.*"[186]

It fell to Justice Field's friend, S. W. Sanderson,[187] also a former Chief Justice of the Supreme Court of California, to make the concluding argument for the Southern Pacific. The other side, he said, had contended "that we are not within the guarantees of the fourteenth amendment, first, because we are not a 'person;' second, because we are not a colored person; and third, because the laws of which we complain are not the laws referred to in that amendment."[188]

The first proposition he found "startling," especially in view of "the number of corporations in the country and the amount and value of their ... property:" some "1600 insurance companies, ... aggregate assets not less than $99,000,000; ... five thousand mining corporations; ... two thousand national banks, with assets [of] more than $2,000,000,000; ... fifteen hundred railroad corporations operating ... 110,000 miles of railroads, with property and assets of not less than $6,000,000,000," besides countless educational, religious and other corporations.

> Now, it may be that all these corporations and all these stockholders are without the protection of the fourteenth amendment; but, if it be so, there should be some surer foundation for such a conclusion than ... emasculating ... the word "person."[189]

The elaborate and now familiar case and text analysis followed—designed to show that "from time immemorial ... corporations [had been] spoken of and treated as legal persons." Then Sanderson too, dramatically played his trump, the dictum from the *Sinking Fund* opinion:

> This Court ... has made no distinction between persons and corporations, but has placed them in the same category.
>
> [Said] Mr. Justice Waite: "The United States, cannot any more than a State, interfere with private rights except for legitimate governmental purposes. They are not included within the constitutional prohibition, which prevents States from passing laws impairing the obligations of contracts; but, equally with the States,

---

[186] Sinking Fund Cases, 99 U.S. 718 (1879).
[187] 1824–1886; Chief Justice, California Supreme Court, January 1864–January 1866; Associate Justice, January 1866–January 1870; resigned to become assistant counsel for Central Pacific Railroad. For a biographical sketch, see Johnson, 25 CAL. STATE BAR J. 105 (1950). Field and Sanderson had both attended Williams College.
[188] Sanderson, PROCEEDINGS, *supra* note 119, at 124.
[189] *Id.* at 124.

they are prohibited from depriving persons *or corporations* of property without due process of law."[190]

The word "corporation," Sanderson continued, appeared in none of the various due process clauses:

> Nowhere in the books, nowhere in Magna Carta, nowhere in any State Constitution, nowhere in the Constitution of the United States, do you find the word . . . in relation to due process of law. And yet no one has ever pretended until now that it does not protect artificial as well as natural persons. The research of counsel upon the other side has failed to find a case in which any distinction has been made, in this respect, between corporations and natural persons.[191]

Daring table turning and hyperbole this was certainly. Since 1871, so far as cases went, *Insurance Co. v. New Orleans* had stood for the proposition that corporations were *not* "persons" within the meaning of Section One, including of course both the Due Process and Equal Protection clauses. In 1879, it is true, Waite had *presumed* the Due Process clause of the Fifth Amendment to embrace corporations. It is likely therefore that both the kindly Chief Justice and his fellow-Ohioan, Justice Woods—who since December, 1880, had been a member of the Supreme Court—listened almost transfixed at the sharp turn Sanderson's argument now took:

> If the Court please, there are some authorities upon this question directly in point, some of which are opposed to the position . . . we take . . . [F]irst . . . is a case decided in Louisiana, in the Circuit Court of the United States, by his honor Mr. Justice Woods.[192]

After stating the facts and quoting the relevant parts of the opinion (already noted in our analysis above) Sanderson continued:

> Now, with all due respect to the learned Judge . . . I think his reasoning is subject to the criticism of Mr. Justice Grier in answering a similar objection in the case of the Baltimore and Ohio Railroad Company, where he said that persons were not to be deprived of their constitutional rights by a syllogism or sophism which deals cunningly with words to the disregard of names and things.
> The reasoning of the learned Judge is this:

---

[190] Sinking Fund Cases, 99 U.S. 718 (1879).
[191] Sanderson, Proceedings, *supra* note 119, at 127.
[192] *Ibid.*

An Innocent Abroad

"Persons are born or naturalized, corporations are not born or naturalized, ergo corporations are not persons."

Now, this is a syllogism, and syllogistic reasoning is unsafe reasoning when we come to ascertain the meaning of the words contained in a statute or Constitution. . . . According to Moses' account . . . Adam and Eve were not born or naturalized; they were created. Vary the syllogism of the learned Judge and apply it to their case. Corporations are not born or naturalized, but created; Adam and Eve were not born or naturalized, but created; therefore Adam and Eve were corporations. Such logic is not safe logic for the purpose of ascertaining the meaning of language as used in a statute or in a Constitution. The Judge says that corporations are not born. It is true that in a literal technical sense they are not, and yet in a legal and figurative sense they are. Bentham says: "Laws and property are born and must die together. Before there were laws there was no property; take away the laws and property ceases."[193]

At this point the sympathetic Justice Bradley, who for eleven years had been Woods' Circuit Justice, interposed:

Do you contend that the first clause of the amendment relates to artificial persons?

Mr. Sanderson: I am not done with that language yet. The confusion, or whatever it may be called, thrown into this amendment in the first clause, is due to the fact that an amendment was tacked on to it which the committee did not report.

Mr. Justice Bradley: I thought you were arguing that, although the word person was used, it might to some extent be applied to corporations.

Mr. Sanderson: Yes, it may. If I understand your honor, I think the construction of the word "person" that the learned Judge [Woods] gives, where it appears in the last two clauses, claiming that it is the same in meaning as the word "person" found in the first, is all wrong, for the reason that the word "person" used in the first clause is accompanied by the associate words "born or naturalized," which are a limitation upon the word "person" as there used, and confines its meaning to those who are born and who are naturalized; while the word "person" in the last two clauses is not associated with any qualifying words at all, but is used in its generic sense, and embraces all persons of all classes. The word "person" in the last two clauses is broader and more comprehensive than the word "person" contained in the first clause. As suggested by my associate, Mr. Edmunds, an examination

---

[193] *Id.* at 127–128.

of the Journal will show that this first clause in relation to citizenship was a political clause, which was not in the amendment at the time it was reported to the House, but was added in the Senate, and has no connection with and was not intended to have any control over the subsequent parts.

To continue . . . The reasoning [in *Insurance Co. v. New Orleans*] interpolates words—adds words to the language of the fourteenth amendment which were not employed by the statesmen who framed it.[194]

After rereading Section One with the phrase "born or naturalized" inserted in all clauses in accordance with Judge Woods' construction Sanderson continued:

To thus interpolate words is not sanctioned by any rule of construction. To thus interpolate words is to make laws and not to construe them. No Court can lawfully do this. *Jus discere non jus dare* is the measure of judicial power. You may declare the law but you cannot make it. Had Congress intended the meaning which the learned Judge has given to the word "person" they would have prefixed to it "such," so that these clauses would have read . . . :

"Nor shall any State deprive any (such) person, etc.; nor deny to any (such) person," etc.

And the fact that no such qualifying words were used conclusively shows that no such limitation upon the meaning of the word "person" was intended.[195]

The game of interpolating missing and needed verbage in Section One, and of "declaring" rather than "making" the law, thus arrived virtually at stalemate. After alluding to the Ninth Circuit decisions, to Judge Drummond's[196] and an Illinois case,[197] Sanderson added: "These decisions"—meaning of course simply those few *prior to 1866*, but not so stating—"we must presume were perfectly familiar to the statesmen who framed the fourteenth amendment. . . . [I]f any layman in either House of Congress had moved to amend by adding the word 'corporation' in addition to the word 'person', every lawyer in the House would have told him that it was entirely unnecessary."[198]

---

[194] *Id.* at 128–129.
[195] *Id.* at 129.
[196] See note 89 *supra*.
[197] Illinois Central R.R. v. City of Bloomington, 76 Ill. 447 (1875). See pp. 450–451, wherein Chief Justice Walker equated the rights of natural persons and corporations rather loosely when invalidating an ordinance that required railroads to bear cost of grade crossings; no constitutional clauses were cited.
[198] Sanderson, PROCEEDINGS, *supra* note 119, at 129.

Sanderson next repeated Conkling's hypothetical case of the Negro partnership turned corporation and back again; then varied the facts to cover a *white* California partnership turned corporation. The anomalous consequences of such "simple transmutations," given the *Slaughter-House*-Negro Race restrictions, were pictured as scandalous and shocking.[199] After recasting the Pomeroy-Field "Corporations-are-composed-of-persons" argument, Sanderson levelled a final barrage at the narrow Negro Race thesis itself. His remarks make strange reading today—indeed, they serve to underscore the current unanimity of the Court in taking a firmer hand[200] to hasten the then-presumed end of public race discrimination under the guarantees of the Amendment: That Sanderson conceived he spoke without guile is as much the measure of our modern duties in this regard as of his own aims and success:

> It is very clear, if we look back over the history of the past twenty years, that this country has done a great deal for [members of] the negro race. . . . It has made them free men; it has endowed them with rights of citizenship, political and civil; . . . it has placed them on a par and equality with the white man. But that is none too much; we do not complain of that. We only say that something should now be done for the poor white man. We ask that he . . . be lifted up and put upon a level with the negro. We ask that this fourteenth amendment be so construed as to concede to the white man equal rights under the Constitution of the United States with the black man. Our claim is for universal equality before the law. . . . [M]y friends upon the other side, by their construction of this amendment, would create a privileged class. They have demonstrated . . . that the negro race . . . stands higher upon the plane of legal rights than the white man; that whenever his rights are invaded he finds a shield and a protection in the fourteenth amendment . . . ; but whenever a white man's rights are invaded, whenever he is outraged by unjust State legislation, we are told . . . that there is no shield for him to be found in the fourteenth amendment; that the white man is without protection in cases where the black man is protected. . . .[201]

This argument, followed by a statistical analysis purporting to show that whites were outnumbered in some Southern states, had precisely its desired effect. It got an immediate rise from Mr. Justice

---

[199] *Id.* at 130.
[200] *School Segregation Cases*: Brown v. Topeka and four other cases, 347 U.S. 483 (May 17, 1954).
[201] Sanderson, PROCEEDINGS, *supra* note 119, at 131-132.

Miller as to the proper interpretation of the *Slaughter-House* decision:

> Mr. Justice Miller: [I]n the Slaughter-House Cases . . . we [said]: "And so, if other rights are assailed by the States which properly and necessarily fall within the protection of these articles, that protection will apply, though the party interested may not be of African descent."
> Mr. Sanderson: I am glad to know that, your honor.
> Mr. Justice Miller: I do not know that anybody in this Court —I have never heard it said in this Court or by any judge of it— that these articles were supposed to be limited to the negro race.
> Mr. Sanderson: But there is a notion out among the people, and our friends on the other side have cited several cases, for the purposes of showing that it was the intention of this Court to give this provision . . . as restricted and limited application as possible.
> Mr. Justice Miller: The purport of the general discussion in the Slaughter-House Cases on this subject was nothing more than the common declaration that when you come to construe any Act of Congress, any statute, any Constitution, any legislative decree, you must consider the thing, the evil which was to be remedied, in order to understand fairly what the purpose of the remedial act was.[202]

This was precisely the opening sought, and Sanderson made the most of it:

> We agree perfectly; and I am not going to urge that there is anything contained in the Slaughter-House Cases which admits of a different construction than your honor now puts upon it. But I must confess that there has been an impression that the Slaughter-House Cases narrowed the provision of the first clause, and also the provisions of the two latter clauses—their scope, as one would naturally understand them from reading their words.
> But, as I was about to show when your honor interrupted me, the Slaughter-House Cases do not justify such an impression. Your honor says, at page 72: "We do not say that no one else but the negro can share in this protection."[203]

Sanderson thereupon continued with the rest of the quotation (which Justice Miller himself had just read), then neatly pointed the whole matter:

---

[202] *Id.* at 132–133.
[203] *Id.* at 133.

I am very glad to have any doubt which has existed in the minds of the profession in regard to the purport and meaning of that decision cleared up by an authoritative opinion, given in this public manner. I understand, then, that we may consider, for the purpose of this case, so far as your honor is concerned, that the color line has disappeared from American jurisprudence; that there are not two Constitutions in this country—one for the black man and one for the white man—and that the white man is at last on an equality with the negro.[204]

At length, and probably in a mood approaching elation, Sanderson arrived at the third and crucial point:

But it is also said that we are not entitled to the benefits of this provision . . . because the laws of which we complain are not . . . the laws to which the fourteenth amendment refers. In other words, it was not intended by the fourteenth amendment to vest the judiciary of the United States with the power of reviewing the revenue laws of the States to ascertain their purpose, or to ascertain whether they were consistent with the Constitution of the United States or not. Where is there a warrant . . . for such an assertion? You do not find it in the language, it is not there; "nor shall any State deny to any person equal protection"—of what? "of the laws" against crime; with respect to the enjoyment of property; in relation to proceedings in Courts of justice; laws relating to conveyancing, and the thousand and one subjects of which laws treat? Not at all. "No State shall deny to any person the equal protection of the laws"—all laws—any law by which a State may deny to any person equal protection with some other person. Now, the subject matter of the law is a matter of the utmost indifference. It is not that against which the Constitution of the United States is to provide protection. No matter what the subject may be, it is as to the law itself—no matter what it relates to. That law must operate equally. Each person must find, who comes in contact with it, equal protection at its hands, no matter in what department of the laws it may be found.[205]

The *San Mateo Case* never was decided on its merits. Two months after these elaborate arguments Justice Field wrote his friend Judge Deady:

---

[204] *Ibid.* **1968:** It is sobering to reread this passage and to reflect that it was addressed to the Court just a few months *before* Mr. Justice Harlan alone of that bench took the positions which Sanderson here assuredly, categorically assumed. All but one of the *Civil Rights Cases* already were before the Court when Sanderson spoke.
[205] *Id.* at 134.

> The argument in the great tax case was, as you say it must have been, full of interest. It was a great argument and the shorthand report of it does not do it justice. The written pages want the fire of the speaker which warmed and illuminated everything that was said.
>
> . . .
>
> The decision of the tax case will not be made this term. The case will be held under advisement until next term, and in the meantime it is probable that other cases exhibiting other features of the tax law of California will find their way to the Court; for there are some forty cases pending at the Circuit.[206]

The following month, on March 28, 1883, Justice Field wrote Professor Pomeroy:

> Some weeks ago, I wrote you with reference to the San Mateo tax case telling you that its decision would not be made until next term, and enclosing you also certain memoranda which had been handed me by two of the Judges. Have you ever received these? They were, of course, intended only for your eye, and I should be glad to know that they have come to your hands.
>
> I shall leave here for San Francisco about the first of June. I

---

[206] Field to Deady, Washington, D.C., February 18, 1883. In the omitted paragraph of this letter Field again outlined to Deady the plan he had been advocating for more than a decade—a functionalized Supreme Court of 21 members (for the hearing of constitutional questions) but sitting in three divisions in the manner of the continental courts of cassation for dispatch of private law cases:

"The Court of Appeals bill is not likely to pass the House. There is too much uncertainty as to the appointment of the Judges for either party to be very anxious that eighteen new offices of so high a grade should be filled. I am inclined to think that eventually the plan, of which I have so often spoken to you and which I have always favored, of increasing the Supreme Court of the United States to twenty one Judges and dividing it into sections will be adopted. One section could then take the equity cases, another section the common law cases, and the third the patent law, admiralty and perhaps the revenue cases also. If a Constitutional question should arise or a question upon the construction of a treaty which would have to be determined for the decision of the case, then the case could be turned over to the full bench. We would thus have one court for the decision of the Constitutional questions and questions arising upon treaties and what would be equivalent to three courts for the hearing of all questions affecting mere property rights. It may be that an amendment to the Constitution will be necessary to carry this plan into effect, but it grows more and more every day into favor. I expect to live to see you one of the Judges of the Supreme Court when this plan is adopted."

The "stream of consciousness" here is most interesting in the light of Field's later acknowledgment that his chief reason for seeking the Democratic nomination for the Presidency had been this "desire to reorganiz[e] the Federal Judiciary, plac[ing] on the Bench able and conservative men . . . thus bring[ing] back the decisions of the Court to that line from which they should not have departed. . . ." See Chapter 3, *supra*, especially n.106. Recollection and re-advocacy of the Court plan in this letter of February 18, 1883, between the two paragraphs relating to the delayed decision in the *San Mateo* case, thus constitutes an interesting association of ideas.

may perhaps stop at Carson City on the way to hold Court for a few days there.

I shall be ready to take up any new tax cases as soon as I arrive, and I hope in whatever case is tried all the facts relating to the mortgage upon the property of the Railroad Company will be shown and also the extent to which its property has been subjected to taxation throughout the State.[207]

Railroad counsel were more than willing to oblige Justice Field in these particulars. In the summer of 1883 the second round of cases, involving many of the old questions, but also including new ones as well as more specific information on the nature and extent of the railroads' mortgages, were rebriefed reargued, and finally, on September 17, again decided by Justice Field and Judge Sawyer in decisions that upheld the companies on nearly every point.[208] Naturally, the elaborate opinion restated and effectively advertised the merits and advantages of the corporate "person," though not even Judge Sawyer, on this occasion, went so far as to hold that a corporation actually was a constitutional "person."[209] Field's opinion again brilliantly exploited the forensic uses of hypothesis and presumption rather than defend his ultimate position:

> Surely [he argued] these great constitutional provisions which have been, not inaptly termed a new *Magna Charta*, cannot be made to read, as counsel contend "nor shall any State deprive any person of life, liberty or property without due process of law *unless he be associated with others in a corporation*, nor deny to any person within its jurisdiction the equal protection of the laws, *unless he be a member of a corporation*." How narrow and petty would provisions thus limited appear in the fundamental law of a great people![210]

---

[207] Field to Pomeroy, Washington, D.C., March 28, 1883, see *supra* at 107.

[208] The Santa Clara Railroad Tax Case: County of Santa Clara v. Southern Pacific R.R., 9 Saw. 165, 18 Fed. 385 (C.C. Cal. 1883). Fields' opinion ran to 41 pages; Sawyer's to 42. Field evaded precise discussion of the amounts of the mortgage per mile, though he gave the aggregate, *id.* at 179, and conceded, *id.* at 209, that the "property is heavily encumbered with mortgages, amount to much more than its actual value." Sawyer conceded the mortgage to be $46,000 per mile and bonds issued $39,000 per mile, *id.* at 246. The assessed valuation contested by the Railroad in the *Santa Clara* case was $15,000 per mile, *id.* at 179.

[209] Whether foreseen and intended or not, the practical result of the reargument of the cases and the failure of the Supreme Court to resolve the question was that Field's and Sawyer's opinions were cited by corporate counsel the country over, 1883–1885; the issue thus went by default. See note 216 *infra*.

[210] County of Santa Clara v. Southern Pacific R.R., 9 Saw. 165, 195, 18 Fed. 385, 404 (C.C. Cal. 1883).

Again appeals were taken. Stipulations meanwhile had made the *San Clara* group of cases the major test;[211] the *San Mateo* case was ordered restored to its original place on the docket. Because of the extreme congestion in the Supreme Court by this date the *Santa Clara*[212] case was not reached until January, 1886. Meanwhile, on November 16, 1885, the Court decided the *Kentucky Railroad Tax Cases*.[213] San Mateo County officials had excellent reason to be encouraged by these decisions. Yet two days later maneuvers were begun to withdraw the suits. At length, the county auditor and treasurer accepted the Southern Pacific's payment of taxes and penalties, then dispatched a telegram, dictated by the Railroad's counsel, Creed Haymond, informing the Clerk of the Supreme Court that settlement had been made, and asking dismissal of the appeals.[214] Over strenuous opposition of state officials, and against the wishes of counsel who had handled the consolidated appeals, these tactics prevailed: On December 21, 1885, just three full years after Conkling's argument, the Supreme Court dismissed the *San Mateo Case* as moot.[215] Arguments in the *Santa Clara Case* were heard the next month. It was then that Chief Justice Waite made his curt announcement that the Court would not rehear argument on whether the Equal Protection Clause applies to "these corporations." "We are all of the opinion that it does."[216]

---

211 See San Mateo County v. Southern Pacific R.R., 116 U.S. 138 (1885).

212 Santa Clara County v. Southern Pacific R.R., 118 U.S. 394 (1886).

213 115 U.S. 321 (1885).

214 See the testimony and documentation in PROCEEDINGS, *supra* note 119, at 174–191; compare Governor Stoneman's letter to the Supreme Court dated November 25, 1885, and similar documentation in REPORT OF THE CONTROLLER OF THE STATE OF CALIFORNIA, 1884–86, 28.

215 San Mateo County v. Southern Pacific R.R., 116 U.S. 138 (1885).

216 Santa Clara County v. Southern Pacific R.R., 118 U.S. 394, 396 (1886). One of the decisive factors in favor of the corporate person—if it met with more than an understandable hesitancy on the part of the Justices—must have been the avidity with which the Field-Sawyer opinions were seized on by an harassed corporate bar, and the speed with which they worked their way into state and federal reports while the *San Mateo* and *Santa Clara* appeals were still pending, 1882–1885, and after the dictum of January, 1886. Justice Field hardly could have been disappointed or surprised at the wave of citation and approval; *viz.*: 1) People v. Fire Ass'n of Philadelphia, 92 N.Y. 311 (1883) (at p. 315 reliance on the *San Mateo* case by Joseph H. Choate; *cf.* the Court's chariness at p. 324. See also the related use by counsel at p. 333); 2) Louisville and N. R.R. v. Railroad Commission of Tenn., 19 Fed. 679 (C.C. Tenn. 1884) (part of a state law voided as a violation of due process by Circuit Judge Hammond); 3) Northern Pacific R.R. v. Carland, 5 Mont. 146 (1884) (Territorial Supreme Court of Montana follows Field on the scope of the Fourteenth Amendment); 4) Stone v. Farmers Loan and Trust Co., 116 U.S. 307, 324 (1885) (indicates due process and equal protection relied on by John A. Campbell for the company, October 13–15, 1885); 5) Missouri Pacific R.R. v. Humes, 115 U.S. 512, 516 (1885) (use by counsel); *cf.* the

An Innocent Abroad 429

SUMMARY–CONCLUSION

What can be said of the doctrines and arguments we have been examining—first from the standpoint of the 1880's, then from our own?

Uppermost in mind, as one attempts an answer, is what an immense difference it makes which viewpoint one adopts! The camera angles have shifted as much between 1882 and 1954 as they obviously did between 1873 and 1882, or from 1866–1873. Emphatically, it will not do to think of Section One, or of corporate personality, as simple absolutes in space and time. Constitutional clauses and doctrines are living things; they are parts of a changing environment, of a complex process of growth and social reasoning. Our transparent little syllogism has as many facets as a crown jewel!

Consider first the larger setting. Section One originally was a synthesis of concepts and clauses possessing a maximum natural rights potential, and hence carrying a maximum charge for protection of the "liberty," "right to earnings," and "property" of "persons" of the Negro race. *Ipso facto* the Section carried the same potential and charge for protecting the *economic* liberty and earning power of other "persons" whenever the occasion should arise—as it presently did.

Hard luck often is an explorer's or inventor's best friend. So it was with corporate personality. Every preferred resource having failed, insurance company lawyers had no choice in 1871 but to try to establish the corporate "person." Syllogisms alone however were not enough; for there were syllogisms and syllogisms, and many of

---

Court's curt rejection of the continued misuse of due process, Field writing the opinion and quoting Justice Miller's "strange misconception" dictum, *id.* at 520; 6) Missouri Pacific R.R. v. Mackey, 127 U.S. 205 (1888) (John F. Dillon for the railroad cites *San Mateo* April 1888); 7) Minneapolis & St. Louis R.R. v. Herrick, 127 U.S. 210 (1887) (C.K. Davis for the Railroad).

Some state courts were slow to appreciate the force of the *Santa Clara* dictum, see Charlotte etc. R.R. v. Gibbes, 27 S.C. 385 (1888); "Corporations are creatures of government . . . hath not the potter power over the clay" etc.

As late as January, 1888, counsel for the State of California in the later Railroad Tax Cases, 127 U.S. 1, 21, 25 (1888), warned of the revolutionary significance of due process and corporate personality used as Field and Sawyer had used them.

It has been overlooked that the *Pembina* and *Beckwith* opinions and dicta clinching the doctrine, see note 24 *supra*, were written by Field. See also his opinion in Charlotte etc. RR. v. Gibbes, 142 U.S. 386 (1892).

Professor Hamilton in *The Path of Due Process of Law, supra* note 45 at 181, has noted that in the form delivered Waite's *Santa Clara* statement was "a dictum [that], oblivious to its lack of authority, . . . began presently to assert its claim as a holding." This is a shrewd and incisive estimate of the matter, but precision of usage and thought was not here the indispensable or priceless ingredient. **1968**: See Chapter 13, *infra*, for recent discoveries and the rationale.

them worked both ways. Moreover, post-war Reconstruction and depression inclined the Courts toward caution in overruling Congress and legislatures.

During the '70's corporations came rapidly of age. No judge could have ignored the benefits they were working; every court was deluged with cases involving their rights against mounting public regulation and interference. Due process was preempted again and again in these arguments. And *Insurance Co. v. New Orleans* naturally acted as a damper on detailed presentation! The protection sought thus was denied, but the status that had been presumed was not. On the contrary, lawyers and judges consciously and unconsciously equated the constitutional with the statutory and common law "person." Chief Justice Waite's dictum marked the climax. Judge Cooley's[217] sounded the dinner bell.

On the broader issues meanwhile, the Court struggled valiantly to escape the destiny thrust upon it. Section One plainly was a universal system conceived for one paramount purpose. But the mesh yielded more than intended; and yielded it, moreover, in very bad order! The haul—early and potential—threatened the craft. Jettisoning the catch was an expedient that worked only until the Court's limited racial text itself finally began to yield results. Then in the light of the universally worded text—"no person"—the anomalies became ludicrous, and the Court itself vulnerable: Judicial self-restraint appeared to be, and was mercilessly caricatured as, judicial distortion and favoritism. So here again, hard luck ultimately proved self-correcting. By 1880 the corporate "person," as shown by the Waite-Cooley dicta and by the "presumed" cases, and above all by *Parrott's Chinese Case*, was coming to be a part of the due process and equal protection complex. All the words of both clauses had grown and were growing because the political and social contexts had grown and were growing. Issues matured—not separately, but in conjunction: the integrity of the taxing power and of legislative control over corporations *versus* the doctrine of vested rights and declining public respect for legislatures. *Equal* protection and *due* process suddenly developed new dimensions and magnitudes.[218] The

---

217 Detroit v. Detroit etc. R.R., 43 Mich. 140, 147 (1880).
218 See the accounts of HAINES, REVIVAL OF NATURAL LAW CONCEPTS 143 ff. (1930); Hamilton, *The Path of Due Process of Law*, supra note 45; TWISS, *op. cit. supra* note 58, c. 4–7 and Corwin, *The Supreme Court and the Fourteenth Amendment*, 7 MICH. L. REV. 643 (1909) all of which stress the mounting pressure of counsel and conservative opinion, the importance of Butchers Union v. Crescent City, 111 U.S. 746 (1884), and the views of its concurring minority. To these perhaps should be added the intertwined, often composite character of the issues, particularly in the series of California

benefits, the advantages, the vulnerability of the corporation at this date far overshadowed its power in the minds of lawyers and judges charged with defending it. Nearly all the emphasis was on these factors. Practically no attention was devoted to the basic problem of the legislature's inherent power to classify and the manner in which such power was related to and affected by Section One. The old Lockean magic blunted analysis,[219] over-simplified problems—pictured the corporation merely as "property," as a simple "partnership," yes, a "tender person!"

Two lines thus merged and reinforced in the *San Mateo Case*: On the one hand, brilliant private exploitation of textual ambiguity and of the anomalies of judicial self-limitation; on the other, mounting public and judicial solicitude for corporate business. The judicial choice, ultimately, came to be a "yes" or "no" on corporate personality. Inherently however, this was "package deal" jurisprudence of a truly momentous kind. Ultimately, the "tied in values" were the payoff. But in 1882 property-as-exchange-value, due-process-as-just-process, and equal-protection-as-substantive-protection were still only gleams in the professional eye or inarticulate premises or dicta in opinions. Some of these have been noted above. Within three years, however, how great the change: *Hurtado v. California*,[220] *Barbier v. Connolly*,[221] and *Yick Wo v. Hopkins*[222]—all Ninth Circuit, and all humanitarian or non-economic cases from California—had rounded out values and literally begun to transmute base metal.[223]

When Justice Holmes declared that "General propositions do not decide concrete cases"[224] he doubtless meant that as a rule they *ought not*. He would have been the last to deny that the Court's alternatives in constitutional litigation often are as limited as the facts and interests are complex; that actually a constitution *is* a series of general propositions; that the judicial reasoning applying them necessarily is brief, elastic, and suggestive rather than explicit;

---

due process-equal protection cases, 1884–1886, cited *infra* notes 220–222, the crowded condition of the Court's docket, new personnel, the illnesses and absences at crucial times of a none too popular or forceful Chief Justice. These are intangible and uncertain factors; their significance can be gauged only when more is known of intra-Court history.

[219] For the double-edged character of this potential, see Chapter 7, *supra*.
[220] 110 U.S. 516 (1884), opinion by Justice Matthews. Hurtado's counsel in this crucial case was A. L. Hart, former Attorney General of California, who had argued against the Railroad in the *San Mateo* appeals.
[221] 113 U.S. 27 (1885), opinion by Justice Field.
[222] 118 U.S. 356 (1886), opinion again by Justice Matthews.
[223] 1968: That is, for all but the freedmen; see the works cited *supra*, note 218.
[224] Lochner v. New York, 198 U.S. 45, 76 (1905).

that in practice therefore, general propositions often must and do decide concrete cases, both judicially and psychologically. Corporate personality is one of the classic examples.

Beyond all this was a fact unfaced in the '70's and '80's because then hardly visible, but increasingly evident today: a corporation is much more than a bundle of "property," or of rights, or of legal relationships. It is also, in many respects, and most importantly in its modern aspect, a going concern, an autonomous unit, and even —in full flower, something of a rival of the state itself.[225] This was the case with the Central Pacific-Southern Pacific system as early as 1882. In number of employees, income, and even in territorial extent (counting public land grants), the Railroads were a match for the State of California.[226] In legal talent,[227] effectiveness of decision making and administration, they were of course far superior. And in some respects, this was fortunate: no railroad could have

---

[225] See the works of BERLE AND MEANS and Timberg, cited *supra* note 1, and U. S. TEMPORARY ECONOMIC COMMITTEE, INVESTIGATION OF CONCENTRATION OF ECONOMIC POWER, FINAL REPORT (1941) especially 675–678, a table and statement comparing the assessed valuations of the states, 1937, with the assets of thirty of the largest corporations, 1935. *Cf.* KAPLAN, BIG ENTERPRISE IN A COMPETITIVE SYSTEM (1954).

[226] Comparisons are striking:
Number of government employees (civil) state, local and federal resident in California, 1880, was 3789 (U.S. Census, 1880, Population Table XXXI, p. 736). This was approximately 200 less than the number of railroad officials and employees resident in California. *Id.* at 737.
Number of employees, in entire C.P.-S.P. system, 1880, was 8,299
1881, was 10,084
1882, was 12,978
(Cal. Bd. of R.R. Commrs., 3d Annual Rept. p. 193, 265; 4th, p. 375, 441; 5th, p. 69, 129). The average annual gross earnings of the C.P.-S.P. system, 1878–1882, were approximately $21 million—almost five times the average annual state income, 1880–1884. *Cf.* 8 U.S. PAC. RY. COMM., *supra* note 117, at 4658; FANKHAUSER, *op. cit. supra* note 155, at 321.
Southern Pacific land grant, authorized, approximately eleven million acres. See 9 Saw. 179.

[227] The "Legal Expense Account" of the Central Pacific Railroad averaged $184,000 per year for the six years, 1878–1883, and amounted to $216,000 in 1882. This was almost exactly the amount spent by the State of California on its judiciary $200,000 per year) and Legal Department (Attorney General's Office, $10,000 per year), 1880–1884 average, see FANKHAUSER, *op. cit. supra* note 155 at 381, 385. Counties paid half the salaries of the judges of the Superior Courts.
At the time of the *San Mateo* arguments in the summer of 1882, names of 17 attorneys or firms appeared regularly on the Railroad's payroll. Eight drew $500 or more per month, and Chief Counsel Sanderson, $24,000 per year. U. S. PAC. RY. COMM., *supra* note 117, at 4710–4736. *Cf.* the $10,000 average annual total expenditures of the Attorney General's office, including the Attorney General's salary of $3,000, FANKHAUSER, cited *supra* this note. Counsel for the State and counties of California in the *Railroad Tax Cases* experienced repeated crises in raising even small sums to carry on the appeals; see San Francisco Chronicle, Nov. 10, 1883, p. 3, col. 7; Nov. 11, 1883, p. 7, col. 1 (crisis involved in raising $2,850 travelling expenses for counsel—prorated at $186 per county!).

operated as the State of California then did, and no State so operating could have built or managed a railroad. The point here is not the comparative merit or efficiency of public and private enterprise, either then or since; it is simply the existent power relationships and the bearing of these relationships on the problem of effective government. As the number and size of corporations has increased it is arguable that there inevitably has occurred a dilution, a pluralization and a "privatization" of government viewed in terms of responsible public controls.[228] Hence, as government's coordinating role becomes more and more indispensable, its burdens heavier, its reach greater, the effectiveness of much of its decision making and capacity for overall control often is correspondingly reduced. To oversimplify: Economic power functionally organized becomes something of a counterpoise, or even "governor," for political power constitutionally organized.[229] This undoubtedly is the challenge which has prompted some modern reservations regarding the corporate constitutional "person." The subject is one that edges off into antitrust law, economic policy, and value judgments about the whole trend and course of modern government and business.

These are fields we need not presently enter. Corporate personality today is much more than an established or an accepted fact. It also is a doctrine—perhaps more accurately, a part of a doctrinal complex—the collective potentialities and misuse of which, in the hands of judges who pushed its elements "to dryly logical extremes,"[230] have proved to a large degree judicially self-correcting. The period from the mid-nineties to the mid-thirties did indeed witness some strange results in the name of a judicial review oriented toward enforcement of "liberty to contract" and substantive due process-equal protection.[231] That these results often were more the products of professional inertia and of social pressures and conditioning in an age of unfettered economic and industrial expansion, rather than of anything superficially identifiable as "judicial bias," would seem to be evident from the materials examined.

The significant point is that perspective, criticism and self-criticism[232] at length brought the Courts to see, long before the public

---

[228] See Timberg, *supra* note 1, at 556 and *passim*.

[229] *Cf.* Berle and Means' suggestion that if corporatization of the economy continues at recent rates corporation law may be the constitutional law of the future! BERLE AND MEANS, *op. cit. supra* note 1, at 356–357.

[230] The phrase is Justice Holmes'?

[231] *Cf.* Pound, *Liberty to Contract*, 18 YALE L.J. 454 (1909); TWISS, *supra* note 58.

[232] *I.e.*, the dissents and writings of Holmes, Brandeis, Stone and Cardozo; and the criticisms of Thayer, Pound, Corwin, Powell and Haines, to mention only those who pioneered the educative process.

clearly did, that to decide complex social and economic issues, ostensibly by these simple rules of logic and inference, yet actually by what was "hostile" or "arbitrary" or "due" or "equal," really was to subvert the principle of representative, responsible government. Constitutional government and judicial review did not—in fact could not—mean judicial censorship or stewardship in matters of social policy and expediency.[233]

Today, therefore, self-knowledge and self-limitation have drawn the teeth of federal substantive due process. In consequence, corporate personality by itself is scarcely a formidable doctrine.[234] One prefers to believe, moreover, that such self-knowledge marks a maturing of judicial review, and hence, practically, has become an unwritten part of the federal Constitution. Surely for a nation so thoroughly committed to judicial review, it would be a strange self-doubt or mistrust that would call at this date for *judicial* renunciation of the corporate person as needed security against future *judicial* misuse. The corporate person too, has come of age and lost its innocence.

EDITORIAL NOTE. Nine harried Noahs in a creaking troubled ark; a forty-year deluge and no relief in sight. Thus members of the Waite Court must occasionally have imagined themselves during the late 1880's. More and more, the business of the Supreme Court—indeed of all the federal courts—was coming to be business, and corporate business, corporate enterprise at that. Yet "The Business of the Supreme Court," as Frankfurter and Landis meticulously have shown, at this period literally was nobody's business. Nobody's business but Congress's, and all Congress could do—all Congress did, in any event—was to continue expansion of federal appellate business, adding new states and districts to the circuits, liberalizing "removals" and "diversity" suits, swelling dockets, and hence arrearages. This melancholy tale Frankfurter and Landis told and documented fully in 1927, the very year of the Beards' *Rise*; and the bearing and the implications today are inescapable. The wonder, indeed, is not that these Justices, like other men, occasionally erred or faltered; rather, that they coped at all, and managed to survive the burdens so heedlessly, so planlessly heaped upon them.

---

[233] See Chapter 3, *supra*.
[234] *Cf.* Chapter 6, *supra*, n.12, 58.

An Innocent Abroad

The crucial facts are that the Court's docket and arrearages doubled each decade from the 1860's through the 1880's, as litigation increased, as cases grew more complex and intricate, suits longer, briefs bulkier, circuits larger, corporate appeals more frequent, constitutional questions more numerous, and seemingly endless.[1] Yet these forgotten harried Justices still lacked even law clerks and adequate libraries; there were yet no "Brandeis briefs" to pinpoint and explore novel issues, to warn of pitfalls and easy presumptions—no more than there yet were *amicae* briefs filed on behalf of Negroes in those momentous suits which decided, not just the rights of the litigants, but of a race—and that, for two generations.

The now obvious point is that there is much more to both "process" and to "protection" than mere deciding—than Supreme Court judging alone. Historians—even constitutional historians—have been slow to make this clear. The matter thus is underscored as we sense belatedly that it was the nation and the generation which gave so little thought to this Court, and to Constitutionalism, treating both in this cavalier fashion—which eventually were pained to discover, as the Supreme Court itself did after 1939, that control over corporations had rather offhandedly, too easily, perhaps half-inadvertently been curbed in the 1880's and 1890's, and curbed first and along with the state taxing power.

Why, during the 1880's, did the state taxing power become the crucial and the controverted power, the focal point of attack via the Fourteenth Amendment? And precisely—or imprecisely—what was the Justices' own role, intent, and attitude in this matter?

If only we had the answers to the second of these questions, as soon, in Chapters 11 and 12, we shall begin to find an answer to the first, how much clearer American constitutional history would be.

Reviewing the ground, and the cases covered in footnotes 97 through 114 *supra*, the student soon appreciates how many fact situations, how many very technical problems of taxation, all with constitutional overtones and undertones, got considered and decided during these years before what eventually came to be the crucial and decisive constitutional point got clearly raised, faced, and decided.

It remains to stress the implications of this fact. "Ripeness" for constitutional adjudication and decision is a vital matter of sophisti-

---

[1] FRANKFURTER & LANDIS, Chapter 2, pp. 56–102, especially the statistics on case loads, pp. 60, 69, and 86. Almost without exception, the justices' correspondence during the Chase and Waite Court period reveals the oppressiveness of expanding dockets and arrearages.

cated judgment and of rather tight discretionary control today.[2] How different the situation here! Given these tremendous pressures and arrearages of the 1870's and 1880's; given the confused *Slaughter-House* and Reconstruction positions generally; calling to mind again the gruff expostulations, and even the oar- and the finger-bashings meted out to counsel and to half-frenzied boarders in *Davidson v. New Orleans*, one senses how rudderless, how much at the mercy of professional and natural elements, this constitutional ark was. It was heroically manned and tended, to be sure; yet dedication and seamanship simply were not enough.

True it was and is that due process–equal protection constitutionalism finally emerged from this very crisis and context; and emerged, we must remember, as a syncretic, decisional tool that made possible a fact-oriented law and constitutionalism. In this job and environment, "inclusion and exclusion of cases," had to be the rule and the solution. No member of the Court apparently mistrusted due process more than Justice Miller, yet it was Miller who accepted and announced that rule, and in the *Davidson* case at that. And why not? What else was available, what else was better, what else was preferable, in this, the second century of American constitutionalism? And at this date (1877 to the mid-80's), it still happily was largely a matter of "exclusion." So far, fine and easy!

Looking back now, with the Court's due process–equal protection log in hand, we seem to see, and to read a charted course. Yet to the judges minding and shifting cargo, taking soundings and punishment, deciding cases at the rate these prophets had to, half the problem was to accept the almost unbearable situation, get on with the job and with the cases, using that tool which seemed to have a judicial and a popular potential. Avoid and evade, in short, don't decide the abstract or the hypothetical. The meaning or upshot of all this is that the factual fundamentals of the cases of the 1880's are peripheral for us now, just as the jurisprudential rationales of the 1860's were largely peripheral then—or got treated so, if possible, and for as long as possible.

This is what makes the genetic history of due process and equal protection so clotted, clouded, and tantalizing. And it also, I submit, is one clue, if not the key, to how and to why so much of what

---

[2] Yet the problem persists. See Davis, *Ripeness of Governmental Action for Judicial Review*, 68 HARV. L. REV. 1122–1153, 1326–1373 (1955), and the updated discussion in K. DAVIS, ADMINISTRATIVE LAW TREATISE (1958), Chapter 21. See also Note, *Federal-Question Abstention: Justice Frankfurter's Doctrine in an Activist Era*, 80 HARV. L. REV. 604–622 (1967).

eventually came to be doctrinaire laissez faire and liberty to contract, got its start and its hold. Questions just came too thick and fast, were too snarled, ramifying, and inseverable; and these rubrics for their disposition and decision (unlike the merits), simply were too broad and too general to enable the Court, in the time and in the premises, to match practice and result on the one hand with the formal opinions, arguments, and rhetoric on the other. When too many questions get rolled into one, courts, like other deciders, are in trouble. Deciding one thing, they appear to be, and sometimes are, deciding or prejudging others. Yet given these overall conditions, who can wonder at the results? Can either the framers, or the Court, be blamed for this situation or breakdown?

These, in 1954-1955, were further queries and reflections as one surveyed the still enigmatic rise of corporate due process and of "judicialized laissez faire." The taxing power obviously was the crucial power, the point of entry, the power for re-study. And it had to be studied in Congress, in the states, in the circuits, not just in the Supreme Court. The Thirty-ninth and the Fortieth Congresses —the period of draftsmanship and ratification of the Fourteenth Amendment—were the point to begin. Perhaps those railroads and insurance companies finally would shed some light.

[CHAPTER 10]

*"Builded Better Than They Knew":
The Framers, the Railroads and
the Fourteenth Amendment*

EDITORIAL NOTE. In limbo, yet still unlaid in 1954–1955, were those wraiths of Beardian *realpolitik* and of my own early "over-circumstanced" case and research. The conspicuous yet still ambiguous and undefined activity of the northeastern insurance and express companies was topped by the gratuitous and still unclarified interest of those Pennsylvania and Ohio railroads; and just what relation did those two groups, and their respective interests and activities, bear to the leading framers of the Fourteenth Amendment, and to the draftsmanship generally? If, as had begun to appear more and more likely, I had researched myself into an absurd historical corner at the outset in the 1930's, it would be some satisfaction and consolation to research out again—to prove that ingenuity at least ran in both directions.

Fortunately, two publications at this point provided unexpected aid, comfort, and stimulus. First, *American Business Corporations Until 1860 with Special Reference to Massachusetts*, by E. M. Dodd (Harvard University Press, 1954). This major posthumous work by the distinguished legal historian and authority on American corporation law provided just the grounding and bases needed for reevaluation of the whole problem, and of the companies' strategy; the more, indeed, since the constitutional position of corporations and legal trends in the northeastern states were specially stressed.

Hardly had I completed my study and review of this work, and of the law it covered, than there appeared in the March, 1955, number of the *Mississippi Valley Historical Review* an article by a visiting English historian, J. F. S. Russell, "The Railroads in 'The Conspiracy Theory' of the Fourteenth Amendment." Russell's research at the Library of Congress, and at the Library of the Bureau of Railway Economics, so well complemented and extended my own, and vice versa, that a final assay and synthesis of the findings of the

1953 Guggenheim trip now progressed rapidly. Two researchers working parallel and independently had at last arrived at similar, negative, and for the most part corrobative conclusions on "framer intent," insofar as the railroads were involved. Russell's essay also showed that "conspiracy" could bedevil English historical thinking as readily as American; and his treatment was seen to be weakest in the discussions of law and politics in a federal system.

Some matters thus finally were severable, perhaps even terminable: How the Conspiracy Theory had evolved; what so long had supported and sustained it even after 1938; the evidentiary and the historiographic implications, particularly as these related to due process development and predilections in general; beyond this, the fascinating tale of those two cities—Philadelphia and Baltimore—and their half century of fierce commercial rivalry. This last was *realpolitik* indeed, even if not quite the constitutional variety envisioned.

Fortunately, too, Pennsylvania during this period had been one of the few states which fully reported its legislative debates; hence discussion in the Pennsylvania legislature and elsewhere of the arbitrary repealers of rival roads' charters, 1864–1869, afforded potentially significant insight, and in fact bore directly on the "original understanding" of due process as related to corporate rights, "persons," and "property."

The denouement certainly is anticlimatic until we remind ourselves again that "Due process is as due process does"; and that in 1865–1866 due process still had "done" very little in this corporate field. Hence legislators still were mute—still failed expressly to anticipate, and to invoke the guarantee, even in one of the likeliest of all situations. Failed and were mute, for quite obvious reasons: Economically and corporately, the due process tradition obviously still lay ahead, still was on the make. Laws deemed bad for business already occasionally were thought, claimed, even inferentially held to violate due process. But not yet—not until courts had made this point much more explicit—could such laws be cited as "bad" because they violated due process. Due, in short, did not *in these premises*, nor to many, yet signify duty—not even judicial duty.

All this is as elementary, as simple, as fundamental as the reversed images we see constantly in the mirror; indeed, this simply is the analogous, reversed, temporal-legal corporate image. How difficult it has been, how hard it is, for laymen—yes, even for lawyers and for historians—to grasp this fact and principle, and grasping, to remember and to apply both.

[CHAPTER 10]

DID the Joint Congressional Committee of Fifteen which in 1866 drafted the Fourteenth Amendment contemplate or understand corporations to be among the "persons" protected by the due process and equal protection clauses? Is there any likelihood corporate citizenship under the privileges or immunities clause also was considered and expressly approved or rejected by the framers?

These and various subsidiary questions have excited interest among judges,[1] lawyers and historians[2] for almost three generations. Before they can be decisively answered, the positive or negative role of two major business groups—railroads and insurance companies—must be clearly determined. This essay will concern itself solely with the potential and role of the railroads and the relations of such roads to the due process and equal protection clauses.[3] Its primary object is to establish the truth or falsity of that impression, first created by Senator Roscoe Conkling in his celebrated argument before the Supreme Court in the *San Mateo Case* of 1882.[4] Conkling, it will be remembered, there let drop a veritable bombshell. Appearing in his joint capacity as counsel for the Southern Pacific Railroad and as one of the surviving members of the Joint Committee of Fifteen which sixteen years earlier had drafted the amendment, he intimated that the word "person" had not been used in section one, solely with the view

---

[1] *Cf.* Wheeling Steel Corporation v. Glander, 337 U.S. 562, 576–581 (1949) (dissenting opinion, JJ. Douglas and Black); Connecticut Gen. Life Ins. Co. v. Johnson, 303 U.S. 77, 87 (1938) (dissenting opinion of Justice Black); (The Santa Clara Railroad Tax Case) County of Santa Clara v. Southern Pacific R.R., 18 Fed. 385 (C.C. Cal. 1883); County of San Mateo v. Southern Pacific R.R., 13 Fed. 722 (C.C. Cal. 1882); Insurance Co. v. New Orleans, 13 Fed. Cas. 67, No. 7052 (C.C. La. 1871); and see Chapter 9, *supra*.

[2] For history and criticism of the thesis that corporations were among the intended beneficiaries of the framers, see Chapters 1–2, *supra*; Boudin, *Truth and Fiction about the Fourteenth Amendment*, 16 N.Y.U.L.Q. REV. 19 (1938); McLaughlin, *The Court, the Corporation and Conkling*, 46 AM. HIST. REV. 45 (1940); Hurst, Book review, 52 HARV. L. REV. 851 (1939). See also note 12 *infra*.

[3] 1968: For a summary of findings and conclusions with reference to the role of the insurance companies, see Chapter 13, *infra*, Editorial Note, p. 552.

[4] 116 U.S. 138 (1885). CONKLING'S ARGUMENT, made December 20, 1882, is analyzed in Chapter 1, *supra*, pp. 35–45; see also Chapter 9, *supra*, at notes 166–186. The ARGUMENT is reprinted in full, with those of other Railroad counsel, in PROCEEDINGS OF THE COMMITTEE ON THE JUDICIARY REGARDING RAILROAD TAX SUITS. CALIFORNIA LEGISLATURE, ASSEMBLY, 28th sess. Journal Appendix, vol. 8, no. 3, pp. 77–111 (1889), the constitutional portions appearing at pp. 83–95. Those portions are reprinted Appendix I, *infra*, pp. 595ff., with the original (1882) paging indicated, and are cited hereafter by that original paging.

to protecting the freedmen, southern loyalists and natural persons, as so long supposed. Rather, it also had been used with an eye toward the plight of corporations—artificial persons—unjustly set upon by state legislatures and state regulation.

"At the time the fourteenth amendment was ratified," he stated—Conkling obviously meant "drafted," or his argument would have been pointless—"individuals and joint stock companies were appealing for congressional and administrative protection against invidious and discriminating State and local taxes. One instance was that of an express company (whose stock was owned largely by citizens of the State of New York) which came with petitions and bills seeking congressional acts in resisting what they deemed oppressive taxation in two states, and oppressive and ruinous rules of damages applied under state laws."[5] No details, no amplification on this crucial and tantalizing point! Simply the unmistakable inference or innuendo that Conkling and his colleagues had taken cognizance of these appeals, and had employed the term "person" in those clauses protecting property rights in contradistinction to the narrower term "citizen" which they had used in the privileges or immunities clause to protect political and civil rights.

Shortly after this argument the Supreme Court began broadening the scope of the equal protection and due process clauses.[6] Substantive interpretations became commoner, first in criminal[7] and humanitarian,[8] then in economic[9] cases. In 1886 corporate personality itself won the Court's *imprimatur* by a curious acquiescence.[10] Under these

---

[5] CONKLING'S ARGUMENT, 25.

[6] See CORWIN, LIBERTY AGAINST GOVERNMENT c. 4 (1948), and works there cited. MOTT, DUE PROCESS OF LAW (1926); Cushman, *The Social and Economic Interpretation of the Fourteenth Amendment*, 20 MICH. L. REV. 737 (1922), reprinted, 2 SEL. ESSAYS CONST. LAW 60 (1938); Haines, *The History of Due Process After the Civil War*, reprinted, id. at 268.

[7] See Hurtado v. California, 110 U.S. 516 (1884).

[8] See Yick Wo v. Hopkins, 118 U.S. 356 (1886); Barbier v. Connolly, 113 U.S. 27, 31 (1885) (dicta). For the backgrounds of these Ninth Circuit Chinese cases, and the role of the so-called "Ninth Circuit law" in spearheading the substantive revolution in due process and equal protection, see Chapter 3, *supra* especially at 137, 143ff.

[9] See *Chicago, M. & St. P. R.R. v. Minnesota*, 134 U.S. 418, 458 (1890) (dictum): "The question of the reasonableness of a rate . . . is eminently a question for judicial investigation, requiring due process of law for its determination." Smyth v. Ames, 169 U.S. 466 (1898); Allgeyer v. Louisiana, 165 U.S. 578 (1897); Reagan v. Farmers' Loan & Trust Co., 154 U.S. 362, 458 (1894).

[10] At the opening of argument in *Santa Clara County v. Southern Pacific R.R.*, Chief Justice Waite announced that the Court would not hear reargument on whether the equal protection Clause applied to "these corporations." "We are all of the opinion that it does," 118 U.S. 394, 396 (1886): thus in effect affirming the two 9th Circuit holdings on corporate personality, see note 1 *supra*, and reversing *Insurance Co. v. New Orleans*, 13 Fed. Cas. 67, No. 7052. See Chapter 9, *supra* note 1.

circumstances, Conkling's argument naturally began to appear, first as a turning point, then as the prime mover. And gradually, as courts expanded their social and economic veto during the years 1890–1910,[11] his statements began to assume something of the character of a revelation: Had a coterie of Republican corporation lawyers perhaps slipped a joker into section one? Had the word "person" been used as a *double entendre* to give corporations and business interests generally increased judicial protection against legislatures? As suspicions of this sort crystallized,[12] they were eventually formulated and given an immense popularity by Charles and Mary Beard in *The Rise of American Civilization*.[13] Wholly undocumented, except for Conkling's *ipse dixit* and a statement by the leading draftsmen, Bingham (which statement[14] proved on analysis to have been made without reference to corporate personality per se)—this so-called "Conspiracy Theory" became in time almost an article of historical faith—challenged if at all, only by a few legal and constitutional historians[15] who objected that substantive due process had not yet developed to a point in 1866 where its use on behalf of corporations could have been readily conceived, or, speaking more accurately, anticipated.

Mounting skepticism and controversy over the Beardian interpretations at length led to a search for evidence in the briefs and con-

---

[11] See note 6, *supra*, also Pound, *Liberty to Contract*, 18 YALE L.J. 454 (1909), reprinted 2 SEL. ESSAYS CONST. LAW 208 (1938) and the useful tables of fourteenth amendment cases and opinions in FRANKFURTER, MR. JUSTICE HOLMES AND THE SUPREME COURT (1938) Appendices I, II. Also see similar summaries, graphs and analyses in Appendices C, E, F of Collins, *The Fourteenth Amendment and the States* (1914).

[12] The "Conspiracy Theory's" topsy-like growth can be traced in BEARD, CONTEMPORARY AMERICAN HISTORY 55–56 (1910); 2 BEARD AND BEARD, THE RISE OF AMERICAN CIVILIZATION 111–13 (1927); FAULKNER, POLITICAL AND ECONOMIC HISTORY OF THE UNITED STATES 416 (5th ed. 1952); HACKER, TRIUMPH OF AMERICAN CAPITALISM 387-92 (1940); HACKER AND KENDRICK, THE UNITED STATES SINCE 1865 (3d ed. 1939); KENDRICK, THE JOURNAL OF THE JOINT COMMITTEE OF FIFTEEN ON RECONSTRUCTION 17–36 (1914); TAYLOR, THE ORIGIN AND GROWTH OF THE AMERICAN CONSTITUTION (1911); WEBB, DIVIDED WE STAND: THE CRISIS OF A FRONTIERLESS DEMOCRACY c. 3 (1937).

[13] Vol. 2, pp. 111–13 (1927).

[14] The "letter for letter and syllable for syllable" quotation relied on by the Beards was from Bingham's speech in the House in 1871. See CONG. GLOBE, 42d Cong., 1st Sess., Appendix 83–85 (1871). Close reading reveals that Bingham was explaining why he had changed from a positive to a negative form of amendment draft in 1866. Yet his remarks frequently have been interpreted as if they avowed—or otherwise revealed —an intention with regard to corporate personality or citizenship. They do no such thing.

[15] Among the confirmed skeptics were Professors Hamilton, *Property—According to Locke*, 41 YALE L.J. 864, 875 (1932), and Chafee, book review, 41 HARV. L. REV. 265, 268 (1927). See also 2 BOUDIN, GOVERNMENT BY JUDICIARY 404 (1932); and E. R. LEWIS, A HISTORY OF AMERICAN POLITICAL THOUGHT FROM THE CIVIL WAR TO THE WORLD WAR 28 (1937).

"Builded Better Than They Knew" 443

gressional debates—and to some startling discoveries.[16] Three in particular put a new face on the problem:

1. It was found that Conkling's elaborate brief and argument of 1882 actually were built upon and around a daring misuse[17] of the Joint Committee's Journal—that document of 1866 which he had produced and employed with such dramatic effect before the Court. This misuse was primarily a misquotation—the substitution by Conkling as he read from the Journal to the Court in 1882, of "citizen" for "person" in the text of one of the primitive drafts of what afterward became the due process and equal protection clauses of 1866.[18] Listeners thus naturally gained the impression, strengthened by other portions of Conkling's argument, that later on, during the Joint Committee's labors in 1866, the word "person" had been reinstated. Offhand, of course, Conkling's innuendo supplied a plausible reason. Yet here was the very official manuscript text from which Conkling purportedly had quoted; it revealed that "person" *always* had been employed in the Committee's drafts—the main reason clearly being that the wordings had been taken from the phraseology of the fifth amendment. Some of Conkling's minor propositions also were dubious,[19] but this one point was crucial, and it cast grave doubt on his entire thesis. For it was past understanding that an advocate with a clear, strong case ever would prejudice it by this brazen historical forgery.

2. Equally baffling was the equivocal, almost sporting character of other contentions and passages in Conkling's argument.[20] Indeed, he not only declined to develop or press this crucial point of the Committee's intent to protect corporations; in the end, he substantially abandoned it. At one point he argued merely that the framers *"must have known* the meaning and force of the term persons"—and spoke in the next sentence of "this surmise."[21] In his peroration, he squarely faced the very obstacle to his thesis which later troubled the legal historians:

> The statesman has no horoscope which maps the measureless spaces of a nation's life and lays down in advance all the bearings

---

[16] See Chapter 1, *supra*.
[17] *Id.*, especially at 35ff.
[18] *Id.* at 42ff., comparing the passage in CONKLING'S ARGUMENT, PROCEEDINGS, *supra* note 4 at 86, with the correct original text in the *Journal* as printed in KENDRICK, *op. cit. supra* note 12, at 51.
[19] See Chapter 1, *supra*, propositions numbered 1, 2, 4 as examined in the discussion at 38ff.
[20] *Ibid.*
[21] *Ibid.* And see CONKLING'S ARGUMENT, 31.

of its career. . . . Those who devised the Fourteenth Amendment may have builded better than they knew. . . . To some of them, the sunset of life may have given mystical lore.[22]

Certainly a strange, equivocal choice of words and arguments, for one deeply and affirmatively committed!

3. More fundamental than either of the foregoing was the further discovery that the privileges or immunities-due process-equal protection trilogy employed by the Joint Committee and by Congress in their drafts in 1866 actually was an old antislavery triad evolved more than thirty years before by the abolitionists and employed repeatedly by them and by others during the constitutional and sectional struggles which culminated in the Civil War.[23] In short, when the Joint Committee set to work in 1865–66 it found in these clauses a ready-made system of constitutional shorthand which already had done yeoman's service for a generation. Bingham and the other drafters had been familiar with it from youth as a bulwark for the civil rights of free Negroes, slaves, and abolitionists.[24] What could have been more natural, accordingly, than that they should prefer to stick to these familiar clauses—as the guarantees of greatest appeal—in order to safeguard the rights of the freedmen? In short, "persons" probably had been used in 1866 for these reasons, and because it had appeared in the fifth amendment, and in most of the state due process clauses, *not* because of any solicitous regard for corporations.

Collectively these three discoveries blighted the whole Conkling-Beard thesis. More likely than not, it seemed that the framers' purposes and understanding in 1866 had been those which antislavery men had shared and had pursued for a generation. That is to say, their purpose had been to outlaw race and color as tests of fundamental rights; to abolish public race discrimination, thus cutting off the roots of bigotry; to enforce nationally the great guarantees of the Bill of Rights which would effectuate these purposes; and toward these great ends, to nationalize citizenship and place civil rights rising out of state legislation and administration under certain national guarantees of equality. More significantly still, and in keeping with the habits of thought and tenets of the times, their purpose had been

---

[22] *Id.* at 34.
[23] For Bingham's use 1856–1866, see Chapter 1, *supra*, at 53ff. For history and evolution of abolitionist theory, and its subsequent bearings, see TENBROEK, THE ANTISLAVERY ORIGINS OF THE FOURTEENTH AMENDMENT (1951), and Chapter 4, *supra*.
[24] Bingham was a student at Franklin College, an abolitionist stronghold, 1837–39, during the peak of the antislavery crusade in Ohio. See Chapter 4, *supra*, at 199 Stevens, Salmon P. Chase, and other influential antislavery leaders were influenced or converted at this time. See *ibid.*, and Chapter 7, *supra* at 301, note 18ff.

"Builded Better Than They Knew"

to declare (via another and cautionary amendment, which would supplement the Thirteenth) that the foregoing *always* had been the *true law* of the Constitution, as still earlier they had been the ideal and the ethical creed of the American people as expressed in the Declaration of Independence and Bills of Rights.[25] If this had been the real orientation of the framers in 1866—and the evidence itself was overwhelming—the corporations angle appeared more and more unlikely and insignificant.

There remained, however, Conkling's factual statements. What about that New York express company? Was it true or not that corporations "had come with petitions and bills" while the Amendment was in draft? If true, what (if any) significance had to be accorded the fact? Search of the congressional journals and *Globe* soon turned up evidence which seemed momentarily to inject new life into Conkling's thesis. Two episodes in particular merited close examination.

First, the initial session of the Thirty-Ninth Congress had witnessed an all-out effort by American insurance companies to fight free of what was to them most oppressive local regulation.[26] A nation-wide petition and write-your-congressman campaign had been launched in 1865–66 against one of the recurrent waves of state license, tax, and bonding laws such as had plagued out-of-state insurance and express companies from the beginning. These petitions, which on their face seemed to meet the requirements of Conkling's statement, were found to have come to attention of individual members of the Joint Committee, including Conkling himself, while the amendment was in draft. Since they related to the right to trade and to be freed from "invidious and discriminating" state and local taxes and "onerous and oppressive rules of damages," it was at first conceivable they might have had some such influence as Conkling intimated.

Second, and potentially corroborative also, and even more suggestive in overall implications, were still other petitions found addressed to Congress by two railroad companies whose charters had been summarily repealed in 1864 by the Pennsylvania legislature.[27] These roads—the Cleveland & Mahoning and the Pittsburgh & Connellsville—thus had lost a furious contest to the entrenched and monopolistic Pennsylvania Railroad. But later, in 1865–1866, lawyers for the Pittsburgh & Connellsville managed to overturn the repealers in the United States Circuit Court[28]—only to be harassed thereafter by a

---

[25] See notes 23, 24 *supra*, and Chapter 6, *supra*.
[26] See Chapter 2 *supra*.
[27] *Id.*, especially at 85ff. See also Chapter 3, *supra* at 123, note 57.
[28] See Baltimore v. Pittsburgh & C. R.R., 2 Fed. Cas. 570, No. 827 (C.C.W.D. Pa., 1865), discussed note 109 *infra*.

series of vexatious suits in Pennsylvania state courts. In a flanking counter-attack the challengers finally sought aid from Congress. Bills sponsored by James A. Garfield and Thaddeus Stevens—the latter the most powerful and influential member of the Joint Committee which then was drafting the Fourteenth Amendment—sought to make both lines national post roads, and a bill actually passed the House which renewed the state-repealed charters on that ground. Conkling, Stevens and Bingham all were found to have voted for these bills, and hence presumably were familiar with the road's plight and problems. Finally, and potentially the most significant fact of all, the Pittsburgh & Connellsville's case had been handled in the federal court by Senator Reverdy Johnson.[29] Johnson beyond doubt was one of the ablest constitutional lawyers in the country; he had participated in the *Dred Scott* case; and he too was a member of the Joint Committee of Fifteen in 1866! Though one of the Democratic minority, he consistently had favored Bingham's due process-equal protection drafts![30] Judge Grier's opinion suggested too, that there had been a rather roundabout use of due process in this case; and still more to the point, it appeared that due process development in Pennsylvania had proceeded far enough so that such use by Grier and Johnson, if studiously considered, could have been made with some latent insight into its potentialities as a judicial shield for business.

But if these facts inclined one to give Conkling the benefit of the doubt, others certainly did not. Indeed, second thoughts hardly were reassuring. It was hard to believe, that if the Joint Committee intended to aid these or other corporations, or if it had intended to afford added judicial bulwarks for corporate and vested rights, and meant to secure a freer right of interstate trade—that these purposes had remained unknown to the beneficiaries. Congressmen rarely are secretive about favors they bestow, and more to the point, businessmen seldom permit them to be. Numerous cases arose in the early post-Civil War years—*Ward v. Maryland*,[31] various railroad tax cases[32]

---

[29] See STEINER, LIFE OF REVERDY JOHNSON (1914); DICT. AM. BIOG.

[30] Johnson was absent from several early sessions of the Joint Committee, and (as a Democrat) voted against reporting out any amendment drafts. He also consistently opposed the "privileges and immunities" wording, and on January 27, 1866, moved unsuccessfully to strike it from an early draft. KENDRICK, *op. cit. supra* note 12, at 57. But in the crucial sessions on April 21, 25, 28, Johnson favored Bingham's due process-equal protection-just compensation phraseology. KENDRICK, *op. cit. supra* at 85, 98, 106. Later, on the floor of the Senate, Johnson avowed his support of a due process clause, but thought the privileges or immunities clause "quite objectionable . . . simply because I don't understand what will be the effect of that." CONG. GLOBE, 39th Cong., 1st Sess. 3041 (1866).

[31] 79 U.S. (12 Wall.) 418 (1871).

[32] *E.g.*, Delaware Railroad Tax Cases, 85 U.S. (18 Wall.) 206 (1874); see arguments in 21 L. Ed. 888 (1874). See also notes 125, 171 *infra*.

and the *Granger Cases*[33] among others, in which, had the framers really anticipated these points, and had they intended, as Conkling later implied, to give interstate business added judicial protection as against the states, one would expect such intentions to have been made known, almost at once—and perhaps first of all in a case like *Ward v. Maryland* involving the commercial rights of *natural* persons. Not a word, however, was breathed for sixteen years! And is it conceivable that *if* Reverdy Johnson, for example, had clearly understood and intended in 1866 that an added due process limitation against the states would constitute a valuable judicial safeguard for business fighting state regulation, that he himself would fail, as he did in 1869 when arguing the hardfought case of *Veazie v. Fenno*,[34] to employ the due process clause *of the fifth amendment* in behalf of a corporate client fighting against a drastic federal law? Johnson was a peerless lawyer. A lifetime at the bar with men like Wirt and Webster and Taney had given him as much insight into the potentialities of due process as any man in the country. Yet here we have him apparently ignoring the guarantee in a manner difficult to reconcile with any clearcut *presumed* insight or intention. In short, this circumstance that sixteen years elapsed before even an inkling was dropped, sticks in the historian's craw. Customarily astute draftsmen and smooth operators do not choose to wait a decade and a half to divulge intentions and reap contemplated gains. Roscoe Conkling himself certainly was not this bashful, patient type.[35] And he would have sensed intuitively that every year's delay made his tale ring less true.

A still more serious and fundamental difficulty inheres in the relation of these Republican leaders to judicial review itself in the fifties and sixties.[36] Bingham,[37] Conkling,[38] Stevens[39] and the others were

---

[33] *E.g.*, Chicago, B. & Q. R.R. v. Cutts, 94 U.S. 155 (1877).

[34] 75 U.S. (8 Wall.) 53 (1869). See 19 L. Ed. 482, 483 (1869) for a summary of Johnson's argument.

[35] CHIDSEY, THE GENTLEMEN FROM NEW YORK (1935) is an unsatisfactory yet revealing biography of Conkling.

[36] See 2 WARREN, THE SUPREME COURT IN UNITED STATES HISTORY 542 (1923); and vol. 3, c. 26, 27, 29, 30, and debates there cited, for Republican attacks on the Court, 1856–1868.

[37] *Ibid.* And CONG. GLOBE, 34th Cong., 1st Sess. Appendix 122 (Jan. 13, 15, 1856); CONG. GLOBE, 36th Cong., 1st Sess. 1839 (April 24, 1860); CONG. GLOBE, 39th Cong., 2d Sess. 250, 501 (Jan. 3, 16, 1867).

[38] See 3 WARREN, *op. cit. supra* note 36 at 69; CONG. GLOBE, 36th Cong., 1st Sess. Appendix 233–236 (April 17, 1860). This speech attacking the Dred Scott decision, the judicial veto and judicial review is one of the strongest reasons for skepticism of the claim that Conkling in the mid-60's anticipated an expansion of judicial review even as against states. See especially *id.* at 233 c. 1, bottom, and 234, c. 3, bottom.

[39] See 3 WARREN, *op. cit. supra* note 36 at 170; CONG. GLOBE, 39th Cong., 2d Sess. 251 (Jan. 3, 1867).

among the severest critics of the Supreme Court and judicial review. One can scarcely avoid the conclusion that it would have constituted a curious—an almost unparalleled case of political schizophrenia—for men of such bent to have consciously and simultaneously *increased* both the powers and discretion of the very Court which they, like most old antislavery men, still viewed with a profound and ever growing mistrust, and which they repeatedly had attacked both in Congress and out.

Finally, *congressional legislation*—not judicial relief, not expanded judicial review—unquestionably, and by Conkling's own statement, was what these corporations themselves had sought in 1866. On its face this point presents perhaps the major obstacle to Conkling's premise. For it certainly is not immediately clear how petitions and bills seeking national *legislative* regulation by Congress somehow influenced that body rather to expand *judicial* power and discretion over the petitioning businesses. Often Congress proves to be callous or indifferent or absent-minded; but rarely is it so gauche, so humble, so precipitate and round-about as this. Even if substantive due process and equal protection are discovered to have been highly enough developed in 1866 to make such a step appear possible, this maneuver and abdication still seem out of character, unlikely, and impolitic. Only if special, overriding considerations are found to have been operative can skepticism reasonably be abandoned here. Together with the general Negro race orientation of sections one and five as a whole, this obstacle is grave and primary.

Clearly, these problems are too important to be left suspended in this unsatisfactory state. *Lately they have been subject of two independent, overlapping, and fortunately, corroborative, studies.* Dr. Russell, an English scholar in the United States under a government exchange fellowship, has spotlighted the role of the railroads. His findings have been reported in the *Mississippi Valley Historical Review*.[40] My own reinvestigations[41] meanwhile have included the parts played by both the railroads and the insurance companies. Though this report is concerned solely with the railroads, the insurance company evidence is equally, or even more conclusive.[42] In the light of the two studies it is hard to avoid a conclusion that Conkling's claim,

---

40 Russell, *The Railroads in the "Conspiracy Theory" of the Fourteenth Amendment*. 41 Miss. Valley Hist. Rev. 601 (1955).

41 Grateful acknowledgment is made to the John Simon Guggenheim Memorial Foundation for a Fellowship, 1953–54, which made possible these and other studies in American constitutional history.

42 For a summary, see Chapter 13, *infra*, Editorial Note.

as accepted and popularized by the Beards, was largely without substance; his equivocations hence were as necessary as they have proved puzzling, and there was more hope than irony or discretion in his remark that perhaps the framers had "builded better than they knew." Too much weight, it now appears almost certain, initially was attached to the mere existence and discovery of the various petitions. *Possibilities* were upgraded and counted as *probabilities*, and Conkling's statements were taken at more than their face value. Much still is obscure, and may remain so, but one at last is confident section one was not *drafted* by its framers, even incidentally, as a boon for business. It is barely possible, however, that section five was so regarded in part—wishfully and hopefully *by* business.

My final hypothesis is that Conkling became a prisoner of his hindsight, his exaggerations, his indiscretions. By the early seventies corporate personality had burst its chrysalis; by the late seventies it already loomed as something of a refuge, if not yet a panacea.[43] With his ego, and his instinct for self-dramatization, Conkling then perceived that in 1866 he and his colleagues on the Joint Committee had stood at one of the crossroads of history. Converging lines had intersected, parallel interests merged. Business, it seemed, had been seeking more than it got, and Congress aiming to give more than some members realized! Old bills and petitions were recalled, re-examined, memories jogged, notes and correspondence compared. Sure enough, it all had been as clear then as it was now: Had not corporations always been "persons"? Conkling's reminiscence was a great comfort to clients and troubled friends in New York and Washington.[44] But his and their will to believe was stronger than ease of proof! Tales out of school to eager, hardpressed clients during the seventies thus led eventually to the morass of inference, conjecture, and misquotation in the *San Mateo* case. Drama there substituted for proof; suggestion for detail; the merely plausible masqueraded as fact. Later, a merciful history all but buried the forgeries. Innuendo and hindsight, together with the trend of judicial review, gave prosaic facts an almost outlandish capacity to deceive. . . . But this is getting far ahead of our story. Here indeed are mystery and romance, a fascinating problem and lesson in historiography.

---

[43] See Chapter 9, *supra*, at 392.
[44] Among others, Justice Field and Conkling were close friends, bound together after 1877, by mutual contempt for President Hayes. See CHIDSEY, *op. cit. supra* note 35, at 204; Chapter 3, *supra* at 136, note 100; Field and Conkling both destroyed the bulk of their correspondence, but evidence of a more than casual friendship is preserved in what remains.

I.

First, a brief preliminary analysis and some cautionary notes.

What we seek is convincing evidence that the due process and equal protection clauses, *contemporaneously understood*, did or did not embrace either (a) corporate "person" or (b) corporate property *as such*. This evidence conceivably may take any one or more of several forms. Most convincing, would be direct evidence that the framers themselves, or other leading congressman, *contemplated* or *understood*[45] that the phraseology applied to corporate persons or to corporate property *per se*. The degree of intention or understanding conceivably might have been either primary or secondary—that is to say, either the dominant motivation, or merely an incidental one. Actually, however, too much is now known and agreed regarding the antislavery backgrounds of this phraseology,[46] and its Negro race motivations, to believe that any intention to embrace and protect corporations in 1866 was other than incidental or secondary.

These same possibilities of course—"contemplated" or "understood"—exist also with reference to the other groups involved—lawyers and business leaders, etc. For example, insurance men, assuming the initiative, might conceivably originate a draft or plan for corporate protection in Congress or the courts. Their sponsorship or activities in its behalf might then make others aware of heretofore unperceived coverage in the amendment. The reverse reflex is equally to be considered: Perhaps Congress was mentor rather than pupil?[47]

Thus far, we have been postulating what generally has been presumed to have been Conkling's meaning, namely that judicial review was what the framers did or did not have in mind. In short, assuming for the moment that the framers *did* have purposes beyond those which were publicly avowed, it is presumed further that those purposes related wholly to the courts and to judicial review. There is, however, another possibility—one already evident from the foregoing discussion—namely, that the added protection which was sought by business, and/or contemplated by Congress, really was for congressional protection under the terms of the amendment, rather than for judicial.[48]

---

[45] The verbs are terms of art; see the Supreme Court's memorandum decision in *Brown v. Board of Education of Topeka*, 345 U.S. 972 (1953), assigning the School Segregation Cases for reargument.
[46] See Chapters 4–7, *supra*.
[47] *Cf.* the various possibilities discussed Chapter 2, *supra*, at 80, 88ff.
[48] *Ibid.*

Sharpening and restating the matter, the issues appear to be these: I. Was corporate business *contemporaneously conceived* to be, along with the freedmen and southern loyalists, the co-beneficiary of an amendment whose *judicial construction* was to afford whatever relief was contemplated or assumed? *Or,* II. Was corporate business rather the co-beneficiary of an amendment which vastly enlarged congressional powers over persons and property, with whatever relief was contemplated or assumed, eventually to be supplied directly by Congress? If the answer is "yes," to either or to both of these questions, then how did the conception originate? A: *Primarily*, in and with Congress itself? *Or,* B: *Reflexively* and *passively*, as a result of the activities and program of business?

These possibilities seem to cover the whole ground, but before pursuing them it remains to note several limitations which exist in practice. The first is that there are reasons for serious doubt that *judicial* protection ever was the remedy sought or intended. The form and source of the petitions themselves are the most serious obstacle. Both the railroad and insurance companies really appealed for congressional relief,[49] and strictly speaking that was all Conkling himself alluded to:—the companies, he said, "came with petitions and bills seeking Acts of Congress." His innuendo was that these somehow had affected the draftsmanship, and that judicial relief had been intended under section one. But it must be remembered that Conkling studiously avoided *saying* this. Moreover, the form in which section one originally was cast—"Congress shall have power to . . . secure to all persons in every state equal protection . . ."[50] is far more consistent, *a priori*, with a postulated congressional relief, than it is with judicial relief. So too, is the final form, provided only that one accepts the conclusions of Flack and others who have reviewed the evidence, that the final negative and restraint form, "No State shall . . . deny . . . any person . . . equal protection," (with section five then giving Congress powers of enforcement by "appropriate legislation,") really was regarded, as Bingham himself later declared, as leaving Congress' powers intact, while providing *also* for direct constitutional and judicial protection *in addition* to congressional protection.[51]

---

[49] *Ibid.* And see Chapter 1, *supra*, at 35ff.

[50] See KENDRICK, *op. cit. supra* note 12, at 46, 51, 56, 60 (drafts and Committee action, Jan. 12–Feb. 3, 1866).

[51] See FLACK, THE ADOPTION OF THE FOURTEENTH AMENDMENT 76, 94–97, 232–237 (1908); Chapter 7, *supra* at 316. Note, for example, that Stevens, in introducing the final amendment to the House, and immediately after having paraphrased section one, added:

In sum, while pursuing our investigation we have to bear in mind that while the Conkling-Beard thesis heretofore presumed only an intended *judicial* relief, this is no longer the sole possibility, nor does it seem now, *a priori*, the most likely one.

A second caution is that since ninety years of historical study of Reconstruction, and almost seventy of mounting controversy over Conkling's thesis, have failed to adduce even a scrap of direct testimony to corroborate his innuendo,[52] we perhaps are obliged to face the likelihood that circumstantial evidence is the best that can be expected here. Yet this, of course, complicates and confuses the historical problem. For as originally stressed in the first chapter on the "Conspiracy Theory,"[53] circumstantial evidence is as dangerous and deceptive as quicksand, applied to a problem involving unavowed purposes and "conspiracy." The reason is that, since the purposes were unavowed, there is silence; silence in turn is easily equated with secrecy, and secrecy then masqueraded in as intent. The circular reasoning is obvious, but the tendency or temptation is inherent in the circumstances. There is no need to labor the point; it is enough if we face it squarely, and recognize the pitfalls and peculiar abuses that *negative findings* accordingly are subject to in situations of this sort. Patently, we must be rigorous in tests of proof and probability. In his original argument Conkling relied heavily on this very confusion, and on the conclusion-hopping faculty of the human mind. The changes in the scope of due process and judicial review which so favored Conkling in 1882 and later, of course, since have been magnified a thousandfold. Hence, so too have our difficulties in viewing these matters in the light that they appeared to men in 1866. Inevitably, we look backward through the large end of a very long and powerful telescope; but our job still is to try to view these matters as they appeared contemporaneously!

Fortunately, recent research into the antislavery backgrounds and Negro race origins of the war amendments has itself served as a help-

---

"I can hardly believe that any person can be found who will not admit that every one of these provisions is just. They are all asserted, in some form or other, in our DECLARATION or organic law. But the Constitution . . . is not a limitation on the States. This amendment supplies that defect, and *allows Congress* to correct the unjust legislation of the States, so far that the law which operates upon the one man shall operate *equally* upon all." (Emphasis added only to the words "allows Congress.") CONG. GLOBE, 39th Cong., 1st Sess. 2459 (1866).

52 Certainly this is an extraordinary situation—the one which in my view most discredits the Conkling-Beard thesis. Granted the difficulties of manuscript research, and the small group involved, this "secret" has been altogether too well kept. "Silence" originally was entitled to no probative value on a point of specific intent; but a near century of silence in the face of persistent search is another matter.

53 See Chapter 1, *supra*, at 46–47.

ful corrective in this respect.[54] No longer are we as naive about the true purposes, nor as gullible, as the public was generally during the period 1890–1935. Then the Conkling innuendo and the Beard thesis appeared to many citizens as a revelation—and to some, almost a pious benediction on the whole course of judicial history. So far, on the other hand, were the actual Negro race purposes of the amendment lost sight of in the twenties and thirties that even historians often were taken in by the corporation thesis—quite oblivious of broader implications.[55] Here, certainly is a final reminder and warning: The fundamental hazard in every situation of this sort is anachronistic thinking—a natural, and at times, almost irresistible tendency, or even temptation, to take simple patterns of favorable circumstance as evidence *of much more than that.* Any constitutional or legal doctrine inevitably is stratified history; it must be read from the bottom up, even when viewed from the top down. Added to this basic difficulty, is the further one here that ambiguity literally has been the making of this view of the amendment—from Conkling's willfully obscure initial argument through to the Beards' terse, undocumented popularization. In short, ambiguity, silence, and arguments from silence are among the major, inherent elements, even though unsatisfactory ones.[56] In the aggregate, these factors complicate our problem immeasurably, may even in the end, render it insolvable. At best, we shall have to work next to and around the problem, even while acknowledging the hazards.

II.

History has made Pennsylvanians acutely conscious of geography. That nearly perfect parallelogram on the map always has mocked at surveyors, congressmen and boards of trade.[57] Cleft almost in two diagonally and corrugated by the Allegheny Plateau, drained by river systems that flow through, or along, then off into other states and which for years made Baltimore the commercial capitol of regions represented at Harrisburg and dominated by Philadelphia, the politics and economics of Penn's woods often were as tangled and confused as its geography.

---

[54] See studies cited notes 23–25 *supra.*
[55] *E.g.,* see WEBB, *op. cit. supra* note 12, c. 3.
[56] On the characteristically negative, ambiguous nature of arguments, both *pro* and *con*, relating to the constitutional corporate "person", see Chapter 9, *supra*, at 376ff.
[57] Two excellent monographs are HARTZ, ECONOMIC POLICY AND DEMOCRATIC THOUGHT: PENNSYLVANIA, 1776–1860 (1948); Clark, *The Railroad Struggle for Pittsburgh: 43 Years of Philadelphia-Baltimore Rivalry, 1838–1871,* 48 PA. MAG. HIST. & BIOG. 1–37 (1924).

Early Philadelphia-Baltimore rivalry[58] for the traffic of the Susquehanna and Potomac basins—a struggle in which Baltimore held strong natural advantages—eventually was transformed by the Erie Canal (and later by the Erie and New York Central Railroads) into an even more complex three-way struggle in which New York City increasingly captured the western traffic to the Lakes via the Mohawk Gap, leaving Baltimore and Philadelphia fighting, first for a rival river-canal route, then for an all-rail route to Pittsburgh and the Ohio. Here, too, Baltimore held advantages of distance and topography—the Potomac valley affording a shorter, easier passage through the mountains to Wheeling or Pittsburgh than did the zigzagging Juniata. The result was a bitter, protracted conflict between the Baltimore and Ohio Railroad, heavily subsidized by the city, state, and commercial interests of Maryland, and the Pennsylvania Central, similarly aided and directed from Philadelphia.[59] During the forties this struggle reached epic proportions; every legislature at both Annapolis and Harrisburg became a free-for-all. In these contests Pittsburgh was both pawn and maverick. The city still was cut off by the Allegheny barrier, and as its leaders repeatedly declared, paying taxes and "tribute" to Philadelphia and the east for "state works" and canals that had benefited it hardly at all. Mistrusted by eastern Pennsylvanians for their geographic ties and natural preference for the Youghigheny-Cumberland-Potomac route to the Chesapeake, the westerners were both bidders and bidden. Baltimore repeatedly capitalized on Pittsburgh's fears of Wheeling as a rival western terminus of the B. & O.;[60] and Pittsburghers in turn sold their own support as dearly as possible—demanding and receiving Baltimore's bond subsidies for their pet western project, the Pittsburgh & Connellsville with its projected extension to meet the Baltimore & Ohio at Cumberland. Construction was slow, costly, beset by failures, panic, repudiation. Yet the main alliances held, and as gaps narrowed, rivalries quickened.

This historic rivalry soon was itself part of a larger process of growth and amalgamation.[61] By 1850 scores of independent local roads, built by home subsidy and capital, often of varying gauges,

---

[58] See LIVENGOOD, THE PHILADELPHIA-BALTIMORE TRADE RIVALRY (1947).

[59] See generally HARTZ and Clark, op. cit. supra note 57; HUNGERFORD, STORY OF THE BALTIMORE AND OHIO RAILROAD, 1827–1927 (1928); BURGESS & KENNEDY, CENTENNIAL HISTORY OF THE PENNSYLVANIA RAILROAD COMPANY, 1846–1946 (1949).

[60] See CLARK, op. cit. supra note 57, at 13–16; also, Crall, A Half-Century of Rivalry Between Pittsburgh and Wheeling, 13 WEST. PA. HIST. MAG. 237-255 (1930). In 1859 Pittsburgh and Allegheny County repudiated their bond support of the Pittsburgh & Connellsville Railroad.

[61] See Clark, op. cit. supra note 57, at 16–20.

"*Builded Better Than They Knew*" 455

began to coalesce and form trunk systems. Among the first to do so were the New York & Erie[62] and the New York Central.[63] With four major lines racing westward for Ohio traffic and connections, the struggle moved swiftly to climax. We have to think, as did the participants, of the northeastern and north central states as a gigantic chess board. Local and state rivalries, indispensable ordinances, and rights-of-way; necessary charter changes—these were the pawns and rooks of strategic play. A rival's state boundaries had somehow to be breached or overshot—one's own, guarded fanatically.

As the two New York roads pushed around Lake Erie from termini at Dunkirk and Buffalo, Pennsylvania's northwestern "Triangle," with its fifty-mile hypotenuse on the Lake jutting up between New York and Ohio—controlled from Harrisburg; or, as cynics had it, from J. Edgar Thomson's and Tom Scott's offices—became one of the capital assets of the new, rapidly expanding Pennsylvania System. The triangle was a more valuable and negotiable asset, since the gauge of Ohio's roads had been set by state law at 4 feet 10 inches.[64] The Erie's was 6 feet; the Pennsylvania's and New York Central's, four feet 8½ inches. As a precaution, the Pennsylvania legislature at first outlawed the two broader "foreign" gauges;[65] then in 1851, it "capitulated" to demands from the Triangle that the town of Erie be made the gauge junction and transfer point. In the interests of interstate comity—not commerce!—the astute legislators simply authorized *both* broad and standard gauge into town from the east, but only the intermediate (Ohio) gauge in from the west,[66] taking good care that depots remained well apart, and that local carters, hostelers and victualers visualized an expansive, indeed, limitless, future.

So began the "Troubles at Erie" or "The War of the Gauges,"[67] 1853–55—one of the forgotten melodramas (or burlesques) of Amer-

---

[62] See Mott, Between the Ocean and the Lakes (1899).

[63] Harlow, The Road of the Century: The Story of the New York Central (1947).

[64] Ohio Laws 40 § 21 (Act of Feb. 11, 1848), 2 Rev. Stat. 1401 (1853).

[65] See Harlow, *op. cit. supra* note 61, at 268.

[66] See Act of March 11, 1851, P.L. 122. Reliance was not solely upon the carters of Erie, however. See Act of April 15, 1851, P.L. 401 § 7, incorporating the Susquehanna & Erie R.R. This section flatly prohibited all Pennsylvania railroads from connecting with the "Ohio and New York State lines," and made violations cause for charter forfeiture.

[67] The best account is in Harlow, *op. cit. supra* note 63, at 267–274; see also Mott, *op. cit. supra* note 62, at 114, 371; Erie: A Guide to the City and County, 45–46 (1938). Newspaper coverage was extensive, and exceedingly critical in Ohio and New York. For examples, see Cadiz (Ohio) Republican, Feb. 2, 9, 16, June 1, 1854; also the digests of Cleveland papers in Annals of Cleveland, 1854, items 1929–1935, Jan. 1854, Jan. 1855; items 3186–3192, Jan. 1855.

ican enterprise, a forcible reminder of how sparingly the federal commerce power, or for that matter, even unaided equity, figured in promoters' schemes while rails literally were outracing laws. At Erie, through travellers and freight made not one, but two transfers in twenty miles; and the town's ultimatum: "No gauge break, no railroad!" was also the current Keystone State formula for national prosperity. "Crossing the Isthmus" in midwinter 1853–54 was a horror experienced by thousands.

The "troubles" dated from April when a guilt-ridden legislature unexpectedly repealed the state gauge law.[68] Erie thus was left, as her mayor said, "singly and alone, to battle for her interests and Pennsylvania's." Valor was not wanting: Nuisance charges were pressed against the two extensions of the Ohio road that had imprudently ventured eastward across the Triangle over a route far sounder economically and topographically than charter-wise.[69] By November, however, New York Central interests had at last won control of these roads and two other shortlines extending eastward from Erie. A "compromise" then was rushed through—one incidentally which left the hoodwinked Erie Railroad at the Central's mercy for years.[70] Shortly, a continuous Ohio gauge was laid down across the Isthmus to the presumed safety of a junction in New York. But the sanguine Yorkers had underrated their opponents; this "stealthy," "foreign and bastard gauge" aroused Erians to fury. Fines and bluster failing, the town constable, aided by a posse of carters, demolished tracks and bridges, restored the vital seven-mile gap, and won plaudits of the Pennsylvania administration from the governor on down. Tracks speedily relaid—including a rerouted line around the embattled junction—also were ripped out repeatedly by hefty baggage smashers, often in feminine attire![71]

Yet law was not mocked; the ensuing litigation occupied the bench and bar for months. The principal actions, significantly, were pressed and won in the name of the Commonwealth. Encroaching roads, the majority of the high state court agreed, had jeopardized their charters by too free and peripatetic a choice of rights-of-way.[72] Presently how-

---

[68] See Act of April 11, 1853, P.L. 239, authorizing "every railroad . . . to construct or change . . . gauges . . . to such width as the directors . . . deem expedient," and repealing "all laws inconsistent with this provision." The latter clause doubtless aimed at § 7, Act of April 15, 1851, quoted note 66 *supra*, but to little effect.

[69] See HARLOW, *op. cit. supra* note 63, at 270. See also Commonwealth v. Erie & N. E. R.R. 27 Pa. 339 (1854); Commonwealth v. Franklin Canal Co., 21 Pa. 117 (1853). For the corporate history of the various Ohio and New York roads, see MOTT, *op. cit. supra* note 62, at 363–364.

[70] *Id.*, at 114, 371–2.

[71] *Ibid.*, and HARLOW, *op. cit. supra* note 63, at 271–273.

[72] See the two cases cited note 69 *supra*.

ever, violence and vigilantism led to a stiffened judicial attitude; decrees were withheld[73] and censure meted out to all parties.[74]

Characteristically, the struggle at this point again shifted to the state legislature. On October 6, 1855, lieutenants rammed through a bill repealing the charters and franchises of the little Erie and North East Railroad, declaring them forfeit for misuse and abuse, and placing the properties in the hands of an executive-appointed manager,[75] one Joseph Casey, reporter of the Pennsylvania Supreme Court. These proceedings were at once attacked by distinguished counsel, including Edwin M. Stanton.[76] On July 16, 1856, a majority of the supreme court, again speaking through the gifted, nimble Justice Jeremiah S. Black,[77] upheld the repealer. The fact that there had been no prior judicial determination of the issue of charter misuse or abuse, Black found immaterial. In this instance clearly there had been misuse and abuse; under the reserved power to alter and amend, the legislature itself might judge. Its power was "not restricted by the rules of pleading and evidence"; hence "the state may act . . . upon a truth which she would have been estopped to show in a court if the legislature had not interfered."[78]

Far different, indeed, was the view taken by Chief Justice Lewis.[79] As in other recent cases,[80] counsel had relied on nearly all the broad "natural rights" provisions of the state constitution, including the law of the land and due course of law guarantees. Cited and quoted specially were the holding and dicta of *Brown v. Hummel*.[81] There,

---

[73] See Commonwealth v. Erie & N. E. R.R., 27 Pa. 339, 378–379 (1856).

[74] *Ibid.* See also Cleveland, P. & A. R.R. v. City of Erie, 27 Pa. 380, 381 (1856).

[75] Act of Oct. 6, 1856, P.L. 656:705: "To repeal the charter of the Erie & North East Railroad and provide for disposing of the same." *Cf.* Act of April 22, 1856, P.L. 586, restoring charter and approving route and connections with the Sunbury & Erie, Pittsburgh & Erie, and authorizing $500,000 in new bonds for the compromise settlement referred to in note 84 *infra*.

[76] 1814–1869, Lincoln's Secretary of War.

[77] See BRIGGANCE, JEREMIAH SULLIVAN BLACK (1934).

[78] Erie & N. E. R.R. v. Casey, 26 Pa. 287, 309 (1856).

[79] The Chief Justice's dissent was not published by Reporter Casey, but appeared later in 1 Grant 274 (Pa. 1856).

[80] See *Sharpless v. Philadelphia*, 21 Pa. 147 (1853), dissenting opinions, 2 AM. L. REG. 27, 85 (1853), and the related case of *Moers v. City of Reading*, 21 Pa. 188 (1853). For the history and background of these cases, cornerstones of the public purpose doctrine of taxation, see Waldron, *Sharpless v. Philadelphia: Jeremiah Black and the Parent Case on the Public Purpose of Taxation*, 1953 WISC. L. REV. 48–75. The dissenting opinions of JJ. Lowrie and Lewis in this case, officially unreported, are in 2 AM. L. REG. 27–43, 85–112 (1853). That of Lewis is of special importance in showing the occasionally strong substantive-natural rights character of due process usage at this date (1853), also the confused, transitional character of the period generally. Lewis, for example, the staunch conservative, would have employed due process to *prevent* municipal aid to powerful corporations—fearing the day free men would become their bondsmen!

[81] 6 Pa. 86 (1847).

nine years before, the Pennsylvania court, in voiding changes made by the legislature in the charter of an orphanage, had upheld counsel's sweeping use of various early due process dicta. Not every act of the legislature was "the law of the land." By that guarantee was meant rather "the law of the individual case, as established in a fair and open trial," and it was "against the principles of liberty and common right to deprive a man of his property or franchises within the pale of the constitution with his hand on the altar without due process of law."[82]

With this view Chief Justice Lewis now (in 1856) wholeheartedly agreed. Due process or due course of law meant first of all *judicial* process; the *Erie* repealers had provided for none, hence "the property of the stockholders" had been taken without the judgment of their peers and contrary to the law of the land. . . . The stockholders are tangible individuals, with rights to protect and defend. They have a right to demand that their property shall not be taken away unless . . . by due course of law as administered by the constitutional tribunals where alone the judicial power is vested."[83] As in *Sharpless v. Philadelphia*,[84] and in the two recent rights-of-way cases,[85] the Chief Justice stated his views emphatically and at length. Significant as they were to be regarded eventually, they afforded cold comfort to the Erie & North East Railroad. The best that hapless road (and the two stymied New York trunk systems standing behind it) could secure, was another "compromise settlement" that restored the Erie & North East's franchises—and of course permitted through traffic— in return for a subscription of $1,300,000 by the three roads to the capital of various Pennsylvania-controlled lines then under construction![86]

Erie and North East Railroad v. Casey is interesting and important today because it marks one of the pioneer uses of due process by a *private* corporation prior[87] to the Civil War. Obviously, no precise nor sophisticated insights were involved. Usage simply grew out of

---

82 *Ibid.*
83 1 Grant 274, 276, 290 (Pa. 1856).
84 Note 80 *supra*.
85 See note 69 *supra*. Lewis, then Associate Justice, dissented in both cases there cited.
86 MOTT, *op. cit. supra* note 62, at 371–2.
87 Such use was far rarer than economic use generally, or use in cases involving *public* corporations; but see note 94 *infra*, concerning arguments in the Ohio Bank tax exemptions. These arguments may have been among the earliest and most extensive applications on behalf of private corporations. See also an apparent unsuccessful use by counsel in *In the Matter of the Empire State Bank*, 18 N.Y. 199, 210, 216 (1858). Characteristically, the talk in all these early cases is of natural persons even though corporations are the parties in interest.

local circumstances and earlier Pennsylvania dicta. And what was *presumed* was far more important than what was argued: "Property" and "deprived," not "person" nor "due process" or "due course of law," were the key words.[88] The big thing from our standpoint is that use of due process by lawyers for business had begun, and had in fact proceeded farther and faster in the eighteen-forties and fifties than the few scattered instances (where counsel carried court majorities with them) have led students to suspect. The extent and significance of such usage will be clear only as more briefs and opinions come to light. It is apparent already, however, that two prevalent assumptions will have to be modified. These are (1) that the New York cases from *Taylor v. Porter*[89] to *Wynehamer*[90] were essentially "sports" and "freaks"; and (2) that the pioneers, in these early applications, necessarily shared nice modern distinctions between "procedure" and "substance."[91] The fact that pioneer usage by and on behalf of business interests actually was sporadic, opportunist, highly controversial, and in the end, disastrously affected by the debacles in *Dred Scott*[92] and the *New York Prohibition* cases,[93] need no longer blind us to the fact that counsel in other jurisdictions[94] also were "pressing their luck," and that doctrinal developments—in retrospect surprisingly like those of the post-Civil War period—did occur, not only in non-corporate, but also corporate cases. What needs to be kept constantly in mind is that these various applications met with no majority judicial acceptance in *corporate* cases; that even the non-corporate substantive-economic or business uses which did win judicial approval, were confined to the scattered New York series and to Taney's *Dred Scott* opinion. All other early uses, including those we

---

[88] On pre-Civil War use and expansion of due process, see Corwin, *The Doctrine of Due Process Before the Civil War*, 24 HARV. L. REV. 460 (1911). Also see his *The Extension of Judicial Review in New York, 1783–1905*, 15 MICH. L. REV. 281 (1917), Chapter 5, *supra*.

[89] 4 Hill 140 (N.Y. 1843).

[90] Wynehamer v. People, 13 N.Y. 378 (1856); regarding the isolated character of this holding, see Corwin, *The Doctrine of Due Process Before the Civil War*, 24 HARV. L. REV. 460, 471 (1911).

[91] See Chapter 5, *supra*.

[92] Dred Scott v. Sandford, 60 U.S. (19 How.) 393, 450 (1857).

[93] See note 90 *supra*.

[94] Though there are no arguments of counsel given in the reports, it appears from various passages in the opinions, and especially from frequent citation of *Taylor v. Porter*, 4 Hill 140 (N.Y. 1843), and *Regents of University of Maryland v. Williams*, 9 Gill & J. 365 (Md. 1838), that due process figured prominently in the corporation's attack on the Ohio bank tax law of 1851. See Mechanics' Bank v. Debolt, 1 Ohio St. 603, 617 (1853); Bank of Toledo v. Bond, 1 Ohio St. 623, 633–634 (1853). Jacksonian state judges in these cases of course challenged even the authority of the *Dartmouth College* decision; see 2 WARREN, SUPREME COURT IN U.S. HISTORY 523 (1923), and WEINBERGER, LIFE OF JUSTICE MCLEAN.

have just noted in Pennsylvania, simply were views of minority judges or contentions of counsel, generally in "tough" or "hopeless" cases; hence their actual and potential importance is easily misread or magnified today.

Out of these checkered, ambiguous backgrounds, then, arose the second great Pennsylvania charter repeal case. The Civil War had given railroads tremendous impetus.[95] It revealed the dangers and weaknesses of state-chartered monopolies, and exposed their hidden social costs. Bottlenecks like those at Erie; strategic counter- and overconstruction, often paired with neglect of other areas, and of the public interest; flagrant state taxation of national commerce;[96] corporate control of state houses and debauchery of legislatures, bad in peacetime, appeared worse in war. Nationalism was now ascendant. Freed of sectional restraints, Congress chartered and subsidized the Pacific Railroad[97] and telegraph,[98] and authorized the President to take possession of any line in certain cases.[99] Leaders meanwhile attacked the states' strangleholds on rail traffic into Washington, pillorying the Camden & Amboy and the Baltimore & Ohio for their inefficiency and passenger taxes,[100] demanding a federal charter for a competing "airline" road to New York,[101] even threatening federal regulation.[102]

---

[95] See, e.g., WEBER, NORTHERN RAILROADS IN THE CIVIL WAR (1952); SUMMERS, BALTIMORE & OHIO IN THE CIVIL WAR (1939); Fish, *The Northern Railroads, April, 1861*, 22 AM. HIST. REV. 778 (1917); Murphy, *Northern Railroads and the Civil War*, 5 MISS. VALLEY HIST. REV. 324 (1918); Russell, *Revaluation of the Period before the Civil War: Railroads*, 15 MISS. VALLEY HIST. REV. 341 (1928).

[96] State decisions, 1861–65, reflected the mounting nationalism in tax matters; see, e.g., Erie Ry. v. State of New Jersey, 31 N.J.L. 531 (1864) reversing, 30 N.J.L. 473. The high court struck down a foreign corporations tax act of 1862 levying a "transit duty" on passengers and freight carried by railroads or canals distances greater than ten miles and excepting movements wholly intrastate. Not until the State Freight Tax Case, Philadelphia & R. R.R. v. Commonwealth of Pennsylvania, 82 U.S. (15 Wall.) 232 (1873) did the Supreme Court strike down such legislation.

[97] Act of July 1, 1862, c. 120, 12 STAT. 489 (later amended and subsidy liberalized by Act of July 2, 1864, c. 216, 13 STAT. 356). See generally, HANEY, CONGRESSIONAL HISTORY OF RAILWAYS IN THE U.S., 1850–1887 (1910).

[98] Act of July 1, 1862, c. 120, 12 STAT. 489–98.

[99] See S. 169, 37th Cong. 2d Sess. (1862), and clarified, H.R. J. RES. 39, 37th Cong., 2d Sess. (1862). A useful supplement to HANEY in tracing these early regulatory measures is REGULATION OF INTERSTATE COMMERCE: HISTORY OF BILLS AND RESOLUTIONS INTRODUCED IN CONGRESS, 1862–1911 (Briggs, compiler, 1912).

[100] See generally the works cited in note 95 *supra*, also HANEY, *op. cit. supra* note 97, 157, 164, 179, 215.

[101] See HANEY, *op. cit. supra* note 97, at 215.

[102] See S. 17, 39th Cong. 1st Sess. (1865), introduced by Sumner, Dec. 6, 1865, and H.R. 11, 39th Cong. 1st Sess. (1862), introduced by Garfield, Dec. 11, 1865. The latter, drastically amended, was the so-called Interstate Communications Act, 14 STAT. 66 (1866). See also the reference to HANEY cited in notes 97 and 100 *supra*; and Garfield's statement, May 31, 1866, CONG. GLOBE, 39th Cong., 1st Sess. 2925 (1866): "I believe the

While these ferments were at work nationally, Pittsburgh supplanted Erie as Pennsylvania's border bastion. Two small roads again posed a threat to the Thomson-Scott empire; one, the Pittsburgh & Connellsville, long had been a vital link in plans of the Baltimore & Ohio for an "airline" from Washington to Pittsburgh via Cumberland and Point of Rocks;[103] the other, the Cleveland & Mahoning,[104] was an Ohio road, but one with a Pennsylvania charter for a route already surveyed to Newcastle.[105] Should this second line ever break through to Pittsburgh, it might afford the Baltimore & Ohio a connection straight to Cleveland. Worse still, by reason of its linkage (present and potential) with both the Erie and New York Central in the booming oil fields of northwestern Pennsylvania, the Cleveland & Mahoning might also ultimately give those two contenders access to Pittsburgh, thus affording Pennsylvania as well as Ohio traffic a competitive outlet to New York,[106] shattering monopoly, perhaps forever.

The showdown came dramatically in 1864. Booming war traffic, and the aggressive leadership of Robert Garrett, a foe in every respect worthy of Thomson and Scott, had made the Baltimore & Ohio a real threat. In alliance with the Latrobes, Garrett overhauled the Connellsville project, succeeded in unfreezing its Baltimore subsidy, pushed lagging tunnel construction, and prepared for triumphant entry to Pittsburgh.[107]

It proved premature. Almost as summarily as nine years before in the Erie fracas, the Pennsylvania legislature, with Tom Scott himself mustering votes on the floor, repealed the franchises of both the Pittsburgh & Connellsville and the Cleveland & Mahoning Railroads, charging failure to fulfill time clauses and other "abuse and misuse" of charter privileges. The properties of the Pittsburgh & Connellsville were turned over to a newly-organized paper subsidiary of the Pennsylvania combine, the Connellsville & Southern Pennsylvania Railroad.[108] Still friendly to the B. & O. affiliate, to which their for-

---

time has come when the General Government must use the authority clearly vested in it by the Constitution 'to regulate commerce . . .' and not allow states and close corporations to block that free commercial intercourse which is the life of industry."

[103] Advantages of the route were stressed by Senator Sherman, CONG. GLOBE, 39th Cong., 1st Sess. 2365 (May 3, 1866). See also Clark, *supra* note 57.

[104] See RUSSELL, *op. cit. supra* note 40, at 606–7; and MOTT, *op. cit. supra* note 62, at 363–365.

[105] Act of Feb. 11, 1853, P.L. 59, § 8. This act forbade construction and branch lines in Erie County.

[106] The Cleveland & Mahoning was the first railroad into the Pennsylvania oil fields. MOTT, *op. cit. supra* note 62, at 363.

[107] See CLARK, *supra* note 57, at 16–20.

[108] See Act of May 4, 1864, P.L. 657 (relative to the Cleveland & Mahoning); Acts

tunes, like Baltimore's, were linked by subsidy, Pittsburgher's rallied to the P. & C.'s aid. In this they were joined by powerful interests in Ohio. Test suits brought by the City of Baltimore as bondholder soon were under way in the United States Circuit Court.[109]

---

of Aug. 19, 1864, P.L. 912, 913, and 914 (relative to the two Connellsville lines). Governor Curtin signed only the C. & M. bill, permitting the others to become law without his approval. The P. & C. repealer carried a "full compensation" clause and provided for appraisal by the Governor's appointees, besides authorizing sale of the company's properties, but neither stockholders nor courts were impressed. See notes 109, 116, 118, 119 *infra*.

[109] See Baltimore v. Pittsburgh & C. R.R., 2 Fed. Cas. 570 No. 827 (C.C.W.D. Pa. 1865). Apparently Senator Reverdy Johnson and J. H. B. Latrobe, chief counsel for the Pittsburgh & Connellsville, were victimized by their own strategy in these cases. As evidenced in note 175 *infra* they contrived to bring the Mayor and City of Baltimore into the case as a plaintiff-bondholder in separate suits against *both* the P. & C. and the Connellsville & Southern Pennsylvania Railway. These actions in equity later were combined, even though the P. & C.'s suit was substantially moot; Justice Grier's decision, and Judge McCandless' later decree, both were made in the consolidated actions. Thus it presently mischanced that when the Connellsville & Southern appealed, the B. & O.'s affiliate—the P. & C.—was dragged along, tarbaby fashion, as a co-appellant with the Pennsylvania's stooge!

In April 1867 the discomfited Johnson and Latrobe moved to effect a severance. But in a memorandum decision, unpublished until 1894, the Supreme Court overruled their motion to dismiss, finding rather that the P. & C. had been "a proper party defendant in the court below, and [that] the appeal in the record appears to have been taken by this defendant, as well as by the others." Connellsville & S.P. Ry. Co. v. Mayor of Baltimore, 154 U.S. 553, app. (decided April 29, 1867). The court did, however, rescind its earlier order assigning the case for argument at that term! Thus matters stood for nearly two years. Finally, on February 16, 1869, the day after Johnson and Latrobe had filed a fifty-six-page brief for the appellees—the Mayor and City of Baltimore—and a full thirteen months after the Scott-Thomson interests had been routed in the state quo warranto proceedings, the Supreme Court, per Chief Justice Chase, issued the following manuscript order: (Supplied by courtesy of Miss Helen Newman, Librarian, Supreme Court of the United States.)

No. 84
Supreme Court of the United States
December Term, 1868

The Connellsville and Southern Pennsylvania Railway Company, The Pittsburgh and Connellsville Railroad Company et al. Appellants vs. The Mayor and City Council of Baltimore—

Appeal from the Circuit Court of the United States for the Western District of Pennsylvania.

This cause came to be heard on the transcript of the record from the Circuit Court of the United States for the Western District of Pennsylvania, and on the stipulation of the Counsel on file, and on the motion of Mr. Latrobe of Counsel for the Appellees. It is now here ordered, adjudged and decreed by this Court, That this Appeal be, and the same is hereby, dismissed with costs.

(Per Mr. Chief Justice Chase)
16 February 1869

Briefs for the appellant Pittsburgh & Connellsville in these cases (No. 413, 1867 term, and No. 84, 1868 term) in the Library of the Supreme Court, along with the official Transcript of Record in 154 U.S. 553 App. (1894) reveal the acute embarrassment of counsel. Johnson and Latrobe appeared nominally for the City of Baltimore,

"*Builded Better Than They Knew*" 463

Directing this attack were Reverdy Johnson,[110] for forty years the B. & O.'s chief counsel, now United States Senator from Maryland; J. H. B. Latrobe,[111] another gifted member of the Baltimore bar; and George Shiras, Jr.,[112] of Pittsburgh, later Justice of the Supreme Court of the United States. Defending the repealers were Jeremiah Black[113] and Walter Lowrie,[114] both former members of the state supreme court, and Black, author of the opinion in the *Erie* case! At the first hearing at Williamsport in June, 1865, Circuit Justice Grier held the repealer "unconstitutional and void under the admissions of the case" as an impairment of the obligations of contract.[115] The properties of the Pittsburgh road had been legislated away without a hearing, without the required *judicial* determination of "misuse or abuse." The *Erie* case, heavily relied on by Black, was brushed aside: The Court there had found, Grier said,

". . . after a full hearing . . . that 'misuse or abuse' did exist, [hence] the act was not void. It cannot, therefore, be any precedent for a case which admits that such facts do not exist. The principles of law, so far as they affect this case, are very clearly and tersely stated by Chief Justice Lewis in his [dissenting] opinion in 1 Grant 275 . . ."[116]

---

appellee, and maintained composure; but underlings arguing for the Railroad conceded their client's satisfaction with the outcome below.

One can readily picture the delight of Jeremiah Black as he contemplated this triumph his friend and rival, the great Reverdy Johnson!

[110] See STEINER, THE LIFE OF REVERDY JOHNSON.

[111] 1803–1891. For his varied career as lawyer, artist, inventor, philanthropist, see SEMMES, JOHN H. B. LATROBE AND HIS TIMES (1917).

[112] 1832–1924. See SHIRAS, JUSTICE GEORGE SHIRAS JR. OF PITTSBURGH, ASSOCIATE JUSTICE OF THE UNITED STATES SUPREME COURT, 1895–1903 (1953).

[113] See note 77 *supra*.

[114] Walter Hoge Lowrie, 1807–1876. District Judge, Allegheny County, 1846–1851; Justice and Chief Justice of Pennsylvania Supreme Court, 1851–1863; subsequently in law practice in Pittsburgh; and at time of death, President Judge of the Judicial District of Western Pennsylvania. See 4 APPLETON'S CYCLOPEDIA OF AMERICAN BIOGRAPHY 46 (1888).

[115] See 2 Fed Cas. 570, No. 827 (C.C.W.D. Pa. 1865). Dr. Russell errs in saying that "The Circuit Court had not yet (May 1866) decided that the repeal of the Pittsburgh and Connellsville's charter was unconstitutional." Russell, *supra* note 40, at 609–610, 617. It is true that Judge McCandless' final decree, following the jury's verdict, did not come until June 1866. Note 119 *infra*. But Justice Grier's opinion of June 1865, which Garfield incorporated in the *Globe* during the House debates (GLOBE 2925) had said "The only question then is the validity of the act," and thereupon proceeded to hold the repealer "unconstitutional and void under the admissions of the case." This fact was widely understood and cited in the various debates. Justice Grier's leave to amend and try the issue of abuse or misuse was dictated by respect for the jurisdiction of the Pennsylvania Supreme Court in which the quo warranto suit was pending.

[116] Baltimore v. Pittsburgh & C. R.R., 2 Fed. Cas. 570, 571 No. 827 (C.C.W.D. Pa. 1865).

Complainants thus were entitled to a decree, but defendants, might if they wished, amend, and the Court would then try the issue of "abuse."[117]

The Pennsylvania system's parallel quo warranto proceedings[118] in the state courts delayed jury trial almost a year. But on June 28, 1866, after a long trial in Judge McCandless' court, followed by a ten-minute verdict, the Pittsburgh and Connellsville at last had its final decree.[119]

Victory, however, was another matter. An appeal was at once taken to the jammed docket of the Supreme Court.[120] Meanwhile, right-of-way acquisition, especially on the Ohio line, was delayed by vexatious suits in local courts.[121] Finally, the quo warranto proceedings in the state supreme court, though eventually decided against the Pennsylvania, dragged and bound almost as badly.[122]

To fight fire with fire in Congress, the Garrett forces, allied now with English capital which was endeavoring to create a trunk system in the Cleveland-Erie sector,[123] enlisted the aid of the friendly Ohio delegation. Senator Sherman and Representative Garfield, with Thaddeus Stevens of Pennsylvania, currently were the main advocates of a nationally-chartered "airline" road from New York to Washington.[124] Such a project naturally held small appeal to the B. & O., with

---

[117] Ibid.
[118] See Commonwealth *ex rel.* Attorney General v. Pittsburgh & C. R.R., 58 Pa. 26 (1868). Information filed May 11, 1865. Opinion by Sharswood, J.
[119] See City of Baltimore v. Pittsburgh & C. R.R., 3 Pgh. Rep. 20, 24–25 (1866). In his instructions to the jury, Judge McCandless declared the case to be "one of great national importance. It was not the design of the wise framers . . . nor is it now the policy of the government and people . . . that any commonwealth . . . be permitted to place restrictions upon commerce between the states. . . . The propriety and necessity of this very road has been recently agitated in Congress, and a bill looking to its early construction has passed [the House] . . . It should be made, [linking] the great west and the lakes . . . with tidewater and the seat of the general government." 23 Pgh. Rep. at 23.
[120] Among various references to this appeal, see, BALTIMORE & OHIO RAILROAD CO., ADDRESS OF JOHN W. GARRETT (December 12, 1866). (22 p., copy in Rare Book Room, Library of Congress). Pages 8 and 9 voice the hope that the Supreme Court might hear the appeal out of order. See also PA. LEGIS. RECORD, Senate, 283 (1867) Speech of Searight.
[121] See the various references in the congressional debates cited notes 124, 128, 129 *infra.* Also BRIEF HISTORY OF THE PITTSBURGH & CONNELLSVILLE RAILROAD CO. AND ITS OBJECT IN ASKING THE INTERPOSITION OF CONGRESS TO AID IN RESTORING ITS VESTED RIGHTS, ASSAILED BY UNJUST AND UNCONSTITUTIONAL STATE LEGISLATION (Baltimore, 1866, 8 pages, copy, Rare Book Room, Library of Congress).
[122] See note 118 *supra.*
[123] Nucleus of which was the Atlantic & Great Western, to which the C. & M. had been leased for 99 years from October 1, 1863. See POOR'S MANUAL 211 (1868–1869); MOTT, *op. cit. supra* note 62.
[124] See H.R. 91 introduced by Stevens, and H.R. 96, by Garfield, both January 8,

"Builded Better Than They Knew" 465

its state freight and passenger taxes and its monopoly of Baltimore-Washington traffic.[125] But the readiness of these aggressive western Republicans to lash at the Pennsylvania, mobilize sentiment, and help break the paralyzing grip on the Pittsburgh-Cleveland sector, offset unpalatable risks. Spring of 1866 thus found commercial interests beating the drums for a "national" Cleveland-Pittsburgh-Chesapeake shortline via Connellsville and Cumberland.[126] Petitions stressed that Pennsylvania had arbitrarily revoked the two rival roads charters, "thus impairing vested rights of citizens of Ohio."[127] Accordingly, Congress was asked to "restore the right to build [those portions of road] within the state of Pennsylvania which had been taken away."

In May, Garfield and Stevens launched two bills[128] which proposed

1866, and both providing for a military and post road organized by the Cookes, Astors, Belmonts, A. T. Stewart and other leading capitalists. Both Congressmen were members of a select committee on the project and pushed the measures relentlessly. See CONG. GLOBE, id. at 2902, 2922. See HANEY, op. cit. supra note 97, at 215.

Garfield also sponsored a bill for a National Bureau of Education (H.R. 276) as well as the revived Interstate Intercourse Bill, see note 132 infra; for Sherman's support of the railroad bills, see CONG. GLOBE, 2365 (May 3, 1866); 2870 (May 29, 1866).

[125] Maryland's gross receipts tax of 20%, or 50 cents on each Baltimore-Washington fare, amounted to a total of $500,000, 1860-70. See 22 L. Ed. 682 (1873). New Jersey and other states had similar arrangements, generally in the form of charter privileges in lieu of other taxes. Counsel for the B. & O. and New Jersey railroads were kept busy defending these and heading off counterattacks through 1860-70. See BRADLEY (later Mr. Justice Bradley), CONSIDERATIONS UPON THE QUESTION WHETHER CONGRESS SHOULD AUTHORIZE A NEW RAILROAD BETWEEN WASHINGTON AND NEW YORK (Wash., 1863); VINDEX (pseud. of C. J. M. Gwinn), THE STEVENS RAILROAD BILL AND HOW IT WILL OPERATE (The Rare Book Room, Library of Congress has two variant editions of this pamphlet by a B. & O. attorney, both dated February 12, 1866, one attacking Congress' power and right to build the competing New York-Washington airline, the other, appealing to Congress to pass the bill for the P. & C. airline to the northwest instead!); VINDEX, THE SHERMAN RAILROAD BILL—AND THE POWERS OF CONGRESS IN RELATION THERETO (1869); MARRIOTT, THE WASHINGTON CONSPIRACY AGAINST THE RAILROAD INTERESTS OF MARYLAND (Wash. 1867).

So unpopular did the Maryland passenger tax become that Reverdy Johnson and Latrobe for the B. & O. finally attacked its constitutionality, citing *Crandall v. Nevada*, 73 U.S. (6 Wall.) 35 (1868), and the commerce clause. This effort failed and Justice Bradley's opinion in the case is very interesting in light of these backgrounds. *Railroad Co. v. Maryland*, 88 U.S. (21 Wall.) 456 (1875).

[126] See e.g., CONG. GLOBE, 39th Cong., 1st Sess. 1925 (1866), petitions submitted by Garfield April 13, 1866, now in vol. 7 of *Thaddeus Stevens Papers, Manuscript Div.*, Library of Congress; CONG. GLOBE, 39th Cong., 1st Sess. 2634 (1866); Memorial of Citizens of Pittsburgh submitted by Sherman, 2635 (May 17, 1866), in National Archives. See also H.R. JOUR. 39th Cong., 1st Sess. 540, 634 (1866).

[127] Petition of the Cleveland & Mahoning Railroad and citizens of Pittsburgh submitted by Garfield, see note 126 supra.

[128] H.R. 527, introduced by Garfield, CONG. GLOBE, 39th Cong., 1st Sess. 2282 (1866), for a line to the northwest, the P. & C. bill, reported back by Stevens and pushed through the House without debate, May 30, 1866; text in CONG. GLOBE, id. at 2902-2903, engrossed copy in National Archives. H.R. 537, the C. & M. Bill, reported back

to do exactly that. In great detail, the rescinded rights were revived and strengthened. Malicious interference and obstructionism such as had prevailed at Erie were penalized and made subject to double damages. Another carefully worded section, submitted later as an amendment, even made the vexatious right-of-way suits against the C. & M. removable to the United States courts![129] These measures eventually failed in the Senate.[130] But they passed the House after hot debate,[131] along with the related Interstate Intercourse bill[132] designed to facilitate trunk connections and forestall further strategic bottlenecks of the Erie type.

The point of crucial interest is that these measures were before Congress while the Fourteenth Amendment was drafting. Thaddeus Stevens, the drivewheel of the Joint Committee (as well as the most influential member of the House in railroad matters) was one of the sponsors. Reverdy Johnson, perhaps the most experienced constitutional lawyer in the country, and also a Joint Committee member, was thoroughly familiar (as winning counsel) with all details of the case. So too, in likelihood, was Jack Rogers, another Democratic minority member and young railroad lawyer whom Republicans baited as representing the "State of Camden & Amboy" in the House.[133] Finally, voting in favor of the bills, were in addition to Stevens, John A. Bingham and Roscoe Conkling![134]

These chapters in Pennsylvania railroad history afford dramatic insight into what was happening in the sixties. Moreover, they illu-

---

and debated the same day and on May 31 and June 16. CONG. GLOBE, *id.* at 2903–2904, 2922–2925. See also CONG. GLOBE, *id.* at 3218–3220 (Rep. Kerr's attack). Engrossed bill is in National Archives.

129 Added at Garfield's motion, May 31, 1866. See CONG. GLOBE, 39th Cong., 1st Sess. 2922 (1866), for the text of sections 9–10. Section 10 as here introduced provided for removal of suits to U.S. Courts, became section 9 of the engrossed Bill 537. For corresponding section (4) of the P. & C. Bill 527, see CONG. GLOBE, *id.* at 2902.

130 CONG. GLOBE, 39th Cong., 1st Sess. 3333 (June 21, 1866). Senator Edmunds of Vermont of the Committee on Commerce, reporting adversely on both H.R. 527 and H.R. 537 related that "the majority held Congress had no constitutional power to authorize a road or railroad within any state . . . without the consent of the state." Edmunds and the minority disagreed. See also CONG. GLOBE, *id.* at 4288 for final Senate action.

131 CONG. GLOBE, *id.* at 2902–3 (H.R. 527); CONG. GLOBE, *id.* at 2922–25 (H.R. 537), vote 77–41, with 65 not voting.

132 Also passed by the Senate in attenuated form. See S. JOUR., 39th Cong., 1st Sess. 472 (1866), and 14 STAT. 66 (1866). The final act, which provided that it should not be construed as authorizing any *new* roads or connections without state permission, was a disappointment to Garfield and Sherman.

133 Rogers was a vigilant defender of the New Jersey monopoly, and his speeches were well sprinkled with constitutional argument and citation. See, *e.g.*, CONG. GLOBE, 38th Cong., 1st Sess. 1238, 1241 (1865).

134 CONG. GLOBE, 39th Cong., 1st Sess. 2925 (1866).

minate the forces and trends which presently were to recast relations between legislatures and the judiciary. Courts long since had acquired the last word, though legislative supremacy had continued in practice. Pre-Civil War cases had established the doctrine of vested rights,[135] and also of strict control of corporations by means of the power to repeal, alter and amend.[136] Economically and politically, change now was at flood. Railroads—and the rush to control and exploit them—had arrayed in combat not only promoters and groups of capital, but whole cities, states, and regions. The result, as just noted, was not town meeting democracy—not even *public* government. Could Jefferson's and Franklin's government of freeholders be yielding at points to government of freebooters? Few courts ever aspired to enter this arena, or to police it; most judges were quite aware of their handicaps. Yet here, springing up as from dragons' teeth, were these "cases and controversies," some of them, already, incidentally employing due process. No one yet thought or talked in sophisticated modern terms of "procedure" or "substance."[137] Primarily in these instances, the matter was deemed one of assuring economic growth, of securing—or saving—the public interest, of protecting municipal and private investors. Conscientious judicial minds had to wrestle with the rights and merits. Litigants and public, moreover, urged that there "had to be" some review, some restraint in such flagrant cases. "Power was not power to destroy or repeal arbitrarily while this court sits," as Justice Holmes later was to put it. There had to be limits—so there began to be! Due process, in short, already is glimpsed standing in the wings—the supremely flexible, open-ended, discretionary guarantee and tool.

These circumstances and social pressures had far more potential significance than did the intent or design of a handful of framers or a multitude of ratifiers. Yet that question insistently recurs: How knowledgeable were the framers and ratifiers? What bearing, *if any*, did this last episode have on draftsmanship of the amendment? The repeals occurred immediately prior to the drafting, and in the states of two major principals, Stevens and Bingham. Resulting bills gained the favorable notice and support of these leaders, as well as of Conk-

---

[135] See Professor Corwin's classic article, *The Basic Doctrine of American Constitutional Law*, 12 MICH. L. REV. 247 (1914), reprinted, 1 SEL. ESSAYS AM. CONST. LAW 101 (1938). Also his *Doctrine of Due Process before the Civil War*, 24 HARV. L. REV. 366 (1911).

[136] See WRIGHT, CONTRACT CLAUSE (1938); DODD, AMERICAN BUSINESS CORPORATIONS UNTIL 1860: WITH SPECIAL REFERENCE TO MASSACHUSETTS (1954); Dodd, "The Reserved Power," in his *Dissenting Stockholders and Amendments to Corporate Charters*, 75 U. PA. L. REV. 582, 592 (1927), and the older work of Stern there cited.

[137] See Chapter 5, *supra*, at 242, 263.

ling and Reverdy Johnson, and perhaps of other Committee members at the very moment the due process-equal protection wording was being hammered out. . . . Here, in short, is a remote truncated pattern of circumstance, one superficially consistent with intent to embrace corporations. Like judicial review as a whole, the corporate person and due process manifestly were being pushed on stage. Certainly, one would think, these framers ought to have considered the status of the corporate person. But did they?

Dr. Russell's handling of this problem and episode is disappointing. For the most part, his article is devoted to the promotional and charter history of the two railroads, and to their strategic or competitive position. These matters are clearly and helpfully treated.[138] The Pittsburgh & Connellsville, he shows to have been in a far stronger position, legally and financially, than its Ohio affiliate. Early defects in its charter had been corrected; it enjoyed the powerful support of the Baltimore & Ohio, and of the cities of Pittsburgh and Baltimore. The Cleveland & Mahoning, on the other hand, was weak and overexposed. Its failure to fulfill time clauses had never been condoned by the Pennsylvania legislature; a lease by the English-controlled Atlantic & Great Western in practice had meant little. Moreover, not until October 1865, Dr. Russell contends, were the fortunes of the P. & C. and the C. & M. firmly linked;[139] and this was *after*, not before, passage of the Pennsylvania repealers.

It is the use Dr. Russell makes of this evidence which is disturbing. Details of charter and promotional history *alone* are made to support conclusions about the intended scope and meaning of the due process and equal protection clauses! Thus, after reciting the differences in the charter situation of the roads, and stressing the weakness of the C. & M. with reference to time clauses and hence its apparent reluctance to challenge the repeals judicially, one encounters this sweeping statement and assumption:

"Under these circumstances it must be concluded that the Fourteenth Amendment *was not designed to assist this railroad*, for the

---

[138] See Russell, *supra* note 40, at 604–610. Dr. Russell's analysis of the strategic relations of the various roads seems less than acute, however. He tends to overlook the seriousness attached by the Pennsylvania to its rivals' pretensions and vice versa, however exaggerated these later proved. He failed to note too, that the counter measures and maneuvers of the C. & M. and P. & C. in Congress were really aimed at the vexatious suits and similar tactics. Far more than a strong *legal* position was needed before out-state railroads gained their ends at this time. Dr. Russell overlooked this crucial difference between a unitary centralized government and a separated federal system. American railroad promoters did not. Thus, much of Russell's criticism of Garfield's efforts in the C. & M.'s behalf is naive. *Id.* at 618.

[139] *Id.* at 604.

intervention of the judiciary under the 'due process clause' of the Amendment would have produced equally unfavorable results."[140] (Emphasis added.)

Plainly, there are oversights and basic confusion here. History has gotten badly out of focus. The main trouble derives from failure to see and place the amendment itself in perspective. Dr. Russell, too, has been taken in by loose talk, and by the fuzzy, undefined terms "conspiracy" and "conspiracy theory." Repeatedly he proceeds as though the question were whether section one was drafted to resolve a crisis *in the affairs of these two railroads*; whether the key clauses —in some undefined fashion—simply grew out of these companies' troubles; whether the amendment was "designed" to help two roads recover their charters![141]

Problems inherent in a federal system, in an emerging judicial review, and in emerging judicial supremacy, are alien to British experience. Yet these clearly are the crux of the present problem. The railroad and charter histories are pertinent, not in and of themselves, but because they *may* reveal and may somehow have helped shape conceptions of "due process" and "equal protection" just before, at, or during the time the phraseology of Section 1 was in draft. This is to say they constitute a valuable historical laboratory for study of these doctrinal developments, and particularly for study of public and professional understanding. Pennsylvania case law and judicial review, we know, possessed all the *potentials* needed for development of the doctrine of corporate personality. The question is how far, how fast, were these potentials currently perceived and realized?

Dr. Russell ignores these phases of the problem entirely. Indeed, he seems at times to regard them as beyond historical investigation.[142] Not a word is said, for example, about either the economic or humanitarian cases in which due process figured prior to the Civil War; nothing about the potential bearing of them; not a word about *Brown v. Hummel* and *Erie v. Casey* in Pennsylvania, nothing about the antislavery backgrounds of the due process and equal protection clauses, nor about the widespread popular usage in the slavery debates of 1830–1860; nothing about the early business cases in New York and Pennsylvania that constituted a parallel economic use of due process, from 1840–1860. More surprisingly still, there is no

---

[140] *Id.* at 611–612.
[141] *Ibid.* And note similar passages and assumptions at 608, top paragraph; 609, last paragraph; 615, top paragraph.
[142] See *id.* at 621, last paragraph.

awareness that the crucial issue here really is one of a *possible* merger, or of joint interest or involvement (perhaps in the person of the same individual draftsmen, Bingham, Conkling *et al.*) of these two strains of due process development and usage—one humanitarian and antislavery, the other economic, by and for business contending against mounting legislative control.

Worst of all, Dr. Russell's thinking about these problems has been short-circuited by misleading connotations of the terms "conspiracy" and "conspiracy theory." Having failed to set his study in perspective, or treat the broader motivation of the amendment, he proceeds as if the question is to determine whether section one was "*designed*" to resolve *specific crises* in corporate affairs.[143] This, obviously, is hindsight distorting with a vengeance. Loose, speculative discussion in the thirties often was as naive as this in its premises,[144] but rarely were matters put so badly.

As a matter of fact, this problem is neither as simple nor as hopeless as Dr. Russell has viewed it. Too much is known today of the main Negro race backgrounds and orientation of the amendment,[145] to invert and "vacuumize" the problem into one of mere relief for certain corporations. The issue now is whether these two railroads' situation, their petitions and bills, and above all, the "due process" angle of their cases in court, ever were sufficiently explored and appreciated, in Congress and out, to raise the point of corporate status or coverage under the due process and equal protection phraseology then currently undergoing draft. "Sufficiently," that is to say, so that one may hazard a guess as to the likelihood of such minimal insights having occurred as the Conkling-Beard thesis seems to presume.

Fortunately, these are matters which can be investigated, at least peripherally and indirectly. Pennsylvania legislative debates of this period were reported in full. Those on the repealers should indicate not only the degree of general public interest, but the manner in which men thought and spoke of the constitutional rights and issues involved. Likewise, the briefs and arguments of Reverdy Johnson and his colleagues in the cases in Judge Grier's, and in the Pennsylvania Supreme Court should indicate to what extent the concepts of the "corporate person," "due process," and "equal protection" were or were not used, singly or in combination. So too, from the

---

[143] See note 132 *supra*.
[144] See, *e.g.*, WEBB, *op. cit. supra* note 12, and such statements as that the framers of 1866 "smuggled" a "capitalist joker" into section one, BATES, THE STORY OF CONGRESS 233–234 (1936).
[145] See notes 23, 24, 25, 51 *supra*.

amount of attention devoted to *Brown v. Hummel* and *Erie & N. E. R.R. v. Casey*, we can get an idea how these cases were contemporaneously regarded, and how much importance was attached to them.

Inquiry pursued in this manner leads to interesting discoveries. The outstanding one is that neither the briefs nor legislative debates reveal even a single instance of an expressly formulated argument to the effect that corporations in general, or these two corporations in particular, were "persons" entitled to due process or due course of law. Indeed—and this is the more surprising and decisive—apparently no argument at all was made on due process per se—not even on behalf of *natural* "persons" or "property" in general. To be sure, the germinal cases and opinions in Pennsylvania and elsewhere, including *Brown v. Hummel* and the *Erie* case, were rather frequently cited and referred to, both in the legislative debates and at the bar, but that marked the current limit of usage. Neither side went beyond it. Due process and the corporate "person" plainly were not yet thunderbolts, or even boomerangs, in corporate practice.[146]

This, however, is but half the story. For it was almost universally agreed, and at times very emphatically argued by friends of the two roads, that "vested rights" had been interfered with, that the repealers were bad and void on that account, and had in fact been so declared by Justice Grier in the *Baltimore* case. Lips, in short, might still be mute, but eyes and minds were alert. Two sets of concepts simply awaited fusion and retagging. A swift review will demonstrate this and re-outline our problem.

In initial debate on the repealers in the Pennsylvania lower house supporters of the Pittsburgh & Connellsville asserted the corporation's rights and appealed that

". . . some respect [be shown] for rights already vested under the guarantees of the state and national constitutions. . . . There are guarantees of vested rights which cannot be taken away in this summary manner [without testimony, hearing or judicial investigation]. It is proposed summarily to legislate this corporation out of existence against the unanimous wish of every stockholder . . . every creditor . . . every person who has been invested [sic] in it."[147]

Only the contract clauses were expressly mentioned, but the *Erie*

---

[146] See *Insurance Co. v. New Orleans*, 13 Fed. Cas. 67, No. 7052 (C.C. La. 1871).
[147] See PA. LEGIS. RECORD 794 (1864), (House, April 21, 1864).

case was several times referred to,[148] and even a prediction made that the federal courts would set the repeal aside in view of Justice Grier's earlier "sledgehammer" blows at "contempt for the forms of legislation."[149] (Running debate established that the power of repeal had been explored at the 1862 and 1863 sessions, and that *then* it had been Pittsburghers who had favored repeal and commutation of the tonnage tax as a weapon against the Pennsylvania Railroad!)[150] "Thank Heaven there were courts," it was said, "if one corporation, with elephant tread, might thus step in, legislate away rights of constituents, and jeopardize a million dollar investment by Baltimore, without hearing, without investigation. The fact of franchise abuse had to be *judicially* ascertained. . . ."[151] Unimpressed, the House passed the repealer 68–28.[152]

Similar debate followed in the state Senate.[153] To Philadelphia apologists, this row simply was one between Pennsylvania and "foreign corporations."[154] The legislature might judge, and in the bill's preamble, it had judged decisively. To Pittsburghers, the row was between the Pennsylvania Railroad and sectional and national progress. The *Erie* case was distinguishable. "No court in the country will sustain our repeal."[155] Corporate franchises could not be so divested. "The Legislature cannot take away a corporate franchise without reference to the courts as to the forfeiture."[156]

That, it will be remembered, is what Justice Grier held just fourteen months later, in June, 1865.[157] Unfortunately, full briefs and arguments have not been preserved in the series of *Baltimore*[158] and

---

148 *Id.*, House, at 793, 795, c. 3. Also *id.*, Senate, at 874 (April 26, 1864), (Penny).
149 *Id.*, House, at 794, c. 2–3. (Bingham).
150 *Id.*, at 795, c. 3 (Smith, referring to his speeches in PA. LEGIS. RECORD, 332 (1863), attacking the positions taken by Thomas Williams of Pittsburgh). Williams was the Radical Republican lawyer and later one of the House managers of the impeachment of President Johnson.
151 *Id.*, 1864 House, at 794, c. 2–3, 799 (Bingham).
152 *Id.* at 799.
153 *Id.*, Senate, at 871–875 (April 26, 1864).
154 *Id.* at 873 (Latta).
155 *Id.* at 874 (Penny).
156 *Ibid.*
157 See note 109 *supra*. See also note 115 *supra*.
158 The chief source in this case (see note 109 *supra*) is a rare pamphlet brief (copies of which are found in the libraries of the Baltimore & Ohio Railroad, Baltimore, and the Bureau of Railway Economics, Washington, D.C.) and whose title page reads: CIRCUIT COURT OF THE UNITED STATES. FOR THE WESTERN DISTRICT OF PENNSYLVANIA. AT WILLIAMSPORT, JUNE TERM 1866. THE CITY OF BALTIMORE VERSUS THE CONNELLSVILLE AND SOUTHERN PENNSYLVANIA RAILWAY CO. ET AL. IN EQUITY (1866). (101 pages.) This pamphlet, hereafter cited as BALTIMORE CASE PAMPHLET, summarizes the four hearings in the case, and apparently was used to publicize the B. & O.—Baltimore

Connellsville[159] cases. Such summaries as are available show clearly the constitutional attack to have been based on the contract clauses, federal and state. It is equally clear however, from citations and passages in the summaries, that Johnson, Latrobe and Shiras, in their successful effort to steer around the holding in the *Erie* case, necessarily relied heavily on Chief Justice Lewis' dissent,[160] citing also, and discussing, *Brown v. Hummel*, and similar early cases that vaguely and tacitly linked corporations and due process. Judging from parallel passages in the briefs and his opinion, Justice Grier followed complainant's reasoning closely in these matters. But his statement, as already noted, was tantalizingly brief: "The principles of law, so far as they affect this case are very clearly and tersely stated by Chief Justice Lewis in his opinion in 1 Grant 275, with a review of the cases and a proper appreciation of that from Iowa,"[161]—the latter[162] being a reference to Chief Justice Lewis' rejection of the reasoning of an Iowa territorial court which had sustained its legislature's power to affect a similar charter repeal.

The prime issue and mystery, of course, are how elaborately Reverdy Johnson and co-counsel had argued these matters—how extensively, if at all—they invoked the requirement of due process. And right here the record fades! It would be dramatic, and surely aesthetically satisfying, if one could say with assurance that a detailed discussion of what constituted due process in such situations as charter repeals, occurred at this point. And it would be more dramatic

---

side of the controversy after the Pennsylvania interests appealed to the Supreme Court. See note 109 *supra*.

Useful aids in running down briefs and pamphlet materials on this and other cases are: BUREAU OF RAILWAY ECONOMICS, WASHINGTON, D.C. LIBRARY. THE BALTIMORE & OHIO RAILROAD AND ITS SUBSIDIARIES, A BIBLIOGRAPHY (1927) which gives locations, is chronologically arranged, and makes use of the earlier LEE, BIBLIOGRAPHY OF THE B. & O., 1827–1879 (London, 1879). The writer is greatly indebted to Mrs. Virginia Reilly, Librarian of the Baltimore and Ohio for aid in the use of these materials.

[159] Cited note 118 *supra*.
[160] See notes 79–84 *supra*.
[161] Baltimore v. Pittsburgh & C.R. Co., 2 Fed. Cas. 570, 571, No. 827 (C.C.W.D. Pa. 1865).
[162] *Miners' Bank of Dubuque v. United States*, 1 Greene 553 (Iowa 1848), opinion by Chief Justice S. C. Hastings, later (1849–51) Chief Justice of the Supreme Court of California, and founder (1878) of Hastings College of Law, San Francisco. The report at 554 shows that counsel for the bank had claimed the repealer void "on grounds of repugnancy to the Constitution of the U.S. and the Ordinance of 1787. The franchise is property, a vested right which . . . cannot be rescinded by the grantor without the default of the grantee," citing the Dartmouth College Case. Apparently no explicit argument was made on due process. For Chief Justice Lewis' caustic criticism of this case, and of frontier jurisprudence generally, see his opinion, 1 Grant 274, 277–8, quoted *infra* at note 190.

and significant still if that discussion could be shown to have revolved about Daniel Webster's classic definition of due process as

> "the general law; a law which hears before it condemns; which proceeds upon inquiry, and renders judgment only after trial. The meaning is that every citizen shall hold life, liberty, property, and immunities, under the protection of the general rules which govern society."[163]

Webster's definition, remember, had originated under roughly parallel circumstances in the *Dartmouth College Case.* Webster there had synthesized not merely Coke's learning and English common law doctrine; but the early American cases involving charter repeals of public corporations: specifically, *Terrett v. Taylor*[164] and *Trustees v. Foy*.[165] Moreover, in 1837, early in his professional career, Reverdy Johnson had been winning co-counsel with Webster in one of the decisive suits in American business history, *Chesapeake and Ohio Canal Co. v. Baltimore & O. R.R.*[166] That great case also turned in part on the contract clause.[167] It—and thirty years of practice since—had provided Johnson with matchless training and background.

Alas! All the bare record of 1865 reveals is that the crucial part of the argument before Judges Grier and McCandless *may have been* quite full and detailed, but *probably* was not![168] Johnson apparently elected to rely on a holding by the Maryland court in the great Canal-Railroad case of thirty years before which perfectly covered his present needs. Judging from the pamphlet summary, he simply condensed and quoted from *Chesapeake and Ohio Canal v. Baltimore & O. R.R.*, 4 Gill & J. 1, 121–122 (Md. 1837).

The passage in the brief read as follows:

> "A Corporation may be dissolved by a forfeiture of its Charter, through abuse or neglect of its franchises, as for a condition broken. But such forfeiture must be judicially ascertained and declared upon direct proceedings against the Corporation for that

---

163 Dartmouth College v. Woodward, 17 U.S. (4 Wheat.) 518, 581 (1819). And see the same case in the state court, 1 N.H. 111 (1817), and SHIRLEY, DARTMOUTH COLLEGE CAUSES AND THE SUPREME COURT OF THE UNITED STATES 158-9 (1879).

164 13 U.S. (9 Cranch) 43 (1815).

165 5 N.C. 58 (1805). *Cf.*, Turpin v. Lockett, 6 Call. 114 (Va. 1804) both discussed in Chapter 1, *supra*. And see Howe, *A Footnote to the Conspiracy Theory*, 47 YALE L. J. 1007 (1939).

166 4 Gill & J. 1 (Md. 1837).

167 *Ibid.* For backgrounds and history of the controversy, see SUNDERLIN, THE GREAT NATIONAL PROJECT: A HISTORY OF THE CHESAPEAKE AND OHIO CANAL (1946).

168 BALTIMORE CASE PAMPHLET, *op. cit. supra* note 158, at 9.

purpose, in order that it might not be condemned unheard for an imputed delinquency."

Canal *vs.* Railroad, 4 Gill & Johnson R. 1–122, citing Rex *vs.* Avery, 2 T.R. 515. Same *vs.* Passmore, 3 T.R. 199. Terrett *vs.* Taylor, 9 Cr. 43. College *vs.* Woodward, 4 Wheat. 518. Slee *vs.* Bloom, 5 Johns. C.R. 366. Same *vs.* Same, 19 Johnson, 456. Trustees *vs.* Hill, 6 Cowan, 23.[169]

The fact that the order and style of citation are here found to be almost identical with that in the Maryland opinion, with only one case omitted at the end, would seem to suggest that while *Terrett v. Taylor* and the *Dartmouth College Case* were cited,[170] their ramifications with regard to due process probably were not discussed. This is not surprising. Johnson and his associates were of course concerned first of all with the character of the reserved power *as it related to the Pittsburgh & Connellsville*; and with the highly factual issue of "misuse or abuse." Any discussion of the character or elements of due process that did occur, arose in that context. Furthermore, the fact that no evidence is found of any citation of either *Trustees v. Foy* or *Regents of the University of Maryland v. Williams*[171]—a case similar to *Foy* in which legislative interference with a chartered university had been voided as a violation of state due process—cautions against presuming too much. Such circumstances as these suggest that the orientation was not toward discussion of

---

[169] Johnson omitted minor ellipsis marks in making the condensation. The official Transcript of Record in the *Baltimore* cases in the Library of the Supreme Court (see *supra* note 109) reveals only a repetition of these arguments and citations—nothing more explicit or additional.

[170] See text at note 192 *infra* for another citation of these cases in the defendant's brief in the quo warranto case in the Pennsylvania Supreme Court.

[171] See 9 Gill & J. 365, 409, 412 (Md. 1838) for very strong and interesting dicta. Johnson of course was thoroughly familiar with this case and in fact later relied on it, along with numerous other contract clause cases, in his OPINION OF . . . REVERDY JOHNSON, ON THE QUESTIONS OF LAW EXAMINED BY GOVERNOR BOWIE IN HIS RECENT MESSAGE RELATIVE TO THE CAPITATION TAX ON THE WASHINGTON BRANCH ROAD OF THE BALTIMORE & OHIO RAILROAD COMPANY 7 (Baltimore, 1870). (Copy in Md. Hist. Soc. Libr.).

The background of this opinion is of interest. Exasperated by the B. & O.'s belated challenge of the in-lieu fare tax of 20% which had benefited it so long (see note 125 *supra*), Governor Bowie proposed that "if the company persists in its refusal to perform its contract and pay [the 20%] that the Legislature repeal all laws exempting [the company's] property from taxation." (Message to the General Assembly, January 1870, 51, 53–54). Johnson's opinion, thus elicited, relied solely on the contract clauses, citing a long list of cases, including both *Canal Co.* and *Williams*, but significantly made no mention of the Fourteenth Amendment, nor of the due process and equal protection clauses ratified just two years before! Certainly this situation provided Johnson with a perfect opportunity to reveal and capitalize the fact, had the P. & C. repealer, or similar incidents, ever figured in the draftsmanship of section one in 1866.

due process per se, but rather toward arguing the broader law of the charter repeal in the light of extant cases.

Overall, then, it appears doubtful that this *Baltimore* case occasioned much discussion of due process or the law of the land as related to charter appeals. Doubt and improbability, however, are not certainty. Moreover, a distinguished lawyer's learning and experience are by no means completely evidenced by his citation of authority in a single case or brief. Indeed, it is quite conceivable that a lawyer of Reverdy Johnson's eminence, whatever his actual course in this particular case, still could have perceived, later on, or even at about this time, as a result of his current experience, implications and possibilities inherent in a due process-equal protection draft, to which other men, even skilled lawyers, were yet blind or indifferent. Of the members of the Joint Committee, therefore, Reverdy Johnson stands as the one most likely to have raised or considered the point of corporate status.[172] In fact, cling to skepticism as one will, vow to concede nothing to conjecture or circumstance, it hardly can be gainsaid that by 1865–66 the constitutional status of the corporation had come nearly full circle. *Whether leaders of the bar or members of the Joint Committee were yet aware of it or not*, the corporate "person" and due process-law of the land phraseology were edging back into a relationship they shared briefly just before Chief Justice Marshall's solution in the *Dartmouth College Case* shunted development in other directions.[173] Already the two halves of the doctrine were viewing one another, if not yet sympathetically, at least at very short range. For one thing, the variety and magnitude of the corporate interest itself had become a fact of supreme importance.[174] So too had the urged necessity for imposing added judicial restraint upon these young corporate giants alternately turned executioner and cannibal, usurping state power. The framers' intention or degree of insight therefore conceivably was of less importance than were these observed general trends.

These conclusions are reinforced by other evidence. Failing to block the repealers in 1864, the two stricken roads tried unsuccessfully for an executive veto. Pamphlets prepared for this purpose,[175]

---

172 See note 203 *infra*.
173 See note 165 *supra*.
174 See generally, Chapters 3 and 9 *supra*.
175 These efforts are best evidenced in GWINN, TO THE GOVERNOR OF THE STATE OF PENNSYLVANIA 6 (Harrisburg, June 1864), a ten page pamphlet in Maryland Historical Society; and are recounted in MEMORIAL OF THE PITTSBURGH & CONNELLSVILLE RAILROAD CO. TO THE MAYOR AND CITY COUNCIL OF BALTIMORE (1864), an eight-page pamphlet in Maryland Historical Society. See especially page 3, stressing the appeal to

"Builded Better Than They Knew" 477

like later memorials addressed to the legislature[176] and to Congress,[177] spoke entirely in terms of "vested rights," of the contract clause, of required judicial determination of the fact of "misuse or abuse,"—never of due process as such, not even due process procedurally limited or related to "property" rather than "persons."

Much the same was true of the later rounds of debate in the Pennsylvania legislature. At the session of 1866,[178] supporters of the two roads repeated all the arguments made originally. They cited and recited Justice Grier's decision[179] but went no farther. Still another vain attempt to rescind the repealers was made at the 1867 session.[180] One speaker saw the matter, not as "a mere struggle between two railroad corporations . . . it involves the honor of the state . . . whether rights of the citizen are equal and coordinate . . .; it is your duty to see that equal and exact justice is meted out to all [Pennsylvania's] people."[181] But he plainly was thinking and speaking of the

---

the principles of state comity and due regard for the vested rights of the City of Baltimore. The prospect of the latter's joining the suit as chief creditor and mortgagee of the road was foreseen as greatly strengthening the P. & C.'s case "technically as well as on the merits." For miscarriage of this strategy, see note 109 *supra*.

[176] See MEMORIAL OF THE PITTSBURGH & CONNELLSVILLE RAILROAD CO. TO THE LEGISLATURE OF PENNSYLVANIA (Harrisburg, January 9, 1865), copies in Library of Congress and Maryland Historical Society Library; the latter signed by J. H. B. Latrobe. See especially page 13 appealing for continued recognition of "the principles of state comity and international freedom of commercial intercourse which have, especially of late years, governed state legislation in regard to internal improvements."

[177] See BRIEF HISTORY, *op. cit. supra* note 121. After recounting the "perfidy" of the vexatious suits and the repeal "secured by means which will not bear the slightest scrutiny," and while "these assaults upon its vested rights" are being redressed in the courts, the company appeals to Congress "for such *remedial* legislation as may effect the object without unnecessary and inexpedient interference with state enactments. The incorporation of a new company is not asked for, but only such an authoritative recognition of the constitutional rights of the existing corporations, chartered for this purpose by the Legislatures of Maryland and Pennsylvania, as will protect them from invasion by unconstitutional state action, by which action, a state, at the instance of a corporation, of her own selection, seeks, by crushing its competitor, to secure to it a monopoly of the trade and travel between the great lakes and the seat of the Federal Government, and forcing it over a route from 70 to 80 miles longer than that of the company whose rights are thus assailed."

[178] See PA. LEGIS. RECORD, 743-745, 801 (House, 1866), on H.B. 1176 (C. & M., killed by 40-30 vote); *id.* at 748-752, on H.B. 1280 (P. & C., killed by 41-39 vote). *Id.* at 916-921, on S.B. 969 (C. & M.). See also the references to numerous petitions urging that the charters be restored. *Id.* at 206-207, 215, 377, 379.

[179] See PA. LEGIS. RECORD, 748 (House, Apr. 3, 1866). (Glass); *id.* at 749 (Ross).

[180] See PA. LEGIS. RECORD, App. cvi-cxxxiii, pp. 257-259, 283, 286 (Senate, Feb. 12-15, 1867). *Id.* at ccclvi-ccclxv (House, Mar. 13, 1867).

[181] *Id.* at cviii (Senate, Stutzman). See also, in the same vein, Senator Graham's minority report declaring that by the 1864 repeal, which was in "utter disregard of vested rights of individuals," the "citizens of several counties of our state are deprived of equal advantages and equal benefits with the balance of our fellow citizens." *Id.* at 257-259.

geographic sections affected, not of the corporation or its shareholders! Another senator blasted the "interference with vested rights" as "without a shadow of justice," cited "6 Barr 92" and quoted the contract clause part of *Brown v. Hummel*, closing with reference to "1 Grant 275," and the proposition: "The stockholders, then, under the charter, have a right to protection of the courts—a right to friendly legislation," in short, to judicial determination of the fact of misuse.[182] Still others wanted a general railroad law like other states'—"their citizens enjoy equal rights and equal protection in all matters of public enterprise and improvement."[183] Speaker after speaker mentioned the battle in the courts, and stressed that Grier had made Chief Justice Lewis' *Erie* dissent the law of the *Baltimore* case.[184] But no one alluded to due process, nor to the Fourteenth Amendment, then before the country!

So it was, too, in 1868,[185] when the legislature (following the ruling in the quo warranto case) finally and unanimously[186] repealed the repealer. Speaking in favor of such action, Senator Graham of Pittsburgh declared:

> "In arrogating to itself the right to repeal this charter the Legislature assumed judicial functions it is incapable of exercising . . . and thereby placed itself in the anomalous position of being accuser and judge, and assumed the right to charge, prosecute, convict, condemn and execute.
>
> ". . . [W]as this legislation right? If this Senate will affirm that it has the constitutional power, of its own mere volition, to deprive any person or body corporate of a natural or vested right or franchise; or if it will hold that is either just, legal, or equitable to decide a grave question of fact involving interests amounting to millions of dollars on the mere suggestion of one party, without notice to or hearing the other, then I must be wrong. But, until they do thus reverse not only the law of the land, but the universal God-like law of right and justice, there can be no justification for refusing to restore to this corporation the charter of which it was deprived by a violation of those principles, revered throughout the world wherever civilization has penetrated.[187]

---

[182] *Id.* at cvix (Senate, Feb. 13, 1867), (White).
[183] *Id.* at cxvii.
[184] *E.g.*, see: *id.* at cxxvi (Senator Bingham); *id.* at ccclvi-x (Reps. Jenks, Mann, Boyle).
[185] See PA. LEGIS. RECORD, 202–206 (Senate, Jan. 30, 1868); *id.* at 213–225 (House, Jan. 30, 1868).
[186] *Id.* at 205.
[187] *Id.* at 203.

"Builded Better Than They Knew" 479

But again, nothing more explicit!

Finally, there were the arguments before the Supreme Court of Pennsylvania. The official report of the quo warranto suit gives only a short list of authorities cited by Johnson, Latrobe and Shiras. This list,[188] however, includes *Brown v. Hummel* and the *Dartmouth College* case among others. A fuller report of arguments is preserved in a pamphlet brief.[189] Signed by Latrobe, Johnson and Shiras, this document reveals that much the same stand was taken in the state as in the federal court: the *Erie* case was carefully distinguished; the Iowa case vigorously attacked. Nearest approach to a due process argument was this:

> "Judge Grier's Opinion of this case in Iowa is expressed in reference to the dissenting opinion of Chief Justice Lewis in the case of Erie & North East R.R. Co. v. Casey, reported in 1st Grant, where it will be found to be properly appreciated. With regard to this case, Judge Lewis remarks in 1st Grant 277: 'The case originating in the territorial transactions of Iowa, when her courts of justice were in a "disorganized condition," is the only one cited which sustains the position that a reservation of power to revoke a charter, in case of abuse, carries with it the additional reservation of judicial power to try and convict the accused corporation of abuse. A few years earlier, the case of Titus Losey was decided by a "Lynch court" of the same territory. He was convicted and sentenced to pay a fine of $800. He appealed from the decision, and as the appellate tribunals of the territory were in a "disorganized condition," the court set up the appeal to the president of a Pennsylvania Common Pleas. He reversed the judgment, and awarded restitution of the fine which had been levied. The "Lynch court," with a proper regard for the due course of law, immediately obeyed the decision. The case is cited, not because it is a better precedent than the one from the same quarter reported in Green's Reports, but merely to show the progress of judicial authority. A few years ago the "popular" tribunals of Iowa were willing to receive the "gladsome light of jurisprudence" from the president of a subordinate court in Pennsylvania. But now, even the irregular struggles of her infant existence furnish a precedent sufficiently potent to shift this ancient and stable commonwealth

---

[188] See Commonwealth v. Pittsburgh & C. R.R. 58 Pa. 26, 41 (1868).
[189] See THE COMMONWEALTH OF PENNSYLVANIA VS. PITTSBURGH & CONNELLSVILLE RAILROAD. IN THE SUPREME COURT OF PENNSYLVANIA IN QUO WARRANTO. DEFENDANT'S BRIEF. MAY TERM 1865. (Cover title, 56 pages, copy in Maryland Historical Society). This brief is dated earlier than the actual arguments, which came after, not before, Grier's decision.

from her constitutional moorings. "The sceptre has" indeed "departed from Judah"!' "[190]

After analyzing an English case, the brief again returned to Judge Lewis' minority views in the *Erie* case of 1856. Elaborate apology was made for pressing "a dissenting opinion on so high a tribunal as the present."[191] But both the three-to-two division in *Erie*, and the fact that Justice Grier in his recent opinion in the federal court had followed Lewis, were cited in justification:

". . . [I]t is difficult [the brief continued] to adduce the weight of Judge Grier's opinion without quoting from Judge Lewis, as reported in 1 Grant 275:
"That a private act of corporation, . . . when accepted and capital expended on the faith of it, is a contract, is too well settled to be denied. That a charter for the construction of a railroad is a private corporation is equally well settled. That the obligation of a contract cannot be impaired by a State, is a principle to be found in the Constitution of the United States, and of the State of Pennsylvania. It follows that a charter to a railroad company, thus accepted and acted on, cannot be annulled against the consent and without the default of the corporators, judicially ascertained and declared, unless the power be reserved in the grant. [Dartmouth College v. Woodward] 4 Wheaton (518 at) 578 [U.S. 1819]; [Fletcher v. Peck] 6 Cr. 88 [i. e. 87] [U.S. 1810]; [New Jersey v. Wilson] 7 [Cr.] 164 [U.S. 1812]; [Terrett v. Taylor] 9 [Cr.] 43 [U.S. 1815]; [Norman v. Heist] 5 W. & S. 101 [i.e., 171] [Pa. 1843]; [Brown v. Hummel] 6 Barr 86 [Pa. 1847]; [Monongahela Navigation Co. v. Coon] 6 Barr 379 [Pa. 1849]; [Bank of Pennsylvania v. Commonwealth] 7 Harris [144 at] 151; [Charles River Bridge Co. v. Warren Bridge] 7 Pick. 344 (Mass. 1829)."[192]

After quoting Chief Justice Lewis further to the effect that the fact of misuse or abuse is not reserved to the legislature, but must be judicially ascertained:[193]

"The conclusions of Judge Lewis are those which the Defendants seek to enforce in arguing their first point, that the repealing act of 1864 is unconstitutional and void."[194]

This brief[195] shows unmistakably the primacy of the contract clause argument; the oblique, shadowy character of the due process

---

[190] *Id.* at 11.
[191] *Id.* at 15.
[192] *Ibid.*
[193] *Id.* at 16–17.
[194] *Ibid.*
[195] *Ibid.*

references; the tendency of counsel to consider and to safeguard corporate rights directly through the relevant cases and citations rather than doctrinally—hence the observed failure to invoke expressly even *procedural* due process. Yet the brief also shows, quite as unmistakably, by the heavy reliance on the Lewis-Grier views, and by the citation of *Brown v. Hummel* (and of the other cases from Chief Justice Lewis' "due process dissent" in *Erie & N. E. R.R. v. Casey*), how and why these matters, still presumed and implicit, soon were to become thoroughly explicit.

Summary Analysis and Concluding Hypothesis

What are we to make of this evidence? What *can* we make of it? At first blush, proof, or even disproof, of Conkling's innuendo seems as elusive as ever. No doubt this is in part because Conkling left so much to suggestibility and imagination that we never can be quite sure or agreed on just what he did mean, or have in mind.

Even a mirage or a rainbow, however, may lead to important discoveries. So it has been here. Nothing has been found which alters the hypothesis that full and equal protection for natural "persons" —including the freedmen, Southern loyalists, aliens, members of disadvantaged and unpopular groups—was the primary and true reason for the choice of this term. The question is whether that reason remained the only one. The content, the form, the sponsorship, the evolution of the phraseology all can be explained without assumed regard for corporations. Conkling's affirmative statement —or inference—still stands absolutely alone, as uncorroborated today by direct testimony as in 1886. This, in itself, must be profoundly disillusioning in view of repeated and extensive search.

On the other side, of course, there remain a few stray, unexplained circumstances: the apparent backing and filling within the Joint Committee over the drafts[196] and the in-again-out-again indecision of committee members, obliged to choose between Bingham's

---

[196] See KENDRICK, *op. cit. supra* note 12, at 37-120. A recent and interesting summary analysis of the voting record of the Joint Committee members as revealed in KENDRICK, is Bickel, *The Original Understanding and the Segregation Decision*, 69 HARV. L. REV. 1 (1955). Mr. Bickel's conjectures sometimes are shrewd, but for the most part undocumented by any new tangible evidence. *Cf.* Professor Kelly's paper, *The Fourteenth Amendment Revisited: The Problem of Intent*, read before The American Historical Association, meeting in Washington, D.C., December 30, 1955, and published as *The Fourteenth Amendment Reconsidered: The Segregation Question*, 54 MICH. L. REV. 1049-1086 (1956).

For Stevens' voting record on the various amendment drafts, see Chapter 2, *supra*, at note 77; for Conkling's record, see, *id.* at note 80.

broadly worded forms and Stevens' strictly racial drafts; the fact that Stevens himself finally voted for Bingham's form in preference to his own; Bingham's trial balloon and talk about curbing the state's taxing power;[197] and always, of course, the fact that corporations *are* "persons" and have always been "persons" in common legal parlance (though this *in itself* does not mean they necessarily were "persons" within the purview of the framers of these constitutional clauses[198] any more than that marriages, being "contracts," were within the purview of the framers of the contract clause in 1787.

What, then, does it all add up to?

1. Disregarding for the moment the more complex issue of the discussions and consensus within the Committee, it seems clear that Reverdy Johnson, one of the three Democrats, is the *individual* member most likely to have "contemplated or understood"—and perhaps even in discussion to have raised the possibility—that Bingham's proposed drafts were so broadly worded even corporations might qualify for federal protection under them. Next most likely candidates in this respect, were Stevens,[199] Bingham,[200] Conkling,[201] Rogers.[202] Unfortunately Reverdy Johnson's correspondence affords no help in clarifying these matters.[203] Furthermore, his later failures to invoke due process in *Veazie Bank v. Fenno* and in his "opinion" on Governor Bowie's proposal, 1870, are still very much a *caveat*.[204]

---

[197] CONG. GLOBE, 39th Cong., 1st Sess. 429 (1866). On January 25, 1866, just as joint committee deliberations were getting under way, and while section one still was in positive form (see KENDRICK, *op. cit. supra* note 12, at 54–62; Minutes of Committee sessions Jan. 24–Feb. 3, 1866) Bingham proposed on the floor of the House that "there should be added" to the primitive draft just reported "the provision that no State in this Union shall ever lay one cent of tax upon the property or head of any loyal man for the purpose of paying tribute or pensions to those who rendered service in the . . . atrocious rebellion. . . . I ask the gentlemen to consider that, as your Constitution stands today, there is no power, expressed or implied, in this Government to limit or restrain the general power of taxation in the States."

[198] See generally, Chapter 9 *supra*.

[199] See CURRENT, OLD THAD STEVENS (1942); WOODLEY, THADDEUS STEVENS (1934). Reverdy Johnson and Stevens served together as counsel in unholding the McCormick reaper patent in 1854. Seymour v. McCormick, 57 U.S. (16 How.) 479 (1853). Correspondence reveals badly strained relations in October 1866, but their professional association was of longstanding.

[200] A forthcoming biography by Dr. Maynard Brichford of the Wisconsin Historical Society promises to clarify Bingham's role. 1968: Unpublished still. A biography is much needed.

[201] But *cf.* his curious voting record on the various amendment drafts, cited note 196 *supra*.

[202] See *supra* note 133.

[203] Johnson's handwriting is so notoriously bad that discovery of further correspondence would not necessarily solve our current problem.

[204] See JOHNSON, *op. cit. supra* note 171.

Nor are the papers of the Garrett family of any more aid.[205] Indeed, it is typical of the false starts and general bathos of the whole search that calendared correspondence in the Library of Congress between President Garrett and congressional leaders during these months proved (upon rather excited examination!) to be acknowledgments of the Baltimore and Ohio's annual passes![206]

2. Turning from individual understandings to the matter of Joint Committee action and discussion—which, after all, is the vital element in Conkling's thesis—several points are in order: First, the blank, inscrutable wall of silence. No caucus records and no supplements to the Journal minutes have come to light.[207] The bare Committee voting records are no help—are open to as many conflicting interpretations as there are personal preferences.[208] All changes in texts and votes can be accounted for without dragging in the corporation as cause.

Viewed in perspective, the most that can be said is this: If we are to attribute scope or efficacy to the railroad evidence, we conclude that *if* the question of corporate status in fact came up, it probably came up incidentally, casually, as a minor, hypothetical point. Conkling, remember, did not *say* otherwise—he simply left the impression! What our railroad evidence suggests is that the Committee members and congressmen privy to the troubles of the Pittsburgh & Connellsville and Cleveland & Mahoning would have been unlikely to have seen any reason in 1866 why such corporations should *not* be permitted to plead the benefits of the proposed constitutional clauses. Plainly, there was yet no clear pattern or weight of precedent in corporations' favor.[209] The whole point still was hypothetical, speculative. And if ever the issue of corporate "citizenship" under the privileges or immunities draft was raised, certainly the conclusion, in the light of the insurance companies' thirty years' failure under the comity clause, must have been overwhelmingly against any likelihood of success in that direction!

---

[205] Grateful acknowledgement is made to Mr. Robert Garrett of Baltimore for permission to consult the *Garrett Papers*, and to Dr. Robert Land and the staff of the Manuscript Division, Library of Congress, for innumerable courtesies.

[206] *Garrett Papers*, January to March, 1866.

[207] So little added light has been thrown on evolution of the fourteenth amendment by research in the major manuscript collections in recent years, that fresh attack is warranted: correspondence of national party leaders (including members of the crucial Republican caucus of late May, 1866) addressed to relatives and political and business confidants in home districts now presents a promising field of search. Ambitious young and local historians, please note.

[208] See Bickel, note 196 *supra*.

[209] See notes 86–94 *supra*. *Cf.* the Johnson-Latrobe-Shiras arguments summarized in the two briefs cited notes 158 and 189 *supra*.

3. So, willy-nilly, we are brought back to the implications of negative evidence in general, and of these findings in particular. Silence, as we observed, had no probative value one way or the other—at the outset of our inquiry: certainly none as proof of an affirmative intention.[210] Now that search has been completed, however, our own consistently negative findings—corroborative of the consistently negative findings of others—gain in weight and significance. Thus the apparent disinterest of business journals and business groups in the amendment,[211] together with the utter absence of any attempt by Democratic opponents of constitutional change to make political capital of the *possibility* that "moneyed corporations" as "persons" *might* become beneficiaries of such phraseology—either in the courts or in Congress—is highly impressive in itself. Certainly nothing would have delighted handicapped Democrats of 1866 more, had there been any inkling (or even suspicion) that corporations might so benefit, than to expose the fact, to raise a great hue and cry. This could and would have been done, one is fairly certain, *even regardless of the Joint Committee's understanding, had the point been readily conceivable.*[212] In other words, universal silence on this score is impressive and now deserves consideration, at least to the extent of warning that this problem is far less simple than has been imagined.

The trouble, clearly, was not with the potentials of these phrases, but with current capacities, contexts, choices. The elements of doctrinal synthesis were there in 1866, right enough; but the synthesis itself apparently still was pending. There were too many distractions, too many counter-possibilities, some highly attractive and very obvi-

---

210 See note 53 *supra*.

211 Examination of the Commercial and Financial Chronicle, and Hunt's Merchant's Magazine, July 1865–July 1866, and the Bankers' Magazine, July 1864–June 1874, reveals no interest in, nor discussion of, a new constitutional amendment as related to business. Notwithstanding extensive case coverage in the latter journal, no mention was made of ratification of the fourteenth amendment, nor of such important early cases as *Insurance Co. v. New Orleans* and *Slaughter-House*. Not even *Hepburn v. Griswold*, or its later overruling, drew attention to due process. *Paul v. Virginia* was simply reported, and with a digest paragraph reading: "A corporation is not a *person* within Article 4 of the United States Constitution." (emphasis added). (v. 24, p. 562). Such monumental myopia and confusion are hard to reconcile with Conkling's thesis!

212 One of the few lawyers who early sensed the jurisdictional, and perhaps substantive, potentialities of the due process clause of the amendment was O. H. Browning, Secretary of Interior in Johnson's Administration; see his letter to W. H. Benneson and H. V. Sullivan published in the Cincinnati Commercial, October 26, 1866, summarized in FLACK, ADOPTION OF THE FOURTEENTH AMENDMENT 146–147 (1908). Yet note that in warning of these potentialities, Browning fixed primarily on the amendment's impact on the *division* rather than the *separation* of powers, and upon the political and social, rather than economic, implications.

ously dominant even in the thinking of hard-pressed counsel and litigants. The main one of course was *congressional* as opposed to *judicial* sanctions and intervention—as witness both the railroads' and insurance companies' strategy! Affirmative exercise of the powers of Congress was the solution sought in each instance. The fact that due process and the corporate "person" are found to appear incidentally in the backgrounds of the two petitioning railroads, and the fact that petitions for enactment of "just and equal laws pertaining to interstate insurances" emanated from the insurance companies, probably means only that the context and content were forming, not that they were yet held clearly in view, or had yet become the basis for even professional insight and understanding.

One submits, then, that this problem is more complex than has been imagined. It is not enough that we today, freed of then current alternatives, distractions, and importunities, can see that certain developments were under way—even assured, given time, perspective and the pressure of experience. The past is clear, but the future was not.

Evidently what we have had here is a classic example of inverted perspective, and of the distortions and confusions that arise out of it. Unconsciously, our generation suspected and presumed more than circumstances warranted. To analogize: we expected to find cave men crying "Fire!" and talking about "conflagrations" and roast beef, on the eve—or during the first month or year of their application of flint to steel! Again: these primitives were presumed to be out looking for gold rings or diamonds. Actually we have discovered them hammering copper and gold and making crude trinkets.

In short, I submit that the discovery, inception, or conception of due process (used in combination with the corporate person)—like the application of flint to steel—was not a matter of momentary, conscious insight or intuition; not a "flash of genius," to use the phrase of the patent lawyers. Rather, it was, and had to be, a matter of collective experience, social growth, trial and error. Only in retrospect can it be said that Socrates employed the "Socratic method." Alexander Graham Bell did not *invent* modern electro-communications—not even the *modern* telephone. Still more to the point, Bell was studying the human voice, seeking better means of teaching the deaf—not searching for (much less talking about) "calling the neighbors," or "calling New York." The real pioneer does not *follow* a blazed trail. Indeed, he generally is unconscious he is blazing one. His object is to explore something, get somewhere himself. *Initially*, the forks of the creek are his *alternatives*, not trails or routes. Usually, he travels them both, unless he is indifferent or lucky. So it was with our pioneers of corporate protection by means of the clauses that made up section one.

To clinch this matter of anachronisms, and get our minds more nearly in the mood of 1866, we have to remember only that the framers and ratifiers of that date proved utterly blind to what eventually proved a glaring loophole in section one as that section was finally adopted. Addition at the last minute in the Senate of the first sentence defining citizenship and making citizenship dual, followed as that sentence was by another which restrained the states from abridging only the "privileges or immunities of *citizens of the United States*," *eventually* made possible the contention, which of course became the basis for the *Slaughter-House* decision emasculating the privileges or immunities clause, that Congress by implication had *not* intended to restrain the states' powers over the privileges and immunities of *citizens of the states!* Now the reason the framers and ratifiers overlooked this potential loophole was that to old antislavery men, and to Unionists and Republicans generally, all the fundamental civil rights were deemed to be privileges or immunities of *citizens of the United States*. The first and obvious purpose of the amendment, therefore, was to *declare* them so. No one dreamed, accordingly, that anyone ever would argue otherwise, much less that the Supreme Court would sustain the argument. The prevalent natural rights-declaratory habits of thinking thus conditioned an outlook that made the alternative view inconceivable.[213] Only after opportunist arguments of Senator Trumbull and others, 1870-71, had suggested the loophole to hardput lawyers in the *Slaughter-House Cases*, did matters change and an apparent flaw develop.[214] Clearly, some such set of factors could have been operative with reference to corporate personality. Indeed, *that* is our hypothesis.

Apply these insights to our problem. Pursue a bit further that analogy of the fire from flint and steel: All the elements are lying around—have been, perhaps, for months and years: the hand, the flint, the steel, the need—even the tinder (and how much of it we can see kicking around Congress and the Joint Committee in 1866!) —everything, in short, but the final fruitful chance, the observation, the insight, the will to repeat. Everything but the spark, then the fire itself. Quite possibly in that dismal cave there even were those who casually knocked things together that last night or month, and

---

[213] See Chapter 7, *supra*.
[214] *Id.* at 295, 330; *cf.* 131 *supra*, note 79.

so got a spark—or who shortly convinced themselves that they had —and the Conklings of course already have thought up the name: "Fire!" But the one thing still lacking was combustion, or, as we have to think of it here, the *corporate* person *hopefully* and *knowingly* associated by counsel and legislators with due process and equal protection to achieve a restraint on legislative and administrative action.

Now there are corollaries of this, and our analogy already has hinted at them. Before there could be clear, general insight into the potentialities of corporate personality and due process, there had to be pretty explicit judicial use. Justice Grier's opinion foreshadowed what lay ahead, but we can see now that it was casual, indirect; too clouded and involved for immediate general insight.[215] It hardly is surprising, therefore, that we find no explicit references in the legislative and congressional debates on the repealers to violation of *due process as such*. The impressive thing today is the amount of talk found of violation of vested rights, the need for prior judicial determination of misuse or abuse, and the view that the legislation was bad for these reasons.[216] Due process, as Professor Corwin made clear years ago, is the rubric under which the doctrine of vested rights achieved ultimate constitutional status.[217] For the present, these repealers were regarded only as impairing obligations of contracts, and as having been "passed without any hearing or judicial determination of the fact of misuse or abuse." *Today* we would say they were unconstitutional *because they violated due process*, and in essence, they did this in 1866, *from our viewpoint*.

What we have to remember is that in 1866 the due process tradition still was on the make.[218] Laws affecting business occasionally were thought and said to violate due process *because they were bad*; or because it was hoped they might be declared bad; not yet, however, were they commonly thought and said to be bad because they violated due process. In short, the remedy still was crystallizing from the matrix.

If we agree that the controlling and popular idea and stage of development at this date was *vested rights*, not due process or equal

---

[215] See notes 109, 161, 168 *supra;* and *cf.* notes 187–189 *supra.*
[216] See notes 121, 127, 147–156, 182, 187 *supra.*
[217] See Corwin, *supra* note 135.
[218] Additional studies like Professor Corwin's *Extension of Judicial Review in New York, supra* note 88, and HARTZ, *op. cit. supra* note 57, together with studies of the determinative role of the Bar, like TWISS, LAWYERS AND THE CONSTITUTION (1942), still are needed to clarify this development. Ohio is a crucial state.

protection, and if we agree that the touchstone in the due process clause was "property," not "person" or "due process," are we not pretty close to saying that even Congressmen who took a dim or outraged view of the Pennsylvania repealers, or of the current insurance and express company laws, were not likely to articulate or pin point their objections using these concepts of a still-future day? Certainly some of these men held and expressed strong opinions on the expediency and injustice of such measures as the repealers, but one simply cannot picture them, nor have we found them speculating in terms still so largely unapplied. That, it seems, is the lesson pointed up by this evidence in the legislative debates.

One concludes then, that while early postwar use of due process and corporate personality in defense of business enterprise certainly was imminent and rapidly approaching, it was not yet an obvious or self-evident proposition. Even the best-informed leaders, lawyers, and legislators still wore the blinkers and check-reins of their time. The answer to our first question therefore would appear to be "No."

There remains the matter of congressional, as opposed to judicial, relief. It is clear beyond doubt that Sherman, Garfield, Stevens and other northern and western nationalists, probably including Bingham and Conkling, did spearhead a drive to gain Congressional relief for certain corporations—relief from what many had regarded as essentially "invidious and discriminating" state laws. It is equally clear that a parallel yet independently motivated drive for constitutional amendments enlarging powers of Congress (and by the later draft, curbing the states) harmonized perfectly with, and in effect facilitated relief in, just such cases as these. It is clear, finally, that this incident dramatized the power and arrogance of state chartered monopolies—was a powerful factor in crystallizing nationalist sentiment, especially in the Midwest and undeveloped parts of the country. The P. & C. and C. & M. propaganda shrewdly addressed itself to such groups and sections—played to the limit Pennsylvania's high-handedness and contumacy of national authority.

Does it follow, then, that the drafts of section one in their original "Congress-shall-have-power" form were perceived or conceived by their framers to cover such situations? The short answer is that there is no evidence of any such understanding or intention; none in the debates, private correspondence, or the press, so far as yet observed. "Vested rights," "the principles of state comity," "the desirability of freedom of commercial intercourse," all were cited and appealed to. There were repeated attacks on the old "exploded and restrictive system designed to confine the channels of trade within the territory of a single state."[219] Yet, nowhere are these objects and subjects articulated, even implicitly, with a new or proposed constitutional amendment, or with the express phrases and doctrines that went into section one. This does not mean of course that such articulation could not have occurred, or categorically that it did not. The harmony of interest and opinion already was too close and striking ever to say that. Yet it is equally hard to believe, if the interrelations of these groups and ideas in 1865-66 were as close or obvious as they became in the immediate post-war period, that Congressmen seeking to rationalize expansion of federal power, or businessmen claiming the need for it and trying to justify it, would not be found, at least occasionally and inferentially, referring to the constitutional expediency, or implying the constitutional mechanics, of such an objective.

All we find of course are these petitions and bills seeking *affirmative action by Congress*—nothing beyond that. And Congress simply was uninterested. The state railroad monopolies already were too powerful, too counterpoised, too mistrustful of federal action and control, for such affirmative legislation to pass. Much the same situation existed with reference to the insurance companies. The industry itself was divided and at loggerheads, and Congress was indifferent. This matter was not really deemed a question of constitutional power, therefore, or of defect of power; but one of policy, defective policy. Congressional leaders of a Congress indifferent to and incapable of exercise of powers already possessed ordinarily are not to be presumed scheming for expansion of those powers. Certainly not with reference to the plight of interests viewed so apathetically. So this second possibility too, smacks of the transpositions and bedevilments of hindsight.

All that can be said is that these two business groups were seeking the help and protection of Congress. Their bills did not pass. They failed in both cases. A few Congressmen were sympathetic, and the companies' general objectives harmonized to some degree with the views and objectives of the Congressional leadership—sufficiently so, perhaps, for Conkling later to remember, then to romanticize and counterpoint, the harmonies.[220]

Once due process began burgeoning again (1869-71);[221] once

---

[219] The quoted phrases are from BRIEF HISTORY, *op. cit. supra* note 121, and from MEMORIAL, *op. cit. supra* note 176.

[220] **1968:** For an updated rationale, see Editorial Note, Chapter 13, *infra.*

[221] See Chapter 9, *supra*, at 393ff. And note, for example, that in *Stuart v. Palmer*, 74 N.Y. 183, 190 (1878), the New York Court of Appeals characterized the due process

Grangers really tightened the screws on railroads generally (1866–75); once insurance leaders had beaten their wits out against the comity and commerce clauses in the courts,[222] and against continued Congressional indifference, grasping finally but futilely at the straws of due process and corporate personality in *Insurance Co. v. New Orleans* (1871)—in short, once sheer physical, mental, and legal exhaustion pretty emphatically had suggested that the due process and equal protection clauses now *might be* the two "last best hopes of Earth" and of judicial review, Conkling *then,* apparently, along with numerous others, completed his "education in the obvious," grew wise and self-assured *after* the event, saw more clearly with every passing month perhaps, how he and his colleagues in 1866, conceivably had "builded better than they knew." Like the celebrated passage in Conkling's argument, this of course is pure "surmise," but what happened later is history.

Overall, the most one is ready to say of this situation in 1866 is that a few men *may have considered* the possibility that corporations might attempt to make use of the text devised for other purposes—as corporations had for years tried without success for a "citizen's" rights of interstate trade under the comity clause. If so, corporate citizenship under section one probably was dismissed as an absurd prospect. Corporate personality, if raised and considered, say by Reverdy Johnson, Thaddeus Stevens or Bingham, in the light of the most advanced use in Judge Grier's court, could have appeared less remote and more attractive. But tender regard for corporations certainly was not the original reason for selection of this phraseology, nor was it ever the primary consideration.

Writing in 1937, Max Ascoli observed that the Civil War and fourteenth amendment celebrated "a marriage" of idealistic and economic elements in our constitutional history.[223] This was an inspired metaphor. It clarified original relationships and now helps us better grasp the implications of current findings. The major qualification one would add today is that this idealistic-economic union, of which the fourteenth amendment was the "supreme celebration," appears to have been, at its consummation in 1866, something of a *liason de convenience,* entered into fortuitously without formal engagement or publication of bans. Moreover, the ultimate

---

clause as the "most important guaranty of personal rights to be found in the federal or state constitutions. It is a limitation upon arbitrary power and is a guaranty against arbitrary legislation."

222 See Chapter 9, *supra*, at 383ff.
223 ASCOLI, INTELLIGENCE IN POLITICS 160–161 (1936).

marriage, at least so far as insurance companies were concerned, actually was to the "deceased wife's sister"! *Persona*—not *Civita*—was her name. Equal protection and due process—not privileges or immunities—were her now undenied charms. Above all, the Supreme Court, not Congress nor the ratifiers, ultimately tied the marital knot. Roscoe Conkling was a brash, over-zealous cupid. Yet if this was essentially a common law marriage, it also proved, for fifty years, a singularly happy one, fruitful, almost Biblical, in its satisfactions and "begats."[224]

Like Ulysses, we have "followed knowledge like a sinking star," and like the Preacher, found mainly "Vanity . . . weariness of flesh." It would be overbold to say that Conkling's thesis is dead. Constitutional history will be insufferably dull and prosaic without the "Conspiracy Theory." The insurance bar may yet move to expunge, or a least amend, its dismal record. These hazards are inescapable and borne with resignation: After years of intermittent search for Conkling's mysterious spook, we waive jurisdiction, plead for judgment on that ancient writ—"Sheriff, bring in the body!"

EDITORIAL NOTE. The concluding paragraph, looking half-ironically and equivocally toward "the insurance bar" for a possible rationale, shows convincingly enough that, as of 1955, bafflement and vexation still hovered heavily over this insurance–express company sector, and indeed over a number of the problems of congressional draftsmanship and "framer" intent. More embarrassingly, the paragraph also shows that I had not yet fully assimilated the "elementary, simple, fundamental" point stressed in the headnote above.

The most promising research paths, moreover, now led away from Congress and back again to the states. That intensive study of "railroad due process" in Pennsylvania, 1847–1869, surely had shown the gains and the leads to be derived from such an attack; the need for re-examining, behavioristically and professionally, "process" and "protection" in other jurisdictions, by other vanguard interests. California, of course, was the "natural" here. In no other state had industrial, legal, and constitutional development been so rapid and accelerated, 1850–1870, nor more recapitulative, crucial and ramify-

---

[224] See note 9 *supra*, and *cf.* the progeny of *Smyth v. Ames* in SHEPARD'S U.S. CITATIONS.

ing, 1870–1890; and nowhere else were to be found an abler bench and bar more widely drawn from diverse jurisdictions. Extensive briefs collections were available, moreover, for these cases and periods; the Los Angeles County Law Library in fact had just acquired another, one of the most illuminating of all.[1] Finally, in California, as nowhere else, the Chinese had acted as veritable catalysts and stimulants, as buffers and bumpers, and acted as such, on both the racial and the economic sides, before the Fourteenth Amendment as well as after, with the police power and the taxing power alike focused and pertinent throughout.

Accordingly California and the midwestern Granger states—Illinois especially—now afforded the most attractive bases for comparative study and attack. In 1957–1958 my Guggenheim Fellowship had been renewed for more work on these and related problems and areas. At the very start, studying briefs in early San Francisco street assessment cases and in various taxing power cases in the Midwest, a curious, now vaguely familiar phenomenon recurred: repeated citation, in these briefs and cases, too, of *Blackwell on Tax Titles*—that same work which, twenty-odd years before (about 1935), had kept popping up, very extravagantly indeed, first in the Chinese habeas corpus briefs preserved and examined among the records of the old United States Circuit Court, and later on in the briefs of Central and Southern Pacific counsel in the various *Railroad Tax Cases*. *Blackwell on Tax Titles*: shelf-checked in amusement at that time, and dismissed as one of the law's minor irrelevancies; yet patently no longer so. Now a missing link indeed—the added frontier key to economic due process and equal protection—as our next two chapters will show.

Researched and drafted, 1958–1960, and here highly condensed, these chapters are based first of all on study of Blackwell's *Treatise*, and on the major Illinois and other northwestern state statutes, cases and experience highlighted by that treatise; secondly, on coverage of the relevant general, state, territorial, public land, economic, financial, fiscal, agricultural histories and documents, working chronologically and jurisdictionally through the standard reference, secondary, and monographic materials, many of which now are conveniently listed in the classed bibliography in Paul W. Gates's admirable survey, *The Farmer's Age: Agriculture, 1815–1860* (1960).

---

[1] The Oscar L. Shafter Collection, briefs in cases heard by the Supreme Court of California during Shafter's term as Associate Justice, January 1, 1864–December 31, 1868, plus cases in which Shafter appeared as counsel before 1873.

The reference list (Appendix III) therefore is rigorously selective, limited to basic and general works, and to those special studies by legal, constitutional, and social historians which best show the nature of the frontier tax problem and syndrome. Footnote documentation likewise is minimal, limited mainly to illustrative material. These chapters are summary and introductory, suggestive only of work to be done and work which cries for interdisciplinary attack. This is another problem which was lost in the shuffle and on the fringes of academic departmentalism. The theme, however, is clear: new frontiers in constitutionalism, constitutionalism on new frontiers.

[CHAPTER 11]

Acres for Cents: The Economic and Constitutional Significance of Frontier Tax Titles, 1800-1890

EDITORIAL NOTE. More media than one, longer and oftener than many can remember, have celebrated and exploited frontier law and administration. Those popular idealized frontiers of course may never have been frontiers at all. What matters, what tickles the historical fancy of constitutionalists in particular, is that even at this late date there still are unexplored sides of these matters; and that these now have for us the highest, special relevance. For it turns out that substantive due process too, and the equal protection of the laws, also won *their* spurs, got *their* start in this same storied, troubled, resurgent environment.

And all the old familiars are "on location." Again and again: Yankee dudes, speculators, and outsiders, even a hated Yankee corporation, the great New York and Boston Illinois Land Company,[1] its managers, successors, and assigns. The white hats and the black, the whites invariably "locals"—locals and losers, but only such until the last happy fadeout. And the "sleepers" and the Samaritans naturally—those necessary "in-betweens"—in this case, and in particu-

---

[1] See (a) its ARTICLES OF INCORPORATION . . . WITH AMENDMENTS (Philadelphia, Printed by I. Ashmead & Co., 1839), Chicago Historical Society Library. (Covers formation of the parent company Nov. 20, 1835; of its successor, the Illinois Land Company, in 1838; and lists the eastern capitalists, their subscriptions and holdings.) (b) its PROCEEDINGS (New York, 1839), Newberry Library, Chicago. (Includes the detailed reports of John Tillson, Jr., the Illinois resident agent and general manager, relating to affairs and plans 1835-1839. In the latter year a projected "domestication" of the corporation as "The Quincy House Company" by the Illinois Act of March 1, 1839 [*id.* pp. 38, 59-64] was frustrated by the Panic.) (c) THE QUINCY HOUSE COMPANY. ACT TO INCORPORATE THE QUINCY HOUSE COMPANY (New York, W.E. Dean, 1839).

In 1838 the company held 907,000 acres of Illinois land, of which 815,000 were in the Military Tract. In 1839 holdings were 850,000 acres valued at $3.66 per acre, including 184,000 acres of patent titles and with chain of title perfected for 538,000 acres of tax titles (PROCEEDINGS pp. 36-37); cash subscribed for stock, and revenue from land sales, totalled $209,000 (*id.*). Daniel Lord was counsel for the company (*id.* pp. 47-52). Chancellor Kent's opinions on tax titles are cited p. 38.

Acres for Cents 495

lar, John Tillson, Jr.,[2] the "good" Quincy land agent and hotel man, who himself lost everything, but who "saved" the Illinois Military Tract,[3] its tax titlists and bounty titlists alike; John Tillson, Jr., agent of the same "hated," "furrin" corporation, who established the needed *private* record system that made it possible to put the Tract's fractured titles together again, yet who lost his own splendid Quincy House (the finest hostelry west of the Alleghenies), built in the 1830's at a cost of $105,000 when Quincy was a town of 1,500. Last, but never least, of course, the lawyers. And what lawyers, what lawyerings these were: None other than Chancellor Kent himself, and Daniel Lord, co-counsel for the great speculators, and for that eastern land company; counsel whose early "chambers opinions" had imprudently raised and dismissed as frivolous a due process argument which then got carelessly published as an *advertisement*[4] in the Illinois press. In this manner due process was picked up by Archibald Williams, N. H. Purple, and J. Butterfield, the hard-pressed Quincy counsel for bounty titlists—that same trio who (never having heard of the golden egg) vainly tried to void *all* "company" tax titles in one fell swoop, in that great "Tract case" of *Rhinehart v. Schuyler*[5] at the time of *Taylor v. Porter* (1843) (as noted *supra*,

---

[2] 1796–1853. For his role, see works cited *supra* note 1; also HISTORY OF QUINCY (edited reprint by Collins, 1905), pp. 49–51; Gates, *The Role of the Land Speculator* (1942), p. 321. The Quincy House was destroyed by fire in 1883.

[3] See generally, CARLSON (1951).

[4] *Quincy Whig*, May 26, June 2, 1838, p. 4, cols. 1–7, "Tax Titles," "extracts from an opinion written by two lawyers in the city of New York," one of whom no doubt was the company counsel Daniel Lord (*supra* note 1). Kent's opinion was solicited by the companies (Robert Schuyler to James Kent, New York, Nov. 23, 1838, Kent Papers, Library of Congress); was favorable to their cause, and cited in the PROCEEDINGS, p. 38. For evidence of further publicity given Kent's views, see *Peoria Register*, Feb. 23, 1839, p. 1, cols. 2–3, quoting a recent number of the *Quincy Whig* and the *Chicago American*, both of which had quoted a letter dated New York, Dec. 8, 1838: "I have the satisfaction to inform you that the opinion of Chancellor Kent on the subject of tax titles [in Illinois] has been given at length and the result is an entire conviction on his part of the validity of these titles. The following is an extract from his opinion, *viz* 'Under all circumstances of the case I am of the opinion that the revenue and road laws above mentioned are constitutional and valid laws, are sound and unimpeachable, provided as the case assumes, that the proceeding and sales for taxes by the state officers, whether auditor, sheriff or clerk, have been regular, in conformity with the state provisions.' Our readers will recollect that Judge Thomas, in one of our recent circuit courts of this state, some time since, decided that the same road and revenue laws were *un*constitutional. The Chancellor we think is quite as good authority as the judge."

[5] 7 Ill. 375; 2 Gil. 473 (1845); discussed Chapter 5, *supra* at notes 60–62. On the Tract title conflicts, see CARLSON, ch. 4, and works there cited; Gates, *Land Policy* (1941); p. 69; *Peoria Register*, Sept. 3, 1841 (formation of the Bounty or Patent Title Association); *id.* May 6, 13, 1842; Aug. 26, Sept. 30, Oct. 7, 1842 (excitement in the tract while the Schuyler case was being heard).

Chapter 5); "Archie" Williams,[6] no less, Abraham Lincoln's beloved friend and fellow member of the legislature, famous as the only man homelier and more ungainly than Lincoln, who kept vainly repeating this due process argument for years, usually in cases in which the "dudes" and the outsiders were represented by O. H. Browning[7]—Browning himself later Lincoln's Secretary of Interior and counsel for Illinois railroads in the *Granger Cases!*

And sure enough: here, finally too, were some vital "long forgotten" unstudied law books. First, the statute books of the early frontier states[8] (the statutes of Virginia and Kentucky, and of the Northwest Territory, and of the territories and the states formed therefrom); then out of these, and out of the chaos therein concealed, congealed, transferred, and so often, and only partially, "remedied," another book, this one a law treatise, the first treatise on the American law of taxation—*Blackwell on Tax Titles*—published in Chicago in 1855, dedicated "To Archibald Williams, Esq., late United States Attorney for the District of Illinois, an able lawyer, the pioneer in tax title litigation. . . ."[9] *Blackwell*, a 700-page elaboration of the Williams-Purple due process briefs which the Illinois court had rejected repeatedly. *Blackwell on Tax Titles*— that seemingly irrelevant work that even the Chinese habeas corpus bar, and the Central and Southern Pacific's tax lawyers, had kept citing and reciting in their briefs to Justice Field and Judge Sawyer in the 1870's and '80's! *Blackwell*, whose first chapter, "Of the Fundamental Principles Which Govern the Taxing Power," is the fullest synthesis of early due process cases, and a fervent plea that this guarantee and tool of a flexible, common-law constitutionalism be made a judicial limitation on the state taxing power, and thus "the inflexible guardian of private property and public rights."[10] *Blackwell*, cited by counsel within a year, and in the same breath with "Solomon's Song of Songs," in that celebrated *Wynehamer* Case[11]

---

6 1801–1863; see A.J. BEVERIDGE, ABRAHAM LINCOLN, 1809–1858 (1928, 2v.) I, 179; BATEMAN, ed., HISTORICAL ENCYCLOPEDIA OF ILLINOIS (Adams County edition, Chicago, 1913), p. 590; and extensive newspaper coverage using the Illinois Historical Library's index of the *Illinois State Journal.*

7 M. BAXTER, O.H. BROWNING, DIARY (Springfield, 1925–1931) 2v.; C.B. LAWRENCE, IN MEMORIAM O.H. BROWNING (1882) (from ILL. STATE BAR PROC., 1882, p. 35).

8 See especially the statutes of Virginia, Kentucky, Northwest Territory and devolute jurisdictions listed in the bibliographic note, Chapter 10, *supra*. The introductions by Pease and Philbrick are indispensable; as is the compilation by N.H. Purple for ready comparison of the Illinois land and tax laws.

9 BLACKWELL, p. iii.
10 *Id.*, p. 5.
11 See Chapter 13, *infra*, note 69.

Acres for Cents 497

(1856). *Blackwell*, the bible of tax lawyers, and of all lawyers stuck with an otherwise hopeless constitutional case, the book that provided the leads and "substance" for countless due process arguments, from Maine to California, during the 1850's, '60's, and '70's.[12] *Blackwell*, cited by Thomas M. Cooley at the head of his own chapter on "Taxation" in *Constitutional Limitations* (1868).[13] *Blackwell*, used especially in the newer states of the west—Michigan, Iowa, Kansas, and California—where the tax title-legislative powers conflicts still were acute; and where able, determined judges (Cooley, Dixon, Dillon, Brewer) led that vain, memorable, and heretofore anomalous attempt, 1868–1875, to frustrate public aid *to* corporations as a violation of due process.[14]

In short, Robert S. Blackwell and Archibald Williams, and their colleagues of the Quincy and Chicago land bars, are the true "prophets and evangels" of "modern," "substantive" due process and equal protection. Blackwell, and not Cooley nor John Norton Pomeroy, is the synthesizer of the antebellum cases that provided the base for the due process–law of the land–police power syncretism which the works of Cooley and Pomeroy subsequently and coincidentally began to effect the very year the Fourteenth Amendment was ratified.[15]

Frontier Illinois, in short, Blackwell's Illinois, now is the setting. The Prairie State and its wild, tax-titled Military Tract, during the territorial years, and from the year of statehood (1818) on through to Abraham Lincoln's inauguration. Lincoln's and Douglas' Illinois, no less. Yet that Illinois tagged and demeaned so often, even by its own residents at this date, as "Suckerland," chiefly because of this searing, decades-long title conflict. Illinois now is "location." And *land*, and *law of the land*, as always, are the recurring themes. The fact, the irony, is that frontiersmen often fighting corporations led the way here. In this instance, too, the bar, the stump, the press were the places where professional and public intoxication began and took hold.

The inescapable fact again is that the American legal profession, and its clients, at length managed to seduce American judges and courts—and not vice versa. Historical scholarship too has to answer again for some outlandish misconceptions and illusions. Due process and equal protection long have been, and today increasingly are,

---
[12] See Chapter 12, *infra*.
[13] P. 479.
[14] See *infra*, at 507, note 25.
[15] Compare B.R. Twiss, Lawyers and the Constitution (1942), pp. 18–41; Corwin, Liberty Against Government (1948), p. 116, and Professor Corwin's earlier works; also my own misconceptions, Chapters 1 and 2, *supra*.

quintessential guarantees of common law constitutionalism. Corporations achieved substantive protection under these clauses years ahead of the acknowledged beneficiaries. Yet this was not the way any draftsmen willed or planned it. Rather, it was the outcome, the resultant, a vectoring of law, prejudice, economics, even frontier forces.

II

Frontiers and constitutionalism, constitutionalism and frontiers—land and the *law of the land*—assuredly are the paramount, unifying themes of nine centuries of Anglo-American history. And land, on the face of it, has been the bridge, the nexus between people and government, between history and law and government, between the economy and government. Land law was the first constitutional law. Land throughout has been "property." Land as property has always spelled power: feudal government and modern federal government alike have been based on it. Jurisdiction, representation, taxation, all have rested on land, risen from land; all in various ways are embodiments and outgrowths of "the law of the land," that *lex terrae*, linked with, or derived from, the *per legem terrae* clause of Magna Carta.

Transitions from feudal to royal to representative-parliamentary government in England; subsequent transitions from colonial to state to federal-representative government of limited, separated, territorially-divided powers in the United States; from Magna Carta and the regressions of the Barons' Wars on through the English and American Revolutions, and the American Civil War, right down to the current drives for civil rights, for reapportionment, for substantial equality in housing, jobs, and education irrespective of race —all these, it can be seen, are in fact parts of one grand continuum, one in which land, "the West," that receding unstable frontier, with its sequential, recapitulative growth on the one hand, and this ubiquitous law of the land, due process of law, and equal protection of the laws on the other, have been the two abiding forces, the parameters, the two changing yet "changeless" constants.

Blackwell is the only book which, in and of itself, unifies and illuminates all this; which does so especially by considering the emergent nineteenth-century land law and the emergent nineteenth-century law of the land, and by considering both of these in relation to the taxing power and land taxation. Which is another way of saying that frontier land taxation,[16] in these American states and

---

[16] For suggestive leads and treatment, see the works of BOGART; HAIG; GATES (1943); HURST (1964); and ISHLLS, vol. 5, index heading "Taxation." See p. 616 *infra*.

Acres for Cents 499

territories, is, as we might well have expected it to be, the tie that binds all this together, as process and as protection, as federalism and constitutionalism, as law and history, both and besides. This one book not only did this 112 years ago; this book also has been utterly ignored since the 1890's, and ignored notwithstanding all that has been written about "the significance of the frontier," notwithstanding all that has been said and written about the rise and the primacy of due process, equal protection, and the law of taxation in American constitutional, legal, and political history.

[CHAPTER 11]

I.

CORPORATIONS, we here observe again, were the whipping boys of Jacksonian politics. "The Bank," "monopolists," "foreign corporations" especially were anathema. And here in the Ohio and Mississippi valleys, in election years especially, "Yankee land companies," "tax title harpies," "engrossers," "speculators" rated as "prairie vermin." This frontier—Andrew Jackson's stronghold—was at once the seedbed and the hotbed of trouble, resentments, antagonisms.

Land hunger here was palpable and overpowering, land speculation universal.[1] And Squatter Sovereignty was a viable doctrine long before Cass and Douglas capitalized it. As an axiom of politics, and as a circumstance conditioning and governing investment, squatter sovereignty meant, in simplest terms, during these days of practical legislative supremacy, *self-enacted preferential treatment for settlers*.[2]

---

[1] See especially Billington; Gates (1941, 1942, 1945). Successful speculators often were the planners of a planless society: the Wadsworths and Ellicotts in New York, Worthingtons and McArthurs in Ohio, Ellsworths in Indiana, were middlemen performing a social function that had been abdicated by government. (See MCNALL, THE AGRICULTURAL HISTORY OF THE GENESSEE VALLEY, 1790–1860 [1952] ch. 2, "Land Agents and their Operation.") Bogue & Bogue, *"Profits" and the Frontier Land Speculator*, 17 J. ECON. HIST. (1957) 1–24, suggest that speculators' profits have been exaggerated, failures ignored.

[2] See especially Tatter; Gates (1962); and the basic treatises of DEMBITZ (1890, 1895) covering the occupying claimants' laws. Until Professor Gates' study (1962) romantic interest in the "claims clubs" overshadowed the basic protections afforded squatters by these equitable laws. Protection accorded by the viscosities of frontier tax administration have been neglected even more. On public lands, squatters were not liable for taxes until they exercised pre-emption rights and made payments. For procedures and the finally settled law, see *Carroll v. Safford*, 3 How. 431 (1845); DONALDSON (2d ed., 1884), 239; 7 TERR. PAPERS OF THE U. S. (INDIANA, 1800–1810) 170, n. 57.

What so much ambiguity and informality in titles and possession meant for assessors and elective officers struggling to determine tax status, especially in times of high

Nonresidents might and did speculate in frontier lands, and pay their assessed taxes. They could not and did not vote. Often, for numerous reasons, they could not and did not pay assessed taxes either. But one of the points to be grasped at the outset, and to be documented at large in this and the next chapter, is that frontier public finance was just as ingenious and timely in its innovations as modern corporate finance so often has been. And the further point is that the frontier land tax bars, like the antislavery and the railroad and the Chinese habeas corpus bars, pioneered substantive due process and equal protection.

During these first decades in the Old Northwest as much as 90 per cent of the cost of state government occasionally was charged to absentee speculators.[3] Resale of lands for tax delinquency for a time constituted an important source of public revenue. Lands thus sold and resold eventually became further sources of speculation, respeculation, and litigation, both individual and corporate. Especially wherever military bounty lands[4] had been allotted far in advance of settlement, and wherever such rights and lands had been assigned over and over (as occurred in Ohio's Virginia Military District[5] at the turn of the nineteenth century, and again in the Illinois Military Tract after 1817[6]), chaos in title recording[7] and tax records was in-

---

absentee ownership and depression, is the phase of the problem that needs to be grasped. The frontier had the advantages of its handicaps, and "squatter sovereignty" —frontier preference—was the collective tag and rationalization for many years.

[3] For details regarding the Northwest Territory and Ohio, see 1 BULEY 603-4; BOGART 21, 71, 73, and tables at 184, 186. For Indiana, see works cited *infra*, Appendix III; for Illinois, see HAIG 62, showing receipts and percentages from nonresidents, 1821-1838. Until 1833, these averaged over 90 per cent. See also 1 BULEY 619-20; PEASE, THE FRONTIER STATE 52-69.

[4] HIBBARD 116-35; Gates (1941); Freund.

[5] Hutchinson.

[6] CARLSON.

[7] Here of course was another source of reverberating record-lack, of confusion compounded by the growth that produced it, with the Illinois Military Tract (1825-1845) again the flagrant exemplar.

Illinois' system of recording deeds and mortgages by counties (readopted from Northwest Territory) obliged absentee speculators and large landholders to deal by frontier post with indeterminable, shifting county seats. At statehood in 1818-1819 most of the Tract had lain in Madison County; Pike County was created in 1821; Fulton, two years later. In 1825 nine counties were added, but only three organized. Resulting confusion and protests led the next legislature to create the office of State Recorder. Nonresidents owning land in several counties were thus extended an option of central recording. Section 6 of the law further required that the state recorder obtain abstracts of deeds previously recorded in the Tract counties, the ultimate goal being a unified title record. By 1829 the magnitude of such an undertaking had become apparent: Section 6 was repealed, but residents as well as nonresidents now were permitted to record at Vandalia. Four years of dual, dispersed listing caused the General Assembly in 1833 to abolish the state office, to return unequivocally to the county system. The luckless Illinois recorder was granted four and a half months

evitable, and often complete. Tax sales then in due course became carnivals for prodigals, mills that ground prairie titles to bits, that shingled whole counties with tax deeds, and which by so doing created decades of confusion and conflict. Equally fundamental, the early specific land taxes in such regions, the flat rates of which were fixed regressively by statute in order to assure maximum return from "outsiders," and to discourage engrossment and speculation,[8] also frequently cut both ways. The practical and compound result thus was that this still remote, land-rich, land-poor Northwest often hocked and even rehocked its excess lands, and its future, in order to launch government and build its first statehouses.

The miracle is that bargains so shortsighted and so exigent as these proved half-fruitful, even benign, nationally, in the long run. Ultimately, in the aggregate, frontier tax policies, frontier public administration, and frontier title wars developed a legal-constitutional feedback. Like slavery's repercussions, during these same decades, this feedback, circuitously and at times erratically, but ultimately just as decisively, helped transform American due process of law—and did so, in this case, by fostering and by nourishing the related

---

to prepare transcripts of his records for the respective counties. Few if any were made, so the next legislature (1835) tackled the problem again: henceforth counties were to prepare their own transcripts, the Governor being authorized to transfer the basic title records from Madison County (as well as those of the abolished state office) to the Schuyler County seat at Rushville for convenience of public and scribes. Not, however, until the Madison recorder had copied his records. The 25 cents per deed allowed for this work proved no inducement whatever. Six years later, when title conflicts already had become acute, the basic records still were in Madison County, still uncopied. Whereupon the legislature repealed the provision for transfer, authorized counties to copy at Edwardsville, and allowed the Madison recorder 12½ cents per deed compared.

On this basis, Tract counties eventually filled out their files. But not without further statutory amendments, three of which are parables in themselves: 1) Transcripts made for Adams County were declared to be admissible as evidence, notwithstanding unauthorized preparation by an *agent* of the appointed commissioner. 2) Specific legislative permission was granted to commissioners, when transcribing deeds covering land in several counties, to omit outside parcels. 3) In 1845, toward the end of the work, commissioners again were admonished—"hereby authorized and required carefully to compare"—transcripts with the records, to correct and certify their work!

At no time before 1845 was there a reasonably complete, consolidated record, even of deeds, in any of the counties of the Military Tract. An independent, equally decentralized and devolute tax record of course compounded the problems. Privatization of records, as an incident of reassembly of title, thus was essential, and indeed a vital part of Tillson's and the great land companies' strategy. See PURPLE for the statutory record of the recording problem; Bigelow, *The Tracing and Recording of Title to Real Estate*, 7 PROC. ILL. STATE BAR ASSN. 76–81 (1884); also Viele, *The Problem of Land Titles*, 44 POL. SCI. Q. 421 (1929); Roberts, *Title Insurance: State Regulation and the Public Perspective*, 39 INDIANA L. J. (1963).

[8] "Tax rigging" in the frontier vernacular; for classic examples, see EVANS; GATES (1943).

concept of the equal protection of the laws. The wonder is that this long-ignored, ramifying conflict over assessment, taxation, sale, and title of frontier lands—especially military bounty lands—not only worked itself out in the end, but worked also to provide a further basis for unplanned, unplannable, yet fundamental changes in constitutional usage and theory, and eventually in constitutional law and judicial review as well. For it was here in the Midwest—and primarily in the Illinois Military Tract—during the years 1820–1860, that popular and professional foundations were laid, constitutional usages advanced and extended, professional associations formed and forensic experience gained, which, *after* adoption of the Fourteenth Amendment, made economic-corporate use of the due process and equal protection clauses so easy and natural.

The Illinois of Lincoln and Douglas thus was the epicenter of two great conflicts, not just one. An organized antislavery-humanitarian due process, and a potentially economic-corporate due process and equal protection here all but intertwined, until the roots and even the trunks are found half joined;[9] and the Whig leadership often is common to both. The various counsel and judges who pioneered corporate use of the Fourteenth Amendment and due process in the *Granger* and *Illinois Railroad Tax* and other cases after the War—Charles B. Lawrence,[10] Orville H. Browning, Burton C. Cook,[11] and Corydon Beckwith[12]—all were associates, adversaries,

---

[9] One of the best papers in Illinois, and modeled on Birney's *Philanthropist*, the Liberty-Free Soil *Western Citizen*, published 1842–1852, edited by Zebina Eastman (1815–1883), best reveals the strong Whig-antislavery affiliations. Weld's and Birney's disciples had moved westward; in the 1840's, for example, they headed both Knox and Illinois Colleges. Quincy was another stronghold. James H. Collins, a leading abolitionist lawyer and a partner of Chief Justice Caton and J. Butterfield, had emigrated to Illinois in 1833 from Oneida County, New York; 2 PALMER, BENCH & BAR OF ILLINOIS (1899, 2 vols.) 608.

[10] Charles B. Lawrence, 1820–1883. Member of the Quincy bar, 1845– ; law partner of Archibald Williams and son, 1847–1856, until his health failed; Justice and Chief Justice, Illinois Supreme Court, June 6, 1864–June 2, 1873, *vice* Corydon Beckwith (January 7–June 6, 1864); spoke for the court in *Chicago & Alton R.R. v. People*, 67 Ill. 11 (1873), voiding Granger law as a due process violation; defeated for re-election, resigned to become counsel for the Chicago and North Western Railroad in the remaining *Granger Cases* (with B. C. Cook). BUCK, THE GRANGER MOVEMENT (1963 reprint) 84–85, 92, 144, 188; 7 PROC. ILL. STATE BAR ASSN., 1884, 53–66; 29 PROC. ILL. STATE BAR ASSN., 1905, pt. 2, 66–87; scrapbook of clippings on Lawrence in Illinois State Historical Library, Springfield. See Chapter 9, *supra*, notes 89, 91–92, 96.

[11] Burton C. Cook, 1819–1894. Republican member of the House, 39–42 Congresses, 1865–1871; sponsor of commercial free intercourse bills, *e.g.*, H.R. 2922, CONG. GLOBE, 41 Cong., 3d sess., 890; resigned to become Solicitor for the Chicago and North Western Railroad (with Charles B. Lawrence). BIOG. DIR. AM. CONG. (1928) 842; BATEMAN, HIST. ENCYC. ILL. (1913); also editorial note preceding Chapter 13, *infra*, notes 19 and 24.

Acres for Cents 503

or partners of the two great lawyers, Archibald Williams and Robert S. Blackwell, who at first unsuccessfully, yet on that account all the more persistently, had advanced and elaborated the due process argument during the "title wars" of 1840–1860.

II.

Frontiers symbolize opportunity. Virgin wealth, the fresh start. Yet we have here to think of them also as self-renewing barriers—and to think particularly of what those successive re-starts meant, in terms of government,[13] for residents and nonresidents alike.

Frontier lands were wealth, property—both "real" and constitutional. Yet all property, including that in land, ultimately is a bundle of legally enforceable, transferable rights; hence a bundle resting on records, on evidence of title, transfer, tax payment, and the like. Transfer of title—conveyancing—was the West's major or "animating pursuit," at times almost its chief industry. Fortunes made and lost buying and selling frontier "title" rarely have lacked celebrants. The frontier tax records and land registers, for obvious reasons, just as rarely have found them. "Insured" and "secure" title—property in the sophisticated modern sense, property as a bundle of adjudicated, or at least adjudicable rights, as yet had little or no existence here—was at first as alien as banking or arbitrage. Speculation continually was overleaping settlement—just as settlement was overleaping government; as government in turn was outdistancing effective central, even effective peripheral or local administration. Frontier government truly was "land office government" —and that phrase today still connotes rush and bustle, haste and waste.

Frontier government was essentially government by statute,[14]

---

[12] Corydon Beckwith, 1823–1890. Law partner of Robert S. Blackwell, Chicago, 1853–1854 (see R. S. B. to J. D. Caton, June 16, 1854, on "Blackwell and Beckwith" stationery, Caton Papers, Library of Congress; Justice, Illinois Supreme Court, January 7–June 6, 1864, resigning to become counsel for the Chicago & Alton Railroad; founder-member of Beckwith, Ayer & Kales, Chicago, 1873– ; leading counsel in the various *Granger* cases, the *Illinois Railroad Tax Cases*, 92 U.S. 575 (1876), and *Northwestern Fertilizing Co. v. Hyde Park*, 3 Bissell 480 (March, 1873) Fed. Cas. #10,336, wherein Circuit Judge Drummond, himself from the Military Tract land bar, held a corporation to be a person within the meaning of the Civil Rights Act of April 20, 1871, 17 Stat. 13. See Chapter 3, *supra*, note 51; Chapter 9, *supra*, note 89; CROSSLEY, COURTS & LAWYERS IN ILLINOIS (1916, 3 vols.) 253–4; 2 ANDREAS, HIST. OF CHICAGO (1885) 465; Letters of Corydon Beckwith to J. D. Caton, 1855–1863; Library of Congress.

[13] "Frontier" historians sadly neglected government, but see these pathbreaking studies by legal and cultural historians: Philbrick (1950: ISHLSS, vol. 5); Blume (1962); Blume & Brown (1962–1963); HURST (1956, 1964); CURTI; HAMILTON (1953).

[14] See generally, in addition to the works cited in note 13, Riesenfeld; Haskins,

frequently by slavishly copied or adopted statute, a statute "adopted" from another state during the earliest territorial period. Frontier government was government and law grounded on statutory presumptions and on statutory assessment; on yeoman-lay administration, with limited, informal adjudication, or during the earliest stages, practically no adjudication at all. The operative restraints on the state taxing power on these frontiers during this period, in other words, emphatically were not constitutional or judicial, but rather political, economic, and geographic. The modern fiction has been that the common law was "received" on the frontier;[15] yet this was so largely in the metaphorical Holmesian sense of the common law as a "brooding omnipresence," a secondary or prospective development that overhung the frontier, and at times greatly depressed it. In each new successive, western jurisdiction, "precedent" had to be created and digested locally. Absentee property owners thus felt—and were—doubly insecure. Speculators, like settlers, were on their own, and they knew it. The interests of these two groups, moreover—both taxwise and otherwise—if not antagonistic for the long pull, popularly were believed to be so, often demonstrably were so, for the short. In this sprawling, peripatetic, speculative society, not only the institution of property but also the principle of federalism at times both seemed to have an Achilles' heel.

Chancellor Kent, for one, became all but certain of this in the 1820's when he learned what had been happening in the Adirondacks:[16] Franklin County trappers while assessing nonresidents' lands, had been paying themselves handsome bounties for destroying wolves "and other noxious animals." Taxation, Kent expostulated in the first edition of the *Commentaries* (1826), ought never to be other than "fair and equal, and in proportion to value." Yet in these distant, backward regions in New York, "and probably in other states," especially in the Far West, there were "wellfounded complaints" that locally elected or appointed assessors had, by such devices, been plundering the property of nonresident landholders. Every man's property, Kent continued, must be secured and protected against such abuses; the Northwest Ordinance, the various state constitutions and enabling acts, all contemplated such protec-

---

Spread of Massachusetts Law in the Seventeenth Century, 106 U. PA. L. REV. 413–7 (1958).

15 On frontier mistrust of the law and the common law, see HOWE, READINGS IN AMERICAN LEGAL HISTORY (1949) 419–26; AUMANN; Utter, *Ohio and the Common Law*, 16 MISS. V. HIST. REV. 321 (1929); ISHLLS, vol. 5, Philbrick Introduction, cccxxxiii–ccclx (1950).

16 2 KENT, COMMENTARIES ON AMERICAN LAW (1st ed., 1826–30) 268–71; 12th Holmes ed., 1873, vol. 2, 331–4, star paging; HORTON, JAMES KENT (1939), Ch. 4.

Acres for Cents

tion; and it was the bounden duty of the state judiciaries to provide it and to keep popular government and majorities in check.

The fact of the matter was simply that for the moment the Chancellor's constraints were strictly and poignantly verbal. The frontier held its own views and counsel on these matters. Isolation in fact worked two ways; the West's animus and instincts both were stronger and sounder[17] than Chancellor Kent ever appreciated.

Immense tracts of land, as Governor Ford of Illinois recalled in 1847,[18] "were then owned principally by nonresidents who were unwilling to sell except at high prices. Every town built, farm made, road opened, bridge or schoolhouse erected by the settlers in their vicinity added to the value of those lands at no expense to the nonresident. The people persuaded themselves that in improving their own farms they were putting money into the pockets of men who did nothing for the country . . . except skin it as fast as any hide grew . . . ."

This "peltry" concept of economic rent thus almost at once found its answer in a "peltry"—or to employ Chancellor Kent's euphemism, "noxious animal"—concept of taxation. Taxwise on the frontier, speculatively held raw land seemed to invite, hence quite often received, rather a raw deal. Flat-rate, specific, regressive taxation was the remedy most frontiersmen prescribed for land engrossment. Such a tax was called for, Governor Ford continued, "to make the nonresident owner contribute his share to the improvement of the country, and thereby burdening the land with taxes render him more willing to sell. A very bad feeling existed toward the nonresident landowners."[19]

The wonder is that the nature and consequences of this conflict have so long gone unprobed. Henry George and his critics, in some respects, were among the most myopic, unoriginal, uninformed of Americans. For actually, *Progress and Poverty* (1879), like Veblen's *Absentee Ownership* (1923), rested on a century of practice and

---

[17] For a justification of frontier Ohio's regressive specific land tax, see ELY & FINLEY 134–6; also Thomas M. Cooley's discussion of the representation problem in his TAXATION (1876) 44–8. Agents often reminded outsiders that road taxes, payable by residents in labor to a maximum of ten or fifteen days a year, justified stiffer taxes on nonresidents' lands. Road-tax equalizing thus engaged countless legislatures; see, *e.g.*, LAWS OF INDIANA TERRITORY, 1809–1816 (1934) 39, 66, 73, 77; HAIG, 51–7; CARLSON 48, 94–5; MCNALL, cited *supra*, note 1, at 46–50. Note also Lincoln's view of the still-unfettered taxing power, 1 COLLECTED WORKS (1953, 9 vols.) 147–8, to W. S. Wait, March 2, 1839; Chief Justice Caton's opinion in People v. Worthington, 21 Ill. 170 (1859), especially 174–8; and the stress placed by HURST (1956) on the frontier view of law as an affirmative social instrument, *passim*.

[18] 1 FORD 262.

[19] *Id.*

complaint. Yet neither George nor Veblen, nor their critics, seem to have cited this pertinent history. Protection for vested rights, moreover, as Professor Corwin long ago pointed out, is "the basic doctrine of American Constitutional law,"[20] and it became such while the frontier was wracked by this colossal, continuing headache. What, if any, then, are the interactions and connections here? Just how easily, carelessly, capriciously, might title vest, divest, or be divested? Again: "No taxation without representation!" is the ancient rallying cry, the common unifying theme of Anglo-American constitutionalism. In this frontier environment and conflict, it can be seen that the cries were raised by both sides, and cut both ways. For the frontier government, anomalously enough, during the earliest territorial period especially, was designed to be, and was bitterly attacked as being highly centralized government, government by executive or legislative appointees and outsiders.[21] Later, during early statehood, it still was hamstrung government—forbidden to tax many lands for three or five years or more, lands that citizens, owners and governments alike dealt with as abstract legal descriptions in makeshift records—squares on unavailable or distant maps —then at other times, as "roosts" for squatters and timberhookers. Under such conditions, who were owners and who agents? Who, what, and which lands were to be taxed, how much, with what representation, safeguards, or the lack of either or both? Finally: the right to fair and equal treatment, the right to be heard, the right to notice—in sum, the rights to due process of law and equal protection of the laws—these too, as so clearly evidenced by the Chancellor Kent–Governor Ford statements, were potentially, controversially reapplicable and reinvolved here, just as they were also in the debates over slavery.

The heart of the matter thus is that that beguiling first chapter of *Blackwell on Tax Titles*, and in fact the whole treatise, stands today as a forgotten bibliographic monument to this conflict which, if not so deep nor so emotional as that over slavery, was, and still is, in its ramifications, almost as fundamental. For Blackwell not only recorded and documented this second, parallel conflict: he also effected a second, reinforcing, antebellum synthesis.

---

20 12 MICH. L. REV. 247–76 (1914).
21 Detailed and documented discussion of these matters will be found in my manuscript study of 1958–1959, cited in Appendix III, *infra*. Attention also is directed to Francis S. Philbrick's 400-page monograph on frontier and territorial government and administration. Printed as the Introduction to ISHLLS, volume 5, 1950, the work has been neglected even by specialists.

Acres for Cents 507

And significantly enough, here was one frontier author who understood intuitively how to introduce and promote an important treatise. A rare advertising leaflet[22] bound at the head of my copy of *Blackwell*—found also at the Library of Congress—shows that galley sheets of the crucial first and early chapters (and later some presentation copies of the entire work) were dispatched to leading counsel and jurists the country over. Of the "testimonials" thus received, twenty-six were then gathered and printed to make up this leaflet. Here is the testimonial which today has truly extraordinary interest:

From Chief Justice Taney. Chief Justice Taney received specimen sheets of the work while indisposed, at "Old Point Comfort"; he therefore was unable to give the work more than a cursory examination. He writes as follows: "So far as I have looked into it, my opinion was a favorable one, and certainly a work on that subject is very desirable."[23]

Within a few months after publication, Blackwell's *Treatise* was used and cited by counsel in the celebrated *Wynehamer* case;[24] and it shortly gained widespread use, not merely in tax title and Prohibition cases, but also in other "policy" fields. Repeatedly challenged were the validity, wisdom, and fairness of special and street assessments, of mortgage taxation, and particularly of state and local tax or bond aid to railroads and other private enterprises.[25] Especially

---

[22] Headed "A Most Valuable Acquisition to every / Lawyer, Real Estate Owner and Conveyancer. / THE GREAT LEGAL WORK. / BLACKWELL ON TAX TITLES." 4p.

[23] *Id.* 2. Relevant facts are that Chief Justice Taney arrived ill at Old Point Comfort, near Norfolk, Virginia, in June, 1855. Judging from Blackwell's letter to Chief Justice Caton, April 13, 1855 (J. D. Caton Papers, Library of Congress), other jurists received their specimen sheets during the months of May and June, 1855. The TREATISE was published October 1, 1855. The *Dred Scott* case was not argued till February 11–14, 1856; was reargued December 15–19, 1856, and Chief Justice Taney read his celebrated opinion, based in part on due process, March 6, 1857. (SWISHER, ROGER B. TANEY [1935] 465–9, 488, 495, 502–3).

In view of early proslave use of due process in the Pinckney Report of 1836, and occasionally thereafter (see Chapter 4, *supra*, notes 186–7, and Chapter 12, *infra*, note 62), no one needs assume it was Robert S. Blackwell who prompted Chief Justice Taney's reliance on the clause in 1857. Yet neither must Blackwell's elaborate published synthesis of 1855 be ignored as a vital part of the antebellum due process context.

[24] See Chapter 13, *infra*, note 69.

[25] It is important to stress again that the principal exploratory or "aberrant" economic-substantive uses of due process, before and during the Civil War, were made, not (as often assumed) by or on behalf of business interests opposing economic regulation; but rather by citizens and interests opposing the public tax and bond aid then being extended to corporations. Extended affirmative government, in short, was the new departure and issue. Public promotion of private enterprise—not public regulation thereof—generally was the form of "state intervention" attacked. (See HARTZ,

in the Midwestern states and California, where adequate law libraries were few or wanting, and where treatise citation still flourished of necessity, *Blackwell* soon became an indispensable favored work,[25a] and, in due course and process of law, a catalyzing, hybridizing one.

ECONOMIC POLICY AND DEMOCRATIC THOUGHT, PENNSYLVANIA, 1776–1860 (1948), part 2; Waldron, *Sharpless v. Philadelphia: Jeremiah Black and the Parent Case on the Public Purpose of Taxation,* 1953 WISC. L. REV. 48–75; Mills, *The Public Purpose Doctrine in Wisconsin,* 1957 WISC. L. REV. 40, 282. Compare the frequently misleading, oversimplified, case- and period-limited studies, MCCLOSKEY, AMERICAN CONSERVATISM IN THE AGE OF ENTERPRISE, 1865–1910; JACOBS, LAW WRITERS AND THE COURTS (1954)).

What many critics have deplored as "judicialized" and "corporatized" laissez faire actually was an end product, a late afterthought. To ignore this, to lump together these reversed positions and interests, is to confuse and falsify development. Conspiratorial interpretations got their start by just such abridgment and surmise.

[25a] Not uncommonly, Blackwell was cited by counsel for both sides: 1) Sears v. Cottrell, 5 Mich. 251 (1858) 252, "Blackwell 31, 32," and by the opposing counsel, James Birney (son of James G. Birney) "Blackwell 2" (probably Chapter 2). 2) People v. Seymour, 16 Cal. 332 (1860) 334, 337–40 (four counsel, seven citations, including four of Blackwell's first chapter). 3) Baker v. Kelly, 11 Minn. 358 (1865–66) 360–1, 363; note the judicial discernment 374–5, also the Blackwell-effected linkages: Taylor v. Porter etc.

For citation by other California counsel and judges, see 1) Hart v. Plum, 14 Cal. 148 (1859) 152, "Blackwell . . . 178, 183." 2) Patten v. Green, 13 Cal. 325 (1859) 326, "Blackwell . . . Ch. 2". 3) Terrill v. Groves, 18 Cal. 149 (1861) 151, "Black. Tax Title, 184, 192." 4) Perry v. Washburn, 20 Cal. 318 (1862), 333, H. H. Haight (later governor of California), citing "Blackwell . . . 205." 5) High v. Shoemaker, 22 Cal. 363 (1863) 365, Robinson & Beatty citing "Blackwell 41;" cf. opinion 369–70 citing "Blackwell . . . cases cited 40, 41," but rejecting attack on a mortgage tax law; overruled, People v. McCreery, *infra* 6) O'Grady v. Barnhisel, 23 Cal. 287 (1863) 289, John Curry citing "Blackwell . . . 93, 94 and the many cases there cited." 7) Haskell v. Bartlett and Weston, 34 Cal. 281 (1867) 283: "Blackwell 243" cited by counsel, also in Judge Sanderson's opinion; a non-constitutional case, but indicative. 8) People v. McCreery, 34 Cal. 432 (1868) invalidating the mortgage tax law and overruling High v. Shoemaker *supra* after extensive due process argument by H. H. Haight; citation of "Blackwell 156" in Judge Rhodes's opinion 442.

Distinguished California counsel, making due process arguments in major cases, continued to cite "Blackwell" as late as the 1880's, even to the Supreme Court; see Hagar v. Reclamation District, 111 U.S. 701 (1884), 28 L. Ed. 569, Belcher & Boalt citing "Blackw. 213" with Cooley and other treatises.

For further evidence of judicial reliance and citation, see Hanson v. Vernon, 27 Ia. (1869) 28, 45–7, in which Judge Dillon expressly holds municipal aid to railroads void on due process grounds, citing "Blackwell on Tax Titles, ch. 1"; cf. Cole's dissent, 83, denying that due process has "any bearing or limitation on the taxing power." The *Hanson* decision was overruled in Stewart v. Board, 30 Ia. 9 (1870). Iowa, Michigan, Wisconsin, California, and Kansas were states in which the public–private purpose debate was most strenuous; due process figured intermittently in all, backed and used by influential judges (Dillon, Cooley, Brewer, but not apparently, in Wisconsin). It is hard to believe that Blackwell and "treatise jurisprudence" were not factors in this assault, nor that the wording of Justice Miller's opinion in Loan Association v. Topeka, 20 Wall. 655, 662 (1874), and later that in Davidson v. New Orleans, 96 U.S. 97 (1877), was unrelated to the struggle. The Supreme Court's eventual solution, in the '80's and '90's with reference to due process and the taxing power, must be viewed in this context. For concise early documentation of leading cases and treatises involved, see THAYER, CASES ON CONSTITUTIONAL LAW (1895) vol. 1, 169–70.

Developments in Indiana best point all this; Blackwell's "testimonial" leaflet again is the clarifying witness, and Judge Samuel E. Perkins, a member of the state supreme court, 1847–1864, is the zealous pioneer and evangelist. Perkins we met at the very start of research as one of the judges who in December, 1856, simply *presumed* a railroad corporation to be a "man" under Section 12 of the state bill of rights which declared "All courts shall be open; and every man, for injury done to him, in his person, property, or reputation, shall have remedy by due course of law." Presumption this was, of high order; but decidedly *not* (yet) a holding of corporate personality (or humanity), for we know that this lead and opportunity long went *un*pursued by the whole corporate bar.[26]

During the past forty years, thanks to the late Charles Warren, Judge Perkins has had a stronger claim to fame. In October, 1855, again two months later, this self-educated Blackstone and brimstone lawyer (who habitually and profusely "cited works on political economy when discussing constitutional questions") twice spoke for the Indiana court in voiding the state's Prohibition law[27]—"lay[ing] down this proposition:

> that the right of liberty and pursuing happiness secured by the constitution, embraces the right, in each *compos mentis* individual, of selecting what he will eat and drink, in short, his beverages, so far as he may be capable of producing them, or they may be within his reach, and the legislature cannot take away that right by direct enactment. If the constitution does not secure this right to the people, it secures nothing of value.

In paragraphs immediately preceding this passage, Judge Perkins had recited provisions of the state bill of rights, including the due course of law clause. Under these guarantees American freemen, unlike the oppressed of Europe, might buy and sell at pleasure.

---

[26] Madison & Indianapolis R.R. v. Whiteneck, 8 Ind. 217 (1856); the "holding" is indeed diffuse, but the premises are not; note also Judge Gookins' opinion, 237, 249. For previous mention of this case, see Chapter 2, *supra*, note 54.

[27] Herman v. State, 8 Ind. 545, 558–9 (Oct. 30, 1855); Beebe v. State, 6 Ind. 501 (Dec. 20, 1855); note the reasons the Beebe case was reported first, page 501. Nothing could be more unwarranted or misleading than the impression and statement of Charles Warren, *The New "Liberty" Under the Fourteenth Amendment*, 39 HARV. L. REV. 431 (1926) 444, that this use of "liberty" by Perkins "seem[s] to have been" unique "prior to 1868." Extravagant, unguarded, Perkins was (see his opinion voiding the state school law, City of Lafayette v. Jenners, 10 Ind. 70 [1858] and earlier opinions there cited, page 80); also 14 DICT. AM. BIOG. 476–7 (1934); Thornton, *Memoir of Samuel E. Perkins*, 4 GREEN BAG 254–5 (1892). But to gain or leave the impression that such usage and premises were unique—even uncommon—before 1868, is to ignore the natural rights orientations and assume that Lockeans were or could be analytical jurisprudents.

Nuisances might be defined and abated, but always under safeguard of judge and jury, and

> by provision of the general law of the land, and not by the tyranny of the legislature whose enactment may not be the law of the land. See numerous cases collected on this point in the first chapter of Blackwell on Tax Titles.[28]

Just a few weeks before decanting these views Judge Perkins, too, we now find, had received and acknowledged a copy of Blackwell's new *Treatise*:

> I have looked with some care through BLACKWELL ON TAX TITLES, and am pleased with the work.
> The branch of the law treated of is . . . thoroughly and systematically examined. . . . The work will be of great practical value to the profession . . . will take its place . . . along side of Angel & Ames' Corporations, "Sedgwick on damages," &c.[29]

This on the face of it is timely, impressive evidence. Our next chapter will examine at length this work which Thomas M. Cooley, fully thirteen years later, cited at the head of his own chaptered discussion of taxation in *Constitutional Limitations* (1868) and again in his *Treatise on Taxation* seven years later. The obvious need at this point is to fit this influential, neglected work into the frontier matrix and syndrome which produced it.

III

The core fact to be grasped is that the frontier revenue structure, like frontier life in general, rested on land, much of which was owned in immense tracts by eastern speculators.[30] Buying in competition with one another, often on credit, speculators placed themselves in competition with the federal government and those western states which still offered immense acreage at about the minimum price of $1.25 per acre. Civilization was rolling westward on economic rent. Speculation lubricated and guided movement. The heaviest, boldest speculators almost always resided "outside." From the original Wyoming counties in New York and Pennsylvania in the 1790's to Wyoming state a century later, many and often most, of the choicest

---

[28] Herman v. State, 8 Ind. 545 (1855), 554–8.
[29] Advertising leaflet, *supra* note 22 (p. 3).
[30] See *supra*, note 21.

lands were absentee-owned. The consequence was that two primary constituencies of frontier society—one political, the other economic—not only failed to match but often were squarely, at times futilely, at odds over tax rates and policy. Lands were the means to fortune; and for absentee owners especially, hostages to it—virtually non-voting stock in risky, distant enterprise. And from the frontier's standpoint, nonresident speculators were silent, indispensable, but quite junior partners, whose tax payments must and could be relied on to get society and government started. Lacking personal jurisdiction, threatened distraint of nonresident lands remained the frontier's sole weapon against tax delinquency. Distraint inherently was a clumsy weapon, and in this case it very soon was blunted. Speculation in land and tax titles, along with agency over-buying and depression, periodically scourged the frontier and speculators alike. Mails and payments were undependable; records were primitive and distant; errors tended to cumulate. Yet with the public domain seemingly unlimited, even the best patent titles often went begging and title itself tended toward the academic, for right of occupancy here constantly infringed and diluted proprietorship. Private and public interests, powers and remedies thus were indeed ingeniously, precariously balanced.

The tax sale, the tax deed, and the tax title were among the hardy fiscal hybrids that bred and flourished in this harsh environment. Specie was scarce; public and private credit limited or unobtainable; capital formation slow and difficult. Local taxation, under such conditions was not merely oppressive; it damped and even penalized frontier development. Wherever possible, and for as long as possible, all fiscal burdens that could be thus were deferred or shifted to nonresidents. *Ad valorem* taxation was an unwelcome and comparatively late comer to all frontiers.

Thus it came to pass that what in the stabler, parent societies of the seaboard had constituted distraint, and there on the whole effectively enforced payment of taxes, presently became, in many of these younger jurisdictions, an interim supplement or a partial substitute for taxes. This, let it be stressed again, was largely happenstance, and a gradual development, not a conscious innovation. But as early as 1810, the Old Northwest had hit upon this way of capitalizing both raw land and raw speculation—of partially financing its original state governments by what amounted to a series of conditional raffles and contingent loans. The controlling fact was that during the early years of statehood in Ohio, Indiana, and Illinois, hundreds—often thousands—of nonresident taxpayers always were delinquent.[31] Population that was "forever moving on" alone assured that. So did the slow, interrupted mails; the lax, derelict, absconding agents and officials; the often half-literate, migrant, defaulting, part-time assessors, collectors, and sheriffs. Frontier government was part-time, one-man, often unmanned government. Tax delinquency and tax sales thus were endemic. On occasion, and particularly at their worst, in the Illinois Military Tract, they were for a time cumulative and self-perpetuating.

What counted for the moment was that men with cash and capital and the frontier flair for risk, would buy a tax title, just as they had bought tickets in the Virginia or Maryland lotteries (often advertised side by side with the domestic delinquent list in the frontier press). What these fractional speculators bought, what the state auditors and county sheriffs sold—never really was "title" as such, not as we think of title today; rather simply chances on title, shares of it, in the form of "tax liens," with a deferred social reckoning, and a world of legislative and judicial trouble. Governmentally and economically, the vital fact was that the local common law had yet to sort out, and to define, the various fragmented, often overlapping rights. Each state could do this only for itself, generally much later, in the course of evaluating and resolving the competing claims and equities incident to reassembly of title. Looking back, it is clear enough that what the frontier at this period really was doing was buying time—and with time, trouble—using its immense land surplus as down payment. The tax titlist, vicariously, and at long range, hoped, like other resident or nonresident speculators, to capitalize the increment which time and population promised to add to land. Institutionally viewed, considering the handicaps, this still must be counted something of a frontier coup. For the result was that these successive land-poor, specie-shy, creditless, raw frontier-state governments managed to skirt insolvency, and at the same time to escape a full measure of domestic taxation—temporarily, by what amounted to a periodic raffling off of absentees' tax delinquent lands —including not infrequently other adjacent or interspersed lands innocently or culpably listed as such.

Fiscally, tax titles thus were the cut-rate, super-speculation of a superlatively speculative era and section. In Illinois during the 1820's and 1830's, they were the cornerstone, with state bank paper, of frontier public finance. That this secondary role has so long gone unnoticed shows merely how completely one generation's fiscal-

---

31 See CARLSON 40–48; also Chapter 12, *infra*, note 38, for delinquency in Illinois.

speculative tastes and diet are lost on successors. In this instance, of course, the deficient or wanting records that spelled trouble for the frontier are still barriers to study and research. Statutes and cases, however, are plentiful, and for our purposes, with Blackwell's treatise, are much more than adequate.

On the frontier, too, assessment and collection procedures were basic, reflecting economic-administrative handicaps on the one hand, contributing to title fission and confusion on the other. Kentucky and Ohio, it happened, first had fumblingly combined the mechanisms which Illinois subsequently perfected. Chief among the elements were the grading of unimproved lands by statute according to quality and location, with legislatively set rates, local rating, and often with separate places, dates, and payment procedures prescribed for residents and nonresidents; rate structures loaded and applied regressively to spur sale and to bring in a maximum return; exemption of improvements and town lots to quicken growth and local development; and finally, as Governor Ford and the statute books bear witness, endless legislative tinkering, and an annual overhaul of dates and details, the results of which, if not the design, served to keep both the fiscal and the record chaos fluid for years.

Frontier tax law and administration thus were strange blends of indulgence and technicality—of sovereign caprice and sovereign grace in bewildering proportions and order. High enough in any event, delinquency often was increased by cupidity as well as by inadvertence, both working almost impartially, on both sides. Taxes as such were not subject to negotiation, but in practice the difficulties of communication, payment, and collection often contributed to that very end.[32]

In the Valley of Democracy tax sales often were a frolic. They were the frontier's way of capitalizing its remoteness, socializing its risks, democratizing even land speculation. In Illinois during the 1820's and 1830's practically the entire cost of state government was borne by nonresidents. The biennial delinquent list advertised from seven to nine thousand quarter sections—up to a million and a half acres for sale—from the Military Tract alone.

Tax purchasers—domestic and foreign alike—thus functioned as volunteer, in lieu, interim, at times multi-duty taxpayers. As such, they gambled on the certainty that they at least stood to get their

---

[32] CARLSON 48. Penalties and back taxes often were waived by statute; see PURPLE, *passim*, and for one example, ILLINOIS REVISED LAWS, 1833, 512, a law of 1827. For criticism of speculators' use of the courts to defeat limitation acts and other measures designed to quiet title, see Moore v. Brown, 52 U.S. 413, 429-34, Catron, J., dissenting.

payments back with interest from redemptioners. At best—in case of death, indifference, or ignorance, on the part of patentees, heirs, or assigns—a tax title might prove as valuable as any, and at roughly one-hundredth of the cost. In the words of a distinguished federal judge of Illinois, Nathaniel Pope, frontier tax titles were the means of getting "acres for cents."[33] Speaking today, and more carefully and accurately, they were a possible means of getting acres for cents. In either case, they inevitably were deplored, decried, and contemned, as well as coveted, all for the same reason. For years the early West itself was of two minds and two interests on this whole matter and problem. Given local conditions, it hardly could have been otherwise. Not till population and wealth increased, and the tax base broadened, not till the illusory gains and the deferred social costs became much plainer and heavier, did the tax sale begin to suffer eclipse and loss of attraction. By then, of course, the damage had been done, the social bill was in. Public sentiment crystallized more from the insights of experience and improvement, than it ever had from principle, conviction, or conscience. Of this there could be no clearer proof than the fact that Archibald Williams, Blackwell's mentor and the Quincy lawyer and bounty-titlists' counsel who again and again in the 1840's and 1850's advanced the rejected due process argument to overturn what he by then regarded as the "iniquitous" tax laws and tax titles of the 1830's, himself had, as one of the ablest of Lincoln's Whig associates in the legislature at Springfield, approved and helped enact the very laws he later attacked.[34]

Summing up, frontier revenue systems reflected the nature and risks of frontier society in general. Specific and regressive rates legislatively applied; capricious changes in penalties, dates, places and procedures of payment; constructive notice and defective records; the repeated fission of counties, and hence the dispersion and duplication of records and diffusion of error: all weighed oppressively on the one side, and made for a fission of title. The saving fact was that these conditions and frustrations, if not inherently self-correcting, were at least time-limited. And even for the interim, they were made tolerable by two compensating developments: one, the presence and

---

[33] Arrowsmith v. Burlingim, Fed. Cas. #563 (1848) at 1188; BLACKWELL 15, 35, 661 (as Arrowsmith v. Burlingame).
[34] Williams represented Adams County in the Senate, 1832–1836; in the Assembly, 1837, 1838; and as delegate in the constitutional convention, 1847. His positions on tax policy are much more clearly defined and documented after 1843, but the legislative journals of the '30's give no inklings of opposition or efforts at reform.

the accomplishments of that frontier marvel and man-of-all-work, the land-and-tax agency or agent; the other, liberal redemption policies which undertook to preserve and safeguard the rights of minor heirs, and of others whose delinquency had resulted from ignorance or inadvertence. On these remote frontiers, representation was personal, not simply geographic or governmental. Agency—traditionally a legal relationship—here developed an institutional-economic side which made it the privatized twin of, and sometimes a surrogate for, government itself. In acute cases, as in the Military Tract, record systems especially tended to become dual, with private initiative and enterprise at first backstopping, then actually taking over for the public systems that had got outdistanced and broken down.

Each of these states of the Old Northwest had its Tiffen, McArthur, Edwards, Tillson, or Stapp—the first three significantly became governors; the others also represented absentee owners by the hundred, paid their taxes, bought and sold and redeemed lands; advised, appeased, and so far as possible, "harmonized" outside and local interests within the Illinois legislature and government. Representation and influence thus were fused, sometimes actually consolidated, along with the offices and powers. One-man, unmanned government thus came to have at least the advantages and the compensations of its handicaps.

A decisive, terminal feedback, moreover, was geared right into frontier growth itself: slowly or rapidly, depending on diverse economic, legal, and political situations and factors, lands shifted to local residents and local ownership;[35] these growing and stabler populations in turn demanded roads and schools; costs of local and state government steadily mounted while the tax payments by absentees declined; local *ad valorem* taxation, so long deferred and dreaded, thus at last became unavoidable, even welcome. Generally this occurred about twenty years after statehood, along with the rise of state appellate reporting, title litigation, and an increasingly professionalized bar and judiciary.

Local and special factors of course quickened or retarded and delayed these shifts. The volume of tax deeds, and of title litigation, was always a prime index of earlier hardships and of the present complications. As a rule, anything which had contributed to the dispersal, inaccessibility, or complexity of basic land title and land tax records, anything which still prevented or interfered with a ready, joint consultation thereof, aggravated and prolonged the adjustments.

---

[35] CARLSON 49–54, 66 ff.

Virginia and Kentucky, Ohio and Illinois, all for long were prime sufferers in these matters; Virginia by reason of its fantastic systems of land grants and "metes and bounds" land description; Kentucky by inheritance of these, and by repeated, prolonged self-indulgence —troubles and chaos bred and compounded by dispersed records, litigation, and conflicts between debtors and creditors, residents and absentees, all stemming in part from the ambiguous Virginia-Kentucky compact, and all intensified by the "Old-New Court War," and by the severe depression of the 1820's. Ohio likewise was ensnared by absentee speculation and by a revenue system patterned (in earliest territorial days) on Kentucky's. Fortunately spared the metes and bounds descriptions (except in the case of prior locations in the Virginia Military District where a frustrating tri-state record system long complicated matters even further), the Northwest Territory and Ohio nevertheless experienced and indeed passed on to their devolute jurisdictions most of the troubles and the problems endemic elsewhere. Yet it was in Illinois, the most remote and hardest-hit territory and state of all, where these problems coalesced and reached their climax. Especially was this true in the Military Tract. There, lands allotted and resold for a generation in advance of settlement, added to the chaos and the entropy, which, at its worst, thanks to the Panics of 1819 and 1837, and to the collapse of rash state banking and public improvement programs in the 1840's, surpassed even that of Kentucky twenty years earlier.

Military bounty lands thus can be seen to have been a perverse common denominator.[36] But chronic and spectacular confusion resulted wherever geography, depression, partisanship, and special registration and conveyancing problems added to the inherent burdens. The ensuing fragmentation of title; the creation of multiple, conflicting interests in the same lands; the tendency for such interests at times to coalesce and to polarize—in-state interests versus out, debtor versus creditor, bounty titles versus tax—all these weighed heavily in the aggregate, and future research in the afflicted jurisdictions and localities must clarify these relations and conflicts.

Several things, however, already are clear. One is that the rise and operation of these largely unstudied frontier revenue systems not only reached to the heart of the problem of law and government generally, but also made for arrearages, cleavages, and conflicts, the resolution of which has marked the Constitution of the United States

---

[36] See works cited *supra*, notes 4–6; also Freund (1946); and counsel's statement on the consequences of record dispersal for lands in the Virginia Military District as late as 1841, Brush v. Ware, 10 L. Ed. 672, 676 (Mason's argument).

to this day. In brief, and in both the general and the special sense, as stressed above, it was land law which profoundly affected and shaped the law of the land. For one thing, acute problems of federalism and of vested rights arose here, chronically and repeatedly, and at first and for long, there was not much that could be done about either! That the confrontations seemingly so stark and implicit in the former, and so disturbing to anxious legal minds like Chancellor Kent's, proved largely, if not always, academic, was due in great measure to the fact that in the second field—vested rights, or, as we might better think of it, as *affirmative protection of property and capital*, capital the frontier's greatest need[37]—frontier courts soon proved as sound and protective as any, thanks in part to the authority of Chancellor Kent's own *Commentaries*.

This is made clear by the fact that once adjudication and reassembly of Illinois' fractured land titles began in the mid-1830's—followed finally by introduction of *ad valorem* taxation in 1839—"Kent" continually was cited against "Kent." One quotation from the *Commentaries* answered another because *at first* no other or better authority was at hand. Chancellor Kent himself moreover, it will be remembered, had been of two minds and taken two positions with reference to frontier taxation—lecturing the Adirondack trappers on their "peltry" predilections, but later sustaining, as counsel for the great New York and Boston Illinois Land Company, the early state tax laws and tax titles, most of which bore some similar taint. In the natural course of events these Kent-Lord solicitors' opinions, including the passages mentioning due process of law, were turned against the eastern capitalists and speculators who had given them wide circulation.[38] This table-turning was first attempted by the frontier land bar at Quincy. Archibald Williams, Charles B. Lawrence, and Robert S. Blackwell in particular invited the judges to overthrow state tax systems of twenty years' standing merely in order to save individual bounty titlists' rights. Opportunism of this order was quite in keeping with an adversary jurisprudence, equally with prevailing Lockean prepossessions and natural rights advocacy. Yet otherwise this was a scandalous, scattergun way to protect a few clients' rights. Illinois courts and citizens were in fact partial to "title direct from the sovereign." Good military bounty or patent titles thus could be (and generally were) upheld without creating utter chaos. Needs and options were shrewdly grasped.

[37] HURST, LAW AND THE CONDITIONS OF FREEDOM IN THE NINETEENTH CENTURY (1956) 10, 20, 23-26, 53, 56; book review, Kutler, 42 N.Y.U. L. REV. 391, 393 (1967).
[38] See Chapter 11 headnote, *supra*, note 4.

There can be no doubt that this frontier bench and bar sensed clearly enough that a merely *syllogistic* due process and equality in such circumstances could be neither *due* nor *equal*. Every man's rights were at stake in such matters. Every man's rights were protected by the same constitutional guarantees. This universality of coverage thus in itself militated against doctrinaire misuse.

Once raised, however, the due process-equality pleas continued to be made against limitation acts, occupying claimants' laws, and most of the devices which the frontier hopefully counted upon to quiet and reassemble title. With a few exceptions such usage was redundant and rejected.[39]

On the larger issues, Illinois thus proved itself as pragmatic and discerning as Kent and its legislatures had been. During the twenty-year recovery period 1840–1860, in the course of which the bar of this once-prostrate state raised itself and Illinois to national leadership of *both* political parties, invested capital and vested rights were upheld along with most of the early acts, rules, and preferences. Title was reconstituted fairly and expeditiously. Not all rights however had vested; and some were not permitted to vest. The chief job was identifying and sorting out the equities and priorities. Individual acquiescence, accommodation, adjudication, gradual buildup of public and private records, aided by the state's rapid growth and by general prosperity in the '50's, accomplished the task—roughly within twenty years.

Our wonder today is twofold: Not that the task was accomplished, but that it was accomplished this soon and well. Not that many constitutional arguments were made and easily rejected, but that these rejected due process–equal protection pleas (and claims) shortly received an enduring synthesis, an ultimately influential restatement. Blackwell's *Treatise on Tax Titles* is another of those phenomenal quixotic works: failing in an originally hopeless use and cause, they nevertheless survive and flourish, advance and reoutfit many others.

To this extraordinary author and work we must now turn attention.

---

[39] See generally, BLACKWELL, *passim*, especially chapters 39 (Statutes of Limitations), 40 (Improvements); also DEMBITZ (1890, 1895); Gates (1962); and the leading Illinois Military Tract cases listed Chapter 12, *infra*, note 38.

[CHAPTER 12]

"Prophet Unhonored": Robert S. Blackwell, Tax Titles, and the "Substantive Revolution" in Due Process and Equal Protection, 1830-1880

EDITORIAL NOTE. Doctrinally the Common Law is a potter's field. Monuments are scarce, and as a rule out of place. Contributions by a single judge, lawyer, case, or treatise are easier to claim than to document or prove.[1] Custom, precedent, *stare decisis*, the adversary system, the interlocking, ramifying character of statutes and decisions, all assure this; all are anti-individualistic, both in operation and result. The "legal author" or the constitutional innovator in many respects thus is as ghostly an abstraction as "economic man." More than History even, Law is a rough, patternless tweed. Our domestic constitutional fabric is surpassingly such, and American due process and equal protection, if not superior to the Donegal or Harris bolts, are just as burry, just as incontrovertibly corporate, cooperative creations. Weavers and designers are problematical at best.

Our chapter title thus unquestionably is anomalous. Once these concessions have been made, how can it be argued, much less established, that a forgotten prairie lawyer, Robert S. Blackwell of the Quincy and Chicago land bars, and his pioneer treatise on *Tax Titles*, played a significant, even a prominent part, in that over-all development which, for lack of better descriptors, we still miscall the "substantive," "laissez faire," or "American revolution in Due Process of Law"? (As if our neat modern distinctions had been foreseen and maintained for all of two centuries; as if there had been no appreciable "substantive" or "laissez faire" use before 1868; as if semantic shifts requiring seven and a half centuries and involving every syllable of a medieval guarantee could be called "revolutions" at all!)

---

[1] "[T]he body of our jurisprudence . . . [is] shaped by . . . powers greater than the greatest individual. . . . The glory of lawyers, like that of men of science, is more corporate than individual." THE OCCASIONAL SPEECHES OF JUSTICE OLIVER WENDELL HOLMES (1962) 57.

Can it really be that Blackwell's or any such volume, first published in Chicago in 1855, and reaching its fifth edition in 1889, not only gave impetus to the professional-popular transformation of due process, but did so, initially, by grooming and nursing rights secured by the companion equal protection concept and clause?

To answer these questions more fully; to detail something of Robert Blackwell's life; how his *Treatise* happened to get written; what its premises, thesis, and main contributions were; how Illinois reassembled its fractured title, and extricated itself, and what the lasting effects were; finally, to point up the personal and professional ties between the antebellum Quincy and Chicago *land bar's* use of due process, and the postbellum Chicago *corporate bar's* use of the same clauses—these are the purposes of the present chapter.

[CHAPTER 12]

EVERY LAW BOOK is a record of conflicts, of lost hopes, of social and personal defeats, misfortunes, and mischances. Yet here is something monumental—over 800 well-indexed pages, 1,100 cases—of concentrated error, incompetence, chicane and abuse, the whole of it treating a conflict that wracked the heart of the American continent. If, as George Dangerfield has phrased it, the period of the 1820's and '30's marked "perhaps the last time in all history when mankind discovered that one of its deepest needs—the need to own—could be satisfied by the simple process of walking towards it,"[1] then this book, written and published in Chicago over a century ago, is more than an American epitaph. Law and national ideals are a crystallization as well as an inheritance; conflicts can advance as well as retard their development. Constitutionalism itself is the product—really the continuing synthesis or an equilibration—of conflict. Truly strong and original minds trained in the method and learning of the common law, unconsciously transcend and transmute their materials. Viewed on this broader scale, individual cases tend to become parts of causes, and failures often are the raw stuff of success. Judges indeed are makers of that tradition and "technique

---

[1] Dangerfield, The Era of Good Feelings (1952) 120.

of utilizing recorded judicial experience,"[2] but they are not the sole makers, much less the sole utilizers. Innovation and creation, in both the common and constitutional law are joint and continuing processes, rarely, if ever, single acts. Yet a single mind, challenged by doctrine and by cases, and dedicated to a mastery and reworking of them, and to a conceived improvement of the law, can expose, criticize, evaluate, re-order—even re-fuse and reconstitute—principles in ways that may turn a stream into new channels, concentrate its flow, make subsequent appropriation much easier than prior, make (in this present instance certainly) *due* process much more significant and attractive than mere due process, and make equal protection of the laws, as ultimately applied to "persons" and taxation, a more appealing, popular, rigorous, yet slowly emergent and always thorny requirement, than the old requirement that taxation be merely "equal" or "uniform."

Blackwell's treatise commemorates a meteoric career at the most interesting and talented—surely the most self-tutored—bar America has known. "A man of rare endowments" struck down at forty by drink and overwork "just when he should have been in the zenith of his fame and usefulness. I became interested in him when he was 13 or 14 . . . a fatherless boy . . . finally took him into my [Quincy] office where he read law [and] afterwards attained to great eminence in his profession." This funeral-day tribute by Orville H. Browning,[3] diarist and United States Senator, with whom Blackwell repeatedly had matched wits in the Military Tract cases of the 50's is significant.

Son of David Blackwell, the pioneer lawyer-editor and Secretary of State who helped defeat the campaign to introduced slavery into Illinois in 1824, Blackwell[4] began to practice as a county attorney in the heart of the Military Tract just as *Rhinehart v. Schuyler* moved towards a showdown. Soon he was the associate of Archibald Williams, the counsel who had developed the due process argument in that case and who gained fame throughout Illinois as the only man homelier and ungainlier than Abraham Lincoln and the lawyer whom Lincoln himself, years afterward, declared to be "the strongest-minded, clearest-headed man he ever saw." This early association

---

[2] Roscoe Pound, *Introduction* to WINFIELD, THE CHIEF SOURCES OF ENGLISH LEGAL HISTORY (1925) xv.
[3] 1 DIARY (1925–33, 2v.) 630; see also *id.* 190, 221, 249.
[4] See 1 BATEMAN, HISTORICAL ENCYCLOPEDIA OF ILLINOIS (1913) 49, and "Blackwell" entries in the Illinois State Historical Library card index of the *Illinois State Journal*, 1851–1860. Neither Robert S. Blackwell nor his *Treatise* gained mention in CHARLES WARREN, HISTORY OF THE AMERICAN BAR (1911), an unusual oversight. He frequently has been confused with his uncle, Robert Blackwell, editor of the *Illinois Intelligencer* (1828) and (with Joseph Hall) of the *Illinois Monthly Magazine* (Vandalia, 1829–31).

with Williams proved professionally decisive. Blackwell appeared in most of the great title cases of the '40's and 50's, and his book bears the dedication: "To Archibald Williams, Esq., United States Attorney for Illinois [1849-1853] . . . pioneer in tax title litigation . . . who by advice and encouragement has materially aided . . . preparation." This book clearly was an expansion of the research done by both men over a decade.

In 1852 Blackwell removed to Chicago, and there attained immediate professional success. One association has had lasting significance and consequences: he had as partner for a time Corydon Beckwith,[5] who after a brief term on the Illinois Supreme Court (1864) moved to front rank in the corporate bar of Chicago, and who, as much as any other counsel, pioneered economic due process in the *Granger* and *Illinois Railroad Tax* cases, 1869-1877. Like most Illinois lawyers, Blackwell entered politics. He was the unsuccessful Whig nominee for Congress in 1854, and one of the founders of the Republican Party. Later he pursued an erratic course that chagrined and embarrassed his friends. Gifted socially and immensely energetic, he served as one of the revisors of the Illinois statutes (1858); and at the time of his death in 1863 had completed four volumes of an abridged edition of the Illinois Reports.

Blackwell's aim and method are implicit even in his Introduction, the first sentence of which was well calculated to catch the attention:

> The subject of the following work is a matter of controlling importance to the landed interest of the United States, . . . it relates to an extraordinary power, which is annually exercised over estates, and which, when well executed, works a complete divestiture of the title against the will of the owner, and oftentimes without his knowledge. This power has been exercised by all the States . . . has, on several occasions, been resorted to by the Federal Government. . . . The principles of law . . . in the new states especially, are of constant application in the regular course of . . . practice.

All this notwithstanding, this subject remained untreated. Already there were upwards of one thousand cases "scattered throughout seven or eight hundred volumes of American reports, thus . . . inaccessible to the mass of the profession." Extensive experience in the Illinois cases, Blackwell explained, had led him, with his "eminent friend's" encouragement and assistance, to perform the needed task. His completed work embraced the entire field of litigation.[6]

---

5 See Chapter 11, *supra* n. 12.
6 BLACKWELL, TREATISE (1855) 3.

"Reducing to a system, the rules which apply to tax sales, and the principles upon which they are founded," had been marked by two major difficulties: first, the conflicting, highly local character of the provisions of the various state revenue systems, and the "peculiar *local policy* which governs their construction;" second, the fact that "the sale of land for nonpayment of taxes, is a proceeding unknown to the common law of England." Feudal tenures indeed had prevented its development; the only involuntary alienation then known was forfeiture for treason; "taxes were collected either by the imprisonment of the delinquent, the distress of his goods and chattels, or an execution against them out of the Exchequer." In modern times the practice of "farming" of the English land tax had forestalled the development. Thus, Blackwell repeated in conclusion:

> the common law is a stranger to the power of sale exercised in this country over landed estates, for the nonpayment of taxes assessed. Yet that law furnishes the principles by which this new power is to be governed. It is the chief excellence of the common law that it is flexible, and constantly expands with the exigencies of society; that it applies to new combinations of circumstances, those rules which are derived from its fundamental principles. In the language of Judge Story, "May it ever continue to flourish here, for it is the *law of liberty, and the watchful and inflexible guardian of private property and public rights.*"[7]

Precisely how "this new power" was to be "governed," how the "flexible" expansive common law was to become "the inflexible guardian of private property and public rights," Blackwell's opening chapter entitled "Of the Fundamental Principles Which Govern the Taxing Power," made immediately clear.

Blackwell began by defining taxes—"The burdens or charges imposed by the legislature of a state upon persons or property to raise money from public purposes"—then distinguished the power of taxation from the power of eminent domain. Both, he explained, appropriated private property to public uses; both were indispensable to government; both were incidents of sovereignty; but eminent domain constituted a special taking for which special compensation had to be provided, while taxation operated upon all, its benefits being deemed inherent in the nature and services of government.[8]

On his next point Blackwell was emphatic yet somewhat equivocal. "There is no limitation upon the power of the Legislature as to the amount or objects of taxation. The interest, wisdom, and justice of

---
[7] *Id.* 5.
[8] *Id.* 7.

the representative body, and its relation with its constituents, furnish the only security against unjust and excessive taxation."[9]

Yet "as to the manner of levying and collecting taxes," there were decided limitations. These next were adverted to. Like most of his generation, Blackwell had mastered his Locke and *Federalist* Number 30. One of the great ends of government was the protection of private property. No citizen entering a governmental compact intended to confer an arbitrary power of taxation upon government, for by doing so he would gain nothing, become merely the "prey . . . of the entire community acting under color of a written constitution. Happily for the people, the power of taxation which they have delegated to their government, is not an arbitrary one, but limited by the words and spirit of the Constitution, and the principles of natural justice."[10]

Blackwell then summarized the constitutional principles of taxation, federal and state, noting specifically, with reference to the latter the requirements of public purpose, periodic assessment, *ad valorem* valuation.

> No one species of property shall be taxed higher than another of equal value. In some of the States by constitution, in others by ordinance or compact, the lands of non-resident proprietors cannot be taxed higher than lands belonging to residents of the state; and it has been held by the Supreme Court of Alabama, that the clause in the Federal Constitution, which declares that "the citizens of each State shall be entitled to all of the privileges and immunities of citizens of the several States," forbade the legislature of that State from imposing a higher tax upon the [slave] property of non-residents than, by the general laws, were imposed upon residents. . . .
>
> By compact made between the Federal Government and some of the new States, it is expressly stipulated that bounty lands, granted, or to be granted by the United States for military services, shall, while they continue the property of the soldier or his heirs, be exempt from taxation for the term of three years from the date of the patent; and that all lands sold by the United States, shall be exempt . . . for the period of five years from . . . day of sale.[11]

Next mentioned were the "Restrictions imposed by the Federal Constitution upon the taxing power of the States"—all federal property and the public domain necessarily being exempt.

---

[9] *Id.* 9.
[10] *Id.* 10.
[11] *Id.* 11-12.

Finally, "The last class of limitations upon the taxing power, as to the manner of levying the tax, are those which have their foundation in natural justice. That such exist is clearly established by the authorities.²"¹²

Somewhat repetitiously there then followed a restatement of the two general principles—"public purpose and just equality." The latter was of course the "governing one" and required both "uniformity" and "periodic valuations":

> The legislature have not the power to exact from a single individual, or class of citizens, or a single county or town, the means of defraying the entire expenses of the State; for if this could be done, the constitutional prohibition could be evaded in all cases, and the legislature could take private property for public use, without compensation, under the vague and indefinite pretence of taxation.
>
> Such are the principles by which the legislative power in this country is controlled in the levy of taxes, as laid down by all the authorities. The difficulty seems to lie in their application to the facts of each particular case. We shall content ourselves with a reference to the adjudged cases, without attempting to reconcile them with each other. [Recitation of all cases last cited, plus 6 Barbour 209; 4 Comstock 419] Thus, in the language of Chancellor Kent: "It is not sufficient that no tax can be imposed on citizens but by their representatives in the legislature. The citizens are entitled to require that the legislature itself shall cause all public taxation to be fair and equal in proportion to the value of property, so that no one class of individuals, and no one species of property, may be unequally or unduly assessed.¹³

It is obvious that Blackwell—even less than Kent—was no one to quibble over substance and procedure. He forthrightly concedes that there are no restraints whatever on the "power of the legislature as to the amount or objects of taxation." For in his book none are needed: every restraint lawyers ever have employed, or can conceive of, is a procedural restraint, even those existing in the "spirit of the Constitution and the principles of natural justice." Indeed, all government is administration, which is simply procedure; all constitutional, all extra-constitutional restraints therefore relate to the manner of its operations. When the Barons and Lord Coke and the Parliamentarians were hedging the royal prerogative, and when

---

¹² *Id.* 12. Blackwell's footnote 2 cited "5 Dana 31; 9 Ibid. 516; 4 N.H. 556; 6 Har. & John 382-3; 6 Barbour 209."

¹³ *Id.* 13-14. Blackwell here cited "2 Kent's Com. 331"—the Adirondacks-"noxious animal" passage discussed Chapter 11, *supra*, n. 16.

the American colonists aimed at the parliamentary taxing power, it was the same: What the right hand gave, the left quickly retrieved. And retrieved not once, but twice:

> Before treating of the rules which govern the courts in the construction of a class of statutes by which rights of property are affected, it may not be deemed inappropriate to consider the principles by which the legislative power is controlled in this country. These principles are to be found in our written constitutions, and are deducible in a three-fold manner. 1) From the declared ends of government. 2) From the particular provisions of the Constitution. 3) From the structure of the government itself. In discussing this subject we shall refer to the Constitution of Illinois, because it is more familiar to us, while at the same time it is substantially like that of every other State in the Union.[14]

Upon examination, "seven great and essential principles" were found to be declared in the various bills of rights:

> 1) That all men are created free and independent. 2) That they possess the rights of life, liberty, reputation and property, independent of human laws. 3) That these rights are indefeasible. . . 4) That all power is inherent in the people. . . 5) That human government is founded upon their authority. . . 6) That government is instituted for their security. 7) That the only end of government is the preservation and perpetuation of these inherent powers and rights.[15]

All "natural" and human rights, moreover, were anterior to government; constitutions merely affirmed them—divided and separated the powers to prevent tyranny and promote justice. In the United States, "neither the whole government, nor any department . . . has any inherent power"; even delegated powers were jealously guarded.[16]

After paraphrasing most of the specific guarantees, Blackwell quoted in full the three he regarded as of paramount importance:

> 1. No freeman shall be imprisoned, or disseized of his freehold, liberties or privileges, or outlawed, or exiled, or in ANY MANNER deprived of his life, liberty or property, but by the JUDGMENT OF HIS PEERS, OR THE LAW OF THE LAND.
> 2. Every person in this State ought to find a certain remedy IN THE LAWS, for all injuries or wrongs which he may receive in his person, property, or character; he ought to obtain justice freely, and without being obliged to purchase it, completely and without

---
14 *Id.* 14-15.
15 *Id.* 15.
16 *Id.* 17-18.

denial, promptly and without delay, conformably to the laws; and
3. The right of trial by jury shall remain inviolate.[17]

By written constitutions, Blackwell continued, Americans had made these guarantees "absolutely binding upon government, and every department thereof." An "independent, impartial judiciary," one that brought "legislative acts to the test of the Constitution" and voided those found wanting, guarded and enforced every restraint.[18] "Conservative power," as Chief Justice Gibson had put it, thus here "is lodged in the judiciary." Americans to be sure always elected their officers; yet this tripartite separation, judicially maintained, was an added "barrier," the chief security "against governmental abuse of power."[19]

"No person or department," he continued, "shall act as legislator, judge, and executioner at the same time." Trouble arose only in "defining with precision the exact limits" of the respective powers. "With due deference to timid judges who seem unable to surmount this difficulty, and therefore give loose rein to legislative power," Blackwell laid it down as "self-evident" that legislative power was in its nature prospective, and "*limited* to the *making of laws*, and not the *exposition or execution of them*." Judicial power, on the other hand, "acts upon past conduct and declares what the law was at the time." "This plain line of demarcation," as Blackwell viewed it, "strictly observed and rigidly enforced," would surmount every difficulty and assure that "the rights of the citizen were more fully secured."[20]

And how was this to be accomplished? Preferably by the correct and creative use of an ancient guarantee:

> Our Constitutions all declare "That no freeman shall be . . . deprived of his life, liberty, or property, but by the JUDGMENT OF HIS PEERS, OR THE LAW OF THE LAND." This clause, on account of its bearing on the subject under consideration, as well as its great importance when properly understood, as a protection against legislative spoliation, also deserves a critical examination.[21]

Thus by a familiar spiraling route, Blackwell at last arrived at his destination. The remaining sixteen pages[22] of this chapter not only "examined" this ancient guarantee, and all important Ameri-

---
[17] *Id.* 19-20.
[18] *Id.* 22-3.
[19] *Id.* 24.
[20] *Id.* 24-6; cf. COOLEY, LAW OF TAXATION (1876) 36-41 for criticism of Blackwell's discussion of the law of the land cases; see also COOLEY, CONSTITUTIONAL LIMITATIONS (1868) Chapters XI and XIV.
[21] BLACKWELL 27.
[22] *Id.* 27-42.

can cases construing it. They also laid the foundations for a running attack on what Blackwell regarded as the evasions, and worse, of the Illinois Supreme Court. In doing this, he effected a synthesis, the consequences of which soon were everywhere evident.

The quoted law of the land clause, Blackwell began, did not "absolutely prohibit" legislative deprivations. It simply required that they be accomplished in one of two ways:

> 1. "By the judgment of his peers," which is universally admitted to mean a judgment rendered upon the verdict of a jury; or,
> 2. "By the law of the land,"—this, in England, where the same language was used in *Magna Carta*, was well understood to require a judgment; and embraced judgments, by confession in criminal and civil causes, upon demurrer, by default, and all other judgments which, by the general laws of the realm, it was legal to render without trial by jury; such as the judgments for contempt, convictions under the military and naval laws of the kingdom, judgments in the ecclesiastical . . . courts, proceedings according to the course of the civil law.[23]

This reference to summary judgments may have been unguarded; certainly for Blackwell it was a sporting concession. But Lord Coke, he continued without interruption,

> said that "to judge a man in a civil or criminal case without affording him an opportunity to be heard in his own defense, would be against this provision."
>
> That this was the meaning of the expression, "LAW OF THE LAND," as used in the great charter of English rights, seems to have been the opinion of all the common law jurists in that country; but that it means the same thing in our own Constitution, has not been so universally agreed. Some judges have been greatly perplexed in attempting to ascertain its true meaning, and have given judgment in entire disregard of it. One judge, at least, admitting that it did not mean and require a *"judgment,"* obviated its force by saying it applied only to criminal cases, and that, unless the clause was so restricted, it would be in opposition to legislative usage.[24]

This reference of course was to the majority opinion in *Rhinehart v. Schuyler*, which Blackwell cited in the margin, and sharply criticized in detail. The Supreme Court of New Hampshire likewise early had decided in the *Dartmouth College Case*, "That all statutes, not repugnant to *any other* clauses of the Constitution, seem always

---
[23] *Id.* 27.
[24] *Id.* 27-8.

to have been considered as 'the law of the land,' within the meaning of *this* clause." But its judgment, Blackwell added, was reversed by the Supreme Court of the United States.

At the outset of his discussion Blackwell thus fairly and ably counterpoised the two approaches to due process—the narrow and historic approach is balanced against the liberal and expansive. He even conceded that in England summary process and judgments had been due process. But he risked little by this, for no one could mistake his conclusion or thesis that things now were to be different in the United States. The next seven pages[25] skillfully assembled passages from the main due process opinions of the Texas, Tennessee, Illinois, Massachusetts, Carolina, New York, Pennsylvania and federal courts, as well as from Webster's *Dartmouth College* argument, all of which, by selection, italics, ellipsis and arrangement, stressed the judicial, common law element, and the "general," "equal," more-than-mere-legislation quality which had been increasingly attributed to the law of the land clause in America. In short, all the pregnant, now-familiar dicta were here marshaled and paraded with telling effect; indeed, Blackwell anticipates here almost every case cited, and every point made at greater length by Cooley in his famous chapters,[26] "Protection to Property by 'the Law of the Land' " and "The Power of Taxation," thirteen years later:

> Upon a careful review of all the authorities [he goes on] it may be safely affirmed as a principle of constitutional law, that the clause in question requires judicial as well as legislative action, before any person can be deprived of his life, liberty or property. Even those who have questioned the correctness of this construction, admit that it is so construed in England, and the only reason assigned for not adhering to the same construction in this country, is, that many acts of the legislature would be inconsistent with it, and, therefore, this cannot be its true meaning; thus bringing the Constitution to the test of the legislation, instead of legislation to the test of the Constitution. Such a position amounts to a virtual abrogation of all constitutional restraints upon the power of the legislature, and makes that body as omnipotent as Parliament itself. On the other hand, the power of the legislature, as limited by the weight of authorities, consists in the power to pass *general* laws for the peace, safety and happiness of the people, directing what they may do or omit, and declaring the consequences of a violation of such laws. Here then power ceases. The application of those laws to the cases of individuals, is assigned to other agents;

---
[25] *Id.* 29-35.
[26] As cited *supra* n. 20.

consequently the legislature has no power, by its own mere action, to deprive any citizen of this property.[27]

This of course was stretching dicta almost beyond recognition. But it was what Blackwell wanted to believe and needed to show, and he continued in an even more dogmatic vein:

> Such are the securities which the people, in the exercise of their inherent powers, have provided against legislative spoliation. It will be seen that every individual has, in the Constitution, an absolute, complete and perfect protection in the quiet use and enjoyment of his property, until it shall be judicially ascertained that he has violated some general law of the land, which authorizes a seizure and divestiture of his right thereto, for such violation. This is most clearly the true reading and exposition of the text of the Constitution. If, however, the requirements of the Constitution must yield to legislative usage, in direct violation thereof, then, of *necessity*, all legislative acts which conflict with these great fundamental principles, should be held, in their construction and application, to the most rigid scrutiny.[28]

That this summary, like most of Blackwell's chapter, was mainly an elaborated restatement of Archibald Williams' extraordinary brief in *Rhinehart v. Schuyler*,[29] that it clearly was aimed at obtuse, erring western courts, especially the Supreme Court of Illinois, became clearer in later passages: "In concluding this branch of the subject it may not be considered improper to make a few suggestions in relation to the constitutional mode of enforcing the collection of taxes." Taxing land and selling it for taxes involved an exercise of the powers of all three departments of government.

> The officer who sells performs an executive function; . . . The legislature declare what facts shall constitute a cause of forfeiture; the judiciary ascertain the facts, apply the rule of law prescribed, and pronounce a judgment of condemnation. For these reasons it has been suggested by an eminent lawyer of Illinois, who has great experience in questions of this character, that "No valid sale of land, for the non-payment of a tax, having the effect of divesting the owner of his estate, can legally take place, unless each of the three great departments of the government concur in the condemnation.[30]

Illinois in 1839 belatedly had revised its procedure to accord with

---
[27] BLACKWELL 35-6.
[28] *Id.* 36-7.
[29] 7 Ill. 375 (1843), discussed Chapter 5, *supra*, n. 60-2.
[30] BLACKWELL 37-8.

these principles, requiring the circuit court's judgment on the Clerk's certified and advertised tax list; and this generally was the law in other states. Even so, the harsh and extraordinary character of the action was not to be overlooked. "No such power as that of selling land for the non-payment of taxes, is to be found in the revealed, natural, civil or common law." But analogous powers, Blackwell conceded, existed in the common law code and in statute law of every civilized nation. One example was the power of eminent domain. Significantly this power required regular judicial inquiry for its exercise. There was

> no difference in principle, between the power of taking land for public use, and the power to tax, and enforce its collection by a sale of the land ... they differ only in degree. Why, then, should not the same solemn forms be pursued in the one case as the other? The only answer is, *state necessity* and *immemorial usage*. The former demands, and the latter sanctions, this departure from the letter and spirit of the Constitution.[31]

Quoting and citing various opinions to this effect, and reluctantly acquiescing for the moment, Blackwell then added that it "undoubtedly [was] a principle of natural justice that every person shall have an opportunity of being heard before he is condemned; and to a hearing every tax payer is entitled—but not before the ministerial officers of the law."[32] Such officers acted at their peril in selling land on which taxes had been paid or were not due; and the taxpayer acted at his peril in risking sale for taxes (and possible redemption and eventual challenge of sale). Not until the taxpayer adopted the latter course was he entitled to a full judicial hearing.

> Thus it will be seen that all of the cases concede that the summary exercise of this power is against the spirit of the Constitution, but defend it upon the ground of immemorial usage and state necessity. But to use the emphatic language of the Supreme Court of Missouri.... "This *very necessity begets another necessity*, that in the execution of such a power the law shall be *strictly and punctiliously* complied with *in all of its requirements.*" Besides, so cautious are the courts in confining the taxing power within the bounds of "state necessity," that they will never permit the enforcement of a penalty, or double tax, in a *summary* manner, under "vague and indefinite pretense of taxation." Taxation includes the power to collect, in a summary mode, the amount levied, from the necessity of the case. This arbitrary, but indis-

---

[31] *Id.* 39-40.
[32] *Id.* 41.

pensable power must be used only to the extent absolutely demanded by the public necessities, and never abused by applying it to the purposes of penal enactments, and under the guise of taxation, to impose penalties which are to be enforced without recourse to the ordinary tribunals. The Constitution protects the citizen from the judgments against his person and property, otherwise than by a jury trial, as heretofore accustomed. . . .[33]

One thus is led to wonder whether Blackwell ever quite made up his mind about some phases of his problem. Or perhaps it would be fairer to say that forensically he needed two strings to his bow, and that the common law had provided those. Certainly American courts never had pooled, still less synthesized, the scattered, fragmentary law of the land cases in any such suggestive, sweeping fashion as this. What they had done, first of all, was to provide these masses—not of precedent, but of dicta—which a creative mind might assemble and repattern to achieve generalized solution of a vexing legal or constitutional problem—a solution that forever after remained in the public domain, and reference now is not to real estate alone, nor even merely to the constitutional law of taxation. Secondly, the courts already had decided a thousand other cases, a large share of which, as Blackwell's last paragraphs implied, treated tax sales and tax titles strictly, indeed with a frank and growing disdain. Blackwell sensed, but never could long bring himself to concede, that past evils—frontier mischiefs—were beyond repair. If in fact it was impossible to extirpate such abominations, it still was the law's duty, as he saw it, to drown them in procedural and statutory technicality.

This was the theme of Blackwell's remaining chapters. Few authors, loathing a subject, have pursued it with such care and detail. The chapter titles reveal the progression: II.) Of the Nature of the Power to Sell Land for the Non-Payment of Taxes, and of the Strictness Required in Such Sales. III.) Of the Onus Probandi. IV.) Of the Election and Qualification of the Several Officers Who Have Anything to Do with the Execution of the Power. V.) Of the Listing and Valuation of the Land. VI.) . . . Levy of the Tax. VII.) . . . Authority to Collect. . . . VIII.) . . . Demand of the Tax. And so on, step by step, through forty-one chapters ending with elaborate discussions of limitation and redemption acts, rules of evidence, *stare decisis*, and fifty pages on statutory interpretation.

Throughout, like a balladist's refrain, ran reminders of the dis-

---

[33] *Id.* 41-2.

reputable features of tax titles, tax deeds, and their purchasers and issuers; astonishment that courts ever had sanctioned such policies; appeals for a strict-pound-of-flesh technicality, for a merciless scrutiny of every step and stage in the summary process. The thesis was that the arbitrary

> nature of the power, the (summary) character of the proceedings, the spirit of the Constitution, the letter of the law, and the true principles of interpretation, all concur in requiring strictness in the execution of this class of powers....[34]

> The principle fairly deducible from the entire field of discussion ... is that *every* requirement of the law, whether *substantial* or merely *formal* in its character, and having the *semblance* of benefit to the owner, which the legislature have said shall attend the execution of the power, ought to be strictly observed by the officers entrusted with its execution, or no title will pass by the sale.[35]

Like other doctrinaires, Blackwell advocated only "true interpretations," but had for himself rather elastic canons. Having at the outset embraced free discretion and extolled the innovating potential of the common law, due process, and the judiciary, all three, singly and in combination, he nevertheless declared himself a literalist (page 72); deplored latitudinarianism and inconsistency (pages 76–77); and demanded strict, inflexible adherence to every requirement:

> In tax titles, the constitutional provisions regulating the taxing power, the statute levying the tax, and prescribing the manner of enforcing its collection, and the acts of those to whom the execution of the power is entrusted, are all essential links in the chain of title—*all of them are matters of record*—and the purchaser is bound to take notice of all omissions or irregularities, which have taken place in the proceedings under which he claims the estate. He is, therefore, to look to it at his peril. The maxim, *caveat emptor*, applies to him with great force.[36]

Ably and eloquently he argued that the burden of proof ought always to be on the purchaser to establish affirmatively that the sale and every thing behind it was regular; this was much easier and fairer than to compel the owner of the land, whose title was sought to be divested, to prove a negative.[37]

---

[34] *Id.* 79.
[35] *Id.* 81.
[36] *Id.* 67.
[37] *Id.* 90-1.

This son of the third Secretary of State of Illinois, nephew of the leading absentee tax agent in the Military Tract, 1825–1840, and counsel for the nonresidents in the great cases of the '40's and '50's, had unique insight into the problem, insight born of family and boyhood experience.[38] Government demanded revenue. But the

---

[38] Robert S. Blackwell's father, David, was territorial auditor in 1817; secretary of state, 1824–1826; and, with his brother Robert (R. S. B.'s uncle), co-editor and co-publisher of the *Illinois Intelligencer* in various partnerships, 1823–1829 (SCOTT, NEWS-PAPERS AND PERIODICALS OF ILLINOIS, 1814–1879 [1910] 340). In 1825 Robert Blackwell & Co. held the state printing contract, publishing not only the state and federal laws but also the auditor's delinquent tax lists, which at this period ran to thirty-eight and forty pages in the *Intelligencer's* special issues. See *id.* Sept. 6, 1823 (9,000 quarter-sections); Oct. 1, 1824 (7,000 tracts sold in Dec., 1823, for taxes 1818–1822); Oct. 7, 14, 21, 1826 (10,000 quarter-sections—the last legislature having advanced the payment deadline from Oct. 1 to Aug. 1 for *both* residents and nonresidents!); Oct. 13, 20, 27, 1827 (9,000 tracts saleable Jan. 1, 1828); Oct. 3, 1829 (8,000 tracts saleable Jan. 1, 1830). See these issues in the "Auditor's Delinquent Tax Volume, 1818–1838," Illinois State Historical Library, Springfield.

From the mid-1820's to the late '30's Robert Blackwell, in partnership with a clerk in the state auditor's office who later (1831–1835) became state auditor, also operated one of the leading land and tax agencies. These partners' business card in the *Intelligencer*, Oct. 7, 14, 21, 1825, announcing 5,000 quarter-sections as saleable Jan. 1, 1826, for accumulated taxes of $4–12 per tract, is a revelation in itself: "The editor of the Illinois Intelligencer in conjunction with J.T.B. Stapp, Chief Clerk of the Auditor's office, where the taxes of nonresidents are liquidated, act as agents for the redemption of land, payment of taxes, recording of deeds, and any other business relating to land agency. Their fees are as moderate as those of any other agent and they will allow the difference of exchange between Illinois money (which is receivable for taxes) and good Eastern funds. All orders on the subject to be postpaid, and letters should be addressed to Blackwell & Stapp, Vandalia, Illinois. Printers throughout the United States are requested to give the above insertion in their respective papers, as many of the lands are yet in the hands of persons who served in the late war. It is hard that their lands should be sold for the want of the proper knowledge in relation to the payment of taxes."

Following the early death of his father, young Robert worked at the tax agency, saw frontier administration at its seamiest, and later, under the tutelage of O. H. Browning and Archibald Williams, drew drastic conclusions and remedies. During the fierce struggle of 1823–1825, in the "era of personal politics," the two elder Blackwells were at odds over slavery. Robert S. in young manhood adhered to his father's free-soil views, but later wavered and reneged.

Leading Military Tract cases in which Robert S. Blackwell appeared as counsel included the following:

(1) Graves v. Bruen, 11 Ill. 431 (1849), co-counsel with A. Williams and C. B. Lawrence against Browning and Bushnell; BLACKWELL 180–3. (2) Irving v. Brownell, 11 Ill. 402 (1849), criticized BLACKWELL 661, 675, 683; cf. 46 Ill. 187 (1867). (3) Ross v. Irving, 14 Ill. 171 (1852), unsuccessfully invoking due process against an occupying claimants statute; here opposed by A. Williams and A. Lincoln, who won reversal on appeal; criticized BLACKWELL 692–3. (4) Harding v. Butts, 18 Ill. 503 (1857). (5) Stearns v. Gittings, 23 Ill. 387 (1860). In these last two cases, Blackwell was the associate of A. Williams, whose briefs vainly stressed due process; Browning and Corydon Beckwith were opposing counsel. Williams' twelve-page printed brief in the last case (#2745) is in the Illinois Archives.

point was that comparatively few delinquencies were perverse and willful:

> Oversight, accident and misfortune, the dishonesty of agents, the neglect of the guardians of infants, and the husbands of women owning separate estates, often interfere to prevent the seasonable payment of taxes. In such cases a sale takes place while the owner is unconscious of the wrong. Shall the innocent owner be protected under these circumstances? Reasonable judges will answer . . . affirmatively. How protected? Not by an immunity from his duty to the government, but by requiring a rigid compliance with the prerequisites of the law.[39]

Blackwell's animus and sympathies thus are everywhere evident. At several points he was perfectly candid about his proposed standards and the intended consequences. *"Very few of these tax sales,"* he quoted a New Hampshire opinion, *"have been found legal; the presumption is, in fact, against their validity."*[40] "Out of one thousand cases of this description, which have found their way into the appellate courts of the country," he noted at another point, "not twenty . . . have been found legal and regular"[41] applying approved and strict tests and standards.

Admitting that government in Illinois never could have operated under such rules twenty years before, he argued that the West had grown up, and pleaded for application of what amounted to the doctrine of changed conditions:

> Railroads traverse the length and breadth of the State; the lands have become valuable; they are either in the hands of actual settlers, or those who are holding them for speculation; the taxes are more promptly paid; the delinquent list . . . instead of requiring an entire newspaper for its publication, has dwindled . . . into a single column; indeed, it may be safely affirmed that the majority of delinquents are now prevented by fraud, accident or mistake, from paying their taxes promptly. Hence the *laxity of strictness* adopted by the courts in early days, on account of the necessities of the government, and the hostility of the settlers to nonresident proprietors—for decisions necessarily partake of the temper of the times in which they are made—is no longer de-

---

[39] BLACKWELL 86–7. Blackwell here was repeating almost verbatim the Williams-bounty-patent titlist argument; and it was oversimplification to say, in the 1850's, that few delinquencies had been willful, or to infer that retrospective acknowledgment of this could resolve existing conflicts and problems. On these matters Blackwell remained a doctrinaire partisan.
[40] *Id.* 92, citing Waldron v. Tuttle, 3 N.H. 340.
[41] *Id.* 93.

manded. It is now safer and wiser, and more in accordance with the spirit of the age, to return to those strict and unbending principles of law which were intended for the security of *private property*, and which the older states know so well how to appreciate.⁴²

On two points Blackwell was tenacious and unquestionably sound and influential. He perceived, as some lawyers and courts had not, the vast difference between making an auditor's tax deed *prima facie* evidence of title, and making it conclusive evidence. To make it conclusive and irrebuttable, either by statute or judicial decision, was in numerous cases to strip the owner of his property, arbitrarily deny him valid defenses, literally take the land of A and give it to B, "the pretended purchaser."⁴³ Secondly, Blackwell saw the equally great difference between decisions which upheld a statute making a tax deed evidence of the regularity and legality of the sale, and between those which extended the statute and force of the deed to cover the authority of the sheriff to sell. On both of these points his analysis and criticisms were penetrating and doubtless contributed to clarification of the issues and law.⁴⁴ The irony was that his arguments were essentially those first advanced by Archibald Williams in *Rhinehart v. Schuyler*. Shorn of the impossible burden of overturning the entire Illinois revenue and title structure dating back to the '20's and '30's, and doing so more for the benefit of speculators than in aid of the unfortunate original owners, the arguments at last exercised greater attraction. Time and judicial erosion already had made academic much of Blackwell's criticism of *Rhinehart v. Schuyler*; but his spirited attacks on that holding⁴⁵ suggest that he and Williams never had reconciled themselves to loss of that great case. *The Treatise* thus is a monument to an acute personal as well as social involvement and frustration.

This fact is of some moment in our inquiry into the sources and pedigree of due process. The "law" in Blackwell's *Treatise* was not simply or even chiefly the law of the reports, or the law of the cases. This learned, self-taught author wrote of law as he wanted it to be, not simply of law as it had been or was. This is the key both to the book's strength and weakness, to its historic significance and present neglect. Much of the "law" in Blackwell's head and treatise never was law in any positivist sense. A great deal of it, the most important part of it—that extraordinary first chapter especially—was in the

---

42 *Id.* 90-1 (a most revealing footnote which begins on page 88).
43 *Id.* 100-3.
44 Marx v. Hauthorn, 148 U.S. 172 (1893) 182.
45 BLACKWELL 28, 107, 179-80; cf. 90-1 as cited *supra* n. 42.

main just "Reason pushing as far ahead as it can." And not Judges' Reason at that! Yet this commoner's Common Law and unpedigreed Reason nevertheless immediately began making, and even remaking, Law. It did so, first, by determining the Bar's approach to the case law of taxation, by helping lawyers and judges find and evaluate the cases. It did so, secondly, by rubbing off the wonderful pollen of due process on the receptive stamen of taxation—then allowing Nature to take its course!

Like the antislavery lawyers and publicists twenty years before— like Ellsworth and Goddard, and Olcott and Birney—Blackwell understood, even better than our generation has at times, the uses, the ways, and the technique of the common law. Like those earlier lawyers, he chose, reforged and employed weapons skillfully, then left them in that armory of experience and ideals which is the common law, for others to use as they saw fit, and as they most certainly, gratefully did.

More and more today we are prone to think of the common law— and of our common law constitutionalism—as something exclusively within the province of the judiciary, something developed only by the judiciary. Constitutional law in other words is professionalized, and in a sense, debilitated. We think of it in terms of briefs, citations, rules, precedents—the technical paraphernalia—smooth, tempered, self-purged of every dictum, only the rules rolling along ball-bearing-like from decision to digest and back again.

Whatever the wonders and the paradoxes of modern automation, it is obvious that this was not the way due process got its start, not the way the Common Law of the Constitution operated in the old Northwest, not even the way it operated once the Lincolns and Fords and Blackwells had grown to manhood and grown a little ashamed of the "JP legal system," of threatened repudiation, and of the vestiges of a "peltry" jurisprudence and economy.[46]

Blackwell, as it happened, was a student and disciple of Lord Coke. Early in the *Treatise* he quoted approvingly Coke's guiding maxim: "In construing a statute we must look to the old law, the mischief and the remedy."[47] For Blackwell as for Coke and Chancellor Kent, the "old law" frequently came first and was a means, not merely of hedging statutes, but of making new law. It was Blackwell's personal maxim, moreover, that where governmental power was by nature "purely arbitrary," as it was where usage and state necessity unconscionably sanctioned summary sale of land for

---

[46] *Id.* 88–91.
[47] *Id.* 60.

taxes, "this furnishes good reason why [that power] should not be exercised in an arbitrary manner."[48] Substance, barred, thus re-entered as Procedure; and dicta were up-graded to rules.

Read in either their cited or their chronological order, the reported cases on which Blackwell based his first chapter are a revelation in this regard: What a vast difference between the rules of those cases and what Blackwell said about and made of them, both individually and in the aggregate. What a vast difference, likewise, between conventional juristic theory about such rules, and about proper use thereof, and between the applications presently made by the profession of passages of this treatise as immediately it began conditioning the Bar's approach to the rules.

In short, it would seem that neither the law as Blackwell found it, nor the law as he left it, nor the law as others came to use it, ever quite squared with the visible antecedents. For one thing, there henceforth was much more accent on the *due*, and on property, and on the possible "spoiliation"[49] thereof, than there was on any mere "process of law." "Mischiefs," in short, now were mainly prospective, not retrospective. "Remedies" were on the make. But this is not surprising. How could we expect to find it otherwise when the problem is to explain how this American guarantee came to rest so far from its "medieval" base and prototype? Perhaps there even was more to the medieval cases than got into the Year Books or *Reports*.[50]

Blackwell obviously had written a best-seller. The professional response was immediate and nationwide. No American treatise had covered any subject more thoroughly for all jurisdictions. Notices were uniformly favorable. The original Chicago edition apparently was exhausted before Blackwell's death in 1863. The second edition, "with 200 cases added," appeared the following year under the Little Brown imprint; the third, with another 400 cases, in 1869; a fourth, with still another 550 cases, in 1875. The fifth and last edition, in two volumes with over 1,200 pages, was published in 1889. These facts record the enduring importance of both book and subject during the thirty years due process was undergoing its greatest transformation.

---

[48] *Id.* 65.

[49] For example, CONKLING'S ARGUMENT, Appendix I, *infra*; and Justice Field's leading opinions from *Slaughter-House* (1873) to the *Income Tax Cases* (1895).

[50] See 2 POLLOCK & MAITLAND, HISTORY OF ENGLISH LAW (2d ed., 1899, 2v.) 31: "The process by which words are specified, by which their technical meaning is determined, is . . . a curious, illogical process. . . . Its course is not circular but spiral; it never comes back to quite the same point as that from which it started. This interplay of reasoning between right and remedy fixes the use of words."

Two distinguished legal authors, Theodore Sedgwick and Thomas M. Cooley, warmly commended the volume. Sedgwick, in his *Statutory and Constitutional Law*, published in 1857, observed that Blackwell had "exhausted the important subject of tax sales. In discussing it he has been led to consider the true boundaries of judicial and legislative power, and his first two chapters contain a close and searching discussion of the whole subject."[51] More critical, and with insights born of more thorough study, Cooley remarked, "Mr. Blackwell . . . has collected the [tax title] cases industriously, and perhaps we shall be pardoned for saying also with a perceptible leaning against that species of conveyance." Yet close reading of Cooley's famous chapters of 1868 reveals how much his own more balanced treatment of "Taxation" and "Protection of Property by the Law of the Land" owed to Blackwell's foregathering of the sheaves.[52] Indeed, Cooley so rarely cited secondary works that his reference to Blackwell at the head of his chapter on Taxation constituted generous acknowledgment in itself.

In retrospect, it is clear that at the time of Blackwell's writing, and even as late as Cooley's writing, there still were the two schools of thought, each representative of a common approach to "the law of the land." One, the conventional, static, or black-letter view, still centered in New England, and took stricter account of the historic procedural and criminal law backgrounds of due process, doubtless reflecting broader knowledge of and readier access to both English sources and professional teaching. The so-called "free" or expansive approach, stronger in the West, South, and rapidly growing commercial states, was more responsive to unhistorical, lay, natural rights, antislavery constructions with their literalist attitude and semantics. Thus, in Massachusetts, even abolitionists remained comparatively earthbound. Charles Sumner, for example, the outstanding black-letter scholar of the movement, resisted temptation to stretch the guarantee, relied rather on the Republican Form of Government Clause and on Equality Before the Law, the latter concept derived as much from French equalitarian theory as from the "self evident truths" of the Declaration.[53]

---

[51] SEDGWICK, *op. cit.*, 357, concluding a discussion of "Summary Judicial and Administrative Proceeding and Tax Sales," 347–57; see also 534–42, 610–2 on due process and law of the land.

[52] See *supra* n. 20.

[53] DONALD, CHARLES SUMNER AND THE COMING OF THE CIVIL WAR (1961) 181–2; L. W. Levy and H. B. Phillips, *The Roberts Case: Source of the "Separate but Equal" Doctrine*, 56 AM. HIST. REV. 510–8 (1956).

The crucial point about Blackwell's *Treatise* is that it tipped this balance decisively in favor of the free or expansive readings. The major due process cases of the '50's and '60's have been treated so often it is enough here to recall that in February, 1856, less than a year after appearance of the book, the two opposing views on the clause were elaborately briefed and argued before the Supreme Court of the United States in *Murray v. Hoboken Land and Improvement Company*,[54] a case involving a form of summary distraint closely related to that in tax sales. Though carefully noting the due process clause of the Fifth Amendment to be a "restraint on the legislative as well as on the executive and judicial powers of the government," and stressing that Congress could not "make any process [it chose] 'due process of law,' by its mere will," the unanimous Court, speaking through Justice Curtis in a decision handed down fifteen days after argument, rejected the "free" construction based on *Taylor v. Porter* and similar authorities, in favor of the conventional black-letter view, ably pressed in this case by the future Justice Bradley as counsel.[55]

Two post-Civil War cases set Blackwell's contribution in perspective. Not till 1893 did the Supreme Court of the United States finally

---

[54] 18 How. 272, 280 (1856). It often has been overlooked that Justice Curtis, sitting at circuit in cases that knocked out the search-and-seizure provisions of the early Rhode Island prohibition laws as violations of procedural due process, relying heavily on and quoting from Judge Bronson's substantive dicta in *Taylor v. Porter*, did much more than anticipate the familiar and so-called "strict" or New England "procedural" definition of due process which he formulated four years later in this case of *Murray v. Hoboken*. Curtis spoke for a unanimous Court in *Murray*. Chief Justice Taney had thought well of the due process usage in the Rhode Island Prohibition cases, *Greene v. Briggs*, Fed. Cas. #5,764 (Cir. Ct., Dist. R.I., 1852, p. 1140); *Greene v. James*, Fed. Cas. #5,766 (Cir. Ct., Dist. R.I., 1853). Yet all were at sixes and sevens over due process in *Dred Scott* 19 How. 393 (1857). "Procedure" and "substance," in short, were insubstantial stuff. See HOPKINS, DRED SCOTT'S CASE (1951) 136-7, and works there cited; also the Maitland quote, *supra*, n. 50.

For another statement of the so-called "strict" or New England view of due process, which likewise reflected the rapid "substantive" development of the 1840's and '50's, see L. A. Jones, *Power of Legislature over Private Property*, 21 MONTHLY LAW REPORTER 449-62 (1858).

[55] Rutgers University's J. P. Bradley Project hopefully soon will be prepared to undertake a full-scale investigation of *Murray v. Hoboken*, a case with fascinating sidelights and personalities, including Samuel Swartwout, one-time associate of Aaron Burr, land speculator, and collector of the port of New York, whose embezzlements and defalcations precipitated the summary distress warrants later at issue in the *Hoboken* case. See 18 DICT. AM. BIOG. (1936) 238; Herskowitz, "The Land of Promise": Samuel Swartwout and Land Speculation in Texas, 1830–1838, 48 N.Y. HIST. SOC. Q. 307-25 (1964). Joseph P. Bradley's participation in this and subsequent *Hoboken* cases obviously gave him extraordinary experience and insights. How far his post-Civil War positions on the scope of due process and equal protection in relation to the taxing power may have reflected this experience is an interesting question.

"Prophet Unhonored": Robert S. Blackwell 541

hold that a state legislature might make a tax deed *prima facie* evidence of the regularity of the sale, of all prior proceedings, and of title in the purchaser; "but as the legislature cannot deprive one of his property by making his adversary's claim to it conclusive, it cannot make a tax deed conclusive evidence of the holder's title to the land."[56] This holding sustained Blackwell in almost his own words, on the point he had labored hardest to establish.[56a] Note also that this decision was rendered (in a case from Oregon!) a full century after the absentees' land problem had first become acute; fifty years after Archibald Williams' argument in *Rhinehart v. Schuyler*; the very year indeed of the Turner thesis on the disappearance and significance of the frontier! The continent was settled, free land gone, when the Court settled the law.

Only three years before, moreover,—in 1890—had the Supreme Court finally held the equal protection clause to be a limitation on the state taxing power.[57] This was sixty years after Kent's homily in the *Commentaries*, and after the first tax sales in the Military Tract; forty-seven years after Williams' original use of Kent; thirty-five years after Blackwell's *Treatise* synthesizing the due process dicta; twenty-four years after the framing of the equal protection and due process clauses of the Fourteenth Amendment, and after Bingham's ambiguous "trial balloon" sounding sentiment for a curbed state taxing power; thirteen years after Justice Miller's testy inference that the due process and equal protection guarantees were *not* limitations on that power; eight years after Conkling's argument and innuendo; even five years after Chief Justice Waite's *Santa Clara* "dictum."

Clearly it was the ancient technical side of due process—notice, hearing, and procedural fairness—that first caught practitioners' interest and attention. As respects the taxing power, and tax sales in particular, this "procedural" side was of immense (but not for long of controlling) importance; it served mainly to link the rights and the guarantee on the one hand, with the broadest power of government on the other. Thenceforth there was to be much less stress on the "law of the land," and much more on *due* process, *just* process, *judicial* process.

Several things are clarified by this book, and by knowledge of its origin. I have repeatedly stressed a lay, popular, nonprofessional element in American due process; more especially the antebellum use

---

[56] Marx v. Hauthorn, 148 U.S. 172 (1893).
[56a] BLACKWELL, Ch. 3, "Of the Onus Probandi."
[57] Bell's Gap R.R. v. Pennsylvania, 134 U.S. 232 (1890); see Chapter 13, *infra*, n. 52.

of the comity-due process-equal protection complex by abolitionist and reformist groups. Such usage nursed and groomed substantive, natural rights concepts, and provided the popular base from which the Fourteenth Amendment was to emerge.

It now is equally clear that this simply is the larger, the ethico-political half, of the story. Side by side with this lay, popular development, we now have found an equally important, equally neglected professional development—one which re-merges, re-nurses, and re-grooms these same elements, clauses, and concepts, and which does this, moreover, in the very areas of the Old Northwest (Ohio and Illinois) and of the northeastern states (New York and Pennsylvania) where the Abolitionist-Prohibitionist movements also were strongest. Taxation was not merely the route by which substantive equal protection-due process made its final entry, 1880–1890; the taxing power was not simply the first power to be curbed after ratification of the Amendment. Taxation also was the field in which the antebellum bar had made its greatest effort and excursus, had made the most prolonged attempt, indeed, to use an inchoate, economic due process-equal protection as a professional ram in the state courts. On the extreme sides, such usage failed utterly. But failure, perversely, was the very thing which in this instance gave impetus and continuity to usage and synthesis. In Illinois, the Archibald Williams-Robert Blackwell-Charles B. Lawrence-Thomas Drummond-B. C. Cook-Corydon Beckwith-O. H. Browning succession and leadership is a revelation in itself; and it appears likely that similar associations and successions are to be found in Ohio,[58] Michigan, and Wisconsin. Ohio and Illinois, at any rate, were foci of this antebellum development, just as they also were foci of the antislavery movement. The two movements reinforced and commingled at Quincy and Chicago in the persons of a number of the Whig-Republican-Unionist leaders listed above,[59] just as the antislavery leadership so often did in the persons of the Birneys, S. P. Chase, John A. Bingham, Thaddeus Stevens, and many others.

Economic no less than humanitarian, due process and equal protection thus had deep antebellum roots. The striking thing, indeed, is how persistently the two concepts seem to have undergone parallel and independent, yet by no means mutually exclusive development; how equal protection cleaves to and reinforces due process in this tax struggle and context, as it did also against slavery; how we find

---

[58] See Chapter 13, *infra*, n. 39.
[59] See Chapter 11, *supra*, Editorial Note, n. 4, 6, and 7; body, n. 10, 11, and 12; and Chapter 12, *supra*, n. 3 and 4.

not only the same principles, but also occasionally the same principals. In both instances, common law constitutionalism ultimately is operating by and through professional practitioners; but in neither is the judicial element yet primary or decisive.

The so-called "great cases," moreover—*Taylor v. Porter, Murray v. Hoboken Land and Improvement Company, Wynehamer v. People, Hepburn v. Griswold,* the *Granger* cases and the *Illinois Railroad Tax* and the *California Railroad Tax* cases—all are linked professionally and doctrinally rather than as mere judicial aberrations or innovations. Thus we have at last a kind of "unified field theory" of due process to supplant or supplement the old "great judges,"—Cooley-Pomeroy-Field—theory of development. In this Blackwell is a pivotal figure. Man and book together, his influence is seen to have been tremendous.

This said, it is important to note the implications and the limitations. We have been tracing and stressing, not a precise, finished, coherent, consistent body of constitutional doctrine, less still an authoritative one; rather, something still inchoate, derivative, opportunist, "sporty and sporting"—hence really a climate of usage, and the sociology and the geography of professional association, influence, and knowledge by which due process and equal protection became what they did, when and how they did. The twisting and the table turnings, the borrowings, the opportunisms, the cross-breedings and the interbreedings, the disparities and the incongruities all are very much a part of this story. We have always had the disconnected cases and citations, the "sporty" dicta, the baffling and puzzling turns. Now we can begin to see more clearly the broader motivations, the professional bases, initiative and leadership, which provided continuity and which assured survival and growth, even in the face of the repeated failures and rejections.

The fallacious idea that many antebellum counsel ever shared modern sophisticated notions and distinctions between procedure and substance when approaching and applying the due process clauses; failure to study usage behavioristically, and to note that the unsuccessful usage was far more extensive than, and just as significant as, the successful; failure to perceive that the linkage and the reinforcement of equal protection and due process extended to tax as well as to racial matters and cases, and antedated the Fourteenth Amendment—these are at once the chief reasons that discoveries have been so long in coming, and springboards for further advance.

More perhaps than any other, due process and Fourteenth Amendment history has suffered from overdoses of false teleology and "presentism." Because this phraseology includes all the universals of Anglo-American constitutionalism, and because it so soon and so thoroughly became the heart of our constitutionalism, we naturally have been predisposed to look at it through current spectacles, interests and prejudices, often reading these back to earlier periods and situations. First came the emasculated, deracialized amendment, then the corporatized-laissez faire one, then the successive reactions to both. It now is time to recognize, as Robert Blackwell and Dean Pound both did in their writings, that the common thread in this whole development has been the common law approach and technique. "Even when we have constitutional texts, we . . . look at them through the spectacles of the common law." Whether we call this approach "common law constitutionalism," "inclusion and exclusion of cases," or "litigation as a substitute for legislation," and for constitutional amendment, the fact is that these two clauses and concepts, by reason of their terms and backgrounds, were best suited to become, and very early became, first the synapses, then the ganglia, then the syncretic lobes, from and through which, first laymen and practitioners, then judges, began to regulate their own, and then our constitutional reflexes and behaviour. Wherever we turn, we find evidence of this, and that is another reason that the anatomy has been so hard to trace out and to chart. And because the axons have long since knit, intergrown, and become a functional complex and system, the tendency has been lately to take the final syncretization for granted, and then busily get on with recording the knee jerks, the brain waves, and more recently, the Rorschachs and couch records.

Going beyond the clinicians, it is plain that the drive for "equality in taxation" (equality as a latent and as a proffered and preferred restraint on the taxing power) extends much farther back into the antebellum period, and has far more significance in the rise of these constitutional restraints, than has been imagined. The lowly tax title and the tax deed had and have a great place in our history. Everyman's Constitution bears lasting marks of it.

Two further reflections occur at this point. One is that Americans obviously gave legislative supremacy a rather thorough, but inconclusive trial down to 1840. Frontier legislatures were supreme in fact, and acted accordingly. The territorial governors of course held the veto; and Illinois had a Council of Revision, 1818–1847.[60] Yet nei-

---

[60] Illinois Constitution, 1818, Art. III, Sec. 19, providing for "a council to revise all bills about to be passed . . . and all bills which have passed . . ." modeled on the New York Council of Revision (New York Constitution, 1777, Art. III; see STREET, THE COUNCIL OF REVISION OF THE STATE OF NEW YORK [1859]).

ther institution served as a substantial check. Neither could. Government at this date had to be free in many of its choices, the legislature untrammelled, in order to cope with the environment. It never will do therefore to tax these legislatures with their handicaps, and argue that this constituted a fair or final test of legislative government under more favorable conditions.

Our main point here, however, is that neither frontier electorates nor their leadership seem to have relished this experience, nor sought to prolong this system. Everywhere the power trends were in favor of the judiciary. Perhaps legislatures in a sense got tarred with the frontier brush, bore the stigma of conditions and chaos which no statutes ever could have caused or cured.

What matters even more, historically, is that once society reached that stage where a more literate bar, the common law, professional adjudication, written opinions and published reports served to make the judiciaries a co-ordinate branch in fact, there then began to be operative these secondary factors that helped make the judiciaries more than co-ordinate. The chief factor, of course, was simply the tactical advantage of having the last word construction-wise, of being the governmental department that had finally to deal with and to resolve such conflicts and headaches as this frontier tax syndrome. But another advantage we can see now, was inherent in this tendency of men trained in use of the common law and use of "precedent" to employ that law, along with natural law, and along with natural law disguised as common law, as auxiliaries to get preferred results in constitutional interpretation.

Here was where the law of the land and due process did double, even triple duty. For the public too participated and acquiesced at these points. Its own political axioms and premises—call them Lockean, Jeffersonian, or simply the American Creed as one chooses —were much the same as the bar's and the judiciaries'. The sum of it is simply that the Bench and Bar thus had the immense advantage of being able to rebuild the foundations of their edifice using political logic and constitutional rhetoric that were here as familiar and acceptable as logs and sod. Since Aristotle's day Justice had been de-

---

For a documented analysis of the Illinois council's revisions, 1826–1827, 1829, see Philbrick, Introduction, ISHLLS, vol. 3, pp. lviii–lxi; PEASE, FRONTIER STATE 63. The council functioned, sporadically at least; some lapses and errors were corrected, thanks chiefly to judicial members; yet very few records were kept, and informal co-operative efforts failed to institutionalize.

A comparative study of these state councils, as related to the development of judicial review and to the Councils of Censors created by the early constitutions of Pennsylvania and Vermont, is overdue.

fined as "giving every man his due." Practically all the constitutions guaranteed every man "due process of law." Due process thus became just process by association and by substitution, not because courts wanted it that way, or at first often construed it that way, but because ordinary citizens already were thinking of it that way, and because the Welds and the Birneys and the Williamses and the Blackwells constantly were capitalizing on the fact and further advancing and popularizing the notion and the trend.

The second reflection is that there is a cosmic, arresting irony in the fact that these two intimate friends of Abraham Lincoln—Archibald Williams and Robert Blackwell—the former the one whom Lincoln called "the strongest-minded, clearest-headed man he ever saw"; the latter, whose license to practice law Lincoln had "perfected" in 1843[61]—should thus be found to have contributed so much to developing and popularizing this due process weapon that Chief Justice Taney in the *Dred Scott*[62] case turned against not only the abolitionists and the Free-Soilers, but against even Senator Douglas' doctrine of Squatter Sovereignty—the doctrine born in the Military Tract—thus committing the irretrievable blunder which more than any other made Lincoln President, brought on the War, the end of slavery, the addition of the Fourteenth Amendment—the latter at last with due process and equal protection clauses. Surely the boomerangs and reverberations of abolitionist usage alone are here compounded infinitely.

The problem no longer is to account for the Chief Justice's usage or error. But one surely would like to know Williams' and Blackwell's reactions to that usage; and we need to comprehend not only these repercussions but also the implications. Certainly one would like to have heard the discussions that took place in these two able lawyers' offices in Quincy and Chicago in March and April, 1857—the discussions throughout the Military Tract for that matter.[63] Was the reaction one of pained surprise? Or simply of bewilderment and consternation? Significantly, Lincoln himself seems never to have made free with due process, either in court or on the stump. But his friends and party[64] did; and in the great debates of 1858 he capital-

---

[61] 2 UNCOLLECTED WORKS OF ABRAHAM LINCOLN (R. R. Wilson, ed., 1948, 2v.) 459; A. Lincoln to Robert S. Blackwell, Springfield, July 24, 1843.

[62] HOPKINS, DRED SCOTT'S CASE 111-40 suggestively, partially reconstitutes early congressional due process usage, placing Taney's dictum in perspective; but see also Chapter 4, *supra, passim*.

[63] See the Quincy *Whig*, March 20, 22, 31, April 1, 13, 14, 25, 1857, for discussion of the case, and criticism of Taney's positions without apparent reference to due process.

[64] See Republican platforms, 1856 and 1860, cited Chapter 4, *supra*, n. 55.

ized Taney's blunder, used Squatter Sovereignty to destroy the "Little Giant of the Tract" politically.[65] But how much did Lincoln see—of what we see today? How much did Williams and Blackwell see? How much could they see?

All one can say is that after a century we now understand well enough that this doctrine and clause were "loaded" long before the time of *Rhinehart v. Schuyler*. They were not the panaceas men thought they were then; and they are not panaceas now. They are no better than the Reason they stand for and the Values they apply. They still are Procedure as well as Substance, still tentative, still imperfect, still chained to the Common Law of Reason rather than wholly liberated by it.

Our findings are another reminder that substantive law is an organic growth, "secreted first in the interstices of procedure." Here again, inertia, arbitrariness, incompatible social objectives, incompetence, sharp practice, and resulting confusion—this time in tax matters on successive frontiers of the West—recreated that old matrix and pattern: Post-frontier lawyers, like their forebears in medieval and revolutionary England, and in colonial America, and like their colleagues and lay-brethern in the struggle against slavery and race discrimination, almost unconsciously "innovated by appeals to pre-existing rights,"—by appeals to a "state of nature" in this instance singularly at odds with the environment whose policies and dross actually had given rise to their attack.

Once the whole American law of due process was commingled with that of taxation—pooled in one volume by Blackwell—something indispensable—at once beneficial and frustrating—was added to each: taxation thenceforth would be (hypothetically at first) less an exercise of naked power; due process thenceforth much more than the historic requirement of notice, hearing, and a day in court (yet again hypothetically at first). Above all, the judiciary, deciding "cases and controversies" in these two fields, automatically was set down (it will no longer do to say "set itself down") for a sizeable extension of its powers, discretion, and responsibilties. This extension still was largely a matter for time and practice to reveal.

What we sense ever more clearly is that the role of the public and the Bar— indeed, of the whole common law tradition—in this process of forever refashioning due process and of giving meaning and vitality to equal protection, has become very badly obscured, and still tends to be underrated—both to the embarrassment of the var-

---

[65] See CREATED EQUAL? THE COMPLETE LINCOLN-DOUGLAS DEBATES OF 1858 (Angle, ed., 1958) 28-9; also the Quincy *Whig*, April 25, 1857, "Squatter Sovereignty."

ious judiciaries and to the deception of the public, for the public in particular obviously fails to grasp its own central role in the constitution-making, constitution-building process. Actually a nation that committed itself, as ours acquiescently yet plainly did, to judicial supremacy and to judicial review under written constitutions, committed itself also to two major corollaries and secondary developments. 1) As precedents accumulated under the Constitution of Powers and under the Constitution of Rights, some more simplified device or formula was certain to be needed and found which would afford a means, not merely of reconciling the precedents in these two areas, but also of reconciling in terms (a) the deference to be accorded the co-ordinate branches with (b) the assumed judicial responsibilities of protecting the private and vested rights of "citizens" and "persons" claiming infringements—some constitutional switching yard or clearance center, in other words, that would combine the needed functions of both a ganglion, and, in racial matters, also a conscience. 2) As ethical perceptions sharpened and became more sensitive in fields like race discrimination, and as legislative, executive, and administrative action increased in scope, judicial review inevitably became more subjective as it became commoner, and this too presumed and required, not merely simplified, less circuitous clearances, but presumed and required also a more sophisticated acknowledgement, eventually, of the still ramifying character of judicial review itself and of the need for a refinement of, and at times for a self-denying limitation on reviewing powers and techniques—in short for a more discretionary, yet self-restrained and controversial judicial review.

These phenomena are in large part those we have had under scrutiny. It now is plain that in matters of race, charter repeals, taxation, eminent domain—in short, even where other constitutional clauses and limitations were available and were freely invoked—the tendency still was toward the coalescence, involvement, and transformation of due process and equal protection. It would appear that as the social mesh becomes progressively finer, so this procedural-substantive accretion or "secretion" necessarily increases along with the higher standards by which government action needs to be, and is, judged. The time accordingly has passed when we can cleave due process down the middle, naively think of one half as "procedural," the other as "substantive." Our fathers were innocent of this barbarism. We alone have been the victims of it. Victims because we so completely compartmentalized learning—divorced law from history, even constitutional law from constitutional history, and virtually bowdlerized them all of both economics and politics, presuming that due process flourished in Lord Coke's day, and down to the *Dartmouth College* Case, then went into hibernation until 1884–1890 except for mysterious stirrings in 1856–1857.

We know better now and can begin to formulate a more rational, unifying hypothesis: "Modern" due process was not something that came on us mysteriously, suddenly, almost unawares during the post Civil War period. It was not a curious aberration of the "new corporate-oriented counsel of the '70's"; still less one of the increasingly corporate-oriented bench of the '80's and '90's; not a formulation or a re-formulation, or an achievement of Mr. Justice Field,[66] nor even of the whole *Slaughter-House* minority—not the result of any single neat or simple cause. Due process and equal protection really are a distillation, an outgrowth, of something more fundamental, more precious, and of much longer duration, than of any or all of these "causes" and "factors." If we must inevitably oversimplify, let us say that the two are the purchase price—on the installment plan—of a written Constitution that is interpreted by laymen, lawyers, and judges—all three—by Everyman trained in the tradition of "utilizing precedent," "Reason," individual and national experience and ideals, the whole of which, historically and textually, is more nearly embodied and expressed in these two quintessential concepts and phrases than in any other single parts of the Anglo-American constitutional heritage. *Per legem terrae*, law of the land, due process of law, equal protection of the laws—this linear progression, succession, and combination, indeed is the longest, largest, most vital and tested common denominator of a common law-minded people determined to live by a law that is just and equal because it is, in its essentials, generally justifiable.

Certainly no better proof of this could be offered than the evidence just reviewed: The Old Northwest was as remote as could be from Westminster. There simply is no more tortuous, watery route than from Runnymede to Plymouth, to the James, to the Hudson, the Mohawk, the Lakes, the Ohio, the Mississippi, the Illinois, and the Sangamon, then back to the state houses and the court houses, and to the Potomac. Yet all these were in their day and still are, frontiers, joining and joined by, a tenuous, indestructible bond—"the tech-

---

[66] Simplistic accounts of the 1930's that made Justice Field the chief architect, and *Slaughter-House* dissent, "revolutionary" or not, the "fountainhead" of constitutional laissez faire (*e.g.*, Chapter 3, *supra*, n. 8) persisted into the '50's, and echo even today: *e.g.*, MCCLOSKEY, AMERICAN CONSERVATISM IN THE AGE OF ENTERPRISE, 1865–1910 (1951, 1964 reprint) 1, 77. Belatedly I disclaim and challenge these views and invite Professor McCloskey's concurrence.

nique of utilizing recorded judicial experience," of transforming and perfecting it into "concepts of ordered liberty." Even the ever-westering frontier, raw and brash though it was, never could forget, nor long lose sight of, its "medieval" inheritance. What Americans brought to the frontier, what the frontier itself re-assimilated, thus was as rare and as vital as the frontier itself. And far more enduring! The fascinations of the Turner thesis sometimes have obscured this. But "Reason pushing as far ahead as it can," or as it dares, had, and must have, innate, overpowering appeal to a people "forever moving on."

EDITORIAL NOTE. Stymied, frustrated, immobilized government—"Government in Ignorance of Law" and of its own processes and decisions—is stark and embarrassing enough in any age. Fifteenth-century England before the introduction of printing; westering American frontiers in throes of overspeculation and hypertrophic growth; even the New Deal United States before establishment of the *Federal Register*:[1] all in turn suffered from this syndrome, a syndrome marked and in part caused by undeveloped, primitive, and sluggish communications.

Contrast now, with these merely chronic, passing, self-liquidating conditions, that pestilent mass affliction and contagion we know as slavery and vestigial racism. Racism still is malignant and retardative precisely because it inbreeds and perpetuates its own bigoted refusal to extend those processes and protections which are the reasons and the bases for government and for social and personal improvement. Mark well this fundamental difference, this all-important contrast between these lesser impasses and that which presently is still our own. Right here is the measure of our difficulty and problem: Any government which fails to function or to govern is in trouble enough; but a government which prolongs, ignores, or condones such failures jeopardizes and destroys itself—destroys its own basis for being. And by this test, racism, as the legacy and the vestige of slavery, plainly constituted, and still constitutes, a unique double threat to any constitutional, representative government resting on consent of the governed. The saving fact, historically, for the Civil War generation, was that slavery—and hence racism—had proved

---

[1] Griswold, *Government in Ignorance of the Law: A Plea for Better Publication of Executive Legislation*, 48 HARV. L. REV. 198–215 (1934).

vulnerable to ethico-moral-religious-constitutional attack, vulnerable to the American ethos and conscience, to the Judeo-Christian conscience and ethic. Here, then, was the hope. And here were the tools.

Everyman's Constitution, thus, was unique merely in this: Its sponsors and its framers sensed—as so many later and still have not—that they as sponsors and framers had to use, and indeed chose to use, in this secular field and emotional borderland, national ideals, national aspirations, national affirmations, and national citizenship historically and legally expressed and declared—had to use these as national pledges, guarantees, and commitments—all to extend the needed protection, to reduce prejudice, to wipe out this odious, lingering race discrimination. These tools were to be what there manifestly *had* to be—the required multipliers and transformers—at once catalysts and reducing agents—means of eradicating this already anachronistic, invidious, menacing system of caste and discrimination.

To all who remain unsympathetic and skeptical, who at first are disposed to quarrel with this reasoned approach, we address one final query: Granted the miscarriages and the difficulties, would caste, customs, mores, and prejudices have yielded, have dissolved any more readily, any more speedily, to any other attack? Would those who have refused to hearken—who still refuse to hearken and to honor these affirmations, commitments, and guarantees—have hearkened to or honored any others, any sooner, any more responsively? If the American Creed and the American Conscience reinforcing religious impulse and religious training and ethical motivation under and within these clauses, did not or does not leaven and enlighten our conduct, our law, and our Constitution, what can, what will?

The fact plainly is that Everyman and his governments, in this one troubled, desperate area, had to remake themselves as they each remade each other. Hopefully Everyman at last can see this.

The American frontier is gone. But the American dilemma remains.

[CHAPTER 13]

The Waite Court and the Fourteenth Amendment

EDITORIAL NOTE. Swift turns and denouements are the prizes and life of research. Everyman's Constitution has known its share. It remains to mention one of the swiftest and most significant.

Humbly, and with delight tempered by acute embarrassment, I realized in 1960–1961 that I at last held convincing proof that Bingham, Conkling, and their fellows of the Joint Committee had not been sophisticated insiders or constitutional cozeners—certainly not tools or allies of those "joint stock companies" which Conkling so ambiguously remarked had come with "petitions and bills," "appealing for congressional and administrative protection against invidious and discriminating state and local taxes."

The beauty of this final discovery lies in its economy and simplicity. It emerged—and that is the proper word precisely—more from a rethinking and restudy than from the turning up of the full texts of those two bills which Bingham (in 1869) had introduced for the companies, and one of which, two years later, he brought to the floor of the House to be quickly and decisively rejected.[1] Some of those texts and bills still are missing. They simply no longer are needed. Bingham's clearance in this matter, and the clearance of other Joint Committee members of the House, is complete, attested by the one man and leader whose knowledge and statement on these affairs, at this point especially, can be accepted as conclusive. That man is C. C. Hine,[2] the same insurance editor and publicist who before and during the Thirty-ninth Congress almost singlehandedly organized and led that stillborn drive for a Federal Bureau of Insurance —and who served as corresponding secretary and volunteer co-ordi-

---

1 See Chapter 3, *supra*, note 54.
2 See Chapter 2, *supra*, notes 63 and 66. Born in 1825, editor of the *Insurance Monitor*, secretary of the International Fire Insurance Company, and publisher of insurance forms and reports, C.C. Hine established himself as a leading insurance publicist and publisher by waging this campaign. Insurance journalism was fiercely competitive in the 1860's. The drive for a national Bureau proved for a time an effective circulation builder; nothing more.

nator during this period when the divided, emergent American insurance industry (as yet a curious example and harbinger of "Triumphant Business Enterprise") still lacked even a trade association.[3]

For nearly two years, Hine had editorialized and lobbied with little success. Congressional indifference to his proffered bills and petitions had been almost complete. His printed circular,[4] dated February 13, 1867, addressed to the supporting companies and various committees, thus provides a fitting climax to our story: From the solicited members of the House, he began,

> Only twenty responses have reached me; of these, six are unfavorable, viz.: Lane and Orth of Indiana; Delano, Ohio; Marvin and Hale, New York; and Cook of Illinois. Mr. Cook is on the Judiciary Committee and personally in favor of the Bill, but says it has no other friend in Committee. [John A. Bingham was a powerful

---

[3] Nothing shows up more strikingly the old notions of an intuitive, clairvoyant, monolithic "capitalism" triumphantly restructuring American constitutionalism and government in its own image and interest, than this insurance-express episode, a vital chapter still in the creation of the national market and economy, but one that must be researched and retold as an integrated whole covering both legislative and judicial development in the states as well as in the federal government. Through the late 1880's, focus remained on the comity and commerce clauses, not on due process or equal protection; judicial, not congressional or business innovation and leadership, was marked and indeed, outstanding. Historians' naïveté and predilections on these matters thus surpassed, and even lately compounded, the corporate bar's. The Justices' role in creating and safeguarding the national market and economy cries for more generous portrayal and acknowledgment, and from these two groups in particular.

[4] The second of two printed circulars prepared and dispatched by Hine as secretary of the Committee of 13; headed "Committee on National Insurance"; bound in a volume of ephemera in the Library of the Insurance Society of Boston; its gold-stamped cover labelled "Nat'l Board F.U. and First Auxillary"; shelved with annual reports of National Board of Fire Underwriters.

Hine's first circular, dated November 15, 1866, had attributed failure to the "unprecedented pressure of political matters" and urged continued effort in behalf of House Bill 738 calling for a national bureau of insurance.

The fourteen favorable responses were from "Hulburd and Griswold of New York; Dixon and Deming, Connecticut; Alley, Massachusetts; Lynch, Maine; Baxter, Vermont; Scofield, Pennsylvania; Julian, Indiana; Upson, Michigan; Ingersoll, Baker, and Farnsworth, Illinois; and Price of Iowa." A hopelessly divided, competitive industry marshalled no more support in the northeast than in the midwest. General agencies in the west indeed were as influential as companies.

"Cook of Illinois" was Burton C. Cook, 1819–1894, Republican from the Ottawa district who served in the Thirty-ninth to Forty-second Congresses, from March 5, 1865, resigning August 26, 1871, to become one of the leading counsel for the Illinois railroads in the *Granger* and other cases. An economic nationalist of a regulative bent, who had seconded Lincoln's nomination at Chicago, and nominated him in 1864, and who also served on the Peace Convention in 1861, Cook is an ideal subject for students wishing to trace interests and continuities from the 1850's on. He sponsored a number of bills important in the early history of the commerce power and free commercial intercourse movements of the 1860's.

member of the Judiciary Committee, so this statement can be taken as doubly exclusive!] Fourteen favorable responses are in my hands, some of them quite encouraging. . . .

The fourteen were then named. Not one was a member of the Joint Committee!

At long last, then, here is the *coup de grâce*. For Roscoe Conkling, and for the Conspiracy Theory as such. Even, hardly less obviously, for that modified "secondary intention" hypothesis insofar as it related to the once-baffling role of the insurance companies. Even for the notion that anything other than achievement of racial protection in fact, and the systematic extirpation of caste and racial inequality in the exercise of fundamental rights, motivated the draftsmen and sponsors of Everyman's Constitution.

My embarrassment stemmed only from the fact that I actually had held this disproof—a transcript of the Hine circular—several years without fully appreciating its implications or significance. So strong were the masking and the camouflaging powers of patterned inference and circumstance. So hardy, tricky, tacky a question-beggar was that lingering notion of "conspiracy" once it had got "seemingly" half-"corroborated" by so many vagrant fortuities!

Hypothesis and the use and interpretation of legal evidence are so central and vital to constitutional history that a denouement which at this point partakes a little of an autopsy may help get these matters and problems in a better focus. When a scholar-statesman as outstanding as Henry Cabot Lodge,[5] and historians of the caliber of the Beards go overboard; when economic and social historians as able as Louis M. Hacker[6] and Harold U. Faulkner[7] also nod; when the leading constitutionalist of the day, A. C. McLaughlin, delicately reprobes these same issues, and also misses—even fails to nail the basic fallacy and confusion—surely it is time to ask and to observe why "theory" and inference here proved even more stubborn than stubborn fact.

The first reason, extenuating or not, concerns the quality and the remoteness of much of the evidence which historians, in lack of better, naturally grasp at, and hence get taken in by. In the instant case of the Conspiracy Theory, even as late as 1958–1959, these va-

---

[5] See *Introduction, supra*, pp. 18–19, and 52 CONG. RECORD, part 2, p. 1158–1159, January 8, 1915.
[6] See Editorial Note, Chapter 3, *supra*, p. 100, note 5.
[7] See his AMERICAN POLITICAL AND SOCIAL HISTORY (3d ed., New York, 1944) p. 388–390.

grants and dissemblers, these over-suggestive, grossly misleading circumstances still embraced and included the following:

1. In one of his earliest speeches of 1866, Bingham, as noted in Chapter 1, spoke ambiguously of need for a curb on the state taxing power.[8] Tendentiously? A trial balloon?

In light of Blackwell's *Treatise* and of the neglected antebellum conflicts over tax equality surveyed above, what significance could have attached to such reference? By 1959–1960, one thing seemed reasonably sure: The corporate "person" no longer had to be postulated as the condition precedent to an economic-substantive use of due process and equal protection, at least not in tax matters. Even conceding the paucity of judicial holdings prior to 1866, there manifestly had been other forces and trends at work, and these now gave the Beards, if not the last word, at least rebuttals and rejoinders. The issue, of course, remained whether Bingham's remark had been made simply with reference to an added power needed to curb tax discrimination against the freedmen and Southern loyalists. (This, I have come to think, was the train of Bingham's thought.)

2. Somewhat less ambiguously, Conkling in his *San Mateo* argument[9] (1882) hinted that addition of the words "taxes, licenses, and exactions of every kind" to Section 16 of the re-enacted Civil Rights bill of 1870 signified not merely congressional understanding that the Fourteenth Amendment in fact had curbed the state taxing power (and that the Court in the 1880's ought to follow the congressional construction), but seemingly also that there may have been subtle, unexplained, unacknowledged *realpolitik* at work here.

3. As a matter of fact, Justice Field in his *San Mateo* opinion at circuit, just three months before Conkling's argument, also had cited[10] Congress' addition of this phrase in support of his own interpretations and positions. Mindful of the Field-Conkling friendship after 1877, the nagging question comes to be whether Conkling had flattered Field by picking up this point and addressing it to the full Court, or whether Field, sometime earlier perhaps, had been "briefed" by Conkling. In either case, as also with that unresolved reference by Bingham, the taxing power had a centrality and focus it previously lacked, and one which made mere dismissal of these questions—and of the notorious insurance-express company activity —not merely difficult, but impossible.

---

[8] See Chapter 1, *supra*, note 63; Bingham's speech of January 25, 1866.
[9] See Editorial Note, Chapter 1, *supra*, CONKLING'S ARGUMENT (original paging p. 33).
[10] The Railroad Tax Case. County of San Mateo v. Southern Pacific RR. Co., 8 Sawyer, 238, 252–253 (Cir. Ct., D. Calif., Sept. 25, 1882).

4. To complicate things further, Conkling had visited San Francisco during the summer of 1869.[11] As senator he there had heard lawyers for the Chinese Six Companies attack California's unconstitutional Foreign Miners' and Passenger taxes, both of which in practice hit only Chinese. At the next session of Congress, Section 16 had been aimed ostensibly at such discriminations. But had its intent and motivation been wholly racial? Or must innuendo, contrived or not, cloud these matters forever?

5. Bingham too had visited San Francisco during the summer of 1871, and his visit had been followed by the *Alta California*'s suggested use of the Civil Rights Acts and of the Fourteenth Amendment against striking miners, against that "Amador Conspiracy."[12]

6. Conkling's elder brother Frederick, it appeared, had been president of the Aetna Fire Insurance Company when the Fourteenth Amendment was drafted and ratified;[13] and William Barnes, the New York state superintendent of insurance[14] who with Elizur Wright pioneered effective state regulation at this time, was the son-in-law of Thurlow Weed and another New Yorker whose role and affiliations excited interest. Where and how was all this to end? What could be the answer?

Rehearsal of such *poseurs* might be much extended, but to little profit. The point is that decades of professional and political association obviously lent themselves to extractive, speculative conjecture, given only those terse, original, suggestive claims and presumptions. Too many associations were too easily extracted and seriously considered—selected almost as if by spotlight, by a still-presumptive luminescence.[14a]

---

[11] San Francisco *Daily Times* and San Francisco *Daily Alta California*, June 25–26, 1869; E. C. Sandmeyer, *California Anti-Chinese Legislation and the Federal Courts: A Study in Federal Relations*, 5 PACIFIC HISTORICAL REVIEW 189–211 (1936). For the position of the Chinese in California, 1867–1874, the years during which Justice Field was confronted with the problem of their protection, see the Bancroft Scraps, Chinese, vol. 6, pp. 34–279, Bancroft Library, Univ. of California, Berkeley.

[12] See Chapter 3, *supra*, notes 63, 67, 68, especially the *Alta California* editorial of July 26, 1871, "The Federal Authority and the Amador Conspiracy," p. 2, col. 1. On the same page, col. 4, appeared the announcement of the California Republican Ticket "Ratification Meeting . . . July 29th . . . Hon. John A. Bingham of Ohio" as speaker! A month earlier, Bingham had been campaigning in the city during the Amador outbreaks; see *Alta California*, June 23, 1871 p. 1, col. 1; cf. also col. 2, "The Amador Communists."

[13] See BIOG. DIR. OF THE AM. CONGRESS, 1774–1927 (Washington, 1928) p. 839.

[14] See Chapter 2, *supra*, note 69; N.Y. DEP'T OF INSURANCE, 5TH ANN. REP'T for 1863, dated March 1, 1864, p. x–xv, for his elaborate comity clause argument, later much used by Hine and others.

[14a] For a striking example, see MOTT, DUE PROCESS OF LAW (1926), p. 188, marvelling again at failure of litigants, judges and commentators to *foresee* the substantive

Only as these irrelevant, misrelated, often plausible, "seemingly" significant facts and conjectures were worked off and discarded, one by one, as they were after 1959, could the situation finally be viewed objectively.

There is no need to rethread these labyrinths. Humility, like charity, begins at home. Though lonely enough, my research odyssey at least was symptomatic, derivative, and now, I think, conclusive: prescience and divination were powers given to gods alone. The good life, liberty, security, and protection are the goals; the noblest, most difficult works and achievements of constitutional man.

"Prejudice," Bierce's *Devil's Dictionary* states, is "vagrant opinion without visible means of support." By no means all prejudice shared and encountered has been racial. In American history, simply the bulk, the worst of it.

A teleology which spuriously and unconsciously imposes itself on historical data or evidence, a false patterning of events that originates in the mind of the author, is the bane of historical writing. This hazard of course becomes much greater wherever and whenever we deal with legal materials, and especially with legal and constitutional cases and ideas. For these, like Law in the aggregate, are precedential and accretional. Hence they often appear, in retrospect, neatly purposive and much more the products of insight and design than ever could have been the case prospectively. Add to this basic hazard the coral-like sociological growth of law; add also this conspiracy hypothesis suffused with suspicion and replete with ambiguity; add finally the viewers' chronic, easygoing disregard for time values and for Negro rights, both over a long century, and their disregard also for the generality and the ambiguity of so many statements and hypotheses—and our rationale, our autopsy, is complete.

It is time, we suggest, that jurists and historians recognize, and make every effort to counter and limit, those mutual hazards of a mutual innocence which are present when each group deals, as both groups must, with the other's specialty and problems. If historians need to "reclaim"[15] much in law that masquerades as history, they need no less—perhaps even more—to master and apply more effectively, the law's rigorous tests for (and distinctions between) fact, presumption, and proof. Judges on their part ought to be equally chary, certainly in major constitutional cases, of misemploying history as a justifier of current policy and decision. Constitutionalism

---

development of due process! Mott in this chapter overlooked Blackwell and his *Treatise*.

[15] See Editorial Note preceding Chapter 8, *supra*, note 2.

and history are complex enough, without adding to either the other's burdens and problems.[16]

* * *

By 1961, the Court, the Corporation, and Conkling no longer were the self-supporting, self-justifying trio they had been in the 1930's. That fact in itself, with the reduced notoriety, was one thing which rekindled professional interest, which demanded an accounting and updating. So it came about that preparation of a paper on this triple theme "revisited," for the American Historical Association meeting in 1961,[17] afforded occasion to recanvass the evidence, to try once again for a final verdict. It was then that the Hine Circular emerged from undeserved obscurity and things fell into proper perspective.

One additional fact—and this, we submit, is the final clincher—produced precisely the same effect. Those long-missing bills which Bingham as a leading member of the House Judiciary Committee introduced and reluctantly sponsored on behalf of the insurance companies, 1869–1871, had, after the Fourteenth Amendment had come into force, sought not protection for corporations as "persons" under the new guarantees; these bills too sought protection for corporations as "citizens" *under the old comity clause!*[18] Moreover, manuscript journals of the House Judiciary Committee, together with the congressional debates and the Hine circular of 1867, leave little doubt that Bingham and Ben Butler simply reported out a substitute bill, and went through the motions,[19] to show insurance men the facts of political life.

"The good old ways, the simple plan," manifestly had held sway

---

[16] See M.D. Howe, THE GARDEN AND THE WILDERNESS (1965).

[17] Graham, "The Court, the Corporation, and Conkling Revisited," a paper read at the American Historical Association Meeting, December 28, 1961.

[18] For these bills, committee action thereon, and the final outcome, see *infra*, Appendix II.

[19] See Chapter 3, *supra*, note 54, regarding the House debate and action Feb. 15, 1871. It is possible that various bills in aid of "free commercial intercourse," 1866–1871 provided the basis for Conkling's innuendo. That corporate *realpolitik* was involved in bills introduced by Representatives Samuel Shellabarger of Ohio and B.C. Cook of Illinois, as well as in those of Bingham and Butler, 1869–1871, is more than likely. Innuendo and inferences drawn from this common-place activity were what got out of hand. See the B.F. Butler Papers, January-February, 1871, Library of Congress, for letters of A.B. Tallman, Isaac Sherman, and W.L. Barnes for examples of businessmen's proposals.

Samuel Shellabarger was one of the Southern Pacific counsel in the *Railroad Tax Cases*. On March 28, 1871, he also had made one of the clearest speeches in Congress on the articulation of the War Amendments, the relations of the various clauses, the intent to grant full power to deal with the racial adjustment. See APPLETONS' ANN. CYCLOPEDIA, 1871, p. 187.

here, but in ways rather different from those historians long imagined. The outcome is a parable for true believers and skeptics alike, no less than for the corporate bar. Government somehow must govern. Ruses and subterfuges pall. Neither legislatures nor courts obligingly emasculate themselves. Neither dares relinquish powers over business to business, or to abolish state lines by acquiescing in a simple syllogism. The Court and Congress accordingly had no choice but to reject again this sterile resurrected corporate "citizen."[20] Both might have gone on rejecting it till doomsday had not this swift congressional rejection—following hard on the New Orleans butchers' successful exploratory arguments in the *Slaughter-House* cases at circuit[21]—happily turned thoughts and pleas in new directions.

Actually the corporate "person" was the final element in this "new" turn and new synthesis, not the first. And even then the "person" was no shoo-in, judicially speaking. That fact counsel for the Continental Life Company shortly learned from Justice Bradley's and Judge Wood's swift rejection in *Insurance Co. v. New Orleans*.[22]

Constitutional choice and protection too are born of experience and perseverance. *Insurance Co. v. New Orleans* and the *California Railroad Tax Cases* evidence that. So too, probably, we are to learn in the present chapter, does Chief Justice Waite's otherwise unexplained, or inexplicable, *Santa Clara* dictum on the corporate "person." In any case, the crucial point, constitutionally, is that another fifteen years elapsed before the Chief Justice even made his apparent concession, and still another four years elapsed before Justice Field, after Waite's death, finally clinched and consolidated that apparent concession. These were the years in which corporations were demonstrating their capacities and transforming the United States. These were the years in which the Justices needed and groped for new, syncretizing, and discretionary tools. These were the years in which due process and equal protection repeatedly were offered as just such tools and devices.

Constitutional protection and innovation are slow business precisely because they are more sociological than verbal; inspiring and inspiriting, but not intuitive, not inspired!

Preparation of a second paper, "California, the Fourteenth Amend-

---

[20] See Chapter 3, *supra*, notes 52–57; Chapter 9, *supra*, notes 50–59.
[21] *Id*.
[22] See Chapter 9, *supra*, notes 57–58. President of the Continental Life Insurance Company (one of the companies that had supported the Hine drive and bills 1865–67) was Justus Lawrence, 1817–1873 (obituary in 36 U.S. INSURANCE GAZETTE p. 177).

ment, and the "Study Pestilence"[23] served to clear up another matter. Whatever the background and purpose of Conkling's allusion to the Civil Rights Act of 1870 may have been, the legislative history and the congressional debates[24] showed clearly enough that the stressed "taxes and licenses" phrase had been expressly added to cover and to outlaw California's unconstitutional taxation of the Chinese. The racial motivations of the framers, of the Amendment, of Congress thus were reconfirmed and rebuttressed. Justice Field's stand against Chinese race persecution won added support and admiration. "Specious," "contrived": these still were the words for Conkling's claims, individually and severally.

During 1963 two major works further clarified roles and attitudes. C. Peter Magrath's *Morrison R. Waite* was the first biography of the Chief Justice based on unrestricted use of the Waite papers. These papers I had spot-checked in 1960, noting especially one exchange between Waite and the Court reporter, J. C. Bancroft Davis, which seemed at last to explain the *Santa Clara* dictum. Later that year (1963) John P. Roche revealed[25] an equally important exchange which showed that Justice Bradley, writing to Circuit Judge Woods in 1870–1871, had at that time held the correct, affirmative, antislavery, "Justice Harlan" view of the scope of equal protection, a view squarely at odds with his *Civil Rights* opinion of 1883.

Here were two more vital missing links—stroboscopic flashes only, but flashes which illuminated and transfixed major cases and shifts.

"The Waite Court and the Fourteenth Amendment" is a review article or chapter, frankly summary and interpretive. In no sense is it offered as the last word—even my own—on Everyman's Constitution. Written during the months of the sit-ins and the Selma showdown—just thirty years after first tackling Justice Field, the Railroads and the Ninth Circuit law, and just as the Court and Congress

---

23 Read before the Berkeley Fellowship of Unitarians, Berkeley, California, February 24, 1963.

24 See Chapter 13, *infra*, note 50; for similar conclusion, see Sandemeyer, *supra* note 11. Samuel Shellabarger's bill of 1866, offered as an amendment to Trumbull's Civil Rights Bill of 1866, (See Trumbull Papers, Library of Congress) had had a "taxes and license" clause; cf. also Bingham's reference to a taxing power curb (*supra* note 8). Such provisions were favored and sponsored by leaders of the "freedom of intercourse" and "freedom of transit" movements in the Thirty-ninth to Forty-second Congresses; and they obviously encouraged the Supreme Court to void such flagrantly unconstitutional restraints as Nevada's stagecoach tax (*Crandall v. Nevada*, 6 Wall. 35, 1868) and Maryland's anti-drummer law (*Ward v. Maryland*, 12 Wall. 418, 1871).

25 See Chapter 13, *infra*, notes 22–24.

together were releasing us from the vices and the vise of state action[26] and national inaction—this essay at least is no snap judgment. It endeavors to draw threads together and focus the major findings and problems.

---

[26] See Chapter 13, *infra*, note 14. This Bradley-Woods correspondence was quoted by Solicitor General Cox in the Supplemental Brief for the United States as Amicus Curiae (pp. 75-76) in the cases reported as *Bell v. Maryland*, 378 U.S. 226 (1964). Note especially Justice Goldberg's concurring opinion at p. 286, 309-310 (text also in POLITICAL AND CIVIL RIGHTS IN THE UNITED STATES 3d ed., 1967, pp. 2098, 2105).

[CHAPTER 13]

CERTAINLY not many lawyers could have stood it, fewer would have, and no one else has had to: Morrison R. Waite alone was "His Accidency"—successor to the great Salmon P. Chase; President Grant's seventh choice for seventh Chief Justice; "that luckiest of all individuals known to the law, an innocent third party without notice."[1] "Dean of Toledo's Bar, A Common lawyer indeed!" Democrats chortled. "A new man that would never have been thought of for the position," Justice Field remarked, "by any person except President Grant . . . an experiment which no President has a right to make with our Court." Named and confirmed, eight-and-a-half months after Chase's death; after, in that incredible sequence, Roscoe Conkling, Hamilton Fish, and Senators Timothy O. Howe and Oliver P. Morton each had declined unsolicited proffers, and after, in the most humiliating climax imaginable, the names of George H. Williams, Grant's incompetent, if not corrupt Attorney General, and Caleb Cushing, an overage (and, opponents claimed, senile) partisan opportunist, each had gone to the Senate, then been withdrawn to escape certain rejection.

"A hard parturition," Secretary of State Fish described it in his diary; and the unfazed Williams, surveying assembled Justices and fellow disappointees at a banquet on the eve of Waite's swearing-in, muttered *sotto voce*, "Did you ever see so many corpses at one funeral!"[2]

---

[1] Quoted from C. PETER MAGRATH, MORRISON R. WAITE: THE TRIUMPH OF CHARACTER (New York: The Macmillan Company, 1963), of which this essay is in part a review.
[2] *Ibid.*

"His Accidency," "experiment" or not, Morrison R. Waite made a good, in some respects outstanding, Chief Justice; served the fourteen years 1874–1888; confounded critics and skeptics alike; won over the colleagues who at first had snubbed him; scorned talk of the Presidency; worked himself literally to death; and managed, without judicial experience, to fill the highest judicial office creditably, at times with a modest distinction.

Rugged, amiable, unpartisan, a small-town property lawyer with thirty-five years of circuit riding and general practice behind him, Waite certainly was not the tyro or the "Jonah" cynics and the public had feared. Unprepossessing, a short, thickset person with very plain—indeed rough features," Field described him, "yet gentlemanly and dignified." "Take the place that belongs to you," he once counseled his nervous wife, "not offensively, but let everyone feel it is yours."[3] Waite had in abundance precisely those qualities he needed most: stamina, poise, a sense of fitness, integrity, capacity for growth. If President Grant might have done better, he might also have done—and too often did—much worse.

Waite's public record at nomination unquestionably was "thin," yet not undistinguished. Son of a chief justice of Connecticut, well educated and studious, a Yale graduate who emigrated at once to the Toledo region, he served single terms in Ohio's House and on the Toledo council, was twice defeated as a Whig-Republican for Congress, and during the Civil War declined appointment to Ohio's court. Successful service as the United States' third lawyer at the Geneva arbitrations brought national recognition in 1873, and he was serving as President of the Ohio Constitutional Convention when the astounding news came that he was Grant's final nominee.

The big job and underachievement thus had never been problems for Morrison R. Waite. Letters written to his ailing wife during the first weeks in Washington reveal almost unbearable strain.[4] "Judge Clifford is the martinetest of all martinetts [sic]."[5] Opinion writing came hard and always remained so. "The difficulty with me is that I cannot give the *reasons* as I wish I could," he once told Field, who suffered no such handicap.[6] Like Beveridge, Magrath has an eye and a gift for portraiture. Glimpses such as these, winnowed by the dozen from the voluminous heretofore-unused Waite Papers at the Library of Congress, make for a striking work. Morrison R. Waite was indeed

---

3 *Id.* at 103.
4 *Id.* ch. 6.
5 *Id.* at 103.
6 *Id.* at 185.

an extraordinary ordinary man. His was "the triumph of Character," —of character over Gilded Age circumstance, the very definition of high and rewarding comedy. This is a judicial biography in every sense, and a portrait of distinction.

Waite concededly was no John Marshall. Yet he was hardly less the man and judge for his times—Chief Justice for a strong Court, as Marshall had been for a weak one; a needed balance wheel; a shrewd judge of men and character (Waite saw through Roscoe Conkling for example, mistrusting and dismissing him as an unsavory boss and "henchman"); a Chief who declined to be pressured or browbeaten by Field,[7] who made full use of Bradley's scholarship and Miller's powers, who held his Court together under the most crushing docket and arrearages of its history, who finally, during an illness in 1885, had the satisfaction of an acknowledgment from Miller that the Chief Justiceship was a far bigger job that he had realized—this from the Justice who ten years before had been more pejorative even than Field ("mediocre," "a sow's ear")[8] yet who, presiding at conferences in Waite's absence (and none too successfully), came to the fairer estimate.[9]

Magrath avoids extended retreatment of the familiar leading cases. Instead there are concise summaries and evaluations of the Court's work in the principal fields: reconstruction, race, economic and corporate regulation. Case law, social setting, monographic literature, letters and memoranda are skillfully synthesized, with focus sharply personal and biographic. Waite and his Court relive in these pages, and there are admirable accounts of intra-Court liaison and one brilliantly researched and written chapter—"Court Packing in the Gilded Age"—details for the first time, from the Garfield and Whitelaw Reid Papers, the pressures that culminated in Stanley Matthews' renomination to the Court in 1881.

Another most significant discovery shows how unhistorical and chancy the decision in the 1883 *Civil Rights Cases*[10] really was. From Mr. Justice Bradley's majority opinion (which in effect declared unconstitutional Sections 1 and 5 of the Fourteenth Amendment)—and certainly from the pother since over the nature and limits of "state" and "private" action—one might guess that the framers of this phraseology were mere logic choppers who regarded slavery as a paper dragon. Actually they were men who knew and dealt with that

---
[7] *Id.* at 258–60.
[8] *Id.* at 107, 271–72.
[9] *Id.* at 273.
[10] 109 U.S. 3 (1883).

institution as one which emancipation had barely touched. Slavery for them was a system of caste—of *institutionalized* race prejudice, disability, and discrimination.[11] Countless cultural residues—"badges, incidents and indicia" were the current tags—remained to be eradicated. Deeply rooted in thought and custom, these could be reached under the federal system only if *both* Congress and the courts were given added constitutional powers to deal with the lingering "abridgments," "denials" and "deprivations." That was the whole purpose and effect of Sections 1 and 5. Many thought the Thirteenth Amendment already had gone the whole way, but Bingham and the moderates thought best to play it safe. Accordingly they "constitutionalized" the Civil Rights Act of 1866, which itself of course specifically reached and voided discriminations grounded in "custom' as well as in laws, statutes, etc.

All this was taken for granted and went without saying in the late 1860's and '70's. It underlay and informed Justice Miller's forceful statement in the *Slaughter-House Cases*,[12] and it repeatedly was made explicit in congressional speeches and papers. Backsliding and hedging developed later and culminated in the sectional bargain or "settlement" of 1877.[13] Justice Bradley's *Civil Rights* opinion thus was indeed "a period piece"[14]—an accommodation to national inertia and letdown, to the absurd belief that if the country only would

---

[11] See generally Chapters 4–7, *supra*, and TENBROEK, THE ANTISLAVERY ORIGINS OF THE FOURTEENTH AMENDMENT (1951); Frank & Munro, *The Original Understanding of "Equal Protection of the Laws,"* 50 COLUM. L. REV. 131 (1950); Kelly, *The Fourteenth Amendment Reconsidered: The Segregation Question*, 54 MICH. L. REV. 1049 (1956).

[12] 83 U.S. 36 (1873). See the passage quoted at note 47 *infra*.

[13] Dr. Magrath's treatment of these matters, and of Waite's relation to Reconstruction and to race problems and cases generally, MAGRATH, *op. cit. supra* note 1, chs. 7–9, will seem to many perhaps the least satisfactory section of his book. The problem —even the biographic problem at this date—is not simply to show that Waite and his colleagues—all able and conscientious men, to be sure—were "men of their times." They were men of their times and of a generation who in the end guessed wrong, who abandoned and betrayed the principles and the constitutional theory which they themselves in many instances had held, understood, and approved—more, or better perhaps, than John Marshall Harlan had at first. The trouble was they did not see, as Harlan did, that to defer this problem, above all to deny Congress power to deal with it, was to aggravate it, to let the *mores* of the slave system and era harden, scatter, and consolidate under freedom. By reason of his apostasy, of his great learning, intellect, and sway over Waite and Woods, Mr. Justice Bradley is a truly tragic figure in our constitutional history; Harlan—patronized by Holmes and others as a commonplace intellect—becomes truly heroic. One must read deeply in both the proslave and antislave arguments, and in the congressional debates, to appreciate fully the soundness, scholarship, and learning of Harlan's *Civil Rights* dissent; the majesty of the prose and the wisdom of the policy judgments today are self evident. See Westin, *John Marshall Harlan and the Constitutional Rights of Negroes: The Transformation of a Southerner*, 66 YALE L.J. 637 (1957).

[14] Roche, *Civil Liberty in an Age of Enterprise*, 31 U. CHI. L. REV. 103, 108 (1963).

ignore vestigial racism (and the then-recent constitutional pledges) the problems might disappear.

What Magrath now brings to light is an exchange of correspondence[15] showing that Mr. Justice Bradley himself, in 1871, was responsible for the wording of one of the clearest and soundest early constructions of the Fourteenth Amendment. Circuit Judge Woods of New Orleans had written him for guidance in the today-too-little-studied case of *United States v. Hall*.[16] A peaceful Republican gathering of Negroes engaged in political discussion had been broken up by armed whites who killed two and wounded more than fifty. Alabama's authority had been involved by the state's failure to provide protection. Perceiving that the Fourteenth Amendment laid an affirmative obligation on the states to protect the freedmen and to secure equality of rights in this regard, Justice Bradley advised Woods:

> Congress has a right, by appropriate legislation, to enforce and protect such fundamental rights, against unfriendly or insufficient State legislation. I say unfriendly or insufficient; for the XIVth Amendment not only prohibits the *making* or enforcing of laws which shall *abridge* the privileges of the citizen; but prohibits the states from *denying* to all persons within its jurisdiction the equal protection of the laws. *Denying* includes inaction as well as action. And denying the equal protection of the laws includes the omission to protect as well as the omission to pass laws for protection.[17]

In his subsequent opinion,[18] Judge Woods incorporated verbatim this passage which begins "Denying includes inaction as well as action." That, in short, in 1871 was still the proper and prevalent view, as is shown by similar statements made in Congress.[19] Today it strikes us as odd at first only because common sense has suffered so long under the state action syndrome. To get back to reality, to sense the mood and the urgency of 1866—to say nothing of 1964— what would we think today, what would the world think, of pleadings or decisions in German or international courts contending that the measures taken in our time against genocide and for purging of racism had no intended place, could have no permitted effect, wher-

---

[15] Excerpted and discussed more fully in Roche, *supra* note 14 at 108–10. See also MAGRATH, *op. cit. supra* note 1, at 121. The Bradley Papers are in the custody of the New Jersey Historical Society, Newark.

[16] 26 Fed. Cas. 79 (No. 15282) (C.C.S.D. Ala. 1871).

[17] Letter from Bradley to Woods (draft), March 12, 1871. The correspondence began with a letter from Woods to Bradley, December 24, 1870.

[18] United States v. Hall, *supra* note 16, at 81.

[19] See, *e.g.*, the remarks of Senator John Pool of North Carolina, CONG. GLOBE, 41st Cong., 2d Sess. 3611 (1870), and the congressional debates on the KKK Act, CONG. GLOBE, 42d Cong., 1st Sess. 575–80, 693–94 (1871).

ever discrimination or outrage were derivative from, or were perpetrated (or perpetuated!) by, "custom," "individual prejudice," "private action"? If "the *mischief* determines and measures the remedy," must not the *evil* do likewise? Can it be supposed rational minds reason, legislators legislate, amenders amend on any other basis? Slavery and its residues were as hateful and repugnant in 1866 as Nazism has been in our time. Governments were deemed governments in 1866 precisely as now. The function, the duty of governments is to protect. The declared function, the declared duty of American governments under this phraseology was then, is now, to protect *equally*. Where, in nine centuries of Anglo-American constitutional and legal history can be found folly, failure, recalcitrance to match this? Had constitutionality of civil rights enforcement been decided in 1871, think what this nation would have been spared!

Turn now to a parallel development. Nowhere in the United States Reports are there to be found words more momentous or more baffling than these:

> Mr. Chief Justice Waite said: The court does not wish to hear argument on the question whether the provision in the Fourteenth Amendment to the Constitution, which forbids a State to deny to any person within its jurisdiction the equal protection of the laws, applies to these corporations. We are all of the opinion that it does.[20]

Measured by apparent repercussions, by generated case law, and by presumed talismanic effects and powers in Populist-Progressive-New Deal America, this oral statement—the *Santa Clara* "rule" or "dictum" of 1886—remains today, even in limbo, the outstanding "holding" of the Waite era. Here are the magic words which served to corporatize Section 1 of the Fourteenth Amendment; which in so doing eventually made Every Businessman His Own Constitutional Lawyer, and more extraordinarily still, made Roscoe Conkling a plausible draftsman-historian in spite of himself. Here, in short, are the words which generated, almost spontaneously, that preposterous, now discredited "Conspiracy Theory"[21] which in turn happily proved the nemesis of what it purported to explain.

For those who wonder what light the Waite Papers have shed in this area, there are two dazzling, stroboscopic flashes. Yet all that these tantalizing glimpses really make clear and certain is that even

---

20 Santa Clara County v. So. Pac. R.R., 118 U.S. 394, 396 (1886).
21 See Chapters 1–2, 9–10, *supra*, and Graham, "The Court, the Corporation and Conkling Revisited," a paper read at the annual meeting of the American Historical Association, Washington, D.C., December 28, 1961.

the recording of this statement was a fluke—the Court reporter's after-thought!

Preparing text for Volume 118 of the U.S. Reports, J. C. Bancroft Davis, the Supreme Court Reporter, cautiously addressed this note to Waite:[22]

> I have a memorandum in the California Cases
>
> Santa Clara County
> v.
> Southern Pacific &c &c
>
> as follows:
>
> In opening the Court stated that it did not wish to hear argument on the question whether the Fourteenth Amendment applies to such corporations as are parties in these suits. All the Judges were of opinion that it does.
>
> Please let me know whether I correctly caught your words and oblige.

Waite replied:

> I think your mem. in the California Railroad Tax cases expresses with sufficient accuracy what was said before the argument began. I leave it with you to determine whether anything need be said about it in the report inasmuch as we avoided meeting the constitutional question in the decision.[23]

"In other words," Magrath concludes, "to the Reporter fell the decision which enshrined the declaration in the United States Reports. Had Davis left it out, *Santa Clara County v. Southern Pac. R. Co.* would have been lost to history among thousands of uninteresting tax cases."[24]

So here at last, "now for then," is that long-delayed birth certificate, the reason this seemingly momentous step never was justified by formal opinion. Think, in this instance too, what the United States might have been spared had events taken a slightly different turn.

---

[22] Davis to Waite, May 26, 1886 (exactly four months after Waite's announcement), Waite Papers, on file in Library of Congress. MAGRATH, *op. cit. supra* note 1, at 223–24.

[23] MAGRATH, *op. cit. supra* note 1, at 224. Letter from Waite to Davis, May 31, 1886, Bancroft Davis Papers, on file in Library of Congress.

[24] MAGRATH, *op. cit. supra* note 1, at 224. The remainder of Dr. Magrath's statement seems to me to suffer from over-compression and from looking at the statement from too many angles and dates simultaneously. He sees and says clearly however that Waite must have regarded his statement as "a fairly routine instruction to counsel . . ." A typographical error, *id.* at 221, misdates the *San Mateo* appeal to the Supreme Court as 1883 (for 1882).

Beyond that, anticlimax and bathos are palpable. Indeed, like ornithologists who have happened on skeletons, fledglings, platypus and dinosaur shells and bones, all in one immense cuckoos' nest, Dr. Magrath and I have come to realize, perhaps better than most, that luck in research sometimes is not all it seems. A series of articles[25] and this judicial biography are not quite the places to unravel mysteries of this order. Still less, doubtless, is a book review. Yet as the explorer who naively wandered into these parts of that Dark (colonized) Continent—Conklinia, Corporataria (as we knew them then) and at length progressed into the "underdeveloped" Antislavery and Negro Territories—yes, that route itself now is a personal and national scandal—and more recently as one who at the opening of the Waite Papers in 1960[26] also met, and not unexpectedly, "Dr. Livingstone, I presume," in the person of this ludicrous Waite-Davis exchange, I shall here briefly set down some reflections and a hypothesis in the perhaps vain hope we may now liquidate this scandalous mystery and get on with the real business of the Fourteenth Amendment.

First the hypothesis. Just how are we to interpret Waite's casual, offhand expressions, "I think," "sufficient accuracy," "leave it with you to determine," as used in his reply to Davis?

One thing seems certain: these emphatically are not the words we conceive a Chief Justice of the United States ever likely to use if he has in mind what he and his associates have understood and intended to be a formally adjudicated, announced, unanimous rule prospectively applicable to corporations generally. This, to be sure, is only a conclusion, an inference; yet it is one few students of the Court, and of the judicial process, will hesitate to draw. Something decidedly less than a general per curiam rule is indicated as being recollected here. Furthermore, "whether anything need be said about it in the report *inasmuch as we avoided meeting the constitutional question in the decision*"—Waite's own clearly manifest doubt—not only underscores this inference, but supplies the further clue: Waite's recollection obviously is of something conditional, something minor, informal, and case-limited, something almost routine for a presiding judge directing oral argument. Waite is thinking, one ventures to suggest, not of a general prospective rule, but of an im-

---

[25] As listed in notes 21 & 11 *supra*, with a third series on frontier taxation, antebellum due process and equal protection being completed.

[26] Using the Waite Papers in April, 1960, I discovered the Davis-Waite exchange, learned of Magrath's forthcoming study, and deferred research and publication accordingly. Our conclusions thus have been arrived at independently.

promptu verbal instruction which he as Chief, on his own knowledge and initiative, as the Court's administrative head, had given "in opening" and "before the argument began"—an informal request to Southern Pacific counsel designed to focus and expedite argument in this one *Santa Clara* case; something perhaps to this effect: "The Court does not wish to hear further argument on whether the Fourteenth Amendment applies to these corporations. That point was elaborately covered in 1882, and has been re-covered in your briefs. We all presently are clear enough there. Our doubts run rather to the substance. *Assume* accordingly, as we do, that your clients are persons under the Equal Protection Clause. Take the cases on from there, clarifying the California statutes, the application thereof, and the merits."

Counsel at least appear to have done exactly that, and the Court, as Waite's reply indicates, once more proceeded to dispose of the cases on nonconstitutional grounds and again in a way that distressed and disappointed Justice Field. Justice Harlan's opinion for the majority upset the taxes, but did so on a technicality that had not been argued or considered at all in the cases at circuit; namely, that the whole assessment was a nullity inasmuch as the State Board of Equalization had included therein the fences along the lines at a value of three hundred dollars per mile, whereas a very detailed statute gave the Board power to assess only "the franchise, roadway, road-bed, rails, and rolling stock."[27] Justice Field concurred in the judgments, but deplored the fact that the Court had not conceived it to be

> its duty to decide the important constitutional questions involved, and particularly the one which was so fully considered in the Circuit Court, and elaborately argued here, that in the assessment, upon which the taxes claimed were levied, an unlawful and unjust discrimination was made between the property of the defendant and the property of individuals, to its disadvantage, thus subjecting it to an unequal share of the public burdens, and to that extent depriving it of the equal protection of the laws .... At the present day nearly all great enterprises are conducted by corporations ... [a] vast portion of the wealth ... is in their hands. It is, therefore, of the greatest interest to them whether their property is subject to the same rules of assessment and taxation as like property of natural persons ... whether the State ... may prescribe rules for the valuation of property for taxation which will vary according as it is held by individuals or by corporations. The

---

[27] Santa Clara County v. So. Pac. R.R., 118 U.S. 394, 412 (1886).

question is of transcendent importance, and it will come here and continue to come until it is authoritatively decided in harmony with the great constitutional amendment which insures to every person, whatever his position or association, the equal protection of the laws; and that necessarily implies freedom from the imposition of unequal burdens under the same conditions. *Barbier v. Connolly*, 113 U.S. 27, 31.[28]

Why the majority had declined to go along with Field is as obvious as his own distress. Dr. Magrath summarizes the evidence in part.[29] Field had repeatedly embarrassed Waite and the Court by close association with the Southern Pacific proprietors and by zeal and bias in their behalf. He had thought nothing of pressuring Waite for assignment of opinions in various railroad cases, of placing his friends as counsel for the road in upcoming cases, of hinting at courses he and they should take, even of passing on to such counsel in the undecided *San Mateo* case "certain memoranda which had been handed me by two of the Judges."[30] His decisions and opinions at circuit in this case moreover had been needlessly broad and economically naive. To hold, as he had, that the mortgage on the Southern Pacific "exceeds $3,000 per mile," when in fact it exceeded $43,000 per mile—nearly three times the contested assessed value—was damning in itself, and doubtless the reason the Court withheld decision in 1883. Later that year Field obligingly heard the second round of cases at circuit. Detailing now the facts of the mortgage situation in his opinion, he still held California's classifications to be a denial of equal protection of the laws, and even soberly advised the state to let the railroad go tax free, to simply assess the mortgages "as in the case of natural persons."[31] Field's associates and subordinates frequently were amused, irritated, or nonplussed by such aberrations, as they were also by his disastrous ventures into Presidential politics,[32] by his plan (if elected) to enlarge the Supreme Court to twenty-one members and pack it with "able and conservative men."[33]

In other respects, Field had been luckier and more successful.

---

[28] County of San Bernadino v. So. Pac. R.R., 118 U.S. 417, 422–23 (1886) (concurring opinion).
[29] The following summary is based primarily on Chapter 3, *supra*.
[30] Field to John Norton Pomeroy, Washington, D.C., March 28, 1883, published as letter III, *supra*, at 106–108.
[31] On the various Railroad Tax cases at circuit, see Chapter 9, *supra*, n.208.
[32] See generally Chapter 3, *supra*, for Field as viewed especially by Judges Sawyer and Deady.
[33] *Id.*; the quotation is from Field's letter to Pomeroy, July 28, 1884, published as letter IV, *supra*, at 108–109.

Commencing in 1874 he had maneuvered ingeniously to give his dissents in the *Slaughter-House*, *Granger*, and *Sinking Fund* cases an independent life and statement in the law of his own Ninth Circuit.[34] In a series of unappealed (generally nonappealable habeas corpus) cases involving rights of the persecuted Chinese minority to employment and equal protection, Field gave much broader scope than the full Court at these dates formally had to the words "person," "liberty" and "property." Consciously or unconsciously, he also replanted and cultivated his "right to pursue the lawful callings" doctrine so that it finally emerged as an inchoate version of "liberty of contract." That Field and his circuit colleagues did all this in defense of a persecuted racial minority (one which, unlike the now deserted freedmen, had powerful steamship, mining, and railroad allies to help wage their constitutional battles) rather obscured orientations at first, may even have won him the majority's wholehearted encouragement.

What happened and mattered was that California bigots asked for and got the judicial intervention under the Fourteenth Amendment others currently were denied, and Field, as always, parlayed his dicta beautifully.[35] When in 1879–1880 the new state constitution and laws prohibited California corporations from employing Chinese, bigotry at last relit and held the candle for the American corporate bar. Timing was equally miraculous and sociological. Nearly nine years before, in 1871, Circuit Judge Woods of New Orleans had ruled, almost simultaneously with his holding in *United States v. Hall*, that foreign insurance companies (which till then had kept stubbornly trying to corporatize citizenship under the old comity clause, and had turned to the Fourteenth Amendment only in desperation) were not "citizens" or "persons" under the new Section 1.[36] In passing we may note that this situation in itself of course is convincing disproof of old notions about "slick" or even "intuitive" draftsmanship.

The significant fact about Woods' holding in *Insurance Co. v. New Orleans* is that it was virtually ignored—honored mainly in the breach. Corporate counsel went right on invoking due process and equal protection, and courts—including the Waite Court—went right on permitting and hearing them, reasoning no doubt, or pre-

---

[34] On the "Ninth Circuit law," see Chapter 3, *supra* at 144ff., and correspondence and materials there cited.

[35] See *id*. at 144, n.125 for the earlier stages of the development; and notes 43 & 48 *infra* for the later stages. Note especially Field's phrasing of the dicta in County of San Mateo v. Southern Pac. R.R., 13 Fed. 145, 149–52 (C.C. Cal. 1882).

[36] Insurance Co. v. New Orleans, 13 Fed. Cas. 67 (No. 7,052) (C.C.La. 1871); for the background and history of this case, see Chapter 9, *supra*, at 382ff.

suming, that if corporations were not "persons," shareholders at least were, and corporate property was "property."[37] Alarmists and critics including Field were repeatedly contending that legislatures and the Court alike were increasingly "hostile" to corporations. So the long-suffering Miller-Waite majority leaned backward, went on hearing arguments, deciding cases on the merits to disprove loose talk. Due process long since had become a favorite and respected weapon, a justifier of legislation. In 1856 the Supreme Court had held, unanimously, that the guarantee restrained all three branches; Congress had not been left "free to make any process 'due process of law' by its mere will."[38] And three years before, in 1853, Waite himself as counsel had invoked due process on behalf of the Toledo Bank[39] in vain to be sure, with no exploration or even mention of corporate personality as such, but like other business counsel with hard or novel cases at this time, making the plea for what it was worth.[40] No one need be surprised therefore that early in his *Sinking Fund* opinion of 1879 Waite observed that while the contract clause did not apply to the federal government, "equally with the States [the United States] are prohibited from depriving persons or corporations of property without due process of law."[41]

And right at this time the new California Constitution forbade corporations to employ Chinese and denied to the Stanford-Huntington railroads the privilege of deducting their mortgages.[42] The corporate "person" thus emerged from hibernation in *Parrott's Chinese Case*,[43] but was fully, approvingly developed only in the *San Mateo*[44] case at circuit and only after the California court[45] had rejected the railroads' due process and equal protection pleas (citing, as a basis, *Insurance Co. v. New Orleans*). Shortly afterward the companies removed to Field's court and later retained Conkling for the show-

---

37 *Id.* at 393, especially nn.89–91

38 Murray v. Hoboken Land & Improvement Co., 18 How. (59 U.S.) 272 (1856).

39 See Bank of Toledo v. City of Toledo, 1 Ohio St. 622, 633–34 (1853); "Waite and Young, attorneys for the plaintiff." See Chapter 2, *supra*, n.12; MAGRATH, *op. cit. supra* note 1, 44–45, 64, discusses the case without reference to due process; sections 1 and 16 of the Ohio Bill of Rights, Constitution of 1851, based on sections 1 and 7 of the Constitution of 1802, were not the conventional due process clause, but rather the "All courts shall be open . . . due course of law . . ." form.

40 See, *e.g.*, the arguments of William Curtis Noyes for various insurance companies in 1854, discussed Chapter 2, *supra*, 77, nn.38–39; see also *id.* at 78, nn.45–47 for Pennsylvania cases of the 1850s, discussed more fully Chapter 10, *supra*.

41 99 U.S. 700, 718 (1879).

42 See Chapter 9, *supra*, 397, and materials therein cited.

43 *Id.* at 393, especially nn.87–88, for background of *In re* Tiburcio Parrott, 1 Fed. 481 (C.C. Cal. 1880); see also Chapter 3, *supra* nn.125–32.

44 See note 35 *supra*.

45 See Chapter 9, *supra*, 398, nn.115–16.

down fight. More crucial and basic than the corporate "person" was whether the equal protection clause had curbed the state taxing power. A dictum Justice Miller had inserted—perhaps as a scarecrow —in his opinion in *Davidson v. New Orleans*[46] implied it had not. Beyond this obstacle was the equally restrictive language of Miller's opinion in the *Slaughter-House* cases: "the one pervading purpose . . ." of this amendment, and indeed of all the war amendments, had been "the freedom of the slave race, the security and firm establishment of that freedom, and the protection of the newly-made freeman from the oppressions of those who formerly exercised unlimited dominion over him."[47]

Where, then, had all this left the Southern Pacific? Precariously exposed seemingly, but not high and dry: "The Ninth Circuit law" now more than proved its worth. Thankful indeed were railroad counsel—including Professor John Norton Pomeroy, who had been retained at Field's suggestion—to cite the growing line of Chinese precedents on the larger scope and "true meaning" of Section 1. Gratified indeed too was Field to be handed such persuasive authority. The circuit opinions in the *San Mateo* case make interesting reading today, but one point tends to get overlooked: Judge Sawyer expressly held corporations to be "persons" under Section 1, but Field, anxious no doubt to avoid headon collision with the now-Mr. Justice Woods, "looked through" the corporation to the individual shareholders as natural persons, while at the same time extolling equal protection and the Fourteenth Amendment as needed bulwarks for corporate property—"a perpetual shield against all unequal and partial legislation by the States."[48]

These of course also were the themes of the celebrated *San Mateo* arguments of December 1882. Conkling in particular recycled, supplemented, and falsely buttressed Field's points.[49] The result was a forgery-riddled *tour de force*—gabled, gilt Hollywood Gothic. Yet, sixteen years after the drafting (and eleven after *Insurance Co. v. New Orleans*) even Roscoe Conkling knew better than to say or hint that he and his colleagues definitely had understood and intended that corporations were "persons" under these two clauses. His argu-

---

[46] 96 U.S. 97, 106 (1878): "[W]e know of no provision in the Federal Constitution . . . which forbids unequal taxation by the States."
[47] 16 Wall. (83 U.S.) 36, 71 (1873).
[48] County of San Mateo v. Southern Pac. R.R., 13 Fed. 722, 741 (C.C. Cal. 1882); see also the earlier opinion denying motion to remand, 13 Fed. 145 (C.C. Cal. 1882).
[49] Compare Chapters 1 and 9, *supra*, and the updated rationale in "The Court, The Corporation and Conkling Revisited," *supra* note 21 (summarized *supra* 15-19, 416, note 177, 558-561).

ment was primarily an attack on the narrow *Slaughter-House* rule and an appeal to the Court to regard the amendment as a curb on the state taxing power, as a bulwark against "unequal taxation." These of course were the indispensable propositions for the railroad. (The corporate "person" merely looked so to us once it had emerged as the doctrinal result of the cases.) Conkling's prime innuendo, which the Beards and all of us so long misread, was that because corporations had been petitioning for relief from discriminatory state taxes while the amendment was being drafted and ratified, the framers and Congress "must have intended" to curb the state taxing power.

Conkling's misquotations from the Joint Committee journal tied in with this argument, and at yet another point he juggled facts and texts to imply that a section which Congress in 1870 had added to the civil rights acts to kill California's discriminatory taxes against the Chinese demonstrated that Congress had understood that the Fourteenth Amendment had been designed to curb all unequal taxation and that the judiciary had in fact been left free to decide what was equal and what was not. This was pure fabrication—innuendo developed obliquely and directly contrary to fact; Congress repeatedly in the 1860's and '70's had refused to curb the states' taxing power, especially in matters involving corporate taxation; and the avowed, the manifest purpose of that section 16 of the act of 1870 had been to kill California's anti-Chinese miners and passenger taxes. Race discrimination, in short, had been the target in 1870, just as it had been in 1866.[50] Conkling misrepresented these matters completely in the course of a rambling stilted attack on California's "invidious" and "despoiling" tax laws.

Justice Field thought the argument "great."[51] What the other Justices thought is unknown. Certainly they saw the economic soft spots and blindspots in Field's circuit opinion, for they refused, even in the *Santa Clara* round, to uphold Field on the substantive issues. Harlan, Waite, Matthews, and perhaps others, had little or no respect for Conkling. The one sure point is that no one bothered to check

---

[50] On this episode, ignored in the original studies, see Conkling's argument reprinted in Proceedings of the Committee on the Judiciary Regarding Railroad Tax Suits, California Legislature, Assembly, 28th Sess., Journal Appendix, v. 8, no. 3, at p. 94 (1889), concerning addition of the phrase "taxes, licenses, and exactions of every kind, and to no other." Compare therewith the legislative history of section 16 of the Act of May 31, 1870. The Enforcement Act, ch. 114, § 16, 16 Stat. 144; section 16 derived from S. 365, 41st Cong., 2d Sess. (1870), introduced by Senator Stewart of Nevada for the steamship companies and Chinese Six Companies January 10, 1870, after the House had passed H.R. 1293, 41st Cong., 2d Sess. (1870). See CONG. GLOBE, 41st Cong., 2d Sess., 1536, 3480, 3658, 3701 (1870).

[51] See Chapter 9, *supra*, 426, quoting Field's letter of Feb. 18, 1883, to Judge Deady.

his committee journal passages or even refer to the Civil Rights debates. Eventually, in 1890, the Court did hold, without hearing other argument, that Section 1 had restrained the state taxing power;[52] yet that point had frequently been assumed by the Justices—or so it appeared at least, from their readiness to hear due process and equal protection invoked in such cases. What we begin to sense now—what the Davis-Waite exchange shows—is that for this pragmatic, overworked Waite Court these "assumptions" did not and do not signify all they once seemed to.

What really counted in the overall development was that by the mid-80's, while the California Railroad Tax cases were before the courts, the anomalies, orientation, and consequences of the "Ninth Circuit law" at last became manifest. Field and his lieutenants had literally gone to the verge. First in the *American Law Review*, then at bar conventions, "certain mischievous tendencies . . . observable in the Federal courts," particularly in those of the Ninth Circuit, gained increasing notoriety. Criticism was not yet of dicta or doctrines, rather of the sheltered and broadened jurisdiction—of one circuit going it alone—of "federal interference and meddling." (On so-called *laissez faire* issues and formulations, Field of course had, and knew that he had, bar leaders behind him, egging him on.[53])

Obviously responding to this criticism, the Court in 1884 partially clipped the Ninth Circuit's wings by holding the habeas corpus jurisdiction of the federal courts to be concurrent rather than exclusive.[54] Circuit Judge Sawyer declared himself "mortified and astonished," especially that Justices Field and Matthews had concurred in the unanimous decision, for both, he confided to the sympathetic Judge Deady, had expressed advance approval of a draft of his now-reversed circuit holding. "So it is now settled," he added philosophically, "that we judges on this coast have been 'elevating our horns' a

---

[52] See Bell's Gap R.R. v. Pennsylvania, 134 U.S. 232 (1890). Note that Justice Bradley here was able to restate for a unanimous Court the views he had expressed as a concurring minority in Davidson v. New Orleans, 96 U.S. 97, 107 (1878); the dicta are most interesting as the law was upheld.

[53] How swiftly and assiduously the bar seized on Field's *San Mateo* holdings at circuit is shown in the N.Y. Tribune, Sept. 16, 1882, p. 2, col. 5, "The Tax on Foreign Corporations." At a meeting called to plan an attack on New York's foreign corporation laws and taxes, George S. Harding, counsel for the Winchester Arms Co., "said that Justice Field had recently given a decision in California that corporations could not be discriminated against in the manner of which those present complained." The reference at this date of course was to Field's decision taking jurisdiction (13 Fed. 145); the main circuit holding did not come until Sept. 25, 1882. Sawyer and Field however for a full month had made no secret of their intentions; see Chapter 9, *supra* —.

[54] See Robb v. Connolly, 111 U.S. 624 (1884); Chapter 3, *supra* n.114.

little too high of late, and will have to take them down."[55] And so they did have to, for by the Act of March 3, 1885, Congress at last restored the appellate jurisdiction of the Supreme Court in habeas corpus cases.[56]

By this date however Justice Field had completed his book. Another flareup of bigotry and economic discrimination, directed chiefly against Chinese laundries, provided the opportunity—and this time in the Supreme Court, while Waite was ill and absent. In the first of the two great San Francisco laundry cases, *Barbier v. Connolly*,[57] speaking for a unanimous Court, and to the surprise of San Franciscans *upholding* the ordinance, Field seized his chance to transfer the fruits of "the Ninth Circuit law" to a majority opinion, including and re-elaborating the lawful callings-liberty of contract dicta, the familiar injunctions against "arbitrary spoliation of property," and formulating the now classic private rights-police power dichotomy from which the "rule of reason" soon was to blossom.

Ten months before this, in the *Hurtado*[58] case, also from the Ninth Circuit but one in which Field took no part, Mr. Justice Matthews at last had begun to make it officially clear that the guarantee of due process of law extended to matters of substance as well as of procedure. Field's nicely phrased and balanced *Barbier* dictum thus completed and articulated what was in effect, if not in intent, a new formulary, an improved circuitry from which counsel and Court alike might take freer readings. The galling thing was that in these vital California Railroad Tax cases the brethren still balked. The consolation was that business counsel and the state and federal judges, more and more of whom came from the corporate bar, or hoped to land there, meanwhile had been citing the circuit opinions on the corporate "person,"[59] as they now began to use this *Barbier* dictum. Also heartening, on this same day of the *Santa Clara* decision, May 10, 1886, the full Court, speaking through Mr. Justice Matthews in

---

[55] *Ibid.*, quoting Sawyer's letter of May 21, 1884, to Deady; opinion by Justice Harlan.

[56] On the jurisdictional bases of the "Ninth Circuit law" see Chapter 3, *supra*—nn.114–15, 117–18; Chapter 9, *supra*—n.85.

[57] 113 U.S. 27 (1885). The Reporter's note, p. v, indicates that Waite was absent when this case was decided Jan. 5, 1885.

[58] 110 U.S. 516 (1884). Hurtado's counsel was A. L. Hart, former Attorney General of California, who had represented the state against the railroad in the *San Mateo* case.

[59] See Chapter 9, *supra* n.216, for examples of such usage during the years 1883–1887.

Yick Wo v. Hopkins, the second great laundry case, struck down San Francisco's outrageous application of its fire ordinances:

> Though the law itself be fair on its face and impartial in appearance, yet, if it is applied and administered by public authority with an evil eye and an unequal hand, so as practically to make unjust and illegal discriminations between persons in similar circumstances, material to their rights, the denial of equal justice is still within the prohibition of the Constitution.[60]

Equal protection thus continued to spearhead due process and the Chinese continued to spearhead equal protection. Business wasn't yet getting what it wanted, but Justice Field finally, more nearly was. "Things really are looking up . . . Brother Matthews[61] . . . a wonderful help . . . strong . . . sound, a man of parts, too close to the Chief perhaps . . . and certainly too close in '77 to 'His Fraudulency,' Hayes . . . but shrewd, astute, a born conciliator . . . Jay Gould's lawyer! . . . a bridge and a bond in our Court. . . . And how strange it is: *he* (not Brother Harlan!) a former abolitionist leader and editor—Birney's and Bailey's successor, Salmon P. Chase's lieutenant, the young Cincinnatian who led the attack on Ohio's Black laws, 1846–48 . . . while I was in Europe . . . that 'Year of the Revolutions' . . . But sound as I am now . . . even on *civil rights* . . . and Brother Bradley[62] too at last . . . But for that dozen years: . . . *Legal Tender* . . . *Munn v. Illinois* . . . The Electoral Commission . . . that dreadful decade . . . But we all came around. Finally. . . . All but Brother Harlan . . . The Kentucky Colonel, as he loves to say, 'is full of corn!' "

This, it hardly is necessary to add, is an imaginary soliloquy. Yet those relationships, associations, resentments, antagonisms, allusions

---

[60] 118 U.S. 356, 373–74 (1886).

[61] Though he served only eight years, evidence points increasingly to Matthews (1824–Mar. 22, 1889) as the swing man of the late Waite Court, in fourteenth amendment matters particularly, bridging the period from the late '40's to the late '80's— from Birney, Chase, Lincoln to Grant, Hayes, Waite, Garfield and Jay Gould—a biography is long overdue. Not to be overlooked, for example, is the fact that Matthews also spoke for the Court—again a unanimous one—in the Kentucky Railroad Tax Cases, 115 U.S. 321 (1885) (involving a number of the same questions as the *California* cases, see Chapter 9 *supra*—). See also MAGRATH, *op. cit. supra* note 1, at 198–200, especially n.84, for Matthews' role in adding the limiting phrases to the Waite opinion in the Railroad Commission Cases, 116 U.S. 307, 331 (1886) (decided just three weeks before Waite's *Santa Clara* announcement). Matthews was responsible here for adding, "This power to regulate is not a power to destroy . . ." etc.

[62] Evidence in the Deady collection and elsewhere indicates that relations between Field and Bradley were strained throughout the '70's. The *Legal Tender* reversal, *Granger* decisions, and "Stolen Election" of 1876, all were Bradley's work in Field's eyes, and moved him at times to fury.

and illusions—all are documented.⁶³ The sum of it is that the old "natural rights" precepts and Lockean rhetoric pioneered by this anti-slavery generation—literally "welded" to due process and equal protection in the 1830's—re-echoed in *Hurtado, Barbier,* and *Yick Wo,* but not in the *Civil Rights Cases.*

One postulates then that if in late May, 1886, Reporter Davis, left to "determine whether anything need be said . . . in the report," queried Brother Field (as the Circuit Justice involved), Field's reply was affirmative. One postulates further that in these Railroad Tax cases the Supreme Court endeavored to do what it generally does and always must try to do—select and decide the crucial appeals with regard for standing law and the merits, avoiding constitutional, collateral, hypothetical questions where possible. To these judges the crucial question never had been, never could have been, simply the corporate constitutional "person" *as such*; never whether corporate "persons" or "property" were to be accorded constitutional protection *in exigent cases*; never whether due process could be applied to such cases. Waite himself, we repeat, had used Ohio's clause in behalf of the Toledo Bank in 1853.⁶⁴ The important words by that date, and increasingly for thirty years thereafter, were "liberty," "property" and "deprived"—not "person" or "due process." American due process had become something different. In the course of it, the judiciary really followed more than it led.⁶⁵ Pragmatist to the core, overwhelmed with pleas, including frivolous ones, the Miller-Waite wing went on winnowing, scrutinizing, "including and excluding," deciding on the merits, saying as little as possible. The sum of it plainly is that what the Court was doing during this transitional period didn't quite accord with what it had said, and what it was saying   ͜ ͜ Supreme Court finally, as elsewhere, practice had got far a͡   ͡ decision in due process matters.

The truth is that we have had, as Dr. Magrath perceives but unfortunately has lacked the space to show,⁶⁶ altogether preposterous

---

⁶³ The Sawyer-Field-Deady, Waite, David Davis, Harlan and other collections are gradually shedding light on the intra-Court relations. See MAGRATH, *op. cit. supra* note 1, chs. 12-15. Harlan, for example, a friend and nominee of Hayes, and as sensitive to his prejudices and to proprieties as Field was insensitive, requested Waite not to assign him opinions in cases decided against Conkling's clients; "from some things I heard last winter" it was Harlan's "impression that Senator Conkling did not feel altogether *kindly* to me." Waite Papers, Harlan to Waite, undated, but attached to a Nov. 29, 1879, assignment slip. Field and Conkling shared a malignant consuming hatred of Hayes.

⁶⁴ Bank of Toledo v. City of Toledo, 1 Ohio St. 622 (1853).

⁶⁵ See Chapter 5, *supra* and Chapters 11-12 *supra*, on Blackwell and frontier taxation.

⁶⁶ MAGRATH, *op. cit. supra* note 1, at 192 and pages following, especially at n.66.

ideas about the so-called Judicial or Laissez Faire Revolution; about the conception, birth, and infancy of so-called modern or economic due process-equal protection; about who and what were responsible for this distinctive American development. Judicial and postbellum storks indeed! These guarantees were in most state constitutions; they early became among the most extensively and loosely used weapons to challenge and to justify governmental power or action—not, as our law school-trained generation has tended to think, to dissect or cleave procedure from substance. Substantive law generally over the centuries has been "secreted at the interstices of procedure." Yet substantive due process somehow burst on us unawares, after the Civil War, with scarcely a hint beforehand!

Nonsense. Probably not one early so-called "substantive" use of due process out of a hundred ever ended up in the headnotes or *Century Digest.* Yet the sparsity there, and the curt judicial rejections, have been the *assumed* measure of usage, and of the whole antebellum development. And it is this illusion that has crippled and stultified so much research and writing in American constitutional history.

Let anyone who is skeptical of this statement and of my positions generally, anyone still convinced that the courts led and misled the bar and public, and not *vice versa;* anyone certain that no "mere" treatise could have been an important factor in these developments before Cooley's *Constitutional Limitations* (published in 1868); everyone puzzled as to why equal protection spearheaded due process after the war, and in these very tax cases; anyone baffled why *Blackwell on Tax Titles* (of all works) appeared continually as a citation in the briefs and opinions, not merely of these postwar tax and even Chinese cases,[67] but in the earlier due process-equal protection cases (including that most important one of all, *Wynehamer v. People*,[68] where it was appropriately cited by counsel in the same breath with Solomon's Song of Songs[69]); let everyone in short who wishes in a

---

[67] Using the manuscript records of the old United States Circuit Court in 1936, I remember laughing at the citation of *Blackwell on Tax Titles* in the briefs of a Chinese habeas corpus case! After years of stumbling over the books, I at last examined it *carefully.*

[68] 13 N.Y. 378 (1856).

[69] See pp. 13–14 of "Points for Plaintiff in Error," by Amasa J. Parker, Wynehamer v. People, *supra* note 68, and "Additional suggestions and authorities . . ." same counsel and case, p. 1; both in New York Court of Appeals, bound briefs, N.Y. State Library, vol. 948, the latter citing on "property" protection: "Blackwell on Tax Titles, 15, 16, 17, 21, 22" along with Taylor v. Porter, "4 Hill, 144" "1 Ohio State R.633'—the Ohio Chief Justice's discussion of Waite's 1853 due process argument in *Bank of Toledo v. City of Toledo,* discussed herein at notes 39 and 64; the original "Points for

few hours to gain a fresh insight into the forces that transformed due process and eventually judicial review—for everyone but the Negro race—let all these get forthwith and read *Blackwell on Tax Titles*,[70] the first edition of which was published in Chicago in 1855, fully thirteen years before Thomas M. Cooley graciously acknowledged his own indebtedness by citing it at the head of his famous chapter on taxation. Read particularly the "Introduction," and Blackwell's enthralling first chapter, "Of the Fundamental Principles Which Control the Taxing Power," in which are gathered and synthesized, and wedded to taxation and equal protection, all the early due process cases. Yes, here is another fountainhead indeed.

To get back to our biography, Dr. Magrath might have clinched his challenge of the facile thesis that the Waite Court bears the chief responsibility for the great shifts we are speaking of by noting three further developments: not until after Waite's death did Field himself finally manage to make the corporate "person" truly explicit in constitutional decisions; not until this same date, 1889–1890, did Justice Bradley, speaking for a unanimous Court, clearly hold section 1 to be a potential curb on the state taxing power;[71] and in 1890 too came the holding[72] that heralded the demise of *Munn v. Illinois*.[73] The late Waite years must doubtless be counted as transitional, but personnel changes which began at this time spelled the major shifts. Between December 1887 and December 1890, Woods, Waite, Matthews and Miller were succeeded by Lamar, Fuller, Brewer and Brown. By December, 1895, Shiras, Jackson, White, and Peckham had replaced Bradley, Lamar, Blatchford and Jackson.[74] Aside from a few limited "concessions," as Magrath notes, the weakened Fuller Court, not Waite's, refashioned due process and equal protection on the economic side. Doctrinaire Fieldian liberty of contract and due process and the corporatized "person," and "property,"

Plaintiff," at p. 14, citing (along with Pliny's Natural History, Herodotus, and Tacitus): "Songs of Solomon, 8, v.12, Psalms, 104, v.14 and 15" in support of this statement on due process: "Under these universally reserved rights, we are to be protected against all sumptuary laws and all interference with personal rights." (Mr. Ernest Breuer, New York State Law Librarian, kindly located and supplied transcripts of these and other rare briefs.)

70 The full title is BLACKWELL, A PRACTICAL TREATISE ON THE POWER TO SELL LAND FOR THE NON-PAYMENT OF TAXES ASSESSED THEREON (1855).

71 See note 52 *supra*.

72 Chicago M. & St. P. Ry. v. Minnesota, 134 U.S. 418, 461 (1890) (opinion by Blatchford, J., Miller, J., concurring; Bradley, Gray, and Lamar, JJ., dissenting).

73 94 U.S. 113 (1877). Magrath has supplemented his chapter on the *Granger Cases* with an excellent article on the *Munn* case in 15 AMERICAN HERITAGE 44 (Feb. 1964).

74 MAGRATH, *op. cit. supra* note 1, at 201–02, makes the point; see 3 WARREN, THE SUPREME COURT IN UNITED STATES HISTORY 482 (1923), for appointment dates.

caught on first in the state and lower federal courts[75] and among those justices who served short and generally rather undistinguished terms. The Fuller and the White Courts, far more than Waite's, must bear the burden.

Another point usually overlooked in assessing the Supreme Court's record in this field is that, at the very least, due process and equal protection and the corporatized "person" were and are infinitely preferable to the corporatized "citizen" and comity clause which the corporate bar so obstinately proffered for eighty years.[76] Here at least was a discretionary formula, flexible and syncretic, a law-fact-embracing tool in the great tradition of common law constitutionalism, two forms which syncretized, as Professor Corwin[77] long ago demonstrated, the constitutional rules and precedent which had developed primarily in the state courts during the first century of judicial review. Like our present-day transistor, due process at least did jobs more efficiently, supplanted more cumbersome apparatus, operated on lower amperages, muted natural law premises, achieved a tighter, tidier solution. Compare with this that absurd automaton and chestnut offered by the insurance and interstate commerce bars!

Three crucial and final points: First, section 1 blanketed the freedmen in; it couldn't and didn't throw others out. Application of these guarantees in defense of Negro and racial rights, in other words, was climactic, normative, additive, not original, unique, or exclusionary. Negroes were to get what others long ago had had. That was the whole thought and point. And it was precisely because the framers looked at the matter in that light that they gave so little thought to constitutional mechanics other than to assuring—or so they thought —the added power necessary to make possible a continuing progressive solution. Second, from our vantage point today it can be seen that Justice Miller's "one pervading purpose-Negro race" rule was over-narrow, imprecise. Race discrimination per se, all race discrimination, not simply that directed against the Negro race, really was the target. Miller tripped over a small point, but he tripped, and the lucky Field capitalized on it for all it was worth. Third, race prejudice and race discrimination being what they are, and mani-

---

[75] See Pound, *Liberty of Contract*, 18 YALE L.J. 454 (1909), reprinted in Ass'n of Am. Law Schools, Selected Essays on Constitutional Law 208 (1938); Paul, Conservative Crisis and the Rule of Law (1960).

[76] See Chapter 9, *supra*, n.97. A study of the insurance and interstate commerce bars' efforts, both in Congress and in the Court, to corporatize the comity clause and citizenship, 1810-1910, especially during the years 1865-1871, will document this point overwhelmingly.

[77] See Corwin, Liberty Against Government 97 (1948), and earlier works there cited.

festing themselves as they did and do—in arbitrary, invidious, often cynical and disguised action—accordingly to give to the judiciary power to decide what was *due* and *equal* and *protection* and what was not in this area *in itself spelled a large and imponderable increase of judicial discretion*. For if courts were not to be dupes they had, willy-nilly, to begin doing, and to continue doing, what they thoroughly dislike to do, and often deny that they do at all: scrutinize legislative-executive motive, purpose, and good faith. Put a little differently, these were qualitative phrases, standards, and tests resting on natural rights premises; as such, they spelled new problems and burdens—many that were not sensed at all at the time. But these difficulties obviously are inherent in the problem and in the objective, not alone in the constitutional forms or texts.[78]

Why has not more of this been seen clearly before? Why indeed, judges and historians may well ask and commiserate one another. Their troubles stem from that common source—common law constitutionalism. Anachronism is bred right into both fields: as the institutionalized method of the one (re-read Dicey's[79] brilliant introduction on the ways and uses of precedent); as the bane, the occupational hazard of the other—especially of legal and constitutional historians whose "sources" (precedents read in reverse) soon come to mean and to cover so much more than ever is originally conceived, intended, or said.

So it chanced that the Beards' Conspiracy Theory, or, speaking more accurately, the Progressive-New Deal generations' Conspiracy Theory, really was anachronized—"Pogo"-ized—history. To quote the learned Walt Kelly,[80] "Incongruity is the nature of the natural .... You develops a good memory, then you reverses the whole process." *Due* process easiest, certainly first, of all! Forty years of constitutional development were misread, and read back into, that one word, "person." The miracle was that the second fluke—the reversed image of the first—helped expose, caricature, in time perhaps, correct the original. Only the Negro race—only the avowed, intended beneficiaries—had to wait still longer.

Fluke, fiction, imposter—constitutionally, historically, historio-

---

[78] This of course is the answer to all talk about "poor draftsmanship."
[79] See DICEY, INTRODUCTION TO THE STUDY OF THE LAW OF THE CONSTITUTION 15–19 (7th ed. 1908).
[80] Quotations of the Okefenokee scholars are from that brilliant series of "Pogo" published Dec. 18, 1963, to Jan. 9, 1964, climaxing: "I predicts that on January first, 1863, A. Lincoln will issue the *Emancipation Proclamation!*" "Man! That's not Future! That's Past!" "Maybe it jus' *seem* like the *Future* sometime. . . ." (Emphasis as in the original.)

The Waite Court and the Fourteenth Amendment 583

graphically. Such is the record and the verdict on the corporate "person." So far as sections 1 and 5 as a whole are concerned, it is clear enough now that history and interpretation, not draftsmanship, were what got sophisticated and misread.

The ultimate irony is that both the Waite Court and the Negro race caught it coming and going. Belabored as "anticorporate," even "communistic," in its own day by business and bar leaders, as Magrath shows, the Waite Court got tagged and re-slandered again in ours as the one that "reneged," "caved in," "reversed itself" on the corporate "person," automatically corporatizing due process and equal protection, completing these framers' *intended* revolution (*i.e.*, a revolution by constitutional amendment!), accomplishing all this by a one-word construction, by "mere acquiescence," when as a matter of fact the shifts and the development of course required decades and literally thousands of cases.

This was the imagined, the postulated, the fictitious Due Process or Judicial Revolution. Yet all the while there also was a real one—flagrant, disastrous, generally ignored: the 1883 *Civil Rights* decision that de-racialized, *instanto*, "by a subtle and ingenious verbal criticism," precisely those protections which Justice Bradley himself so clearly had seen and regarded as necessary and appropriate in 1871. The haunting realization thus is that the corporate fluke, the eventual hypertrophy of the Fourteenth Amendment on the economic side, completely overshadowed and obscured the misreading, the reneging, the stasis and paralysis that developed on the racial side. Inaction ignored, inaction instutionalized, inaction alibied (as even Dr. Magrath is too ready to alibi it—Waite simply was "a man of his era") became inaction indeed. De-racializing equal protection, not corporatizing it—this was our national catastrophe.

Underscoring so much while leaving so much unsaid, this book is a powerful plea for post-1937 trends and constructions—not merely in the Supreme Court, but now in Congress. How does the nation, the Court, the Congress, make good a lost century? Chief Justice Waite's triumph—decidedly more modest in my estimation than in Dr. Magrath's—was that he dared, tried, succeeded—at least by half. The country's failure was that it so long did not—has not yet—even by half.

Twenty years and three constitutional amendments after emancipation too many of our forebears, including all members of this Court except the former Union colonel and converted slaveholder, Mr. Justice Harlan, let themselves be persuaded, as too many others have since, that American governments still lacked the mandate and the power to do, after emancipation and amendment, in behalf of "liberty," what those same governments originally, for three quarters of a century, had been able to do, and had done, against "liberty," in defense of slavery and slave "property." No mandate and no power to protect the "li[ves], liberty and property" of "persons" at last free, nor of those newly-made "Citizens of the United States" for whose double, triple, above all, *equal* protection, these three overlapping guarantees and clauses again had been employed, both affirmatively and negatively, as they had been employed incessantly for two generations. No mandate and no power to protect as *free* "persons," and as "Citizens of the United States," those whom this antislavery generation at least, believed governments had the *power* and the *duty* to protect even as enslaved "persons."

Four years short of the Fourteenth Amendment centennial, let us speak no more of the "failures" and of the "miserable draftsmanship" of that Joint Committee of Fifteen. John A. Bingham and his colleagues did very well indeed. The date, remember, was *1866*.

[CHAPTER 14]

Everyman's Constitution: A Centennial View

"THE complexities of history deserve our respect."[1] Constitutionalism, and Everyman's Constitution at centennial, are complexities indeed. Venerated paragons no less. Commands and guarantees unequivocal on their face. Resisted still; still half realized; widely misunderstood; for long differentially applied.

What are the answers and what the lessons?

It is clear today that framers and draftsmen of Everyman's Constitution were obliged to undertake—and did undertake—something unparalleled and prodigious, something still unique, something now urgent beyond all reckoning because that prescribed remedy went so long unheeded, unfulfilled. In one field of endeavor, we must remember, not in others.

Constitutionalism is the common law and the common sense of history and politics, the now *proven* way of "building better" than Everyman *sometimes* knows. Law, essentially, at best, is a rational, principled, sovereign rule and choice. The Law of the Constitution is the paramount (or "supreme") rational, principled, sovereign rule and choice. Race discrimination, overt or covert, is a tacit, personal, irrational choice, which, if neglected, condoned, and unchallenged socially, operates in the mass extra-officially, as a rule of custom, to deny personal political and economic rights and opportunities to those victims whom it irrationally, collectively condemns and stigmatizes as "racial inferiors."[2] Acquiescent, inert, passive government,

---

[1] MARK DEWOLFE HOWE, THE GARDEN AND THE WILDERNESS (1965), p. 176.

[2] On "racial inferiority" as the product and vestige of slavery as viewed in recent scholarship, see K. M. STAMPP, THE PECULIAR INSTITUTION: SLAVERY IN THE ANTE-BELLUM SOUTH (New York, 1956); S. M. ELKINS, SLAVERY: A PROBLEM IN AMERICAN INSTITUTIONAL AND INTELLECTUAL LIFE (Chicago, 1959); D. L. DUMOND, ANTISLAVERY, THE CRUSADE FOR FREEDOM IN AMERICA (Ann Arbor, 1961) 2 vols. (Vol. 2: A BIBLIOGRAPHY OF ANTISLAVERY IN AMERICA); L. F. LITWACK, NORTH OF SLAVERY: THE NEGRO IN THE FREE STATES, 1790–1860 (Chicago, 1961); D. B. DAVIS, THE PROBLEM OF SLAVERY IN WESTERN CULTURE (Ithaca, N.Y., 1965); W. D. JORDAN, WHITE OVER BLACK: THE DEVELOPMENT OF AMERICAN ATTITUDES TOWARD THE NEGRO, 1550–1812 (Chapel Hill, N.C., 1968).

in this one flagrant, frightening situation, thus does deny and deprive persons and citizens of their most precious rights—the protections of law and of government—does "deny" and does "deprive" them arbitrarily, insidiously, without hearing, or statute, or judgment—and does this in the face of Everyman's Constitution. The "classification" is covert, to be sure, but all the more arbitrary, irrational, insidious, and *invidious* for that.

Statesmen are men with the largest, longest views. America's constitutional statesmen are the Justices of the Supreme Court of the United States with the nearest total views, not merely of instant "cases and controversies," but of what can, what must be accomplished, by and through the processes of law and the protections of government, as these stand revealed and extended in decisions involving the powers of government on the one hand and the "life, liberty, and property" of Everyman on the other.

Due process of law and the equal protection of the laws, their antecedents and cognates, naturally have been preferred tools in this difficult "constitutionalizing" process and enterprise. Preferred tools of American constitutional statesmanship, for good and clear reasons. These clauses came to the fore—and remained there—because they encouraged, facilitated, and sanctioned large and long views—did this so well, and in part, because Everyman himself continually was getting into the effort and the act, using the same formulae and shorthand, taking equally large, long (or short) views, "nudging the judging" so to speak, nudging the dicta, conscience, and elbows. These clauses, were, if not the ideal, at least the preferred jurisdictionalizers, syncretizers, constitutionalizers, which afforded America's judicial statesmen the greatest decisional choice and freedom, the greatest responsibilities and opportunities, within a six or seven-century tradition, and within the current contexts, constraints, and emerging consensus. Beyond this, these clauses also made possible a jurisprudence of constitutional fact,[3] which has been at once the

---

[3] On the umpiring-syncretizing role of the Supreme Court, and its "task of mediation between large principles and particular problems, the task of interposing intermediate principles more tentative, experimental and pragmatic," see Freund, *Umpiring the Federal System*, 54 COLUM. L. REV. 561 (1964): "[J]udicial review is not merely a derivative from a society in agreement on fundamentals; in itself it is an educative and formative influence which, like the idea of a fair trial, may have consequences beyond its immediate applications for a people." On due process syncretism in particular, see Bundy, *A Lay View of Due Process*, in GOVERNMENT UNDER LAW (Cambridge, Mass., 1955); Hastie, *Judicial Method in Due Process Inquiry*, id.; Kadish, *Methodology and Criteria in Due Process Adjudication—A Survey and Criticism*, 66 YALE L.J. 319-363 (1957); Newman, *The Process of Prescribing "Due Process,"* 49 CALIF. L. REV. 214-239 (1961).

A Centennial View 587

means of keeping almost the whole Constitution viable, and of reconciling, by syncretism those often competing, often conflicting choices, under the ever-lengthening lines of "precedent," on the two sides of the Constitution—Powers and Rights. These clauses thus made possible something that any student, or any "decider" with a spark of insight or empathy, will see to have been essential—indeed inevitable—if the Supreme Court and American judicial review were to function effectively during their second and third centuries. No other phraseology, in short, embraced, affected, or effected one half so much. And none, significantly, mustered a fraction of the usage, interest, and application.[4]

The paradox is that these two extraordinary clauses nevertheless have been persistently underrated and misunderstood, in part because study of the constitutional process so long was thoughtlessly, arbitrarily restricted to study of constitutional rules and litigation as such—restricted simply to the judicial and the decisional side and process, rather than embracing the due process as a whole. (Imagine serious or prolonged study of American technology similarly restricted to the rules and the decisions of the Court and the Patent Office!)

Failure thus to take seriously, and to trace out the extrajudicial aspects of American constitutionalism has created serious misunderstanding of the Fourteenth Amendment, and of the Court's own role and relation thereto. The history of antebellum due process and equal protection in particular reveals two great issues—slavery and frontier taxation—in both of which lay, professional, and extrajudicial exploration and usage combined to nurture, anticipate, and ultimately to prompt and reinforce the growing judicial usage. Most important of all, it now has become painfully clear that America's race problem can be solved in no other way than by application of these constitutional powers and remedies—legal process and legal protection—just as framers of this Amendment contemplated.[4a]

Ignoring Everyman's Constitution, ignoring the pledged due process and equal protection, looked, and long was, easy enough. Ignoring texts and commands of any constitutional provision would

---

[4] See estimates in the *Preface, supra* p. ix, based on volume analysis of the "Constitutional Law" sections of the U.S. DIGEST and the DECENNIAL DIGEST, 1897 to date.

[4a] On "Process" and "protection" as related to race relations and here conceived as the indispensable means of actualizing and enforcing constitutional guarantees and corrective social action, see Ginger, *Legal Processes, Litigation as a Form of Political Action*, in LEGAL ASPECTS OF THE CIVIL RIGHTS MOVEMENT, ed. by D. B. King and C. W. Quick (Detroit, 1965) 195-217; see also SOUTHERN JUSTICE, ed. by Leon Friedman (New York, 1966).

have been easy in the premises. Our constitutional crisis presently derives from the fact that we no longer are free to ignore the repercussions and the consequences of those past ignorings. Besides, there now is this grave unforeseen "unforeseeable" complication: historically and judicially, due process nearly always has been slow process.[5] (Slow but steady, slow but continuous and progressive—that, remember, was the great advantage and attraction of Bingham's draft and plan, considered as part of the program which presumed continuance of the Freedmen's Bureau and similar means of easing the racial transitions and adjustments.[6])

The shock of recognition is that due process and equal protection so long overdue, so long unequal and deferred, dare not any longer be scant or slow. That quandary, like Everyman's Constitution, now is Everyman's indeed.

American due process and equal protection, we repeat, are not solely, nor even chiefly, judicial or professional creations. They never have been, and that, in this area, is their strength more than their weakness. Everyman early and persistently proved himself a more alert, innovative, successful constitutionalist than he or his critics and admirers have admitted or imagined. The pity is that after the Civil War the United States snarled, then lost, these threads of its constitutional development, and in part because law and scholarship ignored the role that the various lay, professional, extrajudicial hands and minds had played in the development—still had to play in it, but then were not, nor for long were encouraged, even permitted, to play. Congressional power in particular was curbed and denied.

Constitutional meaning and protection have to embody and reflect a great deal besides case law. Extra judicial factors have been and are the keys to Everyman's Constitution. And this is true on both the racial and the economic sides and fronts. So long as these central facts are ungrasped, the problem of achieving needed, intended affirmative racial protection remains difficult indeed. "Intent," for one thing, continues to be an ever-movable removable road block that delays and frustrates—something we observed it seldom was or did,

---

[5] For an early example, see Barnes, *Due Process and Slow Process in the Late Elizabethan-Early Stuart Star Chamber*, 6 AM. J. LEGAL HIST. 221-249, 315-346 (1962).

[6] Recent distinguished works clarifying the Reconstruction years and process are E. L. MCKITRICK, ANDREW JOHNSON AND RECONSTRUCTION (Chicago, 1960); J. H. FRANKLIN, RECONSTRUCTION AFTER THE CIVIL WAR (Chicago, 1961); B. P. THOMAS and H. M. HYMAN, STANTON: THE LIFE AND TIMES OF LINCOLN'S SECRETARY OF WAR (New York, 1962); L. and J. H. COX, POLITICS, PRINCIPLE, AND PREJUDICE, 1865-1866 (New York, 1963); K. M. STAMPP, THE ERA OF RECONSTRUCTION, 1865-1877 (New York, 1965).

for long, protectively, on the economic or the corporate fronts, 1880–1940.[7] An abstract, legalistic, "original understanding" thus still gets warped in, and placed ahead of, racial understanding, even though a broad racial understanding and adjustment unquestionably was the objective—the very sum and substance—of that original understanding.

One thing more about that "original understanding" deserves reemphasis. The ones who held it in 1866–1868, the ones who made it, the ones who added it to the Constitution by these clauses, were members of the antislavery generation. It is time we quit apologizing for their numbers, their manners, their woeful want of tact in speaking of slaveholders, benevolent or otherwise. Admit simply, and forthwith, that on one point—the need to treat people as people, persons as "persons," and not as chattels, not as second class citizens or persons—the framers and the antislavery generation have been proved absolutely right, as recent events and experience testify.

These things, then, at last are crystal clear: Racial inequality is slavery's vestige and vengeance. Racial inequality has been constitutionally outlawed for a century; it is individually, morally, and socially repugnant; nationally disgraceful, and internationally menacing. Hence racial inequality unquestionably is the gravest threat, "the gravest brutality of our time." And time itself finally has run out.

Mark DeWolfe Howe's resume and indictment thus stand, and they must immediately and powerfully remotivate. It is just as overwhelmingly clear that American government—federal and state, executive, legislative and judicial; American business, labor, and education—every institution of moment, conscience, and integrity—must unite with citizens of every faith and party, in all-out attack upon this long underrated, long deferred constitutional-social problem.

In marshaling forces, and in executing this attack one resource looms ever larger and larger; and almost certainly will prove decisive: American Business, American Corporate Enterprise, as shown above, is itself the colossal and almost fortuitous monument, to this Fourteenth Amendment—to constitutional process and protection munificently but not at all expressly, or even at first intentionally, extended. A monument, in short, to the proposition that individual and corporate opportunities *can* be thus created and extended, and even in the face of stubborn prejudice and badgering hostility.

---

[7] See Chapter 6, *supra*, notes 19–22 for these contrasts.

This, moreover, is no singular outcome, no uncommon historical experience. In the centuries-long development of constitutionalism, in the protection and the safeguarding of human rights—the rights of Englishmen in particular—in the making of the English Constitution, too, we have it from the greatest of constitutional historians, Bishop William Stubbs,[8] that "Opportunity is as powerful as purpose." The judicial and the extra judicial history of Everyman's Constitution thus reproves this point beautifully. Understanding and opportunity, in other words, are the ends of constitutionalism, seldom the "originals." They both are created and creative, and providentially, the two are correlative and reinforcing. Given the chance, and the start, they pay back and pay off. Each generates the other; the two go hand in hand. Recall again simply, as the heart of this corporate principle and parable, the lot, and the wonderful symbiosis, of the California Chinese and the Southern Pacific Railroad. Prejudice was crippling both. Prejudice was vitiating. Prejudice was vulnerable. Understanding and achievement in each case came with opportunity—with that protection which Justice Field, almost alone at first, supplied.

To quote the late Thomas Reed Powell again, "Due process is as due process does." Nothing else does so much, so well, except the equal protection of the laws—that equal protection of the laws which in this Chinese-corporate interlude in California, served as spearhead, just as due process earlier originally had done, for equal protection in the antislavery and frontier tax episodes. Mutuality again, in short, mutuality often. The mutuality of opportunity, of opportunity and understanding.

Statesmanship in our time has come to be as much economic as political; managerial and entrepreneurial, therefore, no less than constitutional and judicial. American Business justifiably prides itself on this. Advertising and public relations ceaselessly exploit and reiterate the point, sometimes perhaps over-capitalize it.

In any event, the chips are down now. In this race relations field, stakes are as high as they possibly can be. The nation's immediate needs fortunately, are needs Business supplies and fills best: jobs and decent housing, above all jobs and job training, with rising independence and security, and, in the aggregate, individual and social opportunity for those who now are outside of industry, and

---

[8] THE CONSTITUTIONAL HISTORY OF ENGLAND (3d ed. Oxford, 1883) II, 536. See also, R. F. NICHOLS, BLUEPRINT FOR LEVIATHAN: AMERICAN STYLE (New York, 1963).

sometimes even outside of welfare programs, at the very bottom of the social pyramid.[9]

The "know-how," leadership, and enterprise which in the 1940's filled and bridged the seas with ships nearly all built by "unskilled" labor, surely can rebuild slums, schools, hospitals; can replant forests, redeem eroded lands, and stop pollution of air and streams by similar methods and programs, as quickly and as well, now that the domestic urgency is as great as the emergency was in World War II. Train the untrained, the "untrainable," school the unschooled, and so protect persons, citizens, and society alike.

Today's giant corporations, "the new 500," we remind ourselves and are reminded repeatedly, rival and surpass the largest states in wealth, income, resources, employees, and the like. Because these corporations now are the peers of states, they must be regarded as states, and act and serve as states.

"Statesmen have no horoscopes." "Futurities are naked to the all-seeing eye,"[10] Conkling himself admitted. The routes and the course of constitutionalism, we have learned and shown are uncharted, and hardly predictable. Yet it is reassuring, nevertheless, to note that there appropriately is one provision of our Constitution, whose history and whose text together do provide the gothic piers and arches for just such achievements as are needed and have been postulated —do provide even a vision of the final possible whole—provided merely that corporate-managerial statesmanship does rise fully to the occasion and moves, voluntarily or otherwise, to assimilate and to reassimilate the Giant Corporation, this rival and surrogate of the states—into the constitutional order in ways commensurate with the corporations' present functions and importance. Proceed pluralistically, in short, on the economic front by and through the once-"private" sector; extend the gains that have to be extended, and do this swiftly, remedially, corporately as well as governmentally.

This constitutional provision just mentioned, of course, is that old comity clause: that very clause corporation lawyers, blind to the salvation at hand, wished and tried so long to make the pillar of their New Jerusalem—for corporate citizens, not corporate "persons."[11] This first clause of Article IV, Section 2 provides, "The

---

[9] For persuasive documentation, see NEWSWEEK, Nov. 20, 1967, p. 32–65, "The Negro in America"; N. E. Long, *The Progress of Poverty and the Poverty of Progress*, 65 UNIV. OF ILL. BULL. no. 28 (The Edmund J. James Lecture on Government, delivered April 12, 1967).

[10] See Chapter 1, *supra*, CONKLING'S ARGUMENT.

[11] See Chapter 2, *supra*, and Chapter 13, Editorial Note, *supra*, at 552.

Citizens of each State shall be entitled to all Privileges and Immunities of Citizens in the Several States."

Where now is the corporation or the labor lawyer, or possibly a Solicitor General or a Chief Justice of the United States, with the vision and the wisdom of a Marshall or a Warren or a Brandeis, who will regrasp these nettles, stand the old evasions on their heads, and fashion not another cat's cradle for the States, or for the Negro race,[12] nor another "perpetual shield" for corporations. Rather now, and instead, a constitutional pack frame, a St. Christopher's sling, a principle and a rule which shoulders fully these burdens and responsibilities, which acknowledges the fact that today's giant corporations are in truth "States," hence their employees, agents, customers, and the like, may, in due course and process of law, be held to be, on some occasions at least, "Citizens entitled to all Privileges and Immunities of Citizens in the Several States," including, by way of example, equal job opportunities, adequate and integrated housing, and the rest.[13]

That word "all"—"all Privileges and Immunities of Citizens in the Several States"—still is hyperbolic, as before, but this time on the side of responsibility and penance, as so long during the nineteenth century, it was the symbol of corporate unstatesmanship—of fatuity and frustration.

Collective bargaining, of course, may already be leading us to something of this sort. Yet Labor itself clearly has skeletons and challenges of its own to be met, as for example, its racially discriminatory apprenticeship policies.[14] The "constitutional" point here is that Labor too is corporate. Organized Labor is also a quasi-state. Thus Labor, too, can, and perhaps soon will be, assimilated into the constitutional order, its racially discriminatory policies reviewed and corrected by analogous reasoning, if not by this same comity formula. Logic and semantics present no problems. Everyman may thus again build better than he knows.

---

[12] See Introduction, *supra*. For signs that the "state action" syndrome is passing, and its days as short-circuiter and emasculator-in-chief of the racially motivated Fourteenth Amendment are ending, see U.S. v. Guest, 383 U.S. 745 (1966); Katzenbach v. Morgan, 384 U.S. 641 (1966) discussed in POLITICAL AND CIVIL RIGHTS IN THE UNITED STATES (3d ed., 1967), pp. 1424, 1485; and see especially Frantz, *Congressional Power to Enforce the Fourteenth Amendment Against Private Acts*, 73 YALE L.J. 1353 (1964).

[13] See Kingman Brewster, Jr., *The Corporation and Economic Federalism*, in THE CORPORATION IN MODERN SOCIETY (ed. E. S. Mason, Cambridge, Mass., 1961), pp. 72–84.

[14] See F. R. MARSHALL and V. M. BRIGGS, JR., THE NEGRO AND APPRENTICESHIP (Baltimore, 1967).

President Brewster of Yale, Professors Berle[15] and Eels[16] of Columbia, and Galbraith[17] and Mason of Harvard, among others, long since gave us our cues in these matters. The history of Everyman's Constitution does precisely the same. The only certainty is that the Constitution during the next century too will be what Everyman makes it.

---

[15] A. A. BERLE, JR., THE 20TH CENTURY CAPITALIST REVOLUTION (New York, 1954); also his THE AMERICAN ECONOMIC REPUBLIC (New York, 1963).

[16] RICHARD EELS, THE GOVERNMENT OF CORPORATIONS (New York, 1962). This is the most comprehensive, fullest-documented survey of the problems involved in "constitutionalizing" the giant corporation.

[17] J. K. GALBRAITH, THE NEW INDUSTRIAL STATE (Boston, 1967).

APPENDIX I

CONKLING'S ARGUMENT

[San Mateo County v. Southern Pacific R.R., 116 U.S. 138. A printed copy of this *Oral Argument of Roscoe Conkling* is preserved in a volume entitled SAN MATEO CASE, ARGUMENTS AND DECISIONS, in the Hopkins Railroad Collection of the Library of Stanford University. Below is a reprint of the constitutional portions of Conkling's argument, with the original paging indicated in boldface.]

[p. 13] The idea prevails—it is found in the opinion of the Court in the Slaughter House cases; it seems to have been in the mind of the court in Insurance Co. vs. New Orleans, (1 Woods, 85); it has found broad lodgment in the public understanding; that the Fourteenth Amendment—nay I might say all three of the latter amendments, the Thirteenth, Fourteenth, and Fifteenth, were conceived in a single common purpose—that they came out of one and the same crucible, and were struck by the same die; that they gave expression to only one single inspiration. The impression seems to be that the Fourteenth Amendment especially, was brought forth in the form in which it was at last ratified by [p. 14] the States, as one entire whole, beginning and ending as to the first section at least, with protection to the freedmen of the South.

Mr. Justice Miller in 16 Wallace, p. 67, speaks of "a unity of purpose" in all three amendments. Again, he speaks, p. 70, referring to the Fourteenth Amendment, of "the proposition" (in the singular) "submitted to amend the constitution," as by the Fourteenth Amendment. Again he says, p. 72, it is impossible intelligently to construe "any section or phrase of these amendments" without recurring to the one original always continuing purpose "which we have said was the pervading spirit of them all, the evil which they were designed to remedy."

It may shed some modifying light on this supposition, to trace from their beginnings the different elements, the different substantive proposals, strangers to each other, independent of each other, originating in different minds, and at different times, not in the order in which they now stand, which finally, by what might be called the attrition of parliamentary processes in the committee and in Congress, came to be collected in one formulated proposal of amendment—put together in sections for convenience and simplicity of submission to the States.

These originally separate, independent propositions, came from a joint committee of the two Houses, a committee most of whose members are dead. Of those who composed it on the part of the Senate, not one is living, save only Mr. Williams of Oregon. Of those who composed it on the part of the House, I believe a majority are gone. The committee sat with closed doors, the injunction of secrecy being often removed as conclusions were reached. A journal of its proceedings was kept by an experienced recorder from day to day.

It seems odd that such a journal has never been printed by order of either House. It has never been printed, however, or publicly referred to before, I believe.

[p. 15] Having consulted some of those whose opinions it preserves, and having the record in my possession, subject to the inspection of our adversaries, I venture to produce some extracts from it, omitting names in connection with votes.

From these skeleton entries—a journal is only a skeleton—your Honors will perceive that different parts of what now stands as a whole—even parts of the clauses supposed to relate exclusively or especially to freedmen and their rights—were separately and independently conceived, separately acted on, perfected, and reported, not in the order in which they are now collated, and not with a single inspiration or design. You will perceive also that before what now constitutes part of the first section was perfected, or even considered, the committee had reported, and lost all jurisdiction and power over, the portion of the amendments which did in truth chiefly relate to the freedmen of the South. The subject of suffrage, the ballot, and representation in Congress, was disposed of before the committee reached the language on which to-day's argument proceeds.

I begin the narrative with the entry of the 9th of January, 1866, the first meeting of the committee at which any proposed amendment of the Constitution was submitted.

"Mr. Stevens submitted a joint resolution, upon which he asked immediate action by the committee, proposing to submit for ratification to the several States the following amendment to the Constitution of the United States:

"Representatives shall be apportioned among the several States which may be included within this Union according to the number of their respective legal voters; and for this purpose none shall be considered as legal voters who are not either natural-born or naturalized citizens of the United States of the age of twenty-one years. Congress shall provide for ascertaining the number of said voters. A true census of the legal voters shall be taken at the same time with the regular census."

Appendix 597

[p. 16] On the same day the chairman of the committee, that is to say, William Pitt Fessenden of Maine, offered, apart from the resolution of Mr. Stevens, the following:

"*Resolved*, That in the opinion of this committee the insurgent States cannot with safety to the rights of the people of the United States be allowed to participate in the government, until the basis of representation shall have been modified, *and the rights of all persons amply secured, either by new provisions or the necessary changes of existing provisions in the Constitution of the United States, or otherwise.*"

I will not stop to ask your honors, most of whom knew Mr. Fessenden, why, if the end to which his mind was reaching out was simply to bespeak protection for the black man of the South, he should choose these general, sweeping, if not inapt words, when he could so easily, plainly, and briefly have expressed exactly the idea on which his thoughts were bent.

"FRIDAY, *January* 12, 1866.

"Mr. Stevens' resolution being under consideration, Mr. Conkling gave notice of the following substitute:

"Representatives and direct taxes shall be apportioned among the several States which may be included in this Union, according to their respective numbers, counting the whole number of citizens of the United States: *Provided*, that whenever in any State civil or political rights or privileges shall be denied or abridged on account of race or color, all persons of such race or color shall be excluded from the basis of representation or taxation.

"Mr. Bingham submitted the following proposed amendment of the Constitution of the United States, and moved that the same be referred to the sub-committee just authorized."

Not as an amendment to any other proposition, I beg to observe, but as a thing substantive, separate, independent, by itself constituting an amendment, a whole, separate amendment, to be proposed to the Constitution—

[p. 17] "The Congress shall have power to make all laws necessary and proper *to secure to all persons in every State within this Union equal protection in their rights of life, liberty, and property.*"

The motion was agreed to; that is, the motion to refer to the sub-committee.

SATURDAY, *January* 20, 1866.

"The chairman from the sub-committee on the basis of representation, reported that the sub-committee had directed him to report the following for the action of the joint committee; the first two as alternative propositions, one of which, with the third proposition, to be recommended to Congress for adoption:

"*Resolved, by the Senate and House of Representatives of the United States of America in Congress Assembled, two-thirds of both Houses concurring,* That the following *articles* be proposed to the legislatures of the several States as *amendments* to the Constitution of the United States, which when *they, or either of them,* shall be ratified by three-fourths of the said legislatures, shall be valid as part of said constitution, viz:

It may not be amiss to remind your honors that the alternative disconnecting words "when they, or either of them, shall be ratified, etc.," were copied from the language in which our fathers submitted to the States the ten several, distinct, amendments to the constitution in 1789.

"ARTICLE—. Representatives and direct taxes shall be apportioned among the several States within this Union according to the respective numbers of citizens of the United States in each State; and all provisions in the constitution, or laws of any State, whereby any distinction is made in political or civil rights or privileges, on account of race, creed or color, shall be inoperative and void."

Alternative article:

"ARTICLE—. Representatives and direct taxes shall be apportioned among the several States which may be included within this Union according to their respective numbers, counting the whole number of citizens of the United States [p. 18] in each State; provided that whenever the elective franchise shall be denied or abridged in any State on account of race, creed, or color, all persons of such race, creed, or color, shall be excluded from the basis of representation."

Now comes the independent article:

"ARTICLE—. Congress shall have power to make all laws necessary and proper to secure to all citizens of the United States, in every State, the same political rights and privileges; and to all citizens in every State"—

I beg your Honors to remark that the term here employed was "all citizens in every State"—

—"*equal protection in the enjoyment of life, liberty, and property.*"

"The joint committee proceeded to consider the report of the sub-committee.

"Mr. Stevens moved *that the last article be separated from whichever of the other two should be adopted by the committee, and be considered by itself.*

"The question was taken by yeas and nays, and decided in the affirmative; yeas, 10; nays 4; absent and not voting, 1.

"The second proposed alternative"—

That is, visiting the loss of representation on the States as a penalty of denying suffrage to the black man,—

"was by vote of the committee considered first."

Appendix 599

"Mr. Stevens moved to amend the proposed article by adding the following:

"And whenever the words '*citizens of the United States*' *are used in the Constitution of the United States, they shall be construed to mean all persons born in the United States or naturalized, except Indians.*

"Pending the consideration of which, Mr. Conkling moved to amend the proposed article by striking out the words 'citizens of the United States in each State' and inserting in lieu thereof the words '*persons* in each State, excluding Indians not taxed.'

[p. 19] "The question was taken by yeas and nays, and it was decided in the affirmative; yeas 11; nays 3; absent and not voting 1.

"So the amendment was adopted."

Mr. Stevens withdrew his amendment.

"The question was upon agreeing to the proposed article as amended"—

which I need not again read.

"The question was taken by yeas and nays, and it was decided in the affirmative; yeas, 13; nay, 1; absent and not voting, 1.

"So the proposed article, as amended, was agreed to."

On motion of Mr. Bingham—

"*Ordered*, That the chairman of the Senate portion of the joint committee (Mr. Fessenden) and the chairman of the House portion of the joint committee (Mr. Stevens) be instructed to report as early as practicable to their respective Houses *the proposed amendment to the Constitution of the United States this day agreed upon by the joint committee, and recommend its adoption by the same.*"

I remind your Honors that when this resolution had been adopted, the joint committee, it being a special committee, had not only acquitted itself of the whole matter of the proposed amendment, to wit, the right to suffrage of the freedmen of the South connected with representation, but *quoad* that subject the committee was *functus officio*. A special committee falls when it reports the subject committed to it, as an insect dies when it stings.

A special committee does not survive its report; it does not revive again unless "the House" recommits the report, or refers a new subject to the committee. Such is the parliamentary law.

After the report was made, the committee continued, only in respect of other matters with which it was charged.

[p. 20] WEDNESDAY, *January* 24, 1866.

"The committee proceeded to the consideration of the following amendment to the Constitution proposed by the sub-committee, on the basis of representation:

"Congress shall have power to make all laws necessary and proper to secure to all citizens of the United States in each State the same political rights and privileges, and *to all persons in every State equal protection in the enjoyment of life, liberty, and property.*"

Motions to amend were made, which I pass over.

"Mr. Blow moved to refer the proposed amendment to a select committee of three to be appointed by the chairman, with instructions to carefully revise the same."

And it was so referred.

It is worth while to observe that the committee to which it was referred was not the sub-committee which had considered the other amendment to the Constitution, but a new and different sub-committee.

The CHIEF JUSTICE—It was a sub-committee of the joint committee.

Mr. CONKLING—Yes, sir; a sub-committee of the joint committee.

"On motion of Mr. Stevens:

"*Ordered,* That the injunction of secrecy be removed so far as to allow any member of the committee to announce in his place in Congress, the substance and nature of *the proposed amendment* to the Constitution of the United States, under consideration by the committee this morning."

That is the amendment I have just read.

"SATURDAY, *January* 27, 1866.

"The committee met pursuant to the call of its chairman.

"Mr. Bingham from the sub-committee on the powers of Congress reported back the proposed amendment of the Constitution referred to them, in the following form:

"Congress shall have power to make all laws which shall be necessary and proper to secure *to all persons in every State* [p. 21] full protection in the enjoyment of *life, liberty and property*; and to all citizens of the United States in any State the same immunities and also equal political rights and privileges.

"The chairman moved to strike out the word 'also' in the last clause.

"The motion was agreed to.

"Mr. Johnson moved to amend the last clause by striking out the word 'any' and inserting 'every,' before the word 'State.'

"The motion was agreed to.

"Mr. Johnson moved to strike out the word 'all,' before the word 'laws.'

"The motion was agreed to.

"Mr. Johnson moved to strike out the last clause of the proposed amendment.

"The question was taken by yeas and nays, and it was decided in the negative—yeas, 4; nays, 6; absent and not voting, 5.

"So the amendment was not agreed to.

Appendix 601

"Mr. Stevens moved that the chairman be instructed to report the joint resolution, as amended, to the Senate, and recommend its adoption by Congress.

"The question was taken by yeas and nays, and it was decided in the negative—yeas, 5; nays, 5; absent and not voting, 5.

"So the motion was not agreed to."

As will be seen, the vote was a tie. The committee was composed of fifteen members. Five of the members voted for it, five members voted against it, and five members were absent—a fact of some significance, when we remember that the preceding amendment commanded a decided majority of the same committee.

WEDNESDAY, *January* 31, 1866.

"The committee met pursuant to the call of its chairman."

The amendment proposed by Mr. Bingham was the unfinished business, but there came back on this morning from the House of Representatives the previous amendment [p. 22] which had been reported to that House and to the Senate, touching suffrage and the basis of representation, recommitted to the committee with all cognate proposals, with all the amendments that the wit of man had suggested in the House. This recommittal reinstated the joint committee in relation to that subject, "revived" it, in parliamentary language, and immediately the returned proposition, to the exclusion of the pending proposition, was taken up and proceeded with. Here is the record:

"Mr. Stevens laid before the committee the joint resolution heretofore reported by the committee proposing an amendment to the Constitution of the United States in relation to the basis of representation, which, together with all propositions upon the same subject offered by members of the House, was by order of the House again referred to this committee without instructions.

"The committee proceeded to consider the joint resolution.

"After discussion—

"Mr. Stevens moved to amend the same by striking out the words 'and direct taxes.'

"The motion was agreed to by yeas and nays, as follows: Yeas, 12; nays, 2; absent and not voting, 1.

"Mr. Johnson moved to amend the proviso so that it should read"—

Here is a curious bit of history—

"*Provided*, that whenever the elective franchise shall be denied or abridged in any State on account of race or color in the election of members of the most numerous branch of the State Legislature, or in the election of the electors for President or Vice-President of the United States or members of Congress, all persons therein of such race or color shall be excluded from the basis of representation."

The purpose was that the freedmen might be excluded as voters in all county, municipal, and other local elections; but unless they were also excluded from elections for mem[p. 23]bers of the State Legislature, elections of members of Congress or presidential electors, the State should for that reason lose no representation.

That motion was lost. Then Mr. Johnson moved the following:

"*Resolved*, That the proposed amendment to the Constitution of the United States in relation to the basis of representation should be so modified as to include among the grounds of disqualification therein referred to in relation to the elective franchise one in regard to former conditions of slavery.

"The question was taken by yeas and nays, and it was decided in the negative—yeas, 6; nays, 7; absent and not voting, 2. So the resolution was not agreed to. Mr. Stevens moved that the joint resolution as modified be reported back to the House of Representatives with a recommendation that the same do pass. The question was taken by yeas and nays, and it was decided in the affirmative—yeas, 10; nays, 4; absent and not voting, 1."

So it went back just as it was reported at first, except that the committee had stricken out the words 'and direct taxes.' So, the States were to be partially denied representation as a penalty of abridging the suffrage, and the existing rule as to direct taxes was left untouched.

SATURDAY, *February* 3, 1866.

"The committee met pursuant to call of its chairman.

"The committee resumed the consideration of the proposed amendment of the Constitution of the United States, reported from the sub committee *on powers of Congress*, the same having been amended when last under consideration by this committee (January 27, 1866,) to read as follows:

"Congress shall have power to make laws which shall be necessary and proper *to secure to all persons in every State full protection in the enjoyment of life, liberty, and property*, and to citizens of the United States in every State the same immunities and equal political rights and privileges.

[p. 24] "Mr. Bingham"—

I beg your Honors to give attention to what now follows, because it seems to me quite significant—

"—moved the following as substitute, by way of amendment:

"The Congress shall have power to make all laws which shall be necessary and proper to secure to the citizens of each State all privileges and immunities of citizens in the States, (Art. 4, Sec. 2.) *and to all persons in the several States equal protection in the rights of life, liberty, and property*. (Fifth Amendment.)"

"After discussion:

"The question was taken by yeas and nays, and it was determined in the affirmative—yeas 7; nays 6; absent and not voting 2. So the amendment was agreed to. The question was upon agreeing to the proposed amendment of the Constitution as amended.

"The question was taken by yeas and nays, and it was determined in the affirmative—yeas 9, nays 4; and absent and not voting 2."

The next day, on the motion of Mr. Stevens this proposition, as a separate and entire amendment of the Constitution—the other amendment having gone, not only from the committee, but beyond its recall, and being pending in the two Houses—this substantive and complete proposition was reported by the committee to the two Houses.

Now, may it please your Honors, obviously the object of the draughtsman of this last referred to amendment in making reference on the face of his resolution to Article 4, section 2, and to the Fifth Amendment of the Constitution, was to remind the committee of the established meaning, and universally accepted import and force, of the words which there stood. May I not affirm if this record shows that the committee understood what was meant, that long afterwards, and after the land had been filled with discussion—"the American people," in the language of Mr. Justice [p. 25] Bradley, "in giving it their *imprimatur* understood what they were doing, and meant to decree what has, in fact, been decreed." (1 Abbott, 397.)

The committee took a week to consider this amendment, thus identified on its face with Article 4, section 2, and with the Fifth Amendment; and on the 10th of February, by a vote of 9 to 5, ordered it reported to the two Houses.

At the time the Fourteenth Amendment was ratified, as the records of the two Houses, will show, individuals and joint stock companies were appealing for congressional and administrative protection against invidious and discriminating State and local taxes. One instance was that of an express company, whose stock was owned largely by citizens of the State of New York, who came with petitions and bills seeking acts of Congress to aid them in resisting what they deemed oppressive taxation in two States, and oppressive and ruinous rules of damages applied under State laws. That complaints of oppression in respect of property and other rights, made by citizens of Northern States who took up residence in the South, were rife, in and out of Congress, none of us can forget; that complaints of oppression, in various forms, of white men in the South,—of "Union men," were heard on every side, I need not remind the Court.

The war and its results, the condition of the freedmen, and the manifest duty owed to them, no doubt brought on the occasion for constitutional amendment; but when the occasion came, and men set themselves to the task, the accumulated evils falling within the purview of the work were the surrounding circumstances, in the light of which they strove to increase and strengthen the safeguards of the Constitution and the laws.

The rights and wrongs of the freedmen, were the chief spur and incentive of the occasion. It may be true, as Mr. Justice Miller has observed, that but for these considerations this amendment never would have been suggested. What [p. 26] then? A particular grievance, some startling illustration of a grievance, is commonly the spur of agitation, and of popular or legislative action—sometimes of revolution. The slaying of his daughter by a Roman father, marked an era in Rome's history, and was the spur to radical changes in Rome's jurisprudence. Swine breaking through a fence is said to have brought on a war. Laying a tax by way of a paltry stamp on paper, sundered the relations of the Colonies and Great Britain. But what then? Did the logic of events, did the changes in jurisprudence, did the spirit of the age, did the principles established, did mutations wrought in relations, did the remedies and redress and general laws secured, confine themselves to the little cause, the particular instance, incident, provocation, or failure of justice, from which the agitation, the movement, the amendment, or the reformation came? It would be hard indeed to explain the second civil rights bill which did pass, and the unnumbered bills of kindred character which were brought forward and did not pass, if the Fourteenth Amendment had for its Alpha and Omega the protection of the dark browed man of the South. I do not forget that the civil rights bill takes the white man and his privileges, as the standard by which to measure the rights of all concerned; declaring that others should have the rights of the white man, such rights being deemed the acme of privilege, immunity, and protection. The men who wrought out the Fourteenth Amendment, were only breaking the way, not for future ages, but for more intrepid legislators; for aftercomers who should march further and with more fearless stride, because supported by a more advanced sentiment, gendered by more revealed necessity. The authors of the Fourteenth Amendment shrank from the idea of taking from the States the power of ascertaining, each State for itself, its own elective body; they paused and cowered before the finality of taking from the States the power to say who should and who should not wield the elective franchise. [p. 27] I say they shrank from such radical amendment. They quailed before the credulity of unbelief—one of the most paralyzing and stupefying of the world's forces. Those who had never seen done what afterwards was done in the southern States, because they had not seen it, did not believe, and would not believe it—they were credulous of their unbelief; and had the Fourteenth Amendment, or any amendment, at that time undertaken by direct Federal force to define, determine, and fix in each State, for the State, and despite the State, the right to vote,

Appendix 605

the concurrence of public judgment, that is to say the approval of a majority, which in a Republic is the force without which no party or administration or congressional policy or organic amendment can succeed, would have been wanting and failure would have frustrated the whole project.

The historic narrative in the famous Slaughter-House cases, omits a great fact, and an ardent sentiment which helped to usher in the Fourteenth Amendment. As I have said, no doubt regard for the rights of the freedman was uppermost in public thought. Uncle Tom's cabin had long been wept over; four million fetters had fallen; and slaves had given a majestic exhibition of temperance and moderation by abstaining from violence and vengeance when the homes of their masters were left unguarded by owners who had gone to the camp and to the field. Black men, on unnumbered fields of battle, had proved that "before man made them citizens, great Nature made them men." All this is true. It is also true that the term "carpet-bagger" had been coined, and a thousand pens had already begun to write "The Fool's Errand." Men who went first to the South carrying knapsacks, when the struggle ended had gone again to engage in the rivalries of peace. From half of the hamlets in the North, the restless foot of adventure had gone out to the South, and everywhere had met with resentment and suspicion, often with overt hostility. Objections to the presence of new comers from the North, had [p. 28] been formulated in the creed of a political party, and had received bloody baptism in leagues and lodges and klans. This was known, not only to the kinsfolk and the neighbors of the vicinage, but to the Representatives and Senators in Congress. In Lord George Gordon's case the court held the cry of the mob admissible in evidence as part of the *res gestae*; and the battle cry of a party against those denounced as "carpet baggers" and intruders—a cry with which the land resounded—was, and is, part of the *res gestae* of the Fourteenth Amendment. Hostility to the privileges and immunities of white men, and to their rights of person, property, and abode, was part of the "very age and body of time."

The elective franchise, citizenship, and the privileges and immunities of citizens, were all undoubtedly associated with the emancipated race, and the two former with that race exclusively. This cannot be said of any other subject matter of the Fourteenth amendment.

At page 72 of the 16 Wallace, Mr. Justice Miller says: "We do not say that none else but the negro can share in this protection. * * * And so, if other rights are assailed by the States which properly and necessarily fall within the protection of these articles, that protection will apply though the party interested may not be of African descent." To these words of grace, may be added the dissenting opinions in the same case, and much in like spirit may be found in Missouri vs. Lewis, 101 U. S., 22; and in U. S. vs. Cruikshank, 92

U. S., 542; and in the Sinking Fund cases. These sayings encourage the hope that this great ordinance will never be dwarfed into a mere remedy for a single wrong, and that of a nature which, with or without constitutional cure, must have been ephemeral in a civilized land in the last quarter of the nineteenth century.

At this point it behoves me to maintain that the Fourteenth Amendment operates upon associations of individuals, [p. 29] that is to say upon *corporations*, as well as upon individuals singly.

The word used to denote those embraced in the amendment, is "persons." This word, as found in the Constitution, and in other solemn instruments, has by long and constant acceptance, and by multiplied judicial construction, been held to embrace *artificial* persons as well as *natural* persons. Law-givers and law writers of the highest authority, have so fixed immemorially the scope of this term.

Corporations of the strictest sect, corporations especially created by royal grant, monopolizing the most exclusive and artificial attributes, have been, in instances without number—it may be said uniformly, held to be within the designation "persons." Coke, Blackstone, Kent, Marshall, Story, and all the galaxy from which in recent centuries has shone "the gladsome light of jurisprudence," again and again declared "persons," to be, and in law to mean, both natural and artificial beings.

The terms "persons," "occupiers," "inhabitants," even "individuals," have each been often held to include corporations or artificial persons.

Some of these cases are referred to in the opinion in the Circuit Court of Mr. Justice Field; others are collected in a note in 13 Federal Reporter, p. 785; still others are given in the brief of my Associate, Judge Sanderson, at pp. 31 to 48.

Among these authorities are instances in which, *in favorem vitae*, the construction was with the strictness applicable to penal statutes; and still "person" was held to include a corporation.

It must be remembered, too, that corporations, as known in England, and also in America, so long as they were created by special grant and charter, were ethically and legally more distinct and independent entities, more substantial and vital "abstractions," than the voluntary associations, which now, under general laws free to all, do business under a corporate or co-operate name, or, in the words of Mr. [p. 30] Justice Grier, "only a fictitious name." Yet it is to such specially created and highly endowed and favored corporations, that most of the authorities referred to relate.

The defendant here, in respect of its property, is in law and in fact but the business style of individual owners united and co-operating in a common undertaking, and who, as mere method and convenience, conduct business through corporate agency. Be it a church, a hospital, a library, a hotel, a mill, a factory, a mine, or a

Appendix 607

railroad, the property and assets of a corporation belong to no one save the creditors and the shareholders.

Suppose, in South Carolina, a society of colored men should incorporate themselves and acquire a hospital, a college, a lyceum, or a church; and this property should, by statute, be confiscated, either by discriminating taxation or otherwise, can it be supposed that the fact of their having formed a corporation, rather than a joint stock company or a partnership, would exclude them from the protection of the Fourteenth Amendment? Could such a cramped construction be given to the amendment, even if the rule of its construction restricted its operation to only the cases known or foreseen by those who chose the language?

The constituents of the corporation, the men and the women who composed it, would be the real parties in interest, and the Court would deal with them—not with names, but with things.

The doctrine here invoked is found in numerous decisions.

Bank of U. S. *vs.* Deveaux, 5 Cranch, 61.
Marshall *vs.* R. R. Co., 16 Howard, 314.
Society, etc., *vs.* New Haven, 8 Wheaton, 464.
United States *vs.* Amedy, 11 Wheaton, 392.
Sinking Fund Cases, 99 U. S., 718.
N. W. Fertilizing Co. *vs.* Hyde Park, 3 Bissell, 480.
Revised Statutes of U. S., ch. 1, sec. 1.
Atkins *vs.* Gamble, 42 California, 86; also, 57 California, 594.
Note and Cases, 13 Federal Reporter, 782.

[p. 31] Suppose colored men in Louisiana should, as a co-partnership or joint stock company, acquire a theatre or baseball ground, and, upon confiscation of their property, should receive the protection of the National courts acting under the Fourteenth Amendment, and afterwards should incorporate themselves for the management of the same property for the same purpose—if a second and like confiscation should occur, can it be that the same courts would say that the right of protection was lost by the act of incorporation, and might be revived again by resuming a copartnership name?

I have put the case of colored men. Let me transpose the illustration. In several States colored men outnumber white men. Suppose in one of these States, laws should be contrived by the colored majority, or a constitution set up, under which the property of white men should be confiscated, surely the Court would not say the Constitution is dumb, but would speak, if only the parties to the record were reversed.

I have sought to convince your honors that the men who framed, the Congress which proposed, and the people who through their Legislatures ratified the Fourteenth Amendment, must have known the meaning and force of the term "persons."

Let me now turn your attention away from this surmise to the real question to be answered. Let me remind you that the scope and effect of a general provision is never to be ascertained by seeking for the particular cases which the author had in thought at the time the provision was drawn or adopted. The court cannot acquit itself as interpreter and expounder by visiting, if the court could visit, the minds, and thoughts and hopes and fears and doubts and expectations and anticipations of those who took part in devising the Constitution. The true question, in exploring the meanings of the Fourteenth Amendment, is not, in a given case, whether the framers foresaw that particular case and acted in reference to it—the inquiry is, does the case fall within the ex[p. 32]pressed intention of the amendment? All cases compassed by the letter of the language, must be included, unless obviously repugnant or foreign to its spirit and purpose.

I ask the Court to listen to the rule of construction as laid down in the Dartmouth College case by a great and rugged magistrate. The words are the words of Chief Justice Marshall, speaking for the Court:

"It is more than possible that the preservation of rights of this description was not particularly in the view of the framers of the Constitution when the clause under consideration was introduced into that instrument. It is probable that interferences of more frequent recurrence, to which the temptation was stronger, and of which the mischief was more extensive, constituted the great motive for imposing this restriction on the State legislatures.

"*But although a particular and rare case may not in itself be of sufficient magnitude to induce a rule, yet it must be governed by the rule when established, unless some plain and strong reason for excluding it can be given. It is not enough to say that this particular case was not in the mind of the convention when the article was framed, nor of the American people when it was adopted. It is necessary to go farther, and to say that, had this particular case been suggested, the language would have been so varied as to exclude it, or it would have been made a special exception. The case being within the words of the rule must be within its operation likewise, unless there be something in the literal construction so obviously absurd or mischievous or repugnant to the general spirit of the instrument, as to justify those who expound the Constitution in making an exception.*" (4 Wheaton, 644–5.)

Could words—even prophetic words, more closely fit the position I maintain?

Who would be so rude as to suggest that committee, Congress, or people, when engrafting the Fourteenth Amendment upon the Constitution, omitted, only because they forgot it, to say that citizens might be stripped of their possessions without due process of law;

Appendix

provided only the spoliation should be under pretense of taxation and the victims robbed in a corporate name?

[p.33] If any man dare affirm such a belief, it must be one ignorant of the fact that Congress, when the amendment had been adopted, declared, in effect, that the shield of "equal protection of the laws" extended to *taxes, licenses,* and the like. This legislative construction was declared in the Civil Rights Act adopted as a substitute of an act passed before the ratification of the Fourteenth Amendment. The first act had not assumed to forbid unequal taxation, but, in the second act, under the warrant of the new amendment, Congress added discriminating taxation, in or by a State, to the list of offenses against the laws of the United States.

Judge Story, who also sat in the Dartmouth College case, and delivered an opinion, reiterates all that I have read from Marshall, in his Commentaries on the Constitution, 1395.

Who has ever gainsayd the canon of construction and interpretation thus plainly spoken from this bench?

With such a key to the import of a provision, how minor and needless become conjectures about what the actors in a past scene knew or thought or expected or believed, as to incidents or events in the future which might invoke the aid of a principle of law.

Man being human, and his vision finite, it is well that saving ordinances need not be shrunken in their uses or duration to the measure of what the framers foresaw.

Truths and principles do not die with occasions; nor do they apply only to events which have cast their shadows before.

The statesman has no horoscope which maps the measureless spaces of a nation's life, and lays down in advance all the bearings of its career.

"*Futurities are naked, before the all-seeing eye.*"

All that wisdom and science in legislation can do, is to establish just principles and laws; this done, every case [p. 34] which afterwards falls within them, is a case for which they were established.

A tree, a fountain, a lamp, set in the public way—a beacon on a cliff—a buoy on the sea, for whosoever sake first thought of or provided, becomes the benefaction and common property of wayfarers, whoever they may be.

To the Mongolian and the Caucasian, as well as to the African, the Constitution says: "*Humani nihil a me alienum puto.*"

"*The hand that rounded Peter's dome,
And groined the aisles of Christian Rome,
Wrought in a sad sincerity,
He builded better than he knew!*"

Those who devised the Fourteenth Amendment wrought in grave sincerity. They may have builded better than they knew.

They vitalized and energized a principle, as old and as everlasting as human rights. To some of them, the sunset of life may have given mystical lore.

They builded, not for a day, but for all time; not for a few, or for a race; but for man. They planted in the Constitution a monumental truth, to stand four-square whatever wind might blow. That truth is but the golden rule, so entrenched as to curb the many who would do to the few as they would not have the few to do to them.

If it be true that new needs have come, if it be true that wrongs have arisen or shall arise which the framers in their forebodings never saw—wrongs which shall be righted by the words they established; then all the more will those words be sanctified and consecrated to humanity and progress.

Before passing to another head of my argument I beg to remind the learned Chief Justice and the Court, of the language of the Court speaking through him in the Sinking Fund cases. Clearly the passage I shall read assumes that corporations are within the protection of the Fourteenth Amendment.

[p. 35] Here it is, 99 U. S., 718.

"The United States cannot, any more than a State, interfere with private rights except for legitimate governmental purposes. They are not included within the constitutional prohibition which prevents States from passing laws impairing the obligation of contracts, *but equally with the States they are prohibited from depriving persons or corporations of property without due process of law.*"

APPENDIX II

COMMITTEE ACTION ON H.R. 142 AND 349 AND RELATED BILLS, 1869–1871

BINGHAM introduced H.R. 142 on March 18, 1869: "a bill to secure and protect the freedom of transit and commerce within the U.S." H.R. 349 was introduced by him on March 31, 1869; both bills were referred to the House Judiciary Committee (Bingham chairman) in the Fortieth Congress. H.R. 349 was "a bill extending to corporations the privileges and immunities guaranteed by the Constitution to citizens of the respective States." The full text read as follows: "Be it enacted by the Senate and House of Representatives of the United States in Congress assembled, That corporations created by, and organized under, the laws of the several States of the United States are hereby declared to be citizens of the several States creating any such corporation; and as citizens shall be entitled to all privileges and immunities of citizens in the several States, as guaranteed by the second section of article fourth of the Constitution of the United States."

From the Docket Book, Committee on the Judiciary (40 Cong. 1st sess. to 41 Cong. 3d sess.), vol. 1939, National Archives, it appears that no action was taken until April, 1870. See also Minute Books of the same committee (40 Cong. 1st sess. to 41 Cong. 2d sess., vol. 1937; and 41 Cong. 1st sess. to 42 Cong. 3d sess., vol. 2002). On April 5 (vol. 1937, p. 232), "Present Messrs. Bingham, Davis, Butler, Cook, Mercur, Loughridge, and Kerr," H.R. 349 "was considered and it was agreed to report a substitute for the same and recommend its passage. Mr. Bingham to report." On April 16, 1870, H.R. 142 "was considered and it was agreed to ask that it be printed and recommitted" (vols. 1937 and 1939; the former lists "Present Messrs. Bingham, Butler, Davis, Cook, Mercur, Loughridge, Eldridge, Kerr and Kellogg").

Bingham was chairman and presided at these meetings. It was at approximately this time that he wrote W. H. Fessenden, Senator Fessenden's son, who replied on April 21, 1870, sending a transcript of the Joint Committee Proceedings of April 28, 1866. This meeting of April 28, 1866, had been the crucial one at which Bingham's drafts, after decisive rejection only three days before, finally gained approval by equally decisive votes. (Cf. KENDRICK, JOURNAL, 1914, pp. 97–100, April 25; and pp. 100–107, April 28, 1866.) The portion of the April 28, 1866, Joint Committee Journal entry copied by Fessenden appears at pp. 106–107 of KENDRICK, thus:

> Mr. Bingham moved to strike out the first section of the proposed amendment to the Constitution which was as follows:
> "Section I. No discrimination shall be made by any State, or by the United States, as to the civil rights of persons, because of race, color or previous condition of servitude."
> and to insert in lieu thereof the following:
> "Section I. No State shall make or enforce any law which shall abridge the privileges or immunities of citizens of the United States; nor shall any State deprive any person of life, liberty, or property, without due process of law, nor deny to any person within its jurisdiction the equal protection of the laws."
> After discussion,
> The question was taken, and it was decided in the affirmative, yeas 10, nays 3, not voting 2, as follows:
> Yeas—Messrs. Johnson, Williams, Stevens, Washburne, Grider, Bingham, Conkling, Boutwell, Blow and Rogers—10.
> Nays—Messrs. Grimes, Howard and Morrill—3.
> Not voting—The Chairman and Mr. Harris—2.
> So the motion of Mr. Bingham was agreed to.

After quoting this passage, Fessenden's letter to Bingham apparently continued (only a carbon copy on newsprint could be found in Mr. Ronsheim's Bingham papers, June 7, 1952) as follows:

> "There was no further discussion on this section in the Committee, and it was reported in this form to Congress. It is supposed that the clause defining citizens at the head of the amendment was added in the house. [ERROR: The sentence was of course added in the Senate.]
> "The meeting of the Committee was held on the 28th day of April, 1866, and the only other meeting that session was on June 6th, which was called to hear the report of the chairman."

All that can be inferred from the above is that some argument made by sponsors of the bills in April, 1870, caused Bingham to write W. H. Fessenden asking what the Committee Journal showed about the final action in the Joint Committee. No further action was taken on either 142 or 349 until the next session when, on December 12, 1870, the Judiciary Committee met and considered H.R. 349 (vol. 2002, p. 3). "Messrs. Bingham, Peters, Mercur, Eldridge, Kellogg, Cook, Loughridge and Butler" were present. It was agreed "to reconsider the order of April 5 last to report a substitute and let the matter rest."

Before the House Judiciary Committee could do this, Chairman Trumbull of the Senate Judiciary Committee asked and got leave on January 17, 1871, to introduce as Senate Joint Resolution 285 (41 Cong. 3d sess., GLOBE, p. 538) as follows:

> "In reference to life insurance companies,
> Be it resolved . . . that no penalty shall be imposed on any life insurance company

Appendix 613

which is authorized by the laws of the United States; nor shall any tax or other condition of doing business be imposed on any such company which is not, by the same authority, imposed upon all life insurance companies."

On January 25, 1871, Senator Trumbull reported adversely on this resolution, and moved indefinite postponement, "which was agreed to." (GLOBE, p. 715; SENATE JOURNAL, pp. 129, 164.)

On January 25, 1871, the House Judiciary Committee also met (vol. 2002) with Bingham, Butler, Cook, Peters, Mercur, Loughridge, Eldridge, and Kerr present. Considering H.R. 142, "Mr. Butler reported a new bill [apparently a substitute for H.R. 349]. Amended and agreed that Mr. Butler to report with amendment. Ask that it be printed and recommitted."

On February 2, 1871, the House Judiciary Committee met again. Present: Bingham, Butler, Cook, Peters, Mercur, Loughridge, Eldridge, Kerr, Kellogg, and Hotchkiss. From the action on H.R. 349, it is clear that the committee reported as a substitute therefor *the same text that had just been rejected in the Senate as Joint Resolution 285*: "Agreed to report a substitute, limiting it to insurance companies and changing the title. Mr. Bingham to report. Mr. Loughridge moved to amend by striking out the words 'or other condition of doing business.'" (An amendment designed to permit the states to continue requiring performance bonds of foreign life companies, while outlawing discriminatory state taxes against such companies.) Voting for the Loughridge amendment, were Cook, Mercur, Loughridge, and Kerr, 4. Nays: Bingham, Butler, Kellogg, Peters, Hotchkiss. The amendment lost therefore, and the substitute bill was reported by an identical 5–4 vote with Bingham and Butler in favor of a bill that would have outlawed both discriminatory taxes and bonds as well as laws requiring foreign life companies to waive their federally secured right to transfer suits from state to federal courts as a condition of doing state business. The Senate already had rejected such a measure as a Joint Resolution (*i.e.*, as a possible constitutional amendment). The Judiciary Committee of the House now was reporting it as a simple bill, a feeler perhaps, or a mere sop to the insurance interest. But Bingham and the Committee would have no truck with the original form of H.R. 349 which had proposed to corporatize the old comity clause by simple declaratory act of Congress. One surmises that Ben Butler of Massachusetts and Peters of Maine pressed for the measure to please insurance constituents. Bingham went along with that and in view of the Supreme Court's later decisions in *Home Insurance Co. v. Morse*, 20 Wall. 445 (1874), and *Doyle v. Continental Insurance Co.*, 94 U.S. 535 (1877), voiding such unconstitutional conditions as this substitute H.R. 349 would have outlawed, his action was sound and statesmanlike, but of no help to the companies. The substitute H.R. 349 was debated February 15, 1871, but quickly smothered by opposition of the West and South.

Bingham and Ben Butler went through the motions without hope of success. (41 Cong., 3d Sess., GLOBE, pp. 1288–90.)

Relevant chronology: H.R. 349 was not brought to the House floor until the Supreme Court had again rejected the commerce-comity clause legerdemain in *Ducat v. Chicago*, 10 Wall. 410, submitted December 20, 1870, decided January 9, 1871; and *Liverpool Insurance Co. v. Massachusetts*, 10 Wall. 566, argued January 11, decided February 6, 1871.

It was only after these final defeats in the Supreme Court, and after the defeat of H.R. 349 in the House, February 15, 1871, and after the Act of February 25, 1871, Sec. 2 (16 STAT. 431) wherein revisors of the statutes had redeclared the rule that the word "persons" may include corporations, that counsel for the Continental Life Insurance Co. of New York attacked a New Orleans ordinance as a denial of due process and equal protection under the Fourteenth Amendment. (*Ins. Co. v. New Orleans*, 13 Fed. Cas. 67, no. 7,052, C.C., La., 1871. The official record for this case shows that proceedings were started February 20-25 and the decree issued April 1, 1871.) February 25, 1871, was "Revelation Day" for the insurance bar, but this was twenty-nine months after the Fourteenth Amendment had gone into force.

Summary and Conclusion. Complete failure of the companies to make headway in the state courts prior to 1866 using the comity-commerce-due process legerdemain prompted Hine and others to seek congressional relief, 1865–1867. Failure of that campaign for the federal bureau, together with failure to gain judicial relief in the Supreme Court of the United States in *Paul v. Virginia* and related cases, led to the attempt in January, 1871, to obtain passage of S.J.R. 285. After Senator Trumbull's rejection of that measure came the perfunctory reporting of a similar bill to the House as a substitute for H.R. 349, and the defeat of this substitute in the House, February 15, 1871. Only then, and only after the nudge from the Revisors of the Statutes, ten days later, did counsel for the Continental Life Company, on their own initiative, decide to try their chances under Section 1 of the Fourteenth Amendment. The corporate "person" under the new dispensation thus was the last point to be raised by counsel and strategists for the insurance companies (acting individually and without central co-ordination). Only after every other attack had failed in Congress and in the courts did counsel raise the argument. John A. Bingham, in particular, pursued an independent course in his relations with the companies, 1866–1871. This is clear from Hine's second circular of February 13, 1867; from Bingham's letter to W. H. Fessenden (April [?], 1870) and W. H. Fessenden's reply April 21, 1870; from the subsequent action of the House Judiciary Committee and the action on the floor of the House, February 15, 1871.

Appendix 615

A final clincher—one which in itself testifies to the labored, sociological movement of constitutional thought and meaning—not necessarily to the nudging powers of statutory revision, is this (doubly significant now in view of the old apparent Bingham *Alta California* "associations"): On May 21, 1871, an editorial in the *Alta California* entitled "Taxation of Personal Property" observed "Corporations are, in a certain legal sense, persons, and they should bear the same burdens in the matter as individuals; no greater, no less." No mention of due process or of litigation; and this was before Bingham arrived in town.

On the face of such a record as this, I find it difficult to believe that Bingham's three-clause form of Section 1 was prompted by solicitude for the insurance interests, or that the insurance interests themselves originally regarded Section 1 with favor. Not every sigh is a desperate longing; and not every reference to the corporate person at this date had to be linked with Bingham. By 1871 the step at last was to be taken. But that step hardly was preconditioned. Corporations too had to learn to walk, and did.

APPENDIX III

THE FRONTIER TAX SYNDROME: BASIC REFERENCES

IN THE FURTHERANCE of needed and hoped-for extended investigations of this frontier tax syndrome, parts of my documented preliminary study (1958–1959), "Frontier Taxation and the Rise of Due Process-Equal Protection, 1790–1890," have been deposited in the Division of Archives and Manuscripts of the State Historical Society of Wisconsin, Madison. That manuscript deals at greater length and in documented detail with the problems of frontier government, taxation, and public administration as highlighted by Blackwell's *Treatise* and by the readings and basic references here listed.

The most useful and revealing state statutory collections are:

Virginia.
VIRGINIA STATUTES AT LARGE, 1619–1792. W. W. Henning, ed. 1823. 13 vols. [Continuation, 1792–1808. 1835–1836. 3 vols.]
VIRGINIA REVISED CODE. B. W. Leigh, ed. 1819. 2 vols. [Appendixes I–IV in vol. 2 reprint the land, forfeiture, and tax sale laws from 1705 to 1819.]

Kentucky.
STATUTE LAW OF KENTUCKY, 1792–1816. William Littell, ed. Frankfort, 1809–1819. 5 vols.

Ohio.
STATUTES OF OHIO AND OF THE NORTHWESTERN TERRITORY, 1788–1833. S. P. Chase, ed. Cincinnati, 1833–1835. 3 vols.

Illinois.
The Illinois State Historical Library Law Series, volumes 1–5, edited and collected editions (cited herein as ISHLLS, VOLS. 1–5), as follows:
Vol. 1. THE LAWS OF NORTHWEST TERRITORY, 1788–1800. Ed. with intro. by T. C. Pease. Springfield, 1925.
Vol. 2. THE LAWS OF INDIANA TERRITORY, 1801–1809. Ed. with intro. by F. S. Philbrick. Springfield, 1930.
Vols. 3–4. POPE'S DIGEST, 1815. Ed. with intro. by F. S. Philbrick. Springfield, 1938, 1940. 2 vols.
Vol. 5. THE LAWS OF ILLINOIS TERRITORY, 1809–1818. Ed. with

Appendix 617

intro. by F. S. Philbrick. Springfield, 1950. [Professor Philbrick's 477-page introduction to this volume remains the most searching and detailed study of territorial and frontier law and government; admirably complemented now by the Blume and Blume-Brown studies listed below. Indispensable in tracing the complexities of Illinois territorial jurisdiction and record devolution—prima facie revelations in themselves—are T. C. PEASE, COUNTY ARCHIVES (1915), and COUNTIES OF ILLINOIS: THEIR ORIGIN AND EVOLUTION, WITH 23 MAPS (n.d.), listed below. [Note also the PURPLE and THRALL collections of land and tax laws.]

Monographic works and articles.

H. C. ADAMS, TAXATION IN THE UNITED STATES, 1787–1816. Johns Hopkins University Studies, vol. 2, nos 5–6. Baltimore, 1884.

F. R. AUMANN, THE CHANGING AMERICAN LEGAL SYSTEM: SOME SELECTED PHASES. Columbus, 1940.

R. A. Billington, *The Origin of the Land Speculator as a Frontier Type*. 19 AGRICULTURAL HISTORY 204–212 (1945).

W. W. Blume, *Legislation on the American Frontier: Adoption of Laws by Governor and Judges: Northwest Territory, 1788–1798; Indiana Territory, 1800–1804; Michigan Territory, 1805–1823*. 60 MICHIGAN LAW REVIEW 317–372 (1962).

W. W. Blume and E. G. Brown, *Territorial Courts and Law: Unifying Factors in the Development of American Legal Institutions*. [2 parts.] 61 MICHIGAN LAW REVIEW 39–106, 467–538 (1962–1963). [Also Blume's earlier studies cited herein.]

E. L. BOGART, FINANCIAL HISTORY OF OHIO. University of Illinois Studies in the Social Sciences, vol. 1, nos. 1–2. Urbana, 1912.

B. W. BOND, THE CIVILIZATION OF THE OLD NORTHWEST. New York, 1934.

B. W. BOND, THE FOUNDATIONS OF OHIO [to statehood]. Columbus, 1941.

S. J. BUCK, ILLINOIS IN 1818. Springfield, 1917.

S. J. BUCK and E. H. BUCK, THE PLANTING OF CIVILIZATION IN WESTERN PENNSYLVANIA. Pittsburgh, 1939.

R. C. BULEY, THE OLD NORTHWEST: PIONEER PERIOD, 1815–1840. Indianapolis, 1950. 2 vols.

T. L. CARLSON, THE ILLINOIS MILITARY TRACT: A STUDY OF LAND OCCUPATION, UTILIZATION AND TENURE. Urbana, 1951.

C. F. CARPENTIER, comp., COUNTIES OF ILLINOIS: THEIR ORIGIN AND EVOLUTION [with 23 maps]. Springfield, n.d.

MERLE CURTI and others, THE MAKING OF AN AMERICAN COMMUNITY: A CASE STUDY OF DEMOCRACY IN A FRONTIER COUNTY. Stanford, 1959.

L. N. DEMBITZ, KENTUCKY JURISPRUDENCE IN FOUR BOOKS. Louisville, 1890.

L. N. Dembitz, A Treatise on Land Titles in the United States. St. Paul, 1895. 2 vols.

Thomas Donaldson, The Public Domain: Its History. Washington, 1884.

R. T. Ely and J. H. Finley, Taxation in American States and Cities. New York, 1888.

P. D. Evans, The Holland Land Company. Buffalo, 1924.

Thomas Ford, A History of Illinois from Its Commencement in 1818 to 1847. Ed. by M. M. Quaife. Chicago, 1945, 1946. 2 vols.

R. Freund, *Military Bounty Lands and the Origins of the Public Domain*. 20 Agricultural History 8–18 (1946).

P. W. Gates, The Illinois Central Railroad and Its Colonization Work. Cambridge, Mass., 1934.

P. W. Gates, *Land Policy and Tenancy in the Prairie Counties of Indiana*. 35 Indiana Magazine of History 2–26 (1939).

P. W. Gates, *Land Policy and Tenancy in the Prairie States*. 1 Journal of Economic History 60–82 (1941).

P. W. Gates, *The Role of the Land Speculator in Western Development*. 66 Pennsylvania Magazine of History and Biography 314–333 (1942).

P. W. Gates, The Wisconsin Pine Lands of Cornell University: A Study in Land Policy and Absentee Ownership. Ithaca, 1943.

P. W. Gates, *Frontier Land Lords and Pioneer Tenants*. Journal of the Illinois State Historical Society (June, 1945).

P. W. Gates, Fifty Million Acres: Conflicts Over Kansas Land Policy, 1854–1890. Ithaca, 1954.

P. W. Gates, *Tenants of the Log Cabin*. 49 Mississippi Valley Historical Review 3–31 (1962).

R. M. Haig, A History of the General Property Tax in Illinois. Urbana, 1914.

W. B. Hamilton, Anglo-American Law on the Frontier: Thomas Rodney and His Territorial Cases. Durham, 1953.

E. W. Hayter, *Livestock Fencing Conflicts in Rural America*. 27 Agricultural History 11–20 (1963).

B. H. Hibbard, A History of the Public Land Policies. New York, 1924.

G. E. Howard, An Introduction to the Local Constitutional History of the United States. Vol. 1: Development of Township, Hundred, and Shire. Baltimore, 1889.

J. W. Hurst, The Growth of American Law: The Law Makers. Boston, 1950.

J. W. Hurst, Law and the Conditions of Freedom in the Nineteenth Century United States. Madison, 1956.

J. W. Hurst, Law and Social Process in United States History. Ann Arbor, 1960.

Appendix

J. W. HURST, LAW AND ECONOMIC GROWTH: THE LEGAL HISTORY OF THE LUMBER INDUSTRY IN WISCONSIN, 1836–1915. Cambridge, Mass., 1964.

W. T. Hutchinson, "The Bounty Lands of the American Revolution in Ohio." Unpublished Ph.D. dissertation, University of Chicago, 1927.

JAMES KENT, COMMENTARIES ON AMERICAN LAW [1st ed.]. New York, 1826–1830. 4 vols.

Thomas LeDuc, *Public Policy, Private Investment, and Land Use in American Agriculture, 1825–1875.* 37 AGRICULTURAL HISTORY 3–9 (1963).

R. L. LOKKEN, IOWA PUBLIC LAND DISPOSAL. Iowa City, 1942.

F. L. PAXSON, HISTORY OF THE AMERICAN FRONTIER, 1763–1893. Boston, 1924.

T. C. PEASE, THE COUNTY ARCHIVES OF THE STATE OF ILLINOIS. Springfield, 1915.

T. C. PEASE, THE FRONTIER STATE, 1818–1848 [Illinois]. Chicago, 1922.

ROSCOE POUND, THE FORMATIVE ERA OF AMERICAN LAW. Boston, 1938.

N. H. PURPLE, A COMPILATION OF ALL THE GENERAL LAWS CONCERNING REAL ESTATE, AND THE TITLE THERETO, IN THE STATE OF ILLINOIS . . . [1776–1848]. Quincy, Ill., 1849.

S. A. Riesenfeld, *Law Making and Legislative Precedents in American Legal History.* 33 MINNESOTA LAW REVIEW 105–144 (1949).

R. M. ROBBINS, OUR LANDED HERITAGE: THE PUBLIC DOMAIN, 1776–1936. Princeton, 1942.

A. E. SHELDON, LAND SYSTEMS AND LAND POLICIES IN NEBRASKA. Lincoln, 1936.

Henry Tatter, "The Preferential Treatment of the Actual Settler in the Primary Disposition of Vacant Lands in the United States to 1841." Unpublished Ph.D. dissertation, Northwestern University, 1932.

WALTER THRALL, A TREATISE UPON THE LAWS RELATING TO THE TITLES OF LANDS WHICH HAVE BEEN SOLD FOR NONPAYMENT OF TAXES [in Ohio]. Columbus, 1847.

P. J. TREAT, THE NATIONAL LAND SYSTEM, 1785–1820. New York, 1910.

W. T. UTTER, THE FRONTIER STATE, 1803–1825 [Ohio]. Columbus, 1942.

W. S. Van Alstyne, Jr., *Land Transfer and Recording in Wisconsin: A Partial History* [2 parts]. 1955 WISCONSIN LAW REVIEW 44, 223.

F. P. WEISENBERGER, THE PASSING OF THE FRONTIER, 1825–1850 [Ohio]. Columbus, 1943.

Index

ABBREVIATIONS

14A = Fourteenth Amendment
dpl = due process of law
epl = equal protection of the laws
∞ = repetition of preceding phrase or entry

ABOLITIONISM. See Antislavery impulse, Antislavery movement.
Adair, Douglas, 26
Adams, Henry, 16
Adamson v. California, 158, 238, 314
Affirmative (applied to law, constitutionalism, and government), 4, 153, 269, 297, 507n, 517
Agency, 515
Alabama: economy, 524
Allgeyer v. Louisiana, 64, 441
"Amador Conspiracy," 125ff, 556
American Antislavery Society: 156, 164, 251, 280, 301; annual reports of, 215n
American conscience, 3, 8, 186ff, 551
American creed, 3, 7, 8, 153, 186ff, 545, 551
American Law Magazine, 260
American Political Science Review, 98
An American Dilemma, 67, 98, 191, 551
Anderson, Alexander, 102
Antislavery impulse (to about 1835): 163, 164, 172, 539; beginnings, 171, 186ff; Biblico-moral, natural-rights appeal, 190-207; British precedent, 164, 204, 209; churches and, 193ff; constitutional contributions of, 171, 239, 589; evangelistic immediatism of, 172, 208; migrations reinforce, 193ff; newspapers, 197; Ohio focus, 197ff; quest for law and protection, 169, 206ff; and slave insurrections, 209-211; reorientation and politicalization, 208, 214ff; South's rejection of, 211-213
The Anti-Slavery Impulse, 66, 156, 163ff
Antislavery movement (from about 1833-1835): antebellum history key to *14A*, 156, 160-162, 170, 186, 278ff; Bingham's constitutional theory rooted in, 161-163, 280; Birney-Weld-Tappan leadership, 164-167; crusade for equal protection, 169ff; in Illinois, 502; Ohio Antislavery Society publications postulate paramount national citizenship, seek *dpl-epl* for free Negroes (1835), 171-176, 278ff; Tappan-hired counsel in *Crandall* case formulators of this theory, 176-184; Birney-edited *Philanthropist* elaborates, turns theory against slavery *per se*, 216-236, 254; propagation by resolutions, petitions, party platforms (1840-1860), 170ff, 255, 280, 301; widening appeal and impact of (1837-1868), 236-241, 542
"Arguments from silence," 159, 276, 484
Articles of Confederation, 192, 219, 278
Ascoli, Max, 94, 490
Ashley, James M., 302
Aves. See *Commonwealth v. Aves*.

BAKER, E. D., 263
Baldwin, Henry, 49
Baltimore and Ohio Railroad, 454ff
Baltimore v. Pittsburgh and Connellesville Railroad, 87n, 462
Bank of Augusta v. Earle, 74-75
Bank of Toledo v. City of Toledo, 73n, 572, 578, 579n
Barbier v. Connolly, 431, 441, 570, 576, 578
Barnard, Chester I., 370
Barnes, Gilbert H., 66, 156, 163
Barnes, William, 84n, 556
Barron v. Baltimore, 56, 58, 84, 238, 248, 308, 314, 316, 320n
Bartemeyer v. Iowa, 134ff
Bates, Edward, 318, 321
Bates, Ernest Sutherland, 33
Beaney, William T., 243
Beard, Charles A. and Mary R.: 19-21, 65, 68, 95, 96, 100, 364, 396, 435, 442, 453, 470, 582; contributions of, 19-21, 26-27; on *14A* intent, 19-21, 23-24, 26, 27-30, 33; thesis criticized, 23, 26-27, 33-35, 442, 453. See also "Conspiracy Theory," Corporate "person."
Becker, Carl L., 337

621

622 Index

Beckwith, Corydon, 121, 394n, 502, 522, 534, 542
Bell v. Maryland, 561
Bell's Gap R.R. v. Pennsylvania, 541, 575
Benezet, Anthony, 191
Bennett, Nathaniel, 102
Berea College, 155
Berle, A. A., Jr., 593
Bill of Rights: 277; as guarantees to be enforced, 254, 444; state, 181, 187, 192, 219, 251 (Mass.), 253 (Ohio), 261, 278, 300, 457ff (Pa.), 509 (Ind.), 526ff (Ill.); U.S. (constitutional amendments 1–8), 278, 380; ∞, viewed by abolitionists as morally binding states, 169, 231-235, 255; ∞, incorporation of, 158, 238, 265, 275, 314n, 320n, 323n, 366, 389; ∞, Justice Field's view of, 405
Bingham, John A.: 12, 18, 19, 24, 32, 70, 79, 80, 83, 96, 126, 155, 199, 236, 276, 301, 305, 313, 316, 442ff, 541, 542, 552, 555, 558, 584; aims of, 32, 47ff, 61-64, 131, 159, 240, 309ff, 444, 564, 588; Beards misread, 33; and Bill of Rights, 47, 240, 314n; in California, 126n, 134, 556; views on comity clause, 61, 161, 281ff, 318; Credit Mobilier and, 123n; denies Supreme Court "final arbiter"; views on *dpl,* 53-63, 162, 280ff, 310n; at Franklin College, 199-200, 232, 256, 280, 280ff; House speeches of, 47-50, 162, 185, 200, 280ff, 309, 313; insurance companies and, 84n, 85, 96, 122, 552-554, 611-615; invokes *dpl* substantively and racially, 35, 50-53, 57n, 161; Justice Miller and, 134n; railroads and, 88, 90-91, 466, 467, 482; vindication of, 552-561, 584, 611-615
Birney, James G.: 156, 165, 251, 502, 537, 542; constitutional theory of, 216-236
Bishop, Joel P., 168n
Black, Hugo, 27, 68, 92n, 100, 123n, 158, 238, 240, 382
Black, Jeremiah S., 78, 457, 463ff
Blackstone, Sir William, 308, 347
Blackwell, David, 521, 534
Blackwell, Robert, 521, 534
Blackwell, Robert S.: 492, 497, 503, 521, 534, 542, 546
Blackwell on Tax Titles: 496ff, 506ff, 517ff, 579; citation and use of, 503; editions, 537; importance of, 536-541, 555
Blaine, James G., 16
Bliss, Philemon, 56, 79, 162, 168, 199, 302

"Bootstrap constitutionalism," 7, 9, 13, 284
Boudin, Louis, 33, 66, 96
Boutwell, George S., 236
Bradley, Joseph P., 11, 12, 105, 126, 137, 240-241, 291n, 297, 384, 403, 421, 540, 559, 560, 561, 563-565, 576ff
Brandeis, Louis D., 113, 592
Brewer, David J., 497, 508
Brewster, Kingman, Jr., 592n
Bronson, G. C., 245, 259, 262
Brown v. Hummel, 72, 86, 351, 457ff, 469ff
Browning, O. H., 263, 484n, 496, 502, 521, 534, 542
Burnett, Peter Hardeman, 102
Butler, Benjamin F., 558, 613, 614

CALDER *v. Bull,* 212
Calhoun, John C., 211, 215, 358
California: 14, 23; hostility to Chinese and corporations, 14, 146, 556, 571, 576; business-economic, 83, 121, 142-147, 150, 491, 508, 572; racial-humanitarian use of *dpl-epl,* 142-147, 150, 559-560, 572; compared with Southern Pacific Railroad, 432
California Railroad Tax Cases (1882–1890): 16, 23, 25, 107, 273n, 398ff, 543, 559; in U.S. Circuit Court, 399-414; in U.S. Supreme Court, 414-428, 566ff, 575
Camp, Edgar W., 79, 96
Campbell, John A., 122, 148, 384
Capitalism: constitutional bulwarks of, 121, 147n
Carpenter, Matthew H., 132-133, 295, 323-333
Caton, John D., 502, 503, 507
Central Pacific Railroad. See Southern Pacific Railroad.
Chafee, Zechariah, Jr., 23
Charles River Bridge case, 245
Chase, Salmon P., 121, 168, 212, 301, 462, 542, 561, 577
Chicago bar, 121, 497, 502-503, 519, 520, 542
Chinese: hostility to in California, 14, 105, 142ff; protected by federal courts, 143-151, 267, 393, 402, 571ff, 590
Citizens (constitutional term): 32, 524, 548; corporations as, 73ff, 381ff, 395n, 407, 558, 571, 581; free Negroes and freedmen as, 170-185, 270, 297, 318, 321; slaves as, 270; of states, 178, 179, 319; of U.S., 61, 175, 278, 296ff, 310ff, 318ff
Citizenship clause, *14A:* 388; addition by Senate, 123n, 131, 160, 296, 318,

Index 623

385, 486; derived from Civil Rights Bill, 309ff, 320; juxtaposition of, misread, 132ff, 296, 318ff, 319n, 385, 388, 486; *Slaughter-House* application of, indefensible, 316n, 319ff, 486
Civil Rights Acts and Bills: 566; (1866) 270, 291n, 295, 305ff, 323ff, 418, 560, 564; (1870) 418, 555, 560, 574n; (1871) 69, 120n, 126, 132, 316, 323n, 394, 395, 556; (1875) 11
Civil Rights Cases: (1880) 397, 402; (1883) 11, 240, 370, 425n, 560, 563, 578
Civil War: 272, 306, 460, 466ff; amendments to Constitution, 26, 156, 157, 270, 405; ∞, antislavery motivations of, 163, 189, 237; ∞, business and, 94n
Clark, Charles E., 68, 346
Classification (constitutional): race and slavery as arbitrary, 10, 189n, 201, 586
Clay, Henry, 194, 218, 359, 363
Cleveland, Grover, 108
Cleveland and Mahoning Railroad, 86ff, 445ff
Clifford, Nathan, 562
Coke, Sir Edward, 525, 528, 537, 549
Colton, D. D., 127n
Comity clause (Article IV, Section 2 of U.S. Constitution): antislavery use of, 173ff, 176, 278ff, 300, 309; Articles of Confederation version, 178-179, 192, 278, 283; Bingham's theory of, 49, 51, 61, 281ff; business-corporate use of (before 1868), 73ff, 373n, 383, 490, 524; ∞ (after 1868), 122, 558, 591ff, 611ff; pro-slave use of, 49, 524; as source of privileges-immunities clause of *14A*, 176ff, 280ff
Commerce clause and power, 49, 84, 342, 348ff, 360ff, 374, 379, 383, 460ff
Common law, 504, 519, 523, 533, 537, 544ff
Commonwealth v. Aves, 252
Communist Manifesto, 119
"Compromise of 1877," 240, 335
Confiscation Cases, 120
Conkling, Frederick, 556
Conkling, Roscoe: 14, 18, 64, 82, 93, 96, 99, 293, 398, 466, 481ff, 561, 563; argues *San Mateo* case, 16, 30, 70, 416ff, 440, 573; characterized, 15-16, 447, 448, 491, 558, 560, 566, 573; member of Joint Committee, 17, 236, 440, 552; ∞, voting record analyzed, 89n; ∞, favors railroads, 88, 466; misuses Joint Committee journal, 17, 19, 38-45, 416, 443, 574; *San Mateo* argument, 17, 24, 26, 68, 82, 273, 352, 416n,

440, 541, 555; ∞, analyzed, 17, 35-45, 96, 352, 416-419, 574; ∞, reprint of, 595-610; visits San Francisco, 556
Connecticut: racial-humanitarian use of *dpl-epl,* 176ff, 185
Connecticut General Life Insurance Co. v. Johnson, 27, 92, 123n, 273, 383, 386ff
Conspiracy, 65, 96, 470, 554, 557
"Conspiracy Theory" of *14A:* 4, 23, 27, 65, 70, 99, 366, 438-439; autopsy and rationale, 26-27, 439, 449, 556ff, 582; circumstantial origins and bases of, 17-18, 23, 26-30, 65, 69, 440ff, 468ff, 555ff; defined, 4, 61-64; disproof of, 19, 93-94, 552ff, 571; fallacies noted, 23, 65, 442ff; investigated, 23-27, 35ff, 68-69, 98-100, 438ff, 491-493, 550-561, 611-615; problems of, 35, 46, 66, 80, 439, 450-453, 481ff, 552ff; railroads and, 438-491; *realpolitik* inflated as, 438, 555, 558, 560n; "secondary intention" hypothesis and, 90n, 96, 122, 450ff, 481ff, 554; underlying premises of, 18, 351, 552-558
Constitution. *See* U.S. Constitution.
Constitutional adjudication, 379-381, 544
Constitutional history, 248, 272, 273, 548, 554, 579
Constitutional law, 247, 248, 272, 285, 548, 585
Constitutional meaning, 26, 366
"Constitutional revolution," 4, 388, 518. *See also* Due process "revolution."
Constitutionalism: 3, 98, 151, 585; American, 20, 150, 152, 239, 267, 435, 519, 549; ∞, adversary jurisprudence in, 267; ∞, *dpl-epl* as preferred tools of, 7, 213, 277ff, 542ff, 586ff; ∞, extrajudicial elements in, 541ff, 549, 587; ∞, "higher law" and, 284ff, 299; "common law," 7, 267, 496, 537, 544, 581, 582; defined, 6, 585; English, 3, 5, 266, 296, 525, 538, 547, 590; frontiers and, 493-551; history and, 3, 20, 337ff, 557, 582; land and, 498ff; natural law and, 6-7, 284ff, 517, 547; printing and, 296, 550; as "process" and "protection," 6-7, 13, 20, 267, 284ff, 549, 588ff; versus racism, 6-9, 20, 585ff
Continental Life Insurance Co. v. New Orleans, 92, 123, 130, 146, 381, 384ff, 398, 415, 420ff, 430, 490, 559, 571, 595ff, 614
Contract clause, 118, 245, 249, 328ff, 374, 379, 404, 474ff
Cook, Burton C., 502, 542, 553, 611-613

Cooke, Jay, 85n
Cooley, Thomas M., 121, 148, 202, 246, 397, 405, 430, 497, 505, 508, 510, 529, 539, 579
Cooper, Thomas, 210
Corfield v. Coryell, 48, 74, 180, 252, 307, 309, 311, 331, 383
Corporate "person" (constitutional): 64, 94, 116, 127, 246, 274, 275, 414n, 555, 559, 575n; congressional relief for corporations and, 450ff, 470, 488ff, 555; doctrine of, 95, 374ff, 566ff; eclipse and recovery of, 130-147, 382ff, 395, 476; Field's views on (1882), 116n, 375, 403-414, 478, 573; (1883), 370, 375, 418, 426-428, 574; (1886–1890), 559, 569ff; judicial review and, 379ff, 433, 450, 468; press comment on, 412-415; state courts and, 428n, 572; Supreme Court and, 395n, 428n, 429, 566ff, 578. *See also* Woods, William B.
Corporations: 13, 17, 23, 146, 150-151, 370ff, 499; as states, 431n, 591-593
Corwin, Edward S., 49n, 54, 59, 69, 77, 99, 244, 299, 365n, 396, 487, 506, 581
Councils of Censors, 545
Crandall, Prudence, 176ff, 252, 278
Crandall, Reuben, 211n
Crosskey, William W.: 240, 299, 338; his *Politics and the Constitution*, 337-366
Cumberland Road, 358ff
Curtis, Benjamin R., 92n, 540
Cushing, William, 193
Custom, 278n, 519, 564, 566

Daggett, David, 180, 184
Daggett, Stuart, 33
Dartmouth College v. Woodward, 71, 118, 257, 293, 404, 418, 474ff, 528, 549
Davidson v. New Orleans, 394, 396, 436, 508, 573, 575n
Davis, J. C. Bancroft, 560, 567, 578
Davis, John W., 273
Deady, Matthew P., 25, 392ff, 411, 425, 575
Declaration of Independence: 3, 55n, 206, 298; as basic American constitution, 55, 187ff, 238, 277, 298; *epl* derives from, 3, 162, 278ff, 445, 539
"Declaratory" (as legal concept and term), 9, 289, 295-334
De facto segregation, 335-336
Delaware Railroad Tax Cases, 446
Dicey, A. V., 582
Dillon, John Forrest, 106, 429, 497, 508
Discrimination, 4ff, 278, 310, 315ff, 585

Dixon, Luther Swift, 497
Doak, Samuel, 195, 198
Doctrine of changed conditions, 292
Dodd, E. M., 438
Douglas, Stephen A., 497, 546
Douglas, William O., 10, 17, 158, 240, 382
Dred Scott v. Sanford, 35, 54, 56, 118, 162, 240, 244, 256, 283, 446, 459, 540, 546
Drummond, Thomas, 121n, 394, 395, 422, 503, 542
Ducat v. Chicago, 92n, 614
Due process of law (*dpl*): clause and guarantee of, 5, 117, 155, 293, 378; academic misconceptions of, 243ff, 264, 380, 497, 507n, 579, 586; affirmative racialized, 153, 242, 290, 297, 588; antislavery use of, 157ff, 251ff; antebellum exploration of, 247-265, 457ff, 509n, 517ff, 540ff, 579; as constitutional shorthand, 255, 277, 377n; as constitutionalized natural law, 249ff, 284ff, 537, 547, 581; corporate use (pre-1868), 70ff, 121, 378, 457ff, 471, 572; ∞ (after 1868), 96, 126, 351, 393n, 394-395, 415ff, 463ff, 570ff; deracialization of, 155, 290n, 291, 544; dynamism of, 291ff, 380; economic use and misuse of, 17, 19, 27, 99, 121, 389, 394, 415ff, 439, 502, 518, 536; extrajudicial, *see* Chapters 4–6, 10–12, 14 *passim*; frontier taxation and, 498ff, 517ff; in 5A, 47-49, 96, 118, 232, 249, 253, 300, 310, 374, 378, 406; judicial review and, 99, 117, 214, 395n, 467, 547-550, 581, 586; Negro race and, 11-13, 150, 267, 290n, 293, 416, 423, 581; in Northwest Ordinance, 56; Pennsylvania legislature's understanding of (1864–1866), 471ff; "persons" protected by, 25, 310n, 375, 418ff, 471, 578; procedural-substantive division and conceptions, 3, 34, 117, 244ff, 467ff, 519ff, 525, 539ff, 543, 547, 576, 579; "profit" secured by, 380n; proslave use of, 253-256; "Rule of Reason" and, 239, 258, 275, 441n, 547ff, 576ff; in state constitutions, 115, 118, 257 (Tenn.), 258, 380, 457ff (Pa.), 526ff, (Ill.), 579; substantiality of purpose test, 229, 547; syncretic potentialities and uses of, 548-550, 581, 586; taxing power and, 435-437, 523ff, 547
Due process "revolution," 26, 27, 239, 242, 243
"Dueness" and "duty," 4, 153, 439
Dumond, Dwight L., 156, 163, 169

Index

Duncan, James, 198
Du Ponceau, Peter Stephen, 262n

EDMUNDS, George F., 88n, 323, 329, 399, 416, 421
Eels, Richard, 593
Electoral Commission (1877), 136, 252
Ellsworth, William W., 177ff, 537
Equal protection of laws (*epl*): concept, clause, guarantee of, 5, 519ff; affirmative, 153, 269, 297; antebellum antislavery use, 157ff, 206ff; antebellum economic roots, 519-550; anti-race discrimination motivation of, 189n, 276, 425n, 581; corporations invoke use of (1870), 391ff, 502; principal beneficiaries of (1886–1940), 274n, 566, 589; Declaration of Independence and, 3, 161, 206, 278; denial by state inaction, 200n, 297, 316n, 565; deracialized, 271, 291, 369, 563, 566, 583, 588; as ethical-moral concept, 292, 304, 582; frontier tax syndrome and, 493-551; natural rights premises of, 186ff, 284ff, 578; "persons" protected by, 271, 375, 425, 566, 582; qualitative rule and test, 304, 582, 586; spearhead for due process, 577; taxing power and, 435-437, 498, 518, 525, 541ff
Erie and Northeast Railroad v. Casey, 78, 79, 86, 456ff, 469
Erie Railroad v. Tompkins, 343, 344, 351
Everyman's Constitution (*14A*, Sections 1 and 5): 4-5, 20, 98, 268, 296, 308, 366, 380, 560, 593; aims, purpose of, 5ff, 313ff, 581; as constitutional shorthand-trinity, 161, 242, 250, 255, 277, 301, 313, 444, 542ff; business invokes and explores, 121n, 126, 351, 393ff, 415; centennial view, 585-593; congressional debates on (1866), 45-53, 303, 320-321; "declaratory" theory and confusion undo, 319-334; in *Slaughter-House Cases* (1873): 330-333; in U.S. Senate (April, 1871), 323-330; defined, 4, 549; form changed from positive to negative, 32n, 83n, 130ff, 171n, 296, 303, 316; "framer intent" and, 275, 450-453, 588; judicial or substantive "revolution," 519ff, 547, 550, 578ff, 583; mini-constitution, 6, 130, 277, 380, 544; "poor draftsmanship" of, refuted, 284ff, 294, 303-304, 430, 550-551, 584; racial purposes of, 5, 274, 276, 425n, 581ff; ∞ acknowledged, 10, 19, 404, 423, 425, 450, 595; ∞ controverted, 157, 275; ∞ evidenced, 19, 157ff, 308, 314, 320, 424, 444, 555, 574, 583-584; ∞ honored, 334, 423, 583; ∞ ignored, 267, 319, 425n, 563ff, 587ff; ∞ miscarry, 293, 318ff; ∞ researched, 157ff, 268, 274ff, 300, 438ff; ∞ resisted, 585; segregation and, 266ff, 335, 585ff; tortured construction of, 11, 268, 294ff, 319ff, 330-333, 351, 415ff, 563, 583-584; uniqueness of, 20, 520-521, 585ff
Ex Post Facto clauses, 328, 348ff

FAIRMAN, Charles, 137, 158ff, 240, 297, 315
Faulkner, Harold U., 554
Federalism, 4, 94n, 88-89, 157, 309, 360, 373, 376, 499, 504, 517
The Federalist, 524
Federalist Party, 344ff
Fessenden, W. H., 611ff
Fessenden, William Pitt, 18, 39, 236, 611
Field, Stephen J.: 14, 15, 24, 99, 110-150, 299, 560; anxiety and bias of, 114ff, 147-149, 407-411, 570ff; brothers of, 14, 109, 120, 128; on California Supreme Court, 114ff; characterized, 110-117, 570, 577ff; views on Chinese exclusion, 105; conservatism of, 106n, 119n; contributions of, 147-150, 370ff, 543, 549, 560, 571, 590; European travels (1848), 128ff; views on *14A*, 24, 25, 110ff, 134ff, 395, 403ff, 569ff; his plan to pack Court, 25, 108, 137ff, 570; judicial motivation of, 114ff, 127, 130, 141ff; Paris Commune and, 116, 124ff; presidential aspirations, 25, 101, 108, 139ff, 570; relations with associates and subordinates, 105, 135, 137-147, 297, 392n, 562, 570, 576ff; Sharon-Hill Divorce Case, 137n; views on state taxing power, 114n, 407-411, 555, 574, 580; Waite and, 135, 136, 562, 570, 577. *See also* Corporate "person."
Finney, Charles Grandison, 163ff
Flack, Horace, 131, 159, 171n, 274, 314
Ford, Thomas, 505, 506, 513, 537
Foreign corporations, 73, 81
Fourteenth Amendment (*14A*): 11, 13, 18, 20-21, 113, 155, 157, 159, 269, 273, 333, 386, 391, 490, 497, 546, 589; Conkling on, 595ff; constitutionalizes Civil Rights Bill, 333; debates in Congress on (1866), 32, 36, 274, 308-313; ∞ (1871), 322-333; early antislavery background of, 152-241, 250ff, 268; genesis (1833–1835), 157-185; system-

ization (1835–1837), 186, 238; historiography of, 23, 66, 68-69, 80, 94-95, 99, 130, 151-161, 240, 264, 268, 276ff, 300, 438-439, 450ff, 467ff, 483, 491-493, 543ff, 552ff; "Declaratory," 295-334; incorporation of Bill of Rights by, 238, 265, 314n; primacy of, ix; school segregation and, 266-294; Waite Court and, 552, 561-584
Framer intent. See "Original understanding."
Frankfurter, Felix: 110n, 240-241; and Landis, 396, 434
Franklin College, 197, 199, 232, 256, 280, 444
Free men, 3, 51n, 56, 66, 173, 310n, 416n, 509
Free Negroes, 60-61, 162ff
Freedmen, 3, 36, 150, 162, 267, 270, 581
Freedmen's Bureau, 291n, 305ff
French Revolution, 118-119
Frontier government and public administration, 494, 500ff, 503ff, 513ff
Frontier law, 494, 513
Frontier revenue systems, 510-518
Frontier tax syndrome, 493ff, 616ff
Fuller, Lon, 284n, 289

GALBRAITH, J. K., 593
Gallatin, Albert, 358
Galloway, Samuel, 302
Garfield, James G., 16, 88, 90, 102ff, 312, 446, 460n, 563
Garrett, Robert, 461ff, 483
Gates, Paul W., 492
General Laws and Liberties of Massachusetts Bay, 154
George, Henry, 113, 505
Gibbons v. Ogden, 360
Gibson, John B., 260, 527
Giddings, Joshua, 55, 80, 162, 168, 199, 218, 301
Goddard, Calvin, 177ff, 252, 537
Godkin, E. L., 125
Goldman, Eric, 26
Good v. Zercher, 258n
Gordon, William, 191n
Gould, Jay, 14, 16, 577
"Government in Ignorance of Law," 550
Graham, John, 224
Granger, A. P., 56, 79
Granger laws and cases, 13, 103, 113, 120, 136, 144, 147, 395, 496, 502, 522, 543, 580
Grant, J.A.C., 62
Grant, Ulysses S., 16, 135n, 136, 561ff

Grier, Robert C., 87, 88, 420, 446, 463, 472ff
Groves v. Slaughter, 49-50, 56, 65n

HABEAS corpus, 25, 142ff, 492, 576
Hacker, Louis M., 100, 554
Haines, Charles G., 62, 69, 245
Hale, Robert S., 83n, 553
Hamilton, Walton, 6, 23, 34, 62, 68, 247, 346, 429
Hamlin, E. S., 199n, 202n
Harlan, John Marshall, 11, 113, 155, 267, 370, 425n, 564, 574, 577, 583
Harris, Ira, 236
Hartz, Louis, 360
Harvey v. Thomas, 260
Hastings, Serranus Clinton, 102, 473n
Hayes, Rutherford B., 16, 136
Haymarket Riot, 117n
Haymond, Creed, 380n, 399-400, 428
Henderson, J. B., 46n
Hepburn v. Griswold, 120, 121, 543, 577
Heydenfeldt, Solomon, 102
"Higher Law," 202, 299, 344
Hine, C. C., 84n, 552, 558
History: misused in constitutional cases, 366. See also "Conspiracy Theory," "Law Office History."
Hoard, C. B., 58
Hoffman, Ogden, 146, 392ff, 406
Hoke v. Henderson, 54, 72, 244, 260, 263
Holmes, Oliver Wendell, 110ff, 113, 431, 564
Horton episode, 194
Hough, Charles M., 246
Howard, Jacob M., 46n, 236
Howe, Mark De Wolfe, i, 97, 585, 589
Huntington, Collis P., 16, 23, 137
Hurst, Willard, 96, 97
Hurtado v. California, 431, 441, 576, 578

ILLINOIS: 502; antislavery in, 226, 502n, 542; economics, 73, 76, 78, 84, 121, 262, 394ff, 422, 542; land titles and taxation in, 494ff, 511ff, 516, 518, 522; ∞ recordation of, 500n
Illinois Council of Revision, 545
Illinois Military Tract, 495, 497, 500ff, 512ff, 521, 534
Illinois Railroad Tax Cases, 395n, 502, 522, 543
"Inclusion and exclusion of cases," 13, 544. See also *Davidson v. New Orleans.*
Indiana: 48; economics, 80, 505, 509, 511
Indians, 267

Index

Insurance Co. v. New Orleans. See Continental Life Insurance Co. v. New Orleans.

Insurance corporations: activity in Congress (1866–1871), 83ff, 122n, 445, 553, 611ff; constitutional position of, 73, 84, 85n, 92; contraverted role of, in *14A*, 92, 611ff; "petitions and bills" of, 84, 92, 552ff, 611ff; seek National Bureau of Insurance, 83ff, 552

Internal improvements, 358ff

Iowa: 94n; economics, 473, 479, 508n

JACKSON, Andrew, 213, 359, 499
Jackson, Robert H., 240, 288n
Jay, William, 168n, 184
Jefferson, Thomas, 7, 195, 345
Johnson, Reverdy: 18, 46, 86, 90n, 81, 91, 93, 96, 123, 124, 351, 446, 463ff; favors due process clause, 87n
Joint Committee of Fifteen on Reconstruction: 12, 16, 93, 236, 250, 283, 313, 351, 440, 446, 482, 552ff, 584; drafts *14A*, 30, 38ff, 552; journal of, 18, 24, 31, 44, 70, 317, 612-613; members from antislavery constituencies, 170, 236, 301-302, 313; "petitions and bills" and, 84n, 94, 445, 465ff, 482ff, 552ff, 611ff
Josephson, Mathew, 33n
Judicial function: 99; Holmes-Field conceptions of, contrasted, 110-117
Judicial power, 242, 448, 527
Judicial review: 4, 101, 239, 244, 247, 395, 433, 450ff, 467ff, 502, 548-550, 587; revolution, 583; supremacy, 548
Judiciary Act: (1789), 328, 344; (1801), 358
Just compensation clause (Fifth Amendment, U.S. Constitution), 33, 59-60, 62, 88n, 90n, 281

KANSAS: due process used in congressional debates on, 54ff, 79, 80,
Kearney, Denis, 15, 371, 397
Kelly, Alfred H., 268, 272n
Kendrick, B. B., 18, 19, 26, 31, 95
Kent, James, 117-119, 259, 495, 504ff, 517, 525, 537, 541
Kentucky: economics, 76, 193, 496, 513, 516
Kentucky Railroad Tax Cases, 428, 577
Kooker, Arthur R., 163
Krulewich v. U.S., 65n

LAISSEZ faire: constitutional, 19, 24, 74, 116, 395n, 544; judicialized, 27, 101, 116, 130, 246, 437, 508; legislative, 374; "revolution," 519ff, 575ff, 579
Land and land law, 498
Land speculation, 499ff, 510ff
Lane Seminary, 165
Latrobe, J.J.B., 463ff, 479
Law: 3, 98, 292, 585; and history, 351
Law of the land, 3, 498ff, 526ff, 549
"Law office history," 268, 276, 337
Lawless, Judge, 226
Lawrence, Charles B., 121n, 394, 395, 502, 517, 534, 542
Lawrence, William, 199n, 311ff, 394n, 395n
Leavitt, Joshua, 167
Legal Tender Cases, 103, 120
Legislative supremacy, 544
Lerner, Max, 33n
Lewis, E. R., 34n
Lewis, Ellis, 78, 87, 457ff, 473, 480
Lewis, Seth, 231
Lex terrae. See Law of the land, Due process of law.
Liberty to contract, 24, 127, 246, 437, 576, 581
Lincoln, Abraham, 12, 14, 263, 297, 363, 496, 505, 521, 534, 537, 546
"Living Constitution," 363
Loan Assn. v. Topeka, 508
Locke, John, 62, 186ff, 245, 298, 302, 517, 524, 545
Lodge, Henry Cabot, 18
Logan, S. T., 263
Lord, Daniel, 494n, 495, 517
Los Angeles County Law Library, 98, 492
Louisiana, 106
Lovejoy, Elijah P., 226
Lowrie, Walter H., 463

MCARTHUR, Duncan, 499, 515
McCulloch v. Maryland, 341, 363
McDuffie, George, 213
McLaughlin, A. C., 67, 73, 100, 123, 272, 554
McLean, John, 56-57
Madison, James, 339, 341, 345, 349, 358
Madison & Indianapolis R.R. v. Whiteneck, 80
Magna Carta, 3, 117, 257, 296, 310, 366, 498, 528
Magrath, C. Peter, 241, 560ff
Maine: economics, 121, 391n, 402
Marshall, John, 293, 338, 340, 363, 370, 404, 418, 563, 592
Marshall, Thurgood, 11, 268
Marx v. Hauthorn, 541

Maryland: economics, 90, 474
Mason, Alpheus T., 243
Mason, E. S., 592-593
Massachusetts: courts, 245; records, 192, 539; economics, 438, 529
Matthews, Stanley, 151, 168n, 563, 574ff, 577
Mayflower Compact, 153
Military bounty lands, 502, 516, 524
Miller, Loren, 99
Miller, Samuel F., 12, 13, 31, 110, 134, 156, 296, 297, 319ff, 333, 373, 402, 405; 423ff, 508, 541, 563, 573, 581
Missouri v. Lewis, 402, 403
Mob action, 225, 226, 297n
Monteith, John, 202n
More, Thomas, 345, 346
Morehead v. Tipaldo, 25
Morrill, Justin S., 236, 302
Morrill, Lot M., 302n
Morrison, Stanley, 240
Morse, Samuel F. B., 361
Mott, Rodney L., 155, 285n
Murphy, Paul, 337
Murray, Hugh C., 102
Murray v. Hoboken Land and Improvement Co., 54, 246, 540, 543, 572
Myrdal, Gunnar, 67, 191, 271

NAACP: 67, 267; memorandum for, 295, 367
Nash, Simeon, 258
National Road. See Cumberland Road.
Natural law (extra-constitutional restraints): interpretations of role of, 3, 7, 56-57, 62, 94, 101, 248, 415, 457, 517, 525
Negro race. See Classification, Custom, Discrimination, Mob action, Prejudice, Protection, Racism, Segregation, Slavery.
Nelson, David, 226
Nevada: economics, 83
Nevins, Allan, 163
New Hampshire: economics, 528
New Jersey: economics, 76
New York: 156; economics, 73, 76-77, 84, 85, 118, 504, 529; courts, 245
New York and Boston Illinois Land Company, 495, 517
New York Central Railroad, 455ff
"Ninth Circuit Law": 14, 24-25, 137, 141ff, 369, 392, 402, 422, 431, 441, 572ff, 575
"No Man's Land" (constitutional), 49
North Carolina: courts, 245; economics, 193, 529

Northwest Ordinance: 504; antislavery clause, 193, 219, 228; *dpl* clause of, 56n, 58n
Northwestern Fertilizing Co. v. Hyde Park, 121n, 394n, 503n
Noyes, William Curtis, 77, 82n, 84n
Nye, Russell B., 237

OBERLIN College, 166
O'Dell, Richard, 195
Ohio: antislavery in, 195ff, 215ff; black laws, 228, 253, 577; constitution, 228ff, 253; economics, 73, 86, 258, 459n, 505, 511, 516, 542, 572; racial-humanitarian use of *dpl-epl*, 66, 173ff, 185, 542
Ohio Antislavery Society, 172ff, 253, 278
Olcott, Charles, 202ff, 537
Oneida Institute, 165
Oregon: 65; racial-humanitarian use of *dpl-epl*, 48, 49, 57-61, 65; economics, 83, 541
"Original understanding," 19, 268, 275, 337, 344, 350n, 356n, 366, 439, 467, 588
Otis, James, 192n

PARIS *Commune*, 124-125
Parker, Amasa J., 77, 579
Parrish, John, 188n
Parrotts' Chinese Case, 315, 393, 430, 572
Paul v. Virginia, 92, 115, 407, 614
Pennsylvania: economics, 72, 73, 78-79, 86, 87, 90, 94, 260, 360, 439, 453ff, 529; racial-humanitarian use of *dpl-epl*, 156
Pennsylvania Railroad, 445ff
Perkins, Samuel E., 509
Persons (legal and constitutional term): 3, 18, 26, 34, 50, 62, 64, 156, 385, 548, 582; classes of, distinguished, 3, 18; Chinese as, 144ff, 147, 392, 572; corporations as, 15, 17, 24, 31, 32, 94-95, 127n, 156, 351, 374ff, 415ff, 450ff, 558, 566, 571, 581, 591, 614-615; Negroes as, 156, 271, 425n; revisors of the U.S. statutes and (1871), 614-615; shareholders as, 381, 427, 572, 573; slavery–antislavery conflict over, 62, 64, 254
"Petitions and bills": 24, 68, 82ff, 441; Conkling's innuendo analyzed, 449-453, 552ff; in *Congressional Globe*, 84n, 92
Philadelphia-Baltimore rivalry, 359, 439, 453ff
Philbrick, Francis S., 506, 617

Index 629

Picketing as "free speech," 389
Pinckney, H. L., 212, 231, 253, 256
Pittsburgh and Connellesville Railroad, 86n, 445, 454, 461ff
Platt, Thomas, 16, 83n
Plessy v. Ferguson, 10, 11, 268, 334
Pomeroy, John Norton, 24, 100, 101, 323, 400-403, 426, 497, 543, 573
Pomeroy, John Norton, Jr., 101
Pope, Nathaniel, 514
Pound, Roscoe, 544
Powell, Thomas Reed, 264, 590
Prejudice: 4, 20, 557, 566; against Negroes, 4, 172, 178, 304; against corporations, 13, 17, 371ff; in California, 14, 371, 590; against Chinese, 14, 590
Prigg v. Pennsylvania, 311
Privileges-immunities clause, *14A*: 384, 407; antecedent theory of, 174-184, 583-584; establishes paramount national citizenship, 303, 318; Supreme Court misinterprets, 319, 330ff, 583
"Process" and "protection" (constitutional terms), 6, 8, 13, 17, 267, 499, 586ff
Property (constitutional term), 56-57, 62, 78, 147, 215, 220, 254, 380, 409ff, 478, 498, 578, 580
Protection: 367; "affirmative," 5, 517; Chinese and Negroes compared, 150; Indians and Negroes lack, 267
"Public purpose" doctrine, 457n, 525
Purple, N. H., 263, 495, 496, 619

QUAKERS, 190, 193, 197
Queue Case, 144-145
Quincy House, 494, 495
Quincy, Illinois: 495, 546; land bar of, 495ff, 517, 519, 542

RACISM, 10, 550, 559, 565
Railroad regulation, 362
Railroads: 460ff; and *14A*, see Chapters 1, 2, 3, 9, 10, 13. See also specific railroads, constitutional cases, clauses, and jurisdictions.
Rankin, John, 198
Reconstruction, 119ff, 132, 143, 271, 285, 304, 564, 587
Republican Party: 55; platforms (1856, 1860), 162; *dpl* plank of, 55, 80
Repudiation Cases (107 U.S. 711), 106
Research (historico-legal), 266, 275ff, 552, 557
Restrictive Covenant Cases, 155, 265n
Rhinehart v. Schuyler, 262, 495, 521, 528, 530, 536, 541, 547

Rhode Island Prohibition Cases, 540
Rice, David, 195
Rights, 3; natural and constitutional related, 3, 7
Rip Van Winkle, 270, 273, 286n
Roberts, Owen J., 25
Roche, John P., 560, 564n
Rogers, Andrew J., 47, 90n, 466, 482
Roosevelt, Franklin D., 25, 137
Rubin, Harris L., 123n
Ruffin, Thomas, 244, 259
Russell, J. F. S., 438, 448, 468-470

SAN Francisco *Alta California*, 125, 127ff, 615
San Francisco *Argonaut*, 107
San Mateo Case, 15, 17, 19, 23, 31, 352, 414-425, 431, 555, 573, 575n
Sanderson, Silas W., 121n, 419-425
Santa Clara Case and "dictum," 414, 426-428, 441, 541, 559, 566ff
Sawyer, Lorenzo, 15, 137, 146, 392ff, 410-412, 573, 575
School Segregation Cases, 268, 269, 273, 292, 300, 334
Scott, Thomas A., 14, 86n, 409n, 455ff
"Security of Private Property," 260
Sedgwick, Theodore, 539
Segregation, 11, 22, 270, 335
"Separate but equal," 11, 154, 274, 291, 539
Sewall, Samuel, 190
Shafter, Oscar L., 492
Sharon-Hill divorce case, 137n
Sharp, Granville, 204
Sharpless v. Philadelphia, 457n, 458
Shellabarger, Samuel, 558, 560
Shiras, George, Jr., 463, 479
Sinking Fund Cases, 144, 397, 418, 419
Skinner, Mark, 79
Slaughter-House Cases, 10, 11, 12, 31, 113, 130, 133, 147, 156, 270, 296, 297, 300, 316, 330-333, 384ff, 391, 402, 416, 423ff, 436, 549, 565, 573, 574, 595ff
Slavery: as arbitrary classification, 189n, 201ff, 302, 586; as institutionalized race discrimination, 5, 284, 304, 564; "badges" of, 8, 270, 274, 305, 313; constitutional status of, in the Dist. of Columbia, 156, 216, 220, 233, 253; in the states, 218ff, 287; in the territories, 57, 80, 118, 220; ∞, Congressional debates on, 62; "higher law" and, 203, 284ff; a "positive good," 210, 272; as racial damnation, 284;

vestiges of, 10, 189, 550, 565, 589; Thirteenth Amendment abolishes, 305
Smith v. Ames, 64, 441n
Sociology of law and research, 266, 543
Sommersett Case, 191n, 204, 209, 252
South Carolina: economics, 529; racial-humanitarian use of *dpl-epl*, 193
Southern Pacific Railroad, 14, 23, 103, 136-137, 409, 492, 496, 590; crisis in affairs of (1880–1882), 14, 140, 397ff, 409n, 573; legal expenses of, 401n, 415n; resources of, 432. *See also California Railroad Tax Cases*, for collective discussion; *San Mateo Case* and *Santa Clara Case*, for major opinions and developments.
Spengler, Oswald, 339, 345
"Squatter Sovereignty," 499, 546, 547
Stanford, Leland, 14, 137
Stanford University, 15
Stanton, Henry B., 167, 207
Stapp, J.T.B., 515, 534
"State action" and inaction, 10-11, 200n, 565, 592n
"States' Rights," 360, 364, 382
Statesmanship, 135, 586, 590, 591
Steamboat regulation, 360
Stevens, Thaddeus, 18n, 77-78, 236, 272, 302, 317, 446, 464ff, 542
Stewart, Alvan, 220n, 255
Storrs, James C., 121n, 393
Stuart, Charles, 165
Stubbs, William, 590
Sumner, Charles, 11, 539
Supreme Court of the United States. *See* U.S. Supreme Court.
Swayne, Noah H., 147
Swayne, Wager, 106
Swisher, Carl B., 24, 101, 272
Syllogistic reasoning, 27, 376-378, 390, 415, 420-421, 429ff, 518, 559

TANEY, Roger B., 57, 62, 75, 80, 118, 162, 245, 254, 256, 507
Tappan, Arthur and Lewis, 164ff, 251, 252
Tax delinquency, 500, 511, 534
Tax sales and titles, 494ff, 511ff, 532ff
Taxing power, state: Bingham and, 48, 50, 482, 541, 555, 560; Blackwell on, 523ff, 580; Chinese and, 556, 560, 574; Congress and, 574; Conkling and, 414, 416ff, 555, 560, 574; insurance industry and, 553, 558; Lincoln and, 505; railroads and, 129, 398, 407ff, 415; U.S. Supreme Court and, 435, 437, 540-541, 560, 573, 575, 578, 580. *See also* Chapters 9 and 10 *passim*.
Taylor, Hannis, 31n, 95
Taylor, John, 370
Taylor v. Porter, 54, 72, 244, 257, 258, 260, 261, 262, 263, 311, 459, 495, 540, 543, 579
Telegraph regulation, 361
Teleology in history, 543, 557
tenBroek, Jacobus, 156, 241, 254, 291, 350n, 356n
Tennessee: economics, 72n, 257; racial-humanitarian use of *dpl-epl*, 193; *dpl* cases, 244, 261, 529
Terry, David Smith, 102, 137n
Tenth Amendment, 342
Tevis, Lloyd, 103, 104, 400
Thirteenth Amendment, 8, 291n, 305, 390, 423
Tiffany, Joel, 168n, 255, 312
Tillson, John, Jr., 495, 501, 515
Towne, A. N., 103, 400
"Transportation Revolution," 359, 365
Trumbull, Lyman, 132-133, 270, 295, 307, 317, 323ff, 614
Trustees of University v. Foy, 71, 244, 474ff
Turner, Nat, 210
Turner thesis, 541, 550
Tuttle, G. M., 258
Twiss, Benjamin, 246

UNITED *States v. Hall*, 291n, 316n, 565, 571,
U.S. Congress: 339ff, 347ff; House Judiciary Committee, 611-614
U.S. Constitution: 3, 298, 516, 525; antislavery argument based on, 217ff; character of, 364; Crosskey on, 337ff, 354; preamble of, 217, 238, 346; proslavery argument based on, 211-215
U.S. Constitutional Convention (1787), 349, 355ff
U.S. Supreme Court: 20, 25, 63, 68, 108, 120, 540, 558, 561ff, 576, 583, 586; business of, 396, 434ff; Crosskey's attack on, 343ff, 352; Ninth Circuit law and, 143ff, 430-437, 573ff; overburdened during 1880's, 434, 575; personnel changes, 397, 580; and Reconstruction, 120, 563ff

Veazie Bank v. Fenno, 93, 96, 447, 482
Veblen, Thorstein, 365, 505
Vermont, 193, 227
"Vested rights": doctrine and protection of, 467, 471, 487, 505, 517ff

Index

Virginia: economics, 106, 155, 496, 516; racial-humanitarian use of *dpl-epl*, 193
Virginia Military District, 500, 516

WADE brothers, 301, 302n
Waite, Morrison R., 13, 17, 135ff, 273, 405, 418-420, 541, 559-584
Walker, David, 209
Walker, Timothy, 217, 258
Walker v. Jennison, 192, 209
Wall, *Ex Parte*, 106n
War Amendments. *See* Civil War.
"War of the Gauges" (1853–1855), 455ff
Ward v. Maryland, 446, 560
Warren, Charles, 24, 344, 509
Washburn v. Perry, 103
Washburne, Elihu, 85, 236
Washington, Bushrod, 74, 180, 252, 309
Webster, Daniel, 74, 118, 474, 529
Weld, Theodore, 156, 165ff, 251
Wells, Alexander, 102
Wells Fargo Express Company, 83, 560
Western Law Journal, 258

Westerwelt v. Gregg, 76, 81, 118
Wheeling Steel Corp. v. Glander, 158, 273n, 387ff
Whiskey Rebellion, 357
Whittier, John Greenleaf, 166
Williams, Archibald, 263, 495ff, 503, 514, 517, 521, 522, 530, 534, 536, 541, 542, 546
Williams, George H., 41, 561
Wilson, James: and "Wilson Doctrine," 340ff, 347, 353
Wilson, James F., 285n, 286, 308ff
Wisconsin, 78, 508n, 542
Wish, Harvey, 66n
Woods, William B., 121n, 126, 130, 291n, 316n, 382ff, 420, 559, 560, 561n, 564ff, 571
Woolman, John, 190n
Wright, Elizur, 167, 368, 556
Wright, John C., 217
Wynehamer v. People, 35, 59, 77, 79, 81, 118, 244, 459, 496, 543, 579

YALE *Law Journal*, 27, 65, 68, 100
Yick Wo v. Hopkins, 431, 441n, 577